The Marshall Cavendish Illustrated Encyclopedia of
WESTERN ART

The Marshall Cavendish Illustrated Encyclopedia of

WESTERN ART

Marshall Cavendish London & New York

Academic Advisor:
Professor Laurence Lerner, M.A.,
Professor of English,
University of Sussex.

Editors:
Michael Bisacre
Richard Carlisle
Deborah Robertson
John Ruck

Published by Marshall Cavendish Books Ltd.,
58 Old Compton Street, London W1V 5PA

© Marshall Cavendish Limited 1975, 1976, 1977, 1979

Some of this material was first published
by Marshall Cavendish Limited in the
encyclopedia *Tree of Knowledge*

First printing: 1979

Printed in Great Britain by Severn Valley Press Limited

ISBN 0 85685 741 6

Introduction

The Illustrated Encyclopedia of Western Art is designed
to cover the whole spectrum of man's cultural achievements and
to provide a treasury of information and ideas about our
artistic heritage. Articles are arranged in two parts: the first
following the development of painting, sculpture and
architecture, the second charting a thousand years of literature,
music and drama.

Part I aims to show the ideas and aspirations which lie
behind the greatest works of art. How were the great medieval
cathedrals built in an age of such limited technical knowledge?
How did Rembrandt, Michaelangelo or Wren reflect their
environments in their work? What is modern art really 'about'?
These are the searching questions the encyclopedia
will answer, as well as offering a comprehensive history of art.
Literature is represented in Part II, from the medieval world of
Chaucer through the turbulent years of Byron and Shelley, to
Hemingway and Scott Fitzergald and finally the novel as it is
known today. Music and the performing arts are also fully
covered in this section, offering a comprehensive guide to the
development of opera, theatre and ballet, as well as the
glittering years of Hollywood.

The book features countless superb colour illustrations of
beautiful paintings, statues and buildings, plus a fascinating
gallery of famous writers and composers, musical instruments,
and theatrical productions throughout the ages. These serve
to complement and endorse an authoritative text and
to provide a volume which will give as much pleasure as it
provides knowledge.

Contents

Part I A Thousand Years of Painting, Sculpture and Architecture

Part II A Thousand Years of Literature, Drama and Music

Part I

A Thousand Years of Painting, Sculpture and Architecture

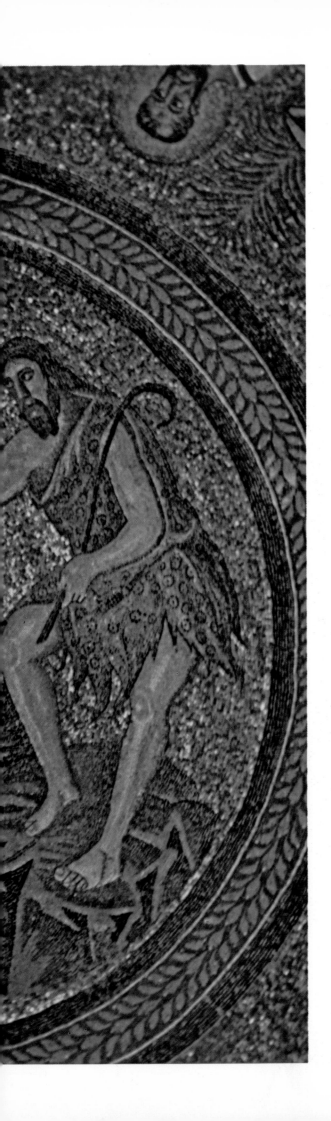

Chapter 1
The Middle Ages

The dome of the Arian Baptistery,
Ravenna. The much restored mosaic
shows a procession of apostles and the
Etiomasia (the gospels enthroned). The
Baptistery is now *Santa Maria in
Cosmedin.*

The title page of the Book of Kells, produced by Irish monks working in Iona – circa 800 A.D.

Its intricate formal portraits are known as 'carpet pages' (see page 14).

The Birth of Christian Art

The art of medieval Europe grew out of the centuries of flux and upheaval that marked the gradual decline of the great Roman Empire. From the fourth to the eighth centuries AD the unity of the ancient world was shattered by internal decline and successive invasions of Barbarian tribes from northern Europe and from the steppelands of Asia.

Historical background

The Roman Empire 'fell' only in the west. In the east it endured, in a gradually weakening condition, until finally succumbing to conquest by the Ottoman Turks in the fifteenth century. In this eastern sector, known as Byzantine, the traditions of Christian art begun in the last centuries of the united Empire continued to develop into the unique and splendid art of the Greek and Russian orthodox churches.

The great western empire, at the dawn of the sixth century, was only a memory. In its place were a group of barbarian kingdoms, their boundaries still fluid and unsettled. The Ostrogothic ruler Theodoric dominated Italy, the Vandals ruled in North Africa, the Visigoths in Spain, Clovis and his Franks were in the process of conquering Gaul (roughly modern France) and the Anglo-Saxon tribes were beginning to settle Britain, driving the native Celts to the fringes of the isles. By 600AD the Ostrogothic kingdom of Italy had collapsed; the north was temporarily held by the Byzantine emperors, and the south was dominated by the progressive invasion of the savage Lombards.

Out of these gloomy centuries of turmoil and bloodshed, a Christian culture, based on a distinctive Western European civilization, was to emerge. The barbarians brought their own qualities, ways of thought, skills and artistic traditions to bear on the relics of classical culture. Christianity was the focal point, the great carrier and synthesizer of traditions, on which this European civilization was founded.

By the year 800AD a new spirit had made itself felt — a barbarian king, Charlemagne of the Franks, had been

Ronald Sheridan

Above: Bronze head of the Emperor Constantine, 4th century, found in Nis, in modern Yugoslavia. In many ways he was the founder of the Christian era in Europe—the first emperor to promote Christianity as a state religion. The head is typical of the Roman feeling for life-like portraiture, but the large eyes and regular patterning of the hair show how imperial artists were beginning to move away from classical realism.

Francis Brunel

Andre Held, Ziolo

Two examples of the early mingling of pagan and Christian art. Above: A section of sculpture from a 3rd century stone coffin shows how the artist has used scenes of idyllic country life, typical of pagan art, to represent Christ as the 'good shepherd'. He carries a lamb across his shoulders. The realistic modelling of the human body and the drapery are still in the tradition of Greek sculpture.

Right: A 6th century mosaic, recently restored, shows Christ in Roman military garb, armed with the cross of martyrdom instead of a sword. He stands supreme over the threatening forces of the lion and the serpent. A similar portrayal of the Egyptian god of healing, Horus, treading down crocodiles, is found on ancient Egyptian stone slabs. Water was poured over these slabs, collected, and used for magical healing. The continuity of pagan images of this kind in Christian art reflects how primitive needs were transferred to the new religion.

Mike Dixon

EGO VERI SVM TASET VIA VITA

Above: The Empress Theodora flanked by attendants—detail from a mosaic in San Vitale church, Ravenna. It dates from c. 547, when much of Italy was in the hands of the barbarian Ostrogoths. Theodora's husband, the Byzantine emperor Justinian, ordered the creation of these impressive mosaics to try to convince the barbarians of the spiritual presence of Byzantium in Italy. Justinian and Theodora are depicted carrying the bread and wine of the mass into the church sanctuary, towards Christ who is seated in the recess, or apse, in imperial robes. The whole church interior is a stunning example of the supreme skill of the Byzantine craftsmen in laying tessarae—tiny cubes of glass glowing with reflected light. Each tessera is set into the wall at a particular angle to create shadows and depth. The large white shapes which form Theodora's head-dress and collar are genuine pieces of mother of pearl, dressing the image as if it were in reality the Empress.

13

Left: Metalwork was the great art of the barbarian tribes. A silver Viking cup displays the typical motifs of bird and intertwined branches that were adapted by Celtic monks for Christian manuscripts. This successful fusion made monasteries like Clonmacnoise (below) founded in 547, cultural outposts in the Dark Ages.

Michael Holford

Trinity College, Dublin

Above: An illuminated page from the Book of Durrow, an Irish manuscript produced towards the end of the 7th century. The intricate interlace pattern uses the common barbarian motif of the self-biting serpent. Incredibly, each serpent in this complex maze can be traced out to its end.

Below: A detail from the Book of Durrow shows the symbol of St. Mark, a lion. The four evangelists were often represented by four winged creatures, suggested by a Bible passage describing Ezekiel's vision. St. John was the eagle, Luke the calf, and Matthew the winged man, or angel.

Snark

The 9th century Viking invasions meant a fresh injection of the traditional art of the northern tribes into European culture. The magnificent carved doorway of the church at Kilpeck, Herefordshire, built around 1150, shows how this tradition was passed into the High Middle Ages. Fighting warriors, sinuous birds and beasts scale the portals, while a chain motif containing the monsters and fishes of the Zodiac decorates the outer arch.

Right: A page from a book of St. Augustine's writings produced in northern Gaul around 750 AD shows the use of barbarian animal images to shape and decorate letters.

Below: The Sutton Hoo purse-cover, found in a 7th century Anglo-Saxon ship-burial. The motifs, picked out in red enamel, are very ancient symbols representing the battle of spirit forces: the man between confronting animals and the eagle seizing a duck.

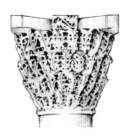

Right: Three decorated capitals (column heads) show the eastern interlace and basketwork effects taken up by European artists. The top two are Coptic (Egyptian Christian) and the third is Byzantine. The migration of monks from eastern and north African monasteries was a major factor in this cultural interchange.

Left: The gospel-writer St. John from the magnificent Irish Book of Kells, produced c. 800. The edges were badly cropped in the 19th century. The figure is completely stylized: the folds of his garment and his hair are reduced to an abstract pattern. A single circle in the distorted feet represents the heel bone. The page is an ideal example of the fusion of traditions. The halo around his head resembles a barbarian metalwork brooch or shield. The border has groups of Coptic interlace, with separate sections of animal interlace in the corners. There is a strong reflection of the discipline of monastic life in the restricting, vice-like border.

Bibliotheque Nationale, Paris

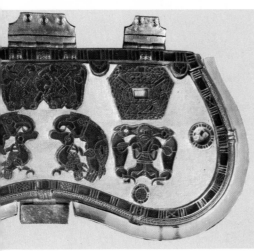

Michael Holford

crowned emperor in the West. He began a policy of re-creating an 'imperial' art and learning, salvaging much that was best of Roman culture for future generations. There were to be further setbacks — the fresh invasions in the ninth century by Vikings and Huns — but the civilization of western Europe was on its way.

The early church and Byzantium
The story of Christian art begins in the latter years of the Roman Empire, in the third and fourth centuries AD before the collapse of the western sector. Before the fourth century Christianity was a persecuted religion, outlawed by the imperial government. But the faith seemed to flourish on the blood of its martyrs; from obscure origins in a remote eastern province of the empire, it continued to spread west and north, attracting a steady flow of converts.

In 312 the Roman emperor Constantine announced his conversion to Christianity, and proceeded to issue a series of edicts which gradually exalted this religion of a hunted minority to a place alongside the official pagan cults. Before the end of the century, it was to become the sole state religion.

The early Christian artists, called upon to decorate the walls of Christian meeting places and the tombs of the faithful, were faced with some very basic problems. They had to draw upon some kind of form and techniques to represent this new subject matter — Christ, the apostles and martyrs, and scenes of Christian inspiration. It is evident that many turned to the traditions of classical art that they already knew. Early tomb decorations and wall paintings show Christ with all the physical perfection and solid presence of a young Greek god.

The mingling of pagan and Christian in the imagination of the people is reflected in this early art: one famous third century mosaic in the tomb of the Julii family in Rome shows Christ depicted like the pagan sun god Helios, riding in a sun-chariot, his head surrounded by rays of light. Wall-paintings in the Catacombs — the Christian cemetery in underground galleries deep in the beds of soft rock near Rome — show how pagan subjects were used and given Christian meanings. Scenes of peacocks and vines, for example, symbolized Paradise and the wine of the Eucharist.

But early Christian art was to absorb and re-vitalize other types of artistic tradition within the late Roman world. In 330 Constantine founded a new capital on the site of the ancient city of Byzantium, to be called Constantinople, modern day Istanbul. This shift in the centre of imperial government, away from Rome, had far-reaching effects on the artistic life of the Empire. The new imperial Christian art was destined to be rooted in the eastern Mediterranean world, not the Roman sphere of the west. Since the conquest of Egypt and the East by Alexander the Great, the Greek world had absorbed into its own culture exotic, eastern religions from Persia, Egypt and other areas.

The spread of these eastern cults, with their emphasis on individual religious experience, and the idea of eternal salvation in a life after death, indicated the popular dissatisfaction with the spiritual bankruptcy of the old pagan religion, and paved the way for the acceptance of Christianity.

The triumph of Christianity, in gaining supremacy over the pagan classical world and in the conversion of the Barbarian tribes, meant that a new philosophy and a whole new system of priorities motivated artists and patrons. Christianity not only taught a social ideal of love, charity and the brotherhood of man, it also emphasized the mysterious spiritual communion between Christ and the faithful.

Christian mysticism, flourishing in the monasteries of north Africa, taught that the visible world was a mere shell concealing the real world of Christ and the Virgin, the angels and saints. Throughout the Middle Ages, artists explored many ways of depicting this heavenly symbolic world, above reason and the senses.

Slowly many of the achievements of Roman wall painting and Greek sculpture were abandoned. The artists of the new religion found those classical skills in depicting men and gods as real people in natural settings were irrelevant to their purposes. It was replaced by an Eastern-Greek desire to depict the spiritual reality which lay behind the visible world.

The flowing folds of classical drapery on a figure were flattened into superficial patterning. When depicting a face, the artists concentrated more on producing an 'other worldly' expression, to represent the man of spirit rather than the man of the flesh. Huge soulful eyes look out at the beholder, or else are cast aside as if concerned with inward thoughts. The Roman art of portrait painting was never totally abandoned, but its goal was changed towards expressing a new kind of spirituality in the face.

The relationship between art and religion caused violent disputes in the early Middle Ages. Large statues of Christ, the Virgin or saints were wholly condemned — they smacked too much of idolatry and the 'graven images' of pagan worship. But painting was regarded rather differently, particularly in the western church. Towards the end of the sixth century, Pope Gregory the Great made this explicit: 'Painting can do for the illiterate what writing does for those who can read.' Pictures were accepted as a useful way of spelling out Christ's teachings, reminding the faithful of the gospel stories and their message for mankind. Conveying the content and message of a sacred story was the aim of the Christian painters and mosaic workers — not a convincing likeness of nature.

In the eastern Empire, the controversy over the use of painting was not so easily solved. There was a strong iconoclastic tradition — a school of thought that was totally against all religious images. In the eighth century the Byzantine emperor Leo III emerged as a convinced iconoclast (literally an 'image-breaker'). Leo's stated reason for his decrees of iconoclasm was that the superstitious use of images — heightened at that time of national insecurity when Constantinople was under siege by Arab armies — was a source of weakness to the Byzantine empire. Leo III ordered the destruction of all religious pictures and images in the eastern Empire, even those which acted as containers for the sacred relics of martyrs, but when iconoclasm ended in 842 there was a great revival of earlier forms of Byzantine art.

The barbarian West

While Byzantine art developed and formalized the Christian tradition of the late Empire, western Europe was taking a very different course. From the fifth century the westward migrations of the barbarian tribes submerged Roman culture. 'Barbarian' was a name the Greeks and Romans applied to a number of different tribes — it originally meant 'stammerer', a speaker of uncouth tongues, a man outside of Roman culture. But these tribes were not without their own sense of beauty and artistic skills. They brought to western Europe a sophisticated, purely decorative art, the sort of art that was natural to people who led nomadic lives. The great statues, paintings and architecture of the Mediterranean world were essentially the art of a settled, agricultural and urban society; they had no place in the life of a wandering tribe.

Instead the barbarians had applied their artistic talents to decorating their tents and weapons, creating jewellery to dress themselves, and decorative trappings for their horses. Their greatest artists worked in metals, precious stones, glass and enamels. Two major elements were injected into European art: a fondness for the bright colours that blazed in these materials, and a strong feeling for art as decoration and design. Where a Mediterranean artist strived for a representation of man and nature, the barbarian used natural forms only as an inspiration for abstract patterns, subjected to symmetry and design.

The kinds of motifs and patterns favoured by the Barbarians have a long and fascinating history, reaching back to the hunting culture of Early Stone Age times. They loved to use animal and bird shapes, and mysterious tortuous patterns of intertwined branches and beasts. The Celts — concentrated in Anglo-Irish areas by the early Middle Ages, but at one time widespread in Europe — contributed the whirling trumpet motif and rounded leaf forms displayed on their brooches and weapons. The Danes and Norsemen, who penetrated the British Isles, brought their own similar patterns, but composed of myriad animals, attacking and self-biting, swelling and intertwining like roots.

These decorative heathen traditions, rooted in ancient spirit-magic, were an important source of artistic inspiration to the early Christian artists in the West. The art of twisting animal and plant motifs into gem-set ornaments was translated from metal to parchment by monastic scribes. The purest early flowering of this decorative Christian art was in the isolated monasteries of northern Europe founded by the Irish church.

In the middle of the fifth century, St. Patrick had undertaken the complete conversion of Ireland to Christianity. The primitive monasticism he introduced was Egyptian in origin, bringing to Ireland the example of Coptic (Egyptian-Christian) art with its own tradition of abstract 'basketwork' interlace.

The Irish monks, in their energetic conversion of the heathen, travelled widely. In 565 Columba founded the monastery on Iona off the west coast of Scotland. In 635 Aidan founded Lindisfarne in Northumbria. Columba headed a mission to convert the Franks in northern Gaul, and nomadic Irish monks set up a cultural outpost as far away as Bobbio in Italy.

Coptic art, the Celtic themes of native goldsmiths, and the gradual impact of barbarian Anglo-Saxon motifs, are all to be found in the unique illustrated manuscripts of the Irish monks. The first masterpiece, the Book of Durrow, was produced at the end of the seventh century in Ireland. It was followed by over a

British Museum

Girandon

Above: A nativity scene from a manuscript made for Bishop Aetholwold of Winchester, c. 980. The artist has rejected the native decorative tradition of Britain— the group of figures is copied from a Carolingian ivory—but a distinctly Anglo-Saxon energy shows through in the complex, lively floral borders.

Left: The Carolingians made a conscious effort to copy classical models, as in this picture of St. Matthew from Bishop Ebbo's Gospel Book, produced c. 820 near Reims. It shows some recovery of the techniques of Roman brushwork and sense of distance in landscape, but charged with the wild nervous energy of the Frankish temperament.

hundred years of creative activity, of which the Lindisfarne Gospels and the Book of Kells (originating in Iona) are the most spectacular surviving products.

They contain complex pages of decoration, aptly known as 'carpet' pages, flat, formalized portraits of the gospel writers that show the human figure reduced to a pattern; huge decorated initials that spill over to occupy a whole page. Their minutely harmonious convolutions perhaps reveal something of the tortuous introspection of the monastic mind.

By the mid-ninth century many Celtic centres of Christian culture had been destroyed by Viking raids, the monasteries pillaged, burnt and left in ruins. But the influence of the Irish artists was to live on — it spread through the monasteries on the continents and through the circulation of manuscripts. It's dynamic lines and intensity of colour passed into the Christian art of medieval Europe.

Charlemagne and European art

From the end of the eighth century the Christian art of a new geographical and political entity — western Europe — really began to take shape. Much of this was due to the efforts of one man, Charlemagne, a great military and political leader, and the first western emperor since the collapse of Rome. The relative stability of his reign made possible the revival of art and literature.

The period, known as the Carolingian Renaissance, saw a renewed interest in Greek and Roman culture, an attempt to recapture the knowledge and skills of antiquity which the barbarians freely admitted were in most ways superior to any of their own achievements. Charlemagne was the great driving force behind this revival. His concern was both to promote better education for priests and monks and to create the sort of cultural environment that befitted his court as the centre of a western empire. While in Italy for his coronation as Emperor, he visited Ravenna and saw the imperial splendours of the Byzantine church of San Vitale. On his return to Aachen he ordered a replica to be built as his own imperial chapel, importing the necessary columns and mosaics from Italy.

His court was the first centre of the revived scholarship. He transformed the Palace School at Aachen into a serious educational enterprise which set standards for the whole empire. He directly encouraged cathedrals and monasteries to expand their educational facilities and improve their scholarship. Scholars and artists were 'imported' from many areas, to form an intellectual elite around the emperor, but his greatest helper was Alcuin of York.

A prolific writer and scholar himself, Alcuin directed the collection, copying and circulation of Latin manuscripts. For this work alone the Carolingian Renaissance can be called a major landmark in cultural history. A mere three or four original manuscripts exist today; all the rest of the great works of antiquity, history, poetry and philosophy, have survived only because Charlemagne had them copied.

The painters of the Carolingian manuscript schools produced beautiful illuminated pages. It is difficult to generalize about the huge variety of lively and interesting manuscript painting that was produced under Charlemagne and his successors; different schools in different areas gave rise to regional traditions and peculiarities. The Carolingian artists copied from Byzantine and late antique models in an effort to recapture Roman techniques. They copied various classical formulae: for example, the gospel-writer, sitting draped in a toga like a Roman poet, becomes a common subject. They placed 'architectural' frames around their pictures in the classical manner, aimed at representing more solid, natural positions and at creating a background with a sense of space and distance.

The original Roman book illustrators had copied the natural illusionist techniques of the Roman fresco-painters, but their successors copied from the books. As books multiplied and circulated, the same naturalistic formulae were copied time after time; they became increasingly stylized and 'unnatural'. Medieval painters completely lost the ability to copy directly from nature. Nevertheless, the Carolingian book painters had achieved an original fusion of the narrative, humanist art of the Mediterranean world with the decorative energy and feeling for colour of their own barbarian past.

Snark

Roger Wood

Left: A 9th century bronze statue, believed to be Charlemagne, is one of the very few pieces of sculpture that survives from Carolingian times. It may have been modelled on a mounted statue of Theodoric the Great that Charlemagne imported from Italy to decorate his palace at Aachen. This 'antique collecting' was typical of his desire to revive imperial art.

Art in the Byzantine Empire and in western Europe went their separate ways in the early medieval period. Left: The painting of the Virgin and Child enthroned between two saints, from St. Catherine's monastery on Mount Sinai, dates from the 6th or 7th century. This is the kind of image that was to dominate in the East. The hypnotic outward stares make this a perfect example of *hieratic* art—art in which the characters address themselves directly to the observer, creating an image to be worshipped.

Right: The other major kind of visual art is *narrative*, pictures which contain a story, and show characters relating to each other. Narrative art was to dominate in the West. The illustration from the First Bible of Charles the Bald, made in Tours c. 846, is a perfect example. One of the first paintings of a historical scene in medieval times, it shows Count Vivian presenting the Bible to Charles.

Hamlyn Group

Romanesque Painting

Painting between the years 1000 and 1300 AD—known as Romanesque—tends to be overshadowed by the awe-inspiring achievements of the cathedral-builders of these centuries. But despite the dominance of architecture as an art form, painting was in fact a flourishing activity. It was considered a useful way of depicting religious principles and stories for the unlearned, of embellishing Bibles and prayer books and decorating church interiors to the glory of God. In western Europe, schools of painting had been encouraged during the ninth century by the Carolingian emperors—the line established by Charlemagne. In the tenth century the German emperors, known as Ottonian, became the dominant power in Europe, and they continued to patronize painting.

Romanesque painting differed in its development from country to country; in France, it was to gradually merge into the great stylistic movement which grew up during the first half of the thirteenth century, known as Gothic—an art which aimed at spirituality, harmony and calmness, making use of graceful postures and serene facial expression, and revealing a love of natural detail. In Italy, on the other hand, where the Gothic was never very prominent, Romanesque art leant more towards Byzantine styles. This

Scala

Below: Illuminated page from a psalter, executed in Trier in Germany in the 10th century for Archbishop Egbert. The artist was a Benedictine monk called Ruodprecht. The vigorous swirling lines of the draperies are Anglo-Saxon in origin, while the Greek key pattern of the border is a survival from classical tradition. The saint is painted against a coloured ground patterned with exotic gold beasts—copied from Byzantine, or possibly Chinese, silks.

Above: An illustration for the entry on music in an encyclopedia, produced c.1023 at the great Benedictine monastery of Monte-cassino. Although very simple in technique compared to the sophistication of the Egbert Psalter, it is one of the few non-religious illuminated works of this period, the subject matter offering the artist a rare chance to use his imagination.

Below: The massive, dramatic quality of Spanish Romanesque art is perfectly captured in this 12th-century wall-painting from San Clemente de Tahull in Catalonia. Christ in Majesty, with the emphasis on his role as awe-inspiring judge, was a favourite subject for decorating the apse. The strong outlines, staring eyes and brilliant colours are typical of Catalan art.

Scala

lasted until about 1300, after which artists began to move more and more towards the realism of the Renaissance.

Throughout Europe, however, medieval painting was primarily religious and closely connected with the church, as it had been since early Christian times. The creations which capture the spirit of Romanesque art most closely are the religious picture-cycles which were painted on the walls of churches. Saint Savin-sur-Gartempe in France, for example, is decorated with four cycles. Very few people at that time could read, and one of the main functions of these cycles was to bring to laymen a greater understanding of Christianity.

The crypt of this church has paintings of the martyrdom of its patron saint, St. Savin, and St. Cyprian; the porch is painted with scenes of the end of the world and the Last Judgement; the vault of the nave is covered with scenes from the first five books of the Bible, culminating in the gallery over the porch where the paintings depict Christ's Passion. The whole scheme has been carefully chosen to illustrate the story of man's redemption, to remind the worshipper that he is ultimately to be judged, but that there is hope because of Christ's sacrifice for mankind.

Apart from a few altar coverings, small scale painting survives mostly in the form of manuscript illumination. This too is nearly all religious. Gospel Books, Psalters and Bibles were all illustrated with religious subjects as an act of devotion, sometimes also hinting at a certain vanity and boastfulness on the part of the patron who had been wealthy enough to commission the book.

Above: Illustration from an early 12th-century manuscript of St. Augustine's writings, probably produced in Canterbury. The rapid, light pen outline with a coloured wash is typical of English work after the Norman conquest. The swirling, detailed patterning indicates the strong decorative tradition in England.

Above: Page from a gospel book prepared for Henry III to present to the cathedral at Speyer. He is shown offering the book to the Virgin, in front of a representation of the cathedral. It is remarkable that a Byzantine artist painted the face of the Virgin— his smooth style clearly contrasts with the hard-lined German painting.

Wall painting was a public art form and so, compared to books, was more limited by the attitudes of the Church in what it could represent. The Church was both rigid and confining; during the twelfth century, for example, wall paintings came under attack by the austere and influential monk Bernard of Clairvaux for being too fanciful in their representations. Manuscripts, as a luxurious, private art form, were permitted greater artistic freedom.

Surviving secular works from this period are rare—at least some of the churches and monasteries have been preserved from the period, but almost no secular buildings of any importance. We know, for example, from the *chanson* of Girart de Roussillon that there were paintings on the walls of castles and mosaics of stags, bulls and peacocks. There are now no western European examples of such work. But although secular painting did exist, it was subordinate to church art and its style corresponded to that of religious art.

The craft of painting, for social and political reasons, was largely practised by monks and by Benedictines in particular. The monasteries were the major centres of culture and artistic endeavour. Patronage by secular rulers depended on their

being politically powerful and enjoying stable positions. The Ottonian emperors of Germany in the tenth and eleventh centuries enjoyed just such power, while the so-called 'do nothing' kings of France did not; thus art in the Ottonian sphere was plentiful and unified, splendid and memorable, while French art of the period is fragmented, consisting of whatever local monastic centres could muster.

Great rulers attracted to them great men, so Ottonian art also had such patrons as Egbert, Bishop of Trier, whose efforts alone were enough to make Trier a thriving artistic metropolis in the second half of the tenth century. Monks and clerics came there from England, Flanders, Holland and France, and from monasteries all over Germany; its fame as a centre of goldsmithing was such that the Archbishop of Rheims asked Egbert to have a gold cross made for him there.

Painting may have been mostly executed by monks but, as the case of Trier shows and as Bernard of Clairvaux complained, this did not mean that they obeyed the monastic rule of staying in one place. There were, for example, many connexions between Spain and Italy, and the most respected member of the scriptorium at the monastery of Cluny in Burgundy in the first half of the twelfth century was a German from Trier.

Manuscripts and pattern books from which artists derived their ideas also moved around relatively rapidly. The Egbert psalter, for example, produced in Trier in the tenth century, was in Russia during the twelfth century and is now in Italy. An exchange of ideas between the various centres of production must have been constant and complex. In common 19

Above: A detail from the wall-paintings at St. Savin-sur-Gartempe, near Poitiers, France, dating from around 1100. It shows Abel offering a lamb to God. The tall, elongated figures, expressive face and hands and the fluttering movement of the draperies present a strong contrast to formal Byzantine style.

Above right: A painting of the Madonna and Child by the mid-13th century Italian artist Coppo di Marcovaldo. Although still heavily influenced by Byzantine art in the use of the gold ground and strong outlines, the painting shows a greater realism in the modelling of the limbs and an attempt to create a feeling of depth.

Below: A Jew at the foot of the Cross, from the frescoes in Assisi painted by Cimabue during the second half of the 13th century. Despite their poor state of preservation, these frescoes are remarkable for their dramatic movement and the sense of solid reality conveyed by the stance of the main figures.

with other medieval craftsmen, very few painters left any clue as to their identity. Even where we do know the name of one of them, as in the case of the Egbert psalter, we can rarely establish more than this basic fact.

The wall-paintings which survive from the period can perhaps give a clearer idea of the variety of styles within Romanesque art. The painting of the enthroned Christ in the Spanish church of San Clemente de Tahull, finished around 1125, is an example of the influence of Byzantine art from Italy on the Romanesque style. This branch of Romanesque is exceptionally vigorous and dramatic, with a massive, almost savage quality. The painting is exaggeratedly linear, with each form surrounded by hard lines, and brilliant, richly-contrasting colours are used which are typical of Spanish art.

The French wall paintings at St. Savin are roughly contemporary with this, dating from around 1100. Here the influence of Byzantine art is almost absent; there is a greater sense of movement than in the Spanish painting, with fluttering, fluid draperies and expressive hands and faces. The colours are also much softer and rely very little on strong contrast.

Janet le Caisne

Scala

Giraudon

Above: 'Jacob blessing the sons of Joseph', an illustration from the *Bible Moralisee*. This sumptuous work was executed by a well-practised studio of French illuminators around 1240. Although still highly stylized, the expressive, soulful faces show the beginnings of the Gothic tradition in painting.

Below: Initial from the *Winchester Bible*. It shows an Egyptian smiting a Hebrew (top) and Moses smiting the Egyptian (below). The artist is nicknamed the 'Master of the Leaping Figures', as he loved to represent lively movement. The plaitwork of the 'H' is Anglo-Saxon; the clinging drapery is Byzantine.

The meaning of medieval art

Romanesque art may seem very hard to understand at first—the distortions of the figures may appear arbitrary and meaningless, the absence of perspective disturbing, the colours sometimes too violent for modern taste. Were the artists of this time incapable of painting realistically or did they merely see things differently? The answer is that their art was not concerned with a natural depiction of the world, but with a twofold principle.

Its first aim was to reveal the idea underlying the mere physical details of a scene. For example, the painting of Christ in San Clemente de Tahull was meant to convey the sense of majesty, awe-inspiring and other-worldly, rather than a natural, life-like being. The abstract art of the twentieth century has much in common with this aim.

The second aim is to do with a decorative consciousness which had been so important in barbarian art. The art of the barbarians was often splendid in its effect, but concerned almost exclusively with surface decoration, a concern that continued even after this style was absorbed into Christian art. The eighth-century Irish illuminated Gospel books are a fine example of this fusion. Right through to the High Middle Ages, barbarian art exerted a strong influence. Although Romanesque art became more figurative, illustrating people and events, the love of patterning and the emphasis on line for line's sake remained: hence the improbable posture and drapery patterns of the figures which decorate initial letters in such manuscripts as the late twelfth-century *Winchester Bible*. This stylization was frequently reinforced by the other

stream in Romanesque painting, coming from the East, Byzantium.

Byzantine art did not, of course, remain unchanged during these centuries, but certain characteristics always predominated: it was a spiritual, schematized art with a deliberately repetitive and rigid system governing its subject-matter. It had conventions for the representation of the facial features, the body beneath drapery, and drapery itself (the last frequently called 'damp fold' because of the way that the material seems to cling to the limbs). These were easily copied by Western artists who already favoured a linear style and who found the sophisticated and splendid art of Constantinople an irresistible magnet. Its attraction reached as far afield as England and dominated Italian art until the end of the thirteenth century.

Two great Italian painters

In the art of Coppo di Marcovaldo, working during the mid-thirteenth century, the first movement away from the Italian Byzantine tradition can be traced. Along with a number of his contemporary artists, he had a complete mastery of Byzantine techniques, but tried to move towards something more expressive, and even realistic. Coppo is also one of the earliest artists about whom we have some biographical details. He was trained by Greeks and Venetians, working first in Siena then in Pistoia.

The oldest known work by him is the San Gimignano crucifix, dating from the years 1255-60, which is a direct copy of a Byzantine model. But the mosaics in the Baptistery in Florence, which were designed either by him or by a close follower, show a violent turmoil of naked figures and demons which is totally un-Byzantine in feeling. Coppo's work was to have great influence in Florence and Siena, where it certainly inspired the early style of the greater painter Duccio.

The tentative innovations brought about by Coppo were carried further by Cimabue, who was born in Florence in 1240 and was working in the second half of the thirteenth century. He too was trained by Greek masters, a fact which emphasizes the mingling of Byzantine with Italian art. Certainly Cimabue's style is rooted in the Byzantine tradition, but he makes it even more dramatic, using looser lines and forms than the austerity of Byzantine art would allow. His art stands at the beginning of the conquest of realism and expressiveness.

One of the mediums which Cimabue worked in was *fresco*, used widely in Italy from the end of the thirteenth century. By this method, colours were applied directly on to wet plaster and actually became fused with it. This is one of the most permanent forms of wall painting known.

As Italy slowly moved towards a new artistic expression, a change was beginning to make itself felt in northern Europe also. With the second half of the twelfth century, monastic influence began to wane as the great universities were founded; the increasingly centralized and powerful courts waxed in artistic importance. By the thirteenth century, interest in the human form and in all aspects of secular life and nature, from flowers to falconry, greatly increased. Secular art became more dominant, and the Romanesque age of abstraction and decoration began to give way to Gothic elegance.

15th century German stained glass, showing the prophet Daniel. The austerity of Gothic interiors was warmed and softened by stained glass, and in German church design great prominence was given to windows and vault, in what were called 'hall' churches.

22

The Art of the Craftsman

The greatest patron of the arts throughout the Middle Ages was undoubtedly the Church. It was the age of faith. The Church commissioned great cathedrals and monasteries, luxurious robes, shrines and reliquaries for sacred relics and vessels for the Mass. No other patron, not even the king, could equal its resources. The rebuilding of a cathedral would receive more in donations from the faithful than any tax could raise and the bishops themselves were often immensely wealthy in their own right.

The great Bishop John Grandisson elected to the see of Exeter in 1327, revealed his luxurious tastes in his will. To his cathedral he left silver-gilt statues of St. Peter and St. Paul, a silver-gilt cross resting on four lions standing on a great enamel base, illuminated books, embroidered vestments, altar cloths and other objects. His purple velvet cope—a processional robe—embroidered with figures was left to the Pope, Urban V. Rich laymen also employed craftsmen for religious work—they commissioned chantry chapels, where masses were sung for their souls, and sculpture for their tombs.

Next to the Church, the king was the most important patron of the arts. He had the right to command every kind of craftsman to come and work for him. In 1343 John de Walworth, a London glazier, was ordered to glaze the windows of the King's Chapel and new chambers in the Palace of Westminster. The king's influence could be very great in establishing or fostering a new craft. To bring tapestry weaving to Bohemia, Charles IV of Germany brought a colony of Persian weavers to Prague, while Henry III's marriage to Eleanor of Provence in 1236 probably caused the introduction into England of the Mediterranean art of paving with inlaid tiles.

The nobles, and by the fourteenth and fifteenth centuries the rising class of rich burghers, were also patrons. They hung their houses with tapestries, drank out of silver cups and washed their hands in enamelled dishes. From the fourteenth century onwards the demand for secular plate and jewellery increased enormously and even commoners' wives had large collections. For example, the last will of the sister-in-law of a Glaziers' guild master shows she owned a golden brooch representing the four points of the compass, a pair of amber rosaries, a silk girdle with roses of silver and a silver cup made in Paris.

Serving an apprenticeship

During the Middle Ages nearly all craftsmen from bakers to silversmiths were gradually becoming organized into professional bodies called guilds or companies. By the middle of the fourteenth century these were mostly well established institutions combining charitable and social activities with their role as professional control bodies.

The guilds laid down how the craftsmen should be trained. The Long Masons' Company, for example, stated in 1360 that

Bulloz

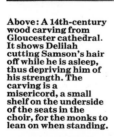

Sonia Halliday

Above: A 14th-century wood carving from Gloucester cathedral. It shows Delilah cutting Samson's hair off while he is asleep, thus depriving him of his strength. The carving is a misericord, a small shelf on the underside of the seats in the choir, for the monks to lean on when standing.

Michael Holford

Left: The kind of tools used by the medieval carpenter can be seen on the craftsman's bench in this 15th-century miniature. Behind him are some 'crocketed' spires which are probably to be used in the making of a choirstall canopy. This is one of four miniatures from a book which has now been lost, showing the Four Conditions of man. In the first he is a hairy savage and in the second a miserable peasant—a sharp contrast with this picture of the industry and prosperity of the carpenter and his wife. The fourth illustration shows him as a nobleman. The artist was Jean Bourdichon, a Frenchman.

Scala

Above: A polychromed (multi-coloured) wooden statuette of the Umbrian school, a style from northern Italy. This Madonna and Child is basically hieratic but there is some attempt to show a human relationship between the Virgin and her son, Christ— her hand holds his foot in a maternal gesture.

Left: A 12th-century crucifix from the church of St. Anna, Pisa. This example is gessoed (the application of a base for painting and gilding) and painted, but some were covered with a sheet of gold. Typically early medieval, the emphasis is on Christ's dignity and mildness rather than his pain.

Far left: A carved angel on the canopy of the choirstall in Chester cathedral. The Chester stalls are some of the finest in the country, with a remarkable range of subjects that show some of the most ingenious ideas of medieval craftsmen, sometimes surprisingly profane.

Scala

Left: An anonymous 14th-century wall painting showing the medieval metal worker at his forge.

Below: The effigy of Geoffrey Plantagenet from Le Mans. It was made sometime between 1151, when he died, and 1160, when we know of the existence of a mausoleum dedicated to **Geoffrey in Le Mans cathedral. It is made out of copper gilt, decorated with *champlevé* enamel of the Limoges type. *Champlevé* enamel involves cutting out a pattern on the copper plate and filling the resulting troughs with glass flux, which becomes enamel when fired. Limoges was famous for this work.**

Above: A reliquary statuette called the Virgin of Jeanne d'Evreux, The round base says that it was given by Queen Jeanne d'Evreux, queen of France, 23rd April, 1339. The virgin is holding a gold fleurs-de-lys enriched with pearls and rubies. The base is enamelled translucently in silver.

Left: This late 12th or early 13th-century German bronze piece was made to contain water for ceremonial occasions, such as mass in the church. This type of pouring vessel was probably derived from middle eastern prototypes, but was very common in northern Germany during this period.

Bottom left: A 14th-century reliquary of St. Sigismund, made in silver gilt and set with jewels. It was made by 'raising up' a flat sheet of silver— the silver-smith moulds the shape of the bust by hammering the sheet. The details are added by 'chasing' with a pointed tool from the outside.

an apprentice should be trained for a period of seven years. Besides the practical training, masters were expected to teach reading and writing and were fined if they failed to do so. On the continent particularly, the apprentice would have to end his tuition by executing a masterpiece. In most German goldsmiths' guilds, he was required to produce a cup, a seal and a ring. If he passed this test, he would be able to take the freedom of the company and become a master himself. Towards the end of the Middle Ages, this system began to break down and in order to restrict the number of masters, the apprentice often had to pay a considerable fee before he was admitted.

Guilds also concerned themselves with craftsmens' working conditions and dealt with the maintenance of professional standards. We read that in 1374 a certain Catherine Duchemin has been making a cloth 'after the manner of Arras' but with linen thread instead of wool. So the warden of the tapestry weavers' guild petitions the court of London aldermen for permission to burn the offending article.

Although the guilds fixed the wages that masters should pay their apprentices and journeymen, the pay the masters themselves received was usually individually negotiated with the employer, the patron.

Patronage was all important to the medieval craftsman. In contrast to the present day, the role of the middleman with a stock of artefacts to be sold retail— such as a modern jeweller's shop—was very limited.

Without middlemen, very little medieval art was produced in quantity, but there were notable exceptions. Large numbers of cheap enamelled copper crosses, reliquaries, basins and so on were produced in the Limoges region of France during the thirteenth century. Many hundreds of alabaster statuettes and altarpieces, sometimes very coarsely carved, were exported from Nottingham, Lincoln and York to other areas of England and the continent in the late fourteenth and fifteenth centuries.

The other great difference between the medieval craftsman and the modern artist is that the craftsman did not regard his own personality as an important part of his work. The artist hardly ever left a signature and was rarely mentioned in the records of the time—a baker, after all, would not dream of signing his loaves. There are isolated and tantalising insights into this almost total anonymity, as when Mathew Paris, himself a painter, took an interest in the decorating of his monastery, and provided a list of some of the painters involved. Generally speaking though, it was thought that there was nothing magical about being a sculptor or a silversmith, but rather, as one guild

Ziolo

Above: The central
section of the rose
window at St. Chapelle,
(right). It shows the
first vision of St. John.
Christ is seated on a
rainbow among seven
candlesticks with a
sword across his face.
The style and imagery of
this glass is derived from
the same 13th-century
manuscript as the
Angers Apocalypse
tapestries. It is possible
that this 15th-century
glass replaced an earlier
window which was
directly based on the
manuscript.

Right: The rose window
at St. Chapelle, Paris.
This is a late form of the
rose window with a
'flamboyant' style of
stone tracery. The glass
shows scenes from *The
Apocalypse*. It was
donated by Charles VIII
(1483-95) and so includes
heraldic glass such as
the gold fleurs-de-lys on
a blue background.

Below: A feathered
angel from an East-
Anglian stained glass
window. The golden
effect is given by the
use of silver stain.

Ziolo

statute said, 'whoever will contribute
both care and concern is able to attain a
capacity for all arts and skills as if by
hereditary right'.

The most prestigious of all the crafts
was that of the goldsmith. He was
frequently a very rich man, in a position
to make loans to kings and nobles which
gave him considerable status. To some
extent he also shared the aura of sanctity
and prestige which surrounded the sacred
vessels and reliquaries he made. Goldsmiths also made and designed coinage,
cut seals and were even sometimes
involved in bronze casting. A great
goldsmith and enameller like Nicholas of
Verdun (c.1180 -c.1230) was in demand all
over Europe: executing a altarpiece in
Klosterneuberg, Vienna, finishing a
shrine in Tournai, Belgium and then

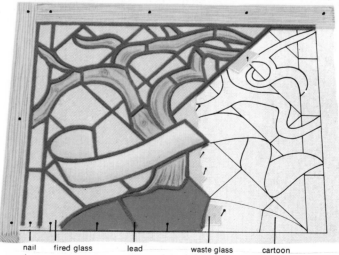

nail   fired glass   lead   waste glass   cartoon

**Above: The design of a
stained-glass window**
was first drawn out on
a piece of paper, called
the cartoon. The shapes
of the individual
pieces were then traced
onto the glass and the
glass cut. Details were
painted on with the
brown, enamel stain
which was fixed by low-
temperature firing in
quick lime. The glass

was reassembled on the
cartoon and joined
by pieces of lead
soldered together. The
lead was cast with an
H-shaped cross-section
and a lathekin (top
right) was run up and
down the core and the
flanges to make them
smooth. The lead was
cut to length with a
cutting knife, which
avoided distorting the

lead. The pieces of
glass were then slotted
between the flanges of
the lead by tapping
them with the end of
the stopping knife. As
the window was built
up, the pieces were
held in place by nails
with waste glass placed
to protect the lead.
Cement or putty was
used to fix the glass
in place.

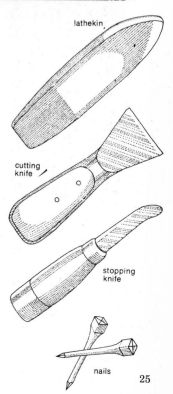

lathekin

cutting
knife

stopping
knife

nails

25

Above and below: Two illustrations of the development of the loom. By the 13th century the horizontal frame had been perfected in Europe and this allowed the frames to be made wider (below). The simple loom (above) is from the 13th century, while the one below is 14th-century.

Above: A scene from the famous Anger Apocalypse tapestries. Commissioned by Louis I of Anjou some time after 1373, the idea may have come from an illustrated copy of *The Apocalypse* he borrowed from his brother, King Charles V. The series of tapestries are on blue and red backgrounds.

Above: A detail from *La Dame a l'Unicorne* one of a series of hangings in the Cluny Museum, Paris. They are thought to illustrate the five senses. This one represents sight, with the unicorn looking at itself in the mirror. The tapestries probably date from 1513 and conform to a general type of weaving known as 'mille fleurs', characterized by few figures and simple backgrounds in which the decorative motifs are freely repeated.

Right: A fine tapestry woven in about 1460 in Flanders, the great centre of weaving in the 15th century. It probably shows Charles d'Orleans and Marie de Clives.

Left: A panel from an English orphrey from the first half of the 15th century. An orphrey is a decorative band on priestly robes. By the 15th century the great heyday of English embroidery had passed, and elaborate work was generally confined to the orphreys. The panel shows St. Lawrence.

Right: A scene of the crucifixion from an early 14th-century embroidered burse. A burse is the stiff square envelope which carries the cloth on which the communion vessels are placed. This shows the standard imagery for the crucifixion with the Virgin and St. John on either side.

Left and Below: Another magnificent piece of English embroidery: the cope (a cloak worn on ceremonial occasions) of Pope Pius II. The whole cope is embroidered with scenes from the lives of St. Margaret, the Virgin and St. Catherine. The detail below shows the birth of Christ and the coronation of the Virgin. The cope is sewn in silver and silver-gilt thread and coloured silks on linen. It was once enriched with a great number of pearls, most of which have now been lost. Made in England c. 1325, it was taken to Italy as a gift to Pope Pius about 100 years later.

making the great reliquary of the Three Kings in Cologne. His work, like that of many silversmiths, is highly sculptural, illustrating the close connection between his art and the mason's.

There is some doubt as to how some work was divided between the different trades. Clearly some of the stone sculpture was done by masons who were often called 'imagers'. Whether this means that the same man who carved decorations on pillars would carve the statues on the cathedral facade is not certain. Choirstalls seem to have been designed by the mason in charge of the building programme, but executed by carpenters. Some craftsmen, towards the end of the Middle Ages, seem to have worked in both wood and stone, but specialized 'kervers' also emerged who concentrated on wooden sculpture.

It is not clear how many carpenters had permanent workshops and how many simply travelled around carrying their tools with them. Rather more is known about the glaziers. They generally had workshops in the larger towns. Their work was transported by water or overland to the church which had commissioned it. In England the great centres of production were London, York, Norwich, Bristol and Oxford.

Stained glass is in fact coloured glass, held together by lead. The only actual stain used was the brownish-black enamel which was used for the finer details. In the fourteenth century 'silver stain' was also introduced which gave a golden colour. Only plain glass was made in England until the fifteenth century so coloured glass was imported.

Glaziers were by no means above using a design more than once. The Parker window at York, for instance has a picture of St. William which is from the same 'cartoon' as St. Nicholas in the Wolveden window. This repetition does not detract from the windows because their effectiveness depends more on the inter-relationship of the various shapes and colours than upon any single detail.

The one craft which was not closely tied to the Church was tapestry weaving. The growing wealth of the laity throughout the fourteenth-century produced a desire for comfort, and these woollen wall-hangings became the most important part of a room's furnishings. Tapestries were sold in what was called a 'chamber' which comprised a canopy, a headboard, a coverlet, and six curtains or wall tapestries. The craft was established in England by Henry III's reign (1216 72), but most tapestries seem to have been imported from Flanders. This was such a great weaving centre that Arras, the name of the main town, became another word for tapestry. The local duke, Philip the Bold, owned so many hangings that he had to have a special stone building put up in Arras to house them all.

Because the hangings were often for palaces and castles, their subject matter was often not religious. They showed episodes from the great tales of the time like the *Roman de la Rose*. By the fourteenth century there were numerous tapestry workers in England, many attracted from Flanders by the Statute of York—a law intended to stimulate the craft. In 1331, the tapestry weavers of London received their statute from the King, but the craft never really took root in England as it did in Flanders.

Medieval Painting

Although the art produced between the thirteenth and fifteenth centuries was mostly Gothic in style, essentially this is a transitional period for the visual arts. During these centuries the aims of artists underwent a radical shift away from the rigid formulas imposed on them by the Romanesque style towards a realistic representation of the world and a desire to master a three-dimensional effect in painting.

The art of this period, however varied in style, was unified by a few common factors. The most important was that art still served a primarily religious function, as it had done since early Christian times. Most painting was still of religious subjects and was designed for religious settings. The majority of frescoes were still in churches and panel paintings, still using subject matter drawn from the Old and New Testaments and the Calendar of Saints, were used to decorate altars. Most illuminated books, too, were prayer books.

But increasingly, aspects of secular life were interwoven with the religious. Quaint and amusing figures or 'drolleries' were often shown scampering along the margins of psalters. Scenes concerned with the elegance and finery of court life were used to decorate the calendar of the Duke of Berry's Book of Hours. In their different ways, these secular details reveal a desire to express all types of emotion, not merely the religious, and to celebrate realistically the variety of contemporary life. Among artists the belief was growing that all activities were in the sight of God and were part of his scheme of things. They were all therefore worth recording.

The second unifying principle was the continuing importance of decorative effect. The backgrounds of paintings were often of gold, on which designs were imprinted with heated tools, a process known as 'tooling'. Sometimes multi-coloured diapering or tessellation (patterns of regular diamond shapes or checks) might be used to fill in the background.

The feeling for elegant design was satisfied by curving draperies and the sway of the human body. No longer were bodies depicted as stiff and puppet-like; limbs and movements were allowed greater fluidity.

Added to these factors was the importance of architectural design. The Gothic painter often framed his pictures with an arch through which the viewer must look as if through a window. Including architectural elements in a painting came to be just as necessary as the niche and canopy framing a Gothic sculpture.

Art's new patrons

In many ways, artistic changes during the high and late Middle Ages were brought about by rapidly changing social conditions. Trade was increasing and towns and cities associated with trade flourished. As a result, not only were the courts more affluent, but richer towns-people and merchants were able to purchase their own works of art. By the

Bodleian Library

Below left: *The Magdalen Reading* (c.1390) by the Flemish artist Rogier van de Weyden. She sits in a contemporary interior with a glimpse of landscape beyond. The folds of her garment are accurately observed and the gold thread in her dress and the light shining through the amber rosary show great technical mastery.

Below: *The Wilton Diptych*, unique of its kind in England. It shows Richard II presented by his patron saints to the Virgin and Child in paradise. The decorative tooled gold ground, softly curved drapery, small feminine features and subtle colours typify the International style which dominated European art around 1400.

National Gallery

National Gallery

Left and below: Two crucifixions that illustrate a development in technique. The early 13th-century *Amesbury Psalter* (left) captures a degree of humanity which the painter of the early 14th-century *Robert de Lisle Psalter* (below) has distorted to increase the effect of emotional intensity, as in the contorted Christ.

The *Amesbury Psalter* is drawn with hard clear lines that emphasize the fluttering drapery, while the later artist has used subtle shadowing to create more fluid drapery. Four different rich textures create an intensely decorative background and the figures are framed like elements in a stained glass window.

Right: 'December', a page from a book of hours painted c.1415 for the Duke of Berry. A book of hours contains the prayers to be read at the various divisions of the day. The artists were the Limbourg brothers. This painting shows their superb mastery of space, with the forest receding rapidly to the tall castles on the horizon.

early fifteenth century every burgher would expect to have his own Book of Hours.

Towns themselves were beginning to patronize the arts. The town council of Siena, for example, commissioned in 1308 a great altarpiece by the Italian master Duccio. It was finished three years later and, to the sound of trumpets and bells and accompanied by the dignitaries of the town and church, it was solemnly carried from the artist's studio to the cathedral where it was placed on the high altar. This was religious art as an expression of civic pride, but civic pride also began to be expressed by purely secular works.

Books were sought after and the most popular, those of courtly love like the *Roman de la Rose*, and the works of the classical writers Terence and Ovid, were illuminated. Studios grew larger as a result of the greater demand for art and were usually grouped in the major centres of government or trade. Altogether, life in many towns in the fourteenth century was becoming more affluent, leisured and refined.

To the new type of patron, anxious to display his wealth and high position in society, the most important aspects of art were the value of the materials used, the quantity of paintings owned and the technical virtuosity they revealed. These concerns are shown in the following letter sent from Avignon to Florence by a merchant acting on behalf of a rich patron: 'Dispatch a panel of Our Lady on a background of fine gold . . . . making a fine show with good and handsome figures, by the best painter and with many figures. Let there be in the centre Our Lord on the cross, or Our Lady, whomsoever you find—I care not so that the figures be handsome and large, the best and finest you can purvey and the cost no more than five and a half florins.'

From this it is clear that the idea of an artist acting on his inspiration and painting subjects to please himself is unheard of during this period. Not until the sixteenth century did this view of the artist gain acceptance. The emphasis was on the painting rather than the artist who, from Romanesque times, was regarded as being rather lowly in the hierarchy of craftsmen—much lower, for example, than the goldsmith.

With the exception of some Italian art, most paintings remained unsigned. Usually paintings are attributed to a certain school rather than to individual painters. Sometimes, if a master's work

became famous, his workshop would continue to paint in his style after his death. But even such masters often remained anonymous, as for example the great Master of Flemalle, teacher of the Flemish painter Rogier van der Weyden, who was only recently identified as Robert Campin.

The status of the artist was, however, changing gradually. In the Middle Ages the great majority were clerics; by the end of the period most were laymen. Some artists who achieved fame were showered with favours by the nobility. The Limbourg brothers, for example, who illuminated the Duke of Berry's Book of Hours, were appreciated so much that the Duke appointed them gentlemen of his bedchamber. Giotto, the great Italian painter living from about 1267 to 1337, was so much admired by the city fathers that he was appointed head of the cathedral works in Florence and city architect. These examples are not typical of all painters, but such recognition would never have occurred in the earlier Middle Ages.

It is impossible to trace a smooth line of development towards realism in the art of these centuries. Innovations made in some parts of Europe might not be accepted by other countries for some time, if at all. Although by the turn of the thirteenth century a few Italian artists had made advances which were later to be recognized as the beginnings of a new age of European art, their ideas were not fully adopted until much later.

Cimabue's work had begun to show some attempts at realism, but in the paintings of the Sienese artist Duccio, who lived from 1255 to 1318, there is a greater flexibility of style and emotional range. His sensitive approach is revealed in the supple movements of his figures, the suggestion of depth and shade and the rich colour range he uses. The decorative element remains in his invariable use of gold as a background, but in his painting, seen at its height in the 'Maesta' altarpiece, a whole new expressive and dramatic range is opened up.

Giotto's break with tradition

A new dramatic quality is uppermost in the frescoes of the most famous of early Italian painters, Giotto. Giotto is to Italian painting what Chaucer is to English literature—a 'father-figure' and a constant source of inspiration. The enormous advance he makes in mastering the effect of space, and the solidity of his figures, is matched by the emotional power

Above: Delightful illustrations from an Italian treatise on falconry, c.1260. They show exceptional attention to detail. Realistic traits began to appear elsewhere, such as the accurately observed birds and animals that decorate the margins of books produced by the East Anglian school.

Below: *Meeting between Joachim and Anna* by Giotto, often regarded as the father of modern European painting. This is part of the great fresco cycle in the Arena Chapel, Padua, painted between 1305 and 1310. It shows his skill at suggesting real substance in his figures and the attempt to show recession in space in the treatment of the gateway.

his figures display. The break with earlier styles is seen most clearly here—Giotto wants to make his figures as human as possible, so that we should feel and sympathise with them. In his great cycle of frescoes in the Arena chapel in Padua, executed between 1305 and 1310, the whole drama of the life of Christ is expressed solely by human beings, their gestures and facial expressions. With his use of simple, uncluttered forms Giotto achieves an effect of monumentality which is truly memorable.

The influence of such revolutionary changes was not, however, felt immediately. Until the end of the fourteenth century, Gothic painting in the rest of Europe absorbed only some aspects of the Italian advances, fusing these with its own stylized and decorative tradition. From this fusion an elegant and sophisticated manner of painting evolved, having as its characteristics a softness of colouring and gentleness of facial expression, flowing lines and elongated, curving bodies. This refined, delicate style of art appealed particularly to courtly taste. Many books were illuminated in this style, with charmingly decorated margins and lively scenes at the base of the page. Through trade connections, through the

dynastic connections of European royalty and through the flow of artists and works of art from country to country, the style spread widely. Because of this, it became known as the International style. It was practised in centres as far flung as London, Avignon, the Rhineland and even Bohemia.

In northern Europe the International style remained static during the second half of the fourteenth century. Significantly, the Limbourg brothers, who worked at the Burgundian court in France and were unusually realistic for French artists in their subject matter and perspective effects, had no immediate followers. The art of the French court was too entrenched in stylization to respond.

In the early fifteenth century certain artists in Italy began to make progress towards greater realism. Here, a striving after realism can be seen in the production of certain treatises which demanded realistic and accurate illustrations for the book to be of use to the reader. For example, during the fourteenth century a number of illustrated editions of a treatise on hygiene written by a man named Albukasem were produced. These had to accurately depict plants so that they might be recognized easily and a tradition grew up of representing them in the context of their landscape. This was the birth of realistic landscape painting and probably inspired the Limbourg brothers' remarkable landscapes in their *Book of Hours*.

Another trend towards realism grew up in a number of Books of Hours and psalters executed for the townspeople of Haarlem and Utrecht. These places were far enough from courts to be unaffected by the style they adopted. What these people wanted was an art reflecting their comfortable standard of living. These book illustrations consisted not of elaborate decorations in gold leaf but often of mere pen sketches with a colour wash, making up for a lack of fine materials with plenty of homely details. This style of faithful depiction of everyday life was adopted by the great painter Rogier van der Weyden who lived from about 1400 to 1464. His painting has some of the precision of colour and form found in the work of his famous contemporary Jan van Eyck but, compared with van Eyck, Rogier is still Gothic in his use of line, stylization and traditional religious symbolism. Nevertheless, his use of homely detail was very influential, contributing to the development of Flemish realism.

National Gallery

Above left: *Virgin and Child* by Duccio, who worked in Siena in the early 14th century. His great achievement was to combine a more flexible style and wider emotional range with the Byzantine tradition. His figures are subtly shaded but lack the solidity of Giotto's. The crimson, blue and black colour combination are typical of Duccio.

Left: Fresco by Simone Martini, dated 1328, showing a victorious general with the castles he has captured. One of the earliest examples of realistic landscape in Western art, documents show that Simone studied one of the castles from life. The encampment on the right has many closely observed details, including tent pegs.

Scala

31

Romanesque Architecture

The term 'Romanesque' was invented in the nineteenth century to describe the architecture of the early Middle Ages that was derived from Ancient Roman models.

At the start of the Romanesque period, in the early eleventh century, western Europe was licking its wounds after a succession of violent invasions by Norsemen, Saracens and Magyars. On the whole it was more peaceful than at any time during the previous 200 years.

With peace came an economic revival and an energetic rebirth of culture, expressed in a great upsurge of church building. As one contemporary chronicler Raóul Glaber wrote: 'Each · Christian community resolved to build sanctuaries more sumptuous than those of its neighbours, as if the world, anxious to cast away its rags, wished to clothe itself in a white robe of churches.'

It is hardly surprising that all the energy and invention of medieval builders should have been channelled into religious architecture. This was an 'age of faith' when Christianity was the exclusive and compulsory religion of European society. The Roman church was a powerful, unifying cultural force in the West. Its sacraments dominated the lives of every member of society from birth to death and its organization was growing in strength and self-confidence.

An energetic church reform movement began in the Benedictine monastery at Cluny in eastern France, in the eleventh century, and eventually involved over 2,000 monasteries throughout western Europe. The monasteries were among the chief patrons of architecture, and the Clunaic emphasis on elaborate and magnificent ceremonial encouraged the development of all the more ornate forms of church art, including architecture on the grand scale.

The intimate links between the church and secular wealth on a local level were a major factor in encouraging church building. Wealthy feudal families expressed their respectability and piety by building churches rather than fine residences for themselves. Partly this was regarded as a financial investment—many younger sons of noble families made profitable careers in the church and monastic orders. But equally it was regarded as a kind of spiritual insurance policy. People from every station in life believed there was a direct relationship between the material honour offered to God and his saints in this world and the chance of reward in the next.

In sheer size and number Romanesque churches stand apart from those of the preceding centuries, although the ordinary parish church was not built in permanent materials before the early twelfth century. It seems likely that the ecclesiastical establishments and lay rulers whose estates contained parish churches only turned their attention to this task when the major religious centres had acquired suitably large and ambitious buildings. Often the church or cathedral was the only stone building for miles around, dominating an area in both real and symbolic terms. Its steeple towers were a landmark to travellers, its bells tolled the hours that marked the events of daily life.

The masons: architects and artists

The skill and imagination of the medieval builders were stretched to the utmost in the task of creating a suitable house for God. The chroniclers of the period, who were nearly all churchmen, tended to give credit for buildings and works of art to the abbots and bishops who commissioned them rather than to the artists who created them. For this reason surprisingly little is known about the eleventh and twelfth century artists, and even the names of the great majority are lost.

Master masons performed most of the same duties as architects today, but unlike architects they were promoted from the ranks of the working masons and not trained purely as designers.

The working masons were divided into 'cutters', who dressed blocks of stone and carved architectural features, and 'setters' who actually put up the building. In the eleventh century it was generally the cutters who were responsible for decorative sculpture, but the great carved doorways of the early twelfth century were certainly the work of skilled specialists.

The Romanesque mason's knowledge of mathematics was very limited by modern standards. The translation of the Greek writer Euclid in the early eleventh century helped to promote a better knowledge of geometry, but the calculation of loads and thrusts seems to have been unknown before the fifteenth century and Romanesque masons must have learnt to gauge the amount of support needed for stone vaults purely by trial and error. Errors there certainly were, as when the vaults in the nave at Cluny crashed in 1125.

The masons of western Europe built on one major tradition which had come down from the early Christian period as the basic form for church architecture in the West. This was the basilica—originally the Roman assembly hall—a spacious rectangular building with columned aisles. The typical basilica-type church of the eighth and ninth centuries had a timber roof, wide internal span, thin walls and an upper range of windows called a 'clearstorey'.

The natural move to dignify and improve on this type of structure was to construct a roof of stone vaults. This development made sense because valuable relics needed protection from the danger

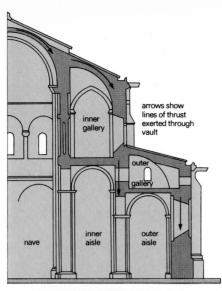

arrows show lines of thrust exerted through vault

inner gallery

outer gallery

nave

inner aisle

inner aisle

outer aisle

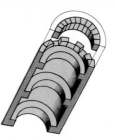

Rapho

Above: Tunnel or barrel vault. This was the simplest kind of vault used in the Romanesque period, strengthened with transverse arches.

Right: The barrel vault in the nave at St. Sernin. The transverse arches join with the half-shafts on the walls to create a powerful rythmical effect.

Above: Groin vault— the other major type of Romanesque vault. Basically it consists of two tunnel vaults at right angles. The 'groins' are the sharp edges produced along the lines where the two tunnels intersect. Over square bays, as above, the groins look like straight diagonal lines from below.

Jean Roubier

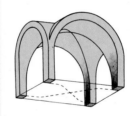

Above: The nave of a medieval church was usually planned as a series of oblong bays. Placing a groin vault over an oblong, instead of a square, produces a twisting curve in the groin. A groin vault, however, with its four sections, gives a better distribution of thrusts than a tunnel vault.

Above: St. Nectaire in the Auvergne—simple, harmonious and solid. This view from the south-east shows the build-up of apse, ambulatory and radiating chapels that is characteristic of French Romanesque.

Right: Plan of St. Sernin at Toulouse shows the layout of a pilgrimage church. The basic cross-shape and semi-circular apse at the alter end go back to the basilica of early Christian times. The extension of side-aisles around the whole of the church is a special feature designed to allow pilgrims to circulate.

Top right: The half cross-section of the nave shows how the thrust of the high barrel vault was led outwards and down by the half-tunnel vaults over the galleries.

Centre right: Interior of Paray-le-Monial shows the splendid effect created within the apse—typical of the Romanesque churches of Burgundy.

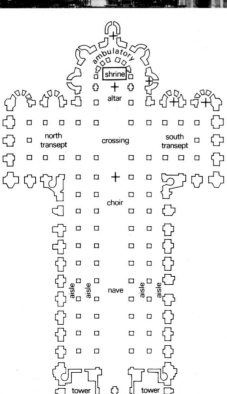

ambulatory
shrine
altar

north transept

crossing

south transept

choir

aisle aisle nave aisle aisle

tower

tower

Above: The rib vault was a solution to the problem of oblong groin vaults. The groins were replaced by thin arches, or ribs, of regular curvature. This method originated with Norman masons in England in the late 11th century, and was used throughout the Gothic period of the later Middle Ages.

of fire from a wooden roof. But the vault also had an immense symbolic significance in church architecture, symbolizing the vault of heaven.

The most perfect vault was the sphere-shaped dome, but domes were extremely difficult to fit above the rectangular shape of the basilican church. Consequently, the masons in the West turned to more suitable Roman models. The two types of vault they copied were the barrel, or tunnel, vault, and the groin vault.

Stone-vaulted churches of the period known as 'first Romanesque' originated in North Italy in the mid-tenth century and quickly spread north and west to Catalonia, the valleys of the Saone and Rhone, Switzerland and Germany. Tunnel vaults, being simpler to construct, were most common. This heavy, rubble-built vaulting (made from blocks of rough, unhewn stone) created low proportions, massive walls and supports and small windows. Clearstoreys were very rare.

In France, masons produced their own development of the Romanesque style, an adaptation to current religious and social needs. One of the earliest and most impressive of these French buildings is the series of churches built along the pilgrimage routes to Compostella in Spain. Compostella was the site of the tomb of St. James (Santiago)—one of the most popular alternatives to far-away Rome and Jerusalem as an object of pilgrimage. The gifts of pilgrims helped to pay for many large churches, as were considered fitting to house valuable holy relics.

The earliest of the series on the route to Compostella, St. Martin at Tours, begun in 997 AD, has been destroyed, but later churches at Conques, Toulouse and Compostella are all intact and remarkably similar in design. They combine the tall proportions of the basilican churches with the barrel vaults of the first Romanesque tradition. The clearstorey was omitted, which meant the naves were lit indirectly via the stone vaulted galleries and aisles. The simple columns of the basilicas were replaced by stouter masonry supports called piers.

The most original feature of the pilgrimage churches was directly linked to their function as shrines for important religious relics. The eastern end of the church—housing the high altar and the tomb of the saint—consisted of a semi-circular recess called an apse. This had been a traditional feature since early Christian times. Now, in the pilgrimage churches, the side-aisles were extended around the apse, forming a semi-circular corridor 33

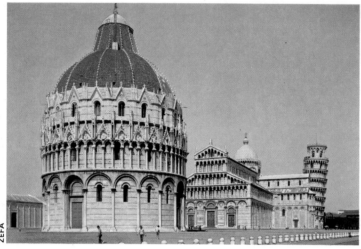

German and Italian architecture of the Romanesque period was notably different from the French.
Above: Speyer cathedral, begun in 1020, is a typical German 'double-ended' church, with towers flanking the apse and transepts at each end. The decorative rows of miniature arches were one of the hallmarks of Romanesque style throughout Europe.

Right: In contrast, the Pisa cathedral complex has a long, hangar-like basilica, with the famous leaning tower and a domed baptistery standing separately. Coloured marble and spectacular tiers of arcading decorate the exterior.

Top and above: Two outstanding examples of Norman architecture in England. The nave at Ely cathedral (top) shows the typical Norman wall-passage above the ground-storey arcade. In this case the roof of the nave is made of wood which is decorated with 19th century paintings. In contrast, the masons at Durham (above) experimented with rib-vaulting in the nave and choir—one of the oldest examples of this. The 'cushion' capitals at the top of the columns are almost universal in English Romanesque—they come from Germany and the Low Countries. The zig-zag carving on the columns was a popular Norman decoration.

called an ambulatory. The purpose of this arrangement was to enable pilgrims to circulate behind the altar and see the shrine of pilgrimage without interrupting services in the central area of the choir.

Not all eleventh century masons were satisfied with the formula evolved in the pilgrimage churches. The omission of the clearstorey was a departure from long-established tradition, and had the practical disadvantage of darkening the nave. The designer of the church of St. Etienne at Nevers, in north-west Burgundy, was bold enough to place a tunnel vault over a clearstorey containing large windows.

The culmination of this line of development, and of the whole Burgundian Romanesque school, was the great abbey church of Cluny, begun in the closing years of the eleventh century but tragically demolished after the French revolution. The 60 m (200 ft) long original church was replaced by a building which in its final form was rather over 180 m (600 ft) long. Its impressive internal height and complexity of double aisles, double transepts, fifteen larger chapels, and six large towers made Cluny a remarkable and imposing building. Its arcades and vault had pointed arches, the first large-scale use of this form in Europe.

The Normans come to England

From the middle years of the eleventh century the most original and advanced churches in northern France were built in Normandy. Through the dynamic and expansionist policies of the feudal nobility of Normandy, this architectural influence spread as far afield as England and Sicily. The abbey church of St. Etienne at Caen—begun by William the Conqueror—illustrates the characteristics of mature Norman style. It has three storeys of which the middle one is a gallery almost as tall as the arcades beneath. In front of the clearstorey windows and within the wall, runs a continuous passage, partly opened out towards the nave as a sort of arcaded verandah. These wall passages became a special feature of Norman architecture. They had no really important use, but were valued purely for the effect of richness and transparency they gave to the upper sections of an interior.

A unique opportunity was given to the Norman masons with Duke William's conquest of England in 1066. By the end of the century almost every cathedral and major abbey in England had replaced, or was in the process of replacing, its small and unambitious Anglo-Saxon structures by a magnificent new church on an enor-

Left: The Dream of the Magi—warned by an angel to avoid King Herod. This sculpted capital from Autun cathedral (c.1125) shows the narrative clarity and disciplined use of the shape of the masonry that is typical of Gislebertus, the sculptor who signed his name on the west portal at Autun.

Left and below: More Gislebertus sculpture at Autun. The right-hand section of the tympanum (left) shows the weighing of souls and the torments of the Damned in Hell. The elongated figures, almost dance-like postures and mastery of emotion show Gislebertus at his most intense. As usual in medieval art the Damned provide scope for more graphic interpretations than the Blessed (below). This freize-like arrangement of figures shows an angel helping resurrected souls from their tombs and the Blessed giving thanks to the great figure of Christ the Judge, situated above, in the centre of the tympanum.

Above and top right: Details of sculpture from the church at Conques. Isaiah holds a tree, an allusion to his prophecy that a branch (Christ) would spring forth from the tree of Jesse. The group of figures represents the Blessed—the Virgin on the right, Peter, next to her, carries his key.

Right: The south portal of Moissac abbey—a splendid example of the complex harmony of Romanesque sculpture. Christ is surrounded by symbols of the evangelists, angels and the 24 elders of the Apocalypse. The central pillars are composed of lions standing one over the other. Statues of Peter and Paul flank the doors.

French Romanesque capital sculpture: at Perrecy-les-Forges (above) by a sculptor who had obviously never seen an elephant; at Vezelay (left) showing a prophet pouring the grain of the Old Law into the mystical mill while St. Paul grinds the pure flour of the New Law; at Moissac (below) in the cloisters.

mous scale. The rate of construction was sometimes very rapid: Canterbury cathedral, for example, was all but finished in about eight years.

The most momentous invention of the Anglo-Norman builders was rib vaulting. The earliest example of this new type of vault dates from 1093 and is found in the choir of Durham cathedral. Pairs of slender arches or ribs, diagonally crossed, provided a framework between which the compartments of the vault could be fitted afterwards. This meant that the curved scaffolding on which vaults were built (called centering) was needed only for the ribs, not for the whole vault as in groin vaults. Rib vaults were usually constructed from carefully shaped pieces of stone rather than rubble embedded in mortar.

Masons working in the Paris region in the mid-twelfth century made rib vaulting more flexible by combining it with pointed arches (whose heights were not so determined by their span) and in the process invented the Gothic style.

At the beginning of the eleventh century large-scale sculpture in stone hardly existed—a century later some half-dozen French churches could boast enormous, richly-sculpted portals which rank among the greatest masterpieces of medieval art. The central feature of these sculptures is a great semi-circular block (the tympanum) enclosing a large seated figure of Christ, usually as part of a scene of the Last Judgement or an Apocalyptic Vision. The compelling force of these compositions must have been even greater when they retained their original brilliant colouring and gilding. The bare stonework of so many Romanesque interiors has little to do with the original intentions of their builders. The walls of medieval churches were invariably painted, whether with simple geometric patterns or with cycles of religious subjects.

Yet stepping inside a Norman or Romanesque church today can still recreate, at least in part, the impact of these impressive interiors on medieval man: the sense of massive solidity and strength, permanent and transcendental; a brilliantly-lit altar relieving the mysterious gloom; ascending storeys topped by seemingly miraculous vaults, towering above like the vault of heaven itself. It was a perfect expression of the image of Christ's kingdom in the medieval mind and, for the great majority of medieval citizens and peasants, their one glimpse of the imaginative world of art and beauty. 35

Gothic Architecture

In more than 3,000 years of European civilization, the 300 years of Gothic architecture were an exceptional period, the most vividly and completely different. The term 'Gothic' is used to describe a particular style of architecture which was current in western Europe between the twelfth and the fifteenth centuries. It was originally used to mean 'not classical' and, in contrast to the monumental simplicity of the Romanesque architecture which preceded Gothic and the classical proportions of the Renaissance period which followed, it does seem very different in spirit.

In is a strange, alien, magical style and, though it shares with Romanesque art the single aim of glorifying God, its approach is profoundly different. In place of the austerity and solidity of Romanesque, Gothic buildings seem fragile structures. The feeling of aspiration, of soaring heavenwards, is conveyed in each feature of the Gothic church, in its lightness, airiness, its slender framework, delicate-seeming decoration and the vertical line of the pointed arch.

Gothic cathedrals reflect exactly the intense, and often joyous, faith that inspired them. For people at that time the cathedral represented the whole of life, both here on earth and after death. Everything was seen in the light of religion—even much of the money earned in trade was given to the churches and monasteries to secure for the donor a fine tomb and, hopefully, a place in heaven.

The spread of Gothic architecture is confined almost exclusively to northern Europe. In some parts of Spain and Italy Gothic ideas were adopted in a modified form and used far less extensively than in France, England and Germany.

The earliest buildings recognizably Gothic were built in the 'Isle de France', that is the area around Paris which came under the immediate sway of the kings of France in the days before the nation as a unified state existed. Here the great cathedrals of Reims, Amiens, Chartres, Paris, Rouen, and Beauvais took shape— all begun in the twelfth century and still the outstanding monuments of Gothic architecture. The style spread quite rapidly in the next half century to England

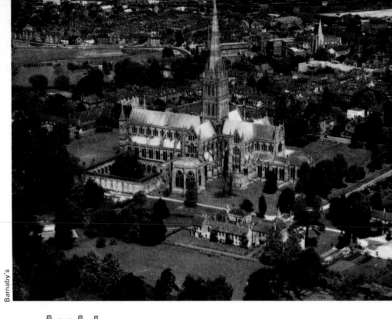

These aerial views of Salisbury cathedral (right) and Chartres (extreme right) show the huge scale of Gothic architecture. Chartres still dwarfs the modern buildings which now surround it. Salisbury has a typical English cathedral close with lawn, trees, and houses for the clergy. Its spire, 123 m (404 ft), is the highest in England. Chartres is very lofty, supported by flying buttresses which are clearly visible. Its rounded apse, typical of the French style, differs from the square English east end. The ground plans (below) show the complexity of Salisbury with its cloisters and chapter-house, in contrast to the compact design of Chartres.

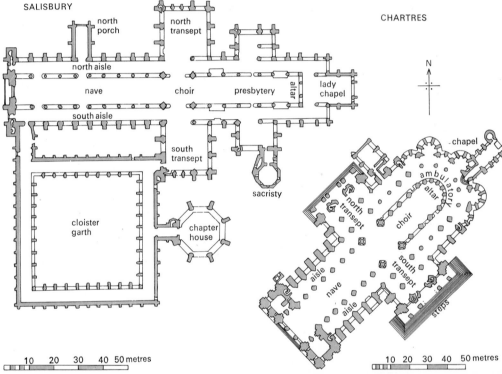

SALISBURY
CHARTRES

Below: In contrast to the fairly plain columns of Beauvais the English cathedral of Wells has clustering decoration on its sturdy arches. Wells is a much broader, less lofty building. The supporting arches added to the crossing in 1338, forming a curved 'X' shape across the nave, are unique to this cathedral.

Right: The elegant interior of the French cathedral of Beauvais shows Gothic building at its most ambitious, achieving an awe-inspiring height and grace. The choir, unlike other parts, did not collapse. Beyond, the rounded apse provides a perfect setting for slender stained-glass windows.

Michael Holford

Barnaby's

Michael Holford

Aerofilms

and to northern and central Germany.

It was during the reign of Henry II, from 1154 to 1189, that the Gothic style gained acceptance in England. Already the ruler of England, Henry gained control of over half of France through his marriage; consequently the two countries came more and more to share a common culture. Ideas on art, music and architecture flowed freely from France to England. Most masons from France worked in England (as at Canterbury and Westminster) and occasionally the reverse, no doubt, occurred.

Gothic architecture is characterized by pointed arches. In roof-vaulting, in windows and in the arcades of columns stretching the length of the church, pointed arches were used.

The simplest form of arch is semicircular, as used in Roman and in Romanesque architecture. But the use of round arches limits the plans of buildings to multiples of square and semicircular bays. As the Romanesque masons discovered, the vaulting of oblong compartments dictated the use of pointed arches—that is arches drawn with the compass point fixed in two or more places. For centuries Moslems had recognized the greater flexibility of arches whose height was not dictated by their width as is the case with the semicircular arch.

In western Europe the great 'breakthrough' which led to the creation of the cathedrals of the Isle de France is usually attributed to Abbot Suger. He organized the rebuilding of the choir roof of the Benedictine abbey at St. Denis near Paris in 1144. However, his masons probably knew of the pointed arch vaults built about 20 years earlier over the ambulatory at Morienval, Oise.

Nearly all of Gothic building in stone, except for the massive castles, was ecclesiastical. The churchmen and their rich patrons were always trying to increase the size, the height, the length, the grandeur of their buildings. The masons were concerned with developing the internal logic of Gothic architecture: making the vaulting ever more light and intricate, spinning webs of stone ribs in more complex patterns. So as the naves of churches became higher and wider, the roofs naturally became heavier and more massive, but the vaults supporting them amazingly grew more delicate—the airy 'vault of heaven' to which the builders aspired. The ribs met in 'stars', carved and gilded bosses, the flat stone between was painted, mostly in blue and red—very different from the massive cave-like barrel vaults of early churches.

The secret of Gothic construction

The development of Gothic towards greater height and slenderness of columns and stone walls between windows was made possible by one simple realization, which is the key to the understanding of Gothic construction. The weight of the stone roofs and vaults operated downwards by the force of gravity and also sideways through the outwards thrust of the arches. Roman and Byzantine builders had dealt with these thrusts by building massive walls, but the Gothic masons transmitted these forces to the ground by constructing other walls or 'buttresses' at right angles to the outside walls of the church, at points corresponding to the places where the ribs of the vaulting met inside the building. These buttresses, 37

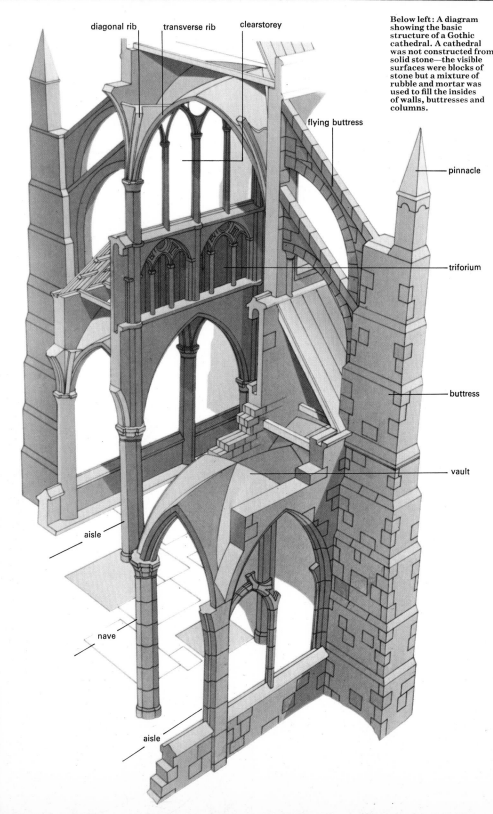

Below left: A diagram showing the basic structure of a Gothic cathedral. A cathedral was not constructed from solid stone—the visible surfaces were blocks of stone but a mixture of rubble and mortar was used to fill the insides of walls, buttresses and columns.

diagonal rib · transverse rib · clearstorey · flying buttress · pinnacle · triforium · buttress · vault · aisle · nave · aisle

Early English 1190-1245

Geometrical decorated 1245-1315

Curvilinear decorated 1315-1360

Perpendicular 1360-1550

Left: Different styles of English window tracery during the Gothic period.

Right and bottom: The contrast in the west face of an English and a French cathedral. The facade of Reims (right) creates a sense of vertical thrust. In comparison, the effect of Wells (below) is squat. Reims has boldly projecting porches, with sculpture standing almost free of the walls, and deep shadowing behind the arcades. The beautiful rose windows lend delicacy to the building. Wells is also sculpted (though much was destroyed in the Reformation) but here the figures are placed in recesses and the effect is flatter; the arcades are filled with stone, making the facade less shadowed than Reims.

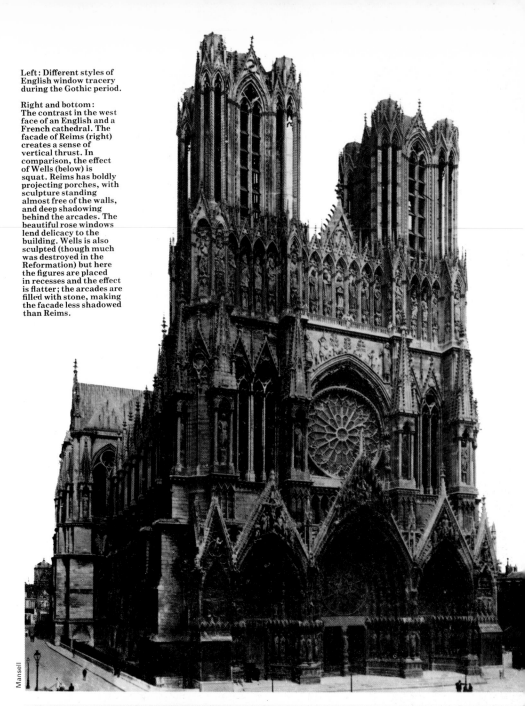

Mansell

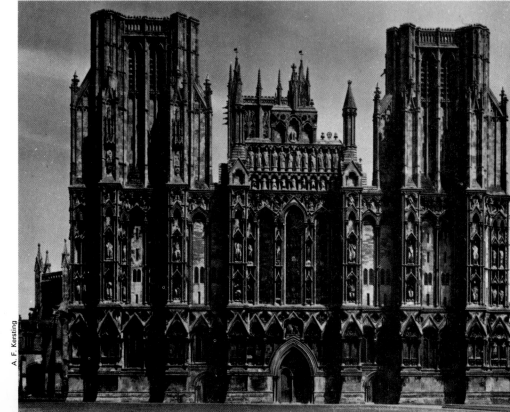

A. F. Kersting

Three examples of Gothic cathedral sculpture. The stone figure at Wells (left) is similar to those at Chartres (right) in pose and elongation, but is far less ambitious in its modelling. It stands in a single niche, and can be seen properly only from the front. The French figures are more rounded and finely detailed; the drapery clings to their limbs, the faces are modelled in depth, even the fingers are sculpted, unlike the stylized hands of the Wells figure. The beautiful sculpted angel from Reims cathedral (above) is still more natural in its graceful curving pose and delightful facial expression. Because of this, it is known as the 'Smiling Angel'.

Below: Tomb sculpture of Edward III in Westminster abbey, c. 1377-1380. This gilt copper effigy, possibly taken from a death-mask, shows some move towards realism. The hair and beard are in the flowing, linear style typical of Gothic, but the shape of the nose, the eyebrows and the lines sketched on his forehead aim at creating a more realistic likeness.

structures of stone built against the lower part of the wall for additional strength, soared upwards separate from the main structure. Arched supports known as flying buttresses connected the roof to the towering buttresses, acting as a kind of stone scaffolding.

Elaborate pinnacles topped the buttresses to give an impression of lightness while in fact adding to the necessary weight or downward thrust. The tall buttresses with their soaring arches gave the same vertical movement to the outside of a building that the ribs and vaults achieved inside. These features combine to give the appearance of delicacy to some of the biggest and heaviest buildings created by man.

In northern Europe the windows stretched from buttress to buttress, providing scope for glowing coloured glass as the major decoration. Masons travelled, copied and competed with each other to build bigger and better windows so that the walls became literally more glass than stone. The invention of stained glass at this time allowed the great windows of the nave and clearstory to become picture books of Bible stories. Although much has been destroyed, enough French stained glass has survived—unlike wall painting —for us to appreciate, at Chartres or Canterbury, for example, what a blaze of colour the cathedrals were.

But the space between and under windows was seldom left blank, it was covered with a lacework of ribbed and arched stonework much like the fluid and decorated stone-ribbed tracery of the windows themselves. The wall niches were filled with carved and often coloured stone figures as the windows were with

stained glass ones. The main columns too were clustered and groined vertically to increase the impression of slenderness and height.

With few exceptions, among these being Salisbury, built between 1220 and 1265, the great cathedrals were built, changed and added to over hundreds of years. Usually a start was made at the east end so that the altar, choir and presbytery could be used for worship first. Work proceeded westward to the 'crossing' with its tower and the transepts at right angles—the smaller arms of the crucifix plan—next the nave with its aisles, and finally the west end with its great window, entrance door and porches, often finished with towers.

Daring experiments of Gothic masons
Generations of craftsmen, working on the building in the same basic style, never hesitated to change the detailed design as fashions in ornament and confidence in more slender structures grew. The approach of the medieval mason and designer was a strange mixture of traditional conservatism and foolhardy experiment. Encouraged by powerful bishops, abbots and priors the masons always aspired to outdo earlier work and build bigger and taller buildings. The result was that vaulting, towers, spires, indeed whole sections of building often collapsed.

The central crossing at Ely did so in about 1320. In France the aspiration was to excel in the height of the vaulting; Reims (1211-90) was 37.8 metres (124 feet) high, Amiens (1220-88) 42.5 metres (140 feet), and Beauvais (1247-1565) over 48 metres (158 feet)—the loftiest in Europe. It has been called the most daring achievement in Gothic architecture. But the builders of Beauvais were over-ambitious, the vaults fell in 1284, and had to be reconstructed with double the amount of support and buttressing.

The Gothic style in Italy dates from the twelfth to the sixteenth century but the dominant vertical line of northern Gothic is generally tempered by horizontal cornices (the projecting ornamental sections along the top of buildings). Roofs, as is usual in southern climes, were flatter, pinnacles and flying buttresses were usually absent. Instead of the intricate carved and recessed mouldings and tracery, decoration usually took the form of strips of coloured marble typical of Italian architecture both before and after the Gothic period. The great exception is Milan cathedral, built later than the greatest northern examples, between about 1385 and 1485, which is somewhat German in character.

German Gothic occurred later than in France or England and was adopted direct from France in the thirteenth century— not evolved out of German Romanesque architecture. Germany was, of course, not one state but many, ruled by either secular or ecclesiastical princes. The styles of building varied, but the most typical are found in the Rhineland, nearest to France, Cologne cathedral being a fine example. The differences in stylistic features which occurred within Gothic architecture were a result of local traditions in worship, the comparative population, wealth and type of stone available in various areas and above all the degree of political stability. Areas ravaged by continual local warfare could not accumulate the wealth needed for great ecclesiastical ventures.

Chapter 2

The Renaissance

Botticelli's *Primavera* (c.1478). Sandro
Botticelli (1444-1510) was one of the
first Renaissance painters to use
mythological as well as purely
religious subjects, prefacing the work
of Michaelangelo and Leonardo.

The Renaissance

In 1338, a year after he had been deeply moved by his first sight of the ruins of Rome, the Italian poet Petrarch (1304-1374) wrote in his poem *Africa*: 'There is perhaps a better age in store; this slumber of forgetfulness will not last forever. After the darkness has been dispelled, our grandsons will be able to walk back into the pure radiance of the past'. The passion for ancient Greece and Rome was thus coupled with the idea that, after the 'darkness' of the Middle Ages, there was about to emerge a golden age, an age of light, of reawakening—in fact a 'Renaissance' or re-birth.

At first, the idea of a rebirth was applied only to the arts, but by the sixteenth century the natural sciences and philosophy had experienced a similar 'rebirth'. It was during this century that the new learning spread north of the Alps to Germany, the Netherlands, France and England.

Italy, where so many of the remains of the Roman Empire were still to be seen, was the natural home for the rebirth of interest in classical civilization. But the commercial and political sophistication of medieval Italy also contributed to the emergence of the new age. From the eleventh century onwards international trade began to revive after centuries of disruption by barbarian and Arab invasions. Italian merchants, situated between routes from the eastern Mediterranean and those to northern Europe, were at the centre of international commerce.

As Italian merchants dominated trade, so Italian bankers dominated international finance. Because of their power and importance, these merchants soon gained political control of their cities; the city-state became the basic political unit all over central and northern Italy in the late Middle Ages.

The wealth and power of these rulers was not all channelled towards political gain. Their desire for fame sought expression in the form of public patronage of all kinds—especially the arts, which flourished in such an atmosphere. But the cultural influence of this powerful class did not extend only to financial patronage. In a profound way, their achievements altered the attitude towards life adopted by the educated men of the time. A new respect for human capability and creativity began to be felt which was expressed in works of art exalting the dignity of man.

Man becomes the focal point

This emphasis on human achievement was gradually taking the place of the medieval view of the universe which was strictly God-centred. But educated men were not becoming less religious; rather their religion was becoming more secular, in the sense that it was focused on this world rather than the next. The belief in human greatness did not detract attention from divine matters. In man's new spirit of creativity, manifested in trade, politics and art, the educated saw a lesser version of God's creativity, revealed throughout the universe.

Whereas most medieval intellectuals had been priests, most of the great figures of the Renaissance were laymen. These men were proud to call themselves 'men of letters', 'poets' or 'artists'. The

M. Pucciarelli

Three Madonnas which show the development from medieval to Renaissance.

Duccio's *Madonna and Child* (above) is typically medieval, a very stylized pose with little movement or naturalism. It is an image intended to arouse the spectator's piety. In contrast, the Renaissance painting by

Raphael the *Tempi Madonna* (below) is highly realistic and humane, with a well-proportioned composition. The later Renaissance painting, Titian's *Pesaro Madonna* (right) is moving away from the regular perfection of Raphael. The composition is much less symmetrical—the Madonna and child are no longer central.

M. Pucciarelli

Right and far right: Two magnificent but very different representations of the Last Judgement. On the right is a 12th-century sculpture by Gislebertus over the doorway of Autun cathedral. The Christ figure is much larger than the others to symbolize his importance he gazes straight at the spectator in god-like

calm. Far right is Michelangelo's Christ from the Sistine chapel in Rome, completed in 1541. Here is the human image on a huge scale; heroic, classical (it is based on a statue of Apollo) and containing a powerful, dramatic movement. It is a wholly individual view of Christ, rather than a work of symbolic piety.

Scala

Mansell

Above right: An allegorical painting entitled *Calumny*, by the 15th-century Italian painter Botticelli. Renaissance artists were unable to copy antiquity directly, as no Greek or Roman paintings were known to them. But here Botticelli imitates antiquity at one remove, for his painting follows the description of a lost picture by the Greek artist Apelles. This painting reflects the atmosphere of the Renaissance; it shows a curious blending of classical, sensuous and Christian elements. For example, next to a naked, classically proportioned figure the bent form of a nun is placed. The architectural setting is elaborately classical.

painter or sculptor, who had traditionally been despised as a manual worker (and was sometimes paid by the yard) now claimed a higher status. Leonardo da Vinci angrily rejected the idea that painting was a 'mechanical art' and declared that painters 'may be called the grandsons of God', sharing, that is, in the divine power of creativity.

Not everyone accepted this new view of the artist's role but some painters, sculptors and architects were rewarded on an unheard-of scale and were treated more or less as equals by their noble patrons. The patrons stopped asking for a 'Madonna' and began to ask for a 'Mantegna' or a 'Raphael'.

Changes such as these form part of a movement known as 'humanism' which developed during the Renaissance. A humanist was an intellectual, often a university teacher, whose interests were centred on five subjects; grammar, rhetoric, poetry, history and ethics. These subjects, considered by contemporaries to be more 'humane' than the rest, were studied through the works of classical authors. Knowledge of these writers had been made possible by Italy's contact—achieved primarily through trade—with the Greek-speaking Byzantine Empire, which had for centuries preserved the works of classical Greek authors unknown in the West.

The central belief of the humanists was that man is distinguished from animals by his power of reason, expressed in his power of speech and his ability to distinguish right from wrong—his ethical ability. Grammar, rhetoric and poetry were all concerned with speech; while history, a fund of moral examples, was associated with ethics. It is noticeable that this list of subjects leaves out logic and theology, so important in medieval times, and the natural sciences, so important in our own. The main interests of the Renaissance humanist were literary and secular.

The new atmosphere of humanism, directed towards secular life rather than the religious, was interpreted in widely different ways by contemporary writers. The Italian nobleman Castiglione incorporates in his book *The Courtier* all those aspects of the Renaissance that dealt with learning, taste and court life. His perfect courtier is a typical Renaissance man—supremely accomplished in the various fields of humanistic studies, art, music, games, hunting and military skills.

The life and writings of Niccolo Machiavelli, who lived from 1469 to 1527, form a strange contrast to the ideal, but shallow and artificial, courtly world of Castiglione. His thinking, concerned with political life, applies and distorts the humanist emphasis on reason to matters of politics and government. His works are a grim reminder that the flowering of culture in fifteenth-century Italy was taking place against a background of violence and war—not only between the different states of Italy, but against foreign invaders also.

In his work entitled *The Prince*, an analysis of the ways by which a ruler can secure and maintain power, Machiavelli divorces reason from any moral basis and uses it as an instrument of manipulation and cynical shrewdness. The successful prince must be willing to use any means, no matter how corrupt, to secure political control.

Machiavelli is often regarded as the first 'modern' political thinker. It comes as a surprise, therefore, to discover how deep was his debt to classical civilization and how naturally he accepted the idea of imitating the ancients, to the extent of basing his famous *Discourses* on the first ten books of the Roman historian Livy.

The idea of imitation
Modelling oneself on older writers may seem an odd practice to the twentieth century, which tends to prize originality, but the respect in which Renaissance writers and artists held the ancient world was so great that it led them deliberately to practise what they called 'imitation'. The English playwright Ben Jonson, who lived from 1572 to 1637, includes this quality among those necessary for a poet; 43

he describes it as the ability 'to convert the substance or riches of another poet to one's own use'. Jonson followed this advice in his own plays. In *Volpone*, for instance, the Renaissance gallant bursts into an eloquent speech in his attempt to seduce the heroine, picks up a lute and sings a song that is a free translation of a famous poem by the Roman poet Catullus: 'Come my Celia let us prove while we can the sports of love'. Educated members of the audience would be expected to recognize the original and admire the skill with which the author had used the substance of the ancient poet for his own purposes.

But the idea of imitation was not only confined to literature. In architecture too there was a return to the use of classical forms. The Florentine architect Brunelleschi, living from 1377 to 1446, is said to have taken measurements of the classical ruins of Rome and made sketches of their ornaments. Many architects after him followed this practice. His Pazzi chapel in Florence, designed in about 1430, presents a striking contrast to the Gothic emphasis on height and intricate tracery. The entrance has classical columns with a pediment over the door. Inside, there are plain white walls with grey Corinthian half-columns.

Knowledge of classical building was greatly increased after 1456 when a manuscript by the Roman architect Vitruvius was discovered, which distinguished the 'orders' or varieties of column used in classical architecture. The most famous architect of the High Renaissance, Bramante, was therefore able to achieve a more correct and severe classicism both in his use of detail and in his ground plans. In the Renaissance, we see not only the simplification of the medieval church's cross-shape, but also the introduction of circular plans.

The Renaissance in the North, however, frequently meant no more than classical decorations (including columns, friezes, pediments and medallions) applied to buildings by craftsmen who continued to build as they had always done. In England, the first real architect (as opposed to skilled mason) is Inigo Jones (1577-1652), who designed the Banqueting House in Whitehall in 1619, nearly two centuries after Brunelleschi's Foundling Hospital, begun in 1421, had announced the new style in architecture.

A new philosophy

During the Middle Ages the favourite ancient Greek philosopher was Aristotle; after the Renaissance it was Plato. The change is revealing; the philosopher who tended to categorize and classify things was replaced by the mystic. For Plato, the world of the senses in which we live is a pale reflection of a more perfect ideal world which the philosopher is constantly striving to understand.

This philosophy was adapted by the Italian philosophers Ficino and Pico della Mirandola and became known as Neo-Platonism. The system sees the world as hierarchical, rising to the increasingly spiritual as man approaches ever nearer to God: angels are more perfect and more spiritual than man, while below man we move from animals and plants down to stones. Man stands at a focal point in this vast order of things: he is the highest of earthly beings but the lowest among those with rational powers. His reason is imperfect because it is subject to the

Left: A fresco by the Italian Pinturicchio, dated 1507, showing the scholar and poet Aeneas Silvius being crowned with the poet's laurel wreath. This man became Pope Pius II—one of the most worldly and learned of all popes. The Renaissance delight in pomp, splendour and the civilized pleasures of the arts are all revealed in this fresco.

Left: A portrait of the Dutch humanist Erasmus, by Hans Holbein. Living from 1466 to 1536, Erasmus was one of the greatest figures of the northern Renaissance. He was famed for the range of knowledge, wit and mastery of the classics shown in his written discourses. A true humanist, he sought to reconcile classical ideals with Christianity.

Below: Niccolo Machiavelli (1469-1527). Regarded as the first modern political thinker, his writings include *The Prince*, a treatise which upholds a ruler's right to maintain power by any means, however corrupt. 'Machiavellian' has since been used to describe political ruthlessness.

Left: The Italian church of S. Maria della Consolazione, built by Caprarola in 1508. This church, perhaps based on a design by the architect Bramante, had an 'ideal' Renaissance plan. Derived from the shape of a Greek cross, it has four equal arms, focussing on a large central area rather than on the altar at the east end, as in medieval churches.

Right: Interior of Santo Spirito church, Florence, by Brunelleschi. Begun in 1435, its round arches and flat roof are in obvious contrast to the Gothic style. The architect has aimed at symmetry and rational proportions; the height of the nave is twice its width and the ground-floor and clearstory are the same height.

Below: Banqueting Hall in Whitehall, London, designed by Inigo Jones and built between 1619 and 1622. Jones, England's first real architect as opposed to skilled mason, had studied in Italy and absorbed the Renaissance interest in classicism. This hall was based on a surviving description of a Roman basilica.

earthly passions (to put the point in Platonic terms) or tainted by sin (to put it in Christian terms).

Platonism was particularly popular during the sixteenth and seventeenth centuries. It was a philosophy which could easily be reconciled with Christianity—a great help to those who saw ancient civilization as a striving towards the truths of Christian revelation, rather than an unredeemed world of sinners. The philosophy appealed only to the educated few. A great deal of Renaissance literature is also addressed to a select minority of educated readers by highly-educated writers.

The Renaissance, as a revival of learning, was in effect a minority movement. Nine-tenths of the population of fifteenth-century Italy remained untouched by the discovery of ancient manuscripts, the revival of the ancient orders and the philosophy of the academics. Their traditional poetry and their oral storytelling continued, shut off from the revival of antiquity. Many people see the Renaissance as a completely new age. But it was hardly this since the movement appealed only to an educated elite, as the humanists themselves admitted.

Neither, perhaps, was the Renaissance as new as it looked. Although the long poem *Orlando Furioso*, written by the Italian poet Ariosto, seems a model of Renaissance classicism, it springs from the tradition of the medieval romances of chivalry. Machiavelli's treatise on the ruler owes more than a little to the medieval writings on the perfect prince which discuss some of the same questions—when should the prince be generous, when should he be merciful? Renaissance painters, like Botticelli and Raphael, took over compositional schemes from their medieval predecessors. Consciously or unconsciously the humanists and artists underestimated their debt to the 'barbarous', 'Gothic' or 'Middle' ages.

Left and far left: Two literary figures of the French Renaissance. The poet Ronsard (far left), 1524-1585, was a member of the *Pleiade*, a group of court poets noted for their attempt to give the French language a new classical dignity. The fame of Montaigne (left), 1533-1592, rests on his *Essays*, which created a new literary form.

Right: Engraved title-page of the playwright Ben Jonson's *Works*, with allegorical figures of the literary genres—satire, pastoral, tragedy, comedy—against the background of a classical monument. The Latin motto 'nor do I work to please the many, content if I am read by the few' testifies to the minority appeal of Renaissance classicism.

A detail from Michaelangelo's *David*, made between 1501 and 1504, after the artist's return to Florence from Rome. The statue became a symbol of Florentine independence from enemy states.

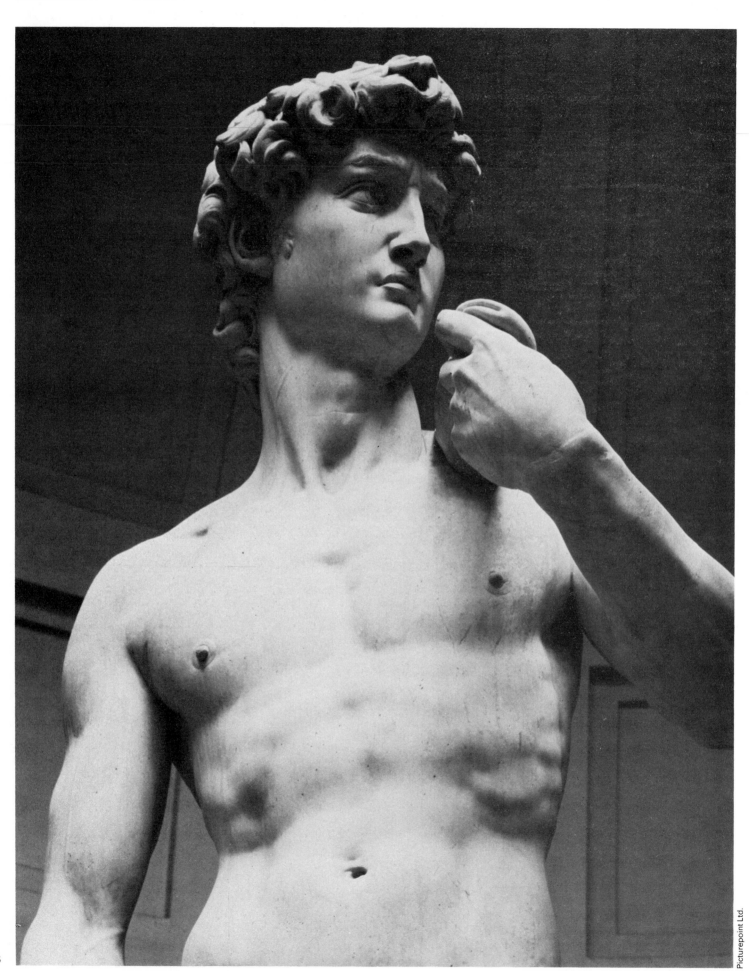

The Renaissance in Florence

It was in Florence that the great cultural revival known as the Renaissance first took root. The intensity of cultural activity in this city in the fifteenth century is perhaps unequalled in history, producing, in little over 100 years, a vast collection of extraordinary artistic wealth.

The city of the Medici

Florence had become one of the great banking centres of Europe, supplying funds at huge rates of interest to the warring kings and nobles of Europe. Trade was growing enormously and the merchants and tradesmen were organizing themselves into strong and ambitious guilds. Sponsoring art was one means of expressing their new wealth and status; such men were willing to encourage the innovations of artists experimenting with rational, unified and naturalistic forms. Their interest was in the material, definable world and this is what they discovered in surviving examples of ancient culture.

As the century progressed, particular families emerged with enormous power—most notably the Medici, who became the ruling party in the city after 1434 and who held political power until the end of the century. Although the temperaments of the generations of Medici (Cosimo, Piero, Lorenzo the Magnificent) differed widely, they were all united in their desire for glory and consequently their lavish patronage of the arts.

Around the Medici a life-style grew up which, in its splendour, was on a par with the courts of kings and princes. As well as building up an enviable reputation for diplomacy, financial and political strength and cultural achievement (with their patronage of philosophers, humanists and artists) the Medici were lavish in their civic patronage; pageants and carnivals were continually being arranged for the citizens of Florence.

But the atmosphere of the city offered some extreme contradictions. The society was full of insecurity and brutality; fear of invasion from neighbouring states was constant and internal strife and conspiracy frequently threatened to disrupt the precarious stability of Florentine life. The luxury and wealth of the powerful families existed side by side with suffering, disease and poverty among the poor. Such contrasts provided fuel for the preaching of the monk Savanarola, in the latter part of the century, whose denunciations of the worldliness, greed and tyranny of his society influenced a great cross-section of Florentines, from the poor to the most renowned intellectuals and artists of the time. His hysterical preachings were a violent reaction to Renaissance excess.

It is not possible to fix an exact date for the start of the Renaissance in Florence. Traces of the movement towards more classical artistic forms—bold, geometric forms in architecture and a solid, naturalistic approach to painting and sculpture—can be seen as early as the twelfth century. San Miniato al Monte, a small church which overlooks Florence from the adjoining hills, has a mathematical

Right: Portrait of Lorenzo de' Medici, known as Lorenzo the Magnificent. One of the most illustrious of the powerful Medici family, Lorenzo lived between 1449 and 1492, becoming absolute ruler of Florence. In political matters Lorenzo was supremely ambitious, revengeful and inclined to tyranny—under his rule, Florence remained a republic only in name. Nevertheless, Lorenzo exemplified the qualities of Renaissance man; besides being a diplomat, financier and politician, he was a versatile intellectual, a skilled prose writer and poet. He gathered around him the most renowned artists, humanists and philosophers of the age, continuing the Medici tradition of patronage.

Below: Detail from *The Journey of the Magi*, a wall-painting in the Medici chapel, Florence, by Benozzo Gozzoli. Heading the procession is the young Lorenzo de' Medici on a white horse. The painting captures the spirit of culture, pageantry and splendour surrounding the lives of the Medici rulers in Renaissance Florence.

Bottom: The *Adoration of the Magi* painted by Sandro Botticelli between 1476 and 1477. Botticelli was given extensive patronage by the Medici. Here, the Medici family are portrayed as the Magi—a fitting tribute to these citizen kings. The man on the far right, gazing out at the spectator, is thought to be Botticelli himself.

clarity of proportion and classical details in its decoration that foreshadows the great Renaissance works of nearly three centuries later. The paintings of Giotto, dating from the early fourteenth century, show an understanding of the depiction of solid forms in space perhaps even more developed than was achieved by many artists in the Renaissance itself. These precedents, however, are isolated. Giotto's initiative was taken up in Siena rather than Florence, and even there his discoveries were not developed further.

The transformation in art

Two dimensional representations of religious subjects in an icon-like style, depending on richness of effect and heavily stylized, dominated painting in 1400. Such pictures do have an abstract beauty, but it must be stressed that the artist's concern was not with the depiction of the real world so much as a symbolic one with its own language and rules. With the great change taking place in Florentine society during the fifteenth century, there was a corresponding desire for change in artistic expression. After centuries of neglect, classical knowledge was taken up as the rallying point of artistic progress, for it contained an emphasis on individualism and human glory rather than on pious, obedient spirituality. Naturally, in being adopted by fifteenth-century Florentines, ancient art was transformed.

The emergence of this new spirit is illustrated by an event which took place in 1401. Two young artists, Lorenzo Ghiberti and Filippo Brunelleschi, took part in a competition for a new pair of bronze doors for the Baptistery of Florence cathedral. Their designs reveal a close attention to classical models. Ghiberti won the competition and spent the next 25 years working on the doors. His sculpture, however, represents only a half-way stage in the emergence of Renaissance art. Although he formed a substantial collection of ancient sculpture and studied the laws of perspective and proportion, he was not entirely at home with the new idiom and much of the linear, two-dimensional nature of a more medieval style remains in his work.

Brunelleschi proved a far more dynamic and innovative figure. After his failure in the competition, he resolved to give up sculpture and went on to become one of the most important figures in the whole history of architecture. His interest in classical art was profound; he apparently set off for Rome in 1402 with the young sculptor Donatello to study the remains of the ancient world at first hand. Brunelleschi also read and formed a sound understanding of the principles of classical architecture described by the Roman writer Vetruvius. The result of this study was a series of buildings in Florence which show a genuine understanding of the laws of proportion and the use of classical ornament. The completion of the dome of Florence cathedral was perhaps his greatest achievement.

Brunelleschi had enormous influence on architecture in the Renaissance, but his discoveries were also of great importance to painters and sculptors. The practical demonstration of classical ideas in the buildings of Brunelleschi led to their written explanation in 1435, in a book entitled *Della Pittura* by another important architect, Leon Battista Alberti.

Artists were beginning to investigate the depiction of space and depth in their work, in other words the working of the third dimension. This is seen most clearly and with the greatest genius in the paintings of Masaccio and the sculptures of Donatello.

Mascaccio was born in 1401. He was probably active as a painter for only about six years, yet his work is of the greatest importance. His frescoes in the Brancacci Chapel in Florence reveal an astonishing contrast to those of his contemporaries and predecessors. Groups of solid figures stand in a real, believable space linked to each other with natural gestures. It is as if the small room of the chapel consists of a series of windows into another ideal and heroic world. Masaccio's extraordinary level of achievement was tragically cut short by his early death at the age of 27.

Donatello—master sculptor

In sculpture, the master was Donatello, who was perhaps the single most influential artist of the early Renaissance. If Michelangelo owes anything to any of his predecessors, it is Donatello. Born in about 1386, Donatello began working in Ghiberti's workshop on the Baptistery doors in about 1403. He then began a series of projects to decorate Florence cathedral and guild church which were to continue for about 30 years. Classical sculpture was arriving in the houses of rich Florentines in increasing quantities from sites in Rome and Donatello was much influenced by these.

He produced a great variety of sculpture, with a consistent intensity and expressive power. He is known to have been an impetuous, excitable man and was a notorious homosexual. His bronze statue of David of about 1434 was probably the first free-standing nude figure made since the fall of the Roman Empire, marking a break with medieval tradition and heralding a new interest in the naked human body as an artistic subject.

The great strides forward made by Brunelleschi, Masaccio and Donatello had an immediate influence on the other artists working in Florence. Fra Angelico (c.1395-1455) adapted the solid figures and spatial depth of Masaccio to a more conventionally devout Christianity. The lyrical religious paintings of this simple monk show clearly how the ideas and techniques of the innovators transformed the outlook of even the more conservative artists.

The intellectual passion for classical knowledge is most clearly seen in the work of Paolo Uccello (c.1396-1475) whose enthusiasm for the mechanics of perspective and foreshortened figures led him to undertake ambitious projects such as the chaotic battle scenes of *The Rout of San Romano* painted in about 1456. Fra Filippo Lippi (c.1406-69) tackled the problem of placing figures in seemingly real space more effectively. He probably studied under Masaccio and was clearly influenced by him, particularly in his use of a single source of light in a picture, allowing light and shade to create the illusion of depth. In the same period, Domenico Veneziano showed the possibilities which the effect of light on colour might have; another discovery to be taken up by artists as the century progressed.

The first half of the fifteenth century thus saw the development of a new language of art. The advances made in

48

Above: Woodcut of about 1486, giving a panoramic view of Florence. The river Arno flows through the city, which is dominated by the cathedral.

Right and far right: Two views of Florence cathedral showing Brunelleschi's dome, built between 1420 and 1436, over the existing cathedral. Many attempts to span the huge arches failed. Brunelleschi's dome was a unique but simple solution to the problem. His study and understanding of ancient Roman building enabled him to devise this structure, a triumph of construction.

Picturepoint

Below: Engraving of the Palazzo Pitti, Florence. This palace, commissioned by the Pitti family in 1458, was probably the work of Luca Fancelli, after designs by Alberti. Its dimension and gigantic size create a sense of sheer power, typifying the aspirations of rich Renaissance families.

Right: A bronze statue of David, sculpted in about 1434 by Donatello. This statue was probably the first free-standing nude figure made since the fall of the Roman Empire. The young David has an elegant, almost feminine pose, revealing to the full Donatello's mastery of the human physique. Though based on classical sculpture, his style remained individual, imaginative and full of dramatic power.

Below right: A panel from the bronze doors of Florence cathedral Baptistery, sculpted by Lorenzo Ghiberti. He worked on these doors for 25 years from 1401. Each panel illustrates a biblical scene in gilded relief. The drapery and solidity of his figures are clearly classical and the receding arches show his understanding of space; but aspects of a linear, two-dimensional medieval style remain.

Left: Panel painting of *The Annunciation* by Fra Filippo Lippi (c.1406-1469). The simplicity and grace of Lippi's composition are allied with soft, subtle colours and a profusion of decorative details.

Right: *Madonna and child* by Masaccio, (1401-1428), the centre panel of a traditional altarpiece. The classical throne and massive, heavy drapery falling over the Virgin's solid, well-defined shape, are Renaissance in style.

Below: *The Flagellation of Christ* by Piero della Francesca, (c.1415-1492). This painting, almost an abstract exercise in perspective, has a clarity and calm achieved by the simple patterns created by the architecture.

these years were so revolutionary that a whole range of new effects became available to later painters.

The most successful of the more rigorously classical artists in the second half of the fifteenth century was Piero della Francesca (c.1415-92). The cool, gentle colouring and perfect geometrical composition of his works give them a silent, timeless beauty. His paintings are planned in series of regularly-spaced vertical and horizontal lines; it is from this that their peaceful quality comes. Piero's work includes some of the most successful abstract exercises in perspective, such as *The Flagellation of Christ* in the Ducal Palace of Urbino.

But, along with the desire for a pure, formal, classical style, went a fascination with the decorative splendour which had formed a part of International Gothic and was now used as a means of expressing delight in the pageantry and pomp of Florentine civic life. Many paintings combined both elements in a subtle blend of classical and decorative—increasingly so as painters began to use subjects from classical mythology. The use of legendary and mythological subjects marks one of the most important breakthroughs of the Florentine Renaissance—the secularization of narrative painting. Up to this point, it had been taken for granted that any major picture would have a religious subject. Now even stories from pagan mythology could be chosen.

The graceful art of Botticelli

The best known mythological paintings are those of Sandro Botticelli, who was born in Florence in 1444 or 45 and died there in 1510. The *Birth of Venus* and the *Primavera*, both commissioned by the Medici, are among Botticelli's most remarkable paintings. They reveal an extraordinary fusion of the graceful linear style of the International Gothic, with its profusion of flowers, and a truly Renaissance outlook, in the depiction of complex mythological subjects inspired by current intellectual studies. The exact meaning of these paintings is unclear, but they are evidence of the almost obsessive study of classical writings that was taking place in the courts of wealthy patrons.

Throughout his career, Botticelli also painted religious scenes and in the last years of his life he underwent a profound religious crisis, influenced by the upheaval in Florentine society caused by the denunciation and prophecies of Savonarola. In their highly-wrought religious feeling, Botticelli's late works

reflect this crisis, and this somewhat 'exaggerated' style is typical of Florence at the end of the fifteenth century.

By this stage, the Renaissance had transformed Italian art. Gradually, however, the driving force was switching from Florence, which was no longer the only city in the sway of the Renaissance. Leonardo da Vinci (1452-1519) and Michelangelo Buonarotti (1475-1564) were the greatest Florentine artists of all, but both worked for most of their careers outside Florence.

Their work represents the summit of a century of ceaseless experimentation and artistic progress. It was no longer necessary to struggle with the rules of perspective, to feverishly study ancient mythology in order to work out a worthy subject, or to gaze at fragments of ancient sculpture to discover the proportions of the human body. These artists had total confidence in the new tradition.

The fifteenth century had seen the fundamental transformation of the meaning of art. As the purpose of artistic endeavour and the basis of patronage had changed, so too had the image of the artist. He was often a talented, learned individual possessing the respect of even the most powerful figures in the state.

Leonardo was not simply a painter, he was a scientist, a philosopher, an inventor. Michelangelo was architect, poet, sculptor and military engineer. The immensity of the achievements of these two men in all these fields is a measure of the legacy of Florence's greatest century.

Right: *The rout of San Romano* by Paolo Uccello, (1396-1475). It is constructed around a geometrical scheme in which the lines of composition recede towards common points in the distance. Uccello's enthusiasm for the laws of perspective led him to attempt extreme foreshortening, as in the corpse lying in the left of the picture.

Below, left and right: Two works by Botticelli. The detail (left) is from the allegorical painting *Primavera*, c.1478. (Right) is the *Birth of Venus*, c.1486. Painted for the Medici, both reflect the intellectual climate of 15th-century Florence with their complex imagery. They are among the most graceful and poetic of Renaissance paintings, deriving harmony from the flowing lines, rhythmic movement and profusion of natural detail used by Botticelli.

The Renaissance in Venice

The Renaissance was firmly established in Florence and Rome before its ideas took root in Venice. Not until the sixteenth century did this city experience a flowering of art on a scale similar to that which had occurred earlier in Florence.

Venice was in many ways separate from the rest of Italy. Physically isolated from the mainland by a lagoon and having strong links with the Greek Byzantine Empire directly to the east, the cultural influences on Venice also differed. The city grew powerful through its sea-trade, becoming a major centre for goods of all kinds, but especially luxuries—such as silks, wool, spices, gold and glass—passing between the East and West. The maritime power of the Venetians reached its height in the first half of the fifteenth century; it then commanded a fleet of over 3,000 vessels, used both for trade and war. Its trade with the East and direct link with northern Europe through a trade route over the Alps made it the most cosmopolitan city in Italy. The power of Venice was carefully fostered by the Council of Ten, the effective governing body of the republic, whose rule amounted almost to a dictatorship. The chief magistrate, the Doge, was by the fifteenth century largely a state figurehead to lead in pageants and formal ceremonies.

In the mid-fifteenth century Venice was a self-sufficient, splendid city, strongly Byzantine in its tastes, but influenced also by the Gothic styles from north of the Alps. The medieval Basilica of St Mark, modelled on a church in Constantinople and decorated with mosaics and inlaid marbles, was still the most influential building in Venice. The making of mosaic and the manufacture of glass—the secrets of which had been learnt from Byzantium—were important Venetian monopolies, closely guarded by the Council of Ten. Palaces were still being built with façades and interior surfaces brilliant with multi-coloured marbles. The practice of mosaic almost certainly helped to delay the development of painting in Venice.

During this period, patronage was confined mainly to the Church and the government, with less private patronage than was usual in Florence. Because of this, there was little demand for wall or panel paintings in private houses; the religious subjects which were commissioned would be executed in an archaic thirteenth-century style. The one large-scale decorative scheme undertaken at this time was the repainting of a room in the Doge's Palace, called the *Sala del Maggior Consiglio*, but the style of this was in no way really new. Indeed its subject matter was very traditional, being concerned with events from Venetian history. The Gothic influence in painting had become firmly rooted in Venice and continued to be practised throughout the fifteenth century; it was the style used by the Vivarini family, whose workshop was one of the most popular in Venice.

During the early fifteenth century there was as yet little sense of ostentatious civic

Giraudon

Above: One of Gentile Bellini's historical paintings which captures the colour and atmosphere of Venice around the year 1500. It shows the saving of the relic of the True Cross, after it had fallen into a canal during a religious procession. The event is recorded in a stiff, almost naive style, with meticulous attention to contemporary detail.

A. F. Kersting

Below: The Olympic Theatre at Vicenza c.1580, designed by Palladio and completed by Scamozzi. Although Palladio's last work, it was his first experiment in classical theatre building. It is based on the ancient Roman idea of a fixed, elaborate architectural stage-setting, with sculptured decoration.

Arborio Mella

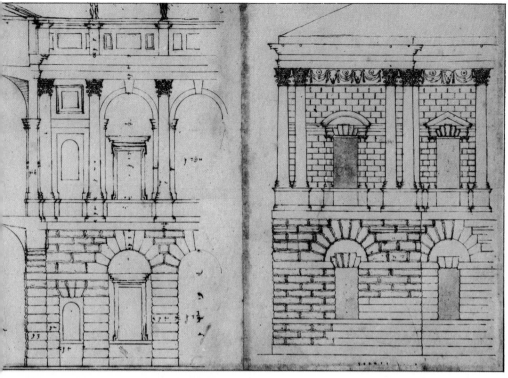

Angelo Hornak

Left: The elegant simplicity of the Villa Maser, designed by Palladio c.1557 for his friend Barbaro's agricultural estate. It is a conscious attempt to rebuild a Roman villa according to descriptions by the Latin writers Pliny and Vitruvius; the central section is an imitation of a temple.

Below: The interior of the church of S. Giorgio, 1565. Its plan is a compromise between the circular temple form favoured by Palladio and the cross shape demanded by the Roman church. The design is of the utmost purity; the curving arches and pale colour create a sense of spaciousness and peace.

Left: Two sketches by Palladio showing different classical facades—designs for a building that no longer exists. Palladio (1508-80) was one of the most influential Renaissance architects, renowned for the pure and harmonious classical style of his buildings. His work is unique in its serenity and elegance.

Below: A 16th-century glass *nef*, or boat-shaped ewer, used to hold salt. Venice held a monopoly in glass manufacture at this time—the secrets of the craft had been learnt from Byzantium. The skill and delicacy of Venetian craftsmanship were famous throughout Europe, for glassware, jewellery and mosaic.

pride and Doges were positively prohibited from starting elaborate and expensive artistic projects. In 1422, for example, the reigning Doge was fined 1,000 ducats for presuming to say that the old palace should be pulled down and a new one built in its place.

Civic pride and patronage

The second half of the fifteenth century, however, saw a crucial change in Venice and the Venetian attitude towards art. The republic began to aspire to more impressive monuments to its wealth and embarked on projects for public buildings that consciously evoked the Roman Empire. In 1483, after a fire in the Ducal Palace, a vote was taken to rebuild it rather than merely repair it. In the entrance courtyard a great staircase was built, with three arches at the top (echoing the style of Roman triumphal arches) and decorated with emblems of the Doge. This supremely self-glorifying venture was not completed until the end of the sixteenth century, when the Venetian architect Sansovino sculpted a giant Mars and Neptune to stand at the top of these stairs, symbols of Venice's dominion over land and sea.

It was also in the second half of this century that each of the four great confraternities, or secular brotherhoods, enormously rich and influential bodies to which everyone in Venice belonged, executed some major building or project. Motivated partly, no doubt, by a desire to keep abreast with the fashion, these projects helped to spread the new style.

In the paintings of the Bellini family, we can see Venetian art emerging from its Gothic roots into a Renaissance manner of its own. The father of the family, Jacopo, (c.1400-1470/1) was evidently a master of late Gothic though few of his paintings have survived. His elder son Gentile (c.1429-1507) is famous for his historical paintings and became so renowned in his own day that in 1479 he was sent to paint for the Sultan in Constantinople as a gesture of good will on the part of the Senate.

Mastery of colour and light

Gentile's brother Giovanni Bellini (c.1430-1516) was the greatest artist of the family. His work was much influenced by the painter Mantegna, who was his brother-in-law. Giovanni was a conservative artist in many ways, rarely departing from religious subjects in his work. Technically, however, he was very advanced. He developed a new style of altar-piece, with the Madonna enthroned and surrounded by saints, a device used by later artists throughout the first half of the sixteenth century. The landscapes in the background of his paintings became increasingly expressive and important in their own right. By 1505 his painting had lost all of its earlier hard-edged quality, developing instead a new softness and a mastery of light and shade.

These qualities were to epitomize the characteristics of Venetian painting during the rest of the century. In explaining the difference between the art of Florence and Venice, the art historian Vasari (himself a Florentine) said that the Florentines excelled at drawing and the Venetians at colour.

The move made by Giovanni Bellini towards the use of colour, light and shadow (instead of drawing) to model forms was explored further by Giorgione (c.1476-1510). This artist's few surviving works are of rather mysterious secular subjects imbued with a sense of nostalgia; his paintings have an 'atmospheric' quality which afterwards became a kind of hallmark of Venetian art. Unfortunately, his life is shrouded in as much mystery as his paintings.

It was Giorgione's art which most influenced Titian (c.1488-1576), the greatest Venetian painter of all. Yet in Titian's mastery of effects of light and shade, and in his attempts to treat conventional composition more freely, he advanced far beyond his teacher.

His fame spread quickly and he was soon befriended and patronized by the most powerful men in Europe. He was commissioned to paint several completely new subjects from classical mythology, which he treated in a rich and sensual way. Such paintings made him famous, as for example the series of *bacchanals* (drunken revels associated with the classical god of wine, Bacchus) executed for the powerful Italian Duke Alfonso d'Este at Ferrara.

The sensuous art of Titian

During his lifetime, Titian painted numerous portraits of Popes and princes, many of them superbly revealing of the sitter's character. Perhaps his highest tribute was being made court painter and knight to Charles V, Holy Roman Emperor and king of Spain, after executing a full-length portrait of him. He became a personal friend of the Emperor, an unheard of honour, comparable only with Michelangelo's relationship with the Popes.

Towards the end of his life, Titian became increasingly concerned with the play of light and shade upon forms; in his use of paint he attempted more dramatic and elusive effects. Vasari described this perfectly when he said that Titian's late works 'are executed in splashes and roughly finished blobs in such a way that they cannot be seen from close up, but from a distance seem perfect'.

Some idea of the way in which Titian actually worked is given in this account by Palma Giovane, who worked in the master's studio: 'He laid in his pictures with a mass of colour which served as a groundwork for what he wanted to express. I myself have seen such vigorous under-painting in plain red earth for the half-tones, or in white lead. With the same brush dipped in red, black, or yellow he worked up the light parts and in four strokes he could create a remarkably fine figure. Then he turned the picture to the wall and left it for months without looking at it, until he returned to it and stared critically at it, as if it were a mortal enemy . . . . If he found something which displeased him he went to work like a surgeon . . . Thus, by repeated revisions he brought his pictures to a high state of perfection and while one was drying he worked on another. This quintessence of a composition he then covered with many layers of living flesh . . .'

During his long career, Titian produced an enormous number of paintings covering a wide and varied range of subjects. He died in Venice during an epidemic of plague in 1576.

During the sixteenth century huge picture cycles in the churches, the *Scuole* (charitable institutions) and the Doge's Palace were undertaken. Probably the grandest and most dramatic painter of these pictures was Tintoretto (1518-1594) a virtuoso in terms of his daring compositions and use of colour. His most important work was a colossal cycle of paintings for the *Scuola di San Rocco*, depicting scenes from the Old and New Testaments. In physical scale they are monumental, showing Tintoretto's style at its most

54 dramatic and 'wild'. His contemporary

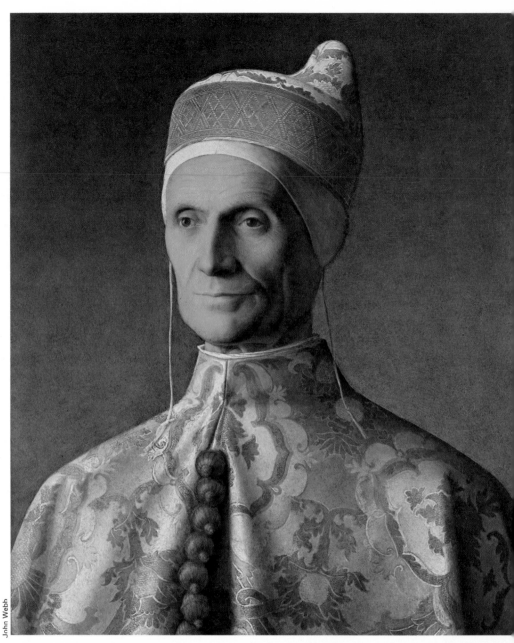

John Webb

John Freeman

Arborio Mella

Left: The Lion of St Mark, patron saint of Venice, painted by Carpaccio for the ducal palace. He specialized in precise narrative paintings with much contemporary detail and a closely observed naturalism. He accurately positions St Marks square and the palace to the left and the new customs house to the right.

Below: *The Tempest* by Giorgione. The atmospheric effect, the lowering storm in the background and the sense of stillness before it breaks have no precedent in earlier painting. The woman staring out at the viewer gives the scene a peculiar immediacy. The painting is said to be of a gypsy and soldier.

Left: *Doge Leonardo Loredano*, by Giovanni Bellini, painted shortly after the Doge's reign began in 1501. This is probably the finest of Bellini's portraits, painted with great delicacy and precision in clear, limpid colours. Swathed in his stiff state robes, the strong personality of the man still emerges, a perfect blending of republican majesty and individual character.

Right: *Portrait of a Lady*, possibly by Titian; it is certainly very close to his style. In some ways it is typical of the numerous portraits painted in Venice during the 16th century, but her state of undress is slightly unconventional and is made even more mysterious by the fact that x-rays have shown her hat to be a later addition.

Below left: Titian's *Bacchus and Ariadne*, painted 1522-3 as part of a series for the Duke of Ferrara. Titian creates a strong sense of movement, with Bacchus leaping from his chariot towards Ariadne, followed by a procession of licentious revellers.

Scala

Scala

Left: *The Venus of Urbino* (1538) by Titian. He probably copied the pose from Giorgione's *Sleeping Venus*. The picture shows how Titian treated subjects from classical mythology in a rich and sensual way. This Venus is no longer a mythical creature but a sensuous woman inviting the spectator to approach. The figure is placed in a luxurious Renaissance room. In the background her maids rummage through a chest, preparing for the lady to rise. In his later work, Titian became increasingly concerned to capture the play of light and shade on forms, making a freer use of paint. A contemporary left this account of his finishing technique: '. . . the final touches he softened, occasionally modulating the highest lights into the half-tones and local colours with his finger; sometimes he used his finger to dab a dark patch in a corner as an accent, or to heighten the surface with a bit of red like a drop of blood. He finished his figures like this and in the last stages he used his fingers more than his brush.'

Paolo Veronese (c.1528-1588) is characterized by his brilliant use of colour. Whereas Tintoretto often makes use of gloom, Veronese's colours are bright, almost jewel-like. His subjects and commissions were often colossal. He did not, of course, physically execute all the painting himself, but had a large and well-organized workshop to paint from his sketches.

While the Senate was concerned with enhancing the interior of the Doge's Palace, the Procurators of St Mark's employed the Florentine architect, Sansovino (1486-1570) to improve the area round St Mark's Square. Numerous houses were pulled down and rebuilt, shacks removed from the Piazzetta, and the great library by the water-front begun in 1536. Basically, the layout of the area around the Basilica, as we know it today, is due to Sansovino.

This desire for grandeur began to make itself felt among the patricians and indeed was common to all the merchant classes of the rich Mediterranean cities. Money which would previously have been invested in trade was spent on acquiring land, on the building of country villas and on much self-glorifying art. This process was encouraged in Venice by the fact that throughout the fifteenth century the city had been acquiring extensive territories on the mainland; thus Venetians were positively obliged to go and live on the mainland for the sake of its administration. This gave Palladio (1508-1580), the greatest architect of the period, his opportunity.

Palladio came from Padua, which was at this time part of Venetian territory and so was closely linked to that city. His education was deliberately classical, supervised by the humanist poet Giangiorgio Trissino, who took him to Rome in 1540 to study ancient buildings. Palladio's style is based on the work of Bramante, but no contemporary was as pure and strict as he in the use of the classical style. From the very beginning his ground plans were rigorously symmetrical and as he went on he simplified his style more and more, aiming for dramatic, elegant, spatial effects. Palladio was widely patronised by the builders of the new villas, his most ambitious design being for the Villa Malcontenta, built between 1551 and 1561. His Villa Maser, built c.1560, is resplendent with Veronese frescoes. Perhaps his most famous design was for the Villa Rotunda which, as its name implies, was built around a circular plan. This elegant building, raised above the gardens which surround it, with each front perfectly symmetrical and approached by great flights of steps, is planned in a style that creates a harmonious link between house and garden.

Palladio was also a writer and, in imitation of Vitruvius, wrote a treatise on architecture called the *Four Books of Architecture* which became a bible for classical architects over the next two centuries. It had a profound influence on the development of English architecture in the eighteenth century, especially on the work of Inigo Jones.

The sixteenth century saw the heyday of Venetian artistic culture. Yet in political and commercial power the city had already declined; her way of life was more pleasure-seeking and prosperous than ever before. By the eighteenth century Venice had become the pleasure resort of all Europe.

Above: *The Saving of the body of St Mark*, painted by Tintoretto between 1562 and 1566. It shows the body of the saint being stolen away by Christians from the pyre on which it was to have been burnt. A hurricane is driving away all the pagans. The painting shows Tintoretto's typically dramatic tricks of composition. The fallen man clutching the curtain in the foreground ushers us into the 'stage' as if in a theatre. The pale, ghostly buildings and figures in the background serve to focus the eye on the main drama and give a feeling of agitation and unreality to the scene.

Left: *Venus and Adonis*, painted by Paolo Veronese c.1580. Adonis is asleep in Venus's lap, while Cupid holds one of the hounds—a reminder that the idyll is about to be shattered when Adonis is killed hunting. The setting sun, with shadowy clouds descending, adds to the sense of advancing doom. Venus is draped in rich damask, typical of Veronese's love of splendid textures.

Leonardo da Vinci

The name of Leonardo da Vinci (1452-1519) is known throughout the western world. The range of his mind was phenomenal. Even during the Italian Renaissance, when devotion to one single art or science was rare, few men could rival Leonardo's achievement in any of the fields in which he occupied himself. He excelled as artist, natural scientist and anatomist; he experimented in studies as diverse and as novel as engineering and town planning, the design of war machines and even theatrical stage design. His paintings the *Mona Lisa* and the *Last Supper* are outstanding even in an age which produced numerous masterpieces. His scientific studies and observations have been seen as anticipating the outlook of modern science.

Nevertheless, in combining science with art Leonardo was a man of his time. Renaissance artists believed that painting must be shown to be associated with science, particularly mathematics, if it was to be a respectable branch of knowledge. At that time painting was not included among the seven liberal arts of arithmetic, geometry, astronomy, music, grammar, logic and rhetoric which were believed to be the basis of all sound learning. Leonardo, however, believed that a connection between art and mathematics (a science that was closely bound up with the magic of perspective and harmony) was highly desirable, to raise the status of painting from a craft to an intellectual pursuit. Hence his intense concern with mathematics. 'Let no one who is not a mathematician read my works.'

His chaotic notebooks indeed show an omnivorous appetite for knowledge of all kinds; as a practising artist he was not only curious to know how things worked, he was also a largely self-educated intellectual who jotted down what interested him from his reading. If painting was to be a branch of knowledge and the painter to be on a par with the philosopher, clearly all branches of natural science, biology, botany and geology were within his range:
'If you despise painting, which is the sole means of reproducing all the known works of nature, you despise an invention, which with subtle and philosophic speculation considers all the qualities of forms: seas, plants, animals, grasses, flowers, all of which are encircled in light and shadow.'

In many ways Leonardo's thinking was typical of his age, an age not yet entirely free from certain medieval casts of mind. Ways of approaching a particular subject did not belong in separate 'compartments' —Leonardo combined observed fact with a vivid imagination, strange fantasy, apocalyptic vision with scientific study, the practical with the impractical in a way that is not now regarded as rational. Yet Leonardo's work also demonstrates the originality of a mind racing ahead of its contemporaries.

Leonardo, this 'universal' man, was born in Vinci near Florence, in 1452. At the age of 20 he passed as a master in the

M. Pucciarelli

Above: Detail from the *Baptism of Christ*, by Verrocchio, showing two angels. The one on the left, more sensitive and subtle, is said to have been painted by Leonardo during his apprenticeship in Verrocchio's studio. The story goes that when the older artist saw that his pupil had surpassed him he gave up painting. The whole panel is in tempera, a medium in which egg yolk or glue is used to bind the colours, but Leonardo used a new oil technique to paint his angel. He failed to understand fully the nature of this medium— one tragic result of this was the decay of his great wall painting, the *Last Supper*.

Below: The unfinished *Adoration of the Magi*, which Leonardo worked on in 1481 for the monastery of San Donato near Florence. The young man looking out of the picture on the bottom right may be a self-portrait. Leonardo is experimenting here with the 'pyramid-shaped' form of composition which he uses in later complex figure groups. The crowded background includes a sketch of a viaduct.

Bottom: One of the multitude of scientific sketches found in Leonardo's notebooks. It shows how a wing could be flapped up and down by the use of a lever mechanism.

Scala

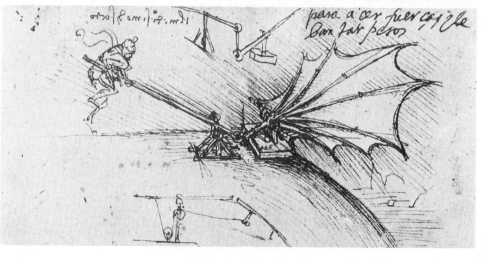

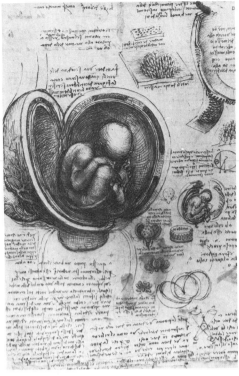

Left: A drawing of an embryo. Leonardo's anatomical drawings were much in advance of his time and are one of his greatest claims to fame and genius. He believed that an understanding of all the forms of nature was essential to the painter and many of his sketches were drawn from dissected specimens. His notes are equally advanced. He wrote about the foetus: 'In the case of this child the heart does not beat and it does not breathe because it lies continually in water. And if it were to breathe it would be drowned, and breathing is not necessary because it receives life and is nourished from the life and food of the mother.'

Below: Pen and ink drawing for a chariot with scythes. Chariots armed with scythes were known to classical literature and used occasionally even in Leonardo's time, but he has added fantasy to fact by giving his machine an overcomplicated rotating drive. This is one of a number of sketches for armoured vehicles and siege machines done in Milan.

matriculation examination of the guild of painters in the exhilarating artistic atmosphere of Medici Florence. It was customary at this time for an artist to learn his trade by helping in the workshop of a famous painter. For example, Leonardo helped his master Verrocchio in the painting of the *Baptism of Christ* by doing one of the two angels. But he showed his artistic independence in an unusual curiosity about the formation of drapery. He made clay figures which he covered with linen dipped in clay and then drew them, carefully studying the way the folds fell.

Moreover in both the angel in Verrocchio's *Baptism* and in the subsequent *Adoration of the Magi* (1481), commissioned for a monastery outside Florence, Leonardo experimented with a new oil technique. He was to use this material disastrously on a plaster wall surface in his *Last Supper*. His failure fully to understand the medium led to the deterioration of this great painting even in his own life time.

Like so many of his works, the *Adoration* was left unfinished. The painting is typical of Leonardo's style in the use he makes of the 'pyramid-shaped' form of composition. This foreshadows his later experimentation with the form in trying to solve the complex figure compositions of the *Virgin of the Rocks* and more especially of the *Madonna and Child with St. Anne*. The mysterious unfinished background of the *Adoration* foreshadows the later landscape in the Mona Lisa portrait. Part of the background consists of an architectural drawing of a viaduct, which anticipates Leonardo's engineering projects in Milan and his concern with the control and diversion of rivers. Indeed he had a lasting fascination with water.

Leonardo in Milan

By 1483 Leonardo had left the republic of Florence for another Renaissance city state, the Duchy of Milan. In the letter introducing himself to its Duke, Ludovico Sforza, he claimed to be a skilled military engineer, mentioning painting only last among his catalogue of accomplishments. The extravagant build-up with plans on a far greater scale than he was to achieve is a revealing personality trait:

'In peace I believe I can give you as complete satisfaction as anyone in the construction of buildings, both public and private . . . I can further execute sculpture in marble, bronze or clay and in painting I can do as much as anyone, whoever he may be. Moreover I would undertake the commission of the bronze horse which will endow with immortal glory and eternal honour the auspicious memory of your father and of the illustrious house of Sforza.'

Leonardo was to work for 16 years on the equestrian statue to the glory of the

58

founder of the Sforza dynasty but, paradoxically, the self-advertised building engineer and inventor of elaborate machinery lacked sufficient technical skill to do the bronze casting for the monument. On the other hand, the drawings of horses which Leonardo made in preparation for his project are unsurpassed.

Leonardo's work in Milan illustrates that strange blend of the scientific with the fantastic. A series of drawings and a sketch for a stage set are evidence of the part Leonardo played in pageants and theatrical performances at the Sforza court. It is now thought that even some of his apparently 'modern' mechanical inventions may have been designed for use in parades or theatrical performances. His sketches for 'armoured vehicles' and siege machines were never built or used in war by Duke Ludovico.

Many of Leonardo's architectural plans and building sketches, however, do strike a more functional note: he drew a house with a double staircase of a similar type to modern concrete designs; a design for a town with roads on two levels indicates a solution to modern traffic problems. The idea of a brothel with three entrances to allow its visitors to enter unobserved would presumably eliminate embarrassment to clients of any period. In Milan Leonardo's preoccupation with water resulted in a practical drawing for the control of a river by means of weirs and sluices.

Two of Leonardo's most famous paintings are associated with his residence in Milan—one of the two versions of the *Virgin of the Rocks* and the *Last Supper*. The latter reveals Leonardo's originality by a break with contemporary treatment of the subject. He offers a 'psychological' rendering of the Apostles' reaction to the crucial moment when Christ declares that one of their number will betray him; the twelve Apostles are arranged in lively interacting groups with Judas sitting among them instead of, as traditionally, separated off across the table.

Natural science and anatomy

In 1499 an invading French army crossed the Alps and captured Milan. Leonardo returned to Florence where he remained on and off for the next six years. Here he spent much time pursuing the studies in anatomy which had begun to occupy him at the Sforza court. Anatomy had been studied by Florentine artists (like Pollaiuolo) since the beginning of the century, but Leonardo's interest appar-

ently exceeded the requirements of an artist. His drawing of a human embryo, for example, indicates that his interest was also scientific.

The mysterious forces of nature, whether in its rock formations, plant life or flowing water haunt Leonardo's paintings as well as his note books. The figures of the *Virgin and St Anne* and the *Mona Lisa*, both painted during this period in Florence, are projected onto rocky scenery similar to that which surrounds the *Virgin of the Rocks*. Plants which have been carefully observed and realistically rendered grow about the feet of both virgins; rivers wind their way into the background behind the *Mona Lisa*. The movement of water which so obsessed Leonardo was sometimes channelled practically into irrigation projects; in drawings it evolved fantastically into the forms of twisting hair and knots and even, in his last years, into a cataclysmic vision of world catastrophe.

In 1502 Leonardo had spent nearly twelve months away from Florence as military engineer to that arch-terrorist Cesare Borgia. He finally left Florence for Rome but after the death of his Medici patron he left for the French court at Amboise—he had already been appointed painter to Francis I in 1517. Two years later he died there, it is said, in the arms of his royal patron.

Leonardo is usually associated with Michelangelo and Raphael as one of the contributors of the High Renaissance—a period in which the whole process of the rebirth of learning culminated in numerous artistic masterpieces. Yet he was 23 years older than Michelangelo and 31 years Raphael's senior. It was he, therefore, who pointed the way to much of the achievement of this time. Although he left only a small number of paintings, few of which were completed, their subtle transitions of tone and sharp contrasts of light and shadow found many imitators but few equals. If he did not quite discover the circulation of the blood, or cast his horse in bronze, get his armoured vehicles into action or his 'aircraft' into flight, he left thousands of drawings for his projects which establish him as one of the world's greatest draughtsmen and a fine anatomist. Closer in outlook to the modern inventor than to the modern scientist, Leonardo's restless, enquiring spirit was opposed to any form of generalization whether medieval or modern. In him, art and science, peace and war, were united in a desire to penetrate nature's secrets and to affirm man's gift of creativity.

Left: Cartoon for the *Madonna and Child with St. Anne*, probably drawn towards the end of Leonardo's stay in Milan. He is continuing to work on the idea of a triangular composition, as in the *Adoration*.

Below left: Leonardo's preparatory drawings for the bronze equestrian statue of the founder of the Sforza dynasty, which ruled Milan while Leonardo was working there. The project only reached the model stage and was destroyed when the French took Milan.

Above: The *Mona Lisa*, one of the most famous portraits in the world. The sitter was the wife of a Florentine official, quite a mature woman. The simplest explanation of the much-discussed smile is that given by Leonardo himself—he kept his model amused with music and reading. Leonardo used subtle colour transitions from light to dark as a means of throwing contours into relief. He wrote in his notes on painting that light and shade should blend 'in the manner of smoke'.

Left: The only known likeness of Leonardo, a self-portrait in old age.

Right: One of a series of visionary drawings of disaster, done in Leonardo's last years, which echo the dillusion and regret expressed in his writings in the same period. He wrote of his visions of man's cruelty: 'Creatures shall be seen upon the earth who will always be fighting one with another . . . when they have crammed themselves with food it shall gratify their desire to deal out death, affliction, labours, terrors and banishment to every living thing . . . there shall be nothing remaining on the earth or under the earth or in the waters that shall not be pursued and molested and destroyed'.

One of five sibyls by
Michaelangelo, on the
ceiling of the Sistine
Chapel. They were
painted on the supports
of the dome, and
represent the revelation
to the gentiles.

DELPH·ICA

Michelangelo

Michelangelo Buonarroti (1475-1564) is an artist whose breadth of attainment testifies to the great aspirations of Renaissance Italy. Although he always considered himself primarily a sculptor, he was also a painter, architect and poet.

Michelangelo was born at Caprese, in Florentine territory, the son of a magistrate of noble stock whose fortunes had declined. In the face of strong parental opposition, he started his apprenticeship as an artist in 1488, at the age of 13. Soon he attracted the patronage of Lorenzo the Magnificent, the powerful head of the Medici family.

In 1492 Lorenzo died; the period which followed was for Florence one of upheaval. Savanarola gained ascendancy and, though Michelangelo was never his close follower, this fanatical friar's books were a life-long influence on the artist. It is probable that Michelangelo began a scientific study of anatomy during these years. Here were the beginnings of what were later the artist's major preoccupations; a reverence for the physical human form and a deeply religious sense and awareness of sin.

Michelangelo's long life—he lived to be 89—was spent between Florence and Rome, patronised in turn by the Popes, the Medici and the Florentine Republic. Many stories are told of Michelangelo's fiery temperament; his broken nose, which disfigured him for life (the result of a youthful fight with a fellow artist) is

just one example of this. His relationship with the Papacy, especially with Julius II, his first great patron, was punctuated by quarrels, for the artist's proud nature rivalled that of his pope.

Some idea of the qualities which Michelangelo was felt to possess is given in the biography by Vasari, a sixteenth-century Italian historian who knew the artist personally;

'The benign ruler of heaven . . . decided to send into the world an artist who would be skilled in each and every craft . . . Moreover, he determined to give this artist the knowledge of true moral philosophy and the gift of poetic expression, so that everyone might admire and follow him as their perfect exemplar in life, work and behaviour . . . . And therefore he chose to have Michelangelo born a Florentine, so that one of her own citizens might bring to absolute perfection the achievements for which Florence was already justly renowned.'

The Renaissance believed that 'true moral philosophy' is required of the artist —he must impart through his works his own view of life. An artist is therefore a man who deals in ideas, and clothes those ideas in outward form, now paint, now stone or marble. Looked at in this manner, there is no disparity between the various aspects of Michelangelo's creative career.

Michelangelo was deeply influenced by the work of earlier artists, especially Masaccio's frescoes and Donatello's powerful psychological sculptures of

Mansell

Scala

Left: A drawing of the *Madonna and Child* by Michelangelo. This study shows clearly the artist's supreme ability in rendering the human body. The infant's torso seems solid and weighty, his flesh almost like marble. The sculptural quality of the drawing is characteristic of the artist's style.

Above: A bronze head of Michelangelo (1475-1564) by an unknown 16th-century sculptor. Michelangelo was adept at several arts; primarily a sculptor, he was also an architect, painter and poet. Before his lifetime, art had been almost a manual craft; he left it a highly-esteemed intellectual discipline.

Below: The *Doni Tondo*, painted by Michelangelo between 1504 and 1506. It reveals his interest in developing tight yet supple compositions, inspired by Leonardo's example. The Virgin resembles a classical goddess rather than a member of the Christian Holy Family; in the background, angels are replaced by nude youths.

religious figures. The study of antiquity was the other enduring influence on his art. His profound interest in the unclothed human figure (so rare in medieval art), his concern with the motifs of classical architecture, and with the remains of antiquity, all made the city of Rome the natural location for the full flowering of his style. He first went there in 1496 and carved his first major work, the *Bacchus*, in a classical manner. He had already made a *Sleeping Cupid* (now lost) which, according to one version of the story, he had buried so that an eager connoisseur might perhaps 'discover' the 'antique'

The heroic human form

During the same visit, he also made the *St Peter's Pieta* (a pieta is a representation of the dead Christ supported on His Mother's lap). This exceedingly intricate, highly 'finished' sculpture established his fame. He returned home to Florence and between 1501 and 1504 made the statue of *David* which is inspired by literary descriptions of huge ancient statues known as *colossi*. No-one before Michelangelo had made such an assured nude on such a scale: its importance was not simply artistic, but political as well, for it stood as a symbol of the Florentine passion for liberty, particularly important at a time when enemy states were threatening the republic's independence.

Michelangelo's first great painting was begun during the same period when, in 1504, he was commissioned to fresco *The Battle of Cascina* for a wall of the Council Hall of the new Florentine Republic, in almost open competition against Leonardo's *Battle of Anghiari*, commissioned earlier. But whereas Leonardo's cartoon for this concentrates on the psychological conflict between men and horses, Michelangelo attempts a scene before the battle, when bathing soldiers are called to arms. This gives him the opportunity to concentrate exclusively on the naked human body, therefore displaying his knowledge of human anatomy.

In 1505 Michelangelo went to Rome and began to design a monumental tomb for Pope Julius II. The *Julius Monument*, as it is called, was dogged by ill-luck. Both the Pope and the artist had fiery temperaments and soon quarrelled. After Julius died in 1513 the project dragged on until finally, after the fifth contract in 1542, it was finished by assistants. The tomb had taken almost 40 years to build and its original design had been drastically cut down in scale and altered. This ruin of a monument was placed in the church of St Pietro in Vincoli, a shadow of the artists original intentions. For the tomb, Michelangelo carved the *slaves*, some of his most impressive sculptures. They reveal, just as in *The Battle of Cascina*, the naked body's ability to convey the range and power of human emotions.

The Sistine ceiling—a vast masterpiece

In 1508, Michelangelo was commissioned to fresco the ceiling of the Sistine chapel. This huge undertaking is made more astounding by the fact that Michelangelo, at first disinterested in the scheme, soon dismissed his assistants and frescoed the entire area alone. For four years, until 1512, he worked on the scheme, often in conditions of great hardship. Most of the time he had to paint lying on his back, too close to the ceiling to ever properly

Below: Michelangelo's unfinished *Pieta*, one of his last works. The style of the detached arm and polished legs indicates his new concern to express a less heroic, more emotional, spirit.

Above: A famous statue, Michelangelo's *David*. Florentines associated this Old Testament hero with the pagan hero Hercules, and Michelangelo has reflected this in the strong, muscular body. Its gigantic size, almost 5 metres high, shows his desire to equal the colossal monuments of the ancient world.

Below: The tomb of Giuliano in the Medici chapel. Michelangelo created a perfect marriage between architecture and sculpture. The combination of cold, angular masses and plain surfaces with delicate ornament and sensuous figures gives the chapel a unique, disturbing quality.

see what he was doing.

In the Sistine ceiling, Michelangelo was able to paint on an immensity of scale impossible in sculpture. The effect of the ceiling is overwhelming; partly because of the great size of the figures, which get bigger towards the altar wall, and partly as a result of its theme. The whole scheme is a tribute to the beauty of man and to the glory of his redemption through the eventual appearance of Christ (seen in *The Last Judgement*, Michelangelo's late work on the altar wall). Michelangelo's subject is no less than the story of the world from the Creation onward; the ceiling is devoted to Old Testament scenes, but Christ's Coming is hinted at by the monumental prophets and sibyls seated down either side of the vault.

The importance of Michelangelo's achievement lies in *scale*—the scale of the figures, of their heroic and forceful bodies, but above all the scale of the artist's powerful imagination. It is not surprising that a view grew up that this artist was endowed with greater than human abilities and divinely inspired; his single-minded genius earned him the title of '*il divino*'—the divine Michelangelo.

Even when he dealt with architecture, Michelangelo treated the stone in a sculptural way, using unusual combinations of classical architectural elements to produce an emotional effect. In his first important commission, the Medici Chapel in the church of St Lorenzo, Florence, (worked on between 1520-34 but never completed) he combined sculpture with architecture. The chapel reveals a blend of tension and lethargy, reflected in the reclining nude figures on the tombs of Guilio and Lorenzo de Medici. During the

same period, he designed the nearby vestibule of the *Biblioteca Laurenziana* (the Medicean Library).

Much of Michelangelo's later life was occupied by architecture, but he also made some sculptures, as private and difficult to understand as his architecture. His last two works were *pietas*, on which he was working in 1563 and in 1564, the year of his death. Their effect is one of tragedy and pathos. This is partly due to the artist's apparent attempt to cut the marble down until it expresses only the spiritual suffering of the religious event, rather than glorifying the beauty of the body. The narrow, emaciated form of the *Rondanini Pieta*, part-polished from an earlier attempt, part rough, with its un-real proportions, testifies to a mind still fertile, ceaselessly experimenting, yet perhaps to a body too feeble to work the marble very finely.

Michelangelo's intentions in these late works are difficult to uncover fully. It is perhaps true to say that he approached work as Leonardo did—as a set of problems to be resolved; once he could see the solution, the interest in actually finishing was diminished.

It was not only in paint and stone that Michelangelo's imagination found expression, but in words also. The sonnets which he wrote are records of a passionate nature, full of religious fervour but deeply fascinated, too, by earthly beauty:

Ravished by all that to the eyes is fair,
Yet hungry for the joys that truly
bless,
My soul can find no stair
To mount to heaven, save earth's
loveliness.

Bulloz

Mansell

Scala

M. Pucciarelli

Above: *The Dying Slave*, one of the figures carved for an early version of the tomb erected to Julius II, captures the final moment of resignation between life and death. In this figure, Michelangelo was much influenced by a classical statue which showed the Trojan priest Laocoon and his sons in their death agony.

Left: The Laurentian Library was a revolutionary piece of architecture, in that Michelangelo totally demolished the classical system in order to produce expressive forms—like this cascading staircase—deliberately ignoring the rules of classical architecture adopted by the Renaissance.

Above: In contrast to the late unfinished *Pieta*, the St Peter's *Pieta* shows Michelangelo's early style. The intricate flowing drapery, together with the high polish given to the marble, makes the work look almost jewelled. The composition broke new ground for sculpture in the grouping of the seated and lying figures.

Right: *The Creation of Adam* from the Sistine Chapel ceiling epitomises the Renaissance interest in physical beauty and classical forms. The figures are highly sculptural, as if Michelangelo the sculptor, frustrated by delays to the Julius monument project, built that monument in paint instead.

Northern Renaissance Painters

The 'Northern Renaissance' was never as clear cut and all-embracing as its Italian counterpart. While the Italians of the fifteenth and sixteenth centuries were experimenting with classical forms and principles, the architects and masons of the period in northern Europe continued to build in a way we still recognize as 'Gothic'. The painters, too, developed in the traditions inherited from the Middle Ages, quickened perhaps by their knowledge of the Italian achievement, but often surprisingly independent of it.

Perhaps the principal feature marking the new spirit of painting in Northern Europe around 1400 is the increasing emancipation of art from an exclusively religious purpose. Whether from piety, tradition or simple convenience, religious subjects were to be treated by artists for centuries to come, but in the early fifteenth century the background of a painting begins to assume a new and increased significance. The landscape, the incidental animals, men, trees, cities, rivers and mountains against which the religious subject is depicted are no longer merely a foil but have a life of their own.

Hand in hand with this discovery of external reality (which was to culminate in the establishment of the landscape and the still life as genres in their own right) goes an increased interest in human personality: more and more the artist sees himself as a unique individual. Nor are the people he depicts merely figures playing a part in a story. Indeed at times the 'story' is incidental to the portrayal of human beings, until by the turn of the fifteenth century portrait-painting emerged as a distinct artistic occupation.

The Netherlands take the lead

Not surprisngly, the Netherlands took the lead in developments in Northern Europe. The Netherlands were in many ways at a stage of development similar to that of Italy: the cities were economically prosperous, their merchant-burghers were interested in new ideas, concerned with their own status, and were wealthy enough to act as patrons of the arts. The country's political organization, a collection of duchies, counties and city states under the over-lordship of the Duke of Burgundy, offered a climate where independence and experimentation might flourish.

The greatest of fifteenth-century painters in the Netherlands was Jan van Eyck (1390-1441) although, like his Italian contemporaries, he never finally mastered perspective. His approach to the depiction of the external world seems to have differed from the Italian method. Instead of acquiring a thorough 'scientific' knowledge of the laws governing perspective, and studying anatomy to understand the human body, van Eyck's technical mastery is based on sheer observation. Detail upon detail is meticulously added to the painting until it faithfully mirrors the world he sees.

Van Eyck's gifts were sufficient to attract commissions from wealthy secular figures and his *Marriage Portrait of Giovanni Arnolfini* is perhaps the most celebrated painting of the age. This fifteenth-century equivalent of a wedding photograph shows Arnolfini, an Italian silk merchant resident in Bruges, standing with his young wife in a room in his house. He strives to re-create the effect of the light which falls from the window and not even the most minute detail escapes the painter's brush, right down to the hair of the dog's coat. This Dutch interior on canvas is the ancestor of the realistic seventeenth-century pictures of everyday life—known as *genre* paintings.

The successors of van Eyck, such as Rogier van der Weyden and Hugo van der Goes, did not immediately develop the secular aspect of his work. Rather, they took his realism and re-applied it to the traditional topics of medieval religious art.

During the first decades of the sixteenth century, the Netherlands produced fewer great masters. This was a period of crisis and change in art, during which the ideas of the Italian Renaissance were being absorbed into existing styles. But between the mid-fifteenth and the mid-sixteenth centuries, two artists, both rather separate from the Italian influences, stand out from their contemporaries.

The first, Hieronymous Bosch (1450-1516) is famed for his symbolic pictures of religious subjects. The theme of his *Hay-Wain* triptych (c.1500) is the progress of the human soul from its first innocence in the Garden of Eden to its temptation by the transient pleasures of earthly desires,

Above: *The Adoration of the Lamb* from the Ghent altar-piece by Jan van Eyck, completed 1432. This religious allegory is given a highly realistic treatment. Van Eyck's marvellously detailed technique is seen in the faces and robes of the crowd, in the flower-strewn meadow setting and the distant Gothic city.

Below: Van Eyck's *Marriage of Giovanni Arnolfini* (1434). The smallest details are faithfully rendered, from the gleaming chandelier to the reflection of the scene in the mirror on the wall. Events from the Passion decorate the mirror frame, echoing other religious images in the picture.

Left: *The Nativity* (c.1475) painted by Hugo van der Goes (c. 1440-82) as part of his *Portinari Altarpiece*. The artist's handling of proportion and space is highly individual (notice the small-scale angels). The three yokel shepherds are sympathetically observed; there is a quality of pathos in the tiny, isolated Infant.

Right: Watercolour of a hare by the German artist Albrecht Durer (1471-1528). Durer excelled in painting, engraving, drawing and woodcuts. A fine, sensitive draughtsman, his subjects ranged through many aspects of nature from landscape watercolours to minutely detailed studies of animals and plant life.

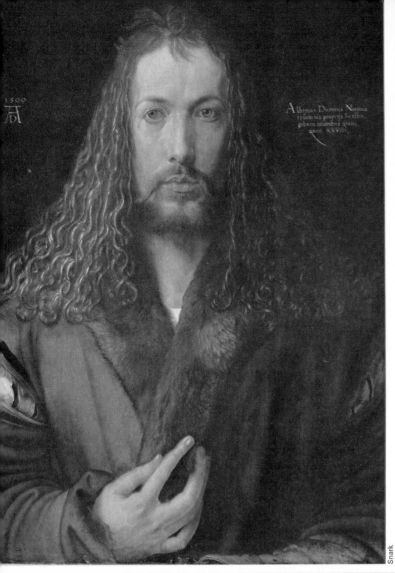

Left: A self-portrait of Durer, dated 1500. During his career, he produced a series of such portraits, a search for a self-image that suggests an increasing curiosity about his innermost nature, not unmixed with a certain personal vanity.

Above: *The Four Horsemen of the Apocalypse*, from a set of woodcuts made by Durer in 1498. His woodcuts and engravings reveal his genius. He perfected the technique of both these art-forms and his work had great influence throughout Europe. The *Apocalypse* series, concerned with the horrors of Doomsday, are a blend of Renaissance realism and Gothic imagery. Here, Durer's powerful, almost visionary imagination is tempered by his careful organization of the packed composition.

and the everlasting agonies in store for those who succumb.

In this, and in the triptych of *The Temptation of St. Anthony* (c.1500), which shows the saint being tormented by weird and evil phantasms conjured up by Satan 'the magician', Bosch reveals the fantastic and grotesque nature of his own imagination. His images seem to embody the religious fears of the medieval mind and even in those paintings which come closest to the realism of van Eyck, the realism is of an exaggerated, menacing kind.

Pieter Breugel the Elder (c.1525/30-1-569) shows the influence of Bosch in his painting known as *Mad Meg* (1562) which is full of the strange imagery of the older artist. But Breugel is mostly remembered for his peasant scenes, intended to be gently satiric and full of sharply observed anecdotes. The good-humoured depictions of simple rustic life, as in the *Peasant Wedding* (c.1568), are by no means 'simple' paintings, but reveal an unerring sense of composition and colour. His evocative landscape scenes of the *Months* (1565) looks forward to the later development of landscape as a fit subject for painting.

Durer: a 'Universal Man'

The new prominence of secular subjects in art seems to appear later in Germany than the Netherlands. Albrecht Durer (1471-1528), is the greatest German artist of the period and, although the legacy of the past is strong in much of Durer's work, he was the closest the Northern Renaissance came to producing a 'Universal Man'.

Durer was not only a major painter, but was expert enough at geometry to produce 65

a treatise on fortifications, to write theoretical works on perspective and proportion, and added to these writings philosophical speculations on the nature of art and the training of artists. Durer was brought up in a craft tradition, his father being a goldsmith. This helped his development in drawing and engraving, fields in which his genius is perhaps better expressed than in his paintings. As a citizen of the rich merchant city of Nuremberg, he accepted with a combination of commercial acumen and artistic integrity the technical challenge to the printer's art involved in producing for a mass market.

Durer's so-called 'master' engravings exhibit a characteristic combination of Gothic and Renaissance elements. The realistically conceived Christian knight in *Knight, Death and the Devil* is placed in an essentially Gothic landscape, where he is threatened by the Devil and Death of medieval tradition. He is, however, utterly realistic in conception and the horse he rides is perfectly proportioned. He is a symbol of the Renaissance belief in the ascendancy of the individual, relying on his own innate strength to conquer the forces of evil and corruption.

In his religious painting Durer imbues Gothic themes with powerful emotion. Such paintings as his *Lamentation of Christ*, the *Feast of the Rose Garlands* or the *Adoration of the Trinity* can only be fully appreciated in the light of medieval tradition, but in all cases he surpasses that tradition in his exploration of human anatomy, technical refinement and selective use of colour, light and shade.

One of the earliest German painters consistently to sign his work, Durer is supremely aware of his own personality. In the course of his life he produced a remarkable series of self-portraits. The intensity of these works derive from Durer's profound self-scrutiny; they reveal an increasing desire on his part to discover the deepest aspects of his nature. Combined with this is a curious degree of vanity and pride in himself, seen at its height in the self-portrait deliberately reminiscent of Christ. Similarly, his portraits of Nuremberg patricians or his charcoal drawing of his mother shortly before her death—extremely powerful in its unflinching, but not unloving realism —show an inexhaustible interest in the mystery of human personality which is wholly Renaissance.

Equally in the spirit of the Renaissance is his exploration of animate and inanimate nature: the unsurpassed sensitivity and realism of his animal paintings or his studies of a piece of garden turf are sufficient to make them worthy of a place in a textbook of natural science.

Holbein: court painter to the Tudors

A German painter of a slightly later date, Hans Holbein the Younger (1497-1543), is best known for his portraits. He was born into the generation most affected by the crisis of the religious Reformation. This forced him to give up his career in painting altar-pieces (at which he excelled) and leave his native country for England. There he became court painter to Henry VIII and produced memorable portraits of the royal household. These restrained and calm portraits, at first meticulously detailed and later much simplified in style, are thoughtful and penetrating in their analysis of personality.

Durer's great contemporary Mathis Neithardt (1470-1528), better known as Grunewald, is more firmly rooted in the Gothic tradition and his work is largely untouched by Italian influences. His most celebrated painting, the *Crucifixion* from the Isenheim altar, is in direct line of descent from the great carved altarpieces of the later Middle Ages, but is infused with a heightened emotional content and an unparalleled dramatic quality. There is no trace in any of the figures of an interest in the beauty of the human body or of a desire to establish a 'just proportion'. Realism is seen in the modelling of the arms, legs and torso of the crucified Christ and in the half-open mouth from which the breath has fled, but

Above: The *Crucifixion* from the Isenheim Altarpiece (1515) by Grunewald (c.1470-1528). In this painting Grunewald is shown to be firmly rooted in the Gothic tradition. His use of proportion and perspective is symbolic rather than realistic; Christ, executed on a larger scale than the other figures, dominates the scene. The painful distortion of his feet, arms and hands reveal the artist's Gothic preoccupation with gory details. This effect is increased by the greenish light bathing the wounded body, dramatic against the gloomy background. The frailty of the other figures emphasizes the intensity of their grief.

Above: *Christ on the Cross*, painted in 1503 by Lucas Cranach (1472-1553). As in Grunewald's work on the same theme, Cranach emphasizes the horrible suffering of the crucified bodies. But his figures are realistic and solid, perfectly proportioned. The drama is set against a finely-detailed rocky landscape, with a threatening sky.

Right: Detail from *The Battle between Carnival and Lent* by Pieter Breugel (c.1525-69), showing a mock joust. This allegorical work reveals Breugel's interest in peasant life. He is celebrated for his good-humoured, gently satiric portrayal of rustic life, full of realistic detail and anecdote.

66

Grunewald operates with a highly unrealistic use of proportion and perspective. In a startling development of medieval tradition, Christ as the dominant figure is executed on a larger scale than the other figures: even the sturdy John the Baptist on the right is small by comparison, while the figures on the left are slight and willowy. The frailty of these figures emphasizes their great anguish.

The work of the members of the 'Danube school' is the most notable sixteenth-century example of how religious pictures were enlivened by human and secular interest. Albrecht Altdorfer (1480-1538) and Lucas Cranach the Elder (1472-1553) both combine the treatment of traditional themes with bold innovations in composition. In Altdorfer's work, in the dream-like quality of his landscapes, whether it is in the soaring background to the *Holy Family* or the swirling foliage of his *St. George and the Dragon*, nature, far from being a mere backcloth, seems to be mysteriously independent of man. In Cranach, however, nature tends to reflect human moods. In his *Christ on the Cross* the Virgin's anguish is closely echoed by nature. The landscape is bleak and isolated under the threat of an impending storm, the dark lowering clouds are luridly lit by lightning.

Cranach was the last member of a remarkable age of German painting. The changed climate of Germany under the impact of the Reformation prevented the emergence of a new generation of major artists and in the coming decades it is once more in the Netherlands that the great names of North European painting are to be found.

Above: The *Ambassadors*, a portrait of French ambassadors at the English court by Hans Holbein the Younger, (c. 1497-1543). Holbein was a German artist who fled to England during the Reformation and became court painter to Henry VIII. In this capacity, he produced many excellent portraits of the Royal Household.

This portrait, with its finely balanced composition and meticulous detail is typical of his style. The ambassadors are shown with symbols of their culture and worldly acquirements. This technique of characterizing his sitters through their setting later gave way to a greater simplicity.

Right: A landscape painting by the German artist Altdorfer (c.1480-1538), one of the first painters to make nature his sole subject. Even his religious works are dominated by imaginative and poetic interpretations of nature. His art reveals a sense of the mystery and grandeur of nature, independent of man.

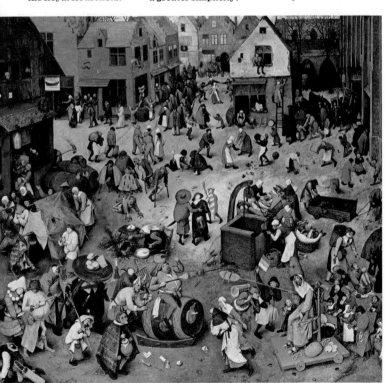

The Spanish Golden Age

In political power and wealth Spain was at its height during the sixteenth century. The discovery and conquest of the New World brought tremendous prestige and riches to the Spanish; their empire included not only the Americas but also parts of Europe and the Far East. It was during this period that the foundations were laid for a 'golden age' in the arts and, as a result of its possessions and connections in Italy and the Netherlands, Spain became familiar with the great cultural developments in the rest of Europe.

The religious background
In literature as in art, the Golden Age in Spain began in the 1580s and lasted for about a century. Spain was a deeply religious country and this faith was directly reflected in the spirit and subject-matter of much of its literature. During the second half of the sixteenth century mystical writings (typifying the religious outlook of Spain) were encouraged by the example of Philip II, a pious and conscientious king, and by the fervent atmosphere of the Catholic Counter-Reformation, which brought a further tightening of the grip of the Inquisition.

Saint Teresa of Avila (1515-82) was one of the most influential of the mystics (a

Above: *St Luke*, the patron saint of artists, painted by El Greco c. 1605 as part of a series of Apostles to hang in Toledo Cathedral. The intense, rapt expression of the saint and the rich tones of the painting place it among the most beautiful of El Greco's works. It has been suggested that *St Luke* is a self-portrait of the artist.

Below: *The Agony in the Garden* by El Greco. In this painting, the artist has abandoned reality to produce a tense, excited, luridly-coloured landscape which conveys the emotion of the subject. Perspective has been minimized in favour of flat pattern and the landscape as well as the figures have movement and passionate intensity. The painting is a strong expression of El Greco's religious conviction.

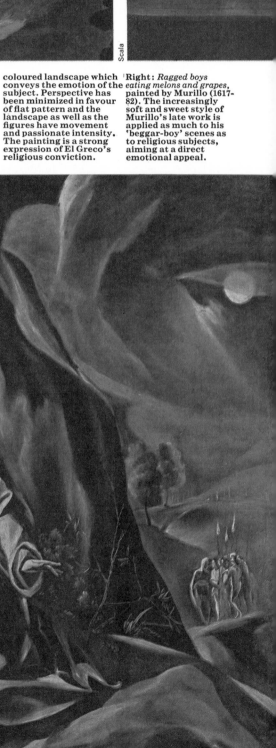

Right: *Ragged boys eating melons and grapes*, painted by Murillo (1617-82). The increasingly soft and sweet style of Murillo's late work is applied as much to his 'beggar-boy' scenes as to religious subjects, aiming at a direct emotional appeal.

John Webb

Bulloz

Scala

Left: Zurbaran (1598-1664) is famous chiefly for his austere, solemn religious scenes, but he was also a fine still-life painter. The impact of this *Still Life with Oranges* derives from his intensely realistic treatment of the three groups, arranged in a simple, deliberate way against a stark background.

Below: *The Trinity* (c.1636) by Ribera (1591-1652). His style is a blend of classical idealism and Spanish realism—with a dramatic use of light and shade. His subjects mirror the religious preoccupations of Spain. This *Trinity* is a devotional image, in which the Father shows Christ to the faithful.

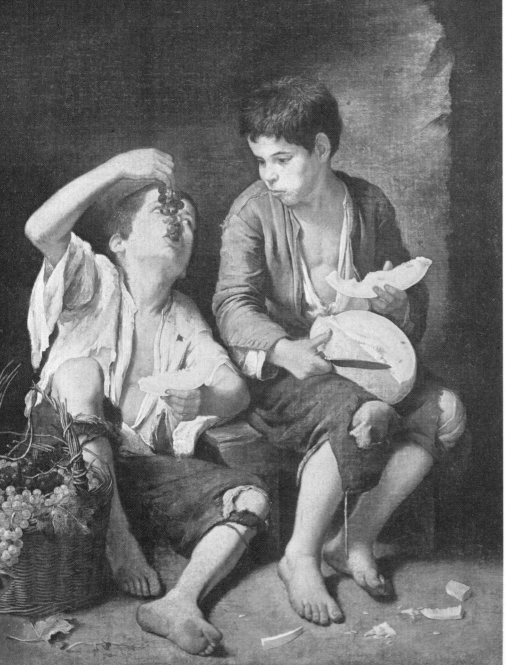

mystic seeks to achieve union with God through contemplation and believes in spiritual truths beyond human understanding). A member of the Carmelite religious order at the age of 19, she became dissatisfied with their laxity and, inspired by religious visions, she founded a reformed group. As Mother Superior, Teresa travelled all over Spain. Her autobiography, together with her many letters of religious instruction and encouragement, combine mystic idealism with practical hints about life, written in a homely style. Her best-known work *The Castle of the Spirit* (1577), describes the soul as a castle with seven suites of rooms radiating outwards. We must progress through these seven rooms (which represent seven stages of prayer) to reach the innermost room, where we find God. St John of the Cross (1542-91), also a member of the Carmelite brethren was the other major religious writer of the period.

In the theatre there was a strong tradition of mysticism, both in the plays performed in the open air and those in the Royal Palaces. Lope de Vega (1562-1635) was the most prolific of Spanish playwrights; a great variety of spectacle poured from his pen (he claimed authorship of 1,800 plays). His *El Arte Nuevo de Hacar Comedias* of 1609 set out his principles: to please the public (he needed money to live as he wished), to keep the outcome of the drama back as long as possible so that the audience stays to the end, and to mix tragedy and comedy. After Lope's death, Calderon de la Borca (1600-81) became the leading Spanish playwright. Having a scholarly training in theology, Calderon wrote a considerable number of *autos sacramentales*—a kind of symbolic mystery play. Like Lope 69 de Vega he also produced plays on the themes of intrigue and honour.

Accompanying the strong theatrical tradition in Spain was an enduring tradition of popular balladry, the *romances*. Plays were mostly written in verse form and many authors, including Calderon and Lope, wrote poetry also. But the straightforward poetry of the ballads gave way, at the beginning of the seventeenth century, to a new style which was obscure and learned, known as *gongorismo* after its originator, Luis de Gongora (1561-1627). In contrast, Francesco de Quevedo (1580-1645), a master of parody and a rather sour observer of the rottenness of contemporary life, advocated simplicity in literary style.

Don Quixote: a great comic novel

In comparison with the cynicism of Quevedo, Miguel de Cervantes' *Don Quixote*, written in two parts, 1605 and 1615, is eminent for its gentle satire and good humour. This novel is the most important and best-loved work to emerge from Spanish literature, having a great influence on the later development of the novel throughout Europe. It combines and satirizes the traditions of the *picaresque* novel (a novel which records the adventures of a rogueish hero) and the romances of chivalry so dear to Cervantes' countrymen.

Don Quixote, a country gentleman, sets out to prove himself a knight-errant, but in his enthusiasm to right all wrongs, he mistakes inns for castles to besiege, windmills for giants, criminals for victims of tyranny. In contrast to his down-to-earth servant, Sancho Panza, Don Quixote sees only the ideal in life. The minor characters in the novel—which is not one continuous narrative but a succession of incidents—present a procession of types from sixteenth-century Spanish society drawn from Cervantes' own richly varied experience.

In the visual arts, first in architecture, then in painting and sculpture, Spain relied far more on foreign influence—the impact of the Italian Renaissance was crucial.

Architecture took a new direction under the initiative of Charles V, who commissioned a new palace in a severe classical style at Granada in 1539. This was followed by Philip II's Escorial near Madrid in 1563. This astonishing monastery, with a centrally-planned church, was also to provide a mausoleum for Charles V. Its grid-like plan has close links with Italian Renaissance theories on the structure of ancient Roman villas.

Philip II was also a connoisseur of painting and enthusiastically commissioned works from Titian which, hanging in the Royal Collections, were to entrance the Flemish painter Rubens on his visits and have a great influence on Spanish artists. At a time when Spanish taste tended towards the Flemish style, these Titians must have looked like visions from another world. They directly shaped the painting of El Greco (1541-1614), who worked in Spain at the end of the sixteenth century.

The haunting art of El Greco

Originally from the Greek island of Crete, El Greco ('the Greek') is said to have been trained in Venice under Titian. El Greco's Byzantine background and his experience of Venetian use of colour combined to

70

M. Pucciarelli

M. Pucciarelli

produce a style which could convey not only the great compositional advances of Renaissance art, but also the inner spiritual experience which was such a vital part of the Spanish religious tradition. His *Agony in the Garden* (c.1595) was made about 20 years after he arrived in Spain and shows clearly the characteristics which were to dominate his style.

His figures are slender and greatly elongated; their forms and those of the landscape background lack a sense of stability, becoming almost flame-like in their wavering, intense quality. The landscape echoes the extreme emotion of the subject, its swirling shapes treated almost as an extension of the drapery. The painting is typical, too, of El Greco's sense of colour: shrill and acid tones of yellow, green and lilac stand out against a moonlit night sky, creating an unreal, eerie atmosphere. The artist is no longer attempting the Renaissance aim of reproducing reality as if seen through a window, but rather the conjuring up in paint of a mystical experience. His images, with their capacity to confront the spectator with fervent religious experiences and inspire feelings of devotion, accord well with the atmosphere of the Spanish Counter-Reformation.

Three years after El Greco's death, a very different kind of artist, Diego Velasquez (1599-1660), finished his training. The greatest Spanish painter of his age, in his early career he followed the 'naturalism' of the Italian artist Caravaggio. His aim was not to create an ideal view of human beauty but to show very real and tangible figures, to represent the reality of 'nature' as faithfully as possible.

The most characteristic works of Velasquez' early career are his *bodegones* or 'kitchen scenes', showing figures with food, drink, cooking pots and other domestic items. *The Old Woman Cooking Eggs* and *The Water Seller of Seville* are two of the best known of these. Velasquez is completely detached from his subject matter, neither sentimental nor mocking about these ordinary people. The objects are so surely painted that they seem real enough to touch; the faces are beautifully observed and a strong, glaring light plays on the figures, contrasting with the very dark, shadowy backgrounds.

When he was just 24, Velasquez' reputation brought him to the attention of the famous. He came to Madrid as court painter and struck up a friendship with the young Philip IV which was to last a lifetime. His father-in-law and former teacher Francisco Pacheco recorded that 'the liberality and affability with which he is treated by such a great monarch is unbelievable. He has a workshop in his gallery and His Majesty has a key to it and a chair in order to watch him painting at leisure, nearly every day.' Whereas El Greco had been primarily an exponent of mystical experience in paint, Velasquez, with his court duties, did little religious work. He was paid to paint portraits of the royal family and their entourage and his work was an instant success at court.

When the great Flemish painter Rubens visited the Spanish court in 1628 he talked with Velasquez and is said to have aroused his enthusiasm for a trip to Italy. The following year he went on this visit, which was to have important effects on his development as an artist. He studied Venetian painting, learning from the way 71

Above: An engraving from the first edition of *Don Quixote* by Cervantes (1547-1616), showing the hero Don Quixote with his down-to-earth servant Sancho Panza. In contrast to his servant, Don Quixote sees only the ideal in life. In spite of the comic plights caused by his enthusiasm, Don Quixote is neither pathetic nor ridiculous; he is made tragic and dignified by the quality of his faith and the breadth of his vision.

Above: A portrait of the versatile Spanish dramatist Lope de Vega (1562-1635) reputed to have written over 1,800 plays.

Right: A view of the interior of the library of the Escorial. Philip II took a close personal interest in the progress of the building. In 1585 he invited Pellegrino Tibaldi from Italy to come and paint a number of frescoes, including these on the library walls.

Below: An aerial view of the Escorial. This immense structure was built by Philip supposedly in fulfilment of a vow to St Lawrence. The plan possibly mimics the gridiron on which St Lawrence was martyred. It served as both convent and palace and contained a mausoleum for the burial of the Spanish kings. This large domed structure—and the whole group design— clearly shows the Italian inspiration behind the architectural style.

the Venetian artists handled space, perspective, light and colour; in particular, Velasquez' mature work shows a much freer technique and a use of brush-strokes that indicates a debt to Titian.

The royal portraits of Velasquez

The years after his return to Madrid were the most productive phase of his career. He continued to produce superlative portraits including the great equestrian portrait of the Count-Duke of Olivares, the power behind the throne. Most typical are the sombre standing portraits, painted in austere greys, browns and olives, enlivened by the occasional glint of white and gold. The massive silhouettes and pale, haughty Hapsburg features were created to both encapsulate and reinforce the autocracy and formality that surrounded the Spanish royal family.

On a second visit to Italy in 1649, where he went on behalf of the king to buy paintings and antiques, Velasquez painted one of his greatest portraits, *Innocent X*, an uncompromising picture that sums up the ecclesiastical and political power of the pope. Velasquez was following in the tradition of Raphael's and Titian's papal portraits, but in technique he moves on in his own right, seen in the almost imperceptible brushstrokes that render the gleaming surface of the Pope's cape

and his confident grasp of the man's expression. The portrait won Velasquez great recognition in Italy.

Returning to Madrid in 1651, Velasquez received further honours and royal offices from Philip. He was much occupied in painting the king's new wife Mariana of Austria and her young children, and in recording the latter years of the ageing king. These portraits complete Velasquez' moving record of the ageing process in his royal master.

In these last years Velasquez painted one of the masterpieces of the seventeenth century, *Las Meninas* (the Maids of Honour). Its subject matter has caused a great deal of speculation. The effect is of looking into the artist's studio—Velasquez is painting the king and queen, who are seen only in reflection in a mirror in the background. Their little daughter and her attendants have come into the room and direct themselves towards the royal presence. We see the scene from the point of view of the two sitters, who stand 'at the invisible border between real and painted space'. This extraordinary painting creates such a strong illusion of involvement that it forces the spectator to question his own sense of reality and to consider the point where 'real' and artistic experience merge.

Two contemporaries of Velasquez, Bartolome Esteban Murillo (1617-1682) and Francisco de Zurbaran (1598-1664) worked with two strongly contrasting styles and types of subject matter. Murillo painted religious subjects and picturesque scenes of everyday life in a style which combined harmonious, flowing compositions with a feeling of pathos and charm. His rather sentimental and sweetly-coloured street urchins and flower girls were much admired in the eighteenth and nineteenth centuries.

Zurbaran is completely different. He was a very fine still-life painter, but is mainly known for his paintings of religious figures—they have a simplicity and austerity which are a reminder of the continuing tradition of strict monasticism in seventeenth-century Spain. Despite the differences in style, his aim, like El Greco, is to reveal the spirit not the flesh. The stark emotion and realistic figures of his paintings have a strong religious purpose —they are meant to lead the spectator into the intensity of mystical experience that the saintly heroes of the compositions actually achieved.

The Water Seller of
Seville by Diego
Velasquez (1599-1660).
Typical of his early
domestic scenes, the
painting demonstrates
a striking use of
chiaroscuro.

Chapter 3

The Baroque Period

The Palazzo Senatorio, part of the
Campidoglio designed by Michaelangelo
and built on the Capitoline Hill, Rome.
The statue of Marcus Aurelius is 2nd
century bronze.

The Baroque Church

Though the term 'Baroque' does describe a particular style of art, it is often used to refer in a general way to a whole period of European culture lasting through the seventeenth and well into the eighteenth century.

As a style, the Baroque originated in Italy just before 1600, springing from a reappraisal of religious feeling within the Catholic church. The Council of Trent, which sat between 1545 and 1563 to discuss the reform of Catholicism, issued only a few edicts concerning art, but these condemned artists who made obscure, licentious or over-decorated works. The Council proclaimed that art had two important functions to fulfil in churches— to instruct and to strengthen piety.

So a new direction was given to religious art and, looking for inspiration to the art of the High Renaissance in Rome, artists created the style known as Baroque. This style is essentially dramatic, highly emotional and 'illusionistic' (concerned to create the greatest possible illusion that a painting is real). Sculpture, painting and architecture would often be used together in one overpowering union, designed to make a direct emotional impact on the spectator.

Where the High Renaissance style had been grand but restrained, the artists of the Baroque sought to involve the

Left: An engraving of the Piazza Navona in Rome, a typical Baroque design for a piazza. Such grand schemes were designed to enhance the effect of the individual buildings.

Far right: The Ecstasy of St Teresa (1645-52) by Bernini. His dramatic and sensuous presentation of this moment is intended to involve the spectator in the emotion of the saint.

Below: The Baldacchino in St Peter's, Rome, which Bernini worked on from 1624-33. This permanent ceremonial canopy over the High Altar of the church was designed by Bernini as a symbol of the renewed power of the Catholic church. The splendour and flamboyance of its bronze and gilt twisted columns, topped by a bronze canopy made to look like heavy cloth, illustrate the Baroque style at its height.

Below right: The facade of the Benedictine Abbey at Melk in Austria, by Jakob Prandtauer. Built 1702-14, its undulating forms and elaborate towers are typical of the Baroque concern for drama and movement in architecture.

Left and below: The dome and facade of the church of *S. Ivo della Sapienza*, Rome (1642-60) designed by Borromini. This architect (1599-1667) was a great exponent of the Baroque and a jealous rival of Bernini. The emotional effect of the architecture (below) derives from the complicated concave and convex curves of the facade, drum and spire. The strange spire is based on reconstructions of the Tower of Babel. Inside, the gold and white decorations of the dome, flooded with light from the spire and windows, create a contrast to the darkness of the church interior. The effect is lighter and more airy than is usual in Italian Baroque.

spectator in the meaning of their work by all the techniques they could muster—making them feel for themselves, for example, the ecstasy of the saint being depicted.

Bernini: the genius of the Baroque

Gian Lorenzo Bernini (1598-1680) dominates Baroque art. The career of this sculptor, painter and architect spans the years when the Baroque style was at its height. Bernini's father was a sculptor and naturally the son's earliest works reveal his father's influence. His sculpture *Aeneas and Anchises* (1618-19) is very detailed and realistic in its treatment of flesh and can be viewed from many angles. Bernini quickly rejected this style in favour of one single viewpoint for his sculpture; he found he could make a more intense, theatrical impact by restricting the spectator's viewpoint. As with a magician on a stage, you are not allowed to view from the back to see how the trick is performed.

Bernini's genius found expression in the various projects for St Peter's in Rome, which occupied him from the 1620s to the 1660s. He was faced with the problem of giving some sense of unity to the immense interior, which measured 183m by 137m (600 feet by 450 feet). Between 1624 and 1633 Bernini worked on a *baldacchino* (a kind of ceremonial canopy), with four richly decorated twisted columns of gilded bronze supporting a luxurious canopy. This marked the liturgical centre of the church.

Much later (1656-66) Bernini designed a monument to mark the throne of St Peter, the *Cathedra Petri*, which the worshipper would see from the entrance of the church, framed by the baldacchino. This monument is an astonishing mixture of actual and sculpted elements. Through a stained glass window depicting the Holy Ghost, real light floods onto brass rods representing rays of heavenly sun, while angels and cherubs carry down the chair on billowing stone clouds.

In its use of a variety of materials, its illusionistic and voluptuous presentation of God's glory, the *Cathedra Petri* can be compared with Bernini's most famous 'stage set' *The Ecstasy of St Teresa* (1645-52). In this depiction of the saint's mystical union with God, the sensuous composition of the pure white marble is intended to convey the experience to the spectator so vividly that he can share in it. Bernini's design follows St Teresa's own description of her experience:

'(*The angel was) very beautiful . . . In his hands I saw a great golden spear, and at the iron tip there appeared a point of fire. This he plunged into my heart several times so that it penetrated my entrails. When he pulled it out, I felt that he took them with it, and left me utterly consumed by the great love of God. The pain was so severe that it made me utter several moans. The sweetness caused by this intense pain is so extreme that one cannot possibly wish it to cease, nor is one's soul then content with anything but God . . .*'

Bernini translates the sexual overtones of the narration into extremely physical terms. The group is typically Baroque in its union of the arts; the sculpted figures are placed in an architectural frame 77

Above: The interior of the pilgrimage church at Birnau, c.1754. Here the grandeur and seriousness of Baroque have given way to an airy, almost playful prettiness—the beginning of 'rococo'. The brilliant white plasterwork is overlaid with a profusion of sculpture.

Below: A statue of *St George* by the German Asam brothers, 1721. Though influenced by the Italian Baroque, their style is more delicate, pretty and less monumental.

Right: St. Paul's cathedral, London (1675-1709) by Christopher Wren. Wren spent many months in Paris in 1665-6 and was much influenced by French Baroque architecture.

which, because it is placed against the wall of the chapel, can only be viewed from the front, like a painting.

Bernini's last work on the St Peter's complex (1655-67) was the most purely architectural, but it clearly showed how architecture can be emotional and expressive. Bernini designed the *piazza*—a large open space—in front of St Peter's with a series of sweeping colonnades. With its curving movement, its changes of level and the glimpses of the church seen through a forest of columns, the design enhances the impact of St Peter's grand but rather dull facade, almost inviting the spectator to move towards the entrance.

The new ideas of Baroque architects

'Movement', both physical and emotional, is a key word in Baroque architecture as a whole. To achieve this effect architects used shapes other than the simple circles and ancient basilican structures previously favoured. Cascading steps, flowing forms, curved walls and bold details such as elaborate towers, are characteristic features of Baroque buildings. The elements of architectural form used in the Baroque church are basically the same as those used earlier in the Renaissance. Yet their scale, the way in which they are put together and the concern of their architects with organizing space in unusual and complex ways are all new features.

Borromini (1599-1667) was the most original genius of Baroque architecture. A comparison between his church of San Carlo and Brunnelleschi's Pazzi Chapel in Florence (c.1429) demonstrates the simplicity and restraint of the earlier work. The plan of the chapel is an oblong with two subsidiary circles, one for the altar alcove, one for the similarly domed area of the entrance portico. The plain inner walls lead the eye to the central dome. The architectural elements do not thrust themselves on the spectator; the mathematical beauty of the architecture can perhaps best be grasped by looking first at the plan and then at a photograph. The design is, in effect, in two dimensions.

Borromini's San Carlo, on the other hand, is made up of elements which grasp hold of space and mould it into exciting and complicated forms—so that the bold columns and curves of the interior and exterior involve the spectator's emotions. For the Baroque, architecture is three-dimensional sculpture—not a collection of flat walls—and for this reason the architects of this period were particularly interested in town planning.

Architects and planners of the seventeenth century were often involved in combining individual buildings within a scheme on a grand-scale. The Piazza Navona, the Piazza of St Peter and Michelangelo's Capitoline Hill (which, designed in 1546, was a great inspiration to the Baroque), are all schemes which act to enhance the grandeur of the individual buildings within them. By comparison, the Pazzi Chapel in Florence is simply an individual building with no part in any planned scheme.

The concern with space and emotional involvement found in this combination of architecture and town planning are also enjoyed in the most spectacular branch of Baroque art—namely illusionistic fresco decoration. Pietro da Cortona was a painter as well as an architect whose *Triumph of Divine Providence* in the Palazzo Barberini (1633-9) marks the beginning of the most exuberant phase of the Baroque style. His ideas were taken up by painters like Gaulli (1639-1709) and Pozzo (1642-1709). Their illusionism was based on the complex art of perspective and foreshortening, which allowed a specialist to paint a framework on the ceiling of a church in such a way that the actual ceiling 'disappeared', to be replaced by a vision of heaven or of saintly works.

Similar kinds of decoration are to be found in eighteenth-century interiors in Germany and Austria, both secular and religious. These are an extension of the Italian Baroque manner, but here sculpture and architecture unite with painting in a manner that is light, pretty and brilliant, lacking on the whole the strong emotional effect of the Baroque of the previous century.

The interior of the village church at Oberammegau. Baroque church architecture, like all Barqoue art, is full of vitality, using structure, space, colour and light to strengthen reverence and faith.

Baroque Art

After the High Renaissance, painting in Italy entered a phase known as Mannerism, replacing the ideal, serene art of the Renaissance by an emotional, restless style. Mannerist painters delighted in complicated compositions, straining, contorted bodies, artificial poses and vivid, unreal colouring and lighting. With its deliberate elegance and obscure subject matter, their art became increasingly a court art.

From the late 1580s, however, in Bologna, Annibale Carracci, his brother and their cousin began to look not to the Mannerist present but to the Renaissance past for their models. They studied the work of the High Renaissance masters and of Titian, producing altarpieces and secular works of simplicity and powerful draughtsmanship. Their work formed the beginning of the Baroque style in art.

Annibale Carracci (1560-1609) went to Rome in 1595 to work for Cardinal Farnese in his palace. There he frescoed the ceiling of the *Farnese Gallery*, finished in 1604. The subject of the ceiling is 'the loves of the gods', and the colouring is bright and natural. The bodies of the figures are healthy and supple, and the atmosphere of the work is vigorously happy; some of the scenes are even humorous.

Its mood contrasts with the solemnity of those High Renaissance schemes which Carracci studied so carefully—Michelangelo's *Sistine Ceiling* and Raphael's *Vatican Stanze*. From these he learnt how to construct strong nudes and impressively clothed figures. But while both Raphael and Michelangelo had been concerned with the salvation of the world (through culture and religion), Carracci sought only to amuse and please. Illusionistic techniques, which were to become a main feature of Baroque decoration, are used only in moderation in this exuberant scheme. Carracci's aim is not to make the painted areas look like extensions of actual space, but only to echo the actual sculpture in niches down the walls by the painted 'sculpture' of the ceiling itself.

Carracci's monumental style can also be seen in his altarpieces, such as the *Christ in Glory with Saints* which he produced soon after his arrival in Rome. The painting is clearly inspired by Raphael. Its composition is strictly based on geometry but, in contrast with High Renaissance work, the figures are fewer in number and bulk larger in the frame; their expressions and gestures are also more theatrical, and light and shade are employed to make them seem even more massive. A lyrical quality is given to many of Carracci's religious scenes by the importance he attaches to their landscape settings.

The vigorous art of Caravaggio

A style equally monumental but different in many ways was that of Caravaggio, whose working life is contemporary with that of Carracci. Caravaggio (1573-1610) was certainly an aggressive and swashbuckling character, whose contempt for most of his fellow artists was well-known. He had a romantic life—he fled from Rome after a stabbing, wandered to Naples, then to Malta, and finally died from fever

on the Tuscan coast—and there is a great temptation to transfer what we know of his life into his art. His pictures seem at once aggressive and uncompromising, scornful of tradition and with the vigour of low life which he was attracted to in real life. The legend easily grew up of a totally new artistic style, owing nothing to the past, which was simple, direct and for the people.

Such an impression is very far from the truth, and misleads us about the nature and intention of his painting. Certainly, he painted direct onto the canvas without preliminary drawing—but so did the Venetians, whose style he knew through an early teacher. In fact, the sources of his style are precisely the same as those of Annibale Carracci—it was from Michelangelo and Raphael that he learnt to use simple and straightforward composition containing a few monumental figures.

His vividly realistic religious scenes, with their use of contemporary settings and costume, and of peasants as models for holy figures, shocked his contemporaries and were rejected by the clergy. Though they use unorthodox methods these paintings are, however, sincerely religious and deeply felt. By using ordinary individuals with common faces and dirty feet, Caravaggio was not trying to make religion merely picturesque or to debase what was considered holy, but to drive home the Christian message in a way that was simple and straightforward.

His first important works were religious canvases to decorate the Contarelli Chapel in S. Luigi dei Francesi, in Rome (1597-1603). *The Calling of St Matthew* shows Caravaggio's dramatic use of lighting known as *chiaroscuro*—the con-

Above: The *Calling of St Matthew* painted by Caravaggio c. 1597, and (below) his *Conversion of Paul*, 1601. These paintings show his development from a rather elegant approach in the *Calling of St Matthew* to a more concentrated and simple presentation in the later work. Both show his interest in large, straightforward compositions made more impressive by the contrast of light and shade (*chiaroscuro*) which sculpts the figures and increases the emotional impact of the scene. Caravaggio's use of contemporary dress and settings, and of peasants as models for holy figures, shocked many contemporaries.

Below: *Apollo and Daphne*, sculpted by Bernini from 1633-5. His virtuosity in handling marble is seen in the way he captures Apollo's balanced pose and in his extremely life-like rendering of the skin of both figures, He shows the fleeting moment when Daphne is turning into a tree—rather than submit to Apollo.

Right: A detail from the ceiling vault of the *Farnese Gallery*, Rome, frescoed by Annibale Carracci between 1595 and 1604. Inspired by Michelangelo's *Sistine Ceiling*, Annibale uses nude male figures (painted to look like sculpture) and a painted architectural framework to separate each mythological scene.

Mansell

Right: The *Trevi Fountain* in Rome, designed by Nicola Salvi and built between 1732 and 1762. This eighteenth-century work is a continuation of Bernini's fountain designs. Sculpted figures emerge from a 'natural' rocky base, dominated by Neptune, standing on a shell drawn by sea-horses.

Below: *The Triumph of Bacchus and Ariadne* from Annibale Carracci's decorative scheme for the *Farnese Gallery* ceiling. Although it derives from High Renaissance schemes, the atmosphere of this work is less solemn—Carracci's intention is to amuse and please. A sense of gaiety pervades this bright, naturally coloured scene.

A. F. Kersting

Mansell

Scala

trast of light and dark. The tones used by earlier artists in their work (with the exception of a few night scenes) had been predominantly light, with the bodies naturally shaded to give them bulk. Caravaggio, as it were, reversed the usual process, and had his figures depicted in light emerging from a generally dark background. Caravaggio's chiaroscuro was a means to underline the high seriousness of his themes and emphasize the splendid, statuesque, slow gestures which his figures make—such as the commanding extended arm of Christ in *The Calling of St Matthew*.

His concentration on low life figures was not, however, appreciated by the ordinary people, who were scandalized rather than impressed. Caravaggio's first altarpiece for the chapel, of *St Matthew writing his Gospel*, had to be replaced by a work he painted in a much more elevated style—possibly because the original version was received with distaste. In the first, the dirty hand of the ignorant saint is guided over the page by an angel so beautiful that the saint appears very clumsy indeed; in the replacement, the saint receives inspiration from heaven in the approved manner.

The illusion of Baroque interiors

The early seventeenth century was a time of lavish, large-scale decorative schemes in which artists could show their virtuosity and stylistic brilliance. Guido Reni (1575-1642) continued Annibale Carracci's ideal and classical style into the mid-century. His ceiling fresco depicting *Aurora* (1613-14) in the Casino Rospigliosi in Rome, can be compared with a ceiling on the same theme, frescoed by his contemporary Guercino in 1623. Whereas Reni 'frames' his fresco just as a canvas would be framed, Guercino attempts to create the illusion that the building is open to the sky. Painted architecture extends up into the 'sky' and the figures are seen from beneath—just as if they are real figures flying across the sky above the spectator.

This scheme heralded the greatest of all Baroque secular ceilings—Pietro da Cortona's *Triumph of Divine Providence* (1633-39) in the Palazzo Barberini in Rome, a dense and complex scheme in which scores of figures seem to be coming into the room itself or floating above it.

This attempt to make painted figures come alive is also a feature of Baroque sculpture, as in Bernini's *Apollo and Daphne* (1622-5). Bernini's virtuoso handling of marble creates a physical,

'living' impression. He captures the moment at which Daphne's skin begins to change into the bark and leaves of a tree as a protection against Apollo's attempted seduction. The two bodies seem to pulsate with life as the light slides over the glossy surfaces.

The sculpture, painting and architecture of the High Renaissance remain detached from the onlooker, occupying their own world. Baroque works, on the other hand, seem to thrust themselves into the space in which we move, always in action, never static. Baroque ceiling paintings are full of this movement and the best Baroque portraits—such as Bernini's sculpted bust of *Cardinal Scipio Borghese* (1632)—convey a vivid impression of life. Rather than a mute statue, this seems to be a person in the act of speaking; his lips move, his eyes twinkle, and his vestments ripple as he breathes.

At the end of the seventeenth century, a different style known as the Rococo developed out of the Baroque. The Baroque had been solemn and serious: the Rococo tended to be light-hearted. Whereas the Baroque employed a monumental figure style to interpret its grand themes, the Rococo was more interested in gracefulness, light and colour. Strong, dark colours give way to delicate pastel tones. Above all, the Rococo is a decorative style, seen to perfection in the works of Giovanni Battista Tiepolo (1696-1770), whose medium was often fresco decoration. He was influenced first by the Venetian tradition of Veronese and then by the long line of Baroque decorators such as Pietro da Cortona.

Tiepolo's splendid frescoes

Tiepolo worked in Spain and Germany as well as Italy. His greatest scheme was the decoration of the Kaisersaal and the Staircase of the Archbishop's Palace at Wurzburg (1750-3). The charm of the scheme resides in its lightness of tone and the beauty of his figures set off by the brilliant white architectural setting with its gilded curves. Throughout his life, Tiepolo's frescoes were in demand, and as late as 1762 he was commissioned to decorate the Royal Palace in Madrid.

The carefree, splendid style which Tiepolo represented was soon, however, to be condemned as frivolous and immoral by followers of a new manner—Neoclassicism. The Rococo was rapidly overtaken by this movement, which looked again to Ancient Greece and Rome for inspiration and sought to give art a new moral meaning.

Above: *Aurora* (c. 1613), a ceiling fresco by Guido Reni in the Casino Rospigliosi, Rome.

Below: Guercino's ceiling, also depicting Aurora, in the Casino Ludovisi, Rome, painted in 1623. Reni treats his scene as if it is an ordinary painting on canvas, contained within a

moulded and gilded frame. Guercino, on the other hand, uses the new Baroque technique of 'illusionistic' painting —creating the impression that the building is open to the sky. This he does by means of painted architecture extending up into the 'sky' with the figures seen from underneath, as if really flying across the room.

Left: *Atalanta and Hippomenes* painted by Guido Reni in 1625. A follower of the Carracci, Reni developed a style of 'ideally' proportioned figures with graceful, exact poses, gestures and expressions.

Right: A ceiling fresco by Pietro da Cortona in the Palazzo Pitti, Florence, 1643-46. Cortona's spectacular illusionistic ceilings were a high point of Baroque technical skill.

Below: *Antony and Cleopatra,* part of the decoration of the Palazzo Labia, Venice, by Tiepolo, completed in 1750. Here, the real architecture is astonishingly extended by imaginary painted architecture creating a strong theatrical impact.

Bottom: A detail from the fresco decorations in the Archbishop's Palace, Udine (1726) by Tiepolo. Baroque schemes were often concerned with both religious and mythological stories. Tiepolo changes these scenes from seriousness to make-believe and splendour, using fairy-tale clothes and light, bright colours.

Isaak van Ostade
(1621–49) of Haarlem,
took the subjects of his
paintings mainly from
peasant life. The
technique of his winter
scenes is characterised
by a fine silvery tone.

Dutch Painting

The seventeenth century saw the emergence of Holland as a major European power. At the signing of the Twelve Years' Truce in 1609 the northern states of the Netherlands became independent of Spanish rule, and entered upon a period of rich cultural, economic and social development. Amsterdam had already taken the place of Antwerp in European trade and economy; it now became a centre for banking. Handsome merchant houses were built along its many canals and the rising class of prosperous traders and burghers created a demand for modest luxury goods. Bulb-growing became an important source of wealth. By mid-century the Dutch navy was beginning to threaten England's mastery of the seas. Despite the setback to art which resulted from the country's break with Catholicism, Dutch painters made a vital contribution to the history of Western art during this century.

The effect of Protestantism on painting was at first catastrophic. In Germany, Holland and England it seemed as if art might not survive. Many Protestants regarded pictures or images of saints in churches as Popish idolatry and painters in these countries lost their most reliable and lucrative source of income—the painting of altar-pieces. Neither could artists (in Holland at least) find employment in the decoration of sumptuous palaces, for the Dutch burghers were sober citizens who disliked what they regarded as the ostentatious pomp of the Catholic south. Book illustration and portrait painting seemed to offer the only means for an artist to make a living, and there was not a large market for either.

Portraits for wealthy burghers

Nevertheless with increasing prosperity the demand for portraiture grew: a worthy burgher who had become a burgomaster would be proud to have himself painted in the insignia of his office; governors of charitable institutions or members of civic bodies—of which there were many in republican Holland—wanted group portraits for their board rooms or for the meeting places of their guilds and companies. Those artists whose work found favour with the public could hope to eke out an existence on this type of painting.

Frans Hals (1580/85-1666) was one such artist. Although Flemish by birth, Hals moved to Holland with his Protestant parents and spent most of his life there. The debts which Hals accrued with his baker and shoemaker demonstrate the adverse conditions of work for a Dutch painter. During his old age (he was over 80 when he died) he was supported by a pittance given by a municipal almshouse, whose board of governors had been pleased by his group portrait. Hal's great

National Gallery/John Webb

Mansell

Above right: *The Courtyard of a House in Delft* painted by Pieter de Hooch (1629-c.1684). De Hooch is best known for his simple, placid household scenes, painted while he lived in Delft. In this tranquil, warm-toned painting, de Hooch displays his interest in the play of sunlight on surfaces and streaming through open doors.

Right: The *Christening Feast* painted by Jan Steen (1626-79). As an innkeeper, Steen had a ready source of subject matter for his humorous paintings, which deal mostly with tavern scenes or visits to respectable households. This bustling scene has many homely details, such as the pots, pans and eggs on the floor.

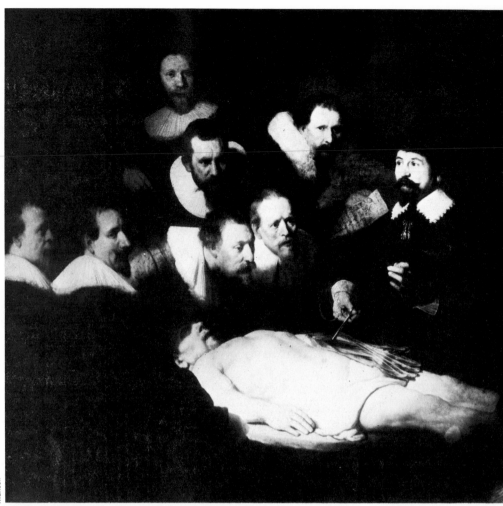

Above: *Self-Portrait* c.
1666 by Rembrandt (1606-
69), one of a series
in which he traces his
progress through to old
age. Rembrandt never
attempted to idealize
his own rather coarse
features, but his frank
and sincere portrayal of
his tragic suffering and
disillusion transcends all
concern for beauty or
ugliness.

Below: The *Night Watch*
by Rembrandt, 1642. This
painting shows a burgher
company marching out to
a parade. Rembrandt
transforms a group
portrait into an
animated assembly. The
strong diagonals of pike,
lance, rifle and banner
emphasize the movement
forward and the contrast
of light and dark areas
add drama to the scene.

Left: *The Anatomy Lesson of Dr. Tulp*, painted by Rembrandt in 1632. This group portrait represents leading members of the Guild of Surgeons. Their mature age emphasizes the importance of the occasion, for the dissection of a corpse was an unusual event. The normal group portrait is made more lively by the various poses and degrees of attention among the doctors. The contrasting effects of light and dark add drama to this scene. The style is more deliberate and 'smooth' than later works. During his life, Rembrandt received various commissions from the Surgeon's Guild. His accurate detailing shows that he must have been present at the public demonstrations and made studies of the corpses being dissected. This work established Rembrandt's fame as a skilled portrait painter.

Right: *A Woman Bathing*, painted by Rembrandt in 1654. This painting, possibly a study for a biblical figure, probably portrays Hendrickje Stoffels, who entered Rembrandt's house as a servant girl after the death of his first wife Saskia. She became his life companion and her warm-heartedness consoled the artist during his later years of financial hardship. This small work is beautifully painted—Rembrandt's sensitivity in rendering expression is seen in the woman's delicately modelled head. A warm light illumines her face and whole body in contrast to the dusky background.

Left: *Jacob Blessing the Children of Joseph*, painted by Rembrandt in 1656. In his religious scenes, Rembrandt increasingly emphasized the inner meaning of the event and the human feeling it involves. Here he conveys compassion by gesture and expression. The scene is lit by the rich, warm colour of Rembrandt's later work.

Below: *The Agony in the Garden*, an etching made by Rembrandt c. 1657. This is the finest of his biblical etchings. In it Jesus, his face full of despair, leans for support on the arms of an angel, aware that he is about to be taken by soldiers. The night scene with its dark shadows conveys a sense of impending tragedy.

gift was for portraiture, especially for his impressionistic, 'snapshot' manner of catching a sitter's expression. The optimistic and jovial mood in which he portrays many of his compatriots perhaps represents the confidence of this first generation of free Hollanders.

A Dutch artist was like a merchant selling the goods the public wanted to buy. If he had no patron he had to rely on the public. Without a talent for portraiture he could not rely on commissions and had to turn to other subjects and to other methods of working. He must first paint his picture and then try to find a purchaser. He would offer his paintings for sale at picture markets or go to a picture dealer. Since competition was stiff, he tended to specialize and concentrate on one type, or *genre*, of painting which he could do well or which the public came to expect of him.

Painters like Adriaen van de Velde (1636-72) or Jan van de Cappelle (c.1642-79), perhaps reflecting the rising importance of Dutch sea power, became famous for their seascapes; Jacob van Ruisdael (c.1628-82) and Meindert Hobbema (1638-1709) for landscapes. Jan Steen (1626-79) on a popular level and Jan Vermeer (1632-75) and Gerard Ter Borch (1617-81) with a greater degree of sophistication and elegance, offered the public domestic interiors with figures usually involved in some little incident. But the greatest painter of the age, Rembrandt van Rijn (1606-69) was not confined to any one of these 'genres'—his vision ranged through many subjects, from portraits to landscapes and religious events.

His career was full of contrasts: happily married, prosperous and known well beyond the confines of his native Holland, his success seemed assured during the 1620s, yet when he died in 1669 he left no other property than his old clothes and some painting utensils. Rembrandt did not paint contemporary prelates and princes, but the people of Amsterdam, members of his family and above all himself. His remarkable series of self-portraits tells us much about the man, from the days of his youth and success to his lonely old age when his face betrayed the tragedy of bankruptcy and human suffering.

Rembrandt never went to Italy, nor travelled widely, yet he was familiar with Italian art and in the days of his prosperity owned Italian paintings. Yet he was not concerned with the beautiful forms of Italian art; indeed his figures, especially his self-portraits, sometimes shock by their unexpected ugliness. In his use of light and shade and in his grouping of figures in a composition, Rembrandt reveals that he did not break with the tradition of Italian art, but, despite these affinities, nothing could be more different in spirit from southern Catholic art than Rembrandt's mature religious paintings.

The profound insight of Rembrandt

As a devout Protestant he was very familiar with the Bible and he penetrated right to the heart of his religious subjects, adhering closely to the text, bringing out the deep inner meaning of the events he depicted and never failing to reveal the genuine humanity of the biblical figures, bringing to them his profound psychological insight.

From the first, Rembrandt's skill as a portraitist brought him success. In 1631 he had left Leyden, where he was born the son of a miller and a baker's daughter, for the busy trading centre of Amsterdam and shortly after established his reputation by his first large-scale group portrait *The Anatomy Lesson of Dr. Tulp*. The painting's forceful composition, in which the figures loom out of a dark background, and its dramatic, direct presentation of the scene indicate the influence of his master Pieter Lastmann who had worked in Italy. Rembrandt's treatment of these figures as a tense, closely-knit group sets this painting apart from other, often dull, contemporary guild portraits.

From now until its climax at the end of the decade Rembrandt's fame increased and simultaneously with professional success came a rapid rise in his social position, through marriage to Saskia van Uylenburg, a member of a wealthy patrician family. Rembrandt bought a house and indulged his extravagant collector's taste for bizarre objects.

After Saskia died in 1642 objections to Rembrandt's increasing use of *chiaroscuro* and to his departure from tradition in the composition of his great group portrait the *Company of Captain Frans Banning Cocq* (the *Night Watch*) produced in that year, contributed to a decline in his popularity with the public. He fell into debt and 14 years later, in 1656, was declared bankrupt; his house was sold and his collection put up for auction. Only the help of his new life companion, Hendrickje Stoffels, and his son Titus saved him from complete ruin, but both died before him and he lived, a lonely man, to the age of sixty-three.

During his middle years after Saskia's death Rembrandt turned to biblical subjects, to landscapes and to studies of the Jews of his neighbourhood, many of which he used in his Bible scenes. His contact with nature resulted in a large number of drawings and etchings of the Dutch countryside in which he developed a 'shorthand' method of recording his impressions which contrasts strikingly with the frequently baroque manner of his painted landscapes.

Rembrandt's later work acquired that natural simplicity, profundity and psychological penetration for which he is renowned and revered. His *Night Watch* of 1642 marks the shift towards his late style; in this painting he broke with the conventions of group portraiture in subordinating some of the individual figures in the interests of a more dramatic and unified composition. Rembrandt chooses the moment when the drum sounds the call to arms and the company of burghers surge forward from all sides to join their leaders. In this way, he transforms a static group portrait into an animated assembly.

Rembrandt's late interpretations of biblical scenes also depart strongly from tradition. The spectacular and ornate gives way to an exclusive concern for the inner, spiritual meaning of the event, as in his *Return of the Prodigal Son*, painted between 1668 and 1669. All the emphasis is placed on the meeting between the father and son, the father's pose, as he bends down over his kneeling son, communicating the utmost forgiveness and tenderness.

The same profound communication of human feeling and the spiritual values of tenderness and trust occurs in another late painting, *The Jewish Bride*, painted

88

Cooper-Bridgeman

Mansell

Above: *A Watermill* by Jacob van Ruisdael (1628?-1682). Ruisdael was born and died in Haarlem but spent much of his working life in Amsterdam, entirely as a landscape artist. He was typical of the trend of 'specialization' in 17th-century northern painting. Sometimes he views the Dutch scene at close quarters, in other paintings he takes in a broad sweep of the countryside. He loved to paint gnarled trees, rushing brooks and stormy clouds with strong effects of light and shade. His realistic landscapes had considerable influence on the development of this type of painting in the 19th century. More than any artist before him he succeeds in expressing his own moods through their reflection in nature.

Right: *Woman at a Virginal* by Vermeer van Delft. The picture is not the most completely successful of Vermeer's paintings—elsewhere he uses the strong lines of geometrical shapes to much more coherent effect —but the range of cool tones and the elegant use of blues and golds is exquisite. The way the scene is bathed in clear light, flooding in through the window, is typical of Vermeer's art.

Left: *The Lacemaker* by Vermeer, reputed to be a portrait of his wife Catharina, aged 35. This is one of a number of portraits by Vermeer showing women at work, engrossed in their occupation. Again, he uses 'sideways' lighting to give depth and shape to the figure.

Left: The *Gypsy Girl* (1628-30) by Franz Hals, one of his most appealing and spontaneous pictures. He uses his impressionistic skill to capture the animal good spirits of his jovial subject. Her smile has been likened to a 'low-life Mona Lisa'.

Right: A later Hals portrait, *A Man in a Slouch Hat* (1661-3), a casual and intimate portrait from the last years of Hals' life. This illustrates one of Hals' most typical subject poses—the seated model leaning one arm over the back of a chair, the face turned towards the observer. The large, rakish hat, which in this portrait is particularly dominant, is another Hals trademark. Hals 'catches' his sitter at a characteristic moment and records it on canvas using deft, free brush strokes to create his images. Compared to Rembrandt, Hals was much more external in his approach to portraits, far less concerned to penetrate the psychological reality of his subject. But technically Hals was superbly skilful; the way he uses his brush is the hallmark of his genius.

Bavaria

Bavaria

in 1665. The love between the married couple is movingly conveyed in their expressions and in the lady's simple gesture of pressing her husband's hand to her heart.

Vermeer's cool interiors

Nothing could be more different to Rembrandt van Rijn than the mentality, manner and productivity of Jan Vermeer of Delft (1632-75). Vermeer's cool objectivity and passive quality is the antithesis of Rembrandt's warmth and human involvement; while Rembrandt had a prodigious output Vermeer was slow in his working methods and had a very small output. Yet superb handling of light and shade is common to both painters' work.

Vermeer was born in Delft when Rembrandt was 26 years old; he thus belonged to the third generation of the great era of Dutch painting. By the middle of the century the Dutch had become accustomed to peace, and the optimistic vitality of an earlier painter such as Hals gave way to a quiet refinement. The cultured enjoyment of music and painting is a frequent theme of Vermeer's work. *The Concert, A Girl interrupted at Music, The Music Lesson, The Artist in his Studio, The Lady with a Lute,* and several paintings of ladies with pearls indicate the more sophisticated nature of Dutch social life.

Similar domestic subjects are treated by Gerard Ter Borch, but, accomplished though he may be in rendering silk and satin, or subtle in his treatment of colour and light, he was no serious rival to Vermeer. The frequency with which Ter Borch repeats certain costumes and accessories suggests that he may have painted pictures in advance, merely adding heads and hands when required.

In 1672 the French King Louis XIV invaded Holland. The French advance was checked by William III but, in spite of this success, Holland was already declining as a world power. This decline was reflected in her artistic output and by the end of the century the 'golden age' of Dutch painting was over.

National Gallery/Michael Holford

89

Peter Paul Rubens (1577-1640) achieved a vast output of work – ceiling paintings, altar pieces, allegorical paintings, portraits and religious subjects such as *The Prophet Elijah receiving bread and water from an angel* (below) – all came within the range of his genius.

Rubens

Peter Paul Rubens (1577-1640) is the complete negation of many popular images of a creative artist. He was not poor, he was not unconventional or unlettered, did not live solely for his art, nor die unrecognized. His self-portraits show us a highly successful, fashionable man, proud of the noble status indicated by his sword. Rubens' vast correspondence, of which the 8,000 letters are probably only a fragment, reveals a highly-cultured man of wide interests ranging from archaeology and architecture to science, literature and theology. He was a competent classical scholar and a collector of antiquities.

Diplomat, courtier and artist

Rubens possessed that rare combination of qualities—creativity and business acumen; he was a sensitive artist and a shrewd man of affairs. He organized an extremely efficient workshop and became a skilled and trusted diplomat, residing at the courts of princes and travelling widely in their service.

Living at a time when the political, religious and social struggles following the Reformation came to a head in the Thirty Years' War on the Continent and the Civil War in England, Rubens worked for peace; but for peace within the old established order. He represented the government of the absolute monarchs and their aristocratic courts; he worked for the glory of the Catholic Church.

Residence in Catholic Flanders gave Rubens artistic advantages denied to his fellow artists in the neighbouring Protestant region of Holland, the United Provinces. Flanders' continued attachment to the Spanish empire after the separation of its northern neighbours in 1609 ensured him the continued patronage of church and court. The Catholic Church made the arts a spearhead of its campaign to revive flagging faith and recapture the heretic. New churches demanded cycles of painting to illustrate the lives of recent saints. Large-scale altar pieces, too, were needed to proclaim the doctrine. The exuberant vitality and sensuous attractions of Rubens' art satisfied the religious need to arouse and teach the faithful—as well as the secular desire for spectacular palace decoration.

Rubens' association with courts and his involvement in diplomacy furthered his career as a painter. His connection with courts began early, being at the age of 14 sent as a page to the household of the widow of a former Regent of Antwerp. His introduction to the court of Mantua in 1600 was crucial to his career both as artist and diplomat. His residence there as Court Painter gave him the opportunity to study the works of Raphael and Titian.

The influence of the heroic, idealized forms of Italian art can be seen in Rubens' major religious commissions of this period. His predecessors in Flanders had mostly painted on a small scale but Rubens had seen the huge canvases decorating Italian churches. He painted his *Raising of the Cross* (1610) for the church of St Walburga, Antwerp, on a large scale with a strong diagonal composition strikingly reminiscent of the Italian painter Caravaggio. *The Descent from the Cross* (1611-14), painted for the chapel of the

Cooper Bridgeman

Above: The *Descent from the Cross*, painted by Rubens (1611-14), now in Antwerp Cathedral. It forms the central panel of an altarpiece commissioned by the Guild of Arquebusiers, whose chief, Nicolaas Rockox, burgomaster of Antwerp, was a friend of Rubens. Rubens' dead Christ has a heroic dignity reminiscent of Italian figures and the white winding sheet strongly emphasizes the diagonal line. The dramatic lighting and tortuous movement are typical of baroque art.

Right: Rubens' self-portrait with Isabella Brant in a bower of honeysuckle, painted in 1609 shortly after their marriage. Isabella was the eldest daughter of Jan Brant, one of the Secretaries of Antwerp. At Isabella's death, Rubens wrote that she had been 'an excellent companion, whom one could love . . . as having none of the faults of her sex. She had no capricious moods, and no feminine weaknesses, but was all goodness and honesty.' Here Rubens' hand rests on his nobleman's sword, which indicates his high social position. In this marriage portrait delicate attention to detail is combined with a simple, bold composition.

Guild of Arquebusiers, shows the influence of Italy in the way he uses light and shade. Of the great decoration begun in 1620 for the Jesuit church in Antwerp only three altar pieces remain—the 39 ceiling paintings were burnt in a fire in 1718. The two altar pieces, *The Miracle of St Ignatius Loyola* and *The Miracle of St Francis Xavier*, show Rubens' response to the pictorial opportunities offered by the life cycles of new Jesuit saints.

By the time of his return from Italy, Rubens' circumstances were flourishing. During this period he was appointed new court painter and adviser to the two Antwerp Regents, Archduke Albert and Archduchess Isabella. He purchased a magnificent Italian-style town residence for the display of his collection of antique sculpture. He married, and the delightful double portrait he painted in 1609 of himself and his bride, Isabella Brant, shows the prosperous, elegantly dressed couple seated in a bower of honeysuckle. Commissions poured in and Rubens had to organize a workshop to help him.

Rubens' vast and varied range
Without his efficient system of delegating work Rubens' vast output could never have been achieved or maintained. Ceiling paintings, large-scale altar pieces, two major picture cycles, allegorical paintings, intimate portraits, romantic landscapes, book illustrations and tapestry designs all came within his range. The artist's method of work is revealed in his letters. He produced the design but the subsequent amount of personal involvement varied. Some pictures the master painted entirely, others were executed by pupils and given the final touches by Rubens; yet others he undertook with the aid of specialists such as Jan Breugel who would concentrate on the garlands of flowers and still-life details. Promising artists like the young Anthony Van Dyck (1599-1641) were glad to collaborate with Rubens.

Van Dyck was the chief assistant in Rubens' workshop for about four years before he went to England in 1620. His master's influence can be seen in the skill with which he rendered textures and surfaces, whether shimmering silk or human flesh. However, a courtly elegance and a hint of melancholy distinguishes Van Dyck's sitters from the robust exuberance of Rubens' heroes and heroines.

Art for the glory of monarchs
Rubens' unrivalled ability in organizing large-scale compositions made his art eminently suitable for the decoration of palaces and the glorification of secular rulers. But when in 1622-5 he decorated the gallery of the Luxembourg Palace in Paris with 21 scenes relating the life story of the Queen Dowager of France, Marie de Medici, he needed all the powers of his fertile imagination to transform an inglorious career into a brilliant mythological pageant. Ignoring the humiliations of the Queen's life he presented her in triumph and produced the greatest pictorial cycle of his career. Allegorical figures and Roman divinities mingle har-

Above: *Helene Fourment with her children*, painted by Rubens c.1636. To Rubens' four children by his first marriage, his second wife Helene added another five. The portraits and sketches Rubens made of his family are among his most attractive smaller works. He excelled in the modelling of heads, making skilful use of light and shade to achieve a natural and lively effect.

Left: The *Arrival of the Queen at Marseilles* from the Marie de Medici cycle painted by Rubens 1622-25. Of the sirens (sea nymphs from classical mythology) shown in this work, the 19th-century painter Delacroix remarked that they 'never seemed to me so beautiful. Abandon and the most complete audacity alone can produce such impressions.'

Left: A detail from the *Fall of the Damned*, a drawing made by Rubens for a painting (c.1620). The jostling, tormented bodies show the energy and vitality of Rubens' style.

Below: *The Judgement of Paris* painted by Rubens c.1638. Rubens' exuberant, earthy treatment of mythology is seen here. He makes the subject vividly real, using a pastureland setting and plump, fair Flemish women as the three classical goddesses, with his young wife in the centre.

moniously with ladies and gentlemen of the court wearing contemporary costume.

Rubens' achievements for Marie de Medici were matched by his work for the English king Charles I and his adviser, the Duke of Buckingham (whom Rubens met in Paris). The *Apotheosis of the Duke of Buckingham* designed for the ceiling of the Duke's house at Osterley Park, and the *Apotheosis of James I*, which formed part of the decoration executed for the ceiling of Charles I's Banqueting House in Whitehall, show Rubens glorifying a 'heretic' government with the symbolism which he had used to present the virtues of the Catholic Church. He depicts both men in the manner of saints in glory. (*Apotheosis* means 'taking up into heaven').

One great sorrow marred Rubens' success. His beloved wife Isabella had died before his visit to England in 1629. On his return to Antwerp in 1630 he married again. His bride, Helene Fourment, was only 16; Rubens was 53. Rubens' portraits of his young wife and her children do not have the poetic or aristocratic qualities of Van Dyck's subjects but instead combine tenderness and warmth in an intimate approach to portraiture.

In 1633 Rubens' faithful patroness, the Archduchess Isabella, died and the painter, aged 56, retired from political life. He bought a castle at Steen near Malines and painted for his own pleasure the landscape around his new home. His rendering of light and atmosphere anticipates the nineteenth-century 'romantic' movement. Evening light was particularly attractive to him and the lengthening shadows captured in his landscape painting produce an elegiac mood befitting the peaceful end of a great career.

Above: *The Castle of Steen* painted by Rubens c.1636. Rubens' most personal landscapes belong to his last years when he retired to this castle surrounded by its great estate. This landscape, radiant with morning light, has an artificially high viewpoint to produce a sense of spaciousness.

Rubens' genius at imparting life and motion to everything he paints is seen here in the drifting clouds, flying birds and crouching peasant and dog.

Below: *Charles I of England* painted by Van Dyck c.1635. In 1632 he became court painter to Charles I. As a young man, Van Dyck had been Rubens' chief assistant. Less forceful in his personality and his art than his master, Van Dyck manages to give the king a natural aristocratic bearing without making use of the outward pomp and splendour which characterizes many of Rubens' portraits of royalty.

The Age of Versailles

In all the arts, the age of Louis XIV was marked by brilliance and splendour. Art was organized by the State for the purpose of increasing the glory of France through the figure of Louis, the Sun King, and the decoration of his private and public buildings. Although such close control of art often results in staleness, official French art of the second half of the seventeenth century is characterized by supreme grandeur and self-confidence.

Ever since the invasion of Italy by Charles VIII in 1494, France had wished to imitate the art of the Italian Renaissance, and the influence of Italians was tremendous throughout the sixteenth century. The palace of Fontainebleau was decorated by Italians (from 1530 onwards) and Italian architects provided designs which greatly influenced native architects. Gradually, from about 1560, France developed a school of architects of her own, but in painting and sculpture foreign artists continued to be used until well into the seventeenth century. French artists tended to go to Italy to be trained and several chose to remain there throughout their careers, including Claude Lorrain (1600-82) and Nicholas Poussin (1594-1665), now considered the greatest French artists of the age.

In 1627, the painter Simon Vouet returned to France from Italy, bringing with him a simplified and less extravagant version of the Italian Baroque style. He trained the artists of the next generation, including Eustache LeSueur (1616-55) and Charles LeBrun (1619-90). LeBrun became virtual dictator of official art under Louis XIV, his work reflecting the pomp and formality of court life. Poussin had met with less success; his visit to Paris in 1640-42 to work for the Crown was an unhappy one, because his austere and thoughtful small-scale paintings could not rival the fashion for Baroque.

By this time Poussin had turned to Christian and classical subjects, in which he explored the nature of human emotion in clear, simple compositions. His belief was that painting should aim to reveal universal truths about Life and Mankind. In his style and philosophical outlook, this artist can be compared with the two great tragic dramatists of the period, Pierre Corneille (1606-84) and Jean Racine (1639-99).

Playwrights of tragedy and comedy
Corneille, in plays like *Le Cid* (1636) and *Polyeucte* (1643), explores the relationship between duty and desire in deliberately precise and analytical language, which has the effect of restraining passion. Racine, whose strict Jansenist background had taught him the depravity of Mankind and the omnipotence of Sin, presents in his plays characters who are much less sure of right and wrong than those of Corneille: they are a prey to their passions (which are seen as mainly destructive), yet they can analyse their struggles in speech which dissects as cleanly as a knife—as in the depiction of jealousy and love in *Phèdre* (1677), or of love and duty in *Bérénice* (1670). The chief characteristic of both writers is the formal, rhetorical quality of their plays. Neither playwright nor painter was confined to his particular age, but was concerned with Man in general: their works are relevant today precisely because of the universal importance of their examination of how Man works.

The same is true of the work of Molière (1622-73), an actor-manager whose

Above and left: The palace of Versailles came to symbolize the power and brilliance of Louis XIV's France. Under the king's direction it was transformed from a hunting-lodge to an establishment big enough to house the entire court. As the scheme progressed, it became more grandiose in scale. The immense garden facade (left) was the work of J. Hardouin-Mansart, from 1678 onwards. The central section alone is 73 m (240 ft) in length. The interior of this section (the Hall of Mirrors, above) epitomizes the luxury of Versailles; mirrors, candles, green marble, ornate gilt mouldings and ceiling paintings by LeBrun—all contribute to the splendid effect.

Left: A portrait of Louis XIV by Hyacinthe Rigaud, principal painter to the French court. The king, dressed in rich, heavy robes, gazes out at the spectator almost condescendingly. By placing the king in such a sumptuous setting, Rigaud has succeeded in conveying an image of self-confident power and nonchalant luxury.

Right: Louis XIV and his court were important patrons of the arts. Entertainments of various kinds were staged at Versailles, including firework displays, masques and plays—such as this performance of Racine's tragedy *Alceste*, given in the Marble Court in 1676, with ballet during the intervals.

comedies (like *Le Misanthrope* of 1666 or *L'Avare* of 1668) aim at the same dissection of Man through a comedy which often reveals a deeply serious tinge. But Parisian society and the court did not survive on a diet of total seriousness. Molière's plays would be lengthened by ballets and masques (in which the King would participate), and firework displays were very popular.

Arts under the Sun King

Louis XIV came to the throne in 1643 at the age of four. His chief minister was at first Mazarin, but at his death in 1661 Louis virtually took over the government of the country himself. Louis is the supreme example of the absolute monarch: his conviction of his divine authority was symbolized in his sun emblem, seen everywhere in the decoration of his palace at Versailles. His reign saw France pre-eminent in Europe; its political power and artistic sophistication was reflected in the court which Louis conducted with rigid formality and ceremony.

A few powerful ministers were retained by Louis, among them Colbert, who was responsible for organizing the arts. During this period France was blessed with academies of architecture, music, inscriptions and dance. The Academy of Painting and Sculpture, founded in 1648, came under the control of Colbert in 1661: he increased its power and made it more exclusive. The idea of the academy was Italian, and took over from the medieval guild-system, with its period of apprenticeship leading up to the production of a 'masterpiece', after which the apprentice became a full member. Colbert established a similar system. Artists were·taught the 'official' style; if they followed it in their own work, they were selected for employment by the State, whether as painters, sculptors, jewellers or joiners.

The 'approved' style of painting during the age of Louis XIV was a modified version of Italian Baroque. Architecture revealed the same influences, seen at work in the scheme to reconstruct the Louvre, the Paris seat of the French kings. The conversion of the building from a medieval castle into a modern palace progressed slowly from 1546 until its completion in 1674 by a team of designers: LeBrun, LeVau and Perrault. Colbert, in his position as Director of Buildings, invited plans for the East Front from leading French architects. Those which were submitted were rejected on various grounds and, finally, plans were sought from Bernini, the master of the Italian

Above: *Louis XIV and his Family* by Jean Nocret. Not content with representing the aristocracy simply as elevated human beings, painters often resorted to allegory, as here, with the royal family pictured as classical gods and goddesses. In keeping with his sun emblem, Louis becomes Apollo, the god of light.

Below: 17th-century French palaces were very large and decorated in a suitably grand style, with rich woods, gilding, tapestries and carpets (a rare luxury). Such a setting would be suitable for this heavy pine dressing-table, with costly *marquetry* (inlaid work) of brass, ebony, ivory and tortoiseshell.

Below right: *Extreme Unction*, painted by Nicholas Poussin 1644-48. Poussin was painting not for the court but for a small group of intellectuals—his style was alien to the fashionable taste for baroque splendour. This painting, in his austere late style, shows his detailed reconstruction of the past.

95

Left: *Self-Portrait* by Nicholas Poussin (1594-1665). Poussin worked for most of his life in Rome. He returned to Paris only once, where he was outspoken in his criticism of French court art. Poussin's own paintings are cool and reflective, governed by reason and restraint in both style and subject-matter.

Above: A scene from Molière's *L'Avare* (The Miser). In Molière's comedies, minor human failings are taken to extremes. By his mania for money, the miser brings misery to himself and his family. Molière's message is always for moderation and against extremes—the gap between the two provides the humour.

Baroque.

In all, Bernini submitted three designs, which were each judged to be out of character with the rest of the building. Bernini's visit to Paris, where he roused the anger of French artists and architects by his low opinion of their work, led to his third and final design being rejected—and with it the full extravagance of Italian Baroque. The East Front as erected still owed something to his plans, being restrained yet festive, but it complements the earlier sections of the building, rather than belittling them, as all Bernini's designs tended to do.

Versailles—symbol of splendour

Members of the same team were employed in the most ambitious architectural scheme of the age—the remodelling of Versailles. Versailles began life as a hunting lodge of very moderate size, the king's private refuge, but was reincarnated as a palace in 1661 to house the entire French court. Its first architect was Louis LeVau (1612-70), who apart from collaborating on the Louvre had designed the great chateau of Vaux-le Vicomte for Fouquet, Louis' Minister of Finance. LeBrun as decorator and LeNôtre, a garden designer, had also worked on the

96

PHÈDRE

chateau. When Fouquet was jailed for embezzlement in 1661 the entire team was re-employed at Versailles.

Today, we can only appreciate LeVau's remodelling of Versailles through prints, for his work was destroyed (from 1678 onwards) by Jules-Hardouin Mansart, who was commissioned to extend the garden front of the building to a length of 402 metres (1,319 ft). On such a scale as this the grandeur verges on monotony.

Mansart's most famous contribution to the interior of the palace is the Hall of Mirrors (1678-84). The mirrors—an expensive commodity used to extravagant profusion—are interspersed by pilasters of green marble; gilded trophies sit on the richly decorated cornice (the projecting ornamental moulding along the top of a wall) and the vaulted ceiling is decorated with paintings by LeBrun. The same qualities of immense scale, colour, richness, and the use of expensive materials are to be seen in the park, where LeNôtre was aided by armies of contractors and labourers. Water and fountains (requiring complicated pumping mechanisms), radiating avenues and *parterres* (ornamental arrangements of flower beds) are all important features in the total effect of order and formality.

In the plan of the scheme as a whole, the authority of the palace seems to radiate outwards to control its surroundings. In the use of Baroque planning principles which this scheme reveals, France discovered a way of expressing her European supremacy.

The furnishing of rooms as numerous and large as those created in palaces like Versailles required a definite organization of the decorative arts. Again, it was Colbert who provided the answer. In 1667 he created the *Crown Furniture Works* at Gobelins just as, three years previously, he had given the factory at Beauvais the title of *Royal Tapestry Works*. The Gobelin family business, founded 200 years before, had in 1662 been taken over for the Crown by Colbert, who declared that henceforth art would serve the King.

The factory at Gobelins, with Charles LeBrun as its artistic director, was to give a home to '. . . painters, master-weavers of high-warp tapestry, founders, engravers, gem-cutters, joiners in oak and other woods, dyers, and other skilled workers in all sorts of arts and crafts . . . .'

The furniture produced during this period was heavy (although rarely as heavy as the suite of solid silver made for the King's study—soon melted down to help military expenses). Marquetry (inlaid work of various coloured woods) and applied decorations in gilt bronze were particularly prized. Curves and scrolls, allegorical and antique motifs were often used. The walls would often be hung with tapestries, which took much longer to make than paintings of similar size, and which might be enriched by gold and silver threads. Carpets woven at Aubusson or Savonnerie would decorate the floors of the palaces.

A style of such magnificence could not survive either the decline in France's fortunes or the death of the Sun King in 1715. The pomp of this age was succeeded by the lightness and pastel gaiety of the eighteenth century. In architecture and the decorative arts as in painting and sculpture the new style, known as Rococo, would rule until challenged by Neo-classical taste after the mid-century.

Françoise Foliot/ Comedie Francaise

Above: The heroine of Racine's tragedy *Phèdre* (Phaedra). Taken from a classical story, the play deals with the relentless course of passion: Phèdre destroys the boy she loves before killing herself with poison. Racine is concerned less with the story of an individual than with the nature of passion itself.

Left: *Equestrian Portrait of the Chancellor Séguier* by Charles LeBrun (1619-90). Séguier was the first patron of LeBrun, who dominated French painting under Louis XIV. This grand, formal portrait marks the occasion of the triumphal entry into Paris of the King and his wife Maria Theresa in 1661.

Right: *Louis XIV's Visit to the Gobelins Manufactory.* Made after a drawing by LeBrun, this tapestry is extremely rich; the wool is heightened with silk, and with gold and silver thread. In the midst of the bustling scene, a variety of objects are being brought forward for the King's approval, including carpets, hangings, furniture and precious metal artefacts.

Bulloz

97

Chapter 4
The Eighteenth Century

Marriage a la Mode (1743-5). William
Hogarth (1697-1764) combined a
satirical sense of humour with delicate
technique, and his 'morality' paintings
were widely popular.

From Wren to Adam

Christopher Wren (1632-1723) was one of the greatest English architects. From the 1660s through to the early years of the eighteenth century Wren was involved to some extent in most of the major building projects in and around London. He had begun by studying mathematics and astronomy but at the age of 30, he began to devote his energies to architecture.

Wren's first work, the Sheldonian Theatre at the University of Oxford, begun in 1664, already demonstrates his characteristic combination of classical influences and technical expertise. The D-shaped plan is derived from that of the Theatre of Marcellus at Rome. The Roman original had been open to the sky, with a canvas awning as its only covering and Wren had to solve the problem of providing a ceiling spanning 21 m (70 feet). He devised an ingenious solution—hanging the ceiling from a system of roof trusses so that no supports were seen.

In 1665 Wren spent several months in France. In Paris he would have been able to see a number of buildings by architects like Francois Mansart and Louis Le-Vau whose style had been influenced by the architecture of the Italian Baroque. Wren was also able to meet the Italian architect Lorenzo Bernini (then working on the Louvre).

On his return from France these influences soon showed themselves in Wren's designs for rebuilding St Paul's Cathedral which (apart from the new West front added by Inigo Jones in the 1630s) was in a state of considerable decay. Many of the new churches Wren would have seen in Paris were surrounded by elegant Baroque domes. Drawing on this experience and on his knowledge of the great Italian works of Michelangelo, Bernini and Borromini (which are the ultimate inspiration for the French works as well) Wren incorporated a dome as the crowning feature of his design. This was, as the diarist John Evelyn remarked 'a form of church building not as yet known in England, but of wonderful grace'.

Wren re-builds London's churches

A matter of days after Wren's design had been accepted the Great Fire had begun destroying more than thirteen thousand houses, a hundred or so churches and the old cathedral itself. The work of reconstruction was enormous and Wren was consulted on many of the major projects, but it was not until 1675 that work on St Paul's could begin. He had in the meantime supervized the design of the 55 new city churches to replace those destroyed in the fire. The churches are very variable in the quality of their decoration and Wren was in most cases not responsible for the detailed aspects of the design (which would have been left to the craftsmen and masons of the parish) but he probably provided most of the plans and, at a later stage, designs for the steeples and towers. Outstanding examples are: St Mary-le-Bow, Cheapside 1670-73, steeple completed 1680; St Vedast,

Above: The entrance front of Chiswick House, London, a villa designed by Lord Burlington (1694-1753), the leading architect of the Palladian movement. Burlington had a large collection of drawings by Palladio and other Italian architects. Chiswick has been described as an architectural laboratory where he tested ideas learned from these earlier masters.

Right: Wren's sketches for the dome of St Paul's cathedral show skilful engineering. The lower, shallow dome is designed to be seen from the inside, surmounted by a tall outer shell of lead and timber, which serves as a landmark.

Foster Lane 1670-73, steeple 1694-97; St Stephen Walbrook 1672-79; and St James, Piccadilly 1682-84.

St Paul's itself was begun in 1675 and completed in 1710. Wren supervized the progress of the building throughout the 35 years. The final appearance of the cathedral is the result of many changes of design. The design of 1673—Wren's own favourite—was for an Italianate centrally-planned church crowned by a fine Baroque dome and with a smaller dome over the western vestibule, modelled closely on Michelangelo's design for St Peter's in Rome. This design (surviving in the Great Model now in St Paul's cathedral) was too revolutionary or perhaps too popish for the churchmen of the day. Wren was obliged to make a more traditional Latin cross plan with a long axis for the nave and choir very much as in a medieval church.

This 'Warrant Design', produced to gain the necessary approvals, has as its main feature an extraordinary combination of dome and spire. The warrant allowed Wren 'the liberty to make some variations rather ornamental than essential as from time to time he should see proper'; he seems to have treated this condition quite freely so that the building as it appears now bears little superficial resemblance to the warrant design. A number of the elements of the final form were re-introduced from the design of 1673, including the dome and the West Front towers. Wren's architecture is complemented by the work of the craftsmen employed to carry out the decorative scheme—the stone carving is by Grinling Gibbons and Edward Pearce; on the inside the magnificent wood-carving,

plasterwork and the wrought iron screens at the east end were executed by the finest craftsmen of the day.

By the end of the seventeenth century resources were again available for major public works and Wren in his various official capacities carried out a large number of important commissions. The most splendid of these later projects was the construction of Greenwich Hospital begun in 1696, where the buildings are laid out symmetrically on either side of a long vista created by parallel colonnades. The fine vista from the Thames between the colonnades is closed by Inigo Jones's Queen's House which Wren was no doubt obliged to keep despite the fact that it is really out of scale with the more monumental buildings he provided.

A. F. Kersting

A. F. Kersting

Wren was assisted at Greenwich by two younger men—Nicholas Hawksmoor and John Vanbrugh, each of whom developed an individual style based on some of the characteristics of Wren's work. With Hawksmoor and Vanbrugh the English Baroque reaches its high-point. Vanbrugh's mercurial character contrasts with the more solid Hawksmoor—who assisted him on many of his projects—and it is probably true that the more flamboyant qualities of these were introduced by Vanbrugh. His country houses—Castle Howard, Yorkshire (1699-1712); Blenheim Palace, Oxfordshire (1705-24); Seaton Delaval, Northumberland (1720-29)—have a massive monumental quality which must have been learnt from such works as Greenwich.

Hawksmoor's buildings like those of Vanbrugh have a monumentality characteristic of the English Baroque but are less theatrical; his architecture shows a greater sophistication. Hawksmoor was a keen student of the architecture of ancient Rome and his buildings reflect this interest. Among his finest works are the London churches of St George, Bloomsbury (1716-27); St Mary Woolnoth (1716-27) and Christ Church, Spitalfields (1749-29).

The Palladian movement

It is perhaps not surprising that the next generation of architects should react strongly against the Baroque of Wren, Hawksmoor and Vanbrugh. Where their predecessors had tended to combine elements derived from the French and Italian Baroque masters with classical and Gothic motifs, the new school developed more rigid, formal rules based

on the works and theories of the Italian architect Andrea Palladio (1518-80) and his follower Inigo Jones (1573-1651).

The first English edition of Palladio's *Four Books of Architecture* was published in 1715 and in the same year Colin Campbell (1682-1754) (architect of some of the earliest English Palladian buildings) published a book of architectural engravings of recent British buildings, *Vitruvius Britannicus*. The introduction was in the form of a statement setting out the significance of Palladio and Jones. Campbell emphasized the qualities of regularity and harmony in their architecture and criticized the excesses of the Italian Baroque which he said could only result in 'the Gothick'. The title was important—just as the Roman architect Vitruvius (whose treatise was the only source of knowledge of classical architectural theory) had inspired Renaissance architects, so this book would be a guide for future British architects.

Mereworth Castle in Kent, begun by Campbell in 1723, demonstrates these new ideas. The source for the design is Palladio's Villa Rotunda at Vicenza (built in the 1550s) and Campbell retained almost all the features of the model—a square plan with a central dome and porticoes on each front so that the composition is symmetrical about both axes. The symmetry is continued on the inside with the regularly shaped rooms disposed around the central circular hall. Campbell's designs are simple and restrained, and by comparison with Vanbrugh's dramatic Baroque, have a more refined grandeur.

The most important architect of the English Palladian movement was Richard 101

**Above: A painting by
Thomas Robins showing
the Chinese Pavilion in
the garden at Woodside,
Windsor, Berkshire
c.1750—a fine example
of mid-18th century
garden design. The
pavilion shows the
development of interest
in exotic, and
particularly Chinese
architecture for garden
buildings.**

**Below: The entrance
hall of Holkham Hall,
Norfolk, by William
Kent (1685-1748). Kent
collaborated with Lord
Burlington on the
design of this huge
country house. He
combines a variety of
classical features to
create a sumptuous
interior contrasting
with the dull brick of
the outside.**

**Right: The Etruscan
Room in Syon House,
Middlesex, designed by
Robert Adam (1728-92)
from 1775-9. The
decoration in reds,
browns, black and
yellow derives from the
early Greek vases then
thought to be the
product of the Etruscan
civilization. It shows
Adam's style at its
most graceful.**

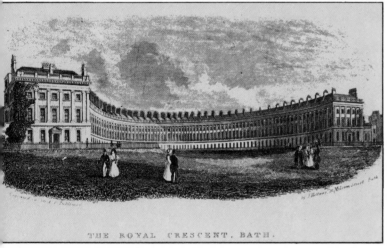

THE ROYAL CRESCENT, BATH.

Above: Somerset House, London, designed by William Chambers (1723-96) in 1776. The building fronted the river before the construction of the Embankment in the 1860s. It was intended as a major public building to house part of the Civil Service and some of the societies under royal patronage.

Left: A view of The Royal Crescent, Bath, designed by John Wood the younger 1767-75. This scheme was one of a number of major 18th century developments of Bath. The idea of treating a group of town houses as a monumental composition was soon taken up elsewhere, notably by Carr at Buxton.

Below: Design for Home House, Portman Square, London by Adam, 1773-9. The scheme, combining sculpture, reliefs, marble and plaster work, is a fine example of Adam's mature style.

collaborated on the design of Holkham Hall in Norfolk for the connoisseur Thomas Coke. Holkham was begun in 1734 and not completed until the 1760s, after both Kent and Burlington were dead. The plain exterior with its vast expanse of brickwork presents a marked contrast to the opulent interiors.

By the middle of the eighteenth century the Palladianism of Burlington and Kent was already being supplanted by new ideas of design less constrained by strict rules of composition. But the influence of the movement was profound, and many provincial architects took up variations of the style both for their country house designs and for town development schemes. Notable for his work in both these categories is John Wood of Bath who employed Palladian principles both in his country houses like Prior Park, 1735, and in his town buildings—Queen Square, Bath begun in 1729. He and his son John Wood the younger were responsible for most of the important eighteenth century development of Bath—notably The Circus, begun 1754 and the Royal Crescent, 1767-75.

Adam's elegant interiors

When Robert Adam (1728-1792) began his practice in London in 1758 the high point of Palladianism had been passed and he was quick to introduce a number of new elements from various sources to enliven the style of Burlington and his followers. Adam had travelled widely in Europe, taking particular care to find examples of ancient domestic architecture. Many more classical sites were being excavated at this time and he was able to use motifs from buildings in Pompeii and Herculaneum as well as from Greece and Asia Minor. The rich decorative style which he made his own was therefore drawn from more sources than that of the Palladians and at the same time more firmly based on antique prototypes.

At Osterley Park, Middlesex, begun 1760, Adam was commissioned to modernize a Tudor house. His principle alteration to the exterior was to replace part of the old building with a *propylon* (an opening formed by two parallel rows of columns surmounted by a pediment) probably based on the Propylaea at Athens, thus providing a grander access to the courtyard and to the building itself. Here and at nearby Syon House (1763-64) Adam created interiors in the sumptuous tradition of Burlington and Kent's Holkham Hall but carried out in a new decorative style. Every element—carpets, furnishings, paintings, plasterwork—is important to the design as a whole and the result is an integrated decorative scheme such as only Adam with his meticulous attention to detail could produce.

The 'Adam style' rests heavily on the decoration employed, for the structures decorated are often of the utmost simplicity. The ease with which others could reproduce the motifs encouraged a number of debased imitations as well as a few significant followers. One of Adam's contemporaries was Sir William Chambers (1723-1796), whose major work was the design for Somerset House in London. This grand public building shows an understanding of many architectural styles—its effect is rich but sober and restrained.

Boyle, Earl of Burlington (1694-1753). Lord Burlington made his Grand Tour of Europe in 1715 and he returned to Italy in 1719 to study Palladio's architecture and collect such of his drawings as could be found. His wealth and influence gave him a major advantage over his fellow Palladians; he actually saw many of Palladio's buildings as well as the Roman structures which are the ultimate source of his style.

Burlington's personal style was thus a somewhat more sophisticated 'Palladianism' than Campbell's. Burlington's own villa at Chiswick demonstrates the differences quite clearly. Like Campbell's Mereworth it derives its basic form from the Villa Rotunda—a square block with a central dome—but where Mereworth follows the model closely, Chiswick House shows a much freer interpretation. At Chiswick Lord Burlington was assisted by William Kent (1685-1748), a painter whom he had met in Rome. Kent's special skills lay in interior decoration and landscape gardening (although later he was to become a significant architect in his own right) and the garden at Chiswick, with its classical temples, statues and canal must be his work. Kent and Burlington also

18th Century Painting

European painting in the eighteenth century shows an extraordinary diversity. Politically the age began with relative peace and prosperity in a Europe which tolerated the divine right of kings and witnessed the rise of the middle classes. The century ended in revolution. Artistically, the seventeenth-century love of splendour slowly yielded to a taste which preferred delicacy to grandeur and which came to view the triumph of reason as the hallmark of the age.

The gracefulness of the period was epitomized in the style known as the *rococo*, applied to interior decoration, sculpture and painting; this was an essentially decorative style which combined curving lines with softness of contour and light, bright colour to produce an effect of prettiness and gaiety. As the century advanced, the concern with reason and empirical science sought to express itself in a return to the rigour and earnestness of classical ideals.

Antoine Watteau (1684-1721) was the finest of the decorative artists to become popular in France. He was strongly

Below: *Colonel Tarleton* by Sir Joshua Reynolds, (1723-92). This portrait illustrates Reynolds' use of bold composition and dramatic set pieces to heighten the grandeur of his work.

Above right: *The Death of the Countess,* from *Marriage a la Mode* by William Hogarth (1697-1764). This series, tracing the disastrous results of a mercenary marriage, combines a delicacy of artistic technique with a keen satirical edge. Here, while the dead Countess is kissed by her diseased child, her valuables are already being taken from her.

Above: *Mr and Mrs Andrews* by Thomas Gainsborough (1727-88), is the masterpiece of this painter's early career. A fresh, natural technique is used in this portrait of a prosperous Suffolk squire and his wife, set in a closely-observed typically English landscape.

Left: Gainsborough's *Morning Walk* is a fine example of his late style. The artist is concerned to express the fashionable elegance of the aristocratic couple: his technique, with its sketchy, graceful brushstrokes, is fluent and sophisticated.

Right: A still life by Jean-Baptiste Chardin (1699-1779). Modest domestic values are preserved and given dignity in such paintings as this, a beautiful, richly toned and textured study of ripe fruits, wineglasses and jug.

influenced by Rubens, yet his work is in marked contrast to the large, healthy and exuberant pictures of his predecessor. The reduced scale and delicacy of Watteau's paintings suggests a very different temperament—and a very different world. A mood of melancholy exists throughout his work; often, as in the *Embarkation for Cythera*, which, despite its title, shows pairs of lovers leaving the island of Cythera after paying their vows at the shrine of Venus, there is a sense of the fleeting, transitory nature of pleasure and a poignant awareness of time passing. This melancholic mood is extended even to his sympathetic portrayal of clowns and wandering players. The world which Watteau's figures inhabit is yet an idealized one—artificial, elegant and refined. It is in his fluid handling of paint and his exquisite brushstrokes that Watteau comes closest to Rubens.

In the paintings of Jean-Honore Fragonard (1732-1806) the rococo reaches its height of frivolity and light-heartedness. Paintings such as the *Swing*, tinged with surreptitious eroticism, portray a fanciful notion of eighteenth-century life.

Much of the painting done in France in the eighteenth century was commissioned by the court. Patronized by Madame de Pompadour, Francois Boucher (1703-70) produced numerous designs for palace tapestries as well as pictures which celebrate the voluptuous beauty of female nudes. He devoted himself to depicting a mythological world which, in its sophistication and advocacy of pleasure, suited the demands of his royal patrons.

By no means all of French painting was devoted to the celebration of artificiality and pleasure. The works of Jean-Baptiste Chardin (1699-1779) con-

tain few of the qualities which characterize his contemporaries. Instead his quiet canvasses depict the intimate and personal aspects of eighteenth-century life. His still-lifes and everyday scenes portray a private world of feeling much in the manner of seventeenth-century Dutch paintings, taking delight in the texture of objects and in undramatic moments of time. With no trace of sentimentality or triviality, Chardin paints the simplest of scenes, whether it be an arrangement of fruit, bottles and kitchen utensils or a housewife returning from the market.

Venetian views

In the eighteenth century Venice was still an important centre of painting, culture and taste. The ability of Venetian painters to handle large-scale decorative commissions led to a demand for their work all over Europe. Following in the great tradition of painters such as Paolo Veronese, they established Italian styles in numerous courts.

The greatest and most famous of these travelling Venetian painters was Giambattista Tiepolo (1696-1770). It was in Wurzburg in Germany that he created a brilliant series of frescoes to adorn the palace of the Prince Bishop between 1750 and 1753. Here in the lavish architectural setting built by Balthasar Neumann, Tiepolo covered vast surfaces with his airy and virtuoso designs executed in pale, bright colours. Gods and men mingle in a sumptuous world which extends the earthly splendours of the Bishop's Residence; ceilings become lofty skies and painted architecture recedes far into the distance.

Although Tiepolo's magnificent decorative cycles found little response in England, a type of Venetian painting arose that excited considerable demand. This was the *veduta* or view painting. Artists such as Giovanni Antonio Canaletto (1697-1768) took the visual splendour of the city of Venice as the subject matter

Above: *The Feast of the Ascension* by Canaletto (1697-1768) captures the vitality of the great Venetian festivals, which were a reminder of more prosperous and opulent times in the city's history.

Below: *Gilles* by Antoine Watteau (1684-1721) reflects the painter's fascination for the life of strolling players. Here the clown's pose and gaze suggest a melancholy typical of Watteau's work.

Right: The *Swing* by Jean Honore Fragonard (1732-1806) is a supreme example of rococo art. The theme of the garden of love is treated in a highly provocative, light-hearted and aristocratic fashion.

for their work. Canaletto's *Stonemason's yard*, an early work, is an intimate view of Venice, showing a run-down, rather than a spectacular, area of the city. Here Canaletto captures perfectly the texture of brick, stone and wood. More typical of his work, however, are his bustling festival and canal scenes.

Francesco Guardi (1712-93) painted many of the scenes which Canaletto had depicted, but his pictures are distinguished by a hazy insubstantiality concerned more to capture the diffused light of the lagoon city than to present solid meticulous townscapes as Canaletto had done. With his free handling of paint and emphasis on air, light and water, Guardi achieves tremendously atmospheric effects.

England: satire and sophistication
In England the painting most in demand during the eighteenth century was portraiture which celebrated the virtues and social status of the propertied middle classes and aristocracy, who could afford the artists' fees.

However, painters like William Hogarth (1697-1764), like popular writers of the day such as Jonathan Swift and Alexander Pope, were by no means blind to the foibles and weaknesses of society. With great verve and wit Hogarth sought to expose precisely those human and social failings that the more elegant French painters had glossed over. He was concerned to depict the strongly defined moral values of the rising middle-class in England, devoting himself to a more realistic appraisal of the quality of eighteenth-century life. He became known chiefly for his moral scenes.

The first of these moral subjects was a series entitled the *Harlot's Progress*, depicting the corruption of a country girl by wicked Londoners. Three more scenes followed, each of them becoming popular and famous; the *Rake's Progress* (1735), *Marriage a la Mode* (1743-5) and the *Election* (1754). The strong satiric and moral element in these is matched by their delicate and sensitive painting. Apart from these series, Hogarth was a fine portraitist—one of his best studies is of the heads of his servants.

In marked contrast to Hogarth's robust manner, the elegance and finesse of Watteau were important in forming the artistic ideals of Thomas Gainsborough (1727-88). As a portraitist he enjoyed the patronage of wealth and royalty. He combined an instinctive ease and fluency in portraying his sitters with a fine sensitivity to English landscape.

Much of his early career was spent in Suffolk. The strongest influence on his work at this time was Dutch seventeenth-century landscape painting. His closely-observed landscapes and even his portraits in landscape settings, such as *Mr and Mrs Andrews*, reflect both this early influence and that of Watteau. After his move to the fashionable town of Bath, the somewhat naive quality of Gainsborough's early work was replaced by a greater sophistication and elegance. He most often painted full-length, life-size portraits of sumptuously dressed people set against imagined landscapes. His technique progressed in fluency; his later paintings show a remarkable sensitivity to materials and textures, executed in feathery, almost sketchy, brushstrokes.

Gainsborough's contemporary and rival, Sir Joshua Reynolds (1723-92), was well-known both as a theorist and as a painter. During the first part of his career, Reynolds was not only a practising artist, but travelled abroad to Italy, where he studied antique art and the High Renaissance painters Raphael and, above all, Michelangelo. On his return to London in 1753 he befriended many well-known figures, including Dr Johnson, Goldsmith, Burke and Garrick. In 1768 the Royal Academy was founded and Reynolds was made its first President. In his *Discourses* to the Academy, given between 1769 and 1790, Reynolds sought to introduce a grand manner into English painting and held that the artist should seek to represent an ideal beauty free from all 'excrescences and deformity of things'.

A similar desire to purify art and to return to the more severe beauty of classical antiquity was felt increasingly in France as the eighteenth century progressed. Inspired by David, artists sought to recapture the grandeur and moral stature of antique art. The *neo-classical* movement which thus arose served as a transition between rococo art and a new revolutionary sensibility. With neo-classicism, David wrote, the 'marks of heroism and civic virtue offered to the eyes of the people will electrify its soul'. The age of Revolution had begun.

Below: *Reclining Girl* painted by Francois Boucher (1703-70). This work, possibly a portrait of a young mistress of Louis XV, illustrates Boucher's ability to handle subjects that are both simple and provocative, with a delight in the sensuous effects of flesh, rich colours and materials.

William Blake

Today William Blake (1757-1827) ranks among England's greatest poets and painters. Yet less than a century and a half ago he was hardly recognized even as an engraver—the craft by which he earned his livelihood.

Youth and apprenticeship

In his life and works William Blake both reflects and rebels against the age in which he lived. He was born in London, the son of a hosier. As a Londoner who spent only three years of his life outside his native city, Blake inhabited and wrote about an outward world familiar to a large number of his contemporaries. But his inner beliefs were less familiar. Blake went without a conventional English education; largely self-taught, his ideas were drawn from a vast range of influences.

Himself a natural visionary, Blake was connected from childhood with the unorthodox religious views of the Swedish mystical theologian Emanuel Swedenborg. From his knowledge of Greek and Oriental philosophy and his interest in Celtic history, Blake created the highly individual (and often incomprehensible) pantheon of gods which people his poetry.

Blake's artistic appreciation was moulded first by five years at a drawing school, and then by his apprenticeship at the age of 14 to the copper engraver James Basire, where he developed a linear Gothic style, derived from the tomb effigies which he copied for his master in Westminster Abbey. For Blake this was the true Christian style, a view which was not widely held in England at the turn of the century. But Blake also admired Michelangelo, although again his view of the great master's art was highly individual. For Blake, Michelangelo's weighty, sculpturesque forms belonged to the earth-bound world from whose restricting laws he wished to be free, but the spiritual energy and spiralling motion of the Italian accorded with his vision of an unfettered world of imagination and spirit.

Politically Blake was a radical, who sympathized with the American and French revolutions and numbered among his friends the revolutionary Tom Paine, author of *The Rights of Man*. Through another friend, the author Mary Wollstonecraft who was acquainted with the works of the French philosopher J. J. Rousseau, Blake acquired advanced ideas on education and even (in common with the Swedenborgians) on free love. Despite his unorthodox views and irrascible, sensitive and quarrelsome temperament, Blake nevertheless enjoyed many years of harmony with his wife Catherine. The illiterate daughter of a Battersea market gardener, she still ardently believed in his genius and helped him in his work, learning to take impressions from his plates and helping with the binding of his books. Blake's relations with his friends were more ruffled: his correspondence reveals public rejection and clashes with contemporaries and social conventions alike.

Blake's 'illuminated printing'

Blake's greatness rests upon the unique

Above: William Blake (1757-1827), poet, painter and mystic, was largely unrecognized during his lifetime and earned his living as an engraver. From his boyhood on, Blake saw visions and relied upon his inner spiritual convictions, believing that 'This World of the Imagination is Infinite and Eternal'.

Below: *The Sick Rose*, an illuminated print from *Songs of Experience* (1794), engraved, coloured and printed by Blake. The worm, secretly destroying the life and beauty of the rose, is Blake's image for Experience—a state of spiritual death in contrast to the joyful, unhindered response to a life of Innocence.

Then the Lord answered Job out of the Whirlwind

The SICK ROSE

O Rose thou art sick.
The invisible worm.
That flies in the night
In the howling storm:

Has found out thy bed
Of crimson joy:
And his dark secret love
Does thy life destroy.

unity of his vision. Blake (unlike his admired Michelangelo) was not simply poet and painter, but a poet-painter and more—for he combined in one activity the arts of poetry, painting, engraving, printing and philosophy.

For whatever reason, whether because his politics were too radical, his religious views too heretical or he preferred to engrave his own works, Blake was without a publisher after the appearance of *Poetical Sketches*, (1783) his first collection of poems. Desiring to produce more work, he began the process of 'illuminated printing', engraving both text and marginal illustrations on the copper plate and then colouring the impression taken from it by hand. In this way he produced all his subsequent writings from the early *Songs of Innocence* (1789)

Above: Blake spent so much of his time earning a living by hack work that his opportunities for original engraving and illustration were greatly reduced. His plates for the *Book of Job* (1825), which include this engraving, 'Then the Lord answered Job out of the whirlwind' combine grandeur of conception with fine craftsmanship. In this biblical text Blake found inspiration for his own vision of man's spiritual life.

Right: In 1793 Blake printed *The Gates of Paradise*, a little book of emblems concerned with the question 'What is Man?' This plate, 'I want! I want!' seems to depict man's desire to encompass all he sees.

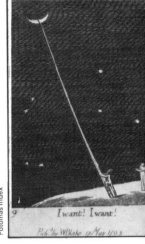

I want! I want!

and *Songs of Innocence and Experience* (1794) to the various Prophetic Books and his late symbolic poems *Milton* (1804-8) and *Jerusalem* (1804-20).

The visual inspiration for Blake's 'illuminated printing' was the beautiful illuminated psalters of the Middle Ages, but the solution to the technical problem of their production Blake, typically, ascribed to supernatural aid. After his favourite brother Robert had died in 1787, Blake had seen his spirit rising 'through the matter-of-fact ceiling, clapping his hands for joy'. This spirit, which had stayed with him, subsequently indicated a way to proceed with his work.

The enchanting coloured volume entitled *Songs of Innocence* was the first major work to be produced in Blake's new manner. To it he added five years later his *Songs of Experience*. The *Songs* differ both in form and intention from the poet's other writings. They follow the rhythms of traditional English nursery rhymes, popular ballads and hymns, attracting by the sheer beauty of their poetry and the simplicity of their symbolism of rose, sunflower, lion or lamb. Taken individually the poems may appear simple, but together they provide an insight into the human condition as well as criticism of

Fitzwilliam Museum

Radio Times Hulton Picture Library

Michael Holford/British Museum

Fotomas Index

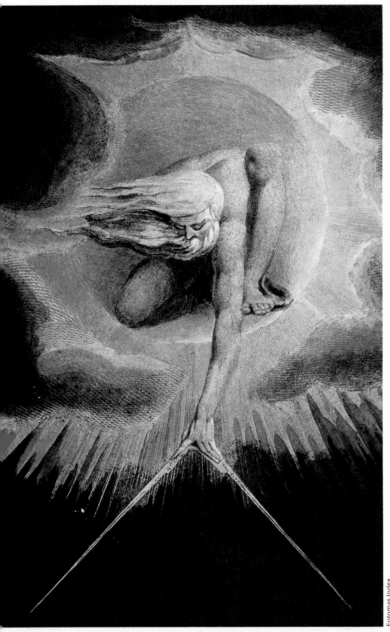

Above: Blake was working on his illustrations to Dante when he died in 1827, at the age of 69. This watercolour depicts the *Whirlwind of Lovers* from Dante's *Hell*.

Left: This colour print of *The Ancient of Days* (1794) formed the frontispiece of Blake's poem *Europe, a Prophecy*. It was inspired by the biblical *Proverbs*, in which the Lord 'sets a compass upon the face of the deep'. The figure is not strictly speaking God, but Blake's mythical being Urizen, the Creator but also (in Blake's view) the symbol of tyranny and rational knowledge.

Below: In common with his contemporary artists, Blake found inspiration in Shakespeare. This colour print entitled *Pity* (1795), executed in a rich, mottled technique, has its source in Macbeth's words as he contemplates murder: 'And Pity, like a naked new-born babe / Striding the blast . . . Shall blow the horrid deed in every eye, / That tears shall drown the wind.'

many eighteenth century attitudes. The *Songs* contain the core of many of Blake's most consistently held views. But there is almost no trace in them of the complex mythological figures of Blake's later writing.

The full title of the complete work is *Songs of Innocence and Experience, showing the Two Contrary States of the Human Soul*. To appreciate Blake's full intention the two sets of *Songs* should be read together and contrasted—many of them are paired—for although they are similar in structure there is yet a distinct difference of character between them. The first set offers an imaginative vision of childlike innocence and the second shows how this is corrupted by experience.

What Blake intended by this contrast and what he understood by 'innocence' and 'experience' is suggested by the motto which he originally wrote for the work:

'*The Good are attracted by Men's
        perceptions,
And Think not for themselves;
Till Experience teaches them to catch
And to cage the Fairies & Elves.*

*And then the Knave begins to snarl
And the Hypocrite to howl;
And all his good friends shew their
        private ends,
And the Eagle is known from the Owl.*

The divine Imagination

Blake despised the mechanical view of the universe offered by philosophers and scientists of the contemporary Enlightenment, with their explanation of the creator who had set the world in motion and then retired from it, leaving it to run on laws of his own devising. Material explanations of the world led, in Blake's view, to spiritual death and ignored the artist's visionary power: the mind was not a passive recorder of impressions gained from without through the senses, but an active, creative force—God himself working within the human soul. For Blake the imaginative life was the only real world: 'This world of Imagination is the world of Eternity; it is the divine bosom into which we shall all go after the death of the Vegetated body.'

Stifling the creative forces which he called 'Fairies & Elves' led to the rigidity of thought that Blake held responsible for the hypocrisy, greed and self-seeking in the world. A state of innocence was for him not a state of ignorance, naivety or 109

even inexperience but spontaneous, un-fettered joy in and response to life. The eagle in the motto is Blake's symbol for the free soaring spirit whose opposite is the bleary night-owl.

For Blake love and compassion, too, must not be confined within the bounds of rationalist thought and morality. In several of the songs the unselfconscious loving and giving of innocence are opposed to the dogmatic, self-interested and calculating attitudes of experience. In the pair of *Holy Thursdays* the simple dignity and 'radiance' of the charity children at Divine Service in St Paul's, the 'flowers of London town' raising 'to heaven the voice of song', is compared with the calculated, self-interested atti-tude of the so-called religious society in the *Holy Thursday* of *Experience*, which dispenses charity with a 'cold and usurous hand' and can allow 'Babes reduc'd to misery' in a 'rich and fruitful land'. The two sets of *Songs* explore, too, the contrast between the forces of power and gentle-ness, the tiger and the lamb. *The Tyger* expresses wonder and awe at the tiger's energy and untamed nature and asks how such apparent opposites as the tiger and lamb can be part of one creation: 'Did he smile his work to see? Did he who made the Lamb make thee?'

The poignant disillusionment which sets apart the 'experienced' songs from the 'innocent' suggests Blake's own harsh contact with reality in the intervening years. In the *Book of Thel* (contemporary with the *Songs of Innocence*), the symbolic figure Thel is appalled by a vision of reality and refuses to accept it. Blake's high hopes of the French Revolution expressed in the prophetic book of that name (1791) were dispelled by the realiza-tion that events were not turning out to his liking. Moreover, his idealistic views of free love caused temporary strife within his marriage.

Visionary and prophet
Shortly after the publication of the set of *Songs*, the mood, imagery and rhythm of Blake's poems change. Prophetic warn-ings and an increasingly Christian (although unorthodox) tone predominates. His poetical world becomes more personal and difficult to understand—deliberately so, for Blake believed poetry should be 'Allegory address'd to the Intellectual powers, while it is altogether hidden from the Corporeal Understanding'.

110

Above: Samuel Palmer was among the young painters who admired and were influenced by Blake during his last years. This *Rustic Scene* is typical of Palmer's pastoral, visionary landscapes.

Right: To *Glad Day* (c.1794), possibly a self-portrait, Blake added: 'Albion arose from where he laboured at the Mill with Slaves: Giving himself for the Nations he danced the dance of Eternal Death.' During Blake's age the power of the machine was growing; the mill, from which the youth breaks away with joyous energy, is its symbol.

In 1800 William and Catherine left London to live at Felpham near Bognor, Sussex, in the cottage of the poet William Hayley, whose work he was engraving. Relations between the two men gradually became strained and after three years Blake and his wife returned to London where they remained until his death.

To this last stage of Blake's career belong the magnificent series of 21 water colours illustrating *The Book of Job*. On his death bed he was still working on his other great series, the illustrations to Dante's *The Divine Comedy*. The wood-cuts which Blake did in 1821 as illustra-tions to an edition of Virgil's *Eclogues* became the inspiration of a type of pastoral landscape for the young Samuel Palmer, one of a small group of artists who at the close of Blake's life recognized the significance of his achievement. Palmer's brooding and vital landscapes owe much of their spiritual intensity to Blake's concept of the unseen world. His *Cornfield by Moonlight* radiates the same cosmic glow.

Blake was a fine creative artist whose painting was of a piece with his poetry and his passion. His sinuous, linear forms, elongated and ethereal, can be recognized today as characteristic of all great spiritual art. For Blake the imagination was man's most divine quality; he spoke of 'Jesus the Imagination'. Above all, his work expresses his belief in unfettered, spontaneous existence and his fervent conviction of the eternal life of the spirit:

He who binds to himself a joy
Does the winged life destroy;
But he who kisses the joy as it flies
Lives in Eternity's sun rise.

Below: After living in obscurity for much of his life, Blake gained a circle of admirers from 1818 onwards. Among them was John Varley, a landscape painter and astrologer, who encouraged Blake to draw 'spirit heads' as a record of the spirits which the poet frequently saw. This drawing, *The Ghost of a Flea* (1819)

was later made into a painting and was said by Blake to be an accurate likeness of the spirit he had seen. As he drew the ghost, he described it to Varley thus: 'There he comes! his eager tongue whisking out of his mouth, a cup in his hand to hold blood and covered with a scaly skin of gold and green.'

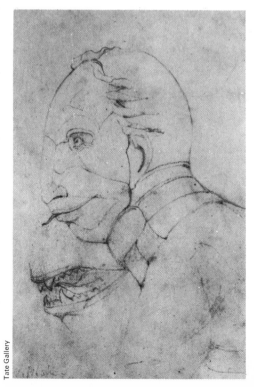

English Landscape Painting

The best of English landscape might never have been painted if it had not been for the Napoleonic wars. Prevented from crossing the Alps by recurring hostilities, the English lord could not pursue the traditional Grand Tour of classical sites, mainly Italy, so he had to look for alternative diversion at home. Similarly, the English artist could no longer visit Michelangelo's Sistine Chapel ceiling nor Raphael's stanze — both considered essential visits for the budding artist of the eighteenth century. Turner, considered by many to be the finest English landscape painter, did not visit Italy until 1819—and by then he was a Royal Academician and some of his best work was already done, inspired by his native landscape.

Rise of landscape painting

Ever since the foundation of the Royal Academy under the presidency of Sir Joshua Reynolds in 1768 the vogue had been for paintings of scenes from the classics; landscape painting had come near the bottom of the artistic hierarchy.

Even when landscape was admired it was not the English scene depicted by English painters but the Italianate landscapes of Claude Lorraine (1600-82) which attracted collectors. This French-born artist was enormously popular for his perfectly balanced compositions. But with the onset of the Napoleonic wars the English were no longer able to view the Roman scene through the eyes of Claude and began to look at their own—hitherto despised—countryside.

An ingenious clergyman, William Gilpin, had conceived the idea of encouraging the English to appreciate the beauty of their own countryside by writing instructive handbooks. *Three Essays: On Picturesque Beauty: on Picturesque Travel: and on Sketching Landscape* was published in 1792, starting a trend for a whole series of 'picturesque' guide books to different parts of Britain.

Dr Monro's Academy

Dr Thomas Monro (1759-1833) was a physician at Bethlehem Hospital (or 'Bedlam', the London lunatic asylum) but he was also a keen amateur artist. With the help of an inheritance from his father, he formed a valuable collection of drawings by artists such as Gainsborough and the eccentric John Robert Cozens (a remarkably able watercolourist who died as one of Monro's patients). By 1794 Dr Monro was living at 8, Adelphi Terrace, London, and it was here that he invited young artists to study and copy his collection on Friday evenings.

J. M. W. Turner (1775-1851) was among the regular young aspirants at Monro's, and alongside him was Tom Girtin—a highly-gifted watercolourist who knew how to contrast cool shadows with brilliant, warm lights. He died at the tragically early age of 27 in 1802. Turner remarked that if Girtin had lived, he

National Gallery

Above: *Landscape with Hagar and the Angel* by Claude (1600-82). From this artist, landscape painters learned that everything in a picture must be subordinate to a single mood. This work was the favourite of Sir George Beamont, (1753-1827), a collector who admired it so much he took it with him everywhere.

Below: *Kirkstall Abbey* by Tom Girtin. This interpretation of the Yorkshire ruin became a popular subject for contemporary artists in search of a romantic subject. Girtin freely created a mood through his use of blurred edges, uneven colour and the relationship of the Abbey to its rural surroundings.

Victoria & Albert Museum

Tate Gallery

Fotomas Index

Tate Gallery

Above: Turner's *Decline of the Carthaginian Empire,* exhibited at the Royal Academy in 1817. This picture is closely modelled on Claude's seaport pictures and could well have been a deliberate attempt to out-bid the master. He requested in his will that it should be hung next to Claude's *Sea Port* and *Mill.*

Right: *Sunset/Rouen?* **(1829).** Turner practised watercolour throughout his life: the fluid medium allows the artist a more immediate and spontaneous record of what he sees. Watercolours like this are now among the most admired of his work but in his own time they were considered mere daubs.

Above: The critics were not enthusiastic about Turner's *The Sun of Venice.* They were used to traditionally gloomy views and this picture of light and colour was appreciated only by John Ruskin, the great art writer, who called it 'the very counterpart of the Sol di Venezia.'

Right: *Snowstorm: Steamboat off Harbour's Mouth*—received by one critic as 'a mass of soapsuds' but seen today as a masterpiece of atmospheric painting. The frail mast makes a lone vertical in the vortex of the storm.

Below: *Norham Castle, Sunrise*—a subject the artist returned to repeatedly in his attempt to capture light on landscape.

(Turner) would have starved.

From Girtin, Turner learned much about watercolour painting and from Monro's collection he became familiar with the most original landscape artists of earlier periods. But with Girtin and other young artists, Turner was encouraged merely to sketch from nature and work up his studies in the studio—a method practised by all nineteenth-century English landscape painters until the revolution of open-air painting introduced by the Pre-Raphaelite Brotherhood in 1848.

Turner's mature works

Turner's precocious talent enabled him to be admitted to the Royal Academy Schools in 1789 and he first exhibited at the RA in 1791. Turner's contemporaries were amazed by his paintings; solid form seems to disintegrate in a sea of light and colour. But the artist had diligently studied the old masters as well as nature; even the freely handled *Interior at Petworth* (c.1837) and the late, unfinished *Norham Castle, Sunrise* (1835-40) reveal Claude's influence, not only in capturing special qualities of light but also in their insistence on structure.

William Hazlitt, the essayist, dismissed Turner's work, saying it consisted of 'pictures of nothing, and very like.' Although meant as an insult there was a grain of truth in this criticism, considering the awesome atmospheric effects Turner was capable of inducing. But in general, awed respect seasoned with incomprehension was the public reaction to Turner. Words like 'extravagant' and 'reckless' recur in reviews of his work.

Having been educated in the tradition of picturesque tours—and having produced, in his youth, many watercolours and oils in that genre (like *Derwentwater*, 1797, and *Plompton Rocks*, c.1798)—Turner never lost his love of travel. He frequently made several tours a year, at first in the British Isles and, after 1819, as far afield as Prague, Vienna, Rome and Naples. Turner was intrepid in his search for new experiences in nature.

This is especially true of the sea pieces in which Turner reinterpreted the long-established European convention through a personal experience of natural conditions. *Snowstorm—Steam boat off a Harbour's Mouth making signals in shallow water and going by the Lead* (1842) features a turbulent vortex of foam and spray in which sky and sea become one. The foundering steamship shows a pathetic mast against a living sky—an experience frozen on canvas: Turner having had himself tied to the mast of that very ship—an event he did not expect to survive.

The place to which Turner most frequently returned, and which is now most closely associated with his achievement as a colourist, was Venice. He visited the city in 1819, 1829, 1833 and

1840, producing masses of watercolour sketches and, eventually, a remarkable series of oil paintings. Turner's familiarity with topographical art and his training with Girtin and others at Dr Monro's stood him in good stead during his first visit to Italy. In four months between August 1819 and January 1820 Turner used 19 sketch books some of which contain detailed studies, others the most delicate and concentrated watercolour washes devoid of recognizable form. These he called 'colour beginnings'.

But not until the 1840s did he find himself able to paint the vaporous atmosphere and prismatic lighting effects of Venice in the more permanent medium of oil in pictures like *The 'Sun of Venice' going to Sea* (1843).

The Sun of Venice, when exhibited, was accompanied by lines from a long unpublished poem written by the artist (called *The Fallacies of Hope*). The ominous sense of impending disaster and the irony which underlies the sunny departure are a feature of many of Turner's works. Like other Romantic artists and writers, Turner was keenly aware of man's frailty in an awesome universe. Pictures like *The Fifth Plague of Egypt* (1800), *The Deluge* (1804-5), *Snow Storm: Hannibal and His Army crossing the Alps* (1812), *The Decline of the Carthaginian Empire* (1817), *Slavers throwing overboard the Dead and Dying—Typhoon coming on* (1840), reflect the reverse side of the general nineteenth-century expansionist optimism. It was with epic landscapes such as these that Turner introduced a tone of moral seriousness into English landscape art. In doing so he effectively challenged the inferior position that landscape had always held in the academy hierarchy.

The challenge of Constable
John Constable (1776-1837) was born in East Bagholt, Suffolk, the son of a well-to-do miller. Although his name is inevitably linked with that of Turner, his background and his major artistic concerns are totally different. He was a late developer (his tentative early efforts show none of the dexterity of Turner's early watercolours, for example)—and he had to strive all his life to achieve the recognition and the patronage which was readily accorded to Turner. It was only in 1829 at the age of 53 that Constable was made a Royal Academician, an honour granted to Turner in 1802 at the age of 27; and Constable never enjoyed the sort of security that a patron like Lord Egremont of Petworth provided for Turner.

Constable never went abroad. His greatest paintings are based on scenes from his boyhood home country in the Stour valley and Hampstead where he lived with his wife from 1820. His father's profession required a familiarity with weather conditions—Constable grew up, therefore, accustomed to view the skies across the flat countryside with special interest.

'It would be difficult to name a class of landscape', wrote Constable, 'in which the sky is not the key note, the standard of scale, and the chief organ of sentiment.' In *Wivenhoe Park* (1817) the sky with its fluffy cotton wool clouds is mainly decorative. During his honeymoon in Dorset in 1816, Constable had paid close attention to weather effects along the coast. *Weymouth Bay* is one result of this study

John Webb/Victoria & Albert Museum

John Webb/Victoria & Albert Museum

Above: *Dedham Vale* (1802) by John Constable, one of the artist's earliest paintings of a scene in the Stour valley which was to dominate his vision for many years. Sir George Beamont had shown the artist Claude's *Hagar and the Angel*; the similarities in composition can be seen clearly in this picture.

Left: Sketch of a tree for Constable's *Valley Farm*. He first painted the farm—or Willy Lott's house as it was sometimes called—in 1812 or 1813. The tree, however, was taken from Hampstead Heath and included in the Valley Farm picture. This composite scene reflects the artist's struggle to convey the 'flavour' of aspects of his past life.

Above right: *Weymouth Bay*, one of Constable's Dorset pictures, painted on his honeymoon in 1816. After a long and stressful engagement to Maria Bicknell the first months of their marriage took him away from the familiar Suffolk countryside and provided him with inspiration for several paintings of Weymouth and Osmington.

Right: In a changing world, with the Industrial Revolution threatening to cut swathes through the countryside, the heart of changelessness for Constable was *The Valley Farm*, or Willy Lott's House. Willy Lott lived there for 80 years without ever leaving it for more than 4 days at a time. Willy Lott was still living there the last time Constable visited the farm; both the man and the countryside became an obsession with the artist. Constable never left England, unlike Turner.

114

and shows a heavy rain-laden sky which —although very much more naturalistic than his earlier skies—shows that Constable had not yet solved the problem of preventing a closely observed sky from dominating the picture. After 1820 in the Hampstead Heath canvases his landscapes were much better balanced.

Studio landscapes

The large series of six-foot Stour scenes on which Constable's reputation has stood were not, despite their naturalism, painted on the spot but in the studio after immensely painstaking studies. *The Hay Wain* (1821), was originally exhibited as *Landscape: Noon.* This shows how Constable's main interest was in the time of day, which controls lighting conditions rather than in what is happening in the picture.

The Hay Wain was the first painting for which Constable executed a full-scale oil sketch. Nobody had done this before—it seems likely that Constable evolved this practice as part of his attempt to co-ordinate overall composition with attention to detail.

Constable's life was by no means easy. The death of his wife shortly after the birth of their seventh child in 1828 was a terrible blow. He also suffered from an increasing sense of failure in his efforts to convince people that, 'in such an age as this, painting should be understood, not looked on with blind wonder nor considered only as a poetic aspiration but as a pursuit, legitimate, scientific, mechanical'. In Constable's late work the confident grasp of reality that characterizes the *View of Dedham* (Stour Valley and Dedham Village, 1815), *Boat Building* (1815), *Scene on a Navigable River* (Flatford Mill, 1817) and *Dedham Lock and Mill* (1820) has waned. Stonehenge and Hadleigh Castle (1829 and 1836) represented for Constable a more dramatic, darker side of nature which preoccupied him with increasing intensity towards the end of his life.

Late works

In 1831 Constable painted *Salisbury Cathedral from the Meadows.* Salisbury was associated with the artist's friendship with John Fisher, the bishop's nephew who had procured for Constable in 1822 a commission to paint *Salisbury Cathedral from the Bishop's Grounds*—the first of a great series of paintings featuring the cathedral—threatening and foreboding.

A similar mood dominates *The Valley Farm* (1835) in which Willy Lott's house is seen from the other side beyond the Hay Wain pool. Constable's art embodies a whole lifetime's response to natural scenery. He had looked scientifically at nature, studied it for its picture-making qualities and valued it for its human associations. In *The Valley Farm* the house is overgrown, the trees dark and gloomy, the bold freshness of *The Hay Wain* has given way to a nervous finicky handling—even the sparkling pool seems silted up. Such comparisons tell us much about an artist who is now acknowledged as one of Europe's greatest landscape artists but who wrote of 'a sad freak with which I have been long "*possessed*" of feeling a *duty—on my part* to *tell* the world that there is such a thing as Landscape existing with "Art"—as I have in so great measure failed to "*show*" the world that it is possible to accomplish it.'

Goya

Goya is recognized as one of the greatest European painters. His pictures express individuality with an intensity that few other artists have equalled. As a result, his life and work have accumulated a mythology of their own: Goya almost died after being stabbed in the back by a jealous husband, he fought in the bullring, he was pursued by the Inquisition, his mistresses were the most powerful women in Spain. There is truth in these stories but it has been embroidered out of all recognition. Goya was, indeed, a powerful and passionate man, but we know this as much from the character of his works as from accounts of his life.

Goya's achievement, in view of the time and place in which he worked, is all the more remarkable. Late eighteenth century Spain did not produce many great artists. Relative to other parts of Europe, the country was backward—politically, economically and culturally. The Church wielded enormous power through the Inquisition and a corrupt, inept court monopolized political power. While elsewhere in Europe and in America new ideas were sweeping away the cobwebs of autocratic monarchies and religious repression, in Spain there was not a hint of change, only stagnation. The art commissioned by the ruling court was frivolous. Dominated by the Rococo style derived from France and Italy, painters produced pleasant diversions for bored and listless aristocrats.

Early life and work

Francisco Goya y Lucientes was born in 1746 near Saragossa. His father was a master gilder and his mother a member of the petty nobility. At 13 or 14 he was apprenticed to a mediocre but reputable provincial painter producing large, Rococo canvasses for churches. In 1766, after two unsuccessful bids to join the Royal Academy, Goya went to Madrid where he entered the studio of Francisco Bayeu. In 1770 Goya was in Italy, possibly to escape the Inquisition which was investigating his reckless and immoral behaviour.

In 1773 he married Josefa Bayeu, the sister of his teacher. This move seems to have been motivated more by ambition than love, although his wife remained a faithful companion until her death in 1812 —despite his numerous affairs. The marriage secured the help of his new brother-in-law who was enjoying considerable success with the court. With Bayeu's recommendation, Goya was commissioned to produce cartoons (or designs) for the Royal Tapestry factory. Modelled on Tiepolo's decorative schemes Goya's cartoons are among the very best of their type, full of luminous colour and freedom of technique, with light brushwork producing fluid, arcadian visions of the life of Spanish peasants and gypsies.

At this time, there was a fashion for *Majos* and *Majas* (members of the underworld of bullfighters and courtesans) to mix freely with the aristocrats of Madrid. Along with the other painters working for the court, Goya concentrated on views of their life-style with a lighthearted and somewhat idealized naturalism, as in *The Parasol* of 1777.

Above: Self-portrait by Francisco de Goya (1746-1828), painter and engraver.

Left: In 1800 Goya was commissioned to paint *Charles IV and his family*. It is difficult to believe that this unpitying depiction of the flabby, chinless King and his uncouth wife met with their approval. But because the likenesses were good and the costumes gorgeous, the royal family were well satisfied. The picture is realistic rather than cruel—Goya paints with a dispassionate vision.

Below: *The Parasol* (1777) is typical of the charm and fluency of Goya's early work.

Arborio Mella

Left: In his portrait of the *Duchess of Alba* (1795) Goya displays his marvellous skill with paint in capturing delicacy of texture. The Duchess, notorious for her liaisons with matadors, had a much-publicized affair with the painter.

Right and below: Goya's pair of paintings *The Naked Maja* and *The Clothed Maja* were probably painted between 1800 and 1805, although stories linking them with Goya's affair with the Duchess of Alba would date them earlier. These pictures reveal a frank sensuality and were remarkably daring for their time. The only previous acknowledged nude in Spanish painting was Velasquez' *Rokeby Venus*. Both the naked and clothed *Maja* show Goya's free handling of paint, the brushstrokes sketchily indicating the heap of pillows and the *Maja's* clinging dress. Goya's art looks both backward—to the styles of Tiepolo and Velasquez—and forward (in its dramatic composition and technical freedom) to Delacroix and the Impressionists.

In 1778 an event of great importance took place in Goya's artistic development. The King invited several artists to enter the private apartments and produce engravings of the royal collection of paintings. Goya was evidently amazed by the native Spanish works of Velasquez which he saw. The drama and majesty of Velasquez and his sharp eye for the characters of his portrait subjects deeply impressed Goya.

In the meantime, Goya's career progressed on the coat tails of his brother-in-law. Bayeu became rector of the Academy in 1780, after which Goya was accepted as an academician. Although he was unpopular with the Academy his success with the court grew steadily. His brusque provincial manner probably appealed to them, and he seems to have been very attractive to the ladies of the court. Eventually in 1789 he was appointed a Royal painter by the new king, Charles IV, and could claim to be the most fashionable artist in Madrid.

A crisis of direction

In 1792, at the age of 46, Goya collapsed with a terrible illness. He was delirious for months, paralysed for part of that time and seemed for a while to be going blind. Goya clearly underwent the most intense torment. When he finally recovered, he was totally deaf. If he had died at this point, as his doctors expected, Goya would be known to us as the finest of several Rococo artists working in Spain, with none of his present enormous reputation. Goya's illness cannot be diagnosed accurately; whether it had a physical or mental origin is not known. All that can be said is that it changed him—and his work—profoundly.

The change is seen in his *Carnival Scene* of 1793 with its new degree of invention and fantasy. Macabre elements had been seen in Goya's earlier pictures, but now there is a certain disgust at the grotesque behaviour of the peasants at their superstitious festival. Goya from this time tried to avoid his duties as an
118 official portrait painter. From 1793 to 1796

Mansell

Below: In *The Second of May*, 1808 Goya expressed the passion of the Spanish revolt against the French. Here, in *The Third of May*, he depicts the tragedy of the reprisals. With dramatic certainty, Goya spotlights a victim of the firing squad, kneeling in a comrade's blood as he throws up his hands in desperation.

Right: In 1808 French troops invaded Spain and overthrew the monarchy. In a series of etchings, *The Disasters of War* (1810-13), Goya showed the brutality of both sides in the war. Here, in a plate entitled *What Courage!* a young woman stands on the heaped-up bodies of the dead men to fire a cannon.

Bulloz

Michael Holford

Below: Giants recur in Goya's imagery. Here in *The Colossus* (c.1812), people and cattle flee in panic from the huge, dreadful—and indifferent—apparition which looms above them. This vision of catastrophe is extremely powerful; its impact is increased by its rapidity and violence of execution.

Above right: In his highly accomplished etchings, Goya gave full rein to his private world of fantasy and invention. Here, in his engraving *Modes of Flight*, Goya constructs a dramatic composition from imagined bird-like men, with beaks and wings attached to them, flying in space.

he produced a series of engravings known as *Los Caprichos*, or *Foolishnesses*. Technically, these still have the lightness of line typical of Rococo drawings but they are shot through with a bitterly individual view of the world. They mock, they reveal weaknesses of character, they despair at humanity. One of them, *The Sleep of Reason Begets Monsters* shows the ghastly fantasies of melancholia, perhaps a memory of Goya's own experience. Some of the drawings have a political message, delivering intense social satire against ignorance, charlatanism and the exploitation of superstition by the Church. Nevertheless, although Goya was involved with the intellectuals and dissatisfied noblemen of the court, he had no political commitment whatsoever. When the Inquisition attacked some of *Los Caprichos*, powerful friends (including his ex-mistress the Duchess of Osuna) protected him. Goya was a liberal of the court, not a revolutionary.

In 1795 he painted the portrait of the Duchess of Alba, one of the richest women in Spain and a celebrated wit. Although he was 16 years her senior and stone deaf, they had a passionate and much publicized love affair. Legend has it that *The Naked Maja* and *The Clothed Maja* were painted for—and of—the Duchess at this time, and a likeness in the model's features is certainly discernible.

Visions of horror
In 1808, Napoleon's troops invaded Spain and replaced the king with Joseph Bonaparte. Goya and others with liberal aspirations looked forward to a new more rational government. They were to be disappointed. Spontaneous riots were brutally crushed by French troops and almost immediately a bloody guerilla war broke out. Goya responded with a new series of engravings called *The Disasters of War* made between 1810 and 1813. The expressive force of *Los Caprichos* is turned in these horrific works towards a more specific subject. Goya, however, did not take sides, he wanted only to show the horror. The brutality of Spaniards and

Frenchmen alike is viewed with a dispassionate gaze.

In 1814 Goya produced his finest works. These are major canvasses into which the whole achievement of the *Disasters* is compressed. *The Second of May*, 1808 and *The Third of May*, 1808 record the events when the people of Madrid rose against the French. On 2 May, French Cavalry charged a rioting crowd and hacked them down with their sabres, killing hundreds. The next day, a series of retaliatory executions took place. The movement and drama in these works is extraordinary. In the freedom of their composition and rich colour they look forward to the Romantics—the French painter Delacroix, for example, was greatly influenced by these pictures. Goya by this stage had totally transcended his eighteenth century background. To the virtuosity of the Rococo decorator, with all the painterly skills of free brushwork and luminous colour, he added a deep, almost savage, sense of pity.

In 1819 Goya retired to a house known as the *Quinta del Sordo* where he began a frenzy of work, covering the walls with hideous, nightmarish visions from his imagination. The series shows devils and monsters, together with representations of all forms of human folly and vice, painted with total abandon. His skilful technique and understanding of composition did not, however, desert him even in this private world of fantasy.

Goya continued to work as a portraitist to the court but most of his late works are personal—of his nightmares and his friends. He fell under official suspicion for his known liberalism in 1824 and went to France, where he died in 1828.

At a time when artists studied the Ancient world with monotonous regularity Goya said 'I have only three masters: Velasquez, Rembrandt and Nature'. In choosing all three of these he was out of his time and much closer to the modern emphasis on individual, subjective experience. Goya's painting presents us with a view of a passionate, intense vitality, a life lived to the full.

119

Ingres' portrait of Napoleon. The artist's skill as a portraitist assured him a living throughout France's political turmoils. He remained a confirmed classicist, painting with meticulous clarity in the tradition of his teacher, David.

Romantic and Neo-Classical Painting

In 1785 women fainted in front of one of the large pictures exhibited at the Paris *salon*. Jacques Louis David's *Oath of the Horatii* was a sensation and the 37-year-old artist immediately became the centre of French artistic activity. This picture is perhaps the best example of the style known as Neo-classicism which was to dominate art for the next thirty years and continue as the official academic style in France for much of the nineteenth century.

The political paintings of David

In the 1780s France was in turmoil. A corrupt and inefficient court was desperately trying to keep control of the country while sections of the aristocracy and the middle classes seethed with discontent. The economic restrictions, aristocratic privilege and political repression of the *Ancien Régime* seemed unbearable. In the face of this, Rousseau, Diderot and Voltaire wrote of a new rationalism, looking back to the philosophy and politics of Ancient Greece and Rome for their model. The encyclopedist Diderot called for artists 'to paint as they spoke in Sparta'. David responded to the call, and in doing so he expressed the ideals of the progressive middle classes as they overthrew their monarchy.

In 1790, a leader of the Revolution called him 'that French patriot whose genius anticipated the Revolution'. In fact David became the official painter of the Revolution, closely identified with the Jacobin party and a friend of Robespierre.

Jacques Louis David (1748-1825) was born the son of a merchant and, thanks to a distant relation, the painter Francois Boucher, he was accepted in the studio of Joseph Vien in 1765. Vien was excited by the discoveries of Roman and Greek art in the excavations of Herculaneum and Pompeii and passed this enthusiasm on to his pupil. In 1775 David won the Prix de Rome, the most important prize for student painters, and went to Rome to complete his studies.

Over the next six years he diligently studied the art of the ancient world. Gradually his works broke away from the style prevalent in France, taking on a serious and austere approach to traditional subject matter from classical mythology and Roman history. While the court entertained themselves with the erotic Rococo paintings of Fragonard, David's *Oath of the Horatii* expressed a heroic patriotism and the highest ideals of Republican virtue.

David became the doyen of Republicanism, and once the Revolution was under way his work assumed a direct relationship with politics. In 1793, for example, David produced *The Death of Marat*, commemorating the Revolutionary leader who was assassinated in his bath. *Marat* is perhaps David's greatest work and is one of the supreme political statements in the whole of art.

Above: With the *Oath of the Horatii* (1785) Jacques Louis David (1748-1825) became France's leading artist. The painting, using a severe and dramatic composition, expresses a new spirit of Republican patriotism. David's return to a classical style, after the frivolity of Rococo art, caused a sensation.

Below: David's *The Death of Marat* (1793) shows the assassination of the Revolutionary leader. Marat is idealized without a trace of sentimentality; the dramatic lighting and restrained colours emphasize his tragic death. No unnecessary details are allowed to detract from the impact of the painting.

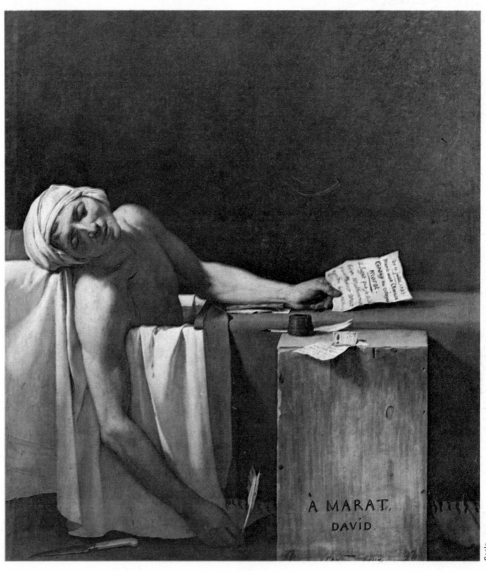

With the fall and execution of Robespierre in 1794, David fell into disfavour and was imprisoned. With the help of his wife and his pupils he was released and in 1779 he produced *The Intervention of the Sabine Women*, again expressing a political message and bringing himself back into official favour. The Directorate, a more conservative government attempting to quieten the revolutionary fervour that gripped France, was hoping to bring about an atmosphere of conciliation. David's painting echoed this by showing the Sabine and Roman heroes prevented from fighting by their women. The certainty of David's earlier vision is lacking in this work—as the representative of a defeated and discredited political group, he needed to find a new identity.

By 1800 he had almost found it. Two contrasting works of that year express the transition; his *Portrait of Madame Récamier* shows the fashionable beauty reclining in the pose of a Greek goddess in a totally simplified and stark setting. Madame Récamier, quite naturally, preferred the more luxurious and sensual portrait produced for her by David's ex-pupil Gerard, so David never completed his version. His portrait of Napoleon crossing the Alps 'calm on a fiery horse' received a much warmer acclaim, however, and initiated David's allegiance to this rising star of French politics.

When Napoleon declared himself Emperor in 1804, David and his followers placed themselves firmly at the disposal of the Government as propagandists. While the style of David's Neo-classicism remained, its spirit was gone. *The Coronation of Napoleon* (1805-7), painted largely by assistants, is a superb feat of organization and composition yet its rich colouring and sumptuous decoration express courtly pomp and grandeur rather than the exactitude and simplicity so essential to David's greatest works.

David's career came to an end after the Battle of Waterloo in 1815 when he fled to Switzerland. Later he retired to Brussels, where he died in 1825.

David was a great teacher and part of his legacy is the work of his pupils, who include Gérard, Girodet, Gros and, most importantly, Ingres. The first three in varying degrees represent the bridge to Romantic painting. Ingres, on the other hand, became the arch-priest of nineteenth century classicism.

Ingres—symmetry and sensuality

Jean Auguste Dominique Ingres (1780-1867) became David's pupil in Paris in 1797. By this time, David's *atelier* (studio) was the most sought after school for young artists and it is a reflection of Ingres' brilliance that he was able to move there from the provincial academy at Toulouse. His early reputation was founded on his skill as a draughtsman—using thin, incisive line to create bold images of total clarity—and his ability to create remarkable likenesses of those who sat for portraits. The next important step for a hopeful young artist was the Prix de Rome, awarded to one student each year by the Academy, enabling the winner to complete his studies in Rome. Ingres won this in 1801 but did not leave for Rome until 1806. His skill as a portraitist was earning him such a reputation that even Napoleon commissioned works from him. After settling in Rome, where he stayed

Ziolo

Right: In 1822-23 Theodore Gericault painted a series of ten moving and realistic portraits of inmates of a Paris asylum. Only five, including this study of an old woman, survive. The paintings were inspired by his friend Georget, who advocated humane treatment of the insane. Gericault's depth of sympathy with his subjects is perhaps due to his own instability; he became increasingly withdrawn until his death in 1824 after a riding accident.

Below: Gericault's *Raft of the Medusa*, exhibited in 1819, combines a vividly naturalistic treatment of the suffering figures with a carefully constructed dramatic composition.

Mansell

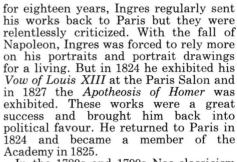

Far left: Baron Francois Gerard (1770-1837) made his reputation as a portrait painter, rivalling his teacher David in popularity. His portrait of *Madame Récamier* is softer and more delicate in approach than the stark simplicity favoured by David.

Left: Baron Antoine-Jean Gros (1771-1835) became David's closest friend and a fervent admirer. Like David, he became a propagandist for Napoleon and painted a series of dramatic portrayals of Napoleon's battles. The purpose of these works was to glorify Napoleon, but they are, at the same time, supremely skilful paintings, full of richness and colour. Here, in *The Battle of Eylau* (1808) the Emperor is shown full of sorrow at the carnage, while a wounded Russian soldier thanks him for his mercy. In reality, it was at this futile battle that Napoleon carelessly counted the dead of his allies in with those of the Russian enemy to secure a more comforting balance of casualties.

Scala

Giraudon

for eighteen years, Ingres regularly sent his works back to Paris but they were relentlessly criticized. With the fall of Napoleon, Ingres was forced to rely more on his portraits and portrait drawings for a living. But in 1824 he exhibited his *Vow of Louis XIII* at the Paris Salon and in 1827 the *Apotheosis of Homer* was exhibited. These works were a great success and brought him back into political favour. He returned to Paris in 1824 and became a member of the Academy in 1825.

In the 1780s and 1790s Neo-classicism had been a progressive movement, allied to the ideals of the 'Enlightenment' that inspired the Revolution. But after 1800 it gradually took on an academic and formal character and became the art of the Establishment. Ingres was a conservative and unimaginative man—Delacroix said his work was 'the complete expression of an incomplete intelligence'.

Ingres' classicism became an obsession and for the rest of his career, until his death in 1867, he took on the role of the defender of artistic integrity against the onslaught of the Romantics. His academic conservatism attracted the patronage of the most staid and authority-bound sections of the French bourgeoisie. The features which relieve his later work are far removed from his theories. His nudes, for example, have a consistent sensuality. At the age of 83 he produced *The Turkish Bath*, a riot of plump female nudes, all carefully drawn and classically posed but altogether expressing an intensely subjective eroticism.

In this sense, despite his academic outrage at their work and his theoretical insistence on the principles of classicism, Ingres was much closer than he realized to the Romantics he affected to despise. Romanticism stressed the primacy of emotions, the importance of immediate experience, and the beauty of nature as it appears to the individual. In the period after 1816, this gradually became the approach to art of younger men looking for personal freedom in an age of growing academic and political repression. This movement, known as Romanticism, spanned all the arts but the two leading painters were Gericault and Delacroix.

The rebellious Romantics

Theodore Gericault was born the son of a wealthy lawyer in 1791. In 1808 he became the pupil of Carle Vernet, a painter of horses rather than history. Already in his choice of teachers, Gericault was showing his preference for nature rather than intellectual classicism. In 1812 he exhibited his famous *Charging Chasseur*, showing a soldier on a rearing horse in a blaze of colour and movement. Although Gericault was an ardent Bonapartist, after Napoleon's fall he joined the liberal opposition. In 1816 he failed to win the Prix de Rome but went to Rome at his own expense. There he produced a series of studies for *The Race of Riderless Horses*, a project which was never completed. He was fascinated by horses, and in these works he combined naturalistic observation, Romantic expression and classical composition with great skill.

In 1819 he exhibited *The Raft of the Medusa*, again incorporating elements of classical composition with acute observation of the suffering figures. The picture, depicting a shipwreck, was a clear political challenge as the government's 123 corruption was held to be responsible for the wreck. In 1820-21 he took the picture to England as a travelling exhibition and there was influenced by the much more advanced naturalism found in English painting. Gericault returned to France with this experience of English art firmly imprinted in his mind, and with a naturalism quite unknown in France at the time produced a series of *Studies of the Insane*.

Gericault died in 1824 and it was left to his chief admirer Eugene Delacroix (1798-1863) to develop his achievements. Because of his short life and concentration on minor subjects (from the point of view of French academicism), Gericault's impact was limited. Delacroix, on the other hand, was at home in the fashionable circles of Paris and became the leader of a new generation of artists, breaking free from classicism.

Delacroix's first salon exhibit *Dante and Virgil crossing the Styx* (1822), was still largely classical in its grouping of figures and restrained colour. The sombre lighting and violent movement, however, looked forward to his mature style. Later, when viewing one of Ingres' pictures, Delacroix was to say Ingres' colours were no more than 'icing on a hardbaked cake'.

Below: This study for the painting *The Death of Sardanapalus* by Eugene Delacroix (1798-1863) contains the vigour and energy so typical of his work. His love of the exotic led him, in 1832, to visit N. Africa, where he found a whole new range of subjects, including scenes from Arab and Jewish life, to inspire him.

Right: Delacroix was the greatest of the Romantic painters. Deeply inspired by literature, he painted scenes from Scott, Shakespeare, Byron and (here) Dante. *Dante and Virgil Crossing the Styx* (1822) was a success, but Delacroix was later attacked for his brilliant colour and free handling of paint.

Colour was to be Delacroix's great contribution to art. In 1827 he was bitterly attacked by the classicists for his *Death of Sardanapalus*, with its erotic and exotic subject matter, brilliant colour and violent movement. Romanticism had arrived.

Subjective, spontaneous freedom for the artist was to be the rule. The value of personal experience was opposed to the intellectual endeavour and study of ancient art demanded by classicism. The artist was to heighten a particular, dramatic moment, with the free use of his imagination. Delacroix was, however, aware of the problems involved in such spontaneity and once he had been inspired by a subject, he would put a great deal of effort into preparatory drawings.

Classical versus Romantic

Throughout the period when their careers overlapped, Delacroix and Ingres engaged in a vigorous controversy. Imaginative, spontaneous Romanticism was set against dry, academic classicism. Moral, intellectually honest classicism was counterposed to excessive, undisciplined Romanticism. Ingres was the patriarch of authority and reaction, Delacroix the apostle of personal liberty and self-fulfilment. In fact, their two styles borrowed freely from one another. Delacroix without his understanding of composition (learned from a classical training) or Ingres (without his flashes of individual, exotic sensuality) would have been lesser artists.

Paradoxically, it is Ingres who has had the most lasting impact. The tradition of his work, with its understanding of the abstract nature of form, has dominated twentieth century art. Delacroix's emphasis on colour and emotion has had its impact too, through the Symbolists to Surrealism, for example. But it is the classicism of David and Ingres that has remained at the centre of Western art.

Above: In *Mademoiselle Rivière* (1805) by J. A. D. Ingres (1780-1867), the curving silhouette made by the girl's dress and fur is echoed in the oval curve of her head, creating a formal symmetry and balance.

Below: Ingres' supreme skill as a draughtsman is seen in this portrait of *The Stamaty family*.

Right: The *Valpinçon Bather*, painted by Ingres in 1808, is one of a long series of female nude studies by him, often placed in Oriental settings. Ingres' classical detachment is here combined with sensuality. The calm voluptuousness of the figure is painted with an almost photographic clarity.

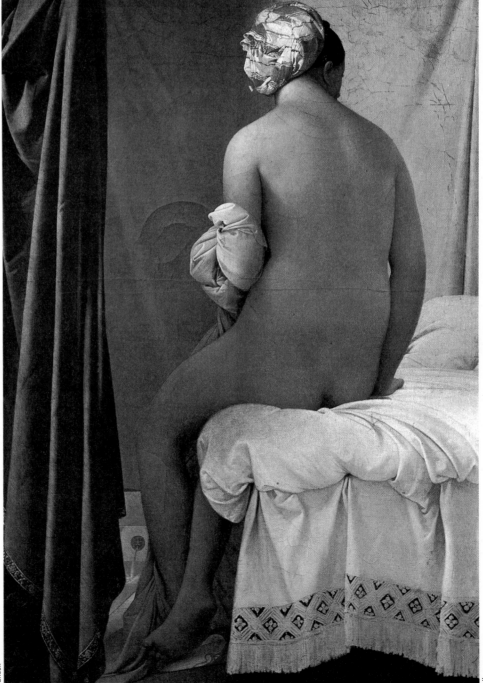

Chapter 5

The Nineteenth Century

At the Circus: Fernando the Ringmaster
by Henri de Toulouse-Lautrec
(1864-1901). Dated 1888, two years
after he settled in Montmartre, it
shows Lautrec's instinct for movement
and gesture. He influenced the 'modern
style' school at Barcelona where
Picasso was beginning to paint.

Early 19th Century Architecture

From the Renaissance to the middle of the eighteenth century, most European architects looked to classical architecture and particularly to the buildings of Ancient Rome as a source of inspiration for their own work. But around 1750 a number of significant changes led to the development of new architectural ideas. Advances in historical and archeological knowledge led architects to experiment with new styles of decoration and to widen the range of design.

Exotic temples and sham ruins

The buildings of the English architect Sir William Chambers (1723-96) illustrate both the continuing taste for classical forms and the growing interest in exotic styles. In his public buildings Chambers followed classical principles, drawing ideas from Palladio and the Italians as well as from his contemporaries. In his gardens and garden buildings, however, he turned to more unusual sources. Frequently these buildings—a Greek or Chinese temple or a Gothic ruin—formed part of one garden, creating small focal points which provided a variety of moods within the scheme as a whole. Such was the case at Kew Gardens, where Chambers and others designed a number of buildings to add variety to the landscape. These included a 'Gothic cathedral' and an 'Alhambra' (in the Moslem style) as well as a Roman Triumphal arch: Chambers himself designed a Chinese pagoda.

'Gothick taste'

It was largely in such frivolous buildings as this that experimentation took place and seeds were sown for a more serious revival of certain historical styles. The 'Gothic' building at Kew Gardens provides one of the early examples of the conscious revival of medieval styles in the eighteenth century. Until the second half of this century, Gothic architecture (although it had not completely died out, appearing in the work of Wren, Hawksmoor and Vanbrugh) was considered as rather barbarous. But the 'Gothick taste' became fashionable once more after 1750. In 1753 the first major example of the application of Gothic decoration to a more formal building was begun—*Strawberry Hill* in Twickenham, the home of Horace Walpole the writer.

Walpole and a number of his friends, inspired by what they took to be the character of medieval life, produced a series of Gothic designs which were, however, little more than elegant ornament imitating medieval prototypes and applied to the basic structure. Not until the next century was the Gothic style copied for both its structural and decorative qualities in the Victorian 'Gothic revival'. Similarly the Greek style which, alongside the Gothic, became fashionable for garden buildings was not revived in earnest until the nineteenth century. Its features were considered primitive by the eighteenth-century Palladians.

Left: In his own house, Sir John Soane (1753-1837) shows a similar concern for light and space as in his Bank of England designs. The Breakfast Room of No. 13, Lincoln's Inn Fields (1812) has light pouring into it from around the edge of the domed hanging ceiling; this light is then reflected by numerous mirrors.

Right: Sussex Place, Regent's Park, London, built in 1822 to the design of John Nash (1752-1835) is part of his finest town-planning scheme. Forming one of the terraces overlooking the park, Sussex Place is characterized by its elegant sweep of colonnades, which unite the individual houses into a pleasing whole.

Below: Long curving terraces combine with groups of villas in one of the largest town developments of the late Georgian period at Clifton, Bristol. The style which John Nash introduced was very influential, and whole areas of Cheltenham, Clifton, Tunbridge Wells, Brighton and Hove were redesigned during the Regency.

Above: The vogue for exotic decoration reached its height in John Nash's Royal Pavilion at Brighton (1815-18), built for the Prince Regent. This extravagant, picturesque scheme employs features taken from Indian and Moslem architecture.

Left: Strawberry Hill, Twickenham, the house of the writer Horace Walpole, was decorated in the Gothic style from 1753 onwards. It is among the earliest 18th century examples of the imitation of medieval Gothic work. This use of Gothic was still, however, playful; Walpole spoke of the 'whimsical air of novelty' it gave to buildings. Not until the 19th century was Gothic revived in earnest.

Fashions in landscaped gardens

Behind these stylistic experiments in small-scale garden buildings lay a growing interest in the art of landscape gardening, fired by admiration for the landscapes of the French painters Poussin and Claude. In their paintings classical scenes are placed in idealized landscape settings which frequently include ruined temples or castles. English landscape gardeners attempted to create a similar mood in the parks of country houses by incorporating appropriate buildings in their schemes.

The eighteenth century saw a number of phases in landscape garden design; formal geometrical layouts had been superceded by the expansive sweeps of parkland with carefully placed trees and lakes characteristic of Capability Brown (1716-83) and his followers. These in turn had been challenged by the 'Chinese' style of Chambers, who had travelled in China and written a semi-serious treatise on Chinese gardening. Towards the end of the century the emphasis again shifted towards a wilder, more natural form of landscaped garden and these ideas became codified as 'the Picturesque taste'.

In architecture the Picturesque led to the design of buildings of irregular plan intended to harmonize with nature rather than standing in contrast to the landscape as would a regular, symmetrically planned classical building.

The 'Picturesque' was part of a larger European movement which took place in the latter half of the eighteenth century towards a more natural, primitive architecture. For architecture, too, shared in the growth of Romanticism in the arts at this time. In England, it took shape in the search for natural forms: in France, the so-called 'revolutionary architects' developed a pure, idealized style based on geometric forms and abstract ideas about design. The two principal figures of the movement, L.-E. Boullée (1728-99) and C.-N. Ledoux (1736-1806), produced a number of designs for monumental buildings based on elementary geometric shapes—massive cubes, pyramids, cylinders and even spheres—with the minimum of decorative detail.

The fantastic schemes of Boullée

Many of Boullée's architectural drawings represent buildings absurdly extravagant for their alleged purpose, and often their shapes are intended to be expressive and symbolic: his design for a cenotaph to Newton is of a huge sphere standing 150 m (500 ft) high and a project for the entrance to a cemetery takes the form of an enormous flattened pyramid flanked by obelisks. These drawings were intended as statements about the nature and role of architecture—which to Boullée was a 'rational' monumental expression of ideals.

Although none of these schemes was ever built, Boullée's influence as a teacher of the next generation of French architects was profound. A few smaller-scale buildings designed by Ledoux survive: their combination of romantic ideals with reasoned design show the intentions of both architects. His Besançon theatre (1775-84) for example, has a massive cube-shaped exterior with a plain un-pedimented portico, while the interior is semi-circular with a continuous colonnade in a Greek Doric style. His Paris toll houses, designed in the 1780s, incorporate a number of different styles but show his continuing interest in simplifying both structure and detail. Ledoux's simple forms became the distinguishing feature of all the great works of Romantic Classicism built throughout Europe around 1800.

Trends in France and Germany

During the lifetimes of Ledoux and Boullée the state of the French exchequer meant that few major public works were undertaken. After 1800, as funds again became available, a series of important public buildings (many glorifying the Emperor Napoleon) appeared in the monumental style of Romantic Classicism. Perhaps the most famous is the Arc de Triomphe in Paris (built in 1806-37), a gloriously magnified Imperial Roman triumphal arch by J. F. T. Chalgrin.

In Germany the Napoleonic Wars did not impose such a severe restriction on building as they had in France. Many French architects went to work in the German states, and buildings appeared there in a mature form of the Romantic Classical style before 1800.

Among the first of these is K. G. Langhans's Brandenburg Gate, Berlin (1789-93), a gateway in the Greek Doric style which with its comparative simplicity was to become a favourite feature of Romantic Classicism throughout Europe. The German version of this style reaches a peak in the works of K. F. von Schinkel, notably in the Altes Museum (1824-28), and the Schauspielhaus (1819-21), in Berlin. The effect of these buildings is still essentially classical but many of the features are devised to suit a modern function and are only loosely based on the Greek prototypes.

Romantic classicism took a rather different form in England, where domestic rather than public architecture had traditionally been the area of innovation. The buildings of John Soane (1753-1837), the most original English architect of the period, share many of the characteristics of French Romantic classicism and particularly the taste for simpler forms, but they also owe much to the Picturesque and to Robert Adam's domestic work.

Soane's first major project was the rebuilding of the Bank of England undertaken from 1788 when he was given the Surveyorship. The need for security, especially after the Gordon Riots of 1780, meant that the building had to be surrounded by huge blank walls. Soane's design, however, makes a virtue of this, interspersing the vast expanse of 129

Above: The church of La Madeleine in Paris (1806-43), designed by Pierre Vignon and completed after his death. In keeping with the aspirations of the Emperor Napoleon, who commissioned the work, the church takes the form of a giant Roman Corinthian temple.

Left: During the 18th century, American architecture developed a new grandeur and, led by Thomas Jefferson, looked directly to antiquity for its style. Jefferson established the pattern for official architecture with his Virginia State Capitol; the Washington Capitol (left) was designed largely by Thornton and Latrobe from 1792-1828, but the Baroque dome was added in the 1850s.

Above: In his own house, *Monticello*, in Virginia, US, (1769), Thomas Jefferson adapted features drawn from English Palladianism. Apart from being an immensely influential architect, Jefferson (1743-1826) was also a statesman, economist and, later, the 3rd President of the US.

Left: The designs of L. E. Boullée (1728-99), based on simple geometrical shapes and representing an ideal rather than an actual architectural style, were an important influence on later architects. The massive simplicity of this project for a cenotaph, designed in the 1780s, is typical of his work.

Right: Napoleon bought Chateau La Malmaison, France, in 1799 and for several years he kept his architects busy remodelling the interiors. This room, the Empress Josephine's bedchamber, is typical of the French Empire style; the furniture incorporates a number of Egyptian motifs—an echo of Napoleonic conquests in the Middle East.

Above: The Arc de Triomphe, situated at the head of the Champs Elysées in Paris, was built between 1806 and 1837 by J. F. T. Chalgrin and others. The huge scale and simplicity of Chalgrin's design distinguish it as part of the Romantic-Classic Classical movement; the arch stands as a symbol of Imperial power.

Right: The Altes (Old) Museum in Berlin, built 1824-28 by K. F. von Schinkel (1781-1841) shows a knowledge of the pure, simple classical style of Ancient Greece, modified to meet modern needs. The Ionic columns of the facade conceal an ingenious arrangement whereby the pictures are lit by diffused light from the windows.

masonry with false windows and making the difficult acute angle formed by two of the walls into a focal point by erecting a semi-circular feature drawn from the Roman temple of Vesta at Tivoli. This corner became known as Tivoli Corner.

The bank's windowless street facades excluded a good deal of light from the main block of offices and Soane was therefore obliged to concentrate his efforts on providing a maximum amount of lighting inside the building; this he did by using shell domes pierced by large areas of glass, through which light flooded down into the interiors. For the interiors, perhaps his finest work, Soane developed a simple decorative style drawn from various classical sources. His free treatment of classical detail shocked the more academic of his contemporaries.

The purely decorative windows used at the Bank appear also in Soane's work at Dulwich—the Art Gallery and Mausoleum (1811-14)—where they are applied to the otherwise plain exteriors. The masses of the building are thus left to provide the principal visual interest.

The elegant English Regency

Where Soane's style was based on a profound and original understanding of both ancient and medieval architecture, that of his great contemporary and rival John Nash (1752-1835) was superficial. Nevertheless Nash showed an ability to adopt a style appropriate for each of the many types of buildings which he designed.

In his country houses Nash used Gothic—as at Luscombe, Devon (1800)—or, for smaller villas, a style based on Italian farmhouses, while at Brighton in the Royal Pavilion, built for the Prince Regent in 1815-18, Nash experimented with Indian and Oriental features, the latticed arches and onion-shaped domes lending an air of fantasy to the palace. In 1811 Nash designed Blaise Hamlet, near Bristol, made up of nine thatched cottages, each planned differently and carefully laid out to give a casual rural quality.

Nash's major achievements, however, were the great urban planning schemes in London, undertaken (like the Royal Pavilion) with the patronage of the Prince Regent, later to become George IV. The most significant of these works of planning was the laying out of Regent Street and the surrounding areas to form a route from Regent's Park in the North through the West End to Carlton House (soon after demolished) in the South. The buildings erected along the new streets are in a style in keeping with the trends of Romantic Classicism; the long terraces of houses are treated as single classical compositions, with colonnades running along their whole length, drawn together by a crowning pediment and one continuous cornice.

Instead of following the traditional pattern for such a triumphal route—a straight wide road connecting important points and flanked by public buildings—Nash's Regent Street curves elegantly away from Piccadilly Circus, and terminates in the terraces and crescents sweeping around the Park, itself dotted with artfully hidden villas. Nash's achievement was thus to unite individual units designed according to the principles of Romantic Classicism in a scheme which, in its irregularity, was fundamentally Picturesque.

Victorian Architecture

Victorian architecture was produced for a rapidly growing and an increasingly industrialized and urbanized population. These rapid changes inevitably led to strains and upheavals in the structure of Britain's building industry. The large contractor and the specialized businessman-architect with his large team of assistants progressively took over from the independent master craftsman and the dilettante architect. Traditional ways of building with local materials began to disappear in the face of new machinery and newly invented materials—iron, plate glass, steel and concrete—which could be produced on a large scale and transported across the country by train and canal.

New architects for a new age

Social changes led to changes in the system of patronage. In Victoria's reign the middle classes acquired the power and the confidence to take the lead from the aristocracy as setters of fashion. They constituted a powerful body of patrons, not only as private individuals, but as members of the numerous building committees directing the construction of schools, offices, banks, hospitals, stations and other large schemes. With the help of guide books and improved transport, middle-class patrons and architects

Above: The British Museum was designed by Robert Smirke (1780-1867) as part of the scholarly Greek revival movement fashionable in the early Victorian era and seen particularly in large-scale municipal buildings. The museum's south front, with its imposing rows of Grecian columns, was built from 1842-47.

Above: In 1834 the Old Palace of Westminster was destroyed by fire. Sir Charles Barry (1795-1860) won the competition to design the new Houses of Parliament with drawings prepared by Pugin. The scheme (built 1839-60) is a successful mixture of classical and Gothic: its symmetrical river facade is offset by a completely assymetrical skyline in a delicate late Gothic style.

Left: A. W. N. Pugin (1812-52) was the major exponent of Victorian Gothic. In the church of St Giles at Cheadle, Staffs (1840-46) Pugin was for once given enough money to realize his vision of a perfect English Gothic church. Most of the work, including this sumptuous interior, was carried out by local craftsmen.

Right: Paddington Station, London (built 1852-54) shortly after its completion. I. K. Brunel designed the three great parallel train sheds and brought in an architect, M. D. Wyatt, to devise appropriate metalwork ornament to integrate the sheds with the platform buildings.

Michael Holford

Michael Holford

Michael Holford

Radio Times Hulton Picture Library

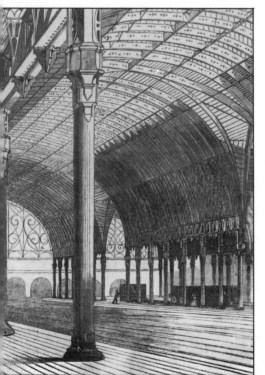

Left: The Victorian age was a great period for municipal building. Grand new town halls were built, many in industrial boom towns such as Birmingham and Liverpool. Leeds Town Hall (1853-59), built by Cuthbert Broderick, expresses civic pride with a splendid array of giant columns, topped by a huge domed tower.

Above: The Palm House, Kew Gardens, designed by Decimus Burton and Richard Turner (1844-48) provided the Victorians with a model for later uses of iron and glass in functional buildings. Here, the materials are used to create an overall smooth glazed surface, shown to advantage in the elegant curves of the design.

jerrybuilders who threatened to exploit the building boom. In the succeeding years a spate of new architectural journals, beginning with the *Builder* in 1842, joined their voices to the RIBA's in the struggle for professionalism. And it was through the pages of these journals that an attempt was made to find a way out of the maze of period styles by asking the question: 'which is the fit kind of architecture for us Englishmen of the nineteenth century?'.

Monuments to industrialism

At various points in the debate it was suggested that the new breakthroughs in engineering, which produced exciting shapes in glass, steel and iron, might provide the basis for a distinctly nineteenth century architecture. But in general architects were so keen on defending the dignity of their new-found professional status that they maintained a rigid distinction between the 'artistic' sphere of architecture and the 'utilitarian' sphere of engineering.

It was, however, in functional building that some of the most spectacular designs of the age were produced. The names of Robert Stephenson (1803-59) and Isambard Kingdom Brunel (1806-59) dominate innovations in bridge-building: Stephenson's tubular Britannia Bridge across the Menai Strait and Brunel's Clifton Suspension Bridge, Bristol, are still impressive monuments to the Victorian railway age. Shells of iron and glass began to be used for exhibition halls and railway stations. Based on greenhouse construction, these buildings were frankly functional. The famous Crystal Palace, built by a former gardener, Joseph Paxton (1801-65) as a temporary hall for the Great Exhibition in 1851, unfortunately does not survive today, but many railway train sheds built by this method can still be seen, among them Newcastle Central (1846-55), King's Cross, London (1851-52) and Paddington, London (1852-54).

But the designs and materials enthusiastically received for utilitarian or temporary buildings were considered totally inappropriate for any building requiring 'artistic' or 'architectural' quality. When the same principles were applied to the design of South Kensington museum (1855-56), its iron naves were ridiculed and had eventually to be removed to Bethnal Green Museum in 1871.

At the beginning of Victoria's reign in 1837 new movements were afoot to give new life to church building after its decline during the eighteenth century. The Oxford Movement, beginning around 1833, and the Camden Society (later the Ecclesiological Society), founded at Cambridge University in 1839, injected a new desire for spirituality into the Anglican church. It was no doubt a little embarrassing for Anglicans that the man who found the right visual means of expressing this new spirituality was a convert to Catholicism—Augustus Welby Pugin (1812-52).

The Gothic ideal

Pugin's most influential book was probably *The True Principles of Pointed or Christian Architecture* published in 1841. The principles—that the structure of a building should not be concealed by its ornament, that it should be manifest in the external appearance of the building

travelled extensively on the Continent, returning with albums crammed with sketches and later with photographs. Equipped also with an increasing number of books which provided scholarly information about the architecture of the past, they felt amply qualified to experiment with a bewildering range of styles. Added to this, there were constant technical advances to be assimilated in such subjects as fire-proofing, sanitation and central heating.

If today Victorian architecture seems confusing in its sheer quantity and variety, to contemporaries it often seemed totally anarchic. There were two main paths which Victorians took in their attempts to restore a sense of order to the architectural scene.

The first took the form of a revolt against industrial society and an attempt to re-establish the honest workmanship and style of building found in medieval England. The leaders of this movement— each a writer as well as an artist—were A. W. Pugin, John Ruskin and William Morris. These men thought that the soullessness, ruthlessness and shoddiness too often seen in industrialized mass production could be replaced by individual pride, social responsibility and high quality if only men would turn their backs on modern capitalism and return to the ideals of pre-industrial society.

The second path was to face squarely the explosion of knowledge and demand and try to find new means of injecting discipline into it. In 1834 the (later Royal) Institute of British Architects was set up as a means of establishing standards and thus defending the status of the new breed of professional architect against the

133

Above: In 1852 Prince Albert decided to build a castle in baronial style at Balmoral in Scotland, designing the whole scheme himself. It was an age dominated by middle-class taste—from fashion to home furnishings. The Royal family were themselves influenced by this shift in taste; a fact reflected in this print of Queen Victoria's sitting room at Balmoral, with its homely, sober interior.

Right: With newly-developed materials such as iron, plate glass, steel and concrete at their disposal, 19th century builders were no longer confined to local brick or stone for their designs. This print, from *The Mechanics Magazine* of 1868, is of Llandrinio House, built at Bickley, Kent; one of the first (or the first) domestic property to use concrete—in the form of hexagonal tubes.

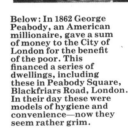

and that it should be adapted to the materials used—were not particularly original. What was revolutionary was Pugin's insistence that these were *Christian* principles, that the Gothic Pointed style of architecture (found in England from Westminster Abbey to the early fourteenth century) was the perfect embodiment of these principles and thus that English Pointed was the only possible style for a Christian Englishman to build in.

Pugin's ideas were widely adopted by Victorian architects, but in his own buildings, Pugin rarely achieved his ideal, usually because of lack of sufficient money. His church at Cheadle, Staffordshire (1846) remains the most complete expression of his aims.

Some architects, however, were unwilling to restrict themselves to the mere imitation of English Pointed Gothic, wanting instead to express the spirit of their own age in an original, Victorian Gothic style. In order to evolve this style they experimented with combining different materials, creating bold coloured patterns which they called *constructional polychromy*, and borrowing elements from Italian and French Gothic styles. The mid-century, as a result, saw the erection of some rather wild-looking buildings. But in the hands of masters like William Butterfield (1814-1900) and George Edmund Street (1824-81) the new eclecticism resulted in some marvellously vigorous yet tightly disciplined designs.

During the Victorian era a great deal of wealth from industry and commerce found its way into country estates, as more and more *nouveaux riches* attained 134 respectability by the age-old method of

Below: In 1862 George Peabody, an American millionaire, gave a sum of money to the City of London for the benefit of the poor. This financed a series of dwellings, including these in Peabody Square, Blackfriars Road, London. In their day these were models of hygiene and convenience—now they seem rather grim.

Right: The over-crowded city churchyards of the 18th and early 19th centuries were squalid and disease-ridden. In the 1830s companies were formed to set up new, pleasant and spacious cemeteries outside the city centres. Highgate Cemetery, London, part of which (a classical row of tombs) is seen here, was opened in 1839.

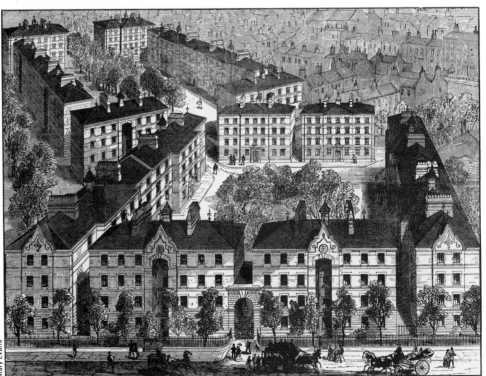

buying their way into the squirearchy. Some of the old landed families, too, found themselves with plenty of money to spare as the result of swelling ground rents from the towns, or the discovery of minerals on their estates.

Changing social requirements encouraged the landed classes to build. In Victorian times the pious and dutiful father figure succeeded the Regency buck as the 'beau ideal' of a gentleman. Encouraged by the climate of philanthropy, he saw his duty as being to build churches, parsonages, schools and model cottages on his estate, and to remodel or build anew his country mansion, so that it might be fitting for his immensely dignified and formal life-style.

The result was the typical large Victorian country house, a complicated machine run by an army of servants. The styles of these stately homes were various. By the 1850s, however, there was an increasing tendency to favour some form of Gothic, considered the native English style, and to drop 'foreign' classical styles.

The 1860s saw a revolt against the Gothic school. Men like Richard Norman Shaw (1831-1912) and Eden Nesfield (1835-88) looked about them and saw that country towns and villages were full of modest but attractive buildings of the late seventeenth and eighteenth centuries which were just as indigenously English as Gothic buildings. So they began to build romantically rambling gabled houses decorated with tiles in what they called their Old English manner, and solid red brick houses with countrified classical details (white-painted sash windows and door surrounds) in what was their Queen Anne manner. These more comfortable and domestic houses suited clients for whom the extreme formality of mid-Victorian life was beginning to seem more than a little absurd.

By the end of Victoria's reign in 1901, changes had been wrought in the landscape which, to an early nineteenth century man, would have seemed incredible. London at night would be bright with the glitter produced by the novel combination of gas lighting and cheap plate glass; new public houses had been built, with great lamps, huge windows and inside a fairyland of cut, embossed and painted mirrors. From the convivial concerts formerly held in the back rooms of pubs had developed great palaces called Music Halls and Variety Theatres. The aristocratic clubland of eighteenth-century St James's had given way to Pall Mall, the clubland of the Victorian middle classes, with its comfortable male preserves contained in stately Italian Renaissance-style mansions. In the city of London, new Venetian Gothic palazzos and glass and iron halls had been erected, containing the offices, banks and commodity exchanges in which the middle classes amassed their wealth.

Railway stations were now firmly established, but the ease of transport provided by trains had given rise to new suburbs, grim back-to-backs for the workers and grand villas in leafy streets for their masters. On the coast new Victorian resorts had grown up, with palatial hotels, promenades and piers complete with entertainment arcades.

The landscape had, for better or for worse, been utterly transformed. That was the achievement of the Victorian.

Above: Bridge-building was one of the most exciting areas of Victorian design. The Royal Albert Bridge at Saltash, Cornwall, was the last engineering feat of I. K. Brunel (1806-59). The bridge, combining suspension principles with tubular arches, curves across the estuary on tall granite piers.

Below: The work of William Burges (1827-81) reveals a fondness for the more whimsical aspects of Gothic art. This detail is of a ceiling from Castell Coch, Glamorgan (1875-90), remodelled by Burges from 13th-century foundations. Its carved wood decoration and finely painted insets are typical of his work.

135

French Realist Painters

Nineteenth century France produced many great painters—among them Delacroix, Ingres, Courbet and Manet. The schools of Romanticism and classicism, exemplified by Delacroix and Ingres, gave way to a concern for the social value of art and a desire to paint the world 'as it is'. Gustave Courbet, in an exhibition he mounted in 1855, gave this new movement the title of *Realism*.

Realism was the outcome of many different artistic tendencies in France in the mid-nineteenth century. It developed in part from the Romantic preoccupation with nature. Artists became concerned to represent what was real and true in the life they saw around them, which gave art a new, directly social link—the opposite of art for art's sake.

France was also at this time dominated by the philosophy of Auguste Comte (1798-1857), the founder of Positivism, which taught that only those things that can be observed or experienced can be known and believed in—a system which excludes all speculative and metaphysical outlooks. The artist, therefore, was to describe accurately by means of a detailed reproduction the objects of nature as he saw them, rather than involve himself in creating a world from his imagination. The view that 'above all one must be of one's own time' (stated by the Romantic writer Emile Descamps) became the fashionable artistic creed.

From these viewpoints emerged an art which rejected its time-honoured role of creating an 'ideal' beauty and looked instead to new subjects from current life to depict, without distorting them in any way. This view of art as a kind of social documentation is justified by Courbet in a pamphlet issued in 1861. In it he declares that:

Painting is an art essentially concrete and can only consist in the representation of real and existing things. An abstract object not visible is not within the domain of painting. Imagination in art consists in knowing how to find the most complete expression of an existing thing . . .

Courbet's social art

Gustave Courbet (1819-77) was born at Ornans in the Franche-Comté region of France and went to Paris in 1840 at the age of 21. Early in his career Courbet decided to work on a large scale: 'Small pictures do not make a name. I must paint a large picture that will make me decisively known at my true nature. I want all or nothing.'

The year 1848 was a time of revolution in France and Europe generally. It also marked the beginning of a crucial period for Courbet. Between 1848 and 1850 he painted four major canvasses, which confirmed him as the father figure of the new pictorial realism: *After Dinner at Ornans; The Stone Breakers; A Burial at Ornans;* and *Peasants of Flagey returning*

Above right: *The Studio* was painted in 1855 by Gustave Courbet (1819-77). This detail—of Courbet himself with a nude model—forms the central scene of a huge canvas which, the artist said, 'represented seven years of my artistic life'. It includes portraits of leading Realist writers and artists, as well as the plebeian models he used in his paintings.

Right: Courbet's *Girls by the Seine* illustrates the painter's vibrant technique. Its glowing colours and thickly-applied paint convey Courbet's delight in richly varied textures.

Below: Courbet's *Burial at Ornans* (1850) caused an outrage because of its sheer size—ordinary people were rarely monumentalized on such a scale.

Above: *Proudhon and his Children*, painted by Courbet in 1865. P. J. Proudhon, a socialist writer and critic, was a close friend of Courbet's and wrote many appraisals of his art.

Left: Expressiveness and keen observation mark the work of Honoré Daumier (1808-79). Using the train to represent contemporary life, Daumier depicts 1st, 2nd and 3rd class travel. Here, in the *3rd Class Railway Carriage*, he paints the poor with no trace of sentimentality. His art is based on the techniques of caricature —it was as a caricaturist that he first earned his living.

Below: The theatrical world fascinated Daumier. Here in *Crispino and Scapino* he paints two comic players.

from the Fair. The critic Théophile Gautier wrote of *After Dinner*, which depicts Courbet's father and friends gathered together: 'M. Courbet can be ranged with that class of realist who takes advice only from nature. His temperament is male, robust and rustic, but with all the healthy peasant qualities.' But Gautier was wrong when he attributed the origin and inspiration of the work solely to nature, for in fact it shows the influence of various artistic traditions deriving from seventeenth-century artists such as Rembrandt and Velasquez. One critic was so provoked by the work that he commented, 'No one could drag art in the gutter with greater technical virtuosity.' It was not so much Courbet's subject matter as his treatment of it that aroused antipathy. For a *genre* work (traditionally a small painting, depicting everyday life and surroundings) *After Dinner* was a very large canvas, a specific moment from Courbet's own life on a monumental scale—not an idealized scene from 'the life of the people', but a commonplace social engagement.

With the *Stone Breakers* and *Burial at Ornans*, the link between realism and social aims came to the fore. Proudhon, the socialist writer and friend of Courbet, called the *Stone Breakers* the first socialist painting—'a satire on our industrial civilization which continuously invents machines to perform all kinds of labour, and yet is unable to liberate man from the most backbreaking toil.' Courbet himself said, however, that he painted the work not for political reasons but because he felt sorry for the stone-breakers. Courbet was sympathetic to social issues, even if he came to see the social implications of his art only when Proudhon pointed them out to him. Proudhon provided Courbet with the political justification of his art—the conviction that he was working for the good of society as well as for his own artistic principles and glory.

The peasant paintings of Millet

The same problem of how far art is intended to carry a social message arises with François Millet (1814-75), many of whose works are concerned with human labour. Peasant naturalism had come into prominence in 1848. In the wake of the 1830 Revolution, liberal reformers and art critics had begun to call for a regional French art rather than the totally traditional classical type. Scenes of peasant life as depicted by artists such as Jules Breton became acceptable and even respectable. However, with the depopulation of the countryside in the wake of the Industrial Revolution, the peasant soon became a controversial political figure.

Millet's work (along with Courbet's) became the focus for new political ideas, although Millet was not militant by nature. He was profoundly moved by the human condition and created an art form to express this and to move others by. Normandy-born, of a prosperous peasant family, he was well read, and after a traditional training he began by painting portraits and mythological works, proceeding to idealized depictions of rural life and from these to rural working scenes. The landscapes of his later years have an almost mystical intensity.

In the Salon of 1850, Millet's *Sower* was exhibited with Courbet's *Stone-*

Breakers and *Burial at Ornans*. This, along with his subsequent *The Gleaners*, aroused much controversy. The themes are not new; Jules Breton and others were already painting peasant scenes which were admired. But the 'stage set' idealization of peasant life common to these works is not found in Millet. He does not paint the peaceful enjoyment of rural life nor depict life on the farm as healthy and contented, but rather as a relentless repetition of tasks, a non-ending struggle for survival.

Because of the political and social upheavals of the day, the struggle between man and his fate, which was the basic concern of Millet, became identified with an outcry against contemporary conditions in society. Millet's own outlook is expressed in a letter of 1851: 'It is the human aspect of things, that which is plainly human, that touches me most in art'. Joy for Millet was to be found only in 'the silence of the forest or near cultivated land.' Paradoxically, Millet's paintings, initially seen as representative of social protest, became symbols of permanence in the following decades of rapid social change. *The Angelus*, for example, painted in 1857 but not exhibited until 1865, became a symbol of bourgeois values, of the ethic of work and religious piety.

Courbet's *Burial at Ornans* seems to suggest a rejection of such values. One critic commented on the people depicted in the painting: 'Is it the painter's fault that material interests, the life of the small town, sordid egotism, provincial snobbishness leave their stamp on the face?' These remarks would not have received much favour with the folk of Ornans. They liked the work. Many members of Courbet's family were depicted in it along with familiar figures of his upbringing within the area. This vast canvas provoked both praise and scorn from its spectators. Death was an integral part of the pictorial tradition when depicted with a sombre sense of an elevated occasion. There is a conspicuous absence of this in Courbet's work—only the freshly dug hole in the ground reminds one of the departed. It was the lack of any seeming respect for man's place in the divine—as opposed to the natural—order that aroused the outcry. Courbet's own grandfather had died in

1848 at the age of 81, and by monumentalizing the commonplace experiences of his personal life, Courbet offended the traditional sense of decorum.

Courbet's huge canvas *The Studio* (1855) concluded the phase of his career most closely associated with Realism in its more social and political aspects. The landscapes, seascapes, still-lifes, nudes and hunting scenes that followed contain no immediate reference to contemporary events, although they do continue Courbet's sense of the physical and immediate as conveyed through the medium of paint. Courbet's personal life, however, became increasingly political: his involvement in the Franco-Prussian War was followed by imprisonment, and he finally fled to Switzerland after his part in the Paris Commune—a workers uprising—of 1871.

Parisian life
In the work of Edouard Manet (1832-83),

usually seen as Courbet's heir, the social realism of Courbet is transformed into a different kind of realism—to do with impressions of city life. His technique (making use of areas of flat, clear colour and strong, dark outline), when added to the subject-matter he chose, caused an outraged reception from the critics. His *Déjeuner sur l'herbe* (1863), although using a traditional theme, was considered immoral because of the combination of clothed and naked figures, and the obviously contemporary setting. A similar outcry was caused by the nude *Olympia*. Manet was primarily concerned with the world of appearances and some of his most beautiful paintings, *Music at the Tuileries* (1862) and *A Bar at the Folies-Bergère* (1882) record his impressions of the society he moved in.

The work of Honoré Daumier (1808-79) perhaps does more than Manet's to reflect the rapid, confused complexities of political, social and artistic changes in

Ziolo

F. Arborio Mella

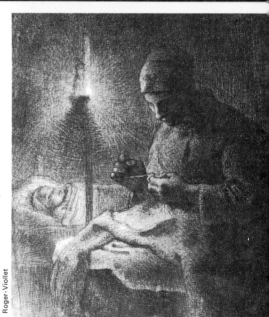

Above: Jean Francois Millet (1814-75) chose as his subject-matter the peasant life of the French countryside. *The Gleaners* **(1857) contains no dramatic incident or anecdote; Millet's concern is merely to depict the non-ending toil endured by the poor. Yet the painting, with its simple composition of heavy bodies modelled against the bright field and the suggestion of rhythmic movement in the figures, achieves a solemn dignity.**

Left: Millet's *The Angelus* **(1857) has become the most familiar of his works. Two peasants recite the** *angelus***, a Catholic devotion in memory of the Annunciation. It is doubtful whether Millet intended the work as the expression of sentimental religious piety that it has become.**

Right: Millet's skill as a draughtsman is seen in this sketch.

Roger-Viollet

Paris during the mid-nineteenth century. After working as a cartoonist he turned to making lithographs for various journals, producing some 4,000 works of bitter political and social satire. In 1832 he had been imprisoned for a cartoon in the weekly *La Caricature*, showing the king as a gluttonous gargantua. During this period, he started to make sculptures and caricature busts out of unfired clay, which, apart from being vigorous works in their own right, greatly strengthened his powers of draughtsmanship. In 1835 *La Caricature* ended and Daumier's association with *Le Charivari* began. From political cartooning of a specific sort he turned to the mirroring of bourgeois society in all its aspects. Court scenes, actors and artists held a special fascination for him, but whatever the subject or situation, his work has a humanity untouched by any concern for the romantic and picturesque. His pen and brush illustrated every aspect of human relationships and of the human condition of his day.

Above: *Dejeuner sur l'Herbe* by Edouard Manet (1832-83) scandalized the public by its daring subject— the juxtaposing of a naked woman with men in contemporary dress. The painting is, however, closely influenced by past art—the theme was used by Giorgione. **Below and right:** The frank realism of Manet's *Olympia* received bitter criticism when it was shown at the 1865 Salon. It became a prime target for caricatures (right) all of which feature the black cat of the original—a symbol of the painting's so-called promiscuity.

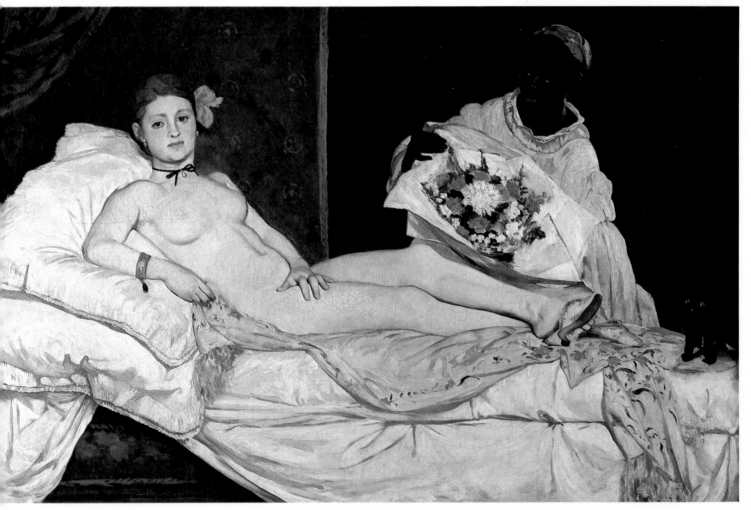

139

Pre-Raphaelite Painting

The Pre-Raphaelite Brotherhood, destined to last only five years, was formed in 1848 in the London studio of John Everett Millais (1829-1896) during the course of a heated discussion of the principles of art. Millais and William Holman Hunt (1827-1910), condemning Raphael's painting of the *Transfiguration*, were dubbed 'Pre-Raphaelites' by the other students present. The label stuck and, fired by the enthusiasm of Dante Gabriel Rossetti (1828-1882), the young artists formed a brotherhood and henceforward signed their works with the initials P. R.B.

The Brotherhood

Although the group consisted of seven artists, the original trio—Millais, Rossetti and Hunt—were the real creative talents. These three established themselves as important artists, although the art of each did develop along very different paths. The avowed aim of the Pre-Raphaelites was the rescue of English art from aesthetic and spiritual triviality; to shake the English art world out of the complacent prettiness, the 'trifles and bombast' of painters such as the Royal Academicians E. M. Ward, William Mulready, Augustus Egg and David Wilkie, whose anecdotal works were fashionable at the start of Queen Victoria's reign. In particular they reacted against obsolete

Above: The depiction of a fallen woman in *Found* (1854) by D. G. Rossetti (1828-82) highlights the Pre-Raphaelite concern with social problems.

Below: *Christ in the House of His Parents* by J. E. Millais (1829-96) was bitterly criticized at the 1850 Royal Academy exhibition.

Above right: Rossetti's drawing of Lizzie Siddal.

Right: A drawing by Millais for Tennyson's poem *Locksley Hall*.

Cooper Bridgeman/Tate Gallery

Above: In his painting of Shakespeare's heroine *Ophelia* (1851-52) Millais used Lizzie Siddal as a model. The beautifully detailed flowers and hedgerows surrounding Ophelia show Millais' keen observation and technical skill; these qualities developed rapidly and came to typify Millais' work.

Below: Rossetti met and fell in love with Lizzie Siddal in 1850 and lived with her until her death in 1863. In *Beata Beatrix* (1863) Rossetti commemorates his dead wife by using her as a model for Dante's dying Beatrice. The picture's haunting, dream-like intensity is enhanced by Rossetti's use of a soft, blurred technique.

Picturepoint

conventions such as using a 'principal light' in paintings; proceeding from dark tones at the edge of the picture to a light centre. English painting was, at the opening of the century, extremely dark in colour—the result of admiration for seventeenth-century masters and the use of *bitumen*, a rich brown pigment which, although producing warm contrasts, is destructive (as it never dries) and soon blackens the painting.

The qualities which the Pre-Raphaelites sought in contrast to this are summed up in Holman Hunt's description of his attempt at painting 'an out-of-door picture, with a foreground and background, abjuring altogether brown foliage, smoky clouds, and dark corners, painting the whole out of doors, direct on the canvas itself, with every detail I can see, and with the sunlight brightness of the day itself'. Determined to banish the gloom characteristic of academic painting, the Pre-Raphaelites developed a technique which gave full scope to light, bright colours—by applying colour very thinly over a white ground. The effect—similar to that of light passing through stained glass—is to give colours brilliance and luminosity.

Moreover, the Pre-Raphaelites revolted against the accepted practice of artists imitating the old masters. Under Sir Joshua Reynolds this practice had become established and the sixteenth-century painter Raphael had become a most revered 'academic' figure. In the words of W. M. Rossetti, the brother of Dante Gabriel and a fellow P. R. B., these young artists were not to be 'bound by rules and big-wiggeries founded upon the performances of Raphael or of any one. They

were to have no master except their own powers of mind and hand, and their own first-hand study of Nature . . .'

The virility and realism of the new movement, its ambitious and idealistic quest for likeness to life, its religious and moral energy was innovatory for England, but a like-minded group already existed in Germany. Called the *Nazarenes*, they too admired Italian painting of the fifteenth century (that is, before Raphael) and produced work which was deliberately archaic, with flat figures and light tones. They were known to the Pre-Raphaelites through the work of Ford Madox Brown (1821-93) who, although never a member of the P.R.B., was the group's acknowledged 'father-figure'.

The 1830s and 1840s saw a growing interest in pre-Renaissance painting. Until this time, English taste was anchored firmly in the art of the sixteenth and seventeenth centuries, from Raphael onwards. But prominent figures such as Prince Albert (whose collection of paintings included early Italian and northern Gothic works by such artists as Van Eyck, Duccio and Fra Angelico) and Sir Charles Eastlake, Director of the London National Gallery, helped to awaken the new interest.

The new brotherhood of young artists was the outcome of all these various influences. Their most clearly defined principles during the first (and most united) years of the movement were, therefore, an admiration for the German Nazarenes, a search for absolute accuracy and attention to detail, deliberate archaism wedded to a new respect for medieval art, and intensity of feeling—for nature, for religion and for literature. 141

It was on one or other of these grounds that Millais, Rossetti and Hunt received such hostile criticism when they first exhibited their work as avowed members of the pre-Raphaelite Brotherhood. Rossetti's simple, naive interpretation of the Annunciation, *Ecce Ancilla Domini* (1849-50) provoked unfriendly reviews when it was shown at the Free Exhibition of Modern Art in April 1850. The artist's imperfect understanding of perspective results in the picture looking truly archaic. But the most bitter attacks were reserved for Millais' painting exhibited at the Royal Academy—again a religious subject—*Christ in the House of His Parents* (1849). According to *The Times* 'the picture is plainly revolting' and to the *Literary Gazette* it was 'a nameless atrocity . . . in which there is neither taste, drawing, expression, or genius'. Possibly the hostility was aroused more by Millais' emphasis on the holy family as ordinary, human beings than on the quality of the painting. Although, as with the Rossetti, the treatment of perspective and space is odd, the painting shows a high degree of realistic detail. It clearly shows that Millais, unlike Rossetti and Holman Hunt who struggled for technical mastery, was a natural painter.

Below: The style of the Pre-Raphaelites was adopted by several minor artists, including Arthur Hughes. His painting *April Love* is typical of his work in its romantic, slightly wistful theme, superb feel for texture and deep, rich colour— seen here in his handling of foliage and silky materials.

Right: The work of Ford Madox Brown (1821-93) profoundly influenced the Pre-Raphaelites. A painstaking and exacting artist, Brown felt impatience for some of the P.R.B. sloppiness of thought and painting technique. Here, in *The Last of England* (1855), he depicts the conflicting emotions of an emigrating couple.

Below: Edward Burne-Jones (1833-98) trained under Rossetti. In his art he developed away from the realism of the Pre-Raphaelites towards the depiction of an ideal world, ethereal and symbolic. He deals frequently with myths, as in *The Beguiling of Merlin* (1874).

Lady Lever Art Gallery/Port Sunlight

City Art Gallery, Carlisle

Manchester City Art Gallery

Left: Of all the Pre-Raphaelites, William Holman Hunt (1827-1910) retained a commitment to exact observation and moral significance. *The Hireling Shepherd* (1851) shows a country lad amusing himself while his sheep encounter difficulties. Hunt uses the strong, pure, acid hues favoured by the movement.

Above: Apart from painting, Burne-Jones produced tapestry and stained-glass window designs in co-operation with his close friend William Morris. The *Voyage to Vinland the Good* (1883) is a cartoon for a window; it shows both his fine draughtsmanship and his feel for stylization and rhythm in design.

Millais and Ruskin

It was Millais who achieved success most readily. His style of painting quickly increased in fluency and became less rigid while retaining its precision of detail. His use of colour also increased in richness. In 1851 he exhibited three more paintings at the Royal Academy, including *Mariana*, from Tennyson's poem of that name, and a religious subject, *The Return of the Dove to the Ark*. Millais was elected an associate of the Royal Academy in 1853, the youngest ever to be admitted except for Sir Thomas Lawrence. Meanwhile Millais had been befriended by the eminent critic John Ruskin, whose letter of support for the P.R.B. in *The Times* is often seen as vital to their subsequent success. In many ways the opinions expressed by Ruskin coincided with Pre-Raphaelite principles. The key to the moral tone of the movement can best be discovered in the writings of Ruskin. Theories of beauty relying on abstract rules of proportion were not for him: 'the whole function of the artist is to be a seeing and feeling creature'. Sensibility and moral feeling went hand in hand and Ruskin praised the Pre-Raphaelites for the honesty and truthfulness of their observation.

Millais accompanied Ruskin and his wife Effie on a holiday in Scotland in 1853. Ruskin had obviously hoped to influence the style of the young artist, and certainly Millais' portrait of Ruskin, begun during this time, shows his influence. But the holiday proved the undoing of this artistic co-operation, for Millais fell in love with Ruskin's wife Effie, who left her husband and after a notorious annullment of their marriage, became Millais' wife in 1855. Millais continued to paint in a Pre-Raphaelite vein for a few years, producing such haunting works as *The Blind Girl* (1856) and *Autumn Leaves* (1856). But gradually he developed into a fashionable and technically polished academic painter of children (such as *Bubbles*), society portraits and popular historical subjects such as *The Boyhood of Raleigh*. Leaving behind his Pre-Raphaelite affinities, Millais later went on to become President of the Royal Academy and a baronet.

Rossetti—poet and painter

Dante Gabriel Rossetti, the driving force behind the Pre-Raphaelite Brotherhood, was both painter and poet. The movement had always been strongly literary; Millais, Rossetti, Hunt and other minor figures returned to authors such as Shakespeare, Keats and Tennyson for inspiration. In the early wave of enthusiasm felt by the brotherhood, it was decided that a magazine should be published. The first issue of *The Germ* (as it was finally called) was published in 1850, but after poor sales the venture had to be scrapped after the fourth issue. *The Germ* was interesting, however, for the poetry it contained. Rossetti published his characteristic poem *The Blessed Damozel* in the 143

Above: *Pegwell Bay, Kent* (1859-60) is a fine evocation of period, mood and landscape by William Dyce (1806-64). Dyce was first influenced by the German Nazarenes; here his keen detail is modelled on the example of Ruskin and the Pre-Raphaelites.

Right and below: In 1861, William Morris (1834-96) founded the firm of Morris and Co. to produce wallpapers, furniture, tapestries, carpets and materials. As a craftsman, Morris emphasized the integrity of individual workmanship and simple, 'honest' design. Typical of the firm's products was the stained-glass window made from a design by Burne-Jones (below). Morris had a life-long friendship with Burne-Jones—who drew the cartoon (right) of Morris at his loom. Morris founded the Kelmscott Press in 1890, and did much to raise the standard of book design and printing. Morris' poems and novels express his socialist theories and his anti-industrialism.

second issue: this poem is full of the mystery and symbolism so much a part of Rossetti's later painting: 'She had three lilies in her hand,/And the stars in her hair were seven.'

In 1850 Rossetti met Lizzie Siddal, who became a model for many paintings not only by him, but by the whole Brotherhood. The two lived together and finally married in 1860. Three years later Lizzie died from an overdose of laudanum and Rossetti commemorated her death in what is perhaps his finest painting, *Beata Beatrix* (1863). After this, his art became increasingly decorative.

Of the founding members of the Pre-Raphaelite Brotherhood, it was William Holman Hunt who changed his style least as he grew older. But the moral tone which he adopted became more dominant and his technique, at first displaying the typical Pre-Raphaelite luminosity and richness of colour, became harsh, even strident. His best paintings were executed during the early 1850s, when the brotherhood still existed and their principles were still fresh. With *The Light of the World* (1853-6), probably the best known of English religious paintings, Hunt began the overt and gloomy moralizing that mars his later painting. In 1854 he left England for Palestine, led by his obsession with painting religious themes to paint in the Holy Land itself.

Hunt's departure for the Holy Land reinforced the break-up of the Brotherhood. Rossetti's relationship with Lizzie Siddal had lessened his involvement with the movement, and Millais' election to the Royal Academy in 1853 had further weakened the bond. Rossetti wrote to his sister Christina, 'Millais, I just hear, was last night elected associate, so now the whole Round Table is dissolved.'

At the end of its first productive five years, the Brotherhood had reached no committed religious position and had made no great moral impact on society, although both themes had been dealt with. As an attempt to halt or at least comment on the excesses of the industrial society of mid-nineteenth century England, the movement did not succeed; it resorted instead to escapism from the harsh problems of the age. The movement was to pass into luxury decoration with the 'second generation' Pre-Raphaelites.

Craftsman and dreamer

Rossetti was the chief figure who continued from the original period into the second phase. Under his influence William Morris (1834-1896) abandoned his architectural studies in Oxford to become a painter, and in 1861 drew all his artistic interests together to form the successful commercial enterprise of Morris, Marshall, Faulkner & Co., producing wallpapers, furniture, tapestries, stained-glass windows, carpets and furnishing materials. In 1890 his founding of the Kelmscott Press did much to encourage and develop the private press.

Morris' friend at Oxford, Edward Burne-Jones (1833-1898), who also learnt to paint under the guidance of Rossetti, provided many of the tapestry and stained-glass designs for Morris as well as illustrations for Kelmscott Press books. Burne-Jones, educated and destined for a career in the church, knew nothing of painting until his friendship with Morris and Rossetti. But by 1859 he was a serious student of Italian art, travelling with Ruskin to Milan and Venice. Burne-Jones produced pictures and designs of langorous beauty as an escape from the hard-hitting commercial life of his mid-Victorian England. 'I mean by a picture', he wrote, 'a beautiful, romantic dream of something that never was, never will be—in a light better than any light that ever shone—in a land no one can define or remember—only desire.' Although they are rooted in Pre-Raphaelitism, Burne-Jones's paintings of the 'ideal' are far removed from the original aims of the Brotherhood. They stand far closer to the 'Aesthetic' movement of the late nineteenth century.

Impressionist Painters

The term 'Impressionism' was first used mockingly, to describe the 1874 exhibition of works by a new generation of French painters—Monet, Renoir, Pissarro, Sisley, Degas and others. Soon the artists themselves accepted the title and gradually Impressionism lost its derisive implications and came to be regarded and praised as a crucial artistic movement. The general opinion of the 1874 exhibition was that if you 'soil three quarters of a canvas with black and white, rub the rest with yellow, distribute haphazardly some red and blue spots, you'll obtain an impression'. One critic, less harsh but more revealing of their work, said 'They are Impressionists in the sense that they render not the landscape but the sensation produced by the landscape'.

The liberation of light

The 'daring' aims shared by the group included the immediate and visually true rendering of a momentary scene; the painting of the whole work in the open air (which entailed abandoning the traditional sequence of preparatory sketches and carefully worked final painting); the use of pure colour on the canvas instead of first being mixed on the palette; the technique, influenced by recent scientific studies, of depicting light in terms of its component colours; the use of small strokes and dabs of brightly-coloured paint and, above all, the use of light and colour as the sole means of unifying a picture, as opposed to the traditional method of building up a painting by outline and modelling with light and shade.

Taken together, these aims represented a whole revaluation of art. And yet, as with so many 'revolutionary' artistic movements, their roots can be found in what went before. The emphasis on painting direct from nature led on from the stress placed on factual data and direct observation by the Realist painters and the followers of the philosophy of Positivism. The Impressionists' use of colour owed much to the findings of the French scientist Chevreul, who observed that juxtaposed colours alter each other and that, when seen from a distance, two different colours placed side by side blend into a single tone. Theories such as these led eventually to the Impressionist practice of placing pure colours on the canvas for the spectator's eye to fuse from a distance.

But this technique had actually been foreshadowed by earlier painters, Delacroix (in France) and Constable (in England), both of whom were revered by the Impressionists. In his journal, Delacroix remarks: 'Constable says that the superiority of the greens in his meadows is due to the fact that they are made up of a large number of different (juxtaposed not mixed) greens. What gives a lack of intensity and life to the ordinary run of landscape painters is that they do it with a uniform tint.' Delacroix himself came to reject earth tones and use pure, unmixed colours and he anticipated the characteristic brushwork of the

Right: *Monet working in his boat* (1874) by Edouard Manet (1832-83). In the summer of 1874 Manet joined Renoir and Monet at Argenteuil on the Seine (where Monet had fitted out a boat as a studio) and there he produced his most Impressionistic work. Manet's art, which so shocked the critics of the 1860s, was deeply admired by the younger Impressionists.

Below: *The Family Reunion* (1867) painted by Frédéric Bazille (1841-71), a friend of Monet. Bazille's career as an Impressionist was abruptly ended by his death in the Franco-Prussian War. His chief aim, as seen here, was the painting of figures out of doors. The stiff formality of this work, despite its lightness of palette, suggests the influence of photography.

Left: Claude Monet (1840-1926) is often considered the leader of the Impressionists. *The Poppies*, seen here, was exhibited at the 1874 Impressionist exhibition. Monet's concern to render truthfully the immediate visual sensation produced by a landscape; his discovery that the eye merged different colours from a distance and that complementary colours (seen here in the red poppies against the green field) intensify each other, are all revealed in this painting.

Below: *Water-lilies: Harmony in green* (1899), one of Monet's first paintings in the series on which he worked until his death. With these water-lily studies he explored further his lifelong devotion to visual sensation—his emphasis on light and colour leading more and more to a dissolution of form.

Right: *Luncheon of the Boating Party*, painted by Auguste Renoir (1841 -1919) in 1881. Renoir's greatest interest was in the human figure and he delighted in portraying people at leisure—in dance halls, cafés or on boating trips. This painting is a superb example of Renoir's use of glowing, pearly colours and fluent, feathery brushstrokes.

Impressionists when he wrote: 'It is well if the brush strokes are not actually fused. They fuse naturally at a certain distance by the law of sympathy that has associated them. The colour thus gains in energy and freshness.' These comments usefully outline the Impressionists' greatest contribution to art—the liberation of light and colour and the attempt to create the sense of the immediate, visual impact of an image.

As a unified movement, Impressionism is really confined to the 1870s. After this decade, the artists developed along more individual paths. The 1860s were formative years for all the future Impressionists, during which a variety of influences shaped their ideas. These influences can best be seen in the career of Claude Monet (1840-1926), the leading member of the group.

Shaping influences

One of the painters whom Monet most respected was Edouard Manet, who was, during the 1860s, an extremely controversial figure: his *Déjeuner sur l'Herbe* (1863) received outraged criticism when it was exhibited at the new *Salon des Refusés* (established for showing works rejected by the official *Salon*). The very qualities for which he was reviled by the critics—spontaneous brushwork, elimination of half tones, lack of smooth modelling and disregard of meticulous transition from light to dark—endeared him to the future Impressionists. Inspired by Manet's painting, Monet himself began a *Déjeuner sur l'Herbe*, spending several months sketching in the forest of Fontainebleau. His intention, however, was different from Manet, for he wanted to paint his picnickers as they appeared in a fleeting moment of sunlight. In the same year as he finished this, 1866,

146 Monet painted *Women in the Garden*,

Phillips Collection, Washington DC/ Cooper Bridgeman

Below: In *The Reader*, Renoir uses light and colour as the sole modelling agent. By rendering the variety of tones of which her complexion and hair are made up when seen in shifting light, Renoir achieves a typically Impressionist effect of vibrancy and vitality.

Scala

with which he began his practice of painting works entirely out of doors.

Monet had, early on in his career, been introduced to painting out of doors by an artist friend Eugène Boudin (1824-98), while living in Le Havre. Monet derived from Boudin a fascination for capturing fleeting atmospheric effects, and his paintings of the harbours and beaches of Normandy are concerned largely with the evocation of the play of light on surfaces.

Monet's developing interest in optical effects are further seen in the series of snow scenes which he painted in and around Honfleur during the early 1860s. By this time his style was being modified by his knowledge of Japanese art. Japanese colour woodcuts were beginning to be known in Europe from the mid nineteenth century, when Japan entered into trade relations with it. Prints of these woodcuts were often used as wrappings and padding for tea, and could be bought cheaply at tea-shops. Many artists in France from the late 1850s onwards collected these prints; they saw in Japanese art a way of revitalizing their own style. Several Japanese motifs corresponded with effects currently being explored in their own environment, for example the cut-off composition, with figures seen from unexpected angles or partly obscured (also a feature of photography), the use of black outline, of large flat areas of colour and of dramatic

perspective foreshortening. This last feature was adopted by Monet in his *Road near Honfleur in Snow* (1867) as it tends to make the picture's impact one of an impression received in a momentary glance.

After this, perspective foreshortening was used repeatedly by the Impressionists, in particular Camille Pissarro (1831-1903) and Alfred Sisley (1839-99) for road scenes, and by Manet again for his river views. Different aspects of Japanese art were taken up by different painters according to their interests: Edgar Degas (1834-1917), more interested in design and drawing than the main Impressionists, was particularly influenced by the uncluttered nature of Japanese art and by the possibilities of the cut-off composition, which he explored most fully in his numerous studies of ballet dancers.

For Manet the attraction of Japanese art lay in its use of colour; his work during the 1860s, with its use of flat areas of bright colour, reflects his knowledge of Japanese prints. Although both Manet and Degas were both, at some stage of their career, influenced by the techniques and findings of the Impressionists, they both held themselves somewhat aloof from the main group—separated by different social backgrounds, by age, by a greater 'sophistication' of outlook, and by different artistic aims.

The growing interest in photography, too, played an important part in Monet's 147

Zi olo

Left: *The Flood at Port-Marly* (1876) by Alfred Sisley (1839-99). His best landscapes, which include this masterly study, were produced during the 1870s. Although he was tremendously influenced by Monet, Sisley's paintings have an entirely personal atmosphere of delicacy, carried through in the use of restrained tones of grey, green and blue.

Below left: *The Red Roofs* (1879) by Camille Pissarro (1831-1903). His early works, with their strong sense of earthiness in colour and 'clotted' texture, gave way in the 1870s to a freer, more spontaneous handling and use of bright, vibrant colour. His work conveys a sense of solidity and firmness lacking in Monet's art.

Below: Henri de Toulouse-Lautrec (1864-1901) used the example of Japanese prints and the art of Degas to develop his own highly personal graphic style, with which he depicted the cafés, dance-halls and brothels of Montmartre. Here he portrays the comedienne Cha-u-Kao, a performer at the famous Moulin Rouge dance-hall.

conception of painting. His depiction of pedestrians in his city scene *Boulevard des Capucines* (1873), in which the people are distorted into mere black dabs, echoes exactly the effects found in contemporary photographs taken on glass plates, which tend to blur moving forms. Sometimes actual photographs were used by the Impressionists; at other times, photography enabled objects and scenes to be viewed from unexpected angles.

Renoir, Pissarro and Sisley
Monet was the link between the different members of the group. He had met Renoir and Sisley in Paris, while studying at the studio of Gleyre, and had befriended Pissarro and Cézanne (a post-Impressionist) at the Académie Suisse, also in Paris. From 1864, these artists

were all working in the Forest of Fontainebleau either independently or together.

Auguste Renoir (1841-1919), although influenced by Monet in his use of bright, flat colour, was more like Manet in his responsiveness to the art of the past. And for him, as for Manet, it is the human figure that remains the most fascinating subject of artistic expression. Throughout the 1860s, Renoir tried to maintain a balance between certain academic standards and the pictorial advances he saw being carried out around him. In its use of deep colour and textured pigment his work at Fontainebleau shows the influence of Courbet. Gradually however— as a result of continual painting out of doors and of Monet's influence—his colours became lighter and his handling

freer. But his interest in the human figure dominates even when he is closest to Monet in theme and style.

In 1868 he and Monet worked together on the River Seine and their individual interpretations of a scene at *La Grenouillère* (a popular bathing place on the River Seine) reveal their contrasting interests—Renoir's in social scenes and human figures, Monet's in the effects of light and water. It was here that Renoir and Monet discovered that shadows are not brown or black (as they were traditionally depicted) but are coloured by their surroundings. They accordingly rejected blacks, browns and earth colours more and more from their palettes.

Along with Monet, it was Pissarro and Sisley who were perhaps the most faithful to Impressionism. Pissarro, though much

Left: *Carriages at the Races* by Edgar Degas (1834-1917). Degas, unlike most of the Impressionists, was not in favour of painting entirely out of doors and his few landscapes were mostly done from memory. This work shows two of Degas' characteristic interests: his close observation of urban society at work and at leisure and his frequent experiments with novel pictorial compositions. The chopped-off small carriage to the left of the canvas, the unexpected angle of the carriage in the foreground and the flat effect produced by the depiction of a dramatically near foreground against a far distant background with no sense of receding space between them—all reveal Degas' huge debt to Japanese prints.

Below: Degas' *Dancer on the Stage* is among his many studies of ballet dancers at rehearsal and in performance. These figures are the starting point for an exploration of form, design and light; of all the new ways in which he could suggest movement and space.

influenced by Monet, reveals a far greater respect for the underlying structure of a painting and for the solid, durable aspects of the earth and countryside. Sisley, almost exclusively a landscape painter, was heavily influenced by Monet in his later works executed during the 1870s. But his landscapes, for example *Misty Morning* (1874), retain a sense of melancholy and delicacy wholly personal to his art.

During the mid 1870s, the Impressionist style reached its peak. The artists associated with it were working in their most characteristic style of small, separate brush strokes, and small dabs of pure colour applied direct to a white primed canvas, with no prior mixing. Their paintings transmit not only a sense of liberation in style, but a true enjoyment of life, their most typical subjects being breakfasts, picnics, promenades and boating trips, and scenes of nature in different moods and in different seasons.

Since 1872 Monet had been living at Argenteuil on the River Seine, where he had fitted out a floating studio, from which he could study and paint the interaction of light and water. Here he painted with Renoir, and in the summer of 1874 they were joined by Manet, whose parents owned a property nearby. This summer marked the height of Manet's involvement with Impressionism: his colours became lighter, his technique looser and he came increasingly to value the experience of working out of doors. His painting *Monet working in his boat* (1874) acts as a tribute to this phase and conveys something of Manet's new-found delight in the spontaneous rendering of the physical aspects of a scene. But although the newspaper critics insisted on talking of the younger artists as 'Manet's gang', Manet himself never wanted to be identified with the Impressionists and refused to take part in any of their exhibitions. Organized by Degas, the first of these Impressionist exhibitions took place in 1874 and was vilified by the critics and the public alike.

Monet's dissolving forms

The group itself, although continuing to hold exhibitions until 1886 had, by the end of the 1870s, begun to split up. Monet left Argenteuil in 1876 and two years later settled at Vetheuil, further from Paris. He began the series of paintings in which he explored one subject under different conditions and times of day: these included the *Poplars* and the *Haystacks*, *Rouen cathedral* and the *Water-lilies*, these last large canvases being painted right up to his death in 1926. They show an increasing dissolution of form and sensuous rendering of light and colour. Renoir, always inclined towards classical art, returned to his basic preoccupation with the human figure and his later work shows an increased attention to form, contour and smoothness of surface. Pissarro became involved with the colour-theories of the neo-Impressionists, led by Seurat, leaving only Sisley of the original group as a pure Impressionist to the end of his life. Thus the 1880s witnessed the original group of Impressionists following their independent styles, and the rise of a new generation—Cézanne, Gauguin and Van Gogh—who, with the Impressionist innovations as their starting point, were to forge a new and more radical art.

Post-Impressionists

During the mid-1880s in France, the style of painting known as Impressionism gave way to more radical—and more individual—advances in art. The artists who made these advances—Seurat, Van Gogh, Gauguin, and Cézanne—had, however, each passed through an Impressionist phase and had found it an important shaping influence.

The work of Georges Seurat (1859-91) can in some ways be seen as a painstaking, systematic extension of the Impressionist interest in light and colour, and for this reason his ideas were soon given the title of *Neo-Impressionism*. Seurat began his art studies in Paris at the age of 15. After military service he returned to Paris in 1880 and his painting at this time was influenced by Millet and Corot. By 1883 his work shows the impact of Impressionism and he started to use suburban and city scenes.

The themes were Impressionist but already his ideas were moving away from the central Impressionist principle of capturing the fleeting sensory moment. Seurat felt far more sympathy for the idea that 'The Artist is charged with the task of recalling to us the ideal . . . of discovering the imperishable character, the pure essence . . .' as expressed by the theoretician Charles Blanc in his *Grammar of Art and Design*. Rather than one brief

Above left: *The White Horse* (1898) by Paul Gauguin (1848-1903). This was painted during Gauguin's last years, which he spent in the Marquesas Islands in the South Seas. Instead of regarding paintings as a mirror of the outer world, Gauguin believed them to be images reflecting man's inner, spiritual nature.

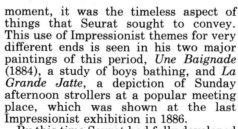

Far left: With *Vision after the Sermon* (1888) Gauguin broke away from naturalism. The vision of the peasant women is set against an unreal background of vivid crimson and the whole work is painted in flat areas of colour enclosed with black outlines—a device stemming from Japanese art and from medieval stained glass.

Below: *The Midday Break* painted by Vincent Van Gogh (1853-1890). One of his many depictions of summer harvests, Van Gogh here conveys the intense heat and sun-drenched atmosphere which had attracted him to Arles in 1888. The intense, vibrant 'beautiful yellow' was, for Van Gogh, the true symbol of the South.

Above left: Van Gogh's *The Fields of Arles* conveys the essence of his later style. The rapid, swirling, almost violent brushstrokes and thickly-applied paint combine to make the fields vibrate with life and serve to impart Van Gogh's intense and passionate identification with all that he painted.

Above: Van Gogh's *Portrait of Dr. Gachet* (1890), who cared for the artist after his spell in an asylum. For the artist who once said 'while trying to go deeper into art I try . . . to go deeper into life, for the two go together' living had become an intolerable strain and soon after this was painted he shot himself.

moment, it was the timeless aspect of things that Seurat sought to convey. This use of Impressionist themes for very different ends is seen in his two major paintings of this period, *Une Baignade* (1884), a study of boys bathing, and *La Grande Jatte*, a depiction of Sunday afternoon strollers at a popular meeting place, which was shown at the last Impressionist exhibition in 1886.

By this time Seurat had fully developed the quasi-scientific method by which colour and light were to be rendered and from *La Grande Jatte* onwards he used these colour theories in each of his canvases. Not only was colour to be broken down into components, with pure pigment applied to the canvas for the eye to mix at a distance, but light itself was to be analyzed and separated out into local colour, the colour of the light, and the interactions between them. According to Seurat's follower Paul Signac (1863-1935) these techniques 'guaranteed all the benefits of luminosity, colour and harmony'.

Seurat's method was to paint in tiny dots or dabs of pure colour, the size of the dabs varying according to the size of the painting and the distance at which it was to be seen. In the degree of careful

analysis and meticulous technique required, this method obviously demanded a completely different approach from the Impressionist ideal of painting the whole work in one sitting. The difference is reflected in output: Seurat painted little more than a handful of major works and, particularly for *La Grande Jatte*, made numerous preparatory studies.

The greater formality of approach was echoed in Seurat's preference for formal, harmoniously proportioned compositions in which the verticals and horizontals are balanced and the figures are placed across the picture plane or at right angles to it—achieving a static, monumental quality at odds with the Impressionist pursuit of movement and changing light effects.

Seurat was influential during the 1880s: not only was the Impressionist Pissarro much swayed by his style, but Van Gogh and Gauguin also felt his impact.

The tormented genius of Van Gogh
Vincent Van Gogh (1853-90) was born in the Dutch Brabant, the son of a Lutheran pastor whose family had artistic connections. After studying theology he was appointed minister to a mining district, The Borinage, in Belgium. During this difficult period of his life he turned to sketching and painting with a great intensity. His life never ceased to be painful and difficult, due largely to his fervently idealistic belief in the inseparability of his social, philosophical and aesthetic ideas from his day-to-day behaviour.

The following few years were spent studying art in Brussels, The Hague and Antwerp and living at home with his family before going to Paris in 1886. Here 151

Scala

Art Institute of Chicago

he came into contact with the current techniques and was attracted more by Seurat's scientific approach than the experimentation of the Impressionists.

Van Gogh owned well over 200 Japanese prints and made many copies from them as well as using them as inspiration for works such as his flowering fruit trees or his pictures of bridges. He also adopted the Japanese method of drawing with a reed pen. It became Van Gogh's desire to set up a community of artists who would provide mutual help and support. But when he invited Gauguin to live with him in Arles in 1888, the results were tragic—the friendship ended and Van Gogh was left in a deeply disturbed state, which led to him cutting off his ear.

For Van Gogh the Provençal town of Arles appeared as beautiful as Japan for its limpid atmosphere and its gay colours. His Arles landscapes fall naturally into three series concerned with aspects of seasonal change. He painted spring orchards in blossom, summer harvests in the blazing sun, and autumnal gardens and fields. His heightened, intense colour and development of writhing, flamelike forms are deeply expressive of his state of mind. But the mental and physical hardships he had endured while at Borinage combined with his intensely troubled personality to create insupportable strains within him. After a year in an asylum at St. Remy in Provence he was cared for by a Dr. Gachet at Auvers near Paris. On July 27 1890 he shot himself and died two days later.

Van Gogh committed suicide probably because he could not accept the limitations and shortcomings of the world. 152 Paul Gauguin (1848-1903) attempted to

avoid limits by escaping from them in order to explore a lost paradise: as with Van Gogh, the result was destruction of the self. Born in Paris in 1848, Gauguin's early childhood was spent in South America. After service in the French navy he entered a firm of stockbrokers and became a weekend painter. Contact with Pissarro provided encouragement for his painting. In 1881 he painted with Pissarro and Cézanne and two years later gave up his regular job for his art.

Gauguin's symbolic world

For Gauguin, a trip to the Caribbean island of Martinique finalized his break away from Pissarro and the Impressionists. His *Vision after the Sermon* (1888), painted in Brittany after his return, marks the break. Gauguin said of it 'the landscape and the struggle exist only in the imagination of these praying people . . . that is why there is a contrast between these real people and the struggle in the landscape which is not real and [is] out of proportion'. The comment describes his move away from realistic representation towards the painting of states of mind, using external objects to symbolize inner feelings, emotions, ideas. The painting shows the influence of Japanese prints, of which he had a large collection and which often appear in the background of his paintings. His elimination of shadow and use of large, flat areas of colour take his art even further from naturalism.

In 1891 Gauguin travelled to Tahiti, returning to Paris in 1893 with 66 canvases. Scenes of everyday Tahitian life and religious beliefs formed the core of the collection, painted in a less flat style than

Above left: *Model in Profile* by Georges Seurat (1859-91). This is one of numerous studies which Seurat made for his large canvas *Les Poseurs* (*The Models*) (1887). Here small dabs of colour define the form, and the model's pensive self-absorption conveys a quality of stillness typical of Seurat's work.

Below: Seurat's haunting work *La Parade* (1886-8) depicts the show held to attract circus customers. Its static quality suggests a permanence that side-shows usually lack. The arrangement of forms is balanced, harmonious and influenced by Egyptian art, whilst the spectators demonstrate Seurat's genius with silhouette.

Metropolitan Museum of Art, Bequest of Stephen C. Clark, 1960.

Above: *Still Life with a Basket of Apples* (1890-95) by Paul Cézanne (1839-1906). Cézanne's search for the inner form of natural objects —to the point of fragmentation—was sensed by the poet Rilke who said that Cézanne's 'fruits ceased to be edible but [became] indestructible in their stubborn presence'.

Above right: *Mont St Victoire* (1904-06) is one of Cézanne's last versions of a theme which he painted more than 60 times. Cézanne himself suggested that 'the logic of organized sensation' was the source of this work, in which interlocking and overlapping areas of colour create a sense of the landscape.

his Brittany works but frequently arranged in a frieze-like way, after the manner of Javanese and Egyptian art. His wish was to convey the simplicity of life and the rich store of religious and mythical belief among primitive, 'unspoiled' peoples. He returned to the South Seas in 1895, where his remaining years were spent in poverty, illness—an attempted suicide—and continual strife with the colonial authorities.

Nature as geometry

Paul Cézanne (1839-1906), alone among the Post-Impressionists, remained uninfluenced by Japanese art, the idea of a paradisical past or an artistic commune in the present. His aim was to formulate a very different order of reality in art and this is what he shares with his fellow Post-Impressionists.

Born in Aix-en-Provence, he came to Paris in the early 1860s against his father's wishes, and soon became acquainted with the Impressionist manner and mode of painting, though his own early works reveal little of their impact. Dark earthy colours applied very thickly characterize his early works. Through his meetings with Pissarro his colours lightened considerably. His concern was with closed and interlocking forms, and the pictorial relationship of objects. His concentration on this led to his rejecting the basic concepts of Western pictorial representation which had prevailed for centuries.

Instead of the traditional single fixed viewpoint, Cézanne introduced multiple and moving viewpoints, for example in *Still Life with a Basket of Apples* (c.1890-95). Only in 1895 did he have his first one

man exhibition; he had ceased to exhibit with the Impressionists in 1877, due to insults from public and critics.

Unlike the Impressionists, Cézanne deeply admired classical art and said that he 'wanted to do Poussin again, from Nature' and that he wanted 'to make of Impressionism something solid and durable, like the art of the Museums'. He referred to his paintings as 'constructions after nature', built out of 'plastic equivalents and colour'.

His idea that the painter must look for the cone, the sphere and the cylinder in nature has been seen as the basis for the twentieth century Cubist movement. This again emphasizes his basic departure from the Impressionist concern with recording the fleeting effects of nature, for a belief in the enduring forms, colours and relationships between these found in the natural world. He painted Mont St Victoire in Provence at least 60 times in his striving for ever deeper perceptions of the underlying natural order, perceptions hardly ever granted to those making a cursory examination of a scene. Landscape, still life, portraits and the theme of *The Bathers* dominated his pictorial explorations of reality. His deep attachment to Aix in Provence and to the South of France in general meant that from 1882 his visits to Paris were brief. When his father died in 1886 he found himself rich and was able to live in seclusion.

With their advances these artists opened the way for twentieth century art, prefiguring in their canvases such modern movements as Symbolism and Expressionism (in the case of Van Gogh and Gauguin) and Cubism (with the work of Cézanne).

153

Art Nouveau

As the nineteenth century drew to its close, a style of art emerged throughout Europe that has become known as *Art Nouveau* (new art). A mood of conscious abandon dominated the artistic and literary centres of Europe. Artists, architects and designers reacted against the rigid standards of the academy and salon, with their emphasis on easily-understood subjects and a representational style—reacted in fact against the whole Classical and Renaissance tradition.

In the place of these aims, artists turned to enigmatic subjects drawn from man's inner life and expressed through symbols—poetry, drama and art all felt the impact of the Symbolist movement. Art Nouveau was part of this trend; in the place of a slavish imitation of nature, its exponents sought beauty, elegance and decorativeness. The elongated female form, heavy eyed and mysterious; convoluted and luxuriant plant life; long-stemmed stylized flowers and curving, intricate patterns—these have become the familiar features of Art Nouveau. They may appear starkly in black and white graphic form, in a colourful poster, in the facade of a building or in an elegantly curved teaspoon or door-handle. For the style, by its very nature, embraced all the visual arts and is seen at its most typical in jewellery, ceramics, furniture and illustration.

The Arts and Crafts movement

The rejection of naturalism by Dante Gabriel Rossetti and Edward Burne-Jones, and the increasing attention to pattern-making in their pictures; the rediscovery of Blake's energetic drawings of human figures and twining foliage; the fascination with a dream world and with exotic experiences among French writers like Charles Baudelaire; all these played their part in forming the style. But perhaps the greatest impetus came from William Morris (1834-96) and his Arts and Crafts movement.

Taking as their ideal medieval standards of design and craftsmanship, these artists passionately believed in artistic unity, in the co-ordination of all parts of a work of art. To this end, they strove to create, say, a building in which decoration, furniture, lighting and even details like cutlery and china would be the result of one harmonizing aesthetic idea. Their ideal of no division between the planner and executor carried over to their actual theories on design: there was to be no division between the function and decorative surface. Decoration was not to be imposed arbitrarily on to the basic design, but instead grow naturally from it.

It was this idea of organic growth which became the hallmark of Art Nouveau. Its designs everywhere reflect a fascination for the fluid, vital forms of nature and an emphasis on sinuous, undulating line shaping itself into plant-like forms. But the practitioners of this style differed in one important respect from their predecessors in the Arts and Crafts movement in that they sought to break away from the past (upon which Morris' group relied so heavily) and introduce a completely modern style. Art Nouveau was essentially a European phenomenon and, for the last decade of the nineteenth century groups of artists all over Europe were exploiting the possibilities of sinuous line and rich ornament.

In Germany Art Nouveau was called Jugendstil after a popular review (*Die Jugend*) founded in 1896. In Austria it was known as Sezessionstil, in Italy it was called Stile Liberty after the store in Regent Street, London, which helped to disseminate Art Nouveau designs, and in Spain the Barcelona version of Art Nouveau was called Modernistica. In Paris, where all things English were the fashion, it was at first known as the Modern Style.

Mackintosh and Beardsley

Probably the most gifted and influential of the generation of young architects of the 1890s was the Scotsman Charles Rennie Mackintosh (1868-1928). His Glasgow School of Art, on which he started work in 1897, can be counted as his masterpiece. The severe and bold simplicity of this design, the way in which the function of the building is reflected in the arrangement of studio windows, and Mackintosh's success in exploiting the steeply sloping site by designing an immense, cliff-like east face, herald twentieth-century architecture.

It is in the detail and interior decoration, the stained glass and the furniture, that Mackintosh employs the sinuous curves and elongations characteristic of Art Nouveau. In the coloured glass doors of the Willow Tea Rooms motifs typical of Mackintosh's work are to be found: stylized rose forms and long, stem-like rods of metal. The near-abstract designs are reminiscent of Celtic art which, with its similar basis in intricate linear patterns and flowing organic plant forms, was an immediate source of inspiration for the exponents of Art Nouveau. Yet, restrained by the influence of the Arts and Crafts movement, Mackintosh never allowed decoration to overflow. The furniture and household objects he designed, often with the collaboration of his wife, Margaret Macdonald, are restrained and controlled.

Aubrey Beardsley (1872-98) was, along with Mackintosh, the most talented British exponent of Art Nouveau. In his birthplace, Brighton, Beardsley absorbed the un-Victorian atmosphere of raffishness and Oriental exoticism that survived in a town whose legacy was the extraordinary Regency pavilion.

Left: Detail of the doors of the Willow Tea Rooms, Glasgow (1903-4) designed by Charles Rennie Mackintosh (1868-1928) and his wife Margaret Macdonald. Carved wood and leaded glass in subtle colours are the medium for his near-abstract plant design based on stem-like vertical lines and stylized rose shapes.

Angelo Hornak

J. L. Charmet

154

It was Burne-Jones, whose stained glass in the Brighton church of St. Michael and All Angels Beardsley probably knew, who launched this precocious young man professionally. In 1891 Beardsley and his sister, Mabel, with whom he lived, visited the great man's studio. There his drawings were admired by Burne-Jones and by the well known author Oscar Wilde (1854-1900), whose book *The Picture of Dorian Gray* was almost the bible of the 'aesthetes' of the day—those who devoted themselves to the pursuit, or creation of, beauty.

The friendship initiated that afternoon was to result in one of Beardsley's most celebrated series of illustrations, for Wilde's *Salome* (English edition 1894). It also had a less fortunate result: Beardsley's name was associated with Wilde's in 1895 during the latter's abortive libel action against the Marquis of Queensberry, who had accused Wilde of a homosexual association with his son, Lord Alfred Douglas. *The Yellow Book*, an illustrated quarterly which was pioneered by Beardsley in 1894 and became a showcase for his work (as well as including contributions by Henry James, Max Beerbohm and others) was a casualty of the libel case when Lane, the publisher, withdrew his support.

Beardsley had admired Burne-Jones's work but soon developed interests widely divergent from those of the older man. Drawing was traditionally seen as a preparatory stage in the production of a finished painting which would be executed in carefully controlled daylight and finally hung in an exhibition room.

Above: Paris metro station designed by Hector Guimard (1867-1942). Iron and glass are used imaginatively to produce the new fluid, organic shapes.

Below: The curving 'whiplash' line recurs throughout the Maison Tassel in Brussels, an Art Nouveau design by Victor Horta (1861-1946).

Right: The church of La Sagrada Familia in Barcelona (1884-1926), designed by the brilliant Spanish Art Nouveau architect Antonio Gaudí (1852-1926). The original plan was for four facades, of which only one was completed. The building integrates fantastically hewn 'natural' sculpture with the actual structure.

F. Arborio Mella

F. Arborio Mella

Beardsley was determined in his rejection of all this. For him, line could suggest everything: movement, weight, mass, even (he suggested) colour. As he was supporting himself until 1894 as a clerk and journalist, Beardsley was familiar with the written word. He early realized his own power of merging visual and literary art and drew upon literature for much of his subject-matter: including Pope's *Rape of the Lock*, Malory's *Morte d'Arthur* and Jonson's *Volpone*. Writing is often incorporated in his designs.

Rejecting tradition, Beardsley regarded drawings as completed pictures, he worked in artificial light and he designed for mass production in illustrated journals or poster form. Unafraid of modern technology, he believed that the poster was an art form that could play an important part in everyday existence. In fact, the strikingly original methods he employed were the only ones that permitted a man with such a short life expectancy to fulfil himself. Beardsley died of tuberculosis in 1898, aged 25.

Left: The Czech-born artist Alphonse Mucha (1860-1933) was a great popularizer of Art Nouveau, whose most successful medium was the poster. Posters were even more popular 60 years later than when they where first produced.

His *Job* cigarette poster of 1897 presents the langourous woman so beloved of the *fin de siècle*, or decadent, artists of the 1890s.

Below, left and right: The most dazzling graphic artist of the age was Aubrey Beardsley (1872-98). Typical of his work is the powerful image (left) of the predatory woman. Strongly influenced by Japanese woodcuts, the figure has a dramatic elegance derived from the exaggerated,

curving silhouette of hat, shoulders and skirt. In its decorative detail, eroticism and ambivalence in terms of size, space and sex, the print (right) is similarly typical of Beardsley's art.

Above: *The Three Brides* (1893) by Jan Toorop (1858-1928). The bride of man (centre), the bride of Christ (left) and the bride of death wearing a chain of skulls (right) are blended into a highly decorative scheme.

Right: Necklace and brooch, designed by René Lalique (1860-1945), which use the flowing shapes and plant motifs of Art Nouveau. Lalique introduced new techniques and new and unusual materials into the making of jewellery.

Nimatallah/Ziolo

European developments

In Paris it was the metro stations, designed by Hector Guimard (1867-1942) between 1899 and 1900, which helped to make Art Nouveau famous. Concoctions of iron and glass, these structures sprout and crystallize in writhing organic shapes. But Guimard's metro designs still retain a unity of design, a total conception to which all detail is subordinate.

In applied arts, France could draw on a rich tradition of eighteenth-century rococo decoration. Some of the most remarkable furniture ever created was designed and constructed in France in the 1890s. In 1895 an art dealer named Bing opened an Art Nouveau shop where the visitor could view glass by the American Louis Tiffany, ceramics by Louis Emile Gallé and jewellery by René Lalique, jeweller to the celebrated actress Sarah Bernhardt.

Victor Horta (1861-1946) and Henry Van de Velde (1863-1957) are the most notable names in Belgian Art Nouveau. Horta built highly decorative and asymmetrical houses for wealthy industrialists while Van de Velde was most disting-

uished as a theorist. He had read Ruskin and Morris and wrote many articles himself which helped to spread ideas on design. In 1894 he married and, in fitting out his new home, endeavoured to put into practice his own ideas just as William Morris had done at the Red House, Bexleyheath, 23 years earlier. Architecturally the house, built at Uccle, near Brussels, is not of great interest. Van de Velde's talents lay in the arrangement of the interior and the design of household items in which he used ornamentation to emphasize the structure.

Van de Velde owed much to English writers on art and design, as did his Dutch contemporary, the painter Jan Toorop (1858-1928) who visited London on several occasions from 1884 until 1889. Toorop spent the first 11 years of his life in Java. His mature art is characterized by rhythmic, linear movements which derive from his familiarity with British Art Nouveau and from a feeling for primitive forms remembered from his childhood.

The cult of woman which is central to Toorop's work was shared by many painters and writers associated with Art

Nouveau and symbolism, ranging from the Frenchman Gustave Moreau (1826-98) and Burne-Jones to the Austrian Gustav Klimt (1862-1918), who excelled in the depiction of sensual, highly stylized and decorative nudes.

In Spain, Art Nouveau appeared as the imaginative architectural expression of one man, Antonio Gaudí (1852-1926), working in Barcelona. In 1884 Gaudí took over the design of La Sagrada Familia (Church of the Holy Family) from the architect Villar. Gaudí's work owes much to his familiarity with Gothic sculpture but, in a new way, the sculpture becomes for Gaudí an integral part of the building. The structure is itself sculpture, combining naturalistic flowers and plants, weird lava flows and Christian motifs. In his civil buildings, Gaudí used daring and eccentric structures, favouring in particular undulating lines and swelling or concave wall surfaces.

Although their achievements were solid and lasting, the Art Nouveau style and movement were essentially luxurious and nowhere did they survive the outbreak of World War I in 1914.

157

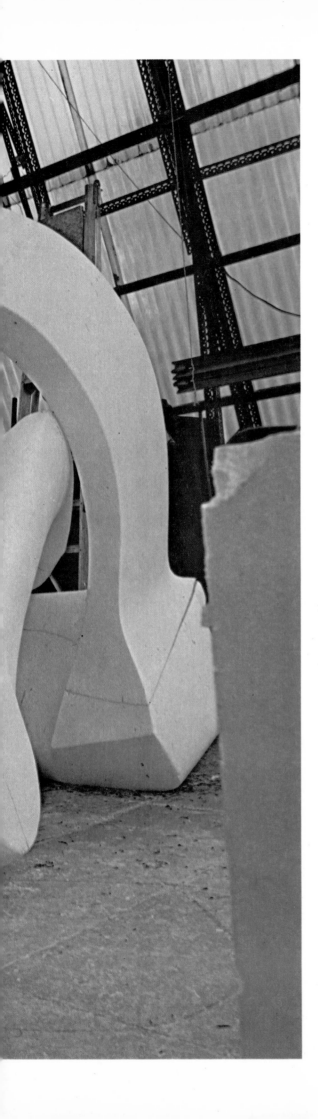

Chapter 6

The Twentieth Century

Henry Moore (b.1898) at work. He has
always shown a mastery of technique,
in wood and stone in the early part of
his career, and since 1940, in bronze.
He has the sculptor's three-dimensional
eye to a rare degree, each work
offering a variety of different views.

Manhattan, looking south towards the Empire State Building. Completed in 1931, the building exemplifies the use of technology in architecture – a steel frame structure means that the weight of the elegant skyscraper need not be carried by the curtain walls.

20th Century Architecture

In the twentieth century, architecture has been forced to develop away from traditional forms to tackle the new demands of an industrialized society. To accommodate the population explosion town planning had to be considered for the first time. Factories and public buildings had to be built on a greater scale than ever before, to give everyone the benefits of well designed buildings. New materials like concrete and steel became available, and amenities such as electric light, air conditioning and heating had to be incorporated into the new designs.

At the end of the nineteenth century, William Morris's Arts and Crafts movement advocated a return to craftsmanship, with the idea that a fresh, more relevant art would spring from an understanding of materials. The movement succeeded in creating design on rational principles and paved the way for a less rigid architecture. The influence of Art Nouveau was also far reaching for modern architecture and design. The free flowing organic style of Art Nouveau focused the possibilities of manipulating space and light, using the modern technology of cast iron and glass.

The skyscraper
In the US new architecture was gaining ground from the stimulus of new technology. However, the greatest and most revolutionary development for architecture in the twentieth century was a breakthrough in construction techniques. With the development of the skyscraper, the curtain wall and reinforced concrete, architects had the capability of building in a way never seen before. New materials such as rolled iron and steel became available during the nineteenth century. The Eiffel Tower, 1887-9, by Gustave Eiffel, an engineer by training, showed very clearly that the new materials could

Angelo Hornak

Above: A model of Vladimir Tatlin's monument to the 3rd International of 1920. The design, which was never realized, was intended as a piece of sculpture as well as a functional building (an assembly hall).

Below: The London factory of Hoover Ltd was designed by Wallis Gilbert and Partners. Built between 1933 and 1938, it is a fine example of the 'art deco' style and shows the influence of Le Corbusier.

be used to produce a new shape. A frame construction in a building, made of steel or reinforced concrete, meant that the weight of the building need not be carried by the walls. The curtain wall could be developed as a non-load-bearing external wall, which could be made in a variety of materials—including glass. A slender, light building utilizing floor space could now be built. The first skyscraper was built in Chicago in 1883; in New York, the Woolworth Building, with fifty-eight stories, appeared in 1912.

Frank Lloyd Wright
It was in Chicago that Frank Lloyd Wright (1867-1959), one of the greatest of the modern architects, built his Prairie series of houses in 1902-10. He revolutionized the house with this series, first in America and later internationally. His houses combined lighting, heating and construction to create a free open space. He abandoned the traditional box-like house by designing large sailing roofs over interconnected spaces in an open plan. He united outside and inside space by creating terraces extending out into the landscape. Frank Lloyd Wright used modern materials and methods of construction, but one of his main sources of inspiration was the traditional architecture of Japan. Wright's knowledge of engineering ensured that his Imperial Hotel in Tokyo, 1922, was one of the few buildings to survive the 1923 earthquake.

HOOVER LIMITED

Angelo Hornak

Left: The home of the Bauhaus school of design at Dessau, now in East Germany. Erected in 1926, the building was designed by Walter Gropius (1883-1969) and was one of the first masterpieces of modern architecture. It has an apparently free plan which is thoroughly controlled—the three major elements, the workshops, living quarters and studios, are divided into separate wings. The Bauhaus brought together artists, craftsmen and architects, and its teachers included the famous artists Paul Klee and Wassily Kandinsky.

Below: This chrome and leather chair was one of the best-known Bauhaus designs.

Left: The interior of the Guggenheim Museum in New York. Designed by Frank Lloyd Wright and built in 1959, its chief feature is a white concrete ramp which ascends in a spiral. This permits the display of paintings or sculptures in an uninterrupted sequence.

Paolo Koch

Elliott Erwitt—Magnum/John Hillelson Agency

Below: Falling Water (1936), Frank Lloyd Wright's famous house at Bear Run, Pennsylvania. It shows the fascination of modern architecture with space and movement. A solid, textured granite-like wall seems part of the mountains while huge spans of reinforced concrete hang over light and airy spaces.

Above: The presidential palace (1956-9) in Brasilia, the modern capital of Brazil. Along with all the public buildings in the new city, it was designed by Oscar Niemeyer (b.1907). A student of Le Corbusier, Niemeyer characteristically built this palace with its curving supports in front of a glass facade.

The German School

In Europe, Germany was the leader in the new styles of architecture. In 1907 an association of progressive manufacturers, architects, artists and writers was formed, called the *Deutscher Werkbund*. They were dedicated to the production of high quality industrial goods and buildings. One of the leading architects, Peter Behrens (1868-1940) designed a turbine factory in 1909 which incorporated steel frame construction and wholly glazed walls, which pointed the way for modern architecture.

The *Werkbund* wished to develop an art and architecture for the new age of machine dominance. It accepted machine production, and Behren's architectural work was chiefly in the industrial field. In 1911 his pupil, Walter Gropius (1883-1969), was co-designer of the first building built wholly to the new principles, the Fagus shoelace factory in Germany. This three storey building had a steel frame supporting the floors, with walls made entirely of steel and glass.

Behrens also had two other great pioneer architects working for him, Mies van der Rohe (1886-1969) and Charles-Edouard Jeanneret, known as Le Corbusier (1887-1966). Le Corbusier went on to work for Auguste Perret (1874-1954), a French architect, who was working using reinforced concrete, particularly in frame construction, an innovative design idea which made concrete a widely used material by all later architects.

The Bauhaus

In 1919, Walter Gropius formed a school of design, building and craftsmanship called the Bauhaus, which had a tremendous impact on all subsequent modern architecture and design. Gropius believed that a building should be designed as a whole—incorporating furniture and all the arts of architecture. The Bauhaus put this into practice by teaching two parallel courses, one devoted to the theories of design and form, and the other to the studies of craft and materials. The basic principles of the Bauhaus meant creating a well designed urban environment that would be pleasant to live in—the greatest possible contrast to the philanthropic 'charity dwellings' erected in the nineteenth century.

The school was closed by the Nazis in 1933, but the teaching of the Bauhaus school has remained one of the strongest influences on modern architecture and design.

The International Style

In 1917 the Dutch *De Stijl* group of artists, designers and architects came together to explore the new ideas of abstract art. The architects were also influenced by Frank Lloyd Wright. The expression of their designs was abstract, anti-natural forms, based on straight lines and flat planes.

By 1920, the city architect of Rotterdam, J. J. P. Oud (1890-1963), an architect of the De Stijl group, had developed a smooth white concrete style of building which became the symbol of an epoch. The culmination of these ideas was at an international exhibition of low cost housing in Stuttgart in 1927, when all the entries used this form of design. After this exhibition, the style, with its predominant white surfaces, cubic shapes and bands of horizontal windows was 163

called the *International Style*. The International Style was again seen at an exhibition in 1932 at the New York Museum of Modern Art, showing the work of Le Corbusier, Mies van der Rohe, Walter Gropius, Frank Lloyd Wright and others.

The International Style did not, however, continue its dominance into the next decade. Hitler in Germany and Stalin in Russia both 'abolished' modern architecture, and world-wide depression meant that little modern building was done.

Aalto's influence

After World War II, the leading architects were able to continue to develop their ideas. Among these were Hans Scharoun (1893-1972), a German architect who rebuilt the devastated centre of Berlin, and Alvar Aalto (1898-1976) of Finland. Aalto, one of the masters of the modern movement, had a love of natural materials, and his buildings reflect his concern for the people who will use them. His attitude was at odds with an emerging school of architecture, particularly popular in the USA, where form and architecture are important above all else, rather than a consideration of the requirements of the building.

The influence of Le Corbusier

One of the most profound influences of Le Corbusier was a concentration on the essential functions of a building. The culmination of this came with the work of the 'Brutalist' school which arose in the 1960s. The Brutalists saw a building as a programme of requirements. 164 The structure of a building was to be

Above: The idealistic movements of the 1920s were concerned with planning new cities for the machine age society. One of the leading writers on the subject was Le Corbusier, who designed Unité d'Habitations (shown here) in Marseilles. Built in 1952, it contains more than 300 dwellings, has shops in the middle stories and recreational facilities on the roof. It was envisaged as a village in the air and heralded post-war architecture.

Above: Sydney Opera House (1956-73). Designed by Jorn Utzon (b.1918), this beautiful sculptured building rises like sails over the sea. It is, however, functionally deficient, and some regard it as a costly white elephant.

Below: The chapel at Ronchamp (1956) is perhaps the most beautiful of all Le Corbusier's buildings. The machine style is modified, and geometrical abstraction gives way to a more fluid, sculptural style.

Above: The engineering block at Leicester University (1963). Designed by James Stirling (b.1926) and James Gowan (b.1923), this striking building has been one of the most influential in post-war Britain.

The exposed frame

Mies van der Rohe (1886-1969), who succeeded Gropius as director of the Bauhaus in 1930, emigrated to the US after the closure of the Bauhaus by the Nazis. Mies developed his style of architecture most fully in his work in the US. After settling in Chicago, he designed a series of buildings for the Illinois Institute of Technology (1940-50). The buildings, using light brick, glass and exposed steel frame, with a perfection of detail, have symmetrical facades, and present a cool, classic appearance. Mies went on to develop this in his Lake Shore Drive apartments in Chicago (1957), and the Seagram Building, New York (1958), with its distinctive bronze facing. Mies' use of the exposed metal frame—echoing the metal frame within—was as much a personal statement as was Le Corbusier's use of reinforced concrete. Mies spare style, summed up in his phrase 'Less is more', influenced architects all over the world.

In Britain, the 50s and 60s were characterized by a large amount of high standard design by municipal authorities. The London County Council built the Royal Festival Hall to mark the Festival of Britain in 1951. Stevenage New Town was started in 1953 as a result of the 1947 Planning Act—the first of several new towns in Britain. This municipal building came as a result of the ideas of the modern movement filtering through from before the war. System building, where all the components are prefabricated in a factory, was developed to provide new schools quickly. Architects and educationalists collaborated closely on what were the needs of a school.

austere in design, with services like pipes and air shafts left unconcealed.

The building which brilliantly expresses this philosophy of design is Le Corbusier's Unité d'Habitation at Marseilles (1947-52). This was a mass housing scheme which gave families privacy combined with maximum space, and achieved Le Corbusier's idea that houses are 'machines for living in'.

The heavy concrete proportions and dramatic roof of Unité are based on Le Corbusier's own system of proportion, called the *Modulor*, which he based on the human figure.

As early as 1922, Le Corbusier designed a plan for a city of three million inhabitants in high rise tower blocks. He used his modular system of proportion—based on the human body—to standardize constructional parts of his buildings, and reinforced concrete structures supported on struts gave greater space at ground level. All these ideas were brought together in his Unité d'Habitation. Le Corbusier's influence was considerable, and many of his ideas were incorporated in the architecture of the fifties and sixties. Eero Saarinen (1910-61) particularly absorbed these influences, as can be seen in his Dulles International Air Terminal (1958-62) with its freely curved roof, and careful consideration of human traffic.

Explosion of building

In the 60s and 70s architecture in Britain celebrated cheap energy and affluence with a rash of building. Universities expanded and became some of the leading patrons of modern architecture. School buildings and housing programmes abounded. But cities suffered because they were caught in the middle of a period of political and economic optimism, and pressures of increasing population and car ownership. New roads carved cities up, and high profits from land speculation nurtured an enormous amount of building, such as office and shopping centres, which owed less to the cities and their needs and more to profit motives.

In common with the general spirit of optimism, many architects considered they were building for a new society, recalling the idealism of the nineteen twenties, and disregarding the existing fabric of cities. Today there has been a reaction against this large scale, 'total plan' thinking, as architects became more aware of existing problems rather than future ideals.

The monumental style of architecture has been discarded. Architects have absorbed the current movement towards self-sufficiency, conservation and personal freedom, and are building on a smaller, more human scale. Designers like Buckminster Fuller (b.1895) have developed a series of structural systems for effective, cheap shelter, quick to erect and capable of covering large areas, known as geodesic domes. These and other similar ideas are being used by architects to solve the problems of shelter in the Third World.

Dr Georg Gerster/John Hillelson Agency

Transworld

Angelo Hornak

Towards Abstract Art

The seeds of modern art were sown in the early years of this century by groups of artists across Europe, who pioneered new and revolutionary attitudes to reality. The fast-developing techniques of photography were able to record the representational world so the artist, if he were to expand his horizons, had to look beyond perspective and three dimensions. This radical change of attitude heralded the advent of an art which no longer used the traditional language of painting to describe its aims. The conception of art since the Renaissance—the representation of reality in terms of form, colour, space and light—was now challenged and replaced by a new language of art that transformed the artist's attitude to the world around him.

The forerunners of this revolutionary abstract movement were a group of artists, working around the end of the nineteenth century, who were themselves in conflict with the art of Impressionism. They saw this movement, radical though it appeared at its birth, as furthering naturalistic attitudes, by recording every nuance of change in the natural world. These Post-Impressionists—Gauguin (1848-1903), Van Gogh (1853-1890), Seurat (1859-1891) and Cézanne (1839-1906)—all experimented with Impressionism but found its means too limited to describe their sensations.

Paul Cézanne, often called the father of Cubism, pioneered an approach to what he termed 'the motif' which sought to explore beyond external reality and describe the structure beneath the surface, and in his later works comes close to abstraction. Paul Gauguin's preoccupation with the two-dimensional quality of his painting, emphasizing with areas of flat, strong colour the decorative nature of the picture, pointed to the near-abstract 'pattern making' of the Art Nouveau movement. Vincent Van Gogh's torments were expressed by violent swirls of expressionistic brushwork which owe more to the artist's mental state than the natural world he described. Each of the Post-Impressionists distorted their vision of the world around them, and used it for expressive ends. The development of the theories and experiments of the Post-Impressionists brought abstraction nearer.

Next, in the early years of this century, came another step forward. *Les Fauves* (meaning literally 'wild beasts') led by Henri Matisse (1869-1954) and André Derain (1880-1954) concentrated on the exploitation of colour for expressive ends; by using pure colour in simplified forms, they employed colour as an end in its own right rather than as purely descriptive of form. The Fauvist movement was not based on theoretical concepts, was comparatively short-lived, and stands as a somewhat isolated period in the history of art. But in its 'abstraction' of colour, and its denial of the 'naturalism' of reality, it is a movement which was a definite influence on abstract art.

Below: *Lac d'Annecy* (1896) by Paul Cézanne (1839-1909). His genius was not recognized until his first big exhibition in 1895. In this later landscape he has used short, abrupt brush strokes to create an almost abstract representation of the material world. These later landscapes anticipate Cubism.

Above: *The Pool of London* (1906) by André Derain (1880-1954). This painting is typical of those produced by the Fauvist movement, which sought to liberate colour from its purely descriptive role. Here Derain, one of the leaders of the Fauvist movement, creates a strange world of green water and vivid boats.

Cubism and Picasso

Then, in 1907, a new movement in art was born. It gave a theoretical and artistic cohesion to the various strands which had been emerging from the developments of Post-Impressionism and Fauvism and was to have an immense impact on the art of the next generation. In the painting called *Les Demoiselles d'Avignon* (1907) by the young Spaniard Pablo Picasso (1881-1973) the new style was born. It was dubbed Cubism.

Based largely on the analytical vision of Cézanne's later painting, Picasso's painting also incorporates his discovery of the anti-naturalistic qualities of Primitive Art, such as African tribal masks. The harsh angularity and distortions of the painting were revolutionary in their impact and far-reaching in their influence. With the explosion of Cubism, led by Picasso and Georges Braque (1882-1963), the move away from representation was advancing rapidly.

The first phase of Cubism (known as 'Analytical') was characterized by the geometrical fragmentation of the subject and the distorted viewpoints adopted by the artist. Freed from the traditional method of translating reality into paint, and being restricted to a specific moment in time and a fixed viewpoint, the artist was now able to concentrate on arranging on the canvas to the new 'abstract' components of picture making. By juggling with the angular planes which constitute the 'architecture' of the painting, Picasso and Braque 'play' with the picture surface and arrive at a definite form of abstraction in this isolation of form from representation. As Picasso said, 'Cubism is an art

Below: *Les Demoiselles d'Avignon* (1907) by Pablo Picasso (1881-1973). Picasso's painting is the starting point for Cubism. It combined the lessons of Cézanne with the influence of African tribal masks to produce a fragmentation of the picture surface and the distortion of the poses which became typical of Cubist art.

Right: *Head* (1915) by Jacques Lipchitz (1891-1973). He attempted to interpret the Cubist theories of distortion into three dimensional sculptural forms.

Below right: *The Yellow Christ* (1889) by Paul Gauguin (1848-1903). His painting had a considerable influence on the Fauvists.

dealing primarily with form, and when a form is realized it is there to live its own life.'

The spread of Cubism
Artists all over Europe felt the impact of Cubism, although many adapted its theories in a highly personal fashion. The Russian artist Wassily Kandinsky (1866-1944) was one of the philosophers of the movement. Although he was mainly concerned with the underlying spirituality and metaphysical qualities of art, Kandinsky crystallized the pioneering abstractionist theories. In his famous treatise *Concerning the Spiritual in Art* (1912) he raises the question of the possibility of totally non-representational painting and, although at the time he had not freed himself wholly from representation, it is in these theories that his great influence lay.

In Italy, the Cubist movement influenced a group of young men under the leadership of the poet Filippo Marinetti (1876-1944), who was concerned with discovering a new art to reflect contemporary society. They called themselves the Futurists—rejecting the art of the past and heralding the future. Their manifesto in 1910 declared 'that a clean sweep should be made of all stale and threadbare subject matter in order to express the vortex of modern life—a life of steel, fever, pride and headlong speed.'

Beyond Cubism
The Futurists, too, were as influential in their theories as in their art itself, and nowhere more so than in Russia. The political ferment in that country in the years around World War I was strong, and the voice of the vociferous Futurists touched a chord in Russian artists. The early paintings of Kasimir Malevich (1878-1935) had already been influenced by the Futurists, and by 1915—adapting the geometric language of Cubism—he produced his first 'Suprematist' painting, *The Black Square*. Suprematist art, declared Malevich, 'found new symbols with which to render direct feelings.' In fact the symbols were the geometric square, triangle and circle. The theory Malevich worked on was that the reality of art was the sensational effect of colour itself. So, by juxtaposing a black square on a white ground, he claimed that the contact achieved was the basis of art. Ultimately he extended this theory to his famous *White Series*, where one white square is placed on another.

Also out of Suprematism grew the Constructivism movement around 1920, which was chiefly concerned with sculpture, architecture and theatre design. Originally it was intended to express the needs of a new socialist society using the techniques of mass production. The Constructivist Manifesto in 1920 announced: 'space and time are the only forms on which life is built and hence art must be constructed'.

Mondrian—the objective painter
In Holland towards the end of World War I a group was formed, which, much as Cubism had done ten years earlier, synthesized the experiments of the various schools of the previous decade. Representation had now broken down almost completely, and with the formation of *De Stijl* (literally 'style') which was also the name of the magazine produced by

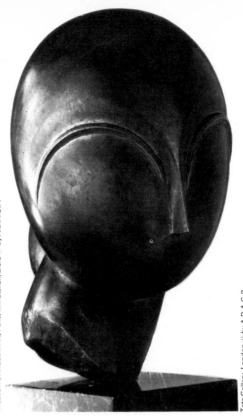

the group, a movement was born whose aims were totally abstract.

De Stijl was founded by Theo van Doesburg (1883-1931) and Piet Mondrian (1872-1944), and Mondrian was to become the painter who developed the objective conception of abstraction to its logical conclusions. Many of his theories were based on the ideas of the Dutch philosopher M. H. J. Schoenmaekers. Mondrian had been an early disciple of Cubism and had responded to the intellectuallism of its philosophy, and in his paintings searched to find an equivalent in paint for the universal truths of life. His method was to reduce the fundamental elements of a picture to the most simple shapes of square, oblong and cube and the primary colours of red, yellow and blue and contrasting white, black and grey.

For Mondrian a horizontal line signified tranquility and eventually death, a vertical line the forces of life, and the right angle signified positive and negative forces. With his experiments in these 'geometric balancing acts' Mondrian perhaps comes closest to the notion of pure abstract art. By this time other artists and other movements were at work developing the art of the next generation, an abstraction based on a far more subjective experience, rather than the objective eye, but using the same tools as abstract art.

Sculpture—the new influences

The revolutionary move to abstraction in painting was also reflected in the field of sculpture. From the break with late nineteenth century naturalism, epitomized by the work of Auguste Rodin (1840-1917) to the work of Henry Moore (b.1898), sculptors responded to the changes in the accepted portrayal of reality. Often developments in sculpture were closely related to the current art movement—sometimes with the painter working as sculptor, as with Picasso's Cubist sculpture. Cubism was also transformed into three-dimensional terms by Jacques Lipchitz (1891-1973).

The work of Constantin Brancusi (1876-1957) bridges the gap between representational and abstract sculpture. His earliest works still reflect a dependence on Rodin but steadily his work came closer to abstraction. In a work like *The Sleeping Muse* he begins to reduce the originally representational image to a near abstract 'essential' shape.

Brancusi opened the door for the work of Jean Arp (1887-1966), whose sculpture is abstract in its origins and treatment. Brancusi was still abstracting from 'something', but Arp created spontaneously from forms of growth like the egg or the sperm, emphasizing the organic quality of his shapes. This interest in natural forms has been crucial to the development of the two sculptors who perhaps most clearly represent abstraction today.

Both Barbara Hepworth's (1903-1974) and Henry Moore's preoccupation with organic forms and their ability to exploit such forms were the result of careful study and assimilation of the teachings of early twentieth century abstraction. In painting and sculpture, the theories, experiments and developments of abstraction in the years between 1905 and 1930 were crucial to the changes in the artist's interpretation of the world.

Above: *Danaide* (1913) by Constantin Brancusi (1876-1957). He rejected the romanticism of Rodin and the intellectualism of the Cubists. Brancusi's abstraction is based on the elimination of any irrelevant detail to achieve a spareness of form and a restraint of expression.

Above left: *Young Girl with a Guitar* (1913) by Georges Braque (1882-1963). In this painting Braque concentrates on the almost totally abstract effect created by using Cubism. The picture surface is made up of a series of planes, set at angles to each other, greatly distorting the subject of the painting.

Far left, above: *Human Concretion* (1934) by Jean Arp (1887-1966). He tried to 'make forms grow' and his sculpture shows his preoccupation with the processes of natural growth and organic forms, so his work looks like a natural object, such as a pebble. The sensuous curves of this highly polished marble sculpture are full of sexual feelings.

Far left, below: *Composition with Red, Yellow and Blue* (1921), by Piet Mondrian (1872-1944). He was the greatest exponent of early abstract art. He used the lesson of abstract art to evolve his austere, geometric compositions, based on straight lines and right angles representing the forces of nature.

Left: *Suprematist Composition* (1915) by Kasimir Malevich (1878-1935). Malevich developed the idea that the reality of art lay in the sensational effect of colour. He created a non-representational art as early as 1913, using the geometric language of the square, triangle and the circle, with a juxtaposition of colour. His influence on graphic design was considerable.

Museum of Modern Art, Paris/Nimatallah/Ziolo © by A.D.A.G.P.

Tate Gallery, London © by A.D.A.G.P.

Stedelijk Museum

Paul in Harlequin costume (1924) by Pablo Picasso. Picasso was a dominant influence on early 20th century painting. He, in turn, had been influenced by Toulouse-Lautrec and shared certain of his favourite subjects – among them clowns, acrobats and dancers.

Picasso

Picasso is probably the best known twentieth century artist. From the early 1900s until his death in 1973, he was a champion of avant garde art, being hailed as a genius by some yet denounced as a charlatan by others. His work is popularly thought of as abstract, but in fact he scarcely ever painted a purely abstract picture.

No collection of modern painting is considered worthwhile without several of his works, and as a result of this demand he became fabulously wealthy. He reputedly bought a château with just one picture. But throughout his long career he never stopped working, producing literally thousands of paintings, drawings, ceramics and sculptures.

Pablo Ruiz y Picasso was born in Malaga in the south of Spain in 1881. His father was an artist who earned his living as a museum curator and teacher. As a child Picasso showed exceptional talent: there is a story that his father, seeing him at work, handed him his own palette and brushes and vowed never to paint again.

In 1900 Picasso visited Paris for a month and the following year he went there to live. The young Spaniard thus thrust himself into the centre of the artistic world. Many of the Impressionists were still alive, but there was a strong move away from their work and Picasso's early works show him responding to a bewildering number of competing styles.

In the next year Picasso established his first entirely personal style. This is known as his 'blue period', for the paintings were done largely in blue *monochrome* (different shades of the same colour), and as subjects he most often chose the poor and destitute. Picasso was indebted at this period to the Symbolists, and through them to nineteenth century Romantic painting.

In 1904 Picasso left Barcelona for the last time and went to live permanently in Paris at the notoriously bohemian Montmartre tenement known as the '*bateau lavoir*' inhabited by many other struggling young artists. He became close friends both with Guillaume Apollinaire, the poet and writer on art, and the playwright Alfred Jarry, whose play *Ubu Roi* is considered to be the beginning of avante garde theatre. Picasso was also now living with Fernande Olivier, who was to be his mistress for some years. She described him at this time: 'small, black, thick-set, restless, disquieting, with eyes dark, profound, strange, almost staring . . . half bohemian, half workman in his dress'.

Picasso's next style, called his 'rose period', continues the theme of the outcast from society but in a much more positive way. The outcasts he now painted were not the starving of the slums but circus people—acrobats, harlequins and their families. The sentimentality of the blue period remains, but an enthusiasm for the life of the mysterious nomads replaces the melancholy.

The birth of Cubism

In 1906 a major exhibition of the works of Cézanne excited great interest in Paris. Cézanne was the Post-Impressionist painter who had made the most decisive break with the naturalistic aims of Impression-

Above: *La Vie*, 1903. Picasso first began working in a new, entirely original style, known as his 'blue period' in 1903. *La Vie* is the most ambitious and complex painting of his 'blue period', owing much to Gauguin and the Symbolists. The picture expresses the cycle of life in a particularly depressing way. A young couple confront a mother and child, their nudity emphasizing their poverty and emaciation. Behind this main group are images of age, at first a couple embracing, and finally at the bottom of the picture, the desolation of old age.

ism in the 1880s and 1890s. Cézanne's paintings distorted reality in accordance with purely artistic criteria.

It was as a result of Cézanne's influence that Picasso was to paint *Les Demoiselles d'Avignon* (see page 1953), a landmark in modern art. The painting started out as an interior of a brothel, with several nude figures, but concern with the subject was rapidly forgotten as Picasso worked on it. The picture is entirely two-dimensional—an arrangement of distorted figures and indeterminate shapes representing a wall and a curtain. Picasso eventually abandoned work on the project and turned the canvas to the wall, but this did not matter. He had made an important discovery and his close associates had seen it.

Picasso and his friend Georges Braque (1882-1962) then set about exploring the

new possibilities. They led the movement that came to be known as *Cubism*. During the next few years Picasso and Braque worked as one artist. By fragmenting the visual image of what they painted, distorting surface and shape into a sequence of interlocking faces of colour and tone, they demolished the first convention of painting since the Renaissance—that of presenting an illusion. In this they claimed they were *more* rather than less realistic, they were getting closer to the object by emphasizing the restructured picture surface rather than an imitation or two-dimensional replica of it.

By 1914 the two artists were drifting apart. The final separation came when war was declared and Braque was drafted into the French army. Gradually Picasso's work changed. On the one hand, he pro- 171 duced large Cubist compositions in broad, flat areas of colour. On the other, he began a series of realistic drawings, usually portraits in the manner of Ingres, the ultra-conservative nineteenth century classicist.

In 1917 Picasso was persuaded by Jean Cocteau to produce the stage designs for the ballet *Parade*, with music by Erik Satie and choreography by Diaghilev. In 1918 he married Olga, one of the dancers in the ballet and soon embarked on a life of high luxury, dressing elegantly, living in expensive hotels and attending the major functions of the social calendar. Braque, returning from the war, was shocked and stayed away.

Picasso was no longer young. He was 38 years old and a successful painter settling down to enjoy the fruit of his labours. Slowly, his work became bound by the formulae he had invented, with still-lifes in two-dimensional Cubist style predominating. He also produced a series of deliberately classical visions of fauns and nymphs, and a series of monumental women, again strongly classical and quite different to the Cubist works. Picasso never lost his energy and enthusiasm for work, but in this period he did lose his sense of direction.

New influences

After this inspirational low point in his career he came into contact with the Surrealists in 1924, and responded with vigour. The Surrealist influence made Picasso create according to the dictates of his subconscious mind and vision. Indeed, in 1925 Picasso's still-life style was transformed with the addition of a

Right: *Three Women at the Fountain*, 1921. Picasso, now an internationally famous artist, experimented with a number of conflicting styles. One of the most surprising for the *enfant terrible* of Cubism was a series of classical or monumental women. In this painting, Picasso is openly acknowledging his debt to the art of the past, specially to three-dimensional antique sculpture. His monumental women express Picasso's vision of a past age.

Below right: *Three Dancers*, 1925, represents Picasso's response to the Surrealist movement, after a period of artistic stagnation. *Three Dancers* is a picture of terrifying force and intensity. The jagged shapes twist and turn in violent movement. Flesh is redefined to become a saw blade, and a face becomes a grimacing mask. Distortion of reality was now common in Picasso's art, but here distortion is employed for a new purpose—to express extreme horror.

Below: *Daniel Henry Kahnweiler*, 1910. By 1910 Picasso and Braque had revolutionized European painting with *Cubism*—the first step in abstract art. The Cubist technique fragmented and distorted the image in accordance with a purely artistic interpretation. In this portrait the features of the sitter, together with his watch-chain and sculpture collection, are just discernable. The emphasis, however, is on abstraction rather than a portrait likeness.

symbolic and expressive aspect. In the same year, he produced one of his greatest works called *Three Dancers*. Contrasting with the static works of previous years, the dancers twist and turn in a violent frenzy, and the figure on the left has a distorted face which must be one of the most horrific nightmarish images in art.

This new approach kept Picasso busy for several years. In 1930 he began work on the *Vollard Suite*, an enormous series of drawings for a limited edition book commissioned by the artistic entrepreneur Ambrose Vollard. This monumental work was finally completed in 1936. They show Picasso assimilating and combining numerous influences, for while many are in his lyrical classical style, others have the tense expressionism that he learned from the Surrealists. The mood of the drawings, too, includes many contrasts—lyrical, violent and erotic.

Guernica and political protest

Later in the 1930s, Picasso took an entirely new turn. He became a political figure. In 1936, with the onset of the Spanish Civil War, Picasso exhibited his works in Spain in support of the Republican Government. In 1937 he agreed to produce a major work to represent Spain at the International Exhibition in Paris.

The picture that resulted is perhaps his most famous: *Guernica*. This commemorates the bombing of the ancient Basque capital of Guernica by German aircraft in the service of the rebel fascist government of Franco. *Guernica* was an immensely self-conscious undertaking.

Despite the political message, the symbolism remains Picasso's own. We see a bull and an anguished horse among the torn and terrified victims of the atrocity. The work shows Picasso using his own stylistic language in a new direction—to express outrage.

During the World War II, Picasso stayed in occupied France. This was a difficult and frustrating time for him, for his work had been denounced as decadent by the Nazis and he was an open opponent of fascism. At the end of the war in 1945 he joined the Communist Party.

Picasso's influence

It has been held that Picasso's genius could do no wrong, that every work was a masterpiece. Such an uncritical approach is no longer accepted and it is now recognised that for some of his career Picasso was a painter without direction.

His successful periods came in response to stimuli outside himself—love affairs, other artists or new surroundings. The Communist Party, however, did not have the same effect; it was too impersonal for his highly subjective and individualistic art. More and more, he turned to the art of the past in his later years, producing pastiches or reworkings in his own manner of the Old Masters such as Titian, Velasquez, El Greco. It is as if they are works by a competent imitator of Picasso's style.

Picasso lived to be 92, remaining firmly in the public eye to the last. For 50 years he had dominated the artistic scene, influencing scores of younger artists. Possibly more than any other artist in history, he had broken down the barriers of the artistic convention, and with extraordinary versatility he showed that there was always something new to be achieved.

Above: *Guernica*, 1937, one of the best known images in 20th century art. Painted by Picasso as a propaganda attack on Franco's fascist Spain, to mark the bombing and destruction of the town of Guernica by German aircraft in 1937. The picture is without colour, the monochrome adding to the expression of anguish and outrage effected by the distorted shapes of terror and death.

Left: *Las Meninas*, 1957, a version of Velazquez's 17th century masterpiece. For all its artistic mastery, the painting looks more like an imitation Picasso.

Below left: *The Mirror*, 1932. In 1932 Picasso began an affair with 17-year-old Marie Therese Walter, inspiring one of his most enthusiastic bursts of artistic activity. In *The Mirror*, Picasso's dominant theme is one of eroticism, portraying the model's face and breasts and the reflection of her buttocks.

Below: Picasso, probably the world's richest and most famous artist, in his workshop at Mougins, France, in 1971.

Developments in Modern Art

At the beginning of the twentieth century, Paris was the centre of the art world. The Impressionist rebellion against academic painting had triumphed, declaring the subjective, visual impressions of the artist to be the subject for the greatest art. Indeed, the force of the rebellion generated by the Impressionists and post-Impressionists set the style for subsequent artists, and opened the way for the new artistic movements of *Expressionism*, *Futurism*, *Surrealism*, and the 'anti-art' of *Dadaism*.

The new generation of artists broke away from the Impressionists' fleeting vision of light and shade, and established the artist's own interpretation as the subject for expression. To achieve this they followed one of two basic approaches. Paul Cézanne (1839-1906) described how the artist must first study the object of his painting and then paint the 'reality' of the subject which lay beneath the surface. The result in Cézanne's work—which had more influence on the development of twentieth century art than that of any other artist—is a structured, balanced image in which the abstract, compositional quality of the painting is predominant.

The alternative approach was that of Paul Gauguin (1848-1903), who concentrated on the expressive qualities of design, drawing heavily on the example of Japanese prints. It also allowed much freer rein to the artist's emotions. Gauguin described how he had produced a large canvas depicting an imaginary Polynesian scene in rich, broad areas of colour. Afterwards, he 'discovered' the meaning of the idea and called the picture *From where do we come? Who are we? Where are we going?* The painting is not a representation of what Gauguin actually saw; it is a representation of what he *felt*. Cézanne painted what he *thought*.

Cézanne's revolutionary ideas provide a link between Impressionism and both Cubism and abstract art in general, the art which came to dominate Paris. Although Gauguin's art was firmly based in nineteenth century Romanticism and Symbolism, it pointed forward to such self-styled 'modern' movements as Expressionism, Futurism and Surrealism.

Expressionism

Expressionism, as a label, can be applied to paintings from the early years of the century right up to the 1950s. It is not the title of a specific group as much as a general term applied to a succession of artists. The Expressionist painter will deliberately distort the shape of the objects he depicts in order to emphasize the emotions he wishes to express in his work, and will intensify their colour to reinforce the exaggerated effect.

Edvard Munch (1863-1944) is often considered to be the first true Expressionist. A Norwegian, he had considerable influence, particularly in Germany. A neurotic and miserable man with a profound fear of women, he allowed his works to express an introspective consciousness of individual isolation. One of

Munch Museet, Oslo

Above: *The Cry*, by Edvard Munch, 1893. This is one of the great paintings of Expressionism. The dramatic colouring and powerful swirling shapes echo the nameless horror in *The Cry*. This evocation of emotion through extreme forms and colour became the dominant theme of Expressionism. Munch's work reflects his unhappy neurotic life and the far-reaching social and economic changes in his native Scandinavia—also observed by the dramatists Ibsen and Strindberg.

Right: *Maria Aegyptica*, by Emil Nolde. It was painted while Nolde was a member of the first German Expressionist group *Die Brücke* (The Bridge) in 1912. Nolde, religious and introspective, painted many biblical scenes, including this interpretation of the whore-saint, revelling with fishermen. The grimacing faces, harsh colours and rough technique add up to a grotesque and uncompromising image.

Federico Arborio Mella

his most famous works, *The Cry* of 1893, concentrates on a single terrified figure, his cry echoed in the brightly coloured sky and swirling landscape. Munch had written in his diary in 1892, 'I stopped and leaned against the railings, dead tired, and I looked at the flaming clouds that hung over the blue-black fjord and the city like blood and a sword. My friends walked on. I stood there, trembling with fright. And I felt a loud, unending scream piercing nature.' The freedom to paint such an intensely personal experience became a basic tenet of Expressionism— while the distorted forms and garish colours became its method.

The first Expressionist group gathered at Dresden in 1905. Known as *Die Brücke* (The Bridge), they were superficially similar to the Fauves in Paris in their use of brilliant colour. While the Fauves were exploring colour as a means towards giving pictures a compositional unity, the young artists of *Die Brücke* wanted colour to have a symbolic meaning as well.

Their works were strikingly original and the contrasts between them are almost more apparent than the similarities. Emil Nolde (1867-1956), for example had a particularly personal vision, painting at this stage of his career a series of religious subjects. He went on to concentrate on landscapes, in which violent and unharmonious colours often create an intensely forbidding atmosphere.

By 1911, the impetus was passing to another Expressionist group, this time in Munich. It was known as *Der Blaue Reiter* (The Blue Rider) after an earlier picture by one of the founders, Wassily Kandinsky (1866-1944). Kandinsky was a Russian, who moved to Munich, giving up a career in law at the age of 30. His intellectual training encouraged him to define his abstract approach to art. In 1908 he produced a water colour that had no representational content whatever. After 1910 he produced a number of abstract paintings in a style which he called 'non-objective', and with these he demonstrated that colour and form could be expressive in themselves. His approach

to the symbolism of colour was relatively precise, particular colours representing specific emotional aspects of experience— blue, for example, is peaceful, yellow is brash.

Der Blaue Reiter also included several artists of note, one of the most daring being Franz Marc (1880-1916). His main interest was in nature, with animals (particularly blue horses) featuring in his landscapes. *The Destiny of Animals* of 1913 demonstrates his intention to investigate the soul of nature, expressing it in an image of aggressively combined form and colour.

While Expressionism is usually associated with Germany, individual artists were to be found pursuing similar paths in Paris. The French artist Georges Rouault (1871-1958) was connected with the Fauves but kept apart from their aesthetic theories, preferring to paint prostitutes and clowns in his bold and dramatic manner. Later, his religious temperament came to the fore and he produced a series of saints and Passion scenes. The Italian

Above: *The Three Judges* (1937-8) by Georges Rouault, a painter who rejected the abstract approach of most modern French painters in favour of Expressionism. Many of his paintings have the intensity and technique of stained glass with their black outlines.

Above right: *Landscape with Church,* Wassily Kandinsky, 1913. The intellectual leader of the German Expressionists, Kandinsky led the way to abstraction through his writings and theories on colour. Here, the bright colours of the landscape express his joy in his own vision of the scene, and his lack of interest in its actual appearance.

Right: Detail of *Dynamism of a Cyclist,* Umberto Boccioni, 1913. One of the leading Futurist painters and theorists, Boccioni produced Futurist paintings which typically represented physical or mechanical force. In this painting, the forms are broken up to express movement.

Hans Hinz/Kunstmuseum Basle

the Futurists wished to symbolize movement and progress—the static, aesthetic searchings of the Cubists were quite alien to them.

World War I broke up the existing groups; some of their number joined the army and several, including Marc and Boccioni were killed. Some took refuge in neutral Switzerland, grouping at Zurich in particular. It was here that the movement known as *Dadaism* was born. Dadaism was out to shock, adopting the motto of the anarchist thinker Bakunin, 'Destruction is also creation'.

Much of what they produced was theatrical, calculated merely to outrage. Marcel Duchamp (b.1887), for example, added a mustachioed version of the *Mona Lisa* to his attack on establishment art. As the international Dadist movement split up in the years after the war, two major trends emerged, corresponding to the two main approaches to art in the twentieth century. On the one hand, artists such as Duchamp merged into, and became leading figures in, the abstract movement. On the other, Surrealism was

Above: *Fate of Animals,* (1913) by Franz Marc, a leading member, with Kandinsky, of the German Expressionist group *Der Blaue Reiter* (The Blue Rider). Inspired by a biblical verse in the Apocalypse, Marc created this most passionate of all his paintings, showing animal life in the forest attacked but unafraid. Marc used colour symbolically to create his animals. He was fascinated by nature, and tried to show 'the soul of the animal to imagine its perceptions . .'

Right: *Nude* by Amedeo Modigliani, 1917. The Italian-born Modigliani provided a link between Expressionism and abstract painting in France. He absorbed the influences of African sculpture, Cubism and Expressionism to create in his sculpture and paintings a vivid portrayal of the elegant, sensuous beauty of his subjects. Modigliani led a wild bohemian life in Paris, being handsome and addicted to drink and drugs.

Amedeo Modigliani (1884-1920), working in Paris, also produced Expressionist works although he leant towards the abstractions of the Cubists.

The Futurists and Dadaism

In Italy a decisive contribution to the development of modern art was made by the *Futurists*. This flamboyant and aggressive group of artists put more importance on manifestos than any other. The poet Filippo Tommaso Marinetti published the first in 1909 and this was followed in 1910 by *The Manifesto of the Futurist Painters*, produced by the artist Umberto Boccioni (1882-1916). These documents proclaimed in grand rhetorical style the Futurist intention to demolish the 'tyranny' of harmony and good taste. The Futurists declared that they were proud to be called madmen, that everything must change, that everything was in constant motion and this was what the artist must represent. 'We proclaim . . . that universal dynamism must be rendered as dynamic sensation; that movement and light destroy the substance of objects'.

In this, they were self-consciously modern. They demanded that the factory, the machine and the technology of industrial society be introduced into the ivory tower of art. The result in painting was images of flickering, dynamic movement in brash, expressive colours. Boccioni's *Dynamism of a Cyclist* of 1913, a garish, fragmented image, really does create a feeling of intense movement and excitement. As with some types of Expressionism, this is not unlike Cubism in the breaking up of the form of the traditional, realistic image. But the intention was again quite different, for

176

Snark/Courtauld Institute Galleries, London

born. For abstract artists, the emphasis was on conscious thought, for the Surrealists only personal experience counted.

Surrealism

The word *Surrealism* was coined in 1917 by the writer Guillaume Apollinaire in the title of a play. In 1919 André Breton used it to describe his experiments with writing, recording on paper everything that came into his head with no thought or organization whatever. In 1920 he invited the Dadists to Paris and by 1922 quite a few of them had gathered around him, publishing the *First Surrealist Manifesto* in 1924. In this, the influence of the psychoanalysis of Sigmund Freud is clearly found. The emphasis was not to be on the artist's conscious expression of the world, but on the *unconscious*. In the spontaneous outpouring of imagery from the deepest recesses of the mind, a special hidden reality would be revealed and the artist (and through him the viewer of the Surrealist picture) would experience the therapeutic benefits of the release.

Philip Halsman/John Hillelson Agency

Snark/ · by A.D.A.G.P. Paris 1977

Left: *The Human Condition*, René Magritte, 1934. A Belgian-born Surrealist, Magritte's haunting paintings dislocate everyday experiences. In this painting, Magritte portrays an enigma, the painting on the easel allowing us to see the landscape behind it exactly. His Surrealist vision is based on reality. 'We must never at any price, depart from the reality of the element which has delivered up its secret to us.'

Above: Salvador Dali typically flamboyant, a style he set in the 1920s and continues to the present day. Dali, always out to shock, delivered a lecture in Paris in 1925 wearing a suit of armour, with his foot in a bucket of goat's milk. It is easy to ignore his art in the face of such clowning. The most capricious of Surrealist painters, he has created many dream-like images in his early work, but in later years he returned to representational art.

In painting, the result was a variety of powerful individual styles, and Surrealism has proved to be one of the most durable modern movements.

However, Surrealism did change. In 1925, Breton added social criticism to its spontaneity, stressing the need in art for a moral purpose. In 1929 he declared a formal alliance with Marxism and was supported in this by many Surrealist painters.

The name of Salvador Dali (b.1901) is synonymous with Surrealism for most people. This is not a view supported by the Surrealists themselves. According to Breton, 'Dali insinuated himself into the Surrealist movement in 1929' and was always guilty of plagiarism, sentimentality and vulgarity. Whatever the truth of this, Dali's images of sunlit deserts littered with melting clocks have an immediate familiarity that must result from something more than the artist's blatant showmanship.

It has become possible to see the patterns emerging in the art of the first four decades of the twentieth century. Before, it seemed that a mass of competing, contradictory styles existed in a state of perpetual excitement and upheaval. Now, it is clear that the two tendencies which have dominated Western art for centuries were still present albeit beneath the surface. On the one side, intellectual, methodical study led Cubists and abstract painters to search for the ideals of Classical harmony. On the other, the spontaneous, expressive capabilities of the individual was stressed by Expressionists, Futurists and Surrealists in the search for personal truth in interpreting the visual world.

Post-war Art

The art of the post-war period reflects the rapid changes in the world and has led to correspondingly fast alterations in the artists' perception of reality. These changes have often resulted in very controversial works, which may appear to many people totally unrelated to art or to reality. Only by examining the period as a whole, and by accepting that the artists are questioning the whole meaning of art, rather than the forms it takes, can we gain any understanding of contemporary art, particularly in its more eccentric forms.

By 1914 abstract art and the *ready made* (from objects readily to hand), were in existence; in 1917 Marcel Duchamp (1887-1968) entered *Fountain*, one of his ready mades, into an art exhibition. It was an ordinary mass-produced urinal which he had signed 'R. Mutt'. Defending his action Duchamp wrote 'Whether Mr Mutt with his own hands made the fountain or not has no importance. He *chose* it. He took an ordinary article of life, placed it so that its useful significance disappeared under the new title and point of view—created a new thought for that object'.

Of equal significance to post-war art were the ideas of the Surrealists who had in the 1920s and 1930s asserted the importance of the subconscious mind and therefore of chance, the irrational and the absurd.

Fired by these ideas, the artists of the *New York School* evolved an art which seeks to communicate mankind's innermost drives and experience. The movement developed during the 1940s and can

Below: A detail from *Convergences* **(1952), by Jackson Pollock.** The painting's content is open to question—a typical example of *Abstract Expressionism*. There is no focal point, no reference to the visible world, the spectator follows the trails of colour built up in layers, as the work came into being.

Right: *Corps de Dame* **(1950), Jean Dubuffet (b.1901).** In the post-war years, artists explored the possibilities of art through intuition. Dubuffet 'discovered' the form of a figure in the intuitive marks which he made on paper, thus breaking out of the conventions of artistic good taste.

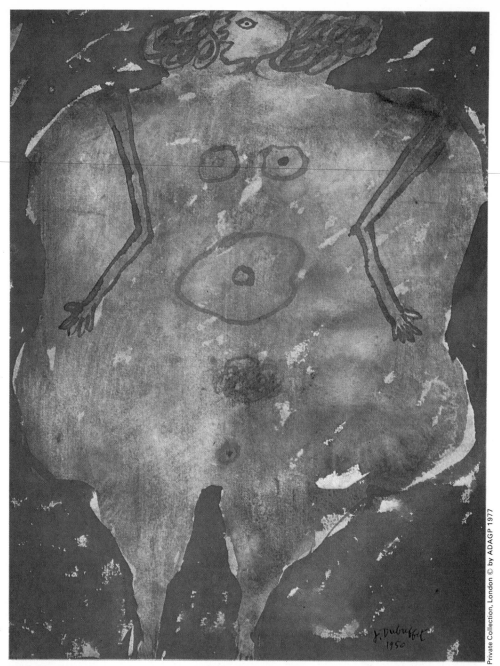

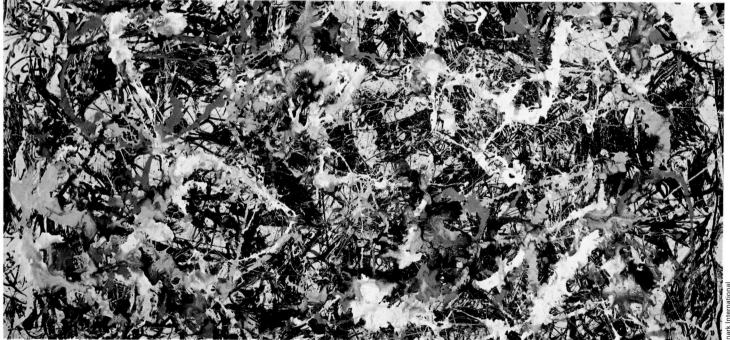

be divided into two groups: *Abstract Expressionism*, seen in the work of Jackson Pollock (1912-56), and *Colour Field Painting*, seen in Mark Rothko's work (1903-70). Pollock created his paintings by using an unstretched canvas laid on the floor, and sticks dipped in paint, which he could then dribble freely into the canvas as he moved all the way round it. Pollock had thus found a way of establishing closer contact with his work, thereby freeing his subconscious from the constraints which a traditional brush and easel would have placed on him. He could, as he said 'literally be *in* the painting'. Pollock's work became the result of a vital encounter between artist and canvas, so his art asserts the importance of spontaneous impulse, the *experience* of painting itself. In a sense its subject is the act of creation.

Rothko's work, on the other hand, is also abstract, but the canvas is stained with colour so that the paintings have an 'all-over' effect which defies analysis into relationships between their parts. Their scale is only *just* too large for us to reach the sides or top, so when viewing a Rothko we have the feeling that we are being absorbed by it.

Environmental art
During the 1950s artists, such as Robert Rauschenberg (b.1925) via his *Assemblages*, took further the role of art as consciousness-raising, by including objects from the everyday world into their works. For instance, one of Rauschenberg's paintings, abstract expressionist in style, included a radio; others are free-standing, consisting of apparently incongruous objects assembled by the artist. These works try to make us more aware of our environment *and* of the narrow line which divides the rational and the irrational. They free our minds from considering our world as fixed and immutable.

One of the developments of the use of assemblage is the breaking-down of barriers between sculpture and painting. In the sense that assemblages are three-

Above: *Marilyn* (1967), Andy Warhol (b.1930). Part of a series produced by pop artist Warhol, who uses the techniques and images of mass culture without comment.

Above right: *Just What Is It That Makes Today's Homes So Different. So Appealing?* (1956), Richard Hamilton (b.1922). Using *collage* (building up the picture by gluing on pre-existing images), Hamilton creates a work which is part criticism, part admiration for the affluent society.

Right: *Monogram* (1959), Robert Rauschenberg (b.1925). His mixture of a stuffed goat girdled by a tyre is calculated to shock, demonstrating the post-war artists' use of disparate objects to create a new art.

dimensional, they can be called sculptures; yet none of the traditional materials or working methods of the sculptor have been used. Post-war sculptors themselves have redefined their work, in terms of their working methods and materials. David Smith (1906-65) extended the boundaries of sculpture in the 1950s by making works from welded metal strips, so making us aware of the landscape which we see through the gaps between the metal of the works themselves. Others, working from a similar impetus to assemblage artists, used the 'junk' of industrial society as material for sculptures. John Chamberlain (b.1927), for instance, makes his works from parts of wrecked cars which he welds together and then paints. His working method of welding is close to that of modern industry, but his use of wrecked cars reminds us of the inherent dangers of the products of society, while the fact that he transmutes this wreckage via paint and the balancing of forms refutes conventional notions of beauty.

The sculptor Anthony Caro (b.1924) has more recently pursued the implications of David Smith's work, making elegant sculptures from ready-made steel parts normally used in industry, which he welds together and sometimes paints a

uniform bright colour. These parts are in themselves slender, though the size of the sculpture is often large. Usually placed in outdoor settings, they have the effect of defining the surrounding space, rather than displacing it, as traditional sculptures do. So again we have an art which makes us more aware of ourselves and our environment.

Environmental art soon took assemblage further again with artists transforming whole rooms into works of art. Edward Keinholz (b.1927), for example, created *Roxy's* (1961), evoking a room in a brothel, with ordinary, rather tatty furniture complete with juke-box playing 1940s tunes, juxtaposed with such surreal objects as a clothed tailor's dummy whose head is replaced by a boar's skull. This evocation of the sordidness of a brothel derives its power from the mixing of the mundane with the incongruous, and is harder hitting because we walk around *in* it rather than being mere outsiders.

Happenings
The desire to involve the spectator and so further dissolve the division between art and life found its consummate expression in the *Happenings* of the late 1950s and early 1960s. In 1959 Alan Kaprow (b.1927) 179

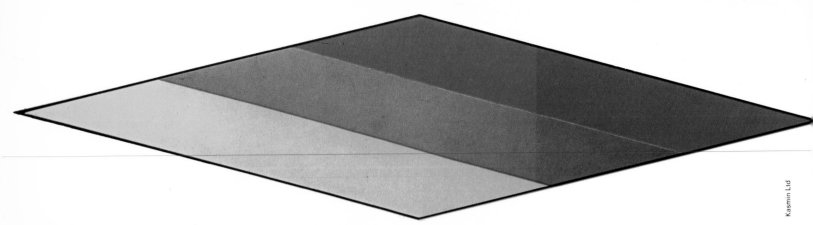

Above: *Bright Ray* (1926), Kenneth Noland (b.1924), is typical of *Post-Painterly Abstraction* in its use of colour and flat canvas, with the colours the dominant force. Noland also experimented with the size and shape of his canvas, creating large paintings where the spectator's eye is surrounded by colour, while the lack of neutral areas or focal points ensure a response to the colour.

Left: *Beth Chaf* (1959-60), Morris Louis (1912-62). One of his series of 'Veils' paintings where he gradually stained the canvas with acrylic paint, without using visible brushstrokes, building up layers of colour. The 'Veils' are of room height, so that they have an overpowering effect and the viewer of the painting becomes engrossed in the experience of colour and size.

presented *13 Happenings in 6 parts* which consisted of three 'rooms' in a gallery whose walls were covered with polythene sheeting, slide projections and various collages. The audience was instructed to change seats several times, thus moving through the 'rooms'. Various actions occurred: two people painted each side of a canvas, another squeezed oranges, an 'orchestra' of toy instruments was to take part. The Happenings differ from theatrical performances in that they have no logical plot and there is no division between participants and audience. The audience extracts its own meaning from the work. By being ephemeral they remove the possibility of their financial exploitation, and by the same token they cannot be reproduced in books or other places, thus stressing the importance of *experiencing* art at first hand.

Pop Art

Modern society is flooded with mass-produced standardized imagery, which has been thought of as too vulgar or mundane to be included within the domain of fine art. The significance of *Pop Art* is that it adopted the artefacts of popular culture as its subject matter, thus forcing us to recognize the effects such culture has on us. Roy Lichtenstein (b.1923) for instance, takes images from pulp comics and meticulously copies them onto canvas on a gigantic scale, complete with the coloured dots used by modern industrial colour printing techniques, as in *Whaam!*, 1963. The effect is to make us look at these images in a new light. Pop Art, by its nature, is possibly the most accessible form of contemporary art, and invites us to look at other artefacts, such as soup cans or even bricks, with less prejudice as to what is art and what is not.

Other artists, such as Richard Hamilton (b.1922), take the trappings of modern consumer society as their subject matter: cars, tinned food, television sets. Previous artists had *interpreted* everyday surroundings but Pop Art used the existing imagery of mass culture. The artist and film-maker Andy Warhol (b.1930) reproduced photographic news images repeated over and over again, using modern photo-mechanical silk screening techniques. These have often been of disturbing subjects like *Race Riots* (1964). By re-producing the images on such a mechanical and dead pan manner, he is pointing to the anaesthetizing effect which the over-exposure of tragic events by the media has on us. Also the work need not be carried out by the artist himself: echoing Duchamp, Warhol locates the importance of the creative act in the ideas or concepts behind the work rather than in his ability to execute it.

Minimal Art

Meanwhile, abstraction had continued to be explored in the works of artists such as Morris Louis (1912-62) and Barnett Newman (b.1905), who painted canvases which were solely concerned with one of the essential elements of painting—colour —and the flatness of the canvas. Known as *Post-Painterly Abstraction*, it stripped art of all extra-visual meaning, asserting the work's right to exist simply by virtue of *being*, as a complete physical object.

In *Minimal Art*, which developed along-side Pop, this concern with reducing art to bare essentials merged with the conceptual aspects of Pop. For instance in *Cuts*, 1967, Carl André (b.1932) used identical pre-cast concrete blocks. These completely covered the gallery floor except for some rectangles which were cut out by removing, in each case, 30 blocks forming differently proportioned but identically sized rectangles. On reflection, its appeal is to the mind rather than to the emotions. The use of the non-expressive form of the bricks ensured that the work simply exists, not making references to anything outside of itself. The anonymous factory-made materials used might lead us to question the trading of art as a valuable, exclusive commodity. Also the responsibility of the work's owner is emphasized as it is dismantled after being exhibited and will alter each time according to the size and shape of the room in which it is shown.

Conceptual Art

Duchamp was one of the first artists to raise the possibility of art created from existing objects. Since the late 1960s this concept has been taken a step further, to an examination of the systems, activities and structures which make up society. This has become known as *Conceptual Art* because of its focus on the concepts behind the works, rather than on the beauty of the physical shape which they take. Because of its all-embracing aims, the forms of Conceptual Art vary enormously. For example, *Les Poseuses* (1975) by Hans Christoph Haacke (b.1936) consists of a reproduction of a famous 19th century painting by Seurat, plus documents showing the painting's history since it left the artist for a small sum, through various financial transactions to its present enormous monetary value for its present owners—Aremis SA—a private company which invests and trades in works of art. The documentation includes the names and financial connections of the firm's board of directors, thus exposing their position of power. The appreciation of this work relies on our understanding, rather than on our senses. We are invited to reconsider our response to art in the light of the place which it has

Right: *Crest* (1964), Bridget Riley (b.1931). Riley evolved a style called *Op Art*, in which she explored optical illusions. Concerned only with the various possibilities of paint and canvas she created paradoxes which are purely visual. In this painting, the black and white lines undulate in a way which suggest constant movement and a curved surface, whereas the painting itself is in fact static and flat.

Below: *The Beanery* (1965), Edward Kienholz (b.1927), an assemblage work of great force. The power of *The Beanery* stems from the fact that it is a life-size evocation of a small, seedy bar. The spectator can actually enter the work, so becoming part of it. Kienholz creates a nightmarish and frightening environment. Here the fellow drinkers are soulless dummies whose heads are nothing but clock faces, shocking the spectator into an increased awareness of the terrors of life.

Left: *Coyote* (1974), Joseph Beuys (b.1921), consisting of a one-week performance in New York, with the artist hidden in a blanket, symbolizing the white man, and the coyote symbolizing everything the white man considers despicable.

Below: *Spiral Jetty* (late 1960s), Robert Smithson (1938-73). An aerial photograph of Smithson's Land Art, which attempts to narrow the gap between art and life by taking art out of museums and galleries.

Bottom: *Fathom* (1976), Anthony Caro (b.1924). Sculptors as well as painters have widened their perceptions. The sculptor Caro welds together pieces of metal together, so avoiding traditional sculpture methods, to create a supple work.

Right: *What does possession mean to you?* (1976), Victor Burgin (b.1941). Political, mass-produced art, in the form of posters displayed on advertising sites in Newcastle.

Caroline Tisdall

What does possession mean to you?

7% of our population own 84% of our wealth

The Economist, 15 January, 1966

Robert Self Gallery

Dr Georg Gerster/John Hillelson Agency

Floyd Picture Library/Goldblatt

acquired in the financial world, something not anticipated by the original artist. Haacke's work itself is devoid of monetary value as it consists of information which can be endlessly reproduced.

Latest trends
A similar desire to widen the content and subject matter of art, and narrow the gap between art and life, have led to the present movement known as *Land Art*, as in the work of Robert Smithson (1938-73), and to *Performance Art*, seen in the work of Joseph Beuys (b.1921). In these the artists work directly with the environment, or with their own bodies, thus escaping from the idea of a work of art as a permanent object.

Robert Smithson works by making alterations to landscape on a large scale. For example his *Spiral Jetty*, 1970, is on the edge of a lake and consists of an extension of the land into the water in a spiral shape 1,500 feet long and 160 feet in diameter.

Beuys' works include performances (or actions) undertaken by the artist before an audience, and are ephemeral in the sense that each work can only be *recorded* on film, but cannot be preserved in its original state. In *Coyote*, 1974, the work consisted of Beuys and a coyote spending a week together enclosed within a screened off area of a gallery. The artist, by actions rich in symbolism, explores the possibility of communicating with the animal, by implication reminding the audience that the possibilities of communication are far wider than those acceptable to present society.

In their various ways, the artists of the post-war years have been concerned with making us more aware of our surroundings, both natural and man-made, and of our inner, subconscious selves. Whether or not individual artists succeed depends very much on the observer: quite often the emotions aroused will be different from those which the artist intended. It could be said that many of the attempts to bring art to a wider audience have failed, since many people would question the validity of such works as 'art'. But even in these cases, perhaps, the works have succeeded by stimulating discussion and argument on what art is all about.

The Cataract Hotel, Aswan **(1978) – crayon drawing by David Hockney. Originally identified with the 'Pop' artists, his more recent** work has used a brittle, figurative style to explore the desperation behind affluent urban life-styles.

Part II

A Thousand Years of Literature, Drama and Music

AD PRELIVM: CON

Chapter 1
The Middle Ages

From the Bayeux Tapestry, showing
the Norman army setting out. The
Tapestry (11th-12th century) is in fact
an embroidery, 230 feet by 20 ins
(70m by 51cms) depicting in more than
70 scenes the Norman Conquest of
England.

The Heroic Age

The great fight is over. Beowulf, the god-like hero with the strength of thirty men (his name, 'bee-wolf', means 'bear'), has crushed the monster Grendel in unarmed combat, wrenching out his arm at the shoulder and sending him to a wretched death in his fenland lair. Now the arm hangs as a bloody monument to Beowulf's deed in the gold-adorned hall of Heorot, pride of the Danish kings, which for twelve years past has been ravaged nightly by Grendel's attacks.

Such deeds are the heart and soul of heroic literature. Now the warriors gather to drink and celebrate, and the poet is on hand to immortalize the act:

> At times a king's thane, a man laden with heroic words, his memory filled with a host of songs and old stories, composed a new poem linked in true metre; or again this man would skilfully fashion verses about Beowulf's exploit, and create with his art a fitting tale, varying his words.

This passage, from the eighth-century Old English heroic poem describing Beowulf's adventures, gives us a glimpse of the oral poet at work before the age of writing. From his vast memory of old stories and verses he honours the hero by reciting traditional legends of past warriors and their triumphs. But he also composes spontaneously in his head, inventing and improvising from a stock of variable phrases and poetic rhythms to create a new work.

When Christianity brought the use of writing to the previously illiterate Anglo-Saxons in the seventh century, the old Germanic Heroic style was used to express religious themes. Some of the ancient tales, including Beowulf, also found their way into monastic manuscripts, while new heroic poems went on being created.

The heroic literature of the northern European peoples of the Dark Ages celebrates the values of the tribal society which preceded and overlapped with the coming of Christianity and medieval feudalism. Under these new cultural and political influences it changed in various ways, and eventually merged into the courtly literature of the Middle Ages.

As the power of the Romans in western Europe declined, the Germanic tribes from northern Europe were on the move. South out of Scandinavia poured Burgundians, Goths and Lombards; Angles and Saxons settled in the British Isles in the early fifth century while Attila the Hun was sweeping into Europe from the East. Late in the eighth century the Vikings began their descent into Europe and their ventures west to Iceland, Greenland and North America. Apart from the Huns, the way of life and language of these tribes were closely related. They were organized into tightly-knit units in which loyalty to kinsmen and allegiance to chieftains were the binding principles; courage and skill in battle the supreme virtues.

Writing in 98AD the Roman author Tacitus describes their military and moral values: 'On the field of battle it is a disgrace to the chief to be surpassed in valour by his companions, to the companions not to come up to the valour of their chief. As for leaving a battle alive after your chief has fallen, that means lifelong infamy and shame. To defend and protect him, to put one's own acts of heroism to his credit—that is what they really mean by "allegiance". The chiefs fight for victory, the companions for their chief.'

This is the heroic code of early Germanic literature in a nutshell. A thousand years after Tacitus, in 991, the same sentiments are found in the Old English poem *The Battle of Maldon*. Byrhtnoth, leader of the East Saxon army, is killed in battle against a band of Vikings. Some cowards take flight but his faithful retainers determine to fulfil their vows of loyalty and avenge his fall. One old warrior sums up the needs of this moment of heroic truth:

> Mind must be the firmer, heart the
> keener,
> Courage the greater as our strength
> grows less.
> Here lies our good leader, hewn
> down to the ground.
> He who flees this battle forever
> will lament.

The demands of a warrior audience, naturally desiring its entertainment to reflect its own tribal traditions and daily struggles, produced in poetry the figure of the idealized hero. Brave, loyal, strong and skilful, he defies Fate by hunting out its challenges and being ready at any time to meet his death. This is the way of honour, the way he gains the reputation which will give him immortality on the tongues of later generations.

Beowulf itself is much more than the tale of one man's battles. Interwoven with the hero's fights against monsters are scenes of glittering ceremony, splendid feasts of welcome and rejoicing, tales of other adventures and fateful references to disaster and the instability of human effort. The rich texture of the poem involves complex shifts in time and place.

Having purged Heorot of Grendel, Beowulf defeats the creature's mother in her lair beneath a monster-infested lake, and later becomes king in his own country. The events of the intervening 50 years, mainly concerned with inter-tribal wars, are described in a series of flash-backs brilliantly intertwined with the hero's last fight.

Beowulf seeks to destroy a dragon who for 300 years has been the guardian of a treasure-mound. Now, disturbed from his long slumber, the beast is ravaging Beowulf's lands. In the fight the old warrior's sword and shield fail him and all but one of his companions flee; he is mortally wounded by the dragon's teeth and flames, but his friend Wiglaf manages to deal the beast a death-blow. Beowulf dies, gazing at the treasure which now goes with him into his burial mound:

> Then around the mound rode twelve battle brave warriors, the sons of princes; they wished to lament their sorrow and mourn the king, to make an elegy and speak of this man . . . they said that among the kings of this world he was the gentlest of men and the kindest, the most gracious to his people, and most eager for fame.

Although *Beowulf* deals exclusively with Scandinavian events of the early sixth century it was first composed in its

Left: A detail from the west door of Hylestad Church in Seterdal, Norway. The carving depicts scenes from the 13th-century story of Sigurd. At the bottom, Regin the smith is at his forge remaking the pieces of Sigurd's father's sword. His father had acquired the sword by pulling it from the trunk of a tree—where the god Odin had fixed it. Regin's first two attempts are in vain. Sigurd is able to break the sword on the anvil with one blow (centre). With the third sword Sigurd fights the dragon, Fafnir, finally killing it (top). Sigurd wins the gold Fafnir was guarding, but before dying the dragon lays a curse upon it. Death and misfortune accompany gold in many of the heroic tales. On another piece of the portal there are scenes of Sigurd roasting Fafnir's heart. Eating the heart and drinking the blood of his enemy was believed to give him the beast's strength and courage.

Right: Four stills from the 1924 Fritz Lang films *Siegfried* and *Kriemhild's Revenge*. He was eager to present the nobility of heroic literature in a modern form. The films were both based on the *Nibelungenlied*, the Song of the Nibelungs. Lang wanted to capture the German spirit, and the heroic legends were an ideal basis for this. The top scene is from *Siegfried* showing the arrival of Brunhild, a fiery Icelandic princess who has come to marry Gunther, a Burgundian prince. The elaborate pageantry, with rows of helmeted soldiers, appealed to German audiences, demoralized after their defeat in the First World War. The lower three stills are from the sequel, *Kriemhild's Revenge*. Kriemhild is showing the bloodstained coat of her dead husband Siegfried to Volker, the minstrel. She is now married to the King Etzel (bottom two pictures) and is plotting to avenge Siegfried's death.

Right: The stories of heroic literature have been used a great deal since they were first written down in the 8th century. German artists particularly have been attracted by the heroism and grandeur of the characters in the tales although the stories are adapted to express the morality of different ages. Wagner used the 13th century *Nibelungenlied*, as the basis for his massive work, *The Ring of the Nibelungs* which was first performed in its entirety in 1876. It comprised four operas: *Rheingold*, *Die Walküre* (The Valkyries), *Siegfried*, and *Götterdämmerung* (The Twilight of the Gods). These two pictures are from the 1974 Covent Garden production of *The Ring*. The top one is from *Rheingold* showing a 20th century version of the giants, common figures in heroic literature. Below is a scene from *Die Walküre* showing Odin, the god of battles, holding his main weapon, the spear.

Kriemhild schenkt Volker den Mantel

Above, left and below: Three extracts from a 15th-century German manuscript of the *Song of the Nibelungs*, which was originally composed in about 1203. The poet's descriptions of bloodstained lances and mutilated bodies are illustrated in explicit detail. The legendary battles of the heroes of the 5th century were updated by the poet, using the settings of jousts and tournaments which figured so much in the courtly romances of the Middle Ages. Jousting was not only a point of honour by this time but also a sport: 'Their pleasure was so strenuous that their good horses' trappings were soaked with sweat.'

present form for a Christian Anglo-Saxon audience. Beowulf's struggles are given a Christian flavour. The monsters are said to be descended from Cain, the first murderer, and the hero fights under divine protection. Christianity found it easy to equate the pagan hero's tasks with some aspects of its own doctrine, especially those of the Old Testament. Allegiance to central authority, the fight against the Devil, and the salvation to be gained by virtuous behaviour are all ideas common to the two beliefs. In the tenth-century Old English crucifixion poem *The Dream of the Rood,* Christ himself is presented as a 'young hero, strong and courageous', eagerly embracing his fate on the cross in order to redeem mankind.

In the French epic *Chanson de Roland* (Song of Roland), composed in about 1100AD, the incorporation of Christianity is complete. Like most epics it looks back to a past age—the Emperor Charlemagne's Spanish campaign of 778—but its atmosphere is that of the early crusades. Roland, a French count, fights equally for king, country and God against the heathen hordes, whose wholesale slaughter is dwelt on in delighted detail.

Another typical heroic feature is the defence of a narrow position, like a bridge or a pass, against overwhelming odds. In Roland's case the action takes place in a Pyrenean mountain pass near Ronceveaux. Roland is in command of the French rearguard when his 20,000 men are treacherously attacked by 100,000 Saracens. (Historically they were in fact Basque tribesmen.) His own valour in battle is almost equalled by that of the warlike Archbishop Turpin, who splits and hacks the foe so ferociously that:

> *The French all cry: A valiant blow*
> *and shrewd!*
> *Right strong to save is our*
> *Archbishop's crook!*

Roland's pride will not allow him to blow his horn to summon reinforcements until it is too late. He dies begging God's mercy.

A different development of the heroic theme is represented by the German *Nibelungenlied* (Song of the Nibelungs), composed about 1203. In dealing with inherited legends whose roots lie partly in the fifth century conflicts between Burgundians and Huns, the poet has transformed them into something like a courtly romance, with lengthy descriptions of ceremony, banquets and tournaments. It is, as one writer puts it, 'like a good hunk of boar's meat smothered in a delicious sauce from the French kitchen'.

The story concerns Siegfried, who slays a dragon, becomes invulnerable to weapons by bathing in its blood, and wins the cursed gold of the Nibelungs. At Worms he woos the Burgundian princess Kriemhild, who 'seemed made for loving'. He then uses his magical powers to impersonate her brother, Gunther, in the feats of strength necessary for the latter to gain the hand of Brunhild, a fiery Icelandic princess. As a result fierce jealousy develops between the two wives. Brunhild incites Gunther's one-eyed retainer Hagen to kill Siegfried, whose immunity is flawed by a weak spot where a leaf fell on his skin during his bloodbath. The second part of the poem deals with Kriemhild's revenge for this act,

Above: An illustration from a 17th-century Icelandic manuscript of Snorri's *Edda*. The original caption reads: 'The goat which is called Heithrun. She stands upon Valhalla, eating buds from the branches of the tree called Laerath. Her udder produces mead for all the Einherjar.' Valhalla is the home of dead heroes chosen by Odin to form an army to fight on the side of the gods at the time of Ragnarok—when the forces of destruction triumph and the entire world is lost in a holocaust. Einherjar means the chosen warriors.

Left: A medieval Viking picture stone showing magical symbols and a Viking boat, the ship of the dead. The stone comes from Lillbjars in Götland.

Below: Medieval Viking picture-stone from Alskog Tjangvide, Götland. It shows the eight-legged horse Sleipnir which is usually ridden by Odin, arriving at Valhalla, the building with a domed roof, top left. There he is welcomed by a female figure with a drinking cup.

Below: A small bronze statuette of the god, Thor. It was found in Iceland and made during the Viking period. He is depicted with a beard, wearing a helmet such as the Vikings would have worn. He is holding his famous hammer, Mjollnir, with which he crushed giants, the enemies of the gods.

Below right: Fuseli's 'Thor fighting the midgard serpent' is a romantic interpretation of the myths. The serpent circles the human world (midgard) like a belt; it is an enemy of the gods. Thor goes fishing with the giant, Hymir, and catches the serpent with an ox-head as bait. He is about to kill it but Hymir cuts the line.

Left: An illustration from the 17th-century manuscript of the *Edda* shows another aspect of Iceland's literary vitality in the Middle Ages. Snorri Sturluson (1178-1241) recorded the ancient mythological lore of the Norse peoples in the *Prose Edda*. In this the gods are treated like the heroes of the sagas. The giant-crusher Thor, the warlike and cunning Odin with his magic arts, the noble Heimdall and Frey, all have superhuman powers, but must nevertheless fight their last battle and die when the forces of destruction overwhelm them at the time of Ragnarok. The picture shows the god, Odin, with his two ravens who are called Thought and Memory (Hugin and Mugin). He sends them out to gather news, essential to his fight against the forces of destruction. Odin is shown with one eye; in his search for knowledge he sacrificed the other to a well in the roots of the mythical tree Yggdrasill, the steed of Odin. The well contained the head of the wise god Mimir, whose wisdom he got in return.

Left: Details from a 13th-century window at Chartres, illustrate the story of Emperor Charlemagne, including scenes described in the Song of Roland.
1 (see key): A battle against the Saracens during Charlemagne's Spanish campaign.
2: During the campaign the Christian French were encouraged by the miracle of the flowering lances. They put their lances into the ground at night and awoke to find that they had burst into flower.
3 and 4: Roland, shown with a halo, fights and kills the giant Ferragut who is with the Saracens.
5: Charlemagne's army leaves Spain at the end of the campaign.
6: His mouth red with blood and his temples burst open, Roland blows his horn, Olifant, finally warning the retreating French army that the rearguard has been attacked, Before the main army can reach him Roland is mortally wounded. To stop his sword, Durendal, being stolen he tries to break it on a rock. The sword is so strong that he tries in vain.

when she is married to the Hunnish king Etzel (Attila).

Similar tales had obviously circulated for centuries among the Germanic tribes. We find the same material written down in Iceland in the thirteenth century, in a collection of mythological and heroic poems known as the *Poetic Edda*. The characters' names are alike (Siegfried is Sigurd, and so on), except that Kriemhild is called Gudrun. Yet where the *Nibelunglied* is detailed and leisurely in its approach, the Norse poems are breathless and densely compressed. The result is a heroic cycle of unequalled force and purity, with savage scenes like the cutting of a man's heart from his living body, and Gudrun's revenge on her husband Atli for the deaths of her brothers. She kills her two sons and serves their cooked flesh to Atli for dinner, then stabs him as he lies drunk and finally sets fire to the hall.

Women of the savage sagas

The Icelandic and German works give much greater attention to women than do *Beowulf* or the *Chanson de Roland*. The same is true of Iceland's thirteenth-century saga literature, with characters like Hallgerd in the *Njals Saga* and Gudrun in the *Laxdale Saga*. Suffering from wounded pride Gudrun forces her husband to kill his closest friend, her former lover. The *Njals Saga* has two very different heroes: Gunnarr is a man of action, his friend Njal a peaceful Christian. Their deaths are the two great climaxes of the saga. Gunnarr puts up a characteristically spirited defence against impossible odds, fighting off his enemies with his mighty bow and a halberd, a spear and battle axe combined. Njal is burnt to death with his wife and sons in the family home after a long feud, refusing an offer of safe conduct 'because I am an old man, and little able to avenge my sons, and will not live in shame.'

These Icelandic works look back to the period of Iceland's settlement and early development from 870 to 1030; nostalgia for a vanished age, especially apt in the bitter and strife-ridden thirteenth century. The sophisticated prose sagas are in some respects like the modern American idealization of the wild west, with its heroes rising to face challenges presented by the lawlessness and disorder of a newly-developing community. The sagas adapt the heroic ideal to a farming society and have an atmosphere of realism far removed from the exaggerations of other epics, yet their heroes are guided by the same principles of family and personal honour. Irony is very central to the sagas and even bloody deaths can give rise to humour: 'These broad spear-blades are fashionable nowadays', observes the victim of a fatal spear-thrust.

On one level heroic literature may be seen as aristocratic and conservative, expressing and supporting the beliefs of the established order. But we can see characters like Beowulf, Sigurd, Roland, Gudrun and Njal outside their immediate historical context as universal moral heroes. In seeking challenges and facing tragic choices they rise above the ordinary limits of fear and knowledge. Christian or pagan, they defeat death by refusing to allow it to dominate their lives, or to inhibit their freedom of action. This is the deeper meaning of the victory over the monster, the symbolic gold and the refusal to live in shame.

Romance and Chivalry

During the twelfth century a new literary form developed in southern France that was to overtake the stern tradition of epic poetry which existed in northern Europe. This poetry was short, lyrical and technically complex, dealing often with personal subjects and especially with loving attachments between the sexes, themes which differed greatly from the warlike, heroic spirit of Germanic literature.

The new lyric poetry reflected the increased sophistication and refinement of feudal life in the twelfth century. It was passionate, gay, often humorous and as inventive as possible in its form and subject-matter. The writers of this poetry were called 'troubadours'. Often they were of noble station, though some were court minstrels. The love lyrics of these French troubadours not only mark the real beginning of modern literature but are also the source of the whole tradition of 'romantic' love in Western Europe.

Codes of love and chivalry

In some ways the new emphasis on love can be explained merely as a device to amuse a class of rich and leisured lords and ladies. But many factors were at work in producing the ideals of courtly love and the code of chivalry with which it is closely connected.

Knightly marriages were often arrangements of convenience and property, with little affection between husband and wife. The husband would frequently be away at the wars, leaving his lady at home, isolated and bored. This kind of lady was to become the central figure in the courtly love tradition.

Much of the significance of courtly love is summed up in the change of meaning of the single word 'lady'. This word derives from the old English *hlaef-dige* (like our words 'loaf' and 'knead') meaning the bread maker, the lady of the household, the partner in marriage of the *Hlaef-weard* or 'guardian of the bread'. As the old household gave way to the feudal court, these words became 'lord' and 'lady' and came to have a very different significance. The lady is no longer merely a bread-maker, but a noble and refined person, who must be treated with respect.

By about the time of Chaucer's death in 1400, 'lady' becomes the word normally used to describe the Virgin Mary. It was meant to convey all the ideas of lover, queenship, inaccessibility, holiness and good. These are the qualities of a courtly lover's lady made perfect.

The early feudal ideals of courage and loyalty, softened by the effect of the Christian religion with its doctrines of duty and charity towards the poor, together influenced the development of a code of chivalry which demanded gallantry and gentility from the knights. Alongside this, an idealized view of love grew up. From Islamic Spain and through taking part in the crusades in Palestine, knights were brought into contact with Arabian literature, which emphasized love as a holy and uplifting emotion. More importantly the knight's every-

Above: 'The offering of the heart', a 15th-century tapestry which captures the essence of courtly love. The troubadours of southern France in the mid-12th century broke new ground in their treatment of intimate personal themes. They excelled in short lyric love poems and by the late 12th century their courtly ideals had spread north to influence longer romance narratives in verse. The heroic epics of the early feudal age had given way to literature composed for a more refined and leisured audience. Their idealization of woman and the concept of 'love' as a passionate emotion, both carnal and spiritual, influenced literature and Western culture itself for centuries to come. The essence of courtly love was absolute loyalty in the knight's service of his lady.

Right: Jousting was the great peace-time sport of knightly soldiers. Fighting each other for the praise of their ladies combined the ideals of victory in battle and service in love. The ideal knight was described as a lion in the field—and a lamb in the bower.

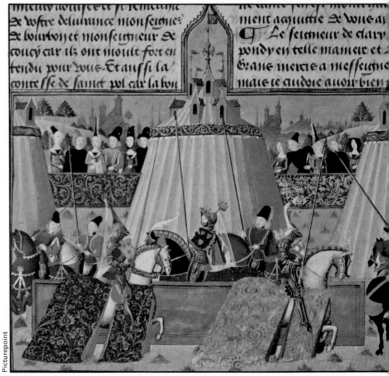

day existence led him to have a special respect for love. For his life centred around a court where he would be expected to practise absolute devotion to his lord and lady, as well as to God and the Virgin Mary. In these circumstances, love and religious feeling became deeply bound together; 'love' to a Christian knight was identified with 'good'.

From these influences developed a whole new set of expectations about love. According to these, the lover falls in love suddenly with a lady who is likely to have a husband already. He will then serve her with devotion, perhaps to the end of his life, although he might never achieve sexual union with her. If he does the love must remain secret, unless marriage is possible. The tradition emphasizes the spiritual aspect of love. The lover often loves only from a distance, and pines in secret. His love is pure, inspiring him to perform good deeds. In spite of the pain and frustration it may cause him, his love is the source of all good in his life. It is clear that courtly love is idealized, taking little account of the real nature of the loved one.

In the 1180s all these ideas were gathered together and written down, perhaps not entirely seriously, at the elegant French court of the countess Marie of Champagne, by Andreas Capellanus in his *Art of Loving*. Andreas tells how it was decided in a debate about love that true love cannot exist inside marriage, because true love requires an intensity of jealousy which marriage weakens. This sounds very much like the game of an idle aristocracy. But Marie also encouraged Chretien de Troyes to write certain romances in which love is more seriously and nobly treated.

The most famous of these romances, concerning the love of Lancelot for King Arthur's wife Guinevere continues the theme of adulterous love. But its main point is to show the extremes of chivalry to which a knight is prepared to go for the sake of his lady. Lancelot endures the humiliation of riding in a dung-cart in order to reach Guinevere more quickly. This incident gives the romance its title of 'The Knight of the Cart'. Such an episode may seem rather exaggerated and perhaps Chretien was gently poking fun at the courtly tradition. But still Lancelot's love shines through pure and passionate.

The Romance of the Rose

A similar code of love and chivalry was described in the 1230s with much delicacy and intelligence by Guillaume de Lorris in his *Romance of the Rose*. The story takes the form of a dream in which a man comes upon a garden where courtly love is played as a beautiful and elegant game.

The figures in the dream are allegorical; Pleasure and Gladness, Beauty and Richness, Idleness, Generosity, Nobility and Youth dance and talk in the presence of the God of Love. The dreamer falls in love with Beauty by seeing, reflected in the fountain of love, a rose bush of great loveliness. After this, it becomes his whole aim to pluck one of the roses. Guillaume de Lorris left the poem unfinished, and it was ended by Jean de Meung, who makes the affair much more earthly, direct and simply sexual.

These two poems, *The Knight of the Cart* and the *Romance of the Rose*, had many imitators in the next 150 years. The love story of Tristram and Iseult, and of King

Left: A scene from the story of Tristram and Iseult, a legend of two lovers which appears in many romance poems.

Below: An ivory relief showing the siege of the Castle of Love, from the *Romance of the Rose*. Knights try to take the Castle, while the god of love shoots down his arrows.

Above: A 14th-century miniature showing the first incident in the poem the *Romance of the Rose* by Guillaume de Lorris. In a dream the lover comes to the garden of Love and is admitted by its portress Idleness. There he plays with Pleasure, Beauty, Youth and others until it is time for him to fall in love in earnest.

Mark, Iseult's husband, was told in several versions during the mid-twelfth century. This romance, handed down from Celtic legends, was re-interpreted in the light of courtly ideals, although the original story is darker and more tragic than anything produced in the chivalric tradition. The overwhelming passion which Tristram feels for Iseult is complicated by the different sort of love he feels for King Mark, his lord, a love arising from duty. The only way in which such conflict can end is with the death of Tristram and of Iseult.

Dante and the Divine Comedy

But the most spiritual effect of courtly love comes in an affair which has a fulfilment beyond death. The Italian poet Dante tells in his *Vita Nuova* or *New Life* how he fell in love with Beatrice in Florence, the town where he was born in 1265 and she in 1266. The emotions he feels for her bring about a great change in his view of life. He at once feels the power of her influence; he tells himself 'Now your blessedness has appeared to you'.

Dante accepts with profound seriousness ideas that may have begun as little more than lighthearted exaggerations. He sees the 'most gentle' Beatrice in a blaze of beauty; he feels that she provides the world with meaning and is the source of all goodness for him. He compares her to the True Light, to Christ; and in the intense misery which her death in 1290 caused him, he had a vision of her in heaven which he expressed in one of the most noble and moving poems ever written, his *Divine Comedy*.

At the beginning of the poem, Dante

Cooper Bridgeman

Cooper Bridgeman

Giraudon

Left: Medieval painting of King Arthur's last battle. Mortally wounded, he tells a knight to throw the sword Excalibur into the lake, where it is received by a lady's hand. Three queens take Arthur to the island of Avalon where he may be healed. Some stories say he dies there, others that he sleeps, to awake in time of Britain's need.

Below: An illustration of Lancelot in battle from a manuscript of *Lancelot du Lac*, a French poem which tells the story of King Arthur, his wife Guinevere and Lancelot—his friend and her lover. Lancelot was the finest knight, but his love for Guinevere caused great dissension and indirectly brought about the death of Arthur.

Above: A 19th-century view of Arthur's death. The legend of Arthur is a compound of historical fact and Celtic myth, embroidered over the centuries by many poets and writers. To the right, a shadowy angel holds the Holy Grail (the cup used by Christ at the Last Supper). The search for the Grail was the quest of Arthur's knights.

Right: *Dante and his Book* by the 15th-century artist Domenico Michelino. On one side of Dante stands the city of Florence—from which he was expelled in a political quarrel after the death of his beloved Beatrice. In his great poem the *Divine Comedy* he tells of his despair at this and how the ghost of the Roman poet Virgil comes to him, sent by Beatrice to show him his way of escape. Dante's hand points to the barren regions of Hell, where Virgil leads him, making him comprehend all the possibilities of human wickedness until he is fit to climb the Mountain of Purgatory. This is shown in the background of the picture. At its summit is the Earthly Paradise in which he is reunited with Beatrice. She takes him through the circles of Heaven to the vision of God and love. Too much, too little or perverted love leads to Hell. The red line of fire at the top of Purgatory is the purging of the excessive love of courtly lovers—but theirs is considered the least of sins.

describes himself as having been lost and isolated in a dark and terrible wood. But there he meets a ghostly figure, the Roman poet Virgil, who tells him that Beatrice has taken pity on him in his despair. Virgil is to lead him through all the possibilities of the human spirit to rediscover Beatrice. The whole poem is about Dante's journey to become united with Beatrice and with God.

First, he must descend through hell, where he meets all kinds of sinners, among them courtly lovers, condemned to ride for ever on a wind through darkness, because in life they abandoned themselves to their passions. Among them are Paolo and Francesca, a self-deceiving couple whose story is nevertheless full of pathos. Their love is almost good: but there is a kind of blindness and selfishness in it which lays open the way through all the circles of hell to the treachery, the cold dark betrayal of Satan himself. But Dante and Virgil go past him to emerge at the bottom of the mountain of Purgatory, the mountain where people are purged of their sins and made free. Lovers, considered to be the least sinful figures in hell, are the nearest to heaven in purgatory.

At the top of Purgatory is the 'Earthly Paradise', the unfallen place of innocence. There Virgil leaves Dante, who is reunited at last with his Beatrice. She leads him through the circles of heaven, in each of which he recognizes her as brighter and more blessed than before, until he can see God himself. The *Comedy* ends with Dante's salvation; his will and mind are taken up in 'The love that moves the sun and the other stars.'

Such a summary cannot do justice to the complexity and beauty of Dante's poem, in which Beatrice and his love for her become the light that illuminates all the detail and life of the universe, and explains all its mysteries.

A new world develops in Italy with Dante's successors, Boccaccio and Petrarch. The loftiness of courtly love has quite gone in Boccaccio, whose tales of love in the *Decameron* and in his *Il Filostrato* are tender at times, but basically represent desire rather than devotion.

Petrarch (born 1304 in Arezzo) expresses all the devotion of courtly love to his mistress Laura. For him, as with Dante and Beatrice, she is the source of grace and the way to heaven. Further, he wrote many sonnets and six *Triumphs*, of Love, Chastity, Death, Fame, Time and Eternity, in which he comes near to Dante's vision of Beatrice in heaven. Perhaps his emotions are less convincing than Dante's, but as a poet and inventor of new poetical techniques Petrarch's influence was tremendous. In a way, courtly love became split, with its earthly side treated by Boccaccio, and its spiritual aspect by Petrarch.

In England, this split was healed somewhat by Geoffrey Chaucer in his version of Boccaccio's *Il Filostrato, Troilus and Criseyde*. But though his Troilus is a perfect courtly lover, his Criseyde is too weak and fickle to be an ideal mistress, and Chaucer subtly criticizes the submissiveness of a courtly lover when his love is directed at such a woman.

Sir Lancelot's illicit love

In the next century, Sir Thomas Malory gave a new and lovely version of the legends of King Arthur and his court, especially of the relationship between Lancelot and Guinevere, in his *Morte D'Arthur*. The legends are concerned with love and chivalry, but their significance goes much further than this. King Arthur's court is a vision of an England unified and at peace, existing through bonds of friendship, chivalry and love. Malory shows how this unity is disrupted and eventually destroyed by a betrayal of these bonds. The fragmentation begins when the knights start putting their personal feelings before the ideal of knighthood. Lancelot's love and loyalty to his king Arthur are divided by his adulterous love for Arthur's wife; in the end Arthur's order of chivalry, the Round Table and his kingdom are destroyed by it. The description of Arthur's death and Lancelot's farewell to Guinevere form one of the most moving scenes in literature. This love ends, as so often in the courtly love tradition, with bitter contrition on the part of the lovers. Guinevere seeks peace in a nunnery and dismisses Lancelot with these words:

Through this man and me hath all this war been wrought, and the death of the most noblest knights of the world; for through our love that we have loved together is my most noble lord slain . . . Therefore Sir Lancelot, I require thee and beseech thee heartily, for all that love that ever was betwixt us, that thou never see me more . . . for as well as I have loved thee, mine heart will not serve me to see thee, for through thee and me is the flower of kings and knights destroyed.

195

The Age of Chaucer

At the time of the Norman conquest, English was rarely used as a written language. Latin had been employed in religious and business matters; now, with the coming of the Normans, French was used for similar purposes. The eventual changeover to English as the major written language coincides with a period of social upheaval caused by the Black Death of 1348. About a third of the population died, including large numbers in the religious orders—who made up a significant proportion of the educated people in England. English quickly became the language used as the medium for communicating new ideas of all kinds. Being the language they were used to speaking, as a written form it expressed more vividly their thoughts and preoccupations.

The basis of modern English literature was being established. The last twenty-five years of the century (approximately the reign of Richard II 1377-1400) saw some of the greatest English writing and three of the very greatest English poets—Geoffrey Chaucer, William Langland, and the anonymous author of *Gawain and the Green Knight*.

Some of the first writing in English was concerned with religious ideas. The religious world was in turmoil with discontent, centred on the activities of the reformer John Wycliffe. There was a movement of dissatisfaction against formal religion in favour of a more personal interpretation of faith, led by Richard Rolle. He and his followers began to rely more on their own emotional responses, and to have faith in supernatural experiences. Several books were written in English concerned with these themes. An unknown author wrote a vivid, racy and compelling work called *The Cloud of Unknowing*, in which he explained that mystical experience is not easily gained; it involves a life of contemplation and we can rarely expect more than to strike with 'darts of love' at what he termed the 'Cloud of Unknowing'. It remains the best English book on meditation. Walter Hilton followed this with his less austere *Ladder of Perfection*. After experiencing a vision of Christ, the nun Julian wrote *The Revelations of Divine Love*, the first English book written by a woman. She writes of a vision of the whole universe, seen to be as small and insignificant as a hazelnut, but lasting forever because God loves it.

The visions of Piers Plowman

William Langland in the poem *Piers Plowman* has something of the same vision of the world as Julian's. But he combines the vision of the mystics with the concern of a social satirist and reformer in a passionate and personal search for truth. Truth is his first name for God. He wrote his poem over 20 or 30 years from about 1365, in three main versions. He tells how he fell asleep by a stream 'on a May morning in Malvern hills and saw beneath him a fair field full of folk'—the whole world about its business, forgetful of the great moral choices which surround it. In his first version he imagines society put to rights by the ordinary good worker, Piers the Ploughman. His poem was taken as a text by the Peasants' Revolt in 1381.

But already in 1377-8 he had written a second part, not denying the first, but convinced that social reform does not go deep enough nor indeed is in any real sense possible, until every man discovers Christ, hidden in himself and his neighbour. An extraordinary range of experience, from a drunkard vomiting in a village ale house to Christ's victory over death is described in vivid detail. Through all, Langland demands, from both society and the individual, repentance for sin and a willingness to alter existing ways of life. His purpose is wholly moral.

Gawain and the Green Knight

Some of the same concerns appear in a group of four poems which may all be by the same author, *Patience*, *Cleanness*, *Gawain and the Green Knight* and *Pearl*. In *Gawain and the Green Knight*, the Green Knight rides into King Arthur's court at New Year, offering to receive a blow from anyone who will stand a return blow from him, a year hence, at the Green Chapel. Gawain strikes off the Knight's head, but the head speaks and tells him to remember his promise and the headless knight rides out.

Gawain sets off through the winter landscape where the birds 'upon bare twigs piteously piped for pain of the cold'. He lodges with a courteous lord who goes out hunting all day and whose wife tries to seduce the guest. This places Gawain in a dilemma, between courtesy and chastity, that we later discover to have been a test, just as the final encounter

with the Green Knight is a test of his courage. The whole poem is a romantic adventure, told in vivid poetry, and at the same time a glimpse of the weakness in Gawain's heart and in the heart of every man.

Among these books only *The Cloud of Unknowing* goes much outside the world of medieval England, or beyond the life of the peasant, the knight and the priest, of courtly love and devotion to Jesus and Mary. With their passion and their gift for vivid detail, sometimes coarsely vigorous, sometimes brightly coloured and sharp like an illuminated manuscript, these works are nevertheless still wise and moving for us today.

Of all medieval English writers, Geoffrey Chaucer (c.1342-1400) is the most well-known and wide-ranging, taking his subjects from all walks of life. He spent his life near the centres of government, as diplomat, customs official and clerk of the King's works. In these capacities he saw much of the world, and in the post of clerk of 'works' must have been involved in the new developments in art and architecture of the fourteenth century.

Before he went to Italy in 1372-3, he was already a fine court-poet, translator of the great French poem of courtly love, the *Romance of the Rose* and author of the *Book of the Duchess*, an elegy for Blanche, wife to Edward III's brother John of Gaunt. When he came back from Italy he brought with him a deep love and knowledge of the great Italian medieval poet, Dante, and of Boccacio and Petrarch, who had already established their native Italian as a literary language. His experience of such different worlds was

perhaps a factor in developing the humour and ironic detachment which is a major element of his poetry.

In the poem *Troilus and Criseyde*, Chaucer takes a story of Boccacio's called *Il Filostrato* which is full of pathos, but not profound, and uses it to treat the great medieval themes of fate and freewill with such a depth of moral passion and concern as to produce one of the most poignant poems ever written. Troilus, a Trojan warrior, wins the love of a young girl called Criseyde who then betrays him by allowing herself to be wooed by one of the Greek soldiers. It creates a bitter sense of loss and the pain of infidelity yet remains a great praise of love. Chaucer leads us to stand inside and outside Troilus and by the end of the poem we have moved with Troilus to a position of detachment from the world. After his death Troilus looks back on his own life from the heavenly sphere, thinking that this world is just a

> *. . . litel spot of erth, that with the sea Embraced is, and fully gan despise This wrecched world, and held al vanite.*

To Chaucer the world is given meaning by love—both sacred and profane. In the more purely medieval *Parlement of Foules*, Chaucer surveys the attitudes of different classes towards love and marriage in the disguise of birds choosing their mates on St. Valentine's Day. In his second great poem *The Canterbury Tales* he continues to explore this theme and many others.

Chaucer's pilgrims and their tales
The characters are a group of pilgrims on

Above: Illustration of a Benedictine nun. Mother Julian was a 14th-century mystic belonging to a Benedictine monastery in Norwich. Her book 'The Revelations of Divine Love', the first in the English language to be written by a woman, was among a group of religious works in which English began to be used in its written form.

Left: A medieval book illustration showing a ploughman at work. In the 14th-century English poem *Piers Plowman*, William Langland takes the ploughman as his model of the ordinary man whose responsibility it is to reform society. This poem was much quoted by the leaders of the Peasants' Revolt in 1381. Piers Plowman includes characters which personify the seven deadly sins, among them Pride (above right) and Gluttony (right). Langland's descriptions are vivid and lively, particularly in the depiction of Gluttony as a drunken, vomiting wretch. But these vices repent after Reason preaches to them, and they eventually follow Piers in trying to make a better society.

Far right: This illustration is from a manuscript of the poem *Troilus and Criseyde*, written around 1380 by Geoffrey Chaucer. It shows Chaucer reading the poem to Richard II and his court. It was far more usual at that time for people to have literature read aloud than to read it for themselves.

the way to the shrine of St. Thomas a Becket of Canterbury. It is agreed that every pilgrim should tell two stories on the way to Canterbury and two on the way back. The poem is unfinished—we have 24 stories in all—but it still constitutes probably the finest collection of tales in the Middle Ages. Every story has a double interest—in its own right, and as a revelation of the man telling it. Chaucer includes himself among the pilgrims—a farcical portrait—and gives himself a dull story to tell. The whole method, with its details of physique, costume, opinion and behaviour, gives us a vivid picture of the world of the fourteenth century.

The Knight tells a story of widom and chivalry, rather like *Troilus and Criseyde*, about the two friends Palamon and Arcite. The tale fits the character of the teller, one

> *That from the time that he first began*
> *To reden out had loved chivalry,*
> *Truth and honour, freedom and*
> *courtesy.*

In violent contrast to the Knight, the Miller tells an immensely funny and bawdy tale.

The wife of Bath's confession and her tale about marriage express her abundant lust for life. The Prioress' story of a little boy killed for his devotion to the Virgin has a sweet, slightly deceptive religious sentiment which again fits the teller's character. One of the most powerful is the eerie, ironic story of the three young drunkards who tried to kill Death, brilliantly conveying the sheer damnation of its teller, the Pardoner, who makes his living from selling false relics to the poor.

As the tale shifts from one character to the next and the laughing cavalcade moves on, the reader begins to ask himself 'Am I like that? How would I fit among those people, and what would they think of me?'

Chaucer succeeds in conveying the sense of a god-like view of life, at once understanding and detached, that Troilus had at the end of *Troilus and Criseyde*. This view is enforced in Chaucer's translation of *The Consolation of Philosophy* by the Roman poet Boethius: it recommends us to rise above our earthly troubles by looking at the world as it would seem from eternity. It is the same kind of view as that of Langland or the nun Julian. It seems to be what Chaucer is looking for, though his means are sometimes painful, sometimes comic. The pilgrimage to Canterbury is a reflection of the pilgrimage to heaven in which we take part.

The literature of this time is not confined to the authors we have mentioned: the English miracle plays are largely a creation of the same time. There was plenty of lyric poetry too, many poems and stories of love, chivalry and magic.

Through it all runs an immense vitality and enjoyment of life. To medieval man this went naturally with a sense of living under God's judgement. Two short, memorable passages from medieval poetry make this clear. The first is from Chaucer:

> *Here is no home, here is but wilderness,*
> *Forth, pilgrim, forth.*

The second is from William Dunbar, a medieval Scottish poet:

> *Man, please thy Maker and be merry,*
> *And give not for this world a cherry.*

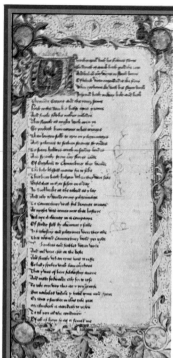

Mary Evans / Bodleian Library

Right: A portrait of Geoffrey Chaucer, which shows a greater degree of realism than was usual for art at that time. The portrait emphasizes the wise, pensive aspect of this great writer, who is often called the 'Father of English Literature'. Chaucer had a profound and witty insight into many aspects of society, which finds expression in his narrative poem *The Canterbury Tales.*

Left: A manuscript of the Prologue from *The Canterbury Tales.* This work was very popular, and many manuscripts of it exist, often beautifully illuminated. The opening lines, illustrated here, give a vivid sense of the re-awakening of life in the spring. Chaucer describes how, after the hardship of winter, people begin to prepare themselves for a pilgrimage. The Prologue is colourful and full of variety, reflecting the assortment of people found on such a journey.

THE MILLER

Ful byg he was of brawn, and eek of bones.
. . . He was a janglere and a goliardeys,
And that was most of synne and harlotries.

He was a very brawny and big-boned man. He talked loudly and told indecent stories, mostly about sin and vulgarity.

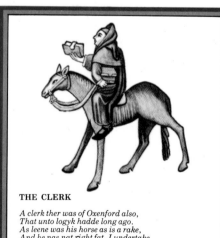

THE CLERK

A clerk ther was of Oxenford also,
That unto logyk hadde long ago.
As leene was his horse as is a rake,
And he nas nat right fat, I undertake,
But looked holwe, and thereto sobrely.

There was also a Clerk from Oxford, who had taken to the study of logic long ago. His horse was as lean as a rake and he was not exactly fat, I declare, but looked gaunt and very grave.

THE WIFE OF BATH

She was a worthy woman all hir lyve:
Housebondes at chirche dore she hadde fyve
. . . In felaweship wel koude she laughe and carpe.
Of remedies of love she knew per chaunce,
For she koude of that art the olde daunce.

She had been comfortably off all her life and had married five times at the church. In company she could share a laugh and joke. She knew all about love and well understood the tricks of that game.

Left: A group of pilgrims setting out from London to Canterbury. Chaucer uses the pilgrimage as the basis for *The Canterbury Tales*, in which a company of pilgrims entertain themselves by each telling a story.

Right: Medieval illustrations which suggest two of the tales. The *Nun's Priest's Tale* is an animal fable, the story of how a cock, Chanticleer, is stolen by a cunning and persuasive fox. He learns his lesson and he in turn tricks the fox into releasing him. The tale includes a witty look at the relations between Chanticleer and his wife Pertelot, and a discussion of the power of dreams and the possibility of foreseeing one's own fate.

The *Wife of Bath's Tale* concerns a knight who reluctantly marries an old witch, only to find her transformed to youth and beauty. The tale has a long prologue on the subject of marriage, famous for its satirical and sympathetic insight, in which the Wife gives a lusty account of her life with five successive husbands and condemns the celibate life.

THE KNIGHT

. . . though that he were worthy, he was wys,
And of his port as meeke as is a mayde,
He nevere yet no vileynye ne sayde
In al his lyf unto no maner wight,
He was a verray, parfit gentil Knyght.

Though he had an important position, he was wise, and bore himself as meekly as a maiden. Never in all his life had he been rude or cruel towards anyone. He was a faithful, courteous, perfect Knight.

THE SQUIRE

Of his stature he was of evene lengthe,
And wonderly delyvere, and of greet strength.
Syngynge he was, or floutynge, al the day;
He was as fresh as is the monthe of May.

He was of average build, wonderfully agile and of great strength. He sang, or played the flute all day, and seemed as fresh as a May month.

THE PRIORESS

That of hir smylyng was ful symple and coy;
Hire gretteste ooth was but by Seinte Loy,
. . . She was so charitable and pitous
She wolde wepe, if that she saugh a mous
Kaught in a trappe, if it were deed or bledde.

She had a very quiet, simple smile, and her strongest oath was by St. Loy. She was so kind and tender hearted that she would weep if she saw a mouse caught in a trap, dead or bleeding.

THE MONK

Of prikyng and of huntyng for the hare
Was al his lust; for no cost wolde he spare.
What sholde he studie and make hymselven wood,
Upon a book in cloystre alwey to poure,
Or swynken with his handes, and laboure,
As Austyn bit?

His sole pleasure was in tracking the hare and hunting; he would spare no expense for these things. Why should he study and send himself mad, always poring over a book in the cloister, or toil and labour with his hands, as St. Augustine bids?

199

Medieval Drama

The drama of medieval Europe was something new. The barbarians who destroyed the Roman Empire were not interested in drama: the Church, probably with reason, disapproved of the triviality and debauchery of the later theatres of Greece and Rome. After the fall of Rome, only wandering players remained, probably doing no more than clowning and singing ballads. There were rituals for the seasons, such as the choosing of a May King and Queen, but we do not know how dramatic these were.

The new drama had its roots in Christianity; particularly the Last Supper. When Christ broke bread and poured wine, his act was symbolic. When his actions were repeated in the mass, they became in fact a 'dramatic' performance, with the priest acting the role of Christ and the congregation replacing the apostles.

Over many centuries rituals were devised to associate the Mass with the particular events in the life of Christ remembered in the annual festivals. At Christmas, a cradle was laid on the altar, on Palm Sunday there was a procession with branches and each Sunday had its own chant. During the sixth century a dramatic sermon was introduced before Christmas, in which all those who were believed to have foretold the coming of Christ were called on to recite their prophecies.

The first actual dialogue seems to come from the ninth century. The choir sang the parts of the angels at Christ's tomb and the three Marys looking for His body:

> Whom do you seek in the tomb,
> people of Christ?
> Jesus of Nazareth who was crucified,
> people of heaven.
> He is not here, He has risen up as He
> foretold. Go tell that He has risen
> up from the tomb.

By the thirteenth century this had been lengthened, and actions (displaying Christ's empty shroud) and costumes (wings for the angels, veils for the women) made it into a real, short play.

The Mystery Plays.
Many other plays were written along these lines, in France and elsewhere. They are partly in Latin, partly in French. The most striking is the *Mystère d'Adam* written either in France or in England around 1150. This was the first play we know to have been performed independently of church services and outside the church.

It is particularly remarkable because of its use of spectacular special effects which were to become essential ingredients of medieval drama. The stage directions for this play indicated smoke belching from the mouth of Hell and later productions used gunpowder, cranes and all sorts of other devices to keep the audience's interest.

One reason for this was probably that the ordinary congregation tended to take less and less part in the ritual of the mass itself. They probably did not understand in any detail what the priests at the altar were saying in Latin. To communicate

the faith to the ordinary people a more comprehensible approach was needed.

The establishment of a new feast in 1265 in honour of the mass, the feast of Corpus Christi, seems to have encouraged the growth of religious drama. The principal feature of the feast was a procession. The medieval world loved ritual pageants; and it is possible that from the start these processions included pageants without words. By 1400, in cities and towns throughout England, the play called Corpus Christi had long been performed. It consisted of a series of dramas, often acted in processional form, telling the story of man from the creation of the world to the Last Judgement. The whole community of each town was involved in the cycles. There was no separation of religion from secular affairs, and the cycles were a civic event. Each play was the responsibility of one of the guilds of the town. Sometimes the guild was appropriate for the special effects; for example, at York, the shipwrights played *Noah* and built the Ark.

The result was often spectacular. The whole history of the world was acted out through a midsummer day, with elaborate stages and special effects. At York the Creation of Light probably took place with the sun rising and the Doom after sun-set. The artificial light of the flames of Hellmouth and the blaze of Heaven would have had great dramatic effect in the dark.

At York, Chester and elsewhere each part of the cycle was performed on a separate pageant wagon. The wagons, often with two storeys, moved in succession through the town, stopping at prearranged points where the audience would remain, enjoying the whole sequence as the wagons arrived. The Cornish too produced cycles in their own language and these, like some in other parts of England, were performed in a single circular space with a number of scaffolds, or 'mansions' around it, which were allotted to the various characters. From here the actors could speak, but if they were involved in the action, they would have to descend into

Above: A spectacular royal procession in Brussels, 1615. The picture, *The Triumph Of Isabella*, shows how impressive the pageant wagons could be. The middle row (from left to right) has floats showing the Nativity (with the angel Gabriel on the roof), the Annunciation and God on his throne.

Right and below: Two works of art apparently inspired by medieval drama. In the alabaster carving (right), c. 1400, the sleeping soldiers are in medieval armour and in the illustration (below) Christ is being nailed to the cross before it is set up—both features typical of the stage performances of the period.

Mansell

Mansell

Left: The title page of the morality play, *Everyman*, written about 1500. Death is shown coming from the graveyard for Everyman, having been summoned by God: 'Where art thou, Death, thou dreadful messenger?' Death, the vices and the virtues were all represented by actual characters on stage.

Below: Part of a modern Corpus Christi procession in Cuzco, Peru. The festival is still a major event in Catholic countries, with large processions and striking crucifixes. The cycles of mystery plays probably developed from just this type of float into the processions of wagons with actors.

ZEFA

Above: A recent reconstruction of the Nativity as it would have been performed inside a cathedral. The shepherds have come to give their presents to Christ. The angel in the pulpit would have done most of the speaking with only a little dialogue, making it more like a dramatic sermon.

Below: Herod and the three wise men from a production of the York cycle at York in 1973. The play was originally performed by the masons and the goldsmiths. The recent revival of interest in medieval drama has produced several modern productions of the cycles.

British Tourist Authority

the central arena. The characters were placed symbolically—God and heavenly personages in the east, the World and the Flesh to the west, and Hellgate to the north. The suggestion was that the round space represented the whole world—a powerful image to the medieval audience.

The language of the plays is vigorous, homely English, including references to local names and to contemporary conditions. The characters appeal directly to the audience and often include them in the action. This gives the impression that everything is happening here and now. It is natural that they should be presented in this way since the theme of the plays is God's relation with man. Man relates to God by choosing or rejecting Him, and choosing or rejecting is something that happens now. The present is the time of grace: later, after death, there will be no time and no grace.

This notion is at once beautiful and terrible, both comforting and threatening. The plays spare no effort to convey all these emotions. On the one hand there is the continual threatening presence of devils, on the other the beauty of the Nativity, the kindness of Christ's healings, and the agony of His sufferings.

But Man is full of weaknesses, and these often provide comedy. There is the comedy of wickedness, like Herod boiling over with ridiculous pride and frustrated anger, or of foolish obstinacy, such as Noah's wife refusing to believe in the Floods, or of humility as when the shepherds offer Christ gifts that include a ball to play tennis.

An element of farce is introduced in a version of the Wakefield cycle, the Towneley manuscript dated about 1425. One of the plays is about Mak the sheep-stealer, who is added to the original Bible story of the three shepherds. The resulting farce is a 'send up' of the Nativity story itself. Mak and his wife, Gyll, steal a sheep from the shepherds. Mak hides the sheep in a cradle and pretends it is a baby. When the shepherds come to look for their sheep they cannot see it, but try to be kind to the 'baby':

MAK
Nay, do way:
He slepys.

THIRD SHEPHERD
Me think he pepys.

MAK
When he wakyns he wepys.
I pray you go hence.

THIRD SHEPHERD
Gyf me lefe hym to kys
And lift up the clowtt.
What the dewill is this?
He has a long snowte.

One of the great aims of the cycles was to persuade men that their lives were given meaning by the Last Judgement when their choice of good and evil would be tested. The same idea is displayed in a quite different sort of play from the same period, the Morality plays. These seem to have been acted by troops of strolling players, and portray the life and death of every man. The universal temptations that he encounters, as well as the virtues that protect him are personified on stage. There are characters like Good Deeds, Knowledge, Flattery and Death himself.

Above: Jean Fouquet's gruesome 'Martyrdom of St. Apollonia' (c. 1460). This is the only contemporary picture we have of a miracle play in performance. In it we can see the scaffolds or 'mansions' around the stage and, although only a semi-circle is shown, they probably continue right round. On the left is Heaven with a ramp leading down to the stage. In the central scaffold is the King's throne which is empty because he has come down to supervise the torture. On the right the mouth of Hell is guarded by demons.

Below: A detail from Pieter Brueghel's 16th-century painting 'Village Festival' shows a farce being performed by wandering players on a portable stage.

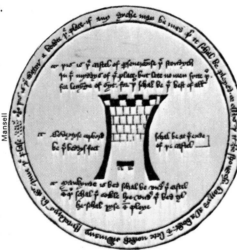

Above: A 15th-century illustration which shows the servant, Malchus, a character in the York and Wakefield cycles, carrying a lamp, suggesting that it is drawn from a production of the mystery plays.

Left: A drawing (c. 1420) of the staging of the morality play *The Castle of Perseverance.* This was performed by travelling players who set up the 'scenery' wherever they stopped. In the middle is the castle in which man takes refuge from the vices that beset him. Most of the action takes place in the circle around the castle; around the circle is a ditch, and the scaffolds where the supernatural figures sit, directing man's fate. The audience would sit among the scaffolds.

The Morality Plays
The finest of the Morality plays is *Everyman.* Written about 1500, it may not have been an English play originally, since there is a Dutch version which is probably earlier. God, seeing that Everyman does not care about his great destiny, summons Death.

When Death arrives, Everyman is deserted by Fellowship (his friends) and Kindred (his relatives) and by all his talents. But there is still Knowledge (the knowledge of the Christian faith) who comes to his aid:

Everyman, I wyll go with the, and be
thy gyde,
In thy moest nede to go by thy syde.

Only Knowledge and Good Deeds (his past good deeds) go with him to judgement.

Everyman is the last of the great medieval plays. The 'interludes' which replaced the moralities and are rather like them, lack their supernatural intensity. They tend to be more secular, dealing with many topics besides religion. They are more down to earth and include some good farces along ancient Roman lines like *Gammer Gurton's needle* and *Ralph Roister Doister.* Despite the name 'interludes', which suggests they were performed in the middle of something else, some of them are full scale plays.

Medieval drama, so closely associated with the pre-Reformation church, died out towards the end of the sixteenth century and was replaced by professional companies of actors playing in purpose-built theatres. Yet even this new, secular drama has links with the medieval tradition: for instance, the circular theatre of the Elizabethans where the actors are almost surrounded by spectators, owes something to the cycles. Shakespeare himself may have seen the last performance of the cycle at Coventry in 1579, when he was fifteen; the medieval intermingling of tragic conflict with the comedy of everyday life lives on in his plays.

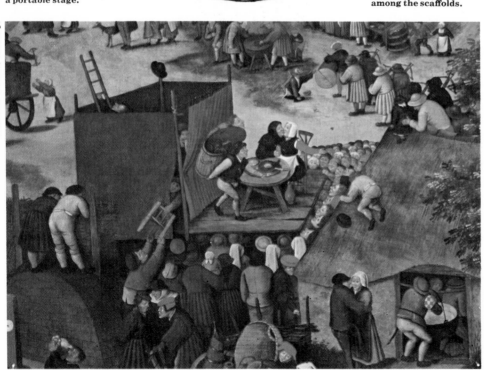

Chapter 2

The Renaissance

Queen Elizabeth I dancing with Lord
Darnley. The painter, Marcus
Gheeraerts the Elder (1521-1604),
settled in England in the latter part
of his life and became a most gifted
engraver, producing the first etchings
to be publicly issued in England.

Renaissance Music

The studies of the humanist teachers of the late fifteenth and early sixteenth centuries brought about a new attitude to all the creative arts—including music. Reading the works of Plato and other Greek philosophers, they were struck by the importance that these ancient writers had attached to music and musicians. They considered the art was not simply a matter of pleasure: it had power to heal the sick, move 'the whole man', affect him morally and spiritually. So the humanists began to prescribe music-making as a worthy occupation for their pupils and the ability to sing well and play an instrument grew to be considered essential accomplishments for the true gentlemen. Many noble homes employed musicians to teach the children of the family and to entertain the neighbouring gentry. For this reason, while the sixteenth century saw the development of instruments of many kinds, there was a special emphasis on those which amateurs could use without too much difficulty.

The most popular instruments

The stringed instruments of the *viol* family became extremely popular. These have *frets* to guide the fingers—strips of wood fixed on the fingerboard which indicate where a string must be pressed for a particular note to be produced. The viol was easier to play than the modern violin, which has no frets, and its quieter tone was well suited to domestic circumstances. The lute, also fretted, was still more universal, since it was well-adapted to accompany the voice. Various instruments related to the lute were even available for customers to use in barbers' shops. Recorders, flutes, crumhorns, and other wind instruments were scarcely less common. Keyboard instruments such as

the harpsichord, virginals and organ became for the first time really efficient, so that elaborate music could be written for them.

To meet the needs of this exciting atmosphere composers had to provide a new kind of secular music in which the amateur could find pleasure without too great a demand on his technical ability. Such music was encouraged by the development of music printing in the period around 1500. Previously, this had been done by a cumbersome method involving wooden blocks, but the invention of a movable metal type by the Italian printer, Ottavio Petrucci, who worked in Venice from 1490 to 1539, allowed publishing to flourish.

These factors help to explain the great development of sophisticated *chamber music* (music for a few performers, suitable for a private gathering rather than a large setting). The most popular music was that written for voices, for two reasons. Firstly, the art of singing was still more highly developed than was the playing of instruments. Secondly, the humanist teachers, believed that the best way of 'moving the whole man' involved unifying the arts of music and poetry. So two musical forms came into being which did precisely this.

The first was the French *chanson*, a type of song for several voices, which became extremely popular in the first thirty years of the sixteenth century. Its poetry was varied, sometimes dealing with courtly love in a sentimental way, sometimes quite down to earth in its depiction of country life, sometimes witty and gay. The composers tried to match the moods

Above: A 17th-century musician playing a lute.

Below: A detail from a painting by Breughel of the first of the five senses, hearing. It shows a carefully-detailed array of musical instruments and pieces of music, or *scores*, used during the late Renaissance. This period saw more varieties of instruments than any other. To the left is a harpsichord with a viol resting against it. Underneath it is a drum and a sackbut (an early type of trombone). A small lute lies on the floor next to a violin. To the right lies a cornetto (a wood or ivory wind instrument), a shawm (an ancestor of the oboe) and a recorder.

PARTHENIA,
OR
THE MAYDEN-HEAD
of the firſt Muſicke that ever was
printed for the VIRGINALLS.

COMPOSED
By three famous Maſters: *William Byrd*, Dr. *John Bull*,
and *Orlando Gibbons*, Gentlemen of his Majeſties Chappell.

Dedicated to all the Maſters and Lovers of Muſick.

Above: The title-page of the first music for the keyboard to be printed in England, in 1651, showing a young lady playing the virginals. The volume, dedicated 'to all the masters and lovers of musick' contained work by William Byrd, John Bull and Orlando Gibbons, the famous composers of the time.

Right: A painting of Queen Elizabeth I dancing with Robert Dudley, accompanied by violins and a viol. Dancing was one of the most popular forms of entertainment during the Renaissance. Some dances, such as this one, were less than stately, the gentleman assisting the lady to jump with his knee.

of the poetry, often managing at the same time to create music which was catchily tuneful, full of lively rhythms and straightforward melody of no great difficulty for the singer. From these principles sprang the Italian equivalent, the *madrigal*, which dominated European secular music for the next 70 or more years.

Exploring new tones and harmonies

Later sixteenth-century composers found the madrigal lacking in the intensity which the ancients were clearly aiming for, and began to expand the form by investigating more unusual methods of expression. Among these were attempts at reviving the ancient Greek scales, one of which was *chromatic*. The difference in effect between a chromatic scale and the medieval scale or mode, is the difference between playing both black and white notes in an octave on a piano and playing just the white notes. This use of more divisions of the octave than hitherto had been thought possible in itself had revolutionary effects.

Another attempt involved the close alternation of fast and slow melody, which allowed violent contrasts to take place. It now became possible, therefore, for a composer to convey detailed changes of emotion, and verse was specially written which encouraged him to do so. 'Word painting' became common, with images such as mountains expressed by ascending scales and valleys by descending ones. In this way, certain forms of music came to be associated with definite moods and emotions. Sadness or anguish was implied by slow moving music with sustained

Right: A detail from a painting of the *Life of Sir Henry Unton*, by an anonymous 16th-century English painter. A wedding feast is taking place, the celebrations being accompanied by music and a 'masque' (an entertainment combining mime, dancing and music, popular during the 16th and 17th centuries).

Playing music to accompany banquets, was one of the most common employments of musicians. Here a group or 'consort' of instruments are playing together, while the procession of mimers, in masks and elaborate costumes, winds up the stairs to pass by the table where the gentry are feasting.

dissonance (the use of chords which have a jarring, discordant effect) while happiness was expressed by quick motion and *consonant* harmonies which made use of chords whose notes seem at rest and in harmony with each other, thus producing an agreeable, satisfying effect.

All this meant that in place of the unity emphasized in earlier times, the music of the High Renaissance concentrates on diversity and contrast. In doing this, it mirrors the variety of human emotions and becomes more capable of expressing personality.

Although the fastest developments in composition were taking place in the more intimate circles of connoisseurs and amateurs, the Renaissance was, above all, an epoch of public show. Saint's days, royal weddings, the relief from plague, a famous victory, the visit of a head of state, all these were celebrated with great pomp and elaborate spectacle. Processions, sometimes called *trionfi* (after the 'Triumphs' of victorious generals in Roman times) would go through the streets of the town on decorated floats, pulled by horses, carrying singers and players performing grand madrigals. To enhance the festivities at the marriage feast of a crown prince perhaps 207 a play would be given, often with splendid intermezzos (musical intervals) between the acts. These would include acted tableaux, with ostentatious music reinforcing the wonders of cloud machines and other marvels of scenic invention.

Of course some of the grandest music written for ceremonial occasions was composed for churches. Most church choirs were not large: the two dozen singers in the Papal Chapel in Rome were considered a large group; the 30 or so in St Mark's, Venice, was even more exceptional. Some quite large cathedrals would have just half a dozen permanent singers, bringing in others for the most festive occasions at Christmas or Easter Day. Usually these were joined by instrumentalists, often members of the local town band (called *waits* in England). They played all kinds of instruments but mainly wind ones, such as cornets and trombones, as these helped to swell the sound of the voices.

Throughout most of the sixteenth century the Catholic church suffered an upheaval, after being challenged by Luther's group of 'protestant' clergy. Among the activities which came under close scrutiny was the role of music and two different attitudes to it emerged. The Roman Church felt that music should be kept simple, and such famous Italian religious composers as Palestrina (c.1525-1594) wrote settings of the Mass which were short and made the words almost completely audible.

At the same time, there were those who thought that the Church should be impressive and convince the populace of its power; a great deal of music was written for this purpose. Towards the end of his life Palestrina came to prefer this manner to the simple devotions of his short Masses, writing huge, rich sounding works to show off the skill of the Papal Choir. His masses, such as the *Missa Assumpta est Maria* achieve an intensity matching the splendour of the newly constructed St Peter's.

Venice: a splendid musical centre

The most splendid music of all was, however, written in the less devout atmosphere of Venice, where the musicians of St Mark's, far from being the servants of the church, were state officials employed to glorify the Republic just as much as Almighty God. As in secular music, the musicians of St Mark's took a particular pleasure in stressing contrast. A group of high voices would be opposed to low ones, instruments against voices, soloists against a choir or orchestra, all being brought together at a climax to produce a massive, glorious sound.

At the turn of the sixteenth century, nearly all the important composers had come from Northern Europe, especially the Low Countries; such men as Josquin des Pres and, a little later, Orlandus di Lassus, held the most important jobs throughout the continent. But by the end of the century it was the turn of the Italians. German monarchs sent their young composers to study with the Venetians, of whom the most famous were the two Gabrielis, Andrea and Giovanni, uncle and nephew, both of whom were composers and organists. Germans showered into Italy even if they were Protestant—the religious tolerance of Venice made it a safe area. Italians tended to be offered posts north of the Alps, to

208

Above: A painting of three musicians, by the Italian painter Costa. Madrigals and chansons were often performed by a small group of voices and instruments. The three singers are accompanied here by a lute, much used for song accompaniment as it could play chords.

Above: A harpsichord made by a great Venetian craftsman, Giovanni Baffo, in 1574. The strings are plucked mechanically, unlike the modern piano, whose strings are struck. Sometimes harpsichords had two keyboards to provide more musical contrasts, for this instrument allowed the player little variation of tone.

Right: An elaborately inlaid wooden *virginal*. Virginals were popular in the 16th and 17th centuries. They were keyboard instruments of the harpsichord family (having their strings plucked) but were smaller and rectangular. The keyboard was placed along the longer side, with the strings stretched parallel to this.

Left: A handsome 16th-century organ. This instrument operates by wind being blown by bellows through a pipe to sound a note. A pedal keyboard (clearly seen at the foot of the organ) is used as well as a manual one. The tone is altered by stops which, when pulled, block the passage of air through a pipe.

Below: A detail from an altarpiece by Jan and Hubert van Eyck, showing angels singing. Church singing became increasingly sophisticated during the Renaissance and many composers achieved fame for their religious music, among them the Englishmen Byrd and Tallis, and the Italian musician Palestrina.

Above: A detail from a painting of *Hell* by the Netherlandish artist Hieronymus Bosch, in which music is visualized as a form of torment. Many of the instruments portrayed are the older type of wind instruments which were played out of doors, such as the hurdy-gurdy on the right of the picture. The hurdy-gurdy was a kind of portable, mechanical viol—played by one hand turning a handle and the other stopping the strings by means of a tiny keyboard. Here two unfortunate victims perform this task ceaselessly, while another is doomed to play the triangle. To the left are a lute and a harp, on which a sinner is actually strung.

increase the prestige of princes and churches. Although it was difficult for foreigners, such as the English, to venture so far afield, they avidly studied Italian madrigals and then imitated them. Some older musicians complained that

'*such be the new-fangled opinions of our countrymen who will highly esteem whatsoever cometh beyond the seas (and specially from Italy) be it ever so simple, condemning that which is done at home though it be never so excellent*'.

This was a 'golden age' in English music too. Such composers as William Byrd, Thomas Tallis, Orlando Gibbons and Dowland created music ranging from complex religious settings to the simplicity of songs for solo voice with lute accompaniment, as well as pieces for keyboard instruments.

It was clear that something new had happened to music. It was no longer a science or an impersonal communication between God and man. It could express the wavering, fluctuating emotions of the individual, and speak from one man to another as never before. It has never been the same since.

Forestier's drawing of the opening of the first Globe Theatre. Many of Shakespeare's plays were originally seen here, produced by The Lord Chamberlain's Men. Performances took place in the afternoon, without lights, although this did not prevent the theatre catching fire in 1613 during a performance of *Henry VIII*.

The Great Age of English Drama

The variety and liveliness of Elizabethan and Jacobean drama is a direct consequence of two things: first, that the dramatists were not particularly concerned about following theories about how plays ought to be written, and second, that English drama had its roots in so many and such diverse traditions. The miracle and morality plays of the medieval church, the 'interludes' which entertained Tudor noblemen, the example of classical playwrights like Seneca and Terence, courtly tournaments and pageantry and the May games and other festivities of country folk—all these played a part in shaping the drama which burst into life during the late sixteenth and seventeenth centuries.

During the early decades of Elizabeth I's reign, before public playhouses came into being, plays were often staged privately at universities, schools or Inns of Court. Intended for educated audiences, these plays followed classical rules fairly closely. But with the emergence of the first generation of playwrights producing work for the public theatre, classical examples began to mingle with some of the other existing traditions.

The name 'University Wits' is sometimes given to the group of young men who wrote the first plays for the public theatre. These were John Lyly, George Peele, Robert Greene, Christopher Marlowe and Thomas Kyd.

The first drama written by John Lyly, the oldest member of the group, was a series of plays for the boy-actors of Paul's, a 'private' theatre with an almost exclusively court audience. Courtly love and intrigue are Lyly's main preoccupations as a dramatist and in a play such as *Galathea* (c.1585) we can see the blending of Lyly's classical interests with local pride when Cupid and Diana of classical mythology are placed in a Lincolnshire setting. *Galathea*, with its pastoral setting, its blend of English and classical elements, its slight but graceful wit and its theme of romantic love and girls disguised as boys, must have provided more than a hint for Shakespeare's romantic comedies.

George Peele's great comic masterpiece, *The Old Wives' Tale*, reveals a considerable poetic imagination and the inner plot, dealing with wandering knights, evil wizards and damsels in distress, is a good-humoured satire on the contemporary taste for romantic dramas. Robert Greene's place in English Literature is secure, rather more because of his unforgettably racy and vivid prose accounts of the London underworld (with which he was intimately acquainted), than because of his plays. Nevertheless at least two of his plays were important in the development of Elizabethan drama.

Friar Bacon and Friar Bungay (c.1591) is a skilfully wrought romantic comedy in which the exploits of a famous English magician are interwoven with a love story. During the play, we encounter

Left: A portrait thought to be of Christopher Marlowe (1564–93). In his life as well as his plays, Marlowe embodies some of the contrasts of his age. A poet with a profound feeling for sensuous beauty, he was also involved in political intrigue and spying. He was killed in a tavern brawl at the age of 30.

Below: The title-page of Marlowe's heroic drama *Tamburlaine*, which transformed Elizabethan theatre. The story of a humble shepherd who succeeds in becoming a mighty monarch emphasizes the sense of limitless human achievement and the richness of the physical world typical of the early English Renaissance.

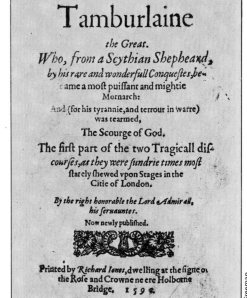

Left: The title-page of *Doctor Faustus* by Marlowe. The woodcut illustrating the page shows Faustus standing within the mystic circle and conjuring the devil. The crude magician of the German Faust legends is transformed by Marlowe into a figure embodying both the heroic and tragic side of Renaissance aspiration.

Below: A scene from a modern production of *Dr. Faustus*. After making his pact with the devil, Faustus is entertained with a pageant of the Seven Deadly Sins, including Gluttony (shown here). This reveals the more medieval aspect of Marlowe's imagination; allegorical figures were a medieval convention.

211

the clown Miles, who is a direct descendant of the comic Vice of medieval drama and Ralph, who foreshadows the more sombre jesters of Shakespeare's plays. In *James IV* Greene set an example much used by his successors in adapting a popular Italian tale of romance and intrigue for the purposes of drama. His combinations of near-tragic incident with a happy ending introduced the tragi-comedy into English drama, a form which was later made popular by Beaumont and Fletcher, two playwrights who collaborated in many plays during the Jacobean era.

Revenge drama
Thomas Kyd's *The Spanish Tragedy* (c.1586) marks the beginning of a greater period of drama. Kyd takes the Latin tragedies of Seneca as his model to create something that was both distinctive and deeply appealing to the Elizabethan imagination. The play opens with the ghost of Andrea seeking revenge for his death and during the rest of the play he witnesses the bloody events which follow. In addition to the vengeful ghost, Kyd uses other Senecan elements, such as a chorus and a messenger who brings extended reports of offstage action. He displays a firmer grasp of the Senecan five-act structure than any predecessor.

But what probably made *The Spanish Tragedy* so strikingly successful with contemporary audiences was its vividly dramatic exploration of the theme of revenge, a theme which for many reasons was of intimate concern to the Elizabethan public. It inspired a whole group of plays such as *The Revenger's Tragedy* by Cyril Tourneur, *The White Devil* by John Webster and, most famous of all, Shakespeare's *Hamlet*, of which Kyd himself may have written an earlier version. In an age when violent death was as familiar as it is in ours, the slow, cumbersome and expensive processes of

law and the importance of personal and family honour made private revenge for real or imagined wrongs seem the only effective response in many circumstances —yet official Christian morality forbade it. It was the tension between these forces which revenge tragedy explored.

Kyd introduced, in the figure of Lorenzo, a character based on popular ideas about the Italian political thinker Niccolo Machiavelli. The stage 'Machiavellian' becomes a character who is totally without moral principles and who acts entirely in his own interests, exploiting the scruples of others while paying lip service to them. Shakespeare's Richard III and Marlowe's Jew of Malta are outstanding examples of such a character.

The great tragedies of Marlowe
Christopher Marlowe is the other great figure in the first phase of Elizabethan tragedy. His first play *Tamburlaine* (c.1587) which may have been written while he was still an undergraduate at Cambridge, took London by storm. It tells the story of a humble Scythian shepherd who, without advantage of birth or fortune, rises to be a world conqueror through sheer self-confidence, ruthless single-mindedness and innate ability. *Tamburlaine* seems to epitomize the splendid energy of Renaissance individualism and its passion for the things of this world, elements which seemed to threaten the older medieval world-view based on hierarchy and obedience. Marlowe's style was as defiantly revolutionary as his material. The opening words of the Prologue proclaim not only the play's theme but the manner in which it is to be expressed:

*From jigging veins of rhyming
mother wits,*
*And such conceits as clownage keeps
in pay,*

*We'll lead you to the stately tent of
war,*
*Where you shall here the Scythian
Tamburlaine*
*Threatening the world with high
astounding terms*
*And scourging kingdoms with his
conquering sword.*

Turning contemptuously aside from the somewhat pedestrian jog-trot of most earlier dramatic verse and the aimless buffoonery of many plays, Marlowe gives to the English drama a voice full of 'high astounding terms' which seem to fully express the strength, the passion and the brutality of one aspect of the Renaissance.

In *Dr. Faustus* (c.1592) Marlowe created his greatest play, where the aspirations of Renaissance man are brought into unforgettable conflict with the moral and religious sanctions which should limit them, in the story of the learned man who sells his soul to the devil in return for 24 years of unlimited power. The last scene, in which Faustus waits in agony while the clock remorselessly ticks away the minutes of his final hour on earth, is a superb dramatic rendering of the splendour and misery of human endeavour.

Ben Jonson's comedies
If Kyd and Marlowe are the founding fathers of Elizabethan tragedy, Ben Jonson can claim pre-eminence in stage comedy. His two early plays *Every Man in His Humour* and *Every Man Out of His Humour* (c.1598) effectively introduced a kind of comedy very different from Shakespeare's romantic comedies, with their pastoral setting, their plots based on disguise and obstacles to the course of true love and their genial tolerance of human frailty. Jonson wholeheartedly embraced the classical view that the purpose of comedy was to correct human folly by holding it up to ridicule. He built

Left: A scene from *The Alchemist* (1610) one of Ben Jonson's finest comedies. Alchemy, the aim of which was to change base metals into gold, was fashionable in Jonson's time. He uses alchemy to symbolize the universal desire to 'get rich quick' and in the swindling characters Face and Subtle he mocks the greed and hypocrisy of Jacobean society.

Right: A scene from a modern production of Webster's sombre tragedy *The White Devil*, showing the adulterous Vittoria with her seducer, urged on by her brother. The melodrama of the plot—including poisoned paintings and disguised stranglers—does not diminish Webster's profound and vivid sense of evil and corruption.

Below: Illustration from *The Triumph of God's Revenge against the Crying and Execrable Sin of Wilful and Premeditated Murder*, a collection of stories about murder and adultery by John Reynolds, published in 1621. One of the stories formed the basis of Thomas Middleton's *The Changeling*. This Jacobean dramatist transforms the crude tit-for-tat morality of the stories into a moving moral tragedy.

his plays by isolating and exaggerating a single obsession in a character until he becomes comically grotesque, monstrous but compelling. These characters are placed in a setting which, while it is recognizable in some details as Jacobean London, has a heightened colour and vividness which matches the larger-than-life quality of the characters.

Of his three best-known plays, *Volpone* (1606), though set in Venice, in many ways recalls Jonson's London. The characters are degraded to the level of beasts by their desire for money and in the end the most cunning of them fall into their own traps. Jonson's other two comic masterpieces, *The Alchemist* (1610) and *Bartholomew Fair* (1614) are both set in London. The first is a marvellously constructed dramatic fable based on the contemporary interest in alchemy, satirising the desire to 'get rich quick' as well as Puritan hypocrisy. The second has as its setting a famous London fair. Though it contains the usual Jonsonian crew of sharpers and their victims, its tone is celebratory rather than satirical.

Harsher satirical comedy dominated the closing years of the sixteenth century and into the reign of James I, exemplified by John Marston and Thomas Middleton. But the plays of Beaumont and Fletcher demonstrate a growing trend for both tragedy and comedy to be softened and 'prettified', largely for the entertainment of the court and aristocracy.

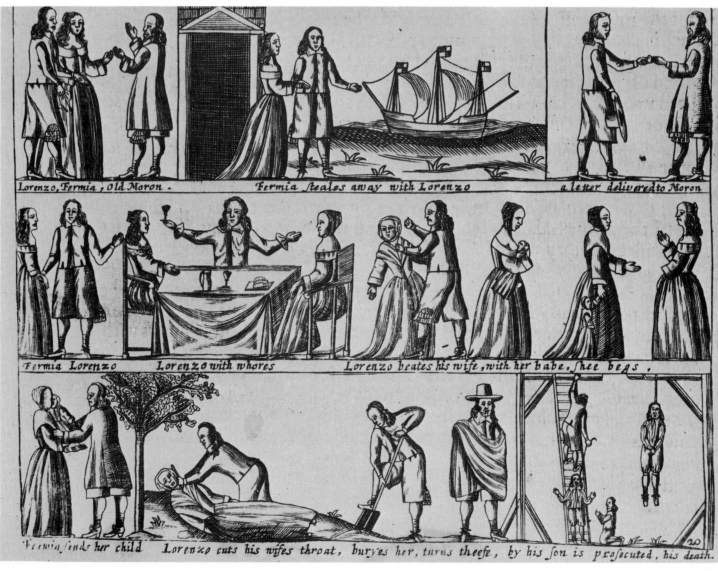

213

Shakespeare

We know very little about Shakespeare's life. He was christened in Stratford on Avon on 26th April 1564. We know that he was the son of a prosperous citizen of the town, who later fell on hard times, and that his mother's family were Roman Catholics. In 1582 Shakespeare married Anne Hathaway, eight years older than himself, and their daughter Susanna was born six months later, followed by twins in 1585; after that nothing is known of Shakespeare, until in the early 1590s he turns up in London as an actor and playwright.

It is uncertain how much education Shakespeare had, whether he travelled in foreign countries, and what took him to London. Even after his career had begun, the only information about his life is found in legal documents (fortunately for the researchers, Shakespeare did not always pay his bills), in the records of his company of actors and in references (not always complimentary) by other writers. Shakespeare's private life is a blank to us. His marriage was possibly unhappy; his family stayed in Stratford while he worked in London, although he retired to Stratford in his last years, when he had made his money.

His work consists of 37 plays, a collection of sonnets, a few lyrics and two long poems, *Venus & Adonis* and *The Rape of Lucrece*, published in 1593 and 1594, when he was still a young man. These poems are no longer widely read, but they may have been the works that gave Shakepeare most satisfaction. Whereas writing plays was thought of as kind of 'script writing' hackwork, (as the writer of film scripts today does not enjoy the prestige of the 'true author'), these poems were the sort of literary performance that aroused admiration among cultivated readers, such as Shakespeare's patron and friend the Earl of Southampton, to whom they are dedicated. They are brilliant examples of sixteenth-century taste, by a poet who has read Ovid (the favourite poet of the age) and is showing his readers how dazzlingly clever he can be.

Shakespearean love stories

For the first half of his career, Shakespeare was primarily a writer of comedy. One of the most famous of these is *The Merchant of Venice*. It combines two traditional stories (like most Elizabethan dramatists, Shakespeare often told two or more stories in one play and sometimes the interacting effects of these double plots can be very subtle). The one is the story of Portia, a young woman who, by the terms of her father's will, has to marry the suitor who chooses correctly between three caskets, of gold, silver and lead. These suitors who want to win her out of mere greed or vanity choose the richer caskets, but Bassanio, the hero, chooses the lead, with a moralizing speech on how 'the world is still deceived with ornament'.

As a love-story it is delightful. Portia's speeches on her love for Bassanio have the spontaneous feeling of the best love-poetry, but the relationship is given deeply ironic overtones by the fact that Bassanio had earlier announced his need to marry Portia for her wealth, so as to

National Portrait Gallery

Mary Evans

Portraits of William Shakespeare (above right) and of the Earl of Southampton (above), Shakespeare's young friend and patron. Some of Shakespeare's sonnets concern a 'dark lady' who causes much unhappiness. A number refer to a young man with intense love and jealousy, whom some scholars believe to be Southampton himself. The sonnet (right) suggests the dark lady and the young man, Shakespeare's 'better angel', together deceived him. A major theme of the sonnets is the awareness of death and decay, of love and beauty eroded by time. Others hint at Shakespeare's self-consciousness about his social origins.

Two loves I have of comfort and despair,
Which like two spirits do suggest me still:
The better angel is a man right fair,
The worser spirit a woman color'd ill.
To win me soon to hell, my female evil
Tempteth my better angel from my side,
And would corrupt my saint to be a devil,
Wooing his purity with her foul pride.
And whether that my angel be turn'd fiend
Suspect I may, yet not directly tell;
But being both from me, both to each friend,
I guess one angel in another's hell:
   Yet this shall I ne'er know, but live in doubt
   Till my bad angel fire my good one out.

Walker Art Gallery

Below: A cartoon of Shylock and Portia from *The Merchant of Venice*, with the great 19th-century actor Henry Irving as Shylock. The character of Shylock, the Jewish money-lender, has always caused controversy; some have seen him as a grotesque villain, others as a wronged and tragic figure.

Right: A scene from Shakespeare's comedy *A Midsummer Night's Dream* by Fuseli. Titania (queen of the fairies), under the influence of a magic potion, falls in love with the ridiculous Bottom, one of a group of workmen rehearsing a play in the forest. He has been given an ass's head by the mischievous fairy Puck.

Angelo Hornak/Victoria & Albert

Bulloz

Below left: Hogarth's painting of David Garrick as Richard III. Shakespeare wrote two sets of four history plays; one deals with the Wars of the Roses and the reigns of Henry VI, Edward VI and Richard III.
A second series moves back in time, looking at Richard II, Henry IV and Henry V.

Below: A scene from a modern production of *Henry IV* Part 1, showing Falstaff with Prince Hal. Falstaff, the corrupt but likeable friend of Prince Hal, is necessarily cast aside when Hal accedes to the throne as Henry V. The theme of the burdens and responsibilities of kingship is central to Shakespeare's histories.

Donald Cooper

recover his failing fortunes. The interaction between love and money, and the problem of establishing true values, is explored throughout the play and is given added complexity by the other half of the plot. This concerns the wicked Jewish usurer Shylock, who tricks his Christian victim into agreeing to have a pound of flesh cut from him if he is late in returning a loan. The two plots are not only linked outwardly (by Portia and Bassanio becoming involed in Shylock's claim) but in a far more fundamental way by their common theme.

As You Like It and *Twelfth Night* are certainly the two most beautiful romantic comedies in English. Both are love-stories in which the hero and heroine are kept apart by obstacles which include disguise and confused identity—the heroine disguises herself as a boy and the hero cannot understand the mysterious attraction that he feels for her. Since female parts were played by boys in the Elizabethan theatre, it was simple and appropriate to use this convention; it was also assumed that the disguise could not be seen through until the characters revealed themselves on stage. The beauty of this convention is that it gives the dramatist a chance to explore with peculiar piquancy

215

Bulloz

Mansell

Bulloz

questions of personal identity, of the
difference between appearance and reality,
and of the existence of unrecognized
feelings and motivations.

As well as comedies, Shakespeare wrote
a number of plays on English history in
the first half of his career. Today his
'histories' are treated as a separate kind
of play, but he probably saw them as
tragedies dealing with the burden of kingship and the tragic situation of the king
on whom responsibility for the whole
kingdom falls. The great theme of the
history plays is the horror of civil war.
Through them runs a conservative belief
in the need for strong government in order
to avoid anarchy—a political position
very acceptable to the Tudor monarchs.
In Shakespeare's hands, however, this
attitude becomes more than mere political
conformism, since he gives it profound
emotional and philosophical implications.

The great tragedies

In the second half of his career
Shakespeare wrote less and changed his
mood. It is not known why he turned to
tragedy: some see it as the natural
development of his art, others as the result
of a personal crisis and a darkening view
of life. Whatever the reason, his tragedies
have made him the world's greatest
dramatist—above all in the five masterpieces, *Hamlet*, *Othello*, *King Lear*,
Macbeth and *Antony & Cleopatra*.

In every case, Shakespeare rewrote an
old play or dramatised an existing story,
but his reshaping of it revealed a profound
originality. For example, Shakespeare's
tragedy *Hamlet* centres around the
popular Elizabethan theme of 'revenge'

and the audience at the Globe theatre no

Mander and Mitchenson

On loan to the National Portrait Gallery from the Tate Gallery

evil characters in the end destroy themselves, but the blameless Cordelia also dies. After the plot against Cordelia's life has been discovered, a messenger is sent to save her, with the line: 'The Gods defend her.' Immediately afterwards comes the famous stage direction: 'Enter Lear with Cordelia dead in his arms.' Such is the value of the gods' protection in this world of hard hearts.

Others may see the spiritual progress of Lear as both the core and 'meaning' of the play. As Lear descends into madness he finds a growing understanding of the sufferings of the poor, of the injustices perpetrated by those in authority and of the hypocrisy of society. Shakespeare shows us 'reason in madness'; the clarity of Lear's vision increases as his grasp on corrupt reality declines. We see Lear, Gloucester and other characters in the play learning humility and love, discovering in effect the moral truths of Christianity in a pagan world.

The vision of the last plays

Shakespeare did not end with tragedy. In his last plays, *Pericles, Cymbeline, The Tempest* and *The Winter's Tale*, he turned to tragicomedy—plays that seem to threaten death and disaster, then at the end offer reconciliation, happiness and a promise of new hope from the next generation. *The Tempest*, possibly Shakespeare's last play, is set on an enchanted island, where an aged Italian duke named Prospero lives with his young daughter Miranda, after being ousted from his rightful throne by his brother. Prospero controls the island by his practice of magic—the spirits of the island are at his command. He causes a storm at sea, by which his usurping brother and his allies are also shipwrecked on the island.

Shakespeare uses this plot to explore the themes of wrong-doing, love and reconciliation through forgiveness; these are brought together to form a solemn, but finally serene and hopeful vision of the world. The play contains some of Shakespeare's finest language; the atmosphere of the island is evoked in some of the most marvellous nature poetry ever written.

The play deals with an old man's vision. Prospero is deeply aware of the transience of all earthly events and the temporary nature of youthful joy. At the end, he gives up his magical art and returns to the kingdom he had once ruled. As he says after summoning up a magical pageant for his young daughter Miranda and her lover, then commanding the ghostly players to disappear:

*Our revels now are ended; these our
        actors
As I foretold you, were all spirits and
Are melted into air, into thin air:
And, like the baseless fabric of this
        vision,
The cloud-capp'd towers, the
        gorgeous palaces,
The solemn temples, the great globe
        itself,
Yea, all which it inherit, shall
        dissolve
And, like this insubstantial pageant
        faded,
Leave not a rack behind. We are such
        stuff
As dreams are made on, and our little
        life
Is rounded with a sleep.*

doubt went along to *Hamlet* expecting the conventional excitements of a revenge play. But as well as these, the play contains many issues at a deeper level; the 'psychological' exploration of Hamlet's relationships, the philosophical puzzlement of the hero unable to bring himself to carry out his task of revenge, the bitter comedy of his pretended madness.

In *King Lear*, Shakespeare once again joined together two different stories to provide the basic plot of his tragedy. Lear, a British king in pre-Christian times, appears in the first scene as a petulant old man who determines to divide his kingdom between his three daughters according to the extent of their affection for him—as displayed in a ceremony before the assembled court. His kingdom goes to Goneril and Regan, who both make a great show of their love for him, while his third daughter Cordelia is banished for her refusal to provide such empty flattery. As the play progresses, we see the full falseness and evil of Goneril and Regan unleashed, while the powerless Lear is brought to an awareness of the wrong he has done Cordelia. Intertwined with this story is the plot concerning one of Lear's nobles, the Earl of Gloucester, who is deceived by a false bastard son into banishing his true son Edgar.

As with most of Shakespeare's plays, King Lear is so rich in its language and ideas that it is open to a number of different interpretations. Shakespeare questions the basis of human wickedness itself; in the words of Lear 'is there any cause in nature that makes these hard hearts?' At times the play seems so pessimistic that it doubts the possibility of goodness surviving in this world—the

Kobal Collection

217

The Elizabethan Theatre

In 1576 James Burbage, a carpenter turned actor, built the first commercial theatre in England. It was called, simply, The Theatre and it stood within the area of Shoreditch, outside one of the northern gates of the city of London. It was therefore beyond the jurisdiction of the city authorities, who were hostile to plays and the acting profession.

After Henry VIII had broken away from the Roman Catholic Church and England was made Protestant, the church authorities became actively hostile to the older medieval drama, which it associated with popery. In spite of deliberate suppression, it took nearly 50 years for this religious drama to be completely stamped out and by that time London already had its first purpose-built theatres and professional actors.

In spite of continued attacks by puritan preachers and city fathers, Burbage's example was followed by many other enterprising business men. During the next sixty years, half a dozen or so public theatres existed in London, until all theatres were finally closed down in 1642. Their survival and continued success were due in part to the patronage of the court and aristocracy, which protected them against civic hostility. But even more important was the fact that they satisfied, throughout a whole range of the population, that taste for drama which had for so long been fed by medieval miracle and morality plays.

Little is known about the exact construction of the first public theatre but there is plenty of evidence, both in the form of direct descriptions (including a sketch by a foreign traveller) and what can be reasonably inferred from the stage action of Elizabethan plays, to tell us what a typical Elizabethan theatre looked like. Most of the theatres of the time probably followed a common pattern, though there might be minor differences.

The playhouse structure

The structure of the Elizabethan playhouse was derived from the kind of buildings in which dramatic and other entertainments had taken place before purpose-built theatres came into existence. These included the banqueting halls of Tudor noblemen, in which 'interludes' were performed during a break between meals, innyards (or the public rooms of inns) and the bull and bear-baiting rings which were popular in Elizabethan London. Like these rings, the outer form of the playhouse was circular or polygonal. One penny admitted you to the building and the performance, though you would have to stand in an open yard to watch it. Surrounding this yard were three tiers of roofed seats, entrance to which required further payment. The sections nearest to the stage, called 'the Lords' Rooms', were even more expensive, roughly corresponding to the boxes of a modern theatre. Seating in tiers was a custom derived from performances in the large inns, which often had two or three storeys, from which the audience could watch.

The acting area consisted of a large

Freeman

Above: An engraving of the famous Globe Theatre c.1612, situated on the Thames Bankside. It was the regular home of the Chamberlain's Men, the acting company to which Shakespeare belonged. It was destroyed by fire in 1613, rebuilt the following year but finally demolished in 1644, two years after English theatres were officially closed.

Below: A portrait of Edward Alleyn (1566-1626), a great Elizabethan actor. He belonged to a company called The Admiral's Men who purchased all Marlowe's plays. Alleyn achieved tremendous success in such roles as Tamburlaine and Dr. Faustus and died rich enough to endow a school and almshouses.

Collection Marquess of Bath

Barnaby's

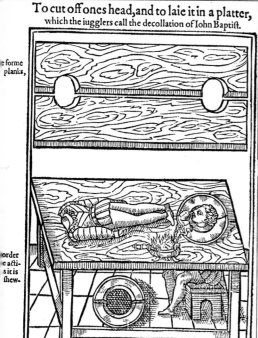

To cut off ones head, and to laie it in a platter, which the iugglers call the decollation of Iohn Baptist.

e forme planks,

order e actisit is ſhew-

Left: An illustration from Reginald Scot's *Discovery of Witchcraft* published in 1584. This device, showing how to 'cut off one's head, and to lay it in a platter', was a popular fairground entertainment. It was probably used in theatrical performances and may have been borrowed from the stage tricks of 'jugglers'.

Right: A costume design for a torch-bearer by Inigo Jones (1573-1652). This design was for one of the many court masques by Ben Jonson for which Jones provided decor and costumes. The two men disagreed over the relative importance of language and visual spectacle, but eventually it was the visual aspect which became more elaborate and ingenious.

Left: A scene from Shakespeare's play *Titus Andronicus*, set in ancient Rome. This is the only existing Elizabethan drawing of a scene from a play. Although the central characters seem to be wearing historical (Roman) costumes, the minor figures are in Elizabethan dress—possibly the usual stage practice of the time.

Right: A detail from a map of London made by a Dutch engraver Claes de Visscher in 1650, showing the octagonal building of the Globe playhouse. Elizabethan public theatres were usually roughly circular, enclosing a yard open to the sky and surrounded by galleries. Play performances took place in daylight.

Radio Times Hulton Picture Library

Michael Holford

Devonshire Collection/Trustees of the Chatsworth Settlement

apron stage which came right out into the yard where the greater part of the audience, known as 'groundlings', stood. Thus the actors were surrounded on three sides by the audience and it was quite usual for young gallants to watch the play seated on benches placed on the stage itself. In addition, there was a balcony over the stage which was sometimes used by musicians, sometimes as part of the playing area and, when it was not required for either of these functions, served as additional seating space. Such informal seating arrangements suggest that there was a close involvement between the actors and the audience. Instead of being separated from the actors by a curtain, and a proscenium arch (a decorated arch framing the stage) the audience could see them at close quarters and from all sides. The fact that performances took place in daylight, from early afternoon to early evening, enhanced the sense of audience and players sharing the same world.

Elizabethan dramatists made impressive use of the image of the theatre as a metaphor for human life. Appropriately enough, the most famous of Elizabethan theatres, the Globe, to which Shakespeare belonged, carried the motto 'All the world's a stage'. Although belief in the medieval Christian world-view was beginning to break up, the idea of human life as a drama played before God was still a powerful force in the Elizabethan theatre. It is no coincidence that the roofed portion of the stage (which was supported by two massive pillars) was known as the 'heavens' and the space below the stage was called 'hell'; this theatre was a miniature image of the universe itself.

The actors entered and left the stage through two doors on either side of the back wall immediately below the balcony. These doors were a regular feature of the great banqueting halls of the Tudor nobility (where interludes were often staged) while the balcony itself may be based on the minstrels' gallery of such halls. The area between the two doors and beneath the balcony was hung with a curtain which could be drawn back to reveal a set scene, such as a cave or tomb. Behind the back wall was the 'tiring house' or dressing rooms while immediately above the roofed stage was a hut housing machinery which could lower elaborate pieces of scenery and even people on to the stage below. At the very top of the building was another hut from which a flag was flown to indicate that a performance was about to take place.

The lavish and colourful stage

Modern reconstructions of Elizabethan playhouses often look austerely functional and even drab. But if the many contemporary references to the original theatres are anything to go by, they were splendidly colourful inside. 'Stately', 'gorgeous', 'magnificent' and similar descriptions are frequently used both by enthusiasts and opponents of the theatre. The two pillars supporting the roof were lavishly gilded and perhaps painted to look like marble, while the underside of the 'heavens' often carried a representation of the zodiac. The rest of the permanent wooden structure was also gaily painted and probably intricately carved. When a tragedy was performed, the sides of the stage would be draped in black while brighter hangings were used for comedies. Splendid costumes, on which large sums of money were often spent, added to the colour and gaiety of the theatre.

Though the Elizabethan theatre had little or no painted scenery, there were a large number of theatrical properties, some of them apparently quite elaborate, which could be used to identify a location when necessary. For example, the inventory of Philip Henslowe, the best known 219 theatre manager of his day, shows that his stock included a 'hell mouth', a 'mossy bank' and a 'city of Rome'. But in general such properties were not used to create a scenic illusion, but only to indicate whether the scene was taking place indoors or out, in day or night time and so on.

While to us this may seem primitive, it had at least two enormous advantages. In the first place, because no elaborate scene changes were involved, the action of the play could flow smoothly from scene to scene if their locations in real life were widely separated one from another. For example, in Shakespeare's *Antony and Cleopatra*, the action moves between Egypt and Rome, land and sea and many different parts of the battle area so rapidly that it would be impossible to stage with any 'realistic' scenic representation. Secondly the near-absence of scenery, as well as the fact that no lighting changes were possible, meant that the dramatist had to create scene and atmosphere through the only means available to him, the spoken word. The result is that Elizabethan drama contains some of the richest and most resonant writing in the language.

The theatre in Shakespeare's day was not only a bright and colourful place, it was also a very lively and noisy one. The audience, as has been noted, surrounded the actors on every side and those who sat on the stage were in the very midst of them. By all accounts, audiences were very demonstrative, not hesitating to express loudly their appreciation or disapproval. Smoking, drinking and munching nuts and apples were a regular part of the afternoon's entertainment, as was the passing of loud comments on the action while it was in progress. The dramatist Thomas Dekker, in his satirical pamphlet *The Gull's Hornbook* (1609) gives a splendid account of how a gallant should behave at a playhouse:

> '*Take up a rush, and tickle the earnest ears of your fellow gallants, to make other fools fall a-laughing; mew at passionate speeches; blare at merry; find fault with the music; whew at the children's action; whistle at the songs; and, above all, curse the sharers (actors) . . .*'

Whatever else the Elizabethan audience may have been, it was not inhibited. The theatre was a truly popular national pastime, drawing into it all classes of society—apprentices and artisans, students and lawyers, courtiers and gentlemen of leisure. Royalty itself regularly patronized the drama through command performances at court of plays that were already successful in the public theatre. Foreign visitors noted with some surprise that respectable women were frequently to be seen in the London theatres—which was not the custom abroad.

Virtuoso acting

As for the actors, they belonged to a profession that was rapidly rising in social esteem as well as in financial prosperity. Some of them such as Richard Burbage and Will Kemp were household names, while at least one, Edward Alleyn, made enough money to endow a college and almshouses in his will. Little is known about just what style of acting the Elizabethans favoured. We do know that

220

Mander & Mitchenson

Above: A portrait thought to be of Richard Burbage (1567-1619), the most distinguished Shakespearean actor in the Elizabethan theatre. He was the leading member of the acting company to which Shakespeare belonged, playing the parts of King Lear, Othello and Hamlet in their first productions.

Below: A 1672 engraving from *The Wits* by Francis Kirkman, showing some of the most popular theatrical characters of the time on stage at the Red Bull Playhouse in Clerkenwell, London. Notice the row of footlights along the edge of the stage; the first depiction of such lighting in an English theatre.

Radio Times Hulton Picture Library

Left: A reconstruction of an Elizabethan theatre. The theatre was probably very colourful inside, often being described as 'stately' and 'gorgeous'. The two pillars supporting the roof were lavishly gilded. The underside of the roof might represent a zodiac, while the rest of the wooden structure was painted and carved.

Right: Edward Kynaston (c.1640-1706), one of the last actors to play feminine roles. In the 16th and early 17th century women did not appear on stage. Later, on the Restoration stage, he played such heroic characters as Henry IV. Samuel Pepys remarked that Kynaston 'made the loveliest lady that ever I saw'.

Mander & Mitchenson

good actors received praise from contemporaries for their naturalness and truth to life, but this is not very helpful as ideas of what is natural and true to life vary a great deal from period to period; anyone who has seen an old film will be able to confirm this. The art of public speaking, known as oratory, which was an art related to acting, in Elizabethan times made use of a series of highly stylized gestures and it is possible that acting, too, was stylized by today's standards. But whatever the technique used, there is no doubt that the best actors carried conviction. When we consider that the roles of women were played by boy actors, it is no small tribute to the actors' art to learn that at Oxford in 1610, the boy who played Desdemona in Shakespeare's tragedy *Othello* 'implored the pity of the spectators by her very face' in the deathbed scene. Certainly, on a nearly bare stage and surrounded by spectators in broad daylight, the demands made on an actor must have been considerable; the plays themselves show that principal actors were also often expected to be singers, fencers, dancers and acrobats. Not surprisingly the profession had its own rigorous system of apprenticeship, with young boys being taken under the wing of older and more experienced players.

In addition to the larger public playhouses, there were also the so-called 'private' theatres which were smaller, completely covered buildings. Because they accommodated fewer people they charged a higher admission price, usually at least a shilling. Gradually these smaller theatres began to attract the more fashionable section of the audience while the public theatres, catering for the larger but poorer section of the audience fell back more and more on tried and tested dramatic formulas. By the time James I died in 1625, there was no longer a single drama that attracted all sections of society and the theatre on which the Puritans brought down the curtain in 1642 was almost exclusively a pastime of the court and its hangers-on.

Features of a Typical Elizabethan Theatre

1 Arena
2 Proscenium
3 Trapdoor
4 Stage doors
5 Inner stage with tiring house (dressing rooms) behind
6 Balcony
7 Hut housing stage machinery

Chapter 3

The Seventeenth Century

The Spinet Concert. The spinet, the ancestor of the upright piano, was particularly popular during the 17th and 18th centuries. It was like a small oblong harpsichord, with a single keyboard and a three octave range.

Milton

John Milton was the most learned of all English poets, one of the most deeply religious and the one who took his calling as a poet most seriously. From his early youth his ambition was to write a great poem. He saw this as something which would bring him immortal fame and also be a way of devoting his talents to the service of God.

Milton was born in 1608 in London. His father was a scrivener, or law-writer, and a musician; the young Milton may have got his love of music and his studious habits from the family atmosphere. He went to Christ's College, Cambridge, in 1625 and as a student he wrote poems in both English and Latin. He felt already that he was destined to write a masterpiece. His own writings tell us that his teachers were enthusiastic about his talents, that the style of the exercises he wrote 'by certain vital signs it had was likely to live'. Both in response to his masters' encouragement and to an 'inward prompting' of his own, he began to think that by a combination of hard work and talent he 'might perhaps leave something so written to after times as they should not willingly let it die'.

Strangely enough, this view of his early ambition comes from a rather unlikely source, a political pamphlet called 'Reason of Church Government' written when he was 33. This is characteristic of Milton's prose; his habit of pausing to speak of his own career and ambitions in the course of a public document means that we know more about him than any other writer of his age—not only the facts of his life but also his innermost thoughts and aspirations. His sense of dedication, the acceptance of hard work as his lot in life, and the conviction that he is a man singled out by God for some high literary task, all emerge. Writing on impersonal themes, he speaks across the centuries with a human, individual voice.

Milton left Cambridge in 1632, and settled in the country. His father had retired to Horton in Buckinghamshire, and there Milton lived for the next six years, reading widely and writing a little. Either at Cambridge or at Horton he wrote a pair of poems, *L'Allegro* and *Il Penseroso* (The Cheerful Man and the Thoughtful Man) comparing the pleasures of Mirth and Melancholy. Their graceful movement and haunting beauty makes them in many ways the most immediately enjoyable of Milton's poems.

Comus: Milton's magical masque

In 1634 Milton's friend Henry Lawes, a musician, wrote the music for a masque to celebrate the appointment of the Earl of Bridgewater, head of the Egerton family, as president of the Council of Wales. The masque was to be performed at Ludlow Castle by members of the family. Milton was invited to write the text—a full-length allegorical story in verse, with songs. He invented as the chief character a figure called Comus (the word means 'reveller'), son of Bacchus, the god of wine and festivity, and of Circe, the enchantress in Greek legend who changed men into pigs. Comus lives in the woods with his troop of wild beasts who were once men and women; his pastime is to capture and seduce unwary travellers.

In the masque, the daughter and the two sons of the Earl of Bridgewater are imagined to be passing through the wood and are accidentally separated. The young men are afraid for their sister's safety when they learn about Comus, but she is quite safe because of her virtue and, though Comus captures her, he is unable to make her drink his magic potion. In the end she is rescued by an Attendant Spirit who has descended from Heaven, with the help of a local river-nymph called Sabrina; the children are then reunited with their parents—who were of course sitting in the audience.

This simple story is clearly meant to represent the trials of the virtuous soul in the wicked world; it is a typical Renaissance work in its blending of Christianity and Greek mythology, and a typical masque in its blending of music, dancing, poetry and moral allegory. We read it today because of the magic of its language. Comus himself speaks with the colourful fascination of so many wicked characters and the speeches of the Lady, fearful and lost in the wood, are expressed with all the power of Milton's romantic imagination. For example, as she follows the elusive sounds of the drunken revellers in

Above and below: 19th-century illustrations from Milton's early lyrical poems *L'Allegro* and *Il Penseroso*, the Cheerful Man and the Thoughtful Man. In this pair of poems, probably written in 1632 when Milton was 23, he contrasts the delights of light-hearted and serious pleasures. He offers such contrasting images as: '... many a youth and many a maid, Dancing in the chequered shade; And young and old come forth to play, On a sunshine holiday ...' '... may at last my weary age Find out the peaceful hermitage, The hairy gown and mossy cell, Where I may sit and rightly spell Of every star that heav'n doth shew ...'

Radio Times Hulton Picture Library

Mansell

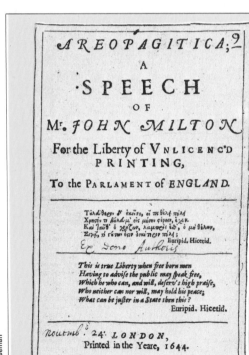

Mansell

Above: Milton as a young man by Jonathan Richardson.

Below: The title page of *Areopagitica*, one of Milton's most famous pamphlets, published in 1644. Unlike most of his political writings, it disagrees with a parliamentary order—that all printed matter must be licensed by Parliament. The pamphlet is a vigorous defence of the right of free speech; the title is derived from *Areopagus*, the hill in Athens which was the meeting place of the Upper Council in ancient Greece. He urges the Lords and Commons not to shackle the 'quick, ingenious and piercing spirit' of the English nation, which is like an 'eagle mewing its mighty youth'.

AREOPAGITICA;
A
SPEECH
OF
Mr. *JOHN MILTON*
For the Liberty of VNLICENC'D PRINTING,
To the PARLAMENT of ENGLAND.

Euripid. Hicetid.

*This is true Liberty when free born men
Having to advise the public may speak free,
Which he who can, and will, deserv's high praise,
Who neither can nor will, may hold his peace;
What can be juster in a State then this?*
Euripid. Hicetid.

November. 24. LONDON,
Printed in the Yeare, 1644.

John Freeman

MILTON'S CONTEMPORARIES

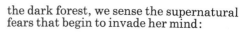

Bulloz

National Portrait Gallery

Above: Oliver Cromwell, Lord Protector of England from 1643-8. Milton was Latin secretary to Cromwell in the 1650s. One of Milton's sonnets, written in 1652 when Cromwell had defeated the Scots and was supreme in England, celebrates the general's victories but urges him now to defend free conscience against those factions who wished to suppress religious freedom:
'. . . yet much remains
To conquer still: peace
     hath her victories
No less renowned than
     war; new foes arise
Threat'ning to bind us
     with secular chains.
Help us to save free
     conscience from the paw
Of hireling wolves whose
     gospel is their maw.'

Above: Andrew Marvell, (1621-78) was Milton's assistant in his government post for a while. Milton and Marvell are the two great Puritan poets of this period. Marvell, was a man of peace and moderation. His *Horatian Ode on Cromwell's Return from Ireland* is one of his greatest poems, a subtle assessment of the political events of the time. It mixes praise of Cromwell's energy with admiration for the graciousness of the executed king. Marvell ends with a cool warning to the all-conquering Cromwell to 'keep thy sword erect' for 'the same arts that did gain a power must it maintain'.

Cooper Bridgeman

Mansell

Above: Edward Hyde, Earl of Clarendon, Royalist and lawyer, whose *History of the Rebellion and Civil Wars in England* established him as a great English historical writer. Much of it was written during periods of exile. In masterly prose, he creates a superb gallery of portraits of his contemporaries and a vivid account of the Civil War. He sums up his discussion of Cromwell: 'he will be looked upon by posterity as a brave bad man', a phrase which typifies the moderate Royalist spirit of the *History* and Clarendon's attempt to give a balanced view of very recent events.

Above: The title page of *Leviathan* (1651), the masterpiece of political philosophy by Thomas Hobbes (1588-1679). He served as a tutor in the Cavendish family for many years but in 1647 he became tutor to the exiled Prince of Wales. *Leviathan* discusses the nature of man, whom Hobbes sees as essentially a selfish competitive creature, whose natural state is one of general war: 'the life of man is solitary, poor, nasty, brutish and short'. To escape this, man establishes certain laws to govern society and gives a sovereign power total authority to enforce those laws.

---

the dark forest, we sense the supernatural fears that begin to invade her mind:

> *What might this be? A thousand*
> *   fantasies*
> *Begin to throng into my memory,*
> *Of calling shapes, and beckoning*
> *   shadows dire,*
> *And airy tongues that syllable men's*
> *   names*
> *On Sands and Shores and desert*
> *   Wildernesses.*

Comus also shows us Milton's admiration of Shakespeare: the wood where the action takes place owes much to the wood near Athens of *A Midsummer Night's Dream*, where Oberon and Titania, king and queen of the fairies, and Puck, the mischievous spirit, also waylay unwary travellers.

In 1637 a young clergyman called Edward King, whom Milton had known at Cambridge, was drowned in the Irish Sea. His friends brought out a volume of verses in his memory, to which Milton was invited to contribute. The poem he wrote has the mixture of the formal and the intensely personal that is typical of much of his other work. He cannot have felt any intense grief, for he had not known King well, and so he calls him Lycidas— a name for a shepherd in Latin poetry. The poem is in the style of a traditional pastoral elegy and, to the modern reader, its conventions seem highly artificial: thus when Milton wants to tell us that he and King studied together at Cambridge, he says that they were shepherds who drove their flocks together to the fields. Yet at the same time, *Lycidas* is one of the most personal and most moving of all elegies, for in writing of the death of the young poet and priest, Milton is thinking of himself. He too has dedicated himself to poetry, he too had once intended to enter the church—will he, also, die young?

Soon after he had written *Lycidas*, Milton set off for Italy. The grand tour, to see the great monuments of European culture, was a normal part of a young man's education. It would usually last a long time, perhaps several years (Milton was away about 16 months); the young man would set off with his tutor, would settle at a number of places, learn the language and meet scholars and writers. Milton was admitted to many learned and artistic circles of Florence and Rome (he visited Galileo, old, blind and the prisoner of the Inquisition). He might have stayed longer, but was called home by the news from England. Charles I had recalled the Long Parliament, the Scots were threatening to invade England and the country was on the verge of civil war.

Pamphleteering for the Puritans
In such a struggle, Milton could not be neutral. His sympathies were all with the Parliamentary side. He disliked the English church, feeling, along with the rest of the Puritan party, that it was still too close to Roman Catholicism: a true Reformation would abolish bishops and elaborate ceremonies. He considered Charles I a tyrant; and he felt it was his duty to join in the struggle—not by fighting, but by writing. Now began a completely new phase in Milton's career, that of pamphleteer.

During the next 19 years, he wrote a flood of tracts—against episcopacy, against censorship (his defence of free speech, called *Areopagitica*, is his most famous prose work, and its eloquence is still relevant today), and in favour of divorce. Milton's reputation has never quite recovered from the fact that he wrote his first divorce tract only six weeks after his first, unhappy marriage. After the execution of the King in 1649, Milton not only wrote defences of the deed, but also became secretary to Cromwell. Between the death of Cromwell and the Restoration of the monarchy in 1660, he returned briefly and vigorously to pamphleteering.

By this time Milton had gone blind. He had already lost his sight when he finally settled to writing the great poem he had so long postponed. He had considered many subjects, some from English history, some from early British legends, some from the Bible; he had toyed with writing a play, or a romantic epic, full of fairies and marvels and allegorical events, like the work of the Italian Ariosto, or his beloved Edmund Spenser, author of the *Faerie Queene*. If he had written this, it would probably have been in the elaborate rhymed stanzas which Spenser used, and might have had much of the magic and mystery of the poetry of *Comus*. But Milton was now a solitary and disillusioned man. He no longer wished to write about this world, so he chose the first and greatest of the Bible stories, the fall of Adam and Eve. His aim, he decided, was 'to justify the ways of God to men'. He wrote an epic in blank verse, which he considered the right medium for an epic or heroic poem. The result was *Paradise Lost*, the greatest poem in the English language.

Paradise Lost: the great masterpiece

Like the epics of Homer and Virgil, *Paradise Lost* starts in the middle—with the expulsion of Satan and his rebel angels from Heaven. Thrown over the crystal battlements, they fall through the vastness of chaos until they find themselves chained on the burning lake of Hell. The first two books tell how they gathered themselves together and held a council of war, like warriors in a classical epic. They decide to avenge themselves on God by seducing his new creature, Man, and Satan sets off to fly to earth and achieve this. The next four books take place in Paradise, and contain Milton's attempt to show us the life of unfallen man.

The earlier events—Satan's rebellion, his battle against the loyal angels and his defeat by the Messiah—are related to Adam by Raphael, the archangel whom God sends to converse with him and to warn him of the dangers of temptation. The story of the Fall itself, the eating of the apple by Eve, then by Adam (and its unhappy consequences) fill Books IX and X. The last two books are a vision of the future, shown to Adam, in which Milton tells the whole story of human history. The poem ends with the expulsion from Eden, in lines of sad inevitability:

> *The world was all before them, where*
> *to choose*
> *Their place of rest, and Providence*
> *their guide;*
> *They hand in hand with wandering*
> *steps and slow*
> *Through Eden took their solitary way.*

Milton wrote two more poems before his death in 1674. It was no doubt natural that, having written *Paradise Lost*, he

Loaned by Mrs. Reeves

Left: A scene from a 1958 production of Milton's masque *Comus* at Ludlow Castle. It was first performed there in 1634. It shows the confrontation between the evil enchanter Comus and the Elder Brother. A kindly spirit has given the two brothers, lost in the wood, a magic herb to protect them against the spells of Comus. Their sister however, defies the temptations of Comus through her own chastity.

Below: An early 20th-century illustration, by Arthur Rackham, showing the people who have fallen under Comus' spell and turned into brutish creatures that 'not once perceive their foul disfigurement but boast themselves more comely than before'.

Cooper Bridgeman

. . . . . . .Hail horrors, hail
*Infernal world, and thou profoundest
Hell*
*Receive thy new Possessor: One who
brings*
*A mind not to be changed by Place or
Time.*
*The mind is its own place, and in
itself*
*Can make a Heav'n of Hell, a Hell of
Heav'n.*
*What matter where, if I be still the
same,*
*And what I should be, all but less
than he*
*Whom Thunder hath made greater?
Here at least*
*We shall be free; th' Almighty hath
not built*
*Here for his envy, will not drive us
hence:*
*Here we may reign secure, and in my
choice*
*To reign is worth ambition though in
Hell:*
*Better to reign in Hell, than serve
in Heav'n.*

Picturepoint

Above: Satan in Council, an illustration by William Blake from Book I of *Paradise Lost*. Both as painter and poet, Blake (1757-1827) was greatly influenced by Milton. He was the first to suggest that Milton's deepest sympathies lay with Satan, not with God: 'Milton was a true poet, and of the devil's party without knowing it'.

Above right: Satan's defiant assertion of ambition from Book I of *Paradise Lost*. Milton uses all his poetic skill to show us what is thrilling and 'heroic' in Satan's pursuit of power, but ultimately reveals its fundamental hollowness. He believes that we can only know good through knowing evil, and the poem offers a clear statement that happiness lies in obedience and salvation through Christ.

Below: Blake's illustration of the Temptation and Fall from *Paradise Lost*. Satan's success in tempting Eve coincides with his own final degradation, forced to assume the shape of a serpent.

Below: The fall of the rebel angels into Hell, by the 19th-century artist Gustave Doré, from Book VI of *Paradise Lost*: '. . . Hell at last Yawning received them whole . . .'. The story of the revolt of Satan and his followers is told to Adam and Eve by the angel Raphael, to alert them to the nature of their enemy.

should also write *Paradise Regained*, but the choice of subject is unexpected. He does not tell the whole story of the Life of Christ, nor does he concentrate on the Crucifixion or the Nativity, the two most significant and famous parts. Instead he chose an episode in the life of Jesus which he may have felt offered parallels with his own sense of dedication; he told the story of the 40 days which Jesus passed in the wilderness, in meditation and prayer, resisting the temptations of Satan; instead of ending on a high religious climax, it ends with him returning quietly to his mother's house.

For his last work, Milton wrote a tragedy, on the model of classical Greek tragedies, based on the Old Testament story of Samson and Delilah. Once again, he must have seen a parallel to his own life. Samson, the chosen hero of God's people, blind and in the hands of his enemies, betrayed by the woman he had loved, is a tragic and moving figure for the old blind Milton to write about. Living in the England of Charles II, feeling that the Puritan revolution had been betrayed, Milton also felt that England was in the hands of God's enemies. There are many passages about blindness in Milton's writing: none of them more direct and powerful than the picture of Samson, 'eyeless in Gaza, at the mill with slaves', telling us how all is now:

*O dark, dark, dark, amid the blaze of
noon,*
Irrecoverably dark, total Eclipse
Without all hope of day.

Samson Agonistes is the last great work of a lonely, pessimistic man.

Museum of Fine Art, Boston

Mansell

Ben Jonson (1573-1637) was a poet, playwright and masque writer. An admirer of the classics, his poetry frequently achieved a classical clarity and strength in both dramatic and non-dramatic verse.

English Poets of the 17th Century

The writings of John Donne (1572-1631) marked the beginning of a style of poetry very different from the pastoral, decorative verse of Elizabethans such as Spenser and Sidney. In 1693 Dryden said of John Donne:

He affects the metaphysics not only in his satires, but in his amorous verses, where nature only should reign; and perplexes the minds of the fair sex with nice speculations of philosophy, when he should engage their hearts, and entertain them with the softness of love.

This description of Donne's poetry stuck, and Donne and his followers have become known as the Metaphysical poets ('metaphysics' meaning abstract philosophical reasoning). Their style is intellectually demanding and rejects the 'softness of love' for an altogether more forthright and argumentative presentation of their major concern: love, both secular and religious.

Poems sacred and profane
Donne abandoned the idyllic settings, nymphs and shepherds of Elizabethan poetry to concentrate instead on invention, wit and passion. Where an Elizabethan poet might begin 'When I admire the rose' or 'Beauty sat bathing by a spring' Donne begins in a far more abrupt, personal way:

For Godsake hold your tongue and let me love

We are forced to sit up and listen, confronted by a drama in miniature.

Sometimes it will be Donne's ingenuity that we are intended to admire. In *The Flea*, for instance, the flea which has sucked his own and his mistress's blood is seen as their 'marriage bed': since their bloods are already mingled in the flea, Donne argues, why should their bodies not also be joined? At other times, he can be frankly erotic, as in his poem *To His Mistress going to Bed*.

Donne's career was varied; after sailing in two expeditions, he took a government post, but lost favour and was briefly imprisoned after he had secretly married his employer's niece. In 1615, after years of insecurity, he entered the Church and in 1621 he became Dean of St Paul's in London where he frequently preached before Charles I. When writing of love he brings in his knowledge of alchemy, science, exploration and religion; when writing of religion he retains more than a hint of his 'profane' loves. He writes:

*For I
Except you enthrall me, never
shall be free,
Nor ever chaste, except you
ravish me.*

This comes from a poem addressed to God, yet it is as violent and as personal as anything he had written previously.

George Herbert (1593-1633) and Henry Vaughan (1622-1695) were also to be

Cooper Bridgeman

Left: A portrait of John Donne (1572-1631). Donne and his followers, known as 'Metaphysical' poets, wrote religious and love lyrics characterized by their wit, passion, learning and invention.

Below: The title page of Henry Vaughan's poems *Silex Scintillans* (the 'flashing flint'). Vaughan often used *emblems*, pictures showing various symbols which would be explained in an accompanying poem. Here the emblem is of God's hand striking a heart-shaped flint from which flames and tears pour. The poem explains how God has broken through the rock of Vaughan's hard heart and made it into flesh, which both weeps and strives for heaven.

Below: The pleasures of the garden are a common theme in 17th century poetry and art. The gardener imposes order on to nature, creating a haven where men can escape the intrigues of politics. There, for Marvell, life is reduced 'To a green thought in a green shade'.

Scala

labelled Metaphysicals, for they both shared certain qualities with Donne. Herbert was renowned for his piety, but his poetry reveals 'a picture of the many spiritual conflicts that have passed betwixt God and my soul'. Herbert's tendency to probe his own actions and emotions links him with Donne, as does his love of working out unexpected connections between things that seem dissimilar.

Throughout his poems, collected together in a volume entitled *The Temple* (1633), Herbert deals with moral conflicts, but seeks always to resolve them. A generation later, Henry Vaughan fully acknowledged his debt to Herbert, whom he frequently imitated. Most of Vaughan's poetry, however, was written at a time when the Anglican Church, to which Herbert had devoted his life, had been torn apart by the Civil Wars. Where Herbert writes with the sense of a great Church tradition behind him, Vaughan frequently writes with a sense of lost innocence.

A different mode of poetry was established by Ben Jonson (1573-1637), who despised decorative and idealising poetry as much as Donne, but reacted by deliberately cultivating the classical tradition. Although Jonson admired Donne's wit he said that Donne 'deserved hanging' for his rough rhythms. Jonson himself aimed at clarity through the use of 'right and natural language'.

Jonson's *Epigrams* demonstrate a wide range of styles, from a witty portrait of a courtier to a moving epitaph on the death of his first son:

Rest in soft peace, and, asked,
say here doth lie
Ben Jonson his best piece of
poetry

Much of his poetry is an attack upon the vices of his age but he gives a vision of a better life in *To Penshurst*, where the aristocratic country house is seen as an embodiment of all the virtues that are threatened by an acquisitive society. Both his love poetry (including the famous 'Drink to me only with thine eyes') and his celebration of the ideal country life strongly influenced the Cavalier poets, a group closely connected with the court of Charles I.

In their lyric poems Thomas Carew (1598-1639), John Suckling (1609-1642), Richard Lovelace (1618-1658) and Robert Herrick (1591-1674) reflect the life and culture of the English aristocracy with a mixture of elegance, sophistication and naivety. Their poems, addressed to court circles rather than the general public, reveal a cultivated interest in subjects such as theology, philosophy and natural science—and, of course, love.

Like the Cavalier poets, Andrew Marvell (1621-1678) has as many links with Jonson as with Donne. Although he sometimes shows an ironic detachment Marvell always retains the metaphysical wit. In his love poetry, he ranges from the pastoral to the magnificent persuasion to love in *To His Coy Mistress*, where his plea to his lady is given added urgency by an acute sense of passing time:

But at my back I always hear
Time's winged chariot hurrying
near.

230

Left: The Royalist camp before the battle of Naseby (1645). Many of the 'Cavalier' poets fought in the Civil War, but their poetry is concerned more with love than with politics.

Below: The Royal Greenwich Observatory in the 17th century. The rise of scientific knowledge had a great impact on poetry—for the Metaphysicals it provided a fund of metaphors; to the Augustans it was evidence of a known and ordered universe.

Above: A portrait of John Dryden (1631-1700). As well as writing political poetry in support of the monarchy, Dryden also wrote lyrics, odes, plays and literary criticism.

Left and above: A drawing of Alexander Pope (1688-1744). Pope (left) continually suffered ill health; an early illness of the spine left his figure distorted and stunted his growth. As a Catholic, he was excluded from university, from voting or holding public office. He wrote poetry from an early age, achieving fame and financial reward with his translation of Homer's *Iliad*. He imitated the epic style of classical writers in his mock-heroic poem *The Rape of the Lock*, which parodies the fashionable life of his day. The illustration (above) shows the climax of the slender plot—the moment when the Baron cuts a lock from Belinda's hair.

The complexities of the age in which he lived lie behind his political and pastoral poetry, which often reveals a conflict between the active and the passive life. Faced with a Cromwellian rule based on violence, the temptation is to retire, like his employer, the Parliamentarian General Fairfax, to the peace of a country estate. *The Garden* takes this theme of retirement from a world of ambition and strife to an extreme, suggesting at first that retirement is most perfect when all human company is left behind.

The beginnings of Augustan poetry

By the time of the Restoration of Charles II in 1660, the personal mode of lyric poetry was already on the wane. After the Civil War, there was an increasing tendency to see individualism in matters of intellect and belief as dangerous and disruptive. A need arose for a literature which would unite men, and uphold public truth. John Dryden (1631-1700) is a crucial figure in the development of English poetry, because he firmly aligned poetry with reason and with public discourse. He looked back to Augustan Rome, the Rome of Horace and Virgil, discovering in that society the restraint and order which had been notably lacking during the Civil War. In doing so, he founded a new age of 'Augustan' poetry.

The order which Dryden valued is carried over into the style of his poetry. Rejecting the roughness of Donne's rhythms and the individual quirks (as he would call them) of Metaphysical poetry, Dryden used instead the smooth, regular rhyming couplet for his poems. Instruction was to be mixed with satire, with its emphasis on the correction of folly.

For Alexander Pope (1688-1744), as for Dryden, poetry was to be guided by 'sense' and the guides of sense were Reason, Truth and Nature. Pope defined 'true wit' as 'What oft was thought but ne'er so well expressed', thus emphasizing poetry as the expression of conventional wisdom. The classical tradition gave Pope a yardstick against which he could measure the follies of his age.

In his early years, Pope wrote mainly pastoral poetry, but in 1712 he published his famous early satire, *The Rape of the Lock*, written in a mock heroic style parodying the vanity and ritual decorum of Augustan society.

In later years Pope 'Stoop'd to Truth, and moralized his song.' His moralising sometimes seems, as more than one victim claimed, the ill-temper of a man deformed in body and mind, but it was not mere personal spite that stimulated Pope to write *The Dunciad* and *The Imitations of Horace*. Like Dryden, he wanted his society to recreate the glories of Augustan Rome, and he saw its potential virtue twisted and distorted by greed and hypocrisy. It was only in his garden at Twickenham that Pope could escape society and re-create the order and stability of a golden age.

The Augustans were never to produce love or devotional poetry as dramatic or witty as that of Donne and Herbert. But they created a mode of their own, for their own different purpose. If the Metaphysicals were masters of the personal lyric, the Augustans demonstrated that the public world was also a fit theme for poetry.

Restoration Theatre

In 1642 the Puritans closed the theatres in England; they were not reopened until the Restoration of Charles II to the throne in 1660. During these 18 years, though the performance of plays was officially prohibited, drama survived in a sort of shadowy half-life. Groups of strolling actors performed 'drolls', or short dramatic entertainments—often with a strong element of ribaldry and acrobatics—in innyards and fairgrounds. Sometimes these were crude abridgements of more serious plays, including some of Shakespeare's. And English actors helped to maintain the continuity of the theatrical tradition by performing Elizabethan and Jacobean plays on the continent.

The Elizabethan and Jacobean roots of Restoration drama, however wounded and withered, were never quite killed off. The plays most often performed during the early years of the Restoration were by the very dramatists, such as Jonson and Fletcher, who had been most popular in the years immediately before the closing of the theatres. These plays had appealed to an increasingly narrow section of society associated with the court, which is one reason why the Puritans were so anxious to close the theatres. The tendency to cliquishness was even more marked after the theatres reopened in 1660. Two types of plays came to be typical of the Restoration stage: the comedy of manners, and its counterpart, the heroic tragedy.

During their long exile in France the king and his entourage had come under the influence of the French court and its drama, and many of the plots of Restoration comedy are adapted from the plays of Molière. The spirit of much of this comedy is touched also by the atmosphere of courtly exile, with its uncertainty about the future and consequent desire to stress the need to make the most of the immediate present.

But the links with the earlier drama are quite clear. The heroines of William Congreve (1670-1729) and William Wycherley (1640-1716) owe much to Shakespeare's Beatrice, Rosalind and Viola. Similarly, while the intrigues of Restoration comedy are much more complicated than those of most Jacobean drama, they are usually of the same kind; so is the intense feeling for London life with its colour and bustle.

Developments in staging drama

In presentation, too, the Restoration theatre developed earlier trends. In the court masques which Inigo Jones designed, the emphasis came to fall increasingly on sets constructed according to strict perspective, artificial lighting and an acting area which was separated from the auditorium rather than surrounded by it. More and more of the stage action came to be framed within the proscenium arch: the 'peepshow' theatre, which was to be the predominant form of theatrical presentation until the beginning of the twentieth century, was born.

There was another important innovation. In the Elizabethan and Jacobean theatre the parts of women had been played by boys but now, for the first time, women began to appear on the public stage. 'The additional objects, then, of real, beautiful women' writes Samuel Pepys, one of the most avid of Restoration theatre-goers, 'could not but draw a proportion of new admirers to the theatre'.

The lavish scenic depiction of locality and the actual presence of women on stage meant that the dramatist need no longer embody through language the sense of place and the 'womanliness' of the boy-actors. Because it was called upon to do so much less, the language of the drama became correspondingly thinner and less rich. Restoration drama is essentially a prose drama, not a poetic one.

Above: A scene from *The Empress of Morocco* by Elkanah Settle (1648-1724), a prolific author of heroic tragedy. The enormous success of this play evoked Dryden's bitter criticism and a controversy developed between the two dramatists. This 1673 illustration based on a stage performance gives a good idea of the spectacular effects employed in the new Restoration theatre.

Right: Thomas Otway's *Venice Preserved*, a famous Restoration heroic tragedy. This scene shows David Garrick (1717-79), the most celebrated actor of the 18th century, with Mrs Cibber. Otway's play reveals the influence of Shakespearean tragedy.

Below: A scene from a modern production of William Congreve's sparkling comedy *The Way of the World*. This play has become even more popular on the modern stage than in Congreve's own day. The polished wit of the dialogue more than compensates for the excessive convolution of the plot.

Above: Hogarth's engraving of *Actors and Actresses Rehearsing in a Barn* gives a vivid impression of the condition of strolling players in the provinces of 18th-century England.

Left: R. B. Sheridan (1751-1816), dramatist, theatre manager and politician, adapted the bawdy of Restoration comedy to suit a more genteel audience. His best-known plays are *The Rivals, A School for Scandal* and *The Critic*.

Right: *Comedy in the Country, Tragedy in London*, a cartoon by Rowlandson (1807), contrasting the social status of the two audiences and their response to drama.

Above: A portrait by Thomas Gainsborough of Sarah Siddons (1755-1851), perhaps the greatest tragic actress England has produced. The eldest of 12 children, she was born into an acting family and appeared on the stage as a child. Her brother John Kemble was also famed as an actor. Mrs Siddons rarely appeared in comedies, but was considered unsurpassed in her portrayal of tragic heroines, most notably Belvedera, in Otway's *Venice Preserved*, and Lady Macbeth. The writer and critic William Hazlitt wrote of her 'She was tragedy personified . . . To have seen Mrs Siddons was an event in everyone's life.'

Paradoxically, this is as true of the so-called heroic tragedy, most of which is written in rhyming couplets or blank verse, as it is of the comedy, which is mainly in prose. The prose dialogue occasionally takes on a sparkle and a rhythmic vitality which brings it close to blank verse, as in the famous bargaining scene between Mirabell and Millamant in Congreve's celebrated comedy *The Way of the World*. But the verse of heroic tragedy nearly always remains stilted, pompous and inane.

Even two of the best examples of the form, John Dryden's *Aurang-Zebe* and Thomas Otway's *Venice Preserv'd*, illustrate this. At his best Otway is full of Shakespearean echoes but his rhetoric and sentimentality make a poor substitute for real dramatic life. As for Dryden, the constraints of rhyming couplets often lead him to banality.

Bawdy Restoration comedies

By contrast, Restoration comedy deals almost exclusively with the problems posed by sustained sexual intrigue. The hero is usually a young gallant, penniless but full of wit and charm, whose one object in life is to conduct as many affairs as he can find time and stamina for without falling into the trap of marriage, which is regarded as a fate worse than death—at least until the final act of the play.

Restoration comedy is witty, worldly wise, cynical and full of a bright and desperate elegance. Its social range is virtually restricted to high society. The plays pay lip service to the satirical thrust, moral severity and didactic intent of Jonsonian comedy.

The best of the Restoration comic dramatists sometimes overcome the dangers of triviality, easy cynicism and merely superficial wit of the comedy of manners. Thus Sir George Etherege (1634-91) in *The Man of Mode* creates a comedy of real depth by portraying as its central character a libertine caught unawares by the depth of feelings his way of life does not permit him to acknowledge. Three of Congreve's comedies also stand above the run-of-the-mill Restoration comedy.

The Way of the World pokes fun not so much at the institution of marriage itself, but at the purely commercial transaction, with women bought and sold like cattle according to considerations of family and property, which marriage in high society had become in Congreve's day. Within the framework of a conventional comedy of manners, *The Double Dealer* and *Love for Love* are both shrewd examinations of the pressures and trivialities of society.

William Wycherley has the strongest claim to be the true heir of Ben Jonson on account of his vigorous satirical strain. In his own time he came to be called 'Manly' Wycherley after the hero of one of his plays, significantly entitled *The Plain Dealer*. But Wycherley's masterpiece is *The Country Wife*. In this play, which concerns a man named Horner who pretends to be castrated while secretly letting society women know that he is not, Wycherley subjects the whole idea of 'reputation' in fashionable society to merciless scrutiny. The play, like most Restoration comedies, is full of bawdy double meanings and unashamed obscenities, but its moral design is always clear and forceful.

233

The beginning of an attempt to broaden the outlook of Restoration comedy while retaining its framework is to be found in the work of Sir John Vanbrugh (1664-1726) and George Farquhar (1678-1707). *The Recruiting Officer*, based on Farquhar's own army experiences in Shropshire, is significant for the fact that, unlike much Restoration comedy the, action takes place outside London. In *The Beaux Stratagem*, Farquhar's finest play, there is a degree of loving observation of life and gentle humour which are much closer to the drama of the eighteenth century than to Restoration comedy of manners.

This new drama, whose chief exponents were John Gay, Richard Steele, R. B. Sheridan and Oliver Goldsmith, was altogether more polite and restrained than its Restoration ancestor. It was designed for the rising middle-class and possessed the bourgeois quality of respectability, not to say dullness. The sexual intrigues, blasphemy and bawdy talk disappeared from the drama, hastened by Jeremy

Above: A cartoon showing John Kemble, his brother Charles and sister Mrs Siddons begging for money as Covent Garden theatre burns in the background. It was during Kemble's management that the theatre burnt down in 1808. When the rebuilt theatre opened the following year, Kemble's attempts to charge higher prices led to the 'OP' (Old Prices) Riots and he was forced to revert to the former charges.

Right: The interior of Drury Lane theatre in London. The first theatre on this site was opened in 1663, after the Restoration. Charles II first heard Nell Gwyn on stage here, and made her his mistress. This illustration shows the tragic actor Edmund Kean on stage in the early 19th century.

Below: A view of Covent Garden and market as it was in 1811.

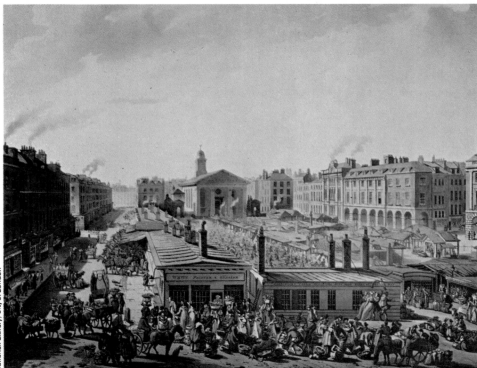

Collier's famous attack, published in 1697, entitled *A Short View of the Immortality and Profaneness of the English Stage*.

In the plays of R. B. Sheridan (1751-1816), including *The Rivals* and *A School for Scandal*, the comedy of manners is domesticated—the wit and sparkle of Restoration comedy are present, but without its licentiousness. Apart from writing plays, Sheridan acquired a share in Drury Lane theatre from the famous actor-manager David Garrick. There he produced his plays until the theatre was burnt down in 1809. Sheridan was also active in politics for much of his life, making several celebrated speeches in his capacity of member of Parliament. With *She Stoops to Conquer* by Oliver Goldsmith (1730-74), poet as well as playwright, we are in a world only distantly related to Restoration drama, though still concerned with comedy. Although it was an age of great acting and Shakespearean adaptation, the latter half of the eighteenth century lacked any playwrights of supreme talent. Only Sheridan and Goldsmith stand above the worthy, respectable and dreary mass of sentimental comedy which held the stage for several decades to come.

Bach and Baroque Music

The term 'baroque', as applied to the music of the seventeenth and early eighteenth centuries, describes a period of musical extravagance, which discovered the delights (and the vulgarity) of virtuosity. Opera singers realized that they could earn small fortunes by travelling round Europe and amazing audiences with their technical skill. Violinists followed suit: the Italians Locatelli, Vivaldi, Geminiani and others found avid audiences in Germany and England. Players of the harpsichord needed a more intimate audience, but Domenico Scarlatti (1685-1757) and François Couperin (1668-1733), composers as well as virtuoso players, delighted the aristocracy of Spain and France respectively.

It was an era, too, of national awareness and conflict. Italians developed their own way of writing and playing music, which the French opposed. In Germany and England, however, the two styles were frequently mixed by composers who liked elements in both, or who did not really appreciate the finer points of difference. And it was an age of religious conflict, which was reflected in music.

Protestant princes who enjoyed the Catholic music of the Counter-Reformation were not satisfied until their own composers had mastered the art of combining its virtues with those of a purely Protestant development—the *chorale* or hymn tune, meant for congregational singing. There has rarely been a time when music was so far in the melting pot.

While ensemble music had been popular during the Renaissance, the Baroque emphasized melody for the soloist, either virtuoso or amateur; it was a period when song flourished. In Italy many volumes of songs, or *arias*, were published, the melody being made tuneful by regular rhythms and a strong sense of key: our modern major and minor scales had by now almost completely superseded the complicated system of the medieval modes.

The arias were accompanied by harpsichord, lute, or guitar. Only the basic harmony for an accompaniment was provided: single bass notes (known as the *basso continuo*) marked with different numbers gave a 'shorthand' method of indicating whole chords. Having to fill in the complete accompaniment from these basic instructions demanded great technical skill on the part of the player; to make his task easier, harmonies were usually kept quite simple. The poems chosen for setting were for the most part love songs, often elegant but rarely passionate. During the second half of the 17th century, arias were often joined together by sung narrations called *recitative*, forming a dramatic entity after the manner of opera. Extended choral pieces of this kind were called *cantatas*, and were especially popular with professional singers, whose skill tempted composers to write quite elaborate and ornamental melodies. The vogue for the aria and cantata was also found in France and in England, where Henry Purcell (1659-95) was a master of the art.

Left: A portrait of the German composer JS Bach (1685-1750). Today considered the greatest composer of his age, during his lifetime Bach's reputation rested chiefly on his skill as an organist. Most of his work was composed as part of his official duties—as a church organist and also at court. Among Bach's huge range of choral and orchestral works are dazzlingly complex pieces for the keyboard. The manuscript (below left) shows part of a prelude from Volume II of *The Well-Tempered Clavier*, completed in 1744. Preludes were often improvised, and when written down were complex and individualistic. Bach's training as a virtuoso organist made him extremely skilful at improvisation.

Below: The frontispiece of Arcangelo Corelli's *Sonate da Camera* or Chamber Sonatas. Corelli (1653-1713) was a violin virtuoso as well as composer. Written for the violin and using dance rhythms and simple harmonies, these sonatas became popular all over Europe.

Arborio Mella

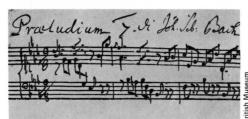

British Museum

M. Pucciarelli

M. Pucciarelli

Above: A portrait of Antonio Vivaldi (1678-1741), Italian priest, composer and violin virtuoso. He wrote works of extreme difficulty, greatly surpassing in brilliance the more modest music of Corelli. A teacher of music, he also travelled widely in northern Europe, producing operas and playing the violin.

Right: François Couperin (1668-1757) was an important French composer of harpsichord music. He held an official post at the court of Louis XIV and much of his keyboard music reflects the wit and sophistication of court life. His *suites*, written in an intimate, delicately ornamented style, were frequently given fanciful titles.

M. Pucciarelli

235

Virtuoso violinists

The equivalent forms for the instrumentalist were the *sonata* and the *concerto*. The violin, a louder and hence more public development of the older viol, became the most popular instrument, and the first generation of virtuosi, led by Arcangelo Corelli (1653-1713), wrote solo violin pieces using harpsichord accompaniment. These were called sonatas, (meaning 'played pieces' as opposed to cantatas or 'sung pieces'). Quite often two violins (or later one violin and one oboe or flute) and basso continuo were combined to form a 'trio sonata'. Two different types of sonata were written, 'church sonatas' (consisting of alternately slow and quick sections or *movements*) and 'chamber sonatas' (consisting mainly of a string of dances).

On grand occasions, when an orchestra was available, the sonata style was adapted to fit the larger resources. This was achieved by contrasting the trio of soloists common in the sonata with the main body of the orchestra; this form became known as the *concerto grosso*, meaning a large body of players.

As the skill of the players increased and the public or semi-private concert came into existence, the tendency was to write for a single player with orchestral

Scala

M. Pucciarelli

accompaniment. These solo concertos were generally composed in three movements, a quick one to grasp the attention of the audience, a slow contrasting section often in the manner of an operatic aria, and then a very fast *finale* for a display of virtuosity. The Italian Vivaldi (1678-1741) was the first great composer of concertos and his works were famous throughout Europe.

Bach—genius of baroque music

Johann Sebastian Bach (1685-1750), generally considered the greatest composer of the period, used all these forms, though usually giving them an unusual twist. He was born of a long line of musicians, his father being a town musician at Erfurt in Germany and then a court musician at Eisenach. The father's death meant that there was pressure on Johann Sebastian to work from an early age, which he did by becoming singer, violinist and then organist at various German towns. His earliest ambition was to become a virtuoso organist, and in 1705

he travelled across most of Germany to Lübeck to study with a great player, Buxtehude.

After this, he obtained a job as court organist at Weimar, where he became one of the finest players of his day, and it was here that Bach composed many of his greatest organ works. A splendid improviser, he wrote *toccatas*, vehicles for virtuoso display; but he also showed an academic interest in the learned form of *fugue*, in which the skill of interweaving a number of different melodic strands and working out the possibilities of a theme were all important. This use of intricate counterpoint was a dying art, and one which immediately alienated Bach from many of his contemporaries.

The other kind of music he had to write as part of his duties was the cantata for church services. Here again Bach's style of writing was extremely individual; he insisted on writing out all the embellishments normally improvised by the performer, which made his music seem very difficult, and occasionally strange.

Cooper Bridgeman

Bildarchiv Kulturbesitz

Deutsches Museum, Munich

Above and right:
A late 17th-century German organist and an organ-maker's workshop. Organs flourished in northern Europe during the Baroque period, with composers such as Buxtehude (1637-1707) and, later, Bach writing vigorous and complex church music, including *toccatas* (short, rapid pieces) and *chorale*

preludes (organ works based on hymn tunes). In the German states and Holland organs often had several keyboards (or *manuals*) with a large number of stops to provide power and variety of sound. In Italy, France and England organs were much smaller, often lacking a pedal keyboard.

Radio Times Hulton Picture Library

So, admired rather than really liked, the more especially because he was not an easy man to work with, Bach decided to take another job in 1717, when he became Director of Music to the prince of the little court of Köthen. This would have been considered by most people to be a promotion, for court musicians were better paid and more respected than church organists. For Bach it meant a complete upheaval. He had no great organ to play, no church for which to write cantatas. Instead he was required to compose orchestral and chamber music of various kinds for the court ensemble. His affection for the organ was transferred to the harpsichord, for which he composed a great range of pieces—suites, preludes and fugues. For the orchestra he composed in the fashionable concerto idiom, producing the set of *Brandenburg Concertos*, written for various combinations of instruments. He also wrote some excellent concertos for the violin, while those for his own best medium, the harpsichord, are unique, demanding great manual dexterity and showing exceptional flair for displaying the sound of the instrument against an orchestra.

It is hard to see why Bach should have wanted to leave Köthen, where he was on the whole at his happiest, but eventually he decided to return to his former profession of church musician, and when the opportunity arose in 1723 to become *cantor* at St Thomas's in Leipzig he accepted. It was an ungratifying post, involving organization of music at two churches, as well as teaching in the attached school. Bach did not get on well with his employers, but his incredibly rich experience, combined with his huge

mastery of *contrapuntal* technique (counterpoint) produced his greatest music. Of this, the church music, cantatas for Sundays and festivals, Passions for Good Friday and a grand Mass, are among the greatest masterpieces of all time.

Devout and dramatic Passions

The Passion music set the words of St Matthew and St John in a dramatic style, describing the story of Christ's crucifixion with graphic, almost horrific realism. Bach's style, combining arias, duets, choruses and solo instrumental parts, was taxing both for players and singers.

Such difficulty was not directed just as the performer. Bach like to set himself abstract problems to solve: such as to write preludes and fugues in all the major and minor keys, a feat which demanded a novel method of tuning the clavier (a word which could mean either harpsichord or clavichord), thus giving the title *The Well Tempered Clavier* to the collection.

Bach's love of the complex and the skilful must not be mistaken for a merely intellectual approach to music. A deeply religious man, his foremost aim was to worship God. He worried little about whether the sound of his music would please his worldly audience, and at times his orchestration and writing for choir are comparatively ineffective. But anyone who has heard or taken part in a performance of one of the Passions will know both the horror of man's sinfulness and the consolation of Christ's sacrifice. The Mass in B minor similarly reveals Bach's certainty of life everlasting. 'Baroque' is a style devoted to man's sophistication and many-sidedness; Bach, by mastering every aspect, was its greatest exponent.

Birth of Opera

Opera was born of the high-minded wishes of some Florentine noblemen to recreate the glories of Ancient Greek tragedy. Drama, they thought, had lost its power and according to their theories this was because the verse was no longer sung, like the Greek, but merely spoken. The remedy was to find a method of combining the two arts. So they experimented by performing a play in which the rhythms approximated to those of speech, while the rising and falling of pitch derived from song. The result was the *stile recitativo*, which was to be used in one form or another until the nineteenth century.

The first operas were given in Florence in the period around 1600. The music was written by two singers, Giulio Caccini and Jacopo Peri, who also invented a way of accompanying this so-called recitative on harpsichords and lutes, using a method known as the *basso continuo*. Because it did not follow the singing line exactly, but played accompanying harmonies, this method allowed the declamation of the singers to be free, and therefore the words to be fully audible. Between the passages of recitative they inserted songs, and this turned out to be a good idea, since recitative by itself could prove little less monotonous than the original verse.

Monteverdi's expressive music

These experiments might have remained the efforts of an elite group without the work of a professional composer, Claudio Monteverdi, who contributed much to the form of opera. Monteverdi (1567-1643) was commissioned to write *Orfeo* (1607) for the courtiers at Mantua, where he was in the employ of the Gonzaga family. He conceived of opera quite differently. Recitative was admittedly necessary if the action of the drama was to be clear; but if emotional power was to be achieved, more obviously musical means must be employed. So the part played by songs increased and even recitative became more melodious and less like speech, with memorable phrases repeated to interest the listener.

In place of the small group of harpsichords and lutes, Monteverdi employed a large ensemble of instruments of many kinds—adding organs and regals (small portable reed-organs) to the keyboard section, and using strings, woodwind and brass to play short but effective interludes. With these he had the resources to give atmosphere to the drama, employing flutes and recorders for pastoral scenes, trombones for the sinister mood of Hades. He also introduced climaxes, writing the most powerful music, appropriately, for the moment where Orpheus has to charm the boatman to let him cross the River Styx, in the attempt to rescue his wife Eurydice.

Orfeo was a great success; but Monteverdi's next opera *Arianna*, written in 1608 to celebrate the wedding of the Gonzaga heir apparent, became one of the most famous pieces of its time. This was largely due to the power of its grand climax, the Lament of the heroine when deserted by her lover, Theseus, which, according to one account, had the ladies in the audience in tears. This was a more human situation than in the allegorical

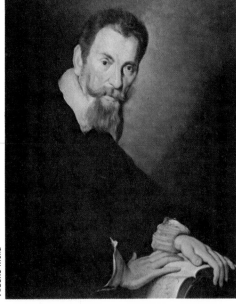

Above: A portrait of Claudio Monteverdi (1567—1643), the first great composer of opera. He held posts at the court of Mantua and later at St Mark's, Venice.

Apart from operas he wrote many madrigals which make use of brilliant, expressive harmonies, ranging in mood from serenity to dissonance and intensity.

Above: Costume designs for the ruling gods and goddesses of the planets from *La Pellegrina*, an *intermezzo* performed in 1589. The intermezzo—staged between the acts of a play—was the predecessor of opera. Such entertainments were often based on classical mythology and involved elaborate scenery and theatrical machines; large numbers of musicians also took part.

Right: An illustration of a temporary amphitheatre built in Bologna, Italy, in 1627. Until the first public opera houses opened in Venice in 1637 opera was performed only on special occasions such as the weddings of nobility, the visits of foreign dignitaries or some special city festival. Most of them were given in halls or temporarily erected theatres, such as this one; their preparation could last many weeks and cost vast sums of money.

Left: A scene from a modern production of Monteverdi's opera *The Return of Ulysses*, written for the Teatro S Cassiano in Venice, one of the earliest public opera houses. Monteverdi brought a new depth and dramatic power to opera by his interest in the portrayal of human character, mood and emotion.

Right: A portrait of the English composer Henry Purcell (1659-95). In the 17th century opera was not yet established in England. Theatres for spoken drama were more popular and so Purcell's main theatrical compositions took the form of *semi-operas*— plays in which a masque or lengthy musical interlude was inserted. His only opera, *Dido and Aeneas*, was written for amateur performance at a girl's school.

Below: An illustration of the 1686 production of *Armide*, an opera by Jean-Baptiste Lully (1632-87). French operas were produced exclusively for the court; they usually involved elaborate sets (as seen here), ballet sequences and lengthy passages of recitative.

Orfeo, and its pathos must have owed a great deal to Monteverdi's own sense of loss at the death of his wife the previous year. Opera had become the direct expression of human emotion.

During the next three decades, activity in the operatic field was sporadic. In Rome, works on religious themes were performed in the palaces of some of the rich cardinals; elsewhere in Italy royal weddings occasionally stimulated the ruling house to commission an opera on a secular or allegorical subject. But the next stage really began in Venice in 1673 when the first public opera house opened.

The splendour of early opera

In that year a group of singers came from Rome (where the political stituation was insecure) and set up a theatre which they financed partly by subscriptions from nobles who rented the boxes for the season, partly from the nightly takings at the door. Their success depended on pleasing the public, and to do this, they presented spectacular entertainments on a grand scale, with splendid scenery and scenic machines. Clouds which moved up and down and opened to reveal Gods and Goddesses were a favourite device.

The only composer with any experience in Venice was the now aged Monteverdi who had become director of music at St Mark's. He wrote several new operas, only two of which, *The Return of Ulysses* and *The Coronation of Poppea*, have survived. They show that his main interest now was in the creation of characters of great humanity, whose changing moods were mirrored in music which varies from the tuneful and gay to the dissonant and intense.

Poppea, written when Monteverdi was 75, is a historical drama taken from Tacitus' *Annals of Ancient Rome*. The 'heroine' is an ambitious woman, mistress to Nero, cruel to her enemies, disdainful of her husband.

Monteverdi presents a real world, quite unlike the allegories of the earlier operas. Fine singers were needed, and the first company to perform it had an absolutely splendid *prima donna*, as well as *castrati* (male singers castrated in order to preserve their unbroken soprano voices) for the principal roles.

The audiences flocked in to the new entertainment. Within a few years there were no less than seven opera houses in Venice and composers had to be found to keep up with public demand. Of these, Monteverdi's assistant and pupil, Francesco Cavalli (1602-76) found he could make twice as much as his annual salary as organist of St Mark's by composing, rehearsing and directing a single opera. He produced at least one opera a year for almost twenty years. His main strength was his melodic gift, shown in tuneful arias which now began to be the principal attraction in place of the strong dramatic sense developed by his master.

After an evening at the opera the English diarist Evelyn said that it was 'one of the most magnificent and expensive diversions the wit of men can invent'. Princes in Austria heard of its success and imported Italian singers and composers to Vienna and Innsbruck. Elsewhere in Italy, and especially in Naples, opera houses began to open, until by about 1680 it was the most popular form of music. The dramas were sometimes enhanced by comic scenes, and the music

ACADEMIE ROYALE DE MUSYQUE

ARMIDE

239

Left: *Farinelli in Walking Dress*, a caricature by Marco Ricci of the famous 18th-century castrato. Castrati were the highest paid artists of their time and enjoyed tremendous social prestige. They were often poor actors but their enormous lung power enabled them to perform long phrases which ordinary singers found too taxing. Farinelli sang in London in many of Handel's operas.

Right: This set is from Cesti's *Il Pomo d'Oro*, produced in Vienna in 1667. It was one of the first truly grand spectacular productions, involving 24 scene changes in the four acts and demanding large numbers of actors on stage for crowd scenes such as this, in which an army besieges a city. The scenery of Italian opera often tried to convey the idea of depth by the use of perspective.

Below: A portrait of the composer G. F. Handel (1685-1759). He wrote many successful operas in the Italian style for the English theatres during the 18th century.

Left: A painting of a scene from an Italian *opera buffa*. Comic scenes were excluded from serious opera in the early 18th century due to the strict ideas on libretto formulated by Metastasio. However, audiences liked them and they eventually developed into a separate form, called opera buffa in contrast to serious opera or *opera seria*.

Right: This 18th century painting of an opera performance captures the opulence of both theatre and scenery.

Below: An engraving of theatre machinery by Diderot. Machines for magic effects were popular in all theatres. Among the favourites were those depicting clouds which, by an elaborate system of pulleys, could be opened to reveal gods. Here the working of such machines is shown, together with the way they appeared to the audience when fully decorated.

frankly dominated by the arias. Little indeed was left of the intentions of the Florentine founders of opera.

The countries which resisted these embellishments were those with a strong tradition of spoken drama, namely England and France. And it was an Italian cardinal, Mazarin, a powerful political figure in France, who introduced the form there. He first of all imported singers and composers from Italy (Cavalli was one of them); but as their performances were in a foreign tongue, they were not very successful, especially as they had to compete with the well-established court entertainment of ballet. But the composer Jean-Baptiste Lully (1632-87), a naturalized Frenchman, saw that—adapted to French taste and in the native tongue—opera had distinct possibilities.

French opera under Lully
In many ways Lully went back to the original concepts of the Florentines. The importance of the verse was restored and, instead of tuneful arias, the words were declaimed in a mixed speech-cum-song, in which there were small snatches of memorable melody but nothing developed for purely musical reasons. In place of

the human drama, the plots resorted once

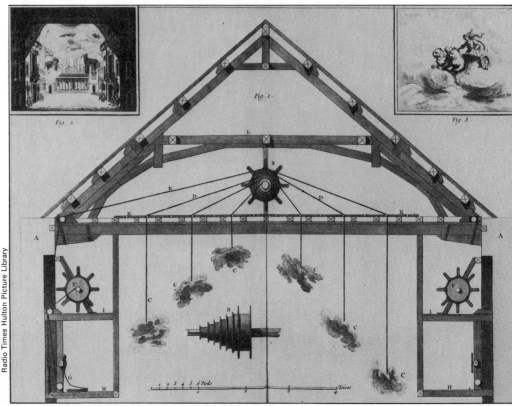

more to allegory, with praise of Lully's employer, the Sun King Louis XIV, always strongly implied.

The main hindrance to the development of French opera was, however, Lully himself. He was not a composer of genius, but his distinct flair for intrigue and politics enabled him to obtain a monopoly of producing operas. This monopoly was transferred to his sons, who effectively prevented any other composers working in the field for half a century. When a great French composer next took to the form, the pattern was still that of Lully. The composer was Rameau (1683-1764), also a harpsichordist, whose genius for evoking situation and atmosphere in vivid orchestral tone pictures was something no Italian could match, and who had the dramatic flair that Lully had lacked.

Meanwhile, Italian opera had changed its style considerably. In the early part of the eighteenth century, the manner of writing the *libretto* (the text of an opera) was given firm directives by the popular poet Metastasio. He abolished the comic episodes and wrote dramas in which there were usually just six characters, all of noble birth. The love interest was complex, with a happy ending after considerable misunderstandings, and usually a conflict in one or more of the characters between their inclinations and their duty to the state. The verse was elegant and meant to be set with the truly dramatic moments sung in recitative, while the emotions of the characters were conveyed in arias.

The music was now the principal enjoyment of the evening, especially as the singers (dominated by the castrati) were brilliant virtuosi with enormously agile voices, who were paid and revered almost as pop stars are today. The arias were written specially to show off their talents, mainly in what is known as *da capo* form. This forms a pattern in which a prolonged opening section is repeated after a contrasting middle one, the singer being expected to ornament his melody during this repeat. There was little purely orchestral music, the evening consisting of a succession of recitatives and arias.

In the hands of an inventive composer, such a formula could add vitality to the drama. The most famous of the Italians was Alessandro Scarlatti (1660-1725) who worked mainly in Rome and Naples, but the greatest composer of operas in this style was a German who settled in England and became a naturalized Englishman— George Frederick Handel (1685-1759).

After studying and producing his first opera in Italy, he came to London in 1710, and for the next 25 years was almost continuously employed writing operas for the English theatres although he also composed orchestral music and oratorios.

Handel's flair for writing really dramatic music, seen at its best in such a work as *Giulio Cesare* (1724), was combined with a gift for melody which expresses the varied emotions of the characters. Not afraid to break from the conventions when the drama seemed to need it, his work in opera dominated the English theatrical scene, even though critics like Dr Johnson called Italian opera an 'exotic and irrational entertainment' and would have liked an opera in the English language.

Handel's genius gained him a fortune, which he lost by bad investments; and if the rivalry of opera companies in London had not finally saturated the market, he might well have gone on to the end of his life composing them. As it was, the vogue for novelty—in London it came in the shape of the *Beggar's Opera*, a mixture of spoken word and song—finally defeated both him and the companies and English grand opera was overtaken by the more popular ballad opera.

241

Chapter 4

The Eighteenth Century

Handel's *Messiah* was first performed in Dublin in 1741. This manuscript was used in a performance at a hospital on April 27th 1758, and the Mr. Wass mentioned received a fee of one guinea.

Henry Purcell (1659-1695) wrote music for court, stage and church. Although little of his work was published during his lifetime, he became a major influence on later 18th century composers.

Music in the 18th Century

Although opera was the most profitable and widespread form of music everywhere in Europe throughout the eighteenth century, concert-giving, too, made great advances. The invention of the commercial concert probably dates back to 1672, when John Banister of London arranged daily programmes of music at his house, financed by the money taken at the door.

In England grander occasions became fashionable on St Cecilia's Day, when a kind of 'festival service' was held in Westminster Abbey. Purcell wrote the music for the royal band, which, with trumpets and drums—and perhaps the boys and men of the Chapel Royal—performed a mighty *Te Deum* and *Jubilate*. The proceeds were given to charity and, since Westminster Abbey was quite often packed on these occasions, these could be considerable.

In France, the Concert Spirituel was held during Lent, when the opera had to shut by order of the Roman Catholic bishops. The orchestra and chorus sang the grand motets of Louis XIV's favourite composers, Jean-Baptiste Lully and Michael Richard de Lalande.

In Italy, the conservatoires in Venice and Naples supported themselves partly by the proceeds from giving elaborate Masses on Saints' Days, and from giving oratorio performances during Lent, when other churches had given up music of any popular attraction until Easter Day. Such oratorios were in effect operas on sacred themes, dealing with episodes in the lives of the Saints. Arias and recitatives formed the main part of them, although there might also be vivid orchestral pieces; and a more important chorus than in opera. Although dealing with religious themes, oratorios were not church music in any sense and were quite often performed in theatres, often in costume.

Handel's great oratorios

It was to this genre that Handel turned when, in 1738, his operatic ventures had finally collapsed. Seeing the success of the St Cecilia's Day celebrations, he decided to model his oratorios on grand church music rather than simply make them a succession of recitatives and arias.

His earliest attempts included *Israel in Egypt*, the story of the Exodus of the Jews told largely in massive choruses, with little operatic music; and the *Messiah*, produced in 1741 in Dublin with enormous success. In this, Handel set biblical texts in a mixture of arias and choruses. The former was operatic in manner, the latter often in the form of anthems. *Messiah* had only a modest reception when it was first given in London, so Handel turned to a more obviously theatrical style, using such dramatic subjects as *Belshazzar*, *Samson* or *Susanna*—all Old Testament stories attracting the support of the wealthy Jewish community and also offering greater opportunities to display Handel's operatic gifts. Not all of these were successful in the composer's lifetime, but enough were popular to give him a fortune, and he died a rich man.

Above: Vienna in the eighteenth century was a major music centre mingling the Italian rococo style of music with the more serious style of the German church. It was a meeting place for musicians of all kinds.

Right: An 18th-century engraving showing brass instruments. As early trumpets and horns had no valves their range was limited. By the time Haydn wrote his *Trumpet Concerto* a new mechanism had made the instruments more agile.

Left: Not all music was performed by professionals, although the standard they set was high. Here the amateur musicians accompany dancing.

Below: Conducting with a baton was unknown at this time; usually the continuo player conducted from his keyboard in a standing position.

National Gallery

Left: Although France was very conservative in the fields of opera and church music, its chamber music was often harmonious, simple and elegant. These musicians using the flute, viol and flute/recorder would produce a highly melodic effect. Orchestral music, however, concentrated on producing a grand effect in the manner of the Concert Spirituel. This mode persisted in France up until the 19th century.

Right: Haydn began life in modest rural surroundings and suffered many hardships before coming to the Esterhazy patronage. His greatest success came at the end of his life when he received many honours.

Left: Lack of more than four octaves and any graduated tone on the harpsichord made it unpopular with the 18th-century composers and singers, who aimed for optimum expressiveness. The piano was evolved to meet this demand; being able to play loudly and softly and make crescendoes and diminuendoes, it was entirely suitable for the delicate, Rococo pieces favoured at the time. Mozart and Haydn wrote much of their music for the piano keyboard.

Right: A gala concert in Venice, painted by Guardi. Venice, no longer a political force, was still an artistic centre. Such concerts were held for visiting heads of state in the Hall of the Procurators in St Mark's Square. The performers were girls from orphanages, or *conservatoires*.

Radio Times Hulton Picture Library

The development of the orchestra

The new wave of concert giving also resulted in the rise of much purely instrumental music and in the constitution of the orchestra becoming stabilized. The Parisian Concert Spirituel helped to establish this trend. The ad hoc groups assembled for the occasion by the virtuoso touring violinists were replaced by a well-rehearsed body which was famous for its splendid sound. To the basic string section, wind instruments (mainly flutes, oboes and bassoons), were added. Harpsichords and other keyboard instruments became inadequate to fill in the harmonies in the manner of the old *basso continuo*, so *corni da caccia* or 'French horns' were introduced for this purpose. Sometimes trumpets and drums were added for special effects, making an orchestra of about 30 or more. Such orchestras, often a shade smaller but essentially the same in the balance of strings and wind instruments, were soon common throughout Europe.

The new forms of music

During the eighteenth century, the forms of the late Baroque—the solo concerto, the suite of dances and the concerto grosso—were all substantially altered. The popularity of dances continued and there was a lot of music using dance rhythms, notably those of the minuet, a modestly paced rhythm which allowed lightly elegant music to be composed. Minuets were usually cast in ternary or A-B-A form, the middle section being called a 'trio' because it was often played by just three instruments. Such dances were frequently included as movements

Below: Frederick, Prince of Wales and his sisters, performing a cantata. He takes the continuo part. The rise of the virtuoso divided music into difficult works for the professionals and easy music for amateurs. It was still quite common, however, for aristocrats to play well, especially on instruments like flute or cello.

National Portrait Gallery

in larger works called 'divertimento', 'cassation' or 'serenade'. The accompanying movements would be marked 'andante' or 'adagio', implying a moderately or even quite slow tempo, and were modelled on the opera aria, with an ornamental melody accompanied by simple harmonies; and 'rondo', a quick piece in which a recurrent tune would be interspersed by contrasted material.

But the most elaborate movement mainly came first and developed out of the overtures to comic operas or *opera buffa*. These were in a fast tempo, with lively themes emphasizing the gayness of a major key, and followed a quite complex pattern. The piece begins with two main themes A and B in the *exposition*, which develop and are *recapitulated* at the end.

The two main themes are often not strongly differentiated (the idea of making them seriously contrasted came later) but the basic difference between them lies in the keys in which they appear. Theme 'A' is always in the main key of the movement; 'B' in the exposition, on the other hand, arrives in a new key and only reverts to the main key in the recapitulation. Thus the composer has to write new or much modified music to achieve a smooth transition in this final section back to the home key. It is the listener's memory of the original section, in contrast to the recapitulation, which gives the feeling of conflict typical of this *sonata* or 'first movement' form, as it is generally known. Similarly the middle 'development' section which splits up the themes into small segments, puts them in a new order and in new keys, contributes also to the sense of argument and tension in the music.

Haydn explores new forms
The composer who did more than any other to explore the possibilities of this new form was Joseph Haydn (1732-1809). Born in modest circumstances in a village in Rohrau, Lower Austria, he was educated in a choir school in Vienna. After a period of poverty, he became a member of the musical establishment at the court of Prince Esterhazy. Haydn remained here until he was about sixty.

The court spent the winters at Eisenstadt, about 30 miles from Vienna and the summers at Esterhazy, in what is now Hungary. Out of touch with the main centres of music and especially cut off from the operatic rat race which was the way most celebrated composers made money, he said 'I was forced to become original' and since he was not a virtuoso player, he chose two media in which he could explore purely musical skills, the string quartet and the symphony.

The quartet was the genre where he could experiment most fruitfully. Written for connoisseurs—both players and listeners—Haydn's style made the most of the new methods of construction. The style naturally needs intense concentration on the part of the listener, a state increased by the subtle way Haydn shares the thematic material among all four instruments. The resulting subtlety of texture, harmony and thematic argument made instrumental music powerful in a novel way, capable of challenging opera or oratorio.

These skills were also transferred to the symphony, although since Haydn had not as fine an orchestra at the Esterhazy court as he could have found in Vienna, his actual symphonic style lagged a little behind that of the quartet. Even so, late in life, when he was first invited to write symphonies for one of the Parisian orchestras and subsequently when he was invited by the impresario Salomon to London in the 1790s, he showed his capacity to put into the symphony the same emotional sophistication as was evident in his chamber music.

It is sometimes said that Haydn was a mainly cheerful composer, fond of jokes (as in the 'Surprise' Symphony with its loud chord to 'frighten the ladies'; or in the 'Clock' with its ticking accompaniment in the slow movement); and it is true that he avoids tragedy. But the great symphonies (from about number 38 onwards) and the still greater quartets contain a wealth of differing emotions, based on an astonishing feeling of energy and health.

He lived on until 1809, and on his deathbed heard the guns of Napoleon's army at the gates of Vienna. In his last years he returned to vocal music, writing two fine oratorios, *The Creation* and *The Seasons*, as well as six extraordinary Masses in a grand manner. Nevertheless his greatest achievement lies in his instrumental music. It was this which inspired and moulded the symphonic styles of Mozart and Beethoven—both of whom he knew and respected—and led eventually to the symphonies of the nineteenth century composers. Haydn's quartets and symphonies showed how the expression of man's thoughts and feelings need not depend on opera or church.

Scala

The Genius of Mozart

Of all the great composers, Mozart appeals to the widest range of people. The reason for this breadth of appreciation lies in his astonishing capacity to absorb other men's music and to combine its virtues with his own originality. During his short life he composed music so varied as to suit the taste of every audience.

Wolfgang Amadeus Mozart (1756-91) was born in Salzburg, Austria. His father Leopold, a musician in the service of the Archbishop of Salzburg, was a man of some distinction, writing a standard text-book on violin playing which was in use for many years. He has sometimes been criticized for exploiting the gifts of his son, but there is no evidence that the tours which the young Mozart and his sister undertook caused them any harm.

Early success

Mozart became an infant prodigy; in 1763 at the age of seven he was taken on an extensive European tour by his father. In many ways he benefitted from such an early start; in London he met J. C. Bach, the son of the great Johann Sebastian, who was in touch with modern tastes, and from him Mozart began at once to pick up the elements of how to please an audience with elegant and graceful melodies in the *galant* (courtly) style. His subsequent tours of Italy, between 1770 and 1773, provided more good experience; apart from composing an opera for the Regio-Ducal Theatre at Milan, Mozart visited the foremost teacher of old fashioned counterpoint, Padre Martini, at Bologna, who awakened his interest in the music of the past. Such journeys were damaging mostly because they encouraged the world to think of Mozart as an interesting prodigy rather than as a genius whose gifts were to develop much further. The last tour of this kind took place in 1778. In many ways it was disastrous. His mother, who had accompanied him, died in Paris. Although he had modest successes as both performer and composer, Mozart was not received with the acclaim he was looking for and the only job he was offered was a minor one as court organist at Versailles, which he turned down. Discontented with his employment with the Prince Archbishop of Salzburg, Mozart was now searching seriously for a way of leaving his home town, which offered no opportunities for musical advancement, having no opera nor even an up-to-date orchestra.

By this time Mozart was a very experienced composer in virtually all the genres of the day: opera; symphonic music (he had written about thirty symphonies and a host of lesser pieces); concertos for violin and piano for his own use and for talented pupils; and church music of all kinds. He was also beginning to receive commissions, the most important of these being for the composition of an *opera seria* for the Munich court theatre. *Idomeneo*, written when Mozart was 25, showed the composer's intuitive understanding of the stage. In a series of letters to the librettist Abbe Varesco, Mozart demanded many alterations to the dying

Above: A silk collage showing Leopold Mozart playing the violin, the young Mozart at the spinet and his elder sister Marianne singing. Brought up in a musical household, Mozart (1756-91) developed early. His father encouraged and exploited his son's talent, arranging for him to tour Europe as an infant prodigy.

Below: A scene from Mozart's comic opera *The Marriage of Figaro* (1786). Here Count Almaviva is seen with his servants Susanna and Cherubino who, together with the manservant Figaro, finally outwit their lustful master. Mozart's musical characterization is supreme: servant and aristocrat alike are treated with sympathy.

Right: A portrait of Mozart, aged 11. A virtuoso pianist and improviser, Mozart wrote 21 piano concertos. These span his career and trace his style as it matures. The later ones, with their rich interplay between soloist and orchestra and wealth of theme and mood, mark a huge advance in the concerto.

Below and right:
Portraits of Mozart as a
young man (right) and
his wife ConstanzaWeber
(below), whom he married
in 1782. Mozart had
already been dismissed
from his post with the
archbishop of Salzburg
and had settled in Vienna.
Marriage increased his
financial difficulties;
although popular and
successful at this time
he failed to achieve
financial security—
through misfortune and,
apparently, extravagance.
An extremely hard-
working man, his output
was enormous: at his
death in 1791 (he was
only 35) he had composed
41 symphonies, 24 string
quartets, several
quintets, concertos,
17 masses, sonatas,
songs and a Requiem.

Scala

Arborio Mella

Right: Mozart's
autograph is clearly
seen on this piece of
music composed in
London when he was 9
years old. Although
during his lifetime his
fame rested chiefly on
his career as an infant
prodigy, Mozart did not
produce work of real
genius until he was
older and his style
had matured.

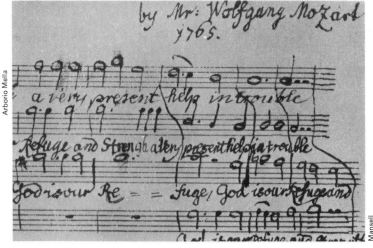

Mansell

form of opera seria to give it a new liveliness; he abandoned the conventional *da capo* arias (in which the first section is repeated after a contrasting one) which had tended to create a static effect, and instead he gave the arias a greater dramatic role. *Idomeneo* proved a magnificent score, and was sufficiently successful to whet Mozart's appetite for opera composition still further and to make his desire to leave Salzburg even stronger. When in the following year he had a quarrel with his employer, largely about a restriction on his movements and musical committments outside the court, he was—quite literally—kicked out of the Archbishop's service and went to settle in Vienna.

The Viennese years
It is often said that thus Mozart became the first free-lance musician, but in fact it was not uncommon for virtuoso players and opera composers to travel round giving concerts or fulfilling commissions and to make a decent, sometimes fairly prosperous living. But Mozart was at a disadvantage: he had never become fully established as a composer in his own right, his reputation still resting to some extent on his career as a prodigy. Additionally,

most composers had some kind of sinecure, which, though often small in value, allowed them to go where and when they wished. Mozart did not obtain one of these (as composer of music for the Emperor) until 1787. In 1782 Mozart had added to his responsibilities by marrying Constanza Weber, who turned out to be an impractical housewife. They had several children and Constanza suffered from a number of miscarriages which necessitated expensive treatment.

Mozart was therefore forced to work extremely hard and to accept commissions which under more favourable circumstances he might have refused. Yet his early years in Vienna also brought his most fruitful commissions. He was almost immediately asked to write a *singspiel*, a mixture of spoken dialogue and music. This was *Die Entfuhrung aus dem Serail*, (The Seraglio) a comedy with a fashionable Turkish setting.

During the next few years Mozart turned to a variety of genres. Still a brilliant pianist, he composed a number of fine concertos, outstanding for their delicate orchestral writing. Light music for social occasions, featuring wind instruments which could play in the open air, was always in demand and he became 249

a connoisseur of this kind of serenade.

While living in Vienna Mozart met and became friendly with the much older Haydn, who said he considered Wolfgang to be the greatest composer of the time—a handsome tribute considering that Haydn was by then a famous figure in Austria while Mozart was distinctly not. Mozart expressed his thanks by dedicating a series of string quartets to Haydn. These were in direct imitation of the latter's very mature quartets of Op 33. Mozart learned a great deal from these quartets about harmony and thematic treatment, though his operatic style of melody and generally greater interest in human emotion gives his own work a warmth which Haydn had so far lacked. The contact with Haydn revitalized Mozart's technical skill, a fact which is evident in his next opera *The Marriage of Figaro* based by Beaumarchais' play.

Don Giovanni and Figaro

Although an *opera buffa*, Figaro is far from purely comic, having serious political overtones which stress the heartlessness and even cruelty of the nobility compared with the shrewdness of the working classes, who finally outwit their masters. It is Mozart's masterpiece of characterization. The women, especially, are given the most subtle expressions of delicately shaded emotion; the sad figure of the deserted Countess and her vivacious but tender maid Susanna beautifully differentiated in music which allows a great range of light, shade and tone. This opera was an enormous and immediate success and was soon taken up by the opera house at Prague, where Mozart was invited to compose another opera. The

Above: A scene from *The Magic Flute* (1791), showing the Queen of the Night. The Queen, a force of darkness and evil, is given music demanding the utmost virtuosity and agility. This opera, with its blend of humour and pathos, and the final joyful triumph of good over evil, seems to reflect Mozart's most deeply-held beliefs.

libretto of *Don Giovanni* was less open to character painting than *Figaro*, but the background to the action—the murder of the Commendatore, which sets the whole action off, and the scene where Giovanni is finally pulled down to Hell—show an extraordinary dramatic power.

The years around the production of *Figaro* (1786) and *Don Giovanni* (1787) were the high spots of Mozart's success, when piano concertos, one or two fine symphonies and a host of attractive minor pieces seemingly came easily and show a mastery of all the musical forms of the time. He was also reasonably prosperous, althoug the amount of work he had to do to maintain this seems today to have been impossibly high. After *Don Giovanni* his difficulties increased. Again there was a gap in obtaining opera commissions, and his good fortune in eventually obtaining a minor post with the Imperial household was tempered by the almost nominal salary. As he said, it was 'too much for what I do, too little for what I could do'.

Mozart's debts in these later years were often considerable, especially to one of his fellow Freemasons, an organization which Mozart had joined largely because it offered an equality between men which was otherwise lacking in the classconscious society of Vienna. To relieve his financial plight he went on a concert tour in 1789 which took him to Berlin, a fruitful visit since it was there that much

of the music of J. S. Bach was preserved. Mozart found it fascinating and was again stimulated to emulate the style of a master —one who in this case was totally unfashionable. As a result Mozart's late music contains far more counterpoint.

Mozart's magical opera

On his return to Vienna, Mozart received opera commissions again, notably for an opera buffa *Cosi fan tutte* and an opera seria *La Clemenza di Tito*. An unexpected commission came from an actor-manager of a troupe which gave *singspiels*, Emanuel Schikaneder, who persuaded him to write the music for a pantomime, *The Magic Flute*, to be performed in a humble theatre on the outskirts of Vienna. But Mozart's music goes far beyond the requirements of such a simple piece. The plot was transformed from a fairy story into an allegory of good and evil with much Masonic symbolism. Like *Figaro* it is a work which can be appreciated on a number of levels—by children, by musicians, by theatregoers of all kinds.

Mozart died in 1791 of an infection, possibly following kidney disease. Because of his debts, he was buried in a pauper's grave. Ironically he was writing a Requiem (the Catholic mass for the dead) at the time. His early death cut short his life's work—he had overcome his most serious setbacks and had he lived would probably have enjoyed success once more. Less abstract and more concerned with humanity than Haydn, Mozart sheds light, and expresses a tolerance and understanding of human behaviour in a way that makes him the most genial of composers, a man for all seasons and moods.

Beethoven

Ludwig van Beethoven's life (1770-1827) spans a period of enormous social, economic and artistic change and his development both as an artist and as a man reflects this.

Beethoven was of Flemish descent; he was born in Bonn of a family of court musicians and was thus brought up in a musical environment where his gifts showed themselves early. Beethoven visited Vienna in 1787 to study with Mozart, but after only a few weeks he had to return home to attend his fatally ill mother. He returned to Vienna in 1792 and was to remain there for the rest of his life. This time Beethoven became Haydn's pupil, an arrangement which turned out to be unsatisfactory for Beethoven who found Haydn was too busy with other work to be sufficiently strict and so the young composer turned to other teachers.

Beethoven was the first great composer to free himself successfully from the old system of court patronage. At one stage he was so reduced in means that he considered becoming *Kapelmeister* (a kind of musical director) at a German court. However, three Viennese noblemen granted him a yearly income on the condition that he remain in Vienna. But behind this financial help lay their recognition of the profound independence of both music and man.

Beethoven lived at a time when the old set rules that society had provided for men were being questioned by the new ideals of, for example, the drafters of the American Constitution and of the supporters of the French Revolution. Above all their desire was for independence, the rights of the individual, liberty, equality and brotherhood—all things that Beethoven, a true man of his age, cared deeply about and embodied in his life and music. There are many anecdotes which reveal this uncompromising independence: when a pupil of his was to give a recital before a group of aristocrats, one had the presumption to talk while the pupil was playing. Beethoven stopped the performance and left the room exclaiming 'We will not play before these swine'. Beethoven had various love affairs, many among the aristocracy, but even though his genius was recognized and respected (it was said that there was 'one God in heaven and one Beethoven on earth') and despite the democratic tendency of the age, this was mixing in a manner inappropriate to his station or class. Possibly this is why he never married, even though he desired to strongly.

In his early compositions it is still just possible for the inattentive listener to confuse Beethoven with Mozart or Haydn. But even his first two symphonies of this period further extend the tendencies already apparent in Mozart's and Haydn's treatment of sonata form. The development section is longer and the *coda* (formerly a brief rounding-off section using previous material) is made increasingly important. This is also apparent in his piano sonatas and quartets. The whole scale of his music is larger, involving a much greater range of emotions —emotions shaped by the new ideas about individual freedom and the struggle needed to attain it.

F. Arborio Mella

Above: In both his life and his music Ludwig van Beethoven (1770-1827) reflects his age—one of revolution and change. His profound belief in man's power to shape his own destiny is expressed in his words 'I will grapple with Fate; it shall not overcome me'. The themes of freedom and fate recur in his work.

Below: From as early as 1799 Beethoven's deafness had plagued him. In 1802 he retired to the country village of Heiligenstadt (shown here) where he wrote a document revealing the spiritual crisis he underwent as a result of his affliction. 'I thank my art', he wrote, 'that I did not end my life by suicide'.

Right: A sketch of the middle-aged Beethoven out walking. The composer was noted for his careless dress and eccentric manner. He carried sketchbooks with him everywhere, in which he noted down musical ideas. Immensely self-critical, he revised his compositions until he was completely satisfied with them.

Mansell

History Museum/Vienna

Left: An illustration of a scene from *Fidelio*, Beethoven's only opera. Fidelio expresses those ideals of liberty and the power of human love to overcome adversity which Beethoven so passionately believed in. Unjustly imprisoned by the tyrannical Pizarro, Florestan achieves freedom through the efforts of his heroic, devoted wife Leonore.

Right: Beethoven experienced at first hand some of the force of Napoleon's military power. Twice during his lifetime Vienna was bombarded and occupied; in the 1805 campaign (right) and in 1809, when Beethoven spent much time in a cellar, his head covered by cushions in an attempt to preserve his hearing.

The struggle with fate

In his second period, Beethoven brings this sense of struggle to a completely unprecedented intensity. There is a speeding up appropriate to a faster moving age; the minuet (usually the third movement of a symphony or quartet) is replaced by the much faster *scherzo*, but there is also a more general sense of greater speed and urgency in the first and last movements of his main works of this period. All this and more is to be found in his third symphony, the *Eroica*, composed 1803-4.

The dimensions of the first movement of the *Eroica* are huge. With its heroic striving and struggles, the movement contains dissonances so extreme that even Richard Wagner, much later, could be led to 'correct' Beethoven's score. Yet Beethoven's sketch books leave no doubt as to his revolutionary intentions. The slow movement is a funeral march for the death of the hero but the spirit of heroism lives on in the final movements. Not surprisingly, the *Eroica* was initially incomprehensible to the contemporary audience. For all but a very few its scale was so great it could not be taken in; what it expressed was so new it could not easily be understood.

Through the need to express his ideals and inner nature in musical terms Beethoven subjected the classical forms he had inherited to increasing strain and distortion. Just as the social forms of life were changing so were the artistic.

It was during the second period that the deafness which had troubled Beethoven from as early as 1799 put an end to his career as a virtuoso pianist and he was unable to be the soloist in his fifth and final piano concerto, the last of his three middle-period concertos. Beethoven was generally not in good health throughout his life and in particular suffered severely from intestinal disorders but the realization that he was losing his hearing, the very faculty that he valued most, drove him almost to suicidal despair. His state of mind and his courageous resolution to accept this challenge of fate is

Above and below right: Beethoven's 3rd symphony the *Eroica*, (1803-4) was originally dedicated to Napoleon and given the title *Bonaparte*. In his early rise to power, Napoleon was seen to realize the ideals of the French Revolution, promoting the cause of liberty and democracy. But by being crowned Emperor, (below), Napoleon seemed to be repudiating his former principles. When news of Napoleon's coronation reached him, Beethoven furiously scratched out the dedication on the score (above). The symphony as it stands is dedicated to the memory of a hero. It marks a huge advance in the whole conception of the symphony.

revealed in a will known as the Heiligenstadt testament (1802).

In fact Beethoven was particularly prolific in the early eighteen hundreds, the time of his struggle with deafness, composing masterpieces in every major musical genre. On 22 December 1808 (at the Theater an der Wien in Vienna) he gave a vast concert which included first performances of his fifth and sixth symphonies, the Choral Fantasy, his fourth piano concerto and several movements from his first mass.

Beethoven's fifth symphony was yet another breakthrough and created a model for many future composers. The first movement (with its famous four-note opening rhythm) was difficult to understand for contemporary audiences because of its entirely new concentration on rhythmic energy rather than melody. The first movement motif was said by Beethoven himself to portray fate knocking on the door. This does not mean, however, that the symphony has any kind of plot, only that in the first movement in C *minor* there is drama and struggle which is eventually resolved in the final movement, which explodes into a victorious C *major*, hammered home again and again at the very end of the work to clinch the

Radio Times Hulton Library

victory. Beethoven's sixth symphony, the *Pastoral*, like his other even-numbered symphonies, is a much more relaxed work and its five movements were given descriptive titles by Beethoven himself. But again the music tells no story; Beethoven disliked any sort of musical picture making and he emphasized himself that the music was a matter of feeling (in this case his love of nature) rather than painting pictures. His fourth piano concerto, the first ever to open with the soloist alone, is a relaxed lyrical piece except for the tense confrontation between soloist and orchestra in the central slow movement. The rhythm of four is present again in the first movement of this concerto, but in a tender melodic way; the same rhythm is to be found in the extremely stormy and dramatic opening movement of the *Apassionata* piano sonata.

As a man, Beethoven was awkward, obstinate and arrogant, yet capable of great affection and generosity and equally of quarrelling violently with even his best friends. Beethoven realized his difficult nature and said of himself that 'Beethoven is only good for music'. His nature became more eccentric still as he grew older and more deaf. Yet with all his arrogance Beethoven believed that inspiration came from a divine source beyond the merely human and that the work of art was greater and more powerful than the artist himself.

It was towards the end of this middle period, from 1813-14, that Beethoven had his biggest public triumphs. Even his only opera, characteristically concerned with freedom, which had been unsuccessful in 1805, was now revised as *Fidelio* and presented with acclaim.

Tragedy and triumph

During his last years Beethoven's work is characterized by a detachment and insight coupled with deepest compassion and lack of any self-dramatization or pity: his victory over fate is won through acceptance. His ninth symphony, the *Missa Solemnis*, the last five of his 32 piano sonatas, his piano variation on a theme of Diabelli and the last five quartets of his 16 belong to this, his greatest period.

His ninth symphony, like the fifth, begins in a sombre minor key and ends in the optimistic major. It was here, in the last movement, that Beethoven felt that music by itself would not be enough and the last variation forms a tremendous setting for choir and four soloists of the German poet Schiller's *Ode to Joy*, a poem expressing ideals close to his own.

Beethoven's *Missa Solemnis* (Solemn Mass) was a setting on a vast scale of the five sections of the Catholic mass. On the score he wrote 'From the heart may it go back to the heart'. This is considered by some to be his single greatest work. His final piano sonatas are remarkable for their variety and their departure from classical form. Perhaps, though, the quartets of his last period, with their reconciliation of conflict, are his greatest achievement. The victory over fate is complete. On the last movement of his final completed work, the quartet opus 135, he wrote 'The decision difficult to take. Must it be? It must be. It must be.'

Beethoven died in 1827, at the age of 57. Passionately believing in freedom himself, he once said that 'he who understands my music shall be free'.

Above: This painting by Friedrich (1774-1840), Beethoven's contemporary, expresses the yearning for nature and solitude typical of Romanticism.

Left: Beethoven on his deathbed, 24 March 1827. It is recorded that among his last words were 'Clap your hands, my friends, the comedy is over.' His funeral was attended by thousands, with Schubert among the pallbearers.

Below: Ear-trumpets used by Beethoven as his deafness increased. When it became absolute, his only means of contact was by 'conversation' books. Cut off from the outer world, his inner life was emphasized and his last works have a new spiritual acceptance.

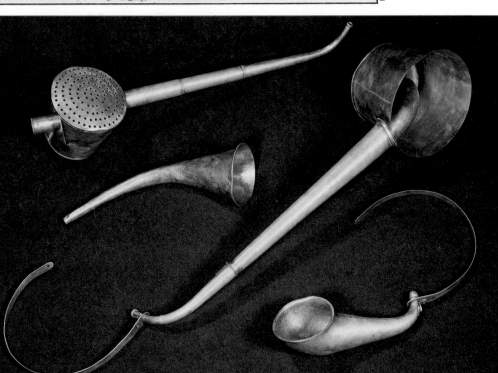

253

The World of
Dr Johnson

Samuel Johnson was the last and the greatest figure of the Augustan Age—that 'classical' period of English literature which began with Dryden in the late seventeenth century and ended with the Romantic revolution 100 years later. Although the term 'Augustan' was first used only in the nineteenth century, these writers consciously took for their model the supreme period of classical Latin literature—the age of Virgil, Horace and Ovid in the time of Augustus Caesar (63BC—AD14).

Johnson and his contemporaries saw themselves in many ways as the direct heirs and guardians of that tradition, a tradition concerned with man's ethical position in the world. Their attitude was essentially backward-looking: they felt that a continuous strand of thought stretched back through Christianity and the Renaissance to classical times. Little new remained to be discovered, it seemed; the main purpose of art and literature was to justify this established system of ethics and knowledge.

The Augustans felt that there could be correct rules for writing and painting just as there were for arithmetic and the newly discovered physical sciences. 'Whatever can happen to man,' wrote Johnson, 'has happened so often that little remains for fancy and invention.' Thus, by the eighteenth century, writers and critics were increasingly concentrating on the way in which these known truths were expressed, rather than on original thought or personal artistic expression.

Johnson's early years

Johnson grew to be the supreme arbiter of taste and style. His unique authority sprang from his learning and his strength of character, both gained in his early years. He was born in 1709 in Lichfield, Staffordshire, the son of the town's bookseller, Michael Johnson. He attended the local grammar school, but probably learnt more by browsing in his father's shop. Certainly by the time he went to Oxford in 1728 he already had a reputation for his learning.

Poverty forced Johnson to leave Oxford after only a year and without a degree. For the next six years he unsuccessfully tried schoolmastering and writing. It was probably sheer need which forced him, in 1735, to marry a widow named Elizabeth Porter, 20 years his senior. With the £700 she had inherited from her late husband, Johnson opened a school of his own, but this too was a failure. Since going to Oxford Johnson had achieved nothing. He then took the major decision of his life: in 1737 he went to London to try to earn his living as a writer.

Johnson got a job on *The Gentleman's Magazine*. Founded in 1731, this was probably the first modern periodical with general articles, reviews, news, poetry and political comment. Cave, its publisher, employed Johnson as one of his regular team of poor, hard-working writers known popularly as 'Grub Street' hacks. It was during this difficult period that Johnson first established a reputation

Radio Times Hulton Picture Library

Mary Evans

Above: A view of Lichfield, Staffordshire in the 18th century. Dr Johnson (1709-1784) was born in the house on the right, the son of a bookseller.

Right: *Samuel Johnson in middle age,* painted by his friend Joshua Reynolds. Physically, Johnson suffered from many defects. This description was written by his step-daughter in 1735: 'His appearance was very forbidding... his immense structure of bones was hideously striking to the eye, and the scars of the scrofula were deeply visible... he often had, seemingly, convulsive starts and odd gesticulations, which tended to excite at once surprise and ridicule.'

Below left and right: A portrait of the Scotsman, James Boswell (left), whose *Life of Johnson* is one of the greatest biographies ever written. The two men met in 1763. A real friendship arose between them, although apart from the tour to Scotland in 1773 they spent little time together. The caricature by Rowlandson (below right) is of the tour. In later life Johnson increasingly enjoyed travel and the study of different societies, an interest reflected in his book *Journey to the Western Isles* published in 1775.

Snark

Arborio Mella

Radio Times Hulton Picture Library

Left: A portrait of Francis Barber, Johnson's servant and companion for 30 years. A slave child in Jamaica, he was brought to Yorkshire by a charitable family and joined Dr Johnson at the age of seven. From then on he was treated almost as a son and was the main beneficiary in Johnson's will.

Below: A portrait of Hester Thrale. Mrs Thrale became Johnson's closest friend in later life and they confided deeply in each other. Johnson moved into the Thrales' house in Streatham in 1765. Hester's remarriage after the death of Henry Thrale in 1781 came as a shattering blow to Johnson.

Below: *Vauxhall Gardens*, a watercolour by Rowlandson. In the box at the bottom left is Dr Johnson with his friends Boswell, Hester Thrale and the poet Oliver Goldsmith. Vauxhall was famous during the eighteenth century as a place of entertainment where people met to talk, eat and listen to music.

with the publication of two works: *London* and the *Life of Richard Savage*.

London was a long poem, published in 1738, in which the poverty, corruption and squalor of the city were described. There is much of Johnson's own misery in it: 'Slow rises worth, by poverty deprest' —the line was printed in capitals—but the poem was immediately noted for its robust style and penetrating comment on London life:

> Prepare for death, if here at Night
> you roam,
> And sign your Will before you sup
> from Home.

In a typically Augustan manner, contemporary material was set into a traditional format and described as an 'Imitation of Juvenal's Third Satire'—a modernized version of a classical Latin work.

The Life of Richard Savage was published in *The Gentleman's Magazine* in 1744. Johnson had formed a close friendship with Savage, a notoriously wild and dissolute poet who also worked for Cave, and who had died in 1743. In this short work we find both the compassion and sympathy which distinguished Johnson, and a vehement and brilliantly written attack on the literary establishment which could let a genius such as Savage die in poverty.

Underlying this is surely Johnson's fear that the same might happen to him. Although he was writing parliamentary reports, dedications, advertisements, catalogues and the monthly articles for Cave, he remained wretchedly poor and had no time or money for the major works

he wished to write. However, his learning and diligence had not gone unnoticed: in 1746 a consortium of seven London publishers commissioned Johnson to write an English dictionary. His fee was £1,575 and, although he had to pay his own assistants from this, he was at last made independent with a regular income; he was even able to buy himself a large new house. The dictionary was to establish his reputation for all time.

The Dictionary

The Augustans regarded formal rules as a necessary part of language. English seemed very haphazard, with its uncertain spellings, unclear pronunciation and imprecise shades of meaning. In his dictionary Johnson sought to give some order to the language. 'Caprice has long wantoned without control,' he wrote of English spelling. There was a need for an authoritative guide to the language and Johnson wrote that by a dictionary, 'the pronunciation of our language may be fixed . . . its purity may be preserved . . . and its duration lengthened.' His words show a typically Augustan emphasis on the preservation of the existing order by establishing rules.

For seven years he toiled, reading a huge number of books to find new words and new meanings, and further extending his vast knowledge of English writing. *The Dictionary of the English Language* was published in 1755. It was immediately recognized as a massive achievement. Previous dictionaries had generally been concerned only with the meanings of difficult words, with spelling or with technical terms. Johnson's dictionary

255

combined all these with quotations showing words used in their proper context. Although some of the derivations were inaccurate and some definitions less than scholarly, the dictionary remained the authority on English for a century and was the foundation on which new dictionaries were based.

Johnson's *Plan of a Dictionary*, a prospectus issued in 1747 to solicit subscriptions, had been dedicated to Lord Chesterfield, an important political and literary figure. The two had some meetings, but Chesterfield soon lost interest and for years did nothing to help Johnson's work. When the dictionary was published, Johnson sent a famous letter to Lord Chesterfield which, as an example of his literary style, is supreme:

The notice which you have been pleased to take of my labours, had it been early, had been kind; but it has been delayed till I am indifferent and cannot enjoy it, till I am solitary and cannot impart it, till I am known and cannot want it. I hope it is no very cynical asperity not to confess obligation where no benefit has been received, or to be unwilling that the public should consider me as owing that to a patron, which providence has enabled me to do for myself.

Such a letter would have been unthinkable 50 years before when authors still depended on patrons for their living. By 1755, however, the growth of the book-buying public enabled professional writers such as Johnson to survive without the help of a patron—defined in the dictionary as 'commonly a wretch who supports with insolence, and is paid with flattery'. The letter to Lord Chesterfield marks the end of an era in literary life.

The middle years

Despite the enormous labour of writing the dictionary, Johnson still found time for much other work. In 1749 his dramatic tragedy, *Irene*, was performed by Garrick's company at Drury Lane, although with little success, and another long poem, *The Vanity of Human Wishes*, was published. In 1750 Johnson undertook the publication of a long weekly essay, *The Rambler*. Here Johnson is in a more relaxed mood, writing for the common reader with amusing good sense. For two years he wrote on a wide range of topics, but the ones which stand out today are those which show his deep humanitarian concern—as in the essay on penal reform.

Johnson was very much a professional writer: 'No man but a blockhead ever wrote except for money', he once said. Even the publication of his dictionary did not solve his financial problems and in the years following 1755 he continued to publish a vast variety of work. A second set of weekly essays, *The Idler* (1758-60), was produced, along with his only novel, *Rasselas*, in 1759—a fable about the vain quest for happiness in this world.

In 1765 another masterpiece—Johnson's edition of Shakespeare—appeared and became a landmark in literary history. Not only did Johnson provide the best text so far, but his assessment of Shakespeare's greatness marked a fundamental turning point. Previously, Shakespeare had been widely criticized for his lack of orthodox style and decorum. But Johnson saw that Shakespeare was 'expressing the course of the world', a world which was not so decorous and disciplined as other, lesser, Augustans liked to think. 'To study Shakespeare', he wrote, 'is to study life' and he emphasized the series of vivid character portraits in the plays. Johnson used his enormous critical judgement to form new opinions which were permanently influential.

Success established

Although Johnson lived for 20 years after the publication of his edition of Shakespeare, his literary output waned and during this time he is associated mainly with conversation. Three factors were responsible: in 1762 George III freed him from the financial need to write by granting him an annual pension of £300 (about £6,000 today); the death of his wife in 1752 had increasingly led him to seek company in clubs and taverns; and his huge reputation made others approach him as a teacher and law-giver. 'The Club' was founded in 1764, largely as a forum in which Johnson could talk to his disciples, who included the poet Goldsmith and the painter Reynolds. These meetings, where Johnson talked with his characteristic common sense and force of expression, are vividly recorded in Boswell's famous 'Life of Johnson' (1791). There were few subjects Johnson was not the master of, few arguments he did not win, few fools he suffered silently. But we also note his humanitarian compassion; and this was not just theoretical, for at this time Johnson filled his house with a strange collection of quarrelsome down-and-outs whom he felt he could not just leave to starve.

Johnson's last years saw two more great works. In 1773 he had travelled in Scotland with James Boswell, his devoted follower and friend. *The Journey to the Western Isles*, published two years later, is notable for its analysis of the social and political distress caused by absentee landlords and government. In his final work, *Lives of the Poets* (1779-81), Johnson returned to literary criticism and wrote a series of introductions to the works of the main Augustan poets. A fine poet himself, he gives us a fascinating survey of the literature of his time.

Johnson died in December 1784, and within a very few years Wordsworth and Coleridge published their first works. The death knell of Augustanism had been sounded, but Johnson's reputation survived. His greatness lay not only in his vast knowledge, his forceful critical judgement and his works, still influential today, but also in his personal integrity, compassion and grandeur.

Above: An engraving of a literary party given at the house of Sir Joshua Reynolds. In 1764 'The Club' was founded, including among its members some of the most eminent men of the time. Sir Joshua Reynolds, Garrick, Burke, Goldsmith and Boswell, as well as Dr Johnson, are seen here at a typical meeting.

Right: An extract from Johnson's *The Dictionary of the English Language* (1755). Johnson lists the word, then its derivation and meaning. This is followed by quotations using the word and drawn from Johnson's vast reading. These quotations help the reader to understand the word and also provide examples of what Johnson considered to be good style and high thought.

Oats. *n. ſ.* [aʒɛn, Sax.] A grain, which in England is generally given to horſes, but in Scotland ſupports the people.

It is of the graſs leaved tribe; the flowers have no petals, and are diſpoſed in a looſe panicle: the grain is eatable. The meal makes tolerable good bread. *Miller.*

The *oats* have eaten the horſes. *Shakſpeare.*

It is bare mechaniſm, no otherwiſe produced than the turning of a wild *oatbeard*, by the inſinuation of the particles of moiſture. *Locke.*

For your lean cattle, fodder them with barley ſtraw firſt, and the *oat* ſtraw laſt. *Mortimer.*

His horſe's allowance of *oats* and beans, was greater than the journey required. *Swift.*

Dr. Johnson in Scotland. After his expedition of 1773, during which he was made a freeman of the city of Aberdeen, he wrote: 'The use of travelling is to regulate imagination by reality, and instead of thinking how things may be, to see them as they are.'

The Age of Goethe

Not until the latter half of the eighteenth century did the literature of Germany secure its place alongside the great literatures of post-Renaissance Europe. The writers that it produced during this time, most notably Goethe and Schiller, exerted a tremendous influence on the whole of European culture during the nineteenth century.

Johann Joachim Winckelmann (1717-68), the man who started this revival of German culture, was in fact not a writer but an art historian. During his lifetime Winckelmann acquired an unrivalled knowledge of ancient art. His masterpiece, the *History of Ancient Art*, issued in 1764, contained the history of Greek art and the principles on which it seemed to be based. Although his knowledge was founded not on the actual Greek art but on Roman copies of it, Winckelmann's enthusiasm and graceful style of description succeeded in directing German artistic taste away from the rococo style towards the more moral and earnest ideals of classicism. The patronage of Cardinal Albani enabled Winckelmann to fulfil his ambition to spend the latter part of his life in Rome. This Italian journey served as a model for the numerous German writers of subsequent generations who shared his longing for the south and his love of the culture of classical antiquity.

The dramatist and critic G. E. Lessing (1729-81) also had unwavering faith in classicism. 'Classic' for him, as for Winckelmann, meant Greek art and literature, not the pseudo-classicism practised in France. Lessing was one of the first German critics to recognize the greatness of Shapespeare, praising his natural genius and lack of artificiality. He urged German playwrights to use the English stage as their model rather than to follow the strict, classical rules of the French drama. In so doing, he paved the way for a revival of original German writing.

Lessing made drama more democratic by taking characters from the middle classes and showing them in situations with which his audiences could identify. His 'domestic tragedies', *Miss Sara Sampson* and *Emilia Galotti*, and the comedy, *Minna von Barnhelm*, are all dramas of marriage, in which Lessing uses his theme to extol the solid virtues of his upright middle-class characters, sometimes in contrast to a corrupt aristocracy.

Another important aspect of the work of Lessing, and one which places him more firmly as a spokesman of the Enlightenment, was his vigorous and controversial writing on religion. After being prevented from publishing further pamphlets on theological subjects, he wrote his last play, *Nathan the Wise*, as a continuation of criticism of the power of established religions, and as a plea for religious tolerance.

Storm and Stress

In his dramatic criticism, Lessing laid the foundations for a movement known as *Sturm und Drang* (Storm and Stress) which developed during the early 1770s.

Above: By his enthusiasm for classical culture, the art historian J. J. Winckelmann (1717-68) formed the artistic taste of an entire generation. He wrote several works, including the *History of Ancient Art* (1764). He saw the 'noble simplicity and calm grandeur' of Greek art as mankind's supreme artistic achievement.

Below: Apart from being an art historian, Winckelmann was a keen archeologist. These temples at Paestum in S. Italy, among the most imposing ruins of the Greek civilization, deeply inspired Winckelmann and were described by him in his book *Observations on the Architecture of the Ancients* (1762).

This movement felt that culture must not base itself on reason alone, but allow full scope to man's emotions. It marked both the climax of Enlightenment concern with freedom and the beginnings of European Romanticism.

Among the most important thinkers associated with Storm and Stress was *J. G. Herder* (1744-1808). Influenced by Rousseau's call for a return to nature, Herder opened the eyes of his contemporaries to the beauty of 'folk' poetry (in which he included Homer, Shakespeare and the Bible); placing this poetry of inspiration and intense emotion above works produced by rational thought.

Herder was to have a decisive influence on the outlook of Goethe. The two men met in 1770 in Strasbourg where the young Goethe was studying law.

The Young Goethe

Goethe (1749-1832) was born in Frankfurt of a prosperous family. By the time of his move to Strasbourg he was already an accomplished poet in the rococo style. But his stay in Strasbourg proved to be a turning point for his entire life and work —during these years he underwent many decisive transforming experiences. The nearby village of Sesenheim was the scene of his first intense love-affair, with Freiderike Brion; and in the landscape of Alsace Goethe discovered the splendours of nature. Together these experiences inspired a number of masterful lyrical poems.

Goethe's great intellectual experience, however, came from his meeting with Herder. Herder's ideas led the way for a whole generation to understand and

Above left: This famous antique statue, *Laocoon*, representing the death-agonies of Laocoon and his sons, crushed by serpents, led in Germany to a controversy over its true interpretation. Part of the controversy was G. E. Lessing's study entitled *Laokoon* (1766) which contrasts the functions of poetry and the visual arts.

Above: This portrait of J. W. von Goethe (1749-1832) shows him in the Italian countryside, to which he fled in 1786. In the range of his genius, Goethe can be compared with the great men of the Renaissance; he was, among other things, a critic, poet, painter, statesman, scientist, playwright and popular novelist.

Below: *Faust*, Goethe's great dramatic poem, was completed just before his death. He had begun it 60 years earlier. Part 1 concerns Faust's despair, his pact with the devil Mephistopheles (shown here) and his love for Gretchen; Part 2 with Faust's life at court, his winning of Helen of Troy and his ultimate salvation.

Above right: In 1770, Goethe went to Strasbourg to study law. There he met the writer and theoretician J. G. Herder (1744-1808). Through him, Goethe developed many new interests, including a respect for German Gothic architecture—a respect fostered by this beautiful cathedral which dominated the city.

appreciate the different contributions of different ages and different nations to the development of mankind, and to value the variety of these contributions. Freedom became the watchword of the age; freedom to develop to the full all the potentialities contained within the individual, and thereby to develop to the full one's humanity, unrestricted by arbitrary and absolute laws. This is the reason for so many great creative, self-assertive characters in the work of the young Goethe; frequently characters who are defeated in their desires by a restrictive society, as in the drama *Gotz von Berlichingen* (1771-3).

This new sense of liberation was, however, matched by intense melancholy and self-doubt in the individual, left as he was without the old rigid scale against which to judge his actions. Nowhere are the extremes of feeling that this conflict produced, the alteration between elation and despair, expressed more powerfully than in *The Sorrows of Young Werther*, (1774) a novel in letters, in which Goethe tells of the love of a gifted, sensitive young man for a woman already happily betrothed to a decent, conventional, and completely different kind of man. The sympathy with which Goethe treated the ultimate suicide of his hero prompted a number of contemporaries to brand the book as immoral.

During the next important period of his life (1775-86), spent in service (as a Government minister) to the Duke of Weimar, Goethe continued writing beautiful poetry, now in a more restrained style. He also began work on scientific subjects and wrote several plays, including *Egmont* and *Iphigenia in Tauris*.

It was partly as a reaction against the frustrations of court life that Goethe virtually fled to Italy in 1786, leaving Karlsbad stealthily early in September, and hastening south under a pseudonym. Here, so Goethe wrote to Duke Karl August, he rediscovered himself as an artist; in the bright light of the southern sky and in patient observation of natural forms and classical works of art, Goethe

259

Die
Räuber.
Ein Schauspiel
von fünf Akten,
herausgegeben
von
Friderich Schiller.

Zwote verbesserte Auflage.

Frankfurt und Leipzig.
bei Tobias Löffler.
1782.

Left: Friedrich von Schiller (1759-1805) as a young man. His fame rests on his poetry and wide range of dramas.

Below: *Wilhelm Tell* 1804, Schiller's last completed play deals, typically, with freedom. This illustration shows the moment when Tell shoots at the apple placed on his son's head.

Above: Schiller's drama *Die Räuber* (The Robbers) established his fame. It was printed at his own expense in 1781. This title page is from the second edition of 1782. The drama is a stirring protest against stifling convention and corruption in high places and was a milestone in the history of German theatre.

developed the controlled, objective style of his maturity, evident at once in the *Roman Elegies*. This cycle of poems celebrating the love, art and nature in an uninhibitedly sensual way was completed shortly after his return to Weimar in 1788.

Another major work of this period is the epic *Hermann and Dorothea* (1797), the first genuinely popular work Goethe had written since *Werther*, and a novel which illustrates Goethe's increasingly conservative attitude in the face of the political upheavals of revolutionary Europe.

In 1794, Goethe met Friedrich Schiller (1759-1805) and formed a deep friendship which lasted until Schiller's death in 1805 when Goethe said he felt he had lost 'the half of his existence'. At a time when Goethe was beginning to feel isolated from his contemporaries, and was devoting himself increasingly to his scientific studies, Schiller encouraged him in the pursuit of literature. The most notable results of this encouragement were Goethe's ballads of the 1790s and his great novel *Wilhelm Meister's Apprenticeship*, which tells of a young man's 'education' in life, developing away from the temptations of a bohemian life for which he is unsuited towards greater social responsibility. Goethe's second major novel, *Elective Affinities*, written after the death of Schiller, is a deeply pessimistic work, which tells of the disruptive effect of the passions on the lives of four people. It is a highly moral work with strong religious overtones. It reflects Goethe's distaste for what he regarded as the unhealthy self-indulgence of the German Romantic movement, which had begun to exercise a dominant influence on the literature of the day.

Goethe lived until the age of 82, without his creative powers appearing to flag, completing *Faust*, a work which had occupied him for almost the whole of his life, less than a year before his death in 1832. *Faust* has been called the greatest work in European literature. It came to reflect all the spiritual stages through which Goethe had passed. In his treatment of this legend in which a man sells his soul to the devil in exchange for earthly power and riches, Goethe poured all the thinking and feeling of a lifetime. In its course, the poem develops the questions of man's relations with God, the individual in relation to society, the modern age in comparison with the ancient world, and the limits of human potential.

Most remarkable of all, perhaps, was his continued ability to write the purest lyric poetry, even love poetry, such as *The Bridegroom* and the *Marienbad Elegy*, right into the last decade of his life.

Goethe is without equal among the major figures of European literature for the range and universality of his genius: few national literatures are so dominated by one single figure as German literature is dominated by Goethe.

Schiller—poet and playwright

A decade younger than Goethe, *Schiller* first achieved fame with *The Robbers* (1781) a drama of freedom and youthful protest against repression and injustice in the *Storm and Stress* style. It is as a dramatist of conflict between man and nature that Schiller owes his enduring reputation and his continued popularity in the theatres of Germany. His second major drama, *Love and Intrigue* (1784), is a domestic tragedy skilfully illustrating the differing moral standards among the social classes in German society, exposing the corruption among 'authority' and showing, like *The Robbers*, the idealism of youth crushed by an imperfect world.

The last decade of Schiller's life saw the completion of a sequence of mature dramas on historical themes, whose greatness is in no way diminished by the way in which Schiller distorted history to suit his own ends: allowing, for example, Joan of Arc to meet her death on the battlefield in *The Maid of Orleans* (1801), and including a highly dramatic meeting between Mary, Queen of Scots, and her adversary, Elizabeth I, in *Mary Stuart* (1800). The greatest of these plays is probably *Wallenstein*, a trilogy (1798-9), almost without equal in German literature for its treatment of the realities of political conflict. As in his earlier works Schiller continued to be obsessed with the theme of man's freedom.

In his early hymn-like poems dedicated to the ideal values of humanity, friendship, harmony and love Friedrich Holderlin (1770-1843) was much influenced by Schiller. In a relatively small number of poems of burning intensity, written during a tragically short creative life, Holderlin repeatedly contrasts the barren present with an idealized past—or otherworld—an age unified and at peace, and looked down upon by a benevolent and divine nature. He suffered an irreversible mental breakdown in 1806 which left him hopelessly insane, and he spent the last forty years of his life in the care of a carpenter in Tubingen. His poetry, much of it complex, did not begin to be fully appreciated until the twentieth century.

Above: An illustration from Goethe's *The Sorrows of Young Werther*. Written in 1774 in the form of an epistolary novel, and based on Goethe's own experiences, it brought him immediate European fame. This tale of disappointed love, ending in the suicide of the hero, exalted the world of the emotions above that of reason.

Below: Heinrich Heine (1797-1856), portrayed with his wife. Heine, one of the best-loved German lyric poets, wrote a generation after Goethe. He expresses disillusionment with man's capacity to achieve lofty ideals. The dreams and yearnings described in his love poetry are accompanied by a sense of irony.

Wordsworth and Coleridge

One day in the 1780s, William Wordsworth, a schoolboy from Hawkshead in the Lake District, out on a solitary ramble, walked over the pass from Langdale and saw the lake and village of Grasmere. It was a moment he never forgot: looking at the scene, he felt the beauty of the landscape, and thought 'What happy fortune were it here to live.' A dozen or so years later, in 1799, Wordsworth (1770-1850) came to live in Grasmere, where he remained for the rest of his life, deriving a small income from a legacy and later from his office as Distributor of Stamps for Westmorland, and devoting himself to writing poetry.

The lifelong influence of nature

Wordsworth's entire life and poetry are deeply bound up with his childhood and youth among the mountains. His greatest poem, *The Prelude*, tells the story of this upbringing, and traces the development of his feeling for Nature.

Poets in the past who set out to compose a great poem had usually devoted themselves to writing an epic, filled with battles, romance and, often, supernatural powers. Wordsworth too felt from early youth that he was meant to dedicate himself to a high poetic task, but he chose as his subject *himself*. This new and more personal conception of literature is still with us today, and in some ways Wordsworth, like Rousseau a generation earlier in France, is the first truly modern writer, the first writer to view his personal experience, his own inner life as a suitable

J. Allan Cash

Radio Times Hulton Picture Library

National Portrait Gallery

She dwelt among th' untrodden ways
  Beside the springs of Dove,
A Maid whom there were none to praise
And very few to love:

A Violet by a mossy stone
  Half hidden from the Eye!
—Fair as a star, when only one
  Is shining in the sky.

She liv'd unknown, and few could know
  When Lucy ceas'd to be;
But she is in her Grave, and oh!
  The difference to me.

Above: Derwentwater, one of the English Lakes. Wordsworth's love for the Lake District led him to write one of the earliest guides to it. Entitled '*A Guide through the District of Lakes in the North of England; with a Description of the Scenery, etc*' it was published in 1810.

Far left: These abbey ruins, on the bank of the river Wye, inspired one of Wordsworth's finest poems, the *Lines Composed above Tintern Abbey*, in which he traces the changing influence of nature upon his life.

Above left: William Wordsworth (1770-1850) proved himself a new and revolutionary poet with *Lyrical Ballads*, published jointly with Coleridge in 1798. To the end of his life, Wordsworth retained his belief in ordinary people, and his wish to be a poet of human nature and simple life— not a learned writer for an elite. He felt that 'One impulse from a vernal wood / May teach you more of man; / Of moral evil and of good, / Than all the sages can.'

Below left: This ballad is from the series of 'Lucy' poems which Wordsworth addressed to a woman whose identity remains unknown. The poems are remarkable for their simplicity and poignance.

subject for poetry.

Wordsworth's aim was to write a long philosophical poem, delivering his opinions on man, on religion and on social problems of the day; and as a preliminary (or *Prelude*) to this, he set out to describe the growth of his own mind. *The Prelude* was completed by 1805, (although it was not published until after his death in 1850) and he then felt ready to begin on his great work. In 1814 he published the first part of this with the title *The Excursion*. Although *The Excursion* is little read nowadays, *The Prelude* is regarded as one of the finest long poems in English. It tells the story of Wordsworth's childhood, his solitary rambles, his closeness to Nature, his conviction that his personality was 'fostered alike by beauty and by fear.' It describes his studies at Cambridge, his reading in the poets, his fascination with mathematics; his walking tour in the Alps when he was 20; and his stay in France during the Revolution.

At first Wordsworth was an enthusiastic supporter of the French Revolution, but he soon became disillusioned. The Reign of Terror and the massacres conducted by Robespierre destroyed all his high hopes, and he began the long reaction that led to the extremely conservative opinions of his later life. At first he was plunged into anxiety and perplexity, feeling so uncertain about politics that he 'yielded up moral questions in despair.' But *The Prelude* describes how he recovers from this despair through his devotion to poetry and through the healing influence of Nature.

In 1795 Wordsworth met Samuel Taylor Coleridge (1772-1834) and their friendship became the most famous in the story of English poetry. The two men were very different in temperament. Wordsworth, lover of the open air, used to

National Portrait Gallery

Above: Although best known as a poet, Samuel Taylor Coleridge (1772-1834) was important also as a lecturer, journalist and critic of literature, theology and philosophy. His *Biographia Literaria* or 'literary autobiography' contains the fruit of his thought on literature and the creative imagination.

Below left: It was from rural life of this kind that Wordsworth drew inspiration for the *Lyrical Ballads*.

Below right: An illustration from Coleridge's *Ancient Mariner* by Gustave Doré. Romantic poets were drawn to the fantastic and supernatural, to old romances and ballads.

Mary Evans

Jouvard   Snark

263
263

Proud Maisie in the wood,
Walking so early;
Sweet Robin sits on the bush,
Singing so rarely.

'Tell me, thou bonny bird,
When shall I marry me?'
—'When six braw gentlemen
Kirkward shall carry ye.'

'Who makes the bridal bed,
Birdie, say truly?'
—'The grey-headed sexton
That delves the grave duly.'

'The glow-worm o'er grave and stone
Shall light thee steady;
The owl from the steeple sing
Welcome, proud Lady'.

Left and below: Sir Walter Scott (1771-1832) (below) dominated the ballad revival of the Romantics. His genius at adapting old ballads often makes it difficult to distinguish between the genuine old ballad and his own work. *Proud Maisie* (left) has all the colloquial style and fierce irony of the ballad tradition.

Above: Scott is perhaps best known as the author of historical novels, immensely popular since the time of their publication. Many, such as *Waverley, Rob Roy, Ivanhoe* and *Woodstock,* have become classics. This illustration is from *Old Mortality* (1816), a tale of religious conflict in 17th-century Scotland.

compose his poems on long walks—and trained his dog to warn him if anyone was coming. Coleridge was a scholar and an incessant reader, a student of German philosophy and (in later years) the author of works in defence of Christian thought. But they were both introspective poets, deeply influenced by Nature, and they both moved from radical opinions in youth to conservatism in later life.

Lyrical Ballads

Their most famous literary collaboration was *Lyrical Ballads*. This was a collection of poems that they planned together, and published in 1798. Coleridge was to choose stories that were supernatural, or at least romantic, and to treat them in such a way as to show their human interest and trace in them 'the primary laws of our nature.' Wordsworth was to choose matter-of-fact subjects from ordinary life, and treat them in such a way as to throw over them a colouring of imagination, so that their familiarity would vanish and they should strike us afresh.

Coleridge's main contribution to the book was *The Rime of the Ancient Mariner*, a long ballad of mysterious adventures on a voyage round the world, told by an old sailor to a wedding guest. The Mariner's ship sails south across the equator, reaches the antarctic regions, and is trapped amid icebergs:

And now there came both mist and
snow,

And it grew wondrous cold:
And ice, mast-high, came floating
by,
As green as emerald.

An albatross comes in sight and leads them out of the ice; but the mariner shoots it for no reason. For this crime against Nature he is punished by a long series of terrifying adventures: the ship is becalmed and a terrible drought afflicts the crew:

Day after day, day after day,
We stuck, nor breath nor motion;
As idle as a painted ship
Upon a painted ocean.

One by one the other members of the crew die, and the Mariner sees their souls fly from their bodies. But eventually the ship moves again, and the Mariner, the sole survivor, reaches home, where he is given penance by a hermit. But still he is compelled to wander from land to

land, telling his story.

The mysterious power of this poem is unique in English: it is like an old ballad, retold by a poet of wild and strange imagination. This poem and *Kubla Khan*, a fragment written after a dream and not forming part of the *Lyrical Ballads* together, reveal the fantastic, visionary aspect of this poet's mind.

Wordsworth's contributions to *Lyrical Ballads* present a great contrast. *Michael*, for example, is the story of a shepherd who falls on difficult times. The story, one of poverty, courage and suffering, is the perfect illustration of the programme that Wordsworth described in his Preface to the second edition of *Lyrical Ballads* in 1800. He has chosen, he tells us, incidents and situations from common life, and told them 'in a selection of the language really used by men'. In this way he hoped to avoid the artificial poetic diction of the eighteenth century, and return to the simple and universal subjects that he believed constituted the true stuff of poetry.

Michael represents one side of Wordsworth's poetry; the other side is personal, introspective, thoughtful, and deeply moving. This is illustrated by *Tintern Abbey*, also in *Lyrical Ballads*, a highly personal meditation on a visit to the banks of the river Wye after an absence of five years. In this poem he traces the growth and development of his feeling for Nature, from his youth in which he felt a physical intensity of contact with mountains, rocks, trees and streams; through his life in London, to the later and more mature vision of Nature that the poem tries to express, in which his love of Nature is blended with a deeper understanding:

For I have learned
To look on nature, not as in the
hour
Of thoughtless youth, but hearing
oftentimes
The still, sad music of humanity.

Wordsworth and Coleridge were friendly with many literary men of the time, but perhaps their closest associate was one who achieved no literary fame of her own—Wordsworth's sister Dorothy, to whom *Tintern Abbey* was written, who accompanied them on their walks, and lived in Wordsworth's home after his marriage. Dorothy shared his passion for nature, and her loving fondness for plants and landscape is recorded in her *Journals*.

Among their contemporaries, the writers William Hazlitt (1778-1830) and Thomas de Quincey (1785-1859) have left us vivid accounts of Wordsworth and Coleridge: Hazlitt in an essay called 'My first acquaintance with poets'—a marvellous description of the spell-binding conversation of Coleridge—and De Quincey in his *Reminiscences of the Lake Poets*. De Quincey, like Coleridge—and like many other nineteenth-century poets—took opium and in his *Confessions of an English Opium-Eater* described the haunting visions that it induced.

Wordsworth survived all his friends and contemporaries, living well into Queen Victoria's reign. In 1843, on the death of Robert Southey, he was made poet laureate (he was then 73), although he had by then virtually ceased to write. He died, old and respected, a survivor from a past age, in 1850.

Wordsworth's home,
Dove Cottage, in
Grasmere. Wordsworth
and Samuel Taylor
Coleridge met in 1795
and formed a close,
creative friendship,
both of them deeply
influenced by the beauty
and tranquillity of the
Lake District.

Chapter 5

The Nineteenth Century

Charles Dickens' comic masterpiece
The Pickwick Papers – the 'transactions
of the Pickwick Club' – grew out of a
publisher's idea for an illustrated
history of an imaginary sporting club,
for which Dickens was to write the
captions. First serialised in monthly
parts, it appeared as a book in 1837.

Shelley, Keats and Byron

The poetry of Wordsworth and Coleridge had introduced Romanticism to England. In place of the eighteenth century concern with reason and decorum, and the study of man in society, these poets had placed a new emphasis on simplicity, the truth of feeling and on individual experience. The young poets of the next generation, Byron, Shelley and Keats, explored different aspects of the new Romantic movement. In their lives as much as in their work these poets represented the rebellion from established society, the sense of longing, the fascination for the exotic and supernatural and the heightened expression of emotion associated with Romanticism.

Percy Bysshe Shelley was born in 1792, the son of a rich Sussex aristocrat. From being a schoolboy at Eton, Shelley went on to Oxford and reacted in fierce opposition to its conventions, developing radical political and religious convictions. In 1811 he was expelled from Oxford for publishing a pamphlet called *The Necessity of Atheism*. This incurred the fury of his father who tried and failed to bring his son back into the fold of respectability by disowning him.

In the same year Shelley fell in love with Harriet Westbrook, a 16-year-old school-girl and, as a liberating act, he eloped with her, himself only 19. For three years they led an unsettled existence, wandering from Edinburgh to York to Keswick (where he briefly dreamed of setting up a Utopian commune), to Ireland (where he distributed his pro-Irish-Republican pamphlets in the streets of Dublin) and to Wales. During this time Shelley wrote his first long poem, *Queen Mab*.

Back in London, with his marriage deteriorating, Shelley found his 'real' soul-mate, he was sure, in Mary Wollstonecraft Godwin, the clever 17 year-old daughter of the political philosopher, William Godwin. In 1814 he eloped with Mary to Switzerland, still hoping that Harriet would join them as their friend and feel free to find a lover of her own. She refused and two years later drowned herself in the Serpentine. Shelley felt the full misery of this increasingly as he grew older.

Shelley's intense idealism, his insistence on the 'free, uncircumscribed' spirit of man and on love as the unifying principle of the universe recurs throughout his work. One of the figures closest to Shelley's own ideals is perhaps Prometheus, who, according to classical myth, stole fire from the gods to give to mankind. This perennial symbol of rebellion against tyranny was the subject of Shelley's four-act lyrical drama, *Prometheus Unbound*, published in 1820. Yet his poetry does not only exist in the realm of lofty ideas; when his indignation was aroused by political and social injustice, Shelley could retaliate with the biting irony of the *Masque of Anarchy*, a poem written after the Peterloo Massacre of 1819.

The greatest work of this doomed idealist, who once wrote 'Alas! This is not what I thought life was' are the poems of his last years, the famous *Ode to the West Wind, Rarely, Rarely comest thou*

Left: This portrait of George Gordon, Lord Byron (1788-1824) in Albanian costume, perfectly expresses his attempt to assume an exotic, romantic role.

Above: Byron's relations with his half-sister Augusta Leigh, (above) added fuel to the scandal of his divorce.

Below: Byron's poetry was a source of inspiration for artists and composers. Delacroix' *Death of Sardanapalus*, drawn partly from Byron's verse drama *Sardanapalus* (1821) shows the Oriental despot ordering his concubines, slaves and horses to be killed before his own suicide.

Spirit of Delight, love lyrics, and *Adonais*. *Adonais*, an elegy (a poem of lament) written in 1821 on the death of John Keats, contains some of Shelley's most persistently held ideas and most haunting images:

> *Life, like a dome of many-coloured glass,*
> *Stains the white radiance of Eternity,*
> *Until Death tramples it to fragments.*

Feeling that he was universally detested in England for his atheism and 'immorality' and deprived of the custody of his children by Harriet, Shelley went to Italy in 1818. Here the Shelleys continued their friendship with Byron, begun in 1816. During the next four years, apart from enduring the deaths of his children,

Shelley developed an increasing sense of isolation as a writer and a deepening sense of the tragic in life.

The Shelley who had once believed that love could and would cure all the evils in life finally admitted in a letter to his wife Mary that 'love far more than hatred—has been to me, . . . the source of all sorts of mischief'. In 1822, not yet 30, Shelley was drowned in a storm off the Gulf of Spezia.

Byron—a legend in his lifetime

Whereas Shelley's opinions were sincere and undisguised, with Byron (1788-1824), according to his friend Medwin, 'it was impossible to know when he was in earnest.' Born of an unhappy marriage, descended from unstable and dissolute forbears—and sensitive about

Left: In 1816 Byron travelled to Switzerland where he stayed with the Shelleys near Geneva (shown here). The scenery inspired both poets. It provided material for Byron's *Prisoner of Chillon*, the tale of a man's imprisonment in the castle of Chillon on Lake Geneva and caused Shelley to write *Mont Blanc*, a poem on Nature's indifference to Man.

Right: A sketch of Lord Byron made in Italy in May 1823, two months before the poet sailed for Greece. Byron's enthusiasm for joining the Greek forces in their war of independence against the Turks soon turned to disillusionment. The poet contracted fever in Missolonghi and died in April, 1824.

Below: Delacroix' vision of the grotesque, nightmarish shipwreck which occurs in Byron's long satirical epic *Don Juan*. Here, as in *Sardanapalus*, it is the dark, horrifying or exotic aspects of Byron's work that the artist visualizes—a trait typical of the Romantic movement.

the club foot which made him lame— George Gordon, Lord Byron took refuge behind a mask of aristocratic ennui enlivened by a desire to shock his contemporaries. Notwithstanding his countless short conquests over Society ladies, (and their maids), his deepest love was stirred by young boys and his half-sister.

In 1815 he married Isabella Milbanke, an heiress, but his wife won a legal separation from him after only one year. Threatened by social ostracism, Byron left England for Italy in the same year, 1816, where he eventually established a life-style of extraordinary decadence. He extricated himself from compulsive promiscuity through his attachment to the young Italian Countess Teresa Guiccioli in 1819. But by 1823 Byron was weary of his life in Italy, and decided to join the Greek revolt against the Turks.

His initial optimism on reaching Greece soon gave way to disillusionment at the corruption and faction-fighting he encountered. Sick and feverish, constantly frustrated in his efforts to unite the Greek leaders, Byron was also suffering from the strain of an unreturned love for his Greek page boy, to whom he addressed his last poems. In April 1824 he died of fever in Missolonghi.

In his own lifetime Byron was a legend. His poetry, although considered immoral, was immensely popular at home and abroad. His lady readers identified him with the gloomy, exotic heroes of his poem —*The Giaour, The Corsair, Childe Harold, Manfred* and *Cain*. To be 'Byronic' was to be filled with *Weltschmerz*—a generalized rebelliousness and melancholy, darkened by the conviction that one was mysteriously branded by destiny to commit unforgiveable crimes. In one of his letters (Byron was a profuse letter-writer, and his letters and journal provide us with a fascinating insight into his personality and outlook) he commented 'The great object of life is sensation—to feel that we exist, even though in pain.'

Byron's other bent—towards anti-Romantic satire—was present from his earliest work. His *English Bards and Scotch Reviewers* (1809) was a fiercely satirical reply to the critics of his first volume of poems. But *Don Juan*, (1819-24) a poem in 16 cantos, is Byron's best and most famous satire. In a sardonic, casual style ('I rattle on exactly as I'd talk/With anybody in a ride or walk') Byron uses 269

Scala

National Portrait Gallery

humour and farce to debunk all values, feelings and ideas which society has ever upheld, extending his satire even to himself:

> I would to heaven that I were so much
> clay,
> As I am blood, bone, marrow,
> passion, feeling—
> Because at least the past were pass'd
> away—
> And for the future—(but I write this
> reeling,
> Having got drunk exceedingly to-day,
> So that I seem to stand upon the
> ceiling)
> I say—the future is a serious matter—
> And so—for God's sake—hock and
> soda-water!

The splendid poetry of John Keats

John Keats (1795-1821) came from the most 'ordinary' background of the three. His father was the manager of a thriving London livery stable who ensured that his eldest son had a good basic literary education at an enlightened school. But Keats was to experience an early break with anything that might be termed care-free childhood. Fatherless at eight, and motherless at 14, Keats had an exceptionally loving relationship towards his younger brothers and sister for whom he now had to take major responsibility. He was apprenticed to a surgeon and apothecary at the age of 14, but spent all the free time of the next five years in an alternative self-apprenticeship to verse-reading, writing and talking about poetry. All his higher education came from his widening circle of friends—Keats had a 270 genius for friendship—which by 1817

included the poets Shelley and Leigh Hunt, the painters Severn and Haydon, the critic William Hazlitt and the future essayist Charles Lamb.

Already in 1817 family worries began to press heavily on him. His brother Tom, with his 'exquisite love of Life', showed signs of consumption. In 1818 his other young brother George emigrated to American to try to improve his fortunes —only to meet with setbacks. It is not surprising that Keats' adolescent poem *Endymion* should escape from the pressures of the real world into a luxurious, imagined world of gods and shepherds in sunlit leafy bowers. What is astonishing is that barely 12 months later Keats had written some of the greatest poems in English. During that time he had nursed Tom until his death and faced anonymous

Above: The fervent idealism found in the poetry of Percy Bysshe Shelley (1792-1822) contrasts poignantly with the details of his actual life. This painting by Joseph Severn, *Shelley amidst the ruins of Caracalla*, emphasizes the youthfulness of this poet, who died in his 30th year. Apart from writing poetry, Shelley was the author of *The Defence of Poetry* (1821). In this he upholds the value and importance of poets to society, for, to him, 'Poets are the unacknowledged legislators of the world'.

Left: Shelley's second marriage was to Mary Wollstonecraft Godwin, the daughter of the anarchist philosopher William Godwin and the feminist Mary Wollstonecraft, author of the *Vindication of the Rights of Woman*. Encouraged by Shelley and Byron, Mary wrote *Frankenstein*, which has since become a classic tale of horror. The monster whom Frankenstein creates, although possessed with superhuman strength and size, is rejected by society because of his hideous appearance. His love repulsed, the monster turns to acts of hate and destruction.

Right: Shelley's first long poetical work, *Queen Mab* (illustrated here by Arthur Rackham) was later dismissed by the poet as juvenile. In it, the fairy queen expounds the causes of misery in the world, attacking authority and established institutions.

Left: Part of a letter written by Keats to his sister Fanny at the onset of his last illness, telling her of his intention of journeying to Italy. He died of consumption in Rome, 1821.

Below left: The poetic development of John Keats (1795-1821) was astonishingly rapid. Within a year of publishing *Endymion* (1818), which received savage reviews, Keats had written some of the great classic poems of English literature. These include his Odes, *The Fall of Hyperion*, *The Eve of St. Agnes* and several fine sonnets.

Below: A silhouette of Fanny Brawne, whom Keats loved and wished to marry.

reviewers sneering at 'the drivelling idiocy of *Endymion* . . . back to the shop Mr John, back to the 'plasters, pills, and ointment boxes'. No writer has ever matured so quickly. Between September 1818 and August 1819 Keats wrote *Hyperion*, *La Belle Dame Sans Merci*, *The Eve of St Agnes*, the *Ode to a Nightingale*, *Ode on a Grecian Urn* and *Ode to Autumn*, *Lamia* and the *Fall of Hyperion*.

The letters that he wrote to his family and friends, which reveal the warmth and intensity of his personality and his keen insight and self-awareness, also trace his development as a poet. 'I hope I am a little more of a Philosopher than I was, consequently a little less of a versifying Pet-Lamb'. In the poems of 1819 and in the group of sonnets he wrote, the former over-abundance of luxuriant detail has given way to a controlled richness. This new style was a perfect vehicle for expressing his fine sensitivity to the world around him and his deepening understanding of human experience. It was also at this period that he fell in love with Fanny Brawne—an experience which heightened his feeling for life immeasurably while it tortured him with its impossibility, ill and poor as he was. By

February 1820 Keats had himself succumbed to consumption. After desperate weeks of illness in London, Keats journeyed to Italy in an attempt to relieve his illness. He reached Rome at the end of 1820, but soon had a relapse. And in February 1821 he died, at the age of only 25.

But the greatest of Keat's poems defy death in their rapture at beauty in art or nature and the truth of love:

'*Thou wast not born for death,*
immortal bird!
No hungry generations tread thee
down;
The voice I hear this passing night
was heard
In ancient days by emperor and
clown:
Perhaps the self-same song that
found a path
Through the sad heart of Ruth,
when, sick for home,
She stood in tears amid the alien
corn;
The same that oft-times hath
Charm'd magic casements, opening
on the foam
Of perilous seas, in faery lands
forlorn.'

271

English Women Novelists

The expansive form of the novel is particularly prone to mirror an author's personality, philosophy and period. It might be expected, therefore, that the novels of five women so different in character as Jane Austen, Charlotte and Emily Bronte, Mrs Gaskell and George Eliot, who lived in a period of great social change, would have little in common but their writers' sex. Nonetheless, their different backgrounds and experience reveal certain similarities which typify the position of women, particularly, in the nineteenth century.

The significance of Christianity throughout the century is underlined by the fact that all five, at least in their early lives, were connected with the Church; nearly all their writings have a high moral tone. All (except Jane Austen, the earliest of these novelists) come from and write about the Midlands or the North of England, an indication of the increasing political and social importance of these areas during the industrial revolution. Strict social conventions, strict etiquette and a male-dominated society are reflected in their novels by an acute awareness of class structure and social comedy and by a marked emphasis on the dangers of careless marriage.

Jane Austen's Regency England

Jane Austen (1775-1817), seventh child of the rector of the parish of Steventon in Hampshire, was the only southerner of the five novelists. 'One has not great hopes from Birmingham' pronounces Mrs Elton in *Emma*, and no northern industrialist darkens Miss Austen's rural doors: '3 or 4 families in a Country Village is the very thing to work on', she wrote to a niece with literary aspirations.

The limited society of a provincial lady formed the substance of her life as well as her art. With the exception of a few visits to London, she saw little of England beyond Bath, Southampton, Chawton in Hampshire, and Winchester, where she died and is buried. A happy childhood, schooldays and family life gave her a personal sense of security from which to judge the society of Regency England (1811-20).

Judge it she did. However apparently trivial or everyday her subject matter— 'domestic life in country villages', or young women finding husbands—moral implications are always brought to bear. Exquisite composition of character and plot produce a vehicle for the author's particular view of life. Marianne Dashwood in *Sense and Sensibility* (1811) flouts Jane Austen's cardinal belief that public behaviour should be rationally controlled; she indulges in an excess of romantic emotionalism and is cruelly jilted. In *Pride and Prejudice* the relationship between the witty and charming Elizabeth Bennet and the proud Mr Darcy illustrate the deceptiveness of appearances.

Fanny Price is the poor relation at everyone's call in *Mansfield Park* (1814); but as the representative of her creator's own views on right behaviour, Fanny

Above: *When the Party Entered*, an illustration by Hugh Thomson for Jane Austen's novel *Pride and Prejudice*.

Below: The Pump Room at Bath, a fashionable meeting place during the Regency period (1811-1820). Jane Austen describes the scene in her first novel, *Northanger Abbey*.

Right: Sketch of Jane Austen by her sister, Cassandra. About 35 at the time, Jane could 'never relax laughing at myself or other people'. Four of her novels were published anonymously in the six years before her death in 1817; her identity was finally revealed with the publication of *Persuasion* in 1818.

receives justice at last. 'Handsome, clever and rich' young *Emma* (1815) is subjected to painful discovery of the truth about herself, while criticism of an oppressive domestic and social order is implied by the frustrated existence of Anne Eliott, the heroine of *Persuasion*, who has broken off an engagement to a penniless naval captain in deference to family and friends.

Reading a Jane Austen novel is often like reading a play: the action moves forward by means of short scenes in dialogue form. Satirical effects are achieved by a lightness of touch combined with minute exterior observation. 'Her business is not half so much with the human heart as with the human eyes', wrote Charlotte Bronte (1816-1855); and this observation sums up a major differ-

ence between the two novelists. Private passions and experiences of the inner life were the mainspring of creativity for Charlotte, and much of her skill as a novelist lay in making autobiography serve art.

The Brontes

Charlotte Bronte was born in Yorkshire in 1816. With her sisters Emily (1818-48) and Anne (1820-1849) she lived a good part of her life in Haworth, a small town on the moors, nine miles from Bradford. Two older sisters, Maria and Elizabeth, died from consumption while still at school; their mother died in 1821, while the girls were still infants, and their only brother Branwell (1817-1848) was a constant source of distress.

All four suffered chronic ill-health and,

Below: A chalk drawing of Mrs Gaskell in 1851. Elizabeth Gaskell was the only mother among this group of women novelists; her family status was extremely important to her. Her novels drew praise from Charles Dickens— *North and South* was first mentioned in his magazine *Household Words*.

Above: Eyre Crowe's famous painting of women factory workers, *The Dinner Hour, Wigan*. Mrs Gaskell's first novel, *Mary Barton*, focused on industrial conditions and brought many attacks from the Manchester factory owners. Mrs Gaskell, however, continued her political involvement and work with the poor.

as the children of a country parson, a lack of financial independence which led them to earn a precarious (and usually unhappy) living by teaching; all died before middle age. Charlotte and Emily studied at the Pensionat Heger in Brussels, as a preparation for running a school of their own. In 1846 the three women published a volume of *Poems* at their own expense, under their pseudonyms Currer, Ellis and Acton Bell.

The sadness of her life provided Charlotte with ample material for fiction. Her frustrated love for M. Heger, the principal's husband at the school where she taught in Brussels, was the inspiration of her first novel *The Professor*, about a young male teacher who falls in love with a pupil. A fictionalized account of her childhood experiences—this time at the school for daughters of the clergy at Cowan Bridge—makes its appearance at the beginning of *Jane Eyre* (1847).

This novel was an immediate success, acclaimed for the sheer power of the author's imagination and the passionate love between Rochester and Jane. A shy, intense orphan, Jane is in autobiographical line with the repressed Lucy Snowe in *Villette*, which describes the loneliness and moral isolation of a foreign and Protestant governess in Brussels—a loneliness Charlotte had experienced herself. Neither Jane Eyre or Lucy Snowe has money, social position or beauty. The emphasis is always on moral and intellectual qualities.

Apart from her passionate and at times mystical poetry, Emily Brontë's fame rests on her novel *Wuthering Heights* (1847). Using two narrators (themselves part of the story) to vary both perspective

and intensity, this strange tale of Heathcliff's demonic and terrifying love for Catherine Earnshaw has a timeless and universal quality. The story of Heathcliff's remorseless struggle to destroy two families for the loss of Catherine, whom he had loved since childhood, is played out in the sombre setting of Wuthering Heights, a bare and forbidding farmhouse over-looking Thrushcross Grange in the rich and sheltered valley below.

Mrs Gaskell's industrial novels

Fulfilment and serenity characterize the work of Elizabeth Gaskell (1810-65). Normally referred to as Mrs Gaskell, her married and family status was undoubtedly an important influence on her work. *Mary Barton* (1848), her first novel, was written in response to her husband's suggestion that writing a novel might help her overcome the loss of a baby son. Like *North and South* (1855) it reflects her work as the wife of a Unitarian minister in Manchester, among the poor victims of northern England's rapidly industrialized society.

Mary Barton is partly a documentary record—careful annotation makes the reader aware of the exact reproduction of dialect words, of contemporary food prices, of the very furniture or lack of it in the cellar homes inhabited by the industrial poor; but it is also a sympathetic and imaginative recreation of the feelings and activities of the poor.

A somewhat melodramatic plot (Mary's cruel choice between her real love for the worker Jem Wilson and her 'gay lover', Henry Carson', the manager's only son) is transcended by the dramatization of individual responses to an urban 273

Right: Branwell Bronte's portrait of his three sisters, Anne, Charlotte and Emily, painted in oils about 1835. His artistic talent, quite marked while he was young, never matured. Failing to make a living as a painter, Branwell began drinking heavily and took to opium in later years. He died of tuberculosis in 1848.

Left: A water colour of a merlin hawk, by Emily Bronte.

Below: *The Bay of Glasstown*, a water colour attributed to Charlotte Bronte. Brought up in an isolated Yorkshire parsonage, the four Bronte children spent hours in imaginative games, producing dozens of tiny books with many such illustrations. They invented a kingdom of Angria, and between them described its history, politics and wars, even detailing the loves and feuds of the aristocracy. In effect these fantasies were training for the later novels, and the books contain the first experiments with themes and situations found in the published works of the three sisters.

environment. Sitting in a cellar room, with her herbs collected in the fields outside the city, old Alice recalls childhood days in her native village; and there is a poignant glimpse of the factory workers walking in Green Heys Fields outside the city in the spring.

The culture and society of mid- and late-Victorian England were affected not only by the growth of industry but by scientific development and an associated questioning of religion. Scientific interests find a pale reflection in *Mary Barton*, with Job Legh's amateur scientific insect collection. Intellectual doubt leads Margaret Hale's father to resign his clerical orders in *North and South*—but the reader is not told the reason for Hale's doubt. Such an omission would not have been acceptable to an enquiring mind like George Eliot's.

The great novels of George Eliot

Mary Anne Evans (1819-1880), better known by her pseudonym of George Eliot, has been called 'the first modern novelist' and her greatest novel *Middlemarch* 'one of the few English novels written for grown-up people.' Her intellectual approach widened the scope of the novel, opening it to theological and philosophical considerations and changing its primary function from entertainment to discussion of the problems of adult life.

Brought up in Warwickshire, where her father was the agent for a landed estate, George Eliot came to fiction late in life; until she was 38 she had written only reviews and translations of books on religion and philosophy. In 1857, however, a series of three tales called *Scenes from Clerical Life* drew attention to her powers of narrative and in particular to her unfailing ear for dialect and speech. In her depiction of men and women transformed by emotional experiences, or unable to see their own weaknesses, she also set a pattern for her later works.

George Eliot frequently introduces characters with contrasting personalities in order to create an argument in the body of the novel. In *Middlemarch*, for example, the idealistic but naive Dorothea marries Casaubon, an elderly scholar and clergyman; gradually realizing her mistake, she is drawn to his attractive young cousin Will. Running parallel to this is the story of Tertius Lydgate, a high-minded young doctor who is brought down by his marriage to the beautiful but totally materialistic Rosamond. By setting the two plots side by side, George Eliot defines more clearly the moral to be drawn from each.

George Eliot's early Calvinistic piety gave way to a rational determinism, a belief in 'the orderly sequence by which the seed brings forth a crop of its kind'. Men and women suffer the consequences of their own actions and weaknesses of character. The fate of the heroes and heroines in her novels thus unfolds logically from her conception of their respective personalities and situations, rather than being thrust upon them in order to provide a happy ending.

George Eliot sets most of her stories in the provinces, and her novels provide a striking portrait of village society being overtaken by the industrial age. The social background is an integral part of all her novels and demonstrates a profound awareness of Victorian society in a state of flux.

Above: An illustration from George Eliot's second novel *The Mill on the Floss*, which draws on the author's own childhood memories. It depicts the end of the book, where Maggie, who has been estranged from her brother Tom since her honour was compromised, is finally forgiven when she saves him from drowning during a terrible flood.

Below left: The school at Nuneaton where the young George Eliot—Mary Ann Evans—boarded from 1828-32.

Below: L. Dickinson's portrait of George Eliot (1872). Raised in the Midlands, she moved to London in 1865 to work as a freelance writer and became the assistant editor of *The Westminster Review*. Soon she met George Lewes, who encouraged her to write fiction, and with whom she lived from 1854. She wrote her last novel, *Daniel Deronda*, before Lewes died in 1878. Two years later she married her financial adviser J. W. Cross, but died shortly afterwards, on 22 December 1880.

Victorian Poetry

*The hills are shadows and they
    flow
From form to form, and nothing
    stands;
They melt like mist, the solid
    lands,
Like clouds they shape themselves
    and go.*

These lines of Tennyson stand as a good introduction to Victorian poetry both because of their characteristic beauty and their theme that the solid foundations of the world had turned out to be changeable and insubstantial. In retrospect the Victorian world seems stable and well ordered, but it was a period of radical and immense change, during which the modern world emerged. The old unbroken course of European development speeded up out of all recognition in the space of a generation. The question of whether 'progress' was worsening the industrial and social conditions depicted by Dickens and Engels, and debasing cultural and moral standards as Matthew Arnold feared, troubled the Victorian mind immensely.

Social and economic doubts were made worse by scientific and religious controversy. While Darwin's *Origin of Species* was not published until 1859, the idea behind the evolutionary theory was well known much earlier, being based on geological studies. Not only was the world far older than was previously thought, but the evidence of evolution undermined the whole Christian interpretation of the world as given in the Bible. Religious and moral values were also, therefore, cast into doubt.

A further blow to the established system came from the weakening of the Church of England. On the one hand nonconformity was spreading among the industrial middle-classes. More seriously, the intellectual class were swayed by the Oxford Movement, a religious group biased towards Roman Catholicism, whose ideas came to a head with the conversion of J. H. Newman, a brilliant intellectual leader and theologian, to Rome in 1845—a shattering blow to Anglicanism.

Tennyson, Arnold and Browning
Alfred, later Lord, Tennyson (1809-92)

Left: W. Holman Hunt's painting of Tennyson's famous poem *The Lady of Shalott*. Alone in her tower, the lady sees the world only through a mirror: 'There she weaves by night and day / A magic web with colours gay. / She has heard a whisper say, / A curse is on her if she stay /To look down to Camelot.'

Above: Alfred, Lord Tennyson (1809-92) as a young man.

Below: An illustration by Doré from Tennyson's Arthurian poems *Idylls of the King*: these trace the foundation of the Round Table ('an image of the mighty world'); its rise to glory and disintegration through betrayal and treachery.

Above: Robert Browning's wife, Elizabeth Barrett Browning, was herself an accomplished poet. The couple met and fell in love in 1845 and, against her father's wishes, the invalid Elizabeth secretly married. The Brownings made their home in Italy until Elizabeth's death in 1861.

Right: A cartoon of the elderly Browning. After his wife's death he returned to England. The 1860s saw many of his greatest poems and he was acclaimed in London literary society.

Below: A page from William Morris's fine edition of Browning's poem for children *The Pied Piper of Hamelin*.

RATS

THEY FOUGHT THE DOGS AND KILLED THE CATS, AND BIT THE BABIES IN THE CRADLES, AND ATE THE CHEESES OUT OF THE VATS, AND LICKED THE SOUP FROM THE COOK'S OWN LADLES, SPLIT OPEN THE KEGS OF SALTED SPRATS, MADE NESTS INSIDE MEN'S SUNDAY HATS, AND EVEN SPOILED THE WOMEN'S CHATS BY DROWNING THEIR SPEAKING WITH SHRIEKING AND SQUEAKING IN FIFTY DIFFERENT SHARPS AND FLATS.

was the most popular of the Victorian poets, in whom every aspect of that age found expression. His poetry covered a vast range of subjects: both contemporary moral and religious problems and, particularly after he became Poet Laureate in 1850, the events of his day—'The Charge of the Light Brigade' and 'The Death of the Duke of Wellington' are two poems of this type in which he captured the emotion of the nation.

Tennyson's most characteristic quality is perhaps the sheer beauty of his verse, his descriptions of the natural world and of landscape—often the Lincolnshire countryside in which he was brought up:

Calm and deep peace on this high
wold,
And on these dews that drench
the furze,
And all the silvery gossamers
That twinkle into green and gold

This fluent, musical and lovely style could be used to recreate remote times; the classical world as in 'Ulysses', or Arthurian legend such as in 'Idylls of the King'. Or this style could be used for more contemporary themes in poems such as 'The Princess' (which is concerned with female emancipation) and 'Enoch Arden', which tells of the rewards of virtue and hard work.

The 'public' side of Tennyson's work is now valued less than his more personal poetry. He deals often with how reality shatters the ideal world—as in 'The Lady of Shalott'—and often a conflict is sensed between the public role and the private man, who publicly had to praise progress but who fundamentally longed for a less materialistic existence. The difference is expressed in his poems 'Locksley Hall' and 'Locksley Hall Sixty Years After', the latter written towards the end of his long career. Frequently, Tennyson's most personal anxieties mirror those of the age. For example, in describing Sir Bedivere's reaction to the death of his lord King Arthur in 'Morte D'Arthur', Tennyson expresses with poignancy the dilemma of the Victorian, caught in the midst of change and with stable traditions fast disappearing; 'For now I see the true old times are dead . . .':

And I, the last, go forth
companionless,
And the days darken round me, and
the years,
Among new men, strange faces,
other minds.

Probably his greatest poem is 'In Memoriam', published in 1850, though written over the previous seventeen years. Its starting point had been the youthful death of Arthur Hallam, his closest friend and soon to become his brother-in-law. This event had led him to question the purpose of life and the importance of death, and to relate this to the religious problems of his day. 'In Memoriam' is almost like a poetic diary—all events are linked to Hallam and to the question of death. It is the very uncertainty of the poem that is poetically moving and typically Victorian. The twentieth century poet T. S. Eliot said of it, 'Its faith is a very poor thing, but its doubt is a very intense experience.' The intensity, the doubt, the beauty: all are typical of Tennyson.

Matthew Arnold (1822-88) was never a popular poet like Tennyson. He felt alien 277

SOHRAB and RUSTUM

An Episode

Left: Matthew Arnold (1822-88) was a shaping influence on Victorian culture. While writing poetry and criticism he led a busy and humdrum life as a school inspector. He wrote several important works on educational reform. His great works of criticism such as *Culture and Anarchy* (1869) placed him in the front rank of European thought.

Above: The title page of Arnold's poem *Sohrab and Rustum* (1853). The poem tells the tragic story of how Rustum, a Persian warrior, slays Sohrab in battle, not knowing until too late that Sohrab is his own son: 'So, on the bloody sand, Sohrab lay dead;/ And the great Rustum drew his horseman's cloak/Down o'er his face, and sate by his dead son.'

Below and right: The poems of Gerard Manley Hopkins (1844-89), shown below as a youth, were not published until this century. Influenced by the Oxford Movement, Hopkins was converted to Catholicism and in 1868 became a Jesuit. A truly original poet, he attempted, with his 'sprung rhythm', to bring poetry closer to the cadences of speech. His poems show his intense response to his faith and to nature. His evocations of nature are joyous and ecstatic: '... what wind-walks! what lovely behaviour/ Of silk-sack clouds! has wilder, wilful-wavier/ Mealdrift moulded ever and melted across skies?' The landscape of Penmaen Pool in Wales (right) was the subject of one of his poems.

help from pain;
And we are here as on a darkling
plain
Swept with confused alarms of
struggle and flight,
Where ignorant armies clash by
night.

The quality of such verse is immediately apparent. It is controlled, beautiful and personal. And throughout Arnold's poetry the reader is moved by what he himself described as 'the eternal note of sadness'.

Arthur Hugh Clough (1819-61) was a close friend of Arnold both at Rugby school and at Oxford. His poetry is today being rediscovered, and found to be witty, intelligent and almost racy. He was a man who espoused causes rapidly and enthusiastically, and was then swayed to doubt by a new cause. But his poem 'Easter Day' sums up, with precision and irony, the chaos of Victorian religion and morality caused by new thinking and scientific knowledge.

Robert Browning (1812-89), like Tennyson and Arnold, felt an estrangement from the reality of the Victorian world. His escape was more physical—he lived for a long time in Italy with his wife the poet Elizabeth Barrett Browning (1806-61). Even when he returned to England after her death, his poetry dealt largely with distant times or lands.

For Browning, as for the other Victorian poets, the world seemed confused; but whereas Tennyson and Arnold felt that there must be an answer, a single idea which might unify the increasingly complex world, Browning believed that there might be no such simple answer. The world, he felt, was multitudinous and random. If this were the case, then there were no easy moral choices or simple morality. His long poem, 'The Ring and the Book' (1868) examines this. Set, typically, in the seventeenth century, it concerns a Rome murder trial; Browning examines the motives and justification of each of the ten participants from their own points of view. They all differ, yet all are personally true. It was this idea of a personal vision that Browning expounded, and his poems tend to deal with psychology rather than action. He dealt with a wide variety of subjects. His love poems, such as 'A Woman's Last Word' or 'By the Fireside', are not poems of rapture and romantic agony, but deal with the psychology of mature love and affection. Other poems deal with the life and role of the artist, and are often in the form of discussions of the lives of painters such as 'Fra Lippo Lippi' or 'Andrea del Sarto'.

Browning's style is also very personal, and is often called slipshod. Certainly it does not have the calculated precision of Tennyson or Arnold at their best. But, successful or not, Browning intended the rapidly changing tenses and syntax, the fluctuations in rhythm and grammar, to reflect the real and confusing experience of life. He was trying, he wrote to Ruskin, 'a putting of the infinite within the finite'—in other words to put the flowing and changing aspects of life into poetry.

The Victorian poets were faced with a society and a moral order in flux. It cannot be said that they found answers to all the questions they asked. But the questioning and the resultant poetry remain vital and beautiful.

from his age; and his great prose works, such as *Culture and Anarchy*, castigate its 'philistinism' and lack of culture and morality. He described his age as an 'iron time of doubts, disputes, distractions, fears'. Out of place, and yet having to live in the world, he is divided against himself, and all he can do in reality is bear this suffering. But such endurance is coupled with nostalgia and a desire to seek new worlds. Poems such as 'Thyrsis' or 'The Scholar Gypsy' yearn for a truer, quieter, more idyllic life in the past.

Above all Arnold felt he had been born in a faithless world, and that this was the fundamental weakness of his age. 'Dover Beach' (1867), regarded as his best poem, expresses this. Arnold is looking out at night over a full sea; he reflects that

The Sea of Faith
Was once, too, at the full ...
But now I only hear
Its melancholy, long,
withdrawing roar,
Retreating ...

Love and faith can alone help in this confused, changing world where there is

Nor certitude, nor peace, nor

'Flash'd all their sabres bare,
Flash'd as they turn'd in air,
Sabring the gunners there,
    Charging an army, while
        All the world wonder'd . . .'

from *The Charge of the Light Brigade*
by Alfred Lord Tennyson.

The Age of Dickens

Charles Dickens' career is one long success story. None of the other great English novelists was so popular, or had such a large and devoted public. On his first visit to America, he described 'the people that line the streets when I go out; the cheering when I went to the theatre; the copies of verses, letters of congratulations, welcomes of all kinds, balls, dinners, assemblies without end.' He meant a great deal to his public; and they meant a great deal to him. He needed the reassurance that many thousands of strangers knew and loved his work: he watched his sales figures anxiously, and worried when they fell off, not just for financial reasons, but because of his emotional involvement with his readers. So to learn about Dickens is to learn about the Victorian public: he understood what causes moved them to indignation or pity, what situations made them laugh and cry.

Charles Dickens was born in Portsea, Hampshire in 1812. His father, a government clerk, was an affectionate but financially incompetent man. Dickens loved him, but could never quite forgive his inability to manage his affairs. When Charles was 11, his father was arrested for debt and spent some time in the Marshalsea prison in London—for it was normal to imprison those who could not pay their debts. During the same period, Charles was taken from school and sent to work in a boot-blacking factory off the Strand. This was a humiliating experience which he never forgot. 'I was so young and childish and so little qualified to undertake the whole charge of my own existence,' he later wrote. He had been a quick, eager, delicate, sensitive child, and now his only companions were his coarse workmates. His bitterness at this episode never left him, and in later life the thought of Warren's Blacking Factory could make him forget his success and wealth. In his most autobiographical novel, *David Copperfield*, he drew directly on his own experiences and retold the story, as fiction.

Dickens inserted into David Copperfield one of two portraits he drew of his father. David lodges for a while with a Mr Micawber and his family, and Mr Micawber, like John Dickens, is unable to manage his finances. He is always waiting for something to turn up, he hints constantly to his wife that her relatives might do something for them, and he too is imprisoned for debt. It is a light-hearted portrait, and the normally cheerful Mr Micawber, with his sudden but brief descents into melancholy, his lack of any talent except for making punch, is one of Dickens' most loved characters.

In a later novel, *Little Dorrit*, Dickens' portrait of his father is far more sombre. He drew once more on his memories for the central character, Edward Dorrit, who is imprisoned for debt and becomes known as the 'Father of the Marshalsea' —living mostly on the charity of his fellow-prisoners and the devoted work of his daughter, and covering up this dependence by developing an elaborate

Above left: A portrait of Charles Dickens (1812-70). Dickens married early in his career and became the father of 10 children; later, however, he separated from his wife. The most popular of English novelists, Dickens was also a social reformer, leading public figure and editor of several influential magazines.

Above: A photograph of Dickens during a public reading. His love of the theatre was satisfied by these readings— enormously successful, they brought him fame and wealth. Dickens' theatrical flair enabled him to hold an audience spellbound. But the strain of the readings ruined his health and led to his early death, aged 58.

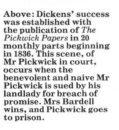

Above: Dickens' success was established with the publication of *The Pickwick Papers* in 20 monthly parts beginning in 1836. This scene, of Mr Pickwick in court, occurs when the benevolent and naive Mr Pickwick is sued by his landlady for breach of promise. Mrs Bardell wins, and Pickwick goes to prison.

Right: Fagin in his cell, an illustration to Dickens' *Oliver Twist* (1837-8) by the famous cartoonist Cruikshank. These, the original illustrations, were closely directed by Dickens and vividly enhance the text. The two men had already collaborated on the illustrated edition of *Sketches by Boz* (1836).

pride. Dickens depicts Edward Dorrit with a brilliant mixture of sympathy and contempt.

Dickens' career

On his father's release, Dickens returned to school and afterwards served as a solicitor's clerk. He taught himself shorthand and became a reporter, first in the law courts and then, in his early twenties, reporting the debates in the House of Commons. He soon began to write sketches of London life which were collected in 1836 as *Sketches by Boz*, his first book. He then began writing *The Pickwick Papers*, the adventures of a group of elderly gentlemen travelling through the south of England. This was first serialized in monthly parts, and appeared as a book in 1837, when Dickens

Below: Marley's Ghost appearing to Scrooge, from the first edition of Dickens' *A Christmas Carol*, published in 1843 with illustrations by the Punch artist John Leech, a close friend of Dickens. The story of how the miserly Scrooge is converted to kindness forms the plot of this immensely popular moral fable.

Left: In *Bleak House* (1852-3) Dickens satirized the muddle and delays of the law. This illustration by 'Phiz' shows Krook the eccentric stationer, nicknamed the 'Lord Chancellor' by his neighbours.

Above: The title page to *David Copperfield* (1849-50), Dickens'

own favourite among his novels, shows Little Em'ly playing outside her uncle's seaside home in Yarmouth.

Below: Uriah Heep (from *David Copperfield*) is among the most memorable —and detestable—of Dickens' creations, with his bristly red hair, constant hand-rubbing and need 'to be 'umble'.

was only 25.

The Pickwick Papers was an enormous success, and from then on Dickens was a popular author. The visit of Mr Pickwick and his friends to Dingley Dell contains the most famous Christmas party in English literature; indeed, it is from Dickens that many of the traditions of Christmas as a family festival are derived. The book has little plot, but much of it is taken up with the law suit of Bardell v Pickwick: Mrs Bardell, Mr Pickwick's landlady, is convinced that Mr Pickwick intends to marry her, and when she is disappointed she is persuaded by unscrupulous lawyers to sue him.

The humorous, convivial world of Pickwick is in strong contrast to Dickens' next novel *Oliver Twist* (1838), which concerns an orphan boy who is brought up in the workhouse.

In his account of the workhouse, Dickens attacked the notorious New Poor Law that had been passed in 1834, and which was deeply hated by the working classes. According to this stern measure the workhouse (last shelter for those without work, or with nowhere to go) was to be made as unattractive as possible, so that no-one would live on poor relief instead of working. Dickens saw in this policy a licence for cruelty, and in the figure of Mr Bumble the Beadle he tried to show the inhumanity with which the poor could be treated by officialdom. The liveliest parts of this dark, melodramatic story are those depicting the criminal gang of Fagin, the old Jewish pawnbroker, and his school for pickpockets.

During the first years of his career Dickens was a prolific writer. Stories and sketches poured from his pen, and he was

282

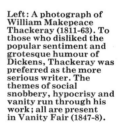

Above: Anthony Trollope (1815-82) was the most prolific Victorian novelist. Although he led a busy life in the Post Office, he wrote over 40 books. He would rise at 5 am and write for three hours before breakfast, producing a thousand words an hour. His novels give shrewd, realistic accounts of 19th-century society.

Left: A photograph of William Makepeace Thackeray (1811-63). To those who disliked the popular sentiment and grotesque humour of Dickens, Thackeray was preferred as the more serious writer. The themes of social snobbery, hypocrisy and vanity run through his work; all are present in Vanity Fair (1847-8).

Above: An illustration by Millais to *Framley Parsonage* (1861), the fourth in the series of Barchester novels by Anthony Trollope. It concerns Mark Robarts, a weak but well-meaning clergyman. Trollope's highly conventional, Victorian view of womanhood is hinted at in scenes of domestic comfort such as this.

often writing more than one novel at a time. His novels were published in serial form in periodicals, and he had constantly to write against the calendar to have his copy ready for the next instalment. Dickens was a man of enormous energy: he lived his stories as he wrote them, acting out the characters of his invention. After *Oliver Twist* came *Nicholas Nickleby* (1838-9), *The Old Curiosity Shop* and *Barnaby Rudge* (both 1841). The latter is a historical novel, set at the time of the Gordon Riots of 1780, the worst riots London had ever seen, in which an anti-Catholic mob burnt and looted for days. The mob scenes in this novel are extraordinarily vivid: led by a wild man, a hangman and an idiot, the mob burns down Newgate prison in a chapter of wild and brilliant prose. Although one part of

Above: A scene from the 1975 film of Thackeray's early novel *Barry Lyndon* **(1844). It is a brilliantly cynical story, told by an utterly unscrupulous Irish fortune-teller.**

Left: Thackeray's *Vanity Fair* **was an instant success on its publication. Here the immortal 'heroine' Becky Sharp—a ruthless, penniless, shameless girl who has to make her own way in the world—attempts to secure the wealthy bachelor Jos Sedley as her husband.**

Right: An illustration to *The Moonstone* **(1868) by Wilkie Collins (1824-89). A close friend of Dickens, he was a pioneer of the popular detective novel.**

Dickens regarded the mob with horror, another side of him clearly identified with —and even relished—it.

The next novel was *Martin Chuzzlewit* (1843-4), which contains the characters of Mr Pecksniff, the self-righteous hypocrite, and Sarah Gamp, the drunken nurse, whose vein of comic language is perhaps richer than anywhere else in Dickens. This novel makes use of Dickens' first impressions of America, and includes a trip to America by the hero in which he loses his money, and almost his life, through the fraud of the Eden Land Corporation, who send him to a miserable swamp. This part gave great offence in America.

After this Dickens' rate of production began to slow down. He still led a life of prodigious energy, editing two successive journals, *Household Words* and *All the Year Round*, making speeches, taking part in reform and philanthropic movements, and helping to bring up his large family. But his books began to grow less light-hearted. He never lost his talent for comedy and for the grotesque, but there is a more careful structure in his later works —a more serious concern with social problems, and also a more condensed and creative use of language.

The middle period of Dickens' career produced *Dombey and Son* (1848), his first serious attack on commercialism; *David Copperfield* (1849-50); and *Bleak House* (1852-3), in which he attacked the long delays of the law. This novel opens with a marvellous description of a London fog: 'Fog everywhere. Fog up the river, where it flows among green aits and meadows; fog down the river, where it rolls defiled among the tiers of shipping,

and the waterside pollution of a great (and dirty) city.' The fog is symbolic of the confusion that reigns over England, and it can be said that throughout the whole book it never really lifts.

Dickens the actor
One main reason for the slower production of novels in Dickens' later years was his public readings. He began these in the 1850s to raise money for charity; then, realising his enormous talent for holding an audience, he began to tour England (and later America) systematically, making a great deal of money, and drawing huge crowds whever he went. He turned some of his most dramatic scenes into material for reading, and his version of the murder of Nancy by Bill Sikes (from *Oliver Twist*) was capable of reducing hundreds of people to terror and hysteria. His health suffered under the strain he imposed on himself, and it seems likely that the readings hastened his early death.

The late Dickens
Dickens' last four complete novels were *Little Dorrit* (1855-7), in which the debtors' prison becomes a symbol for the whole of society; *A Tale of Two Cities* (1859), his second historical novel, set during the French Revolution; *Great Expectations* (1860-1) and *Our Mutual Friend* (1864-5).

Great Expectations is perhaps his masterpiece: certainly it is almost entirely free from the sentimentality and crudeness that seem an unavoidable part of his popular genius. It tells the story of Pip, a boy brought up in Essex by his shrewish sister and her kindly husband, Joe the blacksmith. It is Dickens' most

subtle study of class distinction—Pip is spoilt by the wealth that is mysteriously endowed on him—but it also opens up a richer and wider world than he could otherwise have known. When he finally realizes that his benefactor is a convict whom he had helped in a bid to escape the prison ships, he is horrified and ashamed but gradually develops sympathy and even love for Magwitch the convict. The passages concerning Pip's childhood, his encounter with the convict on the marshes, his meeting with the proud Estella and her obsessed aunt Miss Havisham are among Dickens' most intense and imaginative writing. *Great Expectations* is rich in comic and grotesque characters, and at the same time offers a coherent and powerful vision of society.

When Dickens died suddenly, in 1870, he had written less than half of his last novel, *Edwin Drood*, which opens with a haunting scene in an opium den. He left no indication how the story would continue, and the promise of mystery in the existing chapters has led critic after critic to speculate on whether, and how, Edwin would be murdered.

Dickens has a strong claim to be considered the greatest of all English novelists. For all his faults (melodrama and sentimentality occur everywhere) his fertile genius in the creation of character and in his handling of language has never been matched. From Mr Pickwick, Sam Weller and the delightful villain Mr Jingle, to Noddy Boffin the Golden Dustman, Mr Veneering the newly rich, and Silas Wegg the wooden-legged villain of *Our Mutual Friend*, Dickens' characters remain alive in the memory of thousands. 283

Nineteenth Century French Novelists

As in England, the nineteenth century in France was a great age of fiction. The novels and short stories of Stendhal, Balzac, Flaubert, Maupassant and Zola brilliantly illustrated the range and vitality of this literary form. Novels had, of course, been produced in the eighteenth century; many of these took the form of exchanges of letters between supposedly real-life people, while others pretended to be the memoirs of persons of 'quality'. Both tend to suggest how uncertain the eighteenth century writer was about the value of mere 'story' telling. The best of these novels, for example Choderlos de Laclos' *Dangerous Acquaintances* (1782), display intelligence, sensibility and an elegant sense of structure; others, such as Marivaux's *The Upstart Peasant* (1735-6), contain lively scenes of low life.

Librairie Hachette

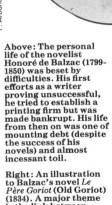

F. Arborio Mella

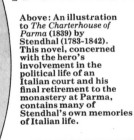

Above: An illustration to *The Charterhouse of Parma* **(1839) by Stendhal (1783-1842).** This novel, concerned with the hero's involvement in the political life of an Italian court and his final retirement to the monastery at Parma, contains many of Stendhal's own memories of Italian life.

Right: Balzac always enjoyed participating in fashionable society. This watercolour sketch shows Balzac (on the left) with two friends, the actor Frédérick Lemaitre and Théophile Gautier. Gautier (on the right) was a fervent Romantic and a popular literary figure: he wrote poems, novels and much art criticism.

Above: The personal life of the novelist Honoré de Balzac (1799-1850) was beset by difficulties. His first efforts as a writer proving unsuccessful, he tried to establish a printing firm but was made bankrupt. His life from then on was one of mounting debt (despite the success of his novels) and almost incessant toil.

Right: An illustration to Balzac's novel *Le Père Goriot* **(Old Goriot) (1834).** A major theme is the link between money and corruption: Goriot lives in penury in order to maintain his two daughters in a fine lifestyle, without realizing that they merely exploit him and are ashamed to own him as their father.

Mansell

But on entering the fictional worlds of Balzac or Flaubert or Zola the reader becomes aware of a more varied and ambitious range of characters, a more vivid and concrete rendering of the physical scene; of the energies and aspirations of individuals in an increasingly complicated society. The realism which became the major convention of nineteenth century French fiction is apparent in the strong sense of fidelity to everyday experience. This feeling for the 'real', for the surfaces of social life, for differences of class, dress, furniture, styles of living is rooted in the great changes which operated in French society from the last decade of the eighteenth century and after.

The break-up of the static society of old monarchical France, which began with the Revolution of 1789, continued under the impact of a late industrial revolution that brought accelerating economic and technological change to France from the 1830s on. And these basic changes had important consequences: they produced large urban centres, helped to create new classes of investor, banker, manager, factory worker and middle-man, and precipitated severe social and political strains culminating in the revolutionary upheavals of 1830, 1848 and 1871. Paris gradually emerged as the capital of pleasure and a magnet for foreign visitors and French provincials. French novels were taken up by tourists, like other Parisian luxury articles, and French writers commanded a wider public among educated people abroad than the writers of any other country. Railway book-stalls increased the sales of novels among the French, emphasizing a trend in the commercializing of literature which began with the introduction of cheap newspapers in the 1830s. Significantly, these early mass-circulation papers tried to boost their sales by printing a daily serial written by a popular novelist of the hour.

Above: *Gare St Lazare,* by the French Impressionist painter Claude Monet. Apart from providing an exciting new fund of subjects for artists and writers, the coming of railways helped to spread literature further afield, and to increase the sales of novels by way of station bookstalls.

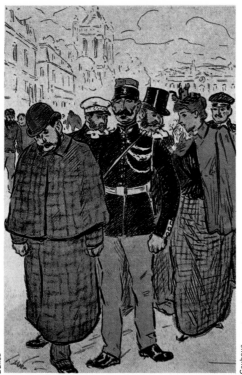

Below: The short story writer Guy de Maupassant (1850-93) wrote some 300 stories and six novels. His stories range over many areas of life, but a tone of ironic detachment is common to them all. This illustration is to his tale *Ce Cochon de Morin,* which first appeared in the journal *Gils Blas* in 1893.

Stendhal—reason and romanticism

Of the major writers of fiction, Stendhal (pseudonym of Henri Beyle, 1783-1842) seems to many the most engaging. Apart from fascinating autobiographical writings, witty, candid and unpretentious, he wrote charming books of travel and highly individual essays on music, painting and politics. His three outstanding novels are: *The Red and the Black* (1830), *The Charterhouse of Parma* (1839) and *Lucien Leuwen* (unfinished and published fifty years after his death, in 1894). All show talented and ambitious young men at odds with hypocritical and conforming society. All favour the qualities which Stendhal, who spent several years in Italy, believed he found in Italian life: spontaneity, vitality, intelligence, responsiveness to beauty. All the heroes and heroines tend to live dangerously in pursuit of the happiness that comes from a reciprocated love. All strive to preserve personal integrity in a shifting and treacherous world and all are recorded with affectionate irony by the author-narrator in a style that is plain, lucid and urbane.

The realism of these novels lies principally in their unflinching scrutiny of human relationships in a world where beauty, power and position are the prizes. Julien Sorel, carpenter's son and restless hero of *The Red and the Black,*

285

Below: An illustration to *Les Misérables* (1862) by the great writer Victor Hugo (1802-85). The book was an immediate success with readers of every type. The main theme in this vast, complex novel, which recreates the life of the Parisian underworld, is of man's ceaseless struggle against evil.

Left: Zola's novel *Germinal* (1885) as it appeared in the periodical *Les Romans Célèbres* (Celebrated Novels).

Below left: In its candid depiction of low life, Degas' painting *The Absinthe Drinker* follows the 'realism' favoured by many 19th century writers.

Above: Portrait of Emile Zola (1840-1902) by Edouard Manet. Zola sought in his novels to analyze the effects of environment and heredity on his characters. This he did in the series 'The Rougon-Macquart Family' (1871-93), whose development over five generations is seen as being conditioned by these factors.

finds power snatched away from him and is finally executed for attempting to murder his former mistress; Fabrice del Dongo of *The Charterhouse of Parma* knows the intrigues of high politics and the love of the beautiful Duchess de Sanseverina before retiring to the great monastery at Parma; Lucien in *Lucien Leuwen* fails to carry off the young widow, Mme de Chasteller, and instead ends up supervizing the ballot-rigging of a series of provincial elections. But all three battle to define themselves *against* society and to find a true identity amid the social and political manoeuvering in which they are involved.

Balzac's 'Human Comedy'

Honoré de Balzac (1799-1850), although a 'realist', was not simply a chronicler of the surface movements of society. Balzac's novels faithfully reflect many aspects of the life of French society under the Restoration and the July Monarchy, but he is also a critic of that society. He has a strongly personal vision of society in which he sympathizes with its go-getting energy and initiative but condemns its materialism, greed and inhumanity.

Balzac's great achievement is the collection of about ninety interlocking novels and stories which he wrote in under twenty years and which constitute the *Comédie Humaine* or 'Human Comedy'. These volumes, which shed light on each other, are held together and given unity by two devices. The first is the use of recurring characters who crop up in different books and are known to each other, so helping to create the impression of a self-sufficient world separate from ours but at least as real. The second device Balzac used was to classify the novels under different groups

—*Etudes de moeurs* (Studies of be-

haviour), *Etudes philosophiques* (Philosophical studies)—and further divide the *Etudes de moeurs* into groups such as *Scènes de la vie privée* (Scenes of private life) and *Scènes de la vie parisienne* (Scenes of life in Paris).

These devices may be helpful in creating the illusion of unity but Balzac's material is so abundant and so varied that it is the great diversity within the 'Human Comedy' that is chiefly striking. This diversity reveals itself in the vast profusion of characters—from judges, lawyers and bankers to journalists, prostitutes and gangsters—who throng the pages of the novels. It appears too in the densely rendered physical settings and furnishings of a whole range of dwellings, from student lodging and smart town house to country mansion and provincial vicarage. Balzac saw background, upbringing, environment all as affecting a person's destiny:

consequently he devotes much time to minute descriptions of the physical details of the world which each character inhabits—the towns and streets in which they live, their houses, their clothes and their mannerisms. The individual is continually influenced by the pressure of outward circumstances, and his own actions, in turn, are seen to involve many others besides himself. Balzac's strength lies in his ability to bring to life a hugely dramatic world, in which sacred and profane, good and evil, crime and punishment seem the natural elements of human activity. Caught up in the author's intensity, the reader moves from the obsessions of the miserly Grandet (in *Eugénie Grandet*, 1833) to the sinister and hidden power of the arch-criminal Vautrin (in *Old Goriot*, 1834); from the corrupt newspaper offices of *Lost Illusions* (1837-43) to the melodramatic poisoning of the retired scent manufacturer Crevel and his mistress (*Cousin Bette*, 1846). Balzac's writing heightens and intensifies the commonplace; together the novels are less a document on French capitalist society than a kind of great symbol of the corruptions of appetite, wealth and power.

Flaubert and Zola

With Gustave Flaubert (1821-80) realism, in the sense of concern with the life of modern society, is most strongly present in his masterpiece, *Madame Bovary* (1857) and in *A Sentimental Education*

(1869), a flawed but deeply interesting study. Although a mass of exact and conscientious research went into Flaubert's grandiose evocation of ancient Carthage (*Salammbo*, 1862), the total effect is one of an impressive monument rather than a living novel. But in *Madame Bovary* Flaubert achieves a perfect fusion of realistic observation of provincial life and a style which shapes and controls human experience in a hauntingly beautiful way.

The story of Emma Bovary, a provincial doctor's wife, who attempts to escape from the monotony and vulgarity of her environment by a series of love-affairs and is finally driven to suicide, gives little inkling of the power of this novel. With superb ironic detachment, *Madame Bovary* condemns not only sentimental illusions but a crass and philistine society that has no room for beauty or individuality or human aspiration.

Much of Flaubert's pessimism and of his preoccupation with vulgarity, mediocrity and hypocrisy is to be found in the striking short-stories of his disciple, Guy de Maupassant (1850-93). There is the same disgust at the philistinism of the bourgeois, the same scepticism about the durability of human relations, the same conviction about the absurdity of human illusions. These find expression in an extraordinary range of stories marked by sharp observation and telling economy, if occasionally a little mechanical in their ironies. The mood can vary

from the robustness of the brothel scenes in 'At Madame Tellier's' to the disenchantment of 'Two Friends' or the bitter irony of 'The Necklace' with its feeling for the dullness and desperation of penny-pinching lives.

Balzac borrowed the theories of the zoologist Geoffroy Saint-Hilaire so as to develop in his novels affinities between human society and the animal kingdom—perhaps to lend a new kind of seriousness and 'objectivity' to the novelist's art. Emile Zola (1840-1902), in a more systematic way, tried to apply some of the theories on environment and heredity which he had found in the writings of the physiologist Claude Bernard and the geneticist Prosper Lucas to the fictional world he invented. From these scientific writers he derives his conception of the novelist as a scientific observer, and the novel as a kind of experimental world in which characters react predictably to the stimuli of their environment and heredity. His careful documentation and emphasis on heredity are certainly expressed in the

Bulloz

Left: This painting of the interior of a Parisian pastry shop by J. Béraud (1889) shows a typical scene of middle class life. The conventions and decorum of the bourgeoisie were dominant in France at this time. It was the more crass and narrow aspects of this society that Flaubert condemns in his novels.

Above: The reputation of Gustave Flaubert (1821-80) rests chiefly on his two masterpieces *Madame Bovary* and *A Sentimental Education*. A slow and fastidious writer, Flaubert sought in *Madame Bovary* to find in the style alone the beauty which he felt does not in fact exist in commonplace reality.

remarkable novels of working-class life which form part of his ambitious series, 'The Rougon-Macquart Family' (1871-93). In *The Dram Shop* (1877) he relates forcefully and with pathos the break-up of a family in the Paris slums; in *Germinal* (1885) he brilliantly evokes the life of a mining community enslaved by the machine and brutalized by their labours. The primitive appetites of the peasant are shown as inseparable from his closeness to the soil in *Earth* (1887). Although Zola's theories tend to produce a fatalistic picture of human activity, this picture is complicated by the visionary and mythical elements that are prominent in his work, as when he lends a kind of monstrous life to the mine in *Germinal*. With Zola the centre of interest in the nineteenth century novel moves away from the individual to the group and its collective sufferings. It is why he has been called 'the poet of the crowd'.

Emergence of American Literature

It was during the nineteenth century that America evolved a literature of its own. The opening years of the century were characterized by endless pleading in the columns of American journals and newspapers for an American literature, one which would make extensive use of the inhabitants, scenery and language of the New World. 'It is hoped,' remarked a distinguished citizen, 'that the free government of America will produce poets, orators, critics, and historians equal to the most celebrated of the ancient commonwealths of Greece and Italy.'

This aspiration was certainly widespread but any swift fruition was hampered by large problems, problems which were to affect the themes and structures of American literature throughout the century. In the first place America was such a busy land, so preoccupied with opening up the continent, building roads, railways, towns and canals, founding industries, apportioning land, that the artist—usually regarded as an élite figure in the Old World—seemed redundant. As late as 1850 the writer Nathaniel Hawthorne (1804-64) made a comparison, only half-jestingly, between himself and his industrious Puritan ancestors: 'No aim that I have ever cherished, would they recognize as laudable; no success of mine . . . . would they deem otherwise than worthless, if not positively disgraceful.' Moreover, while American writers could certainly claim that they were surrounded by novel and abundant material for literature, one after another attested to a significant lack of traditions, places and customs richly encrusted with what Washington Irving (1783-1859) called 'the charms of storied and poetical association'.

The hesitant attempts of American writers to break away from European models were hampered by the lack of an international copyright agreement between Great Britain and the United States (an agreement not finally ratified until 1891). This meant that British writers need be paid no royalties and so pirated copies of English novels flooded the market and made it very difficult for American writers (who had to be paid royalties) to publish their work.

The early novelists

Literary successes early in the century tended to emerge from various adaptations of European models rather than refutations of them. Charles Brockden Brown (1771-1810), in a series of quickly-written novels which included *Wieland* (1798), *Ormond* (1799) and *Edgar Huntly* (1799), transformed the typical features of the European Gothic novel—the crumbling castle and the subterranean passages—into an often crude but surprisingly complicated examination of the unsettled nature of the New World, where madness and evil lie just below the hugely optimistic surface.

Above: *The Return of Rip Van Winkle,* painted in 1829. In this famous story by Washington Irving (1783-1859) Rip sleeps for 20 years and so misses the American Revolution. On his return, he has doubts as to his identity— signifying perhaps America's own uncertain cultural identity during this period.

Below: Thomas Cole's painting illustrating a scene from *The Last of the Mohicans* by James Fenimore Cooper (1789-1851), which concerns the maturity of Natty Bumppo, or 'Hawkeye'. The American landscape, depicted by Cooper as at once beautiful and awesome, here dwarfs the human figures by its colossal grandeur.

Above right: *Sioux Indians Pursuing a Stag* by George Catlin (1796-1872). Catlin began an eight-year journey into the American wilderness in 1830. He emerged with a knowledge of 48 Indian tribes and a unique folio of paintings of all aspects of Indian life. During the 19th century the depiction of Indians in American literature varied from sentimentalizing them as 'noble savages' to portraying them as bloodthirsty animals.

Right: Illustration to *The Fall of the House of Usher* (1839) by Edgar Allan Poe, in which the neurotic, intellectual hero succumbs to the horror of a union with his 'dead' sister.

Above: Edgar Allan Poe (1809-49) is regarded as one of the greatest American writers: his intuitive knowledge of abnormal psychology allowed him to capture brilliantly the morbid and terrifying excesses of the imagination.

Below: Following the logic of nightmare, Poe's tale *The Pit and the Pendulum* concerns a prisoner of the Inquisition who escapes the razor sharp pendulum blade but is forced, by the shrinking of his cell, towards a pit edge.

Above: *The Virginian Partridge* **painted by John James Audubon (1785-1851), part of his massive work** *The Birds of America* **(1827-38). This included colour plates of every known American bird.**

Left: *The Peaceable Kingdom,* **painted by the Quaker Edward Hicks (1780-1849). He made nearly 100 versions of this allegorical work— a vision of an idyllic, innocent and unified America. Illustrating the biblical text 'the wolf also shall dwell with the lamb, and the leopard shall lie down with the kid' it shows, in the background, a treaty being signed between the white settlers and the native Indians.**

Right: **Walt Whitman (1819-92) was the self-styled poet-prophet of an 'ideal' America. In** *Leaves of Grass* **Whitman sees himself as embodying the diversity of the new nation: 'Of every line and caste am I, of every rank and religion, /A farmer, mechanic, artist, gentleman, sailor, Quaker, /Prisoner, fancyman, rowdy, lawyer, physician, priest'.**

Washington Irving achieved one of America's first international literary successes with *The Sketch Book* (1819-20). This work was seriously important for two reasons. In the character of the narrator, Geoffrey Crayon, Irving created the diffident American bachelor-artist, fascinated by the Old World experience yet both unwilling and unable to enter into it, a prototype of many later fictional heroes found in the work of Nathaniel Hawthorne, Herman Melville and Henry James. Though most of the material in *The Sketch Book* is description of English landscape 'scenes' the book does contain two enduring and endearing American stories, 'Rip Van Winkle' and 'The Legend of Sleepy Hollow'. In the first, Irving deals with the problem of the artist's role in the bustling New World in

terms of a myth. Rip conveniently sleeps for 20 years and misses the troubled years of the War of Revolution. He returns to a changed world, having lost his old identity but with a secure niche as a storyteller in touch with history.

The American novel took a major step forward with the creation, by James Fenimore Cooper (1789-1851), in five novels written between 1823 and 1841, of Natty Bumppo, also known as 'Deer-slayer', 'Hawkeye' and 'Leatherstocking'. The best known of these is probably *The Last of the Mohicans* (1826). In Natty, a hunter, Cooper embodies his own divided feelings about the development of democracy in America. For Natty, a 'back-woodsman' (or unsophisticated country-man) is a noble figure, fated to assist an expanding, avaricious society whose

progress means the end of his way of life and that of his Indian companion, Chingachgook. Despite his over-elaborate natural description and passages of sermonizing, Cooper is often an admirable, gripping story-teller whose depiction of the tensions between the individual and society in the United States left a huge legacy to American culture—not least the development of the 'western'.

The period 1830-60 was a particularly rich one in American literature and may usefully be divided between the 'yea-sayers' and the 'nay-sayers': that is, between those who took an optimistic view of man's place in the New World and his ability to attain a harmonious relationship with his society and surroundings and those who concentrated on the darker problems of this emergent

Bettman Archive

Left: An illustration to *Moby-Dick*, the masterpiece of Herman Melville (1819-91). Concerned with the relentless hunt for the great white whale Moby- Dick by Ahab, the whaler captain, the book has been seen as symbolic of American enterprise, the search for self-discovery and for heroic leadership.

Below: *The Adventures of Tom Sawyer* (1876), illustrated here, was written by Mark Twain (1835-1910) and is essentially a boy's book. Despite some sharp criticism of American small town society, it is written with a nostalgic glow, and its worst terrors never go beyond the confines of secure adult society.

Bettman Archive

society: on the individual's sense of alienation from the society he lived in and his feelings of guilt and sin. These writers saw that, as Herman Melville (1819-91) said of Hawthorne: '. . . the other side (of the soul)—like the dark half of the physical sphere—is shrouded in a blackness, ten times black.'

The Transcendentalists
The chief spokesmen amongst the optimists were Ralph Waldo Emerson (1803-1882) and Henry David Thoreau (1817-1862). These writers were part of a group known as the *Transcendentalists*, who believed that God, whom they chose to call the 'Over-Soul', is present everywhere—within man's soul and in every aspect of nature—so that all things were part of a great cosmic unity. This unity,

they believed, could be perceived by *every* man through his imagination and intuition. Such ideas were bound to be popular with a developing democratic nation, for they emphasized the ability of the common man to achieve fulfilment: furthermore they did not rely on past traditions and were therefore free of Old World influence. Thus the individual in the New World could be seen as an heroic figure shaping and fitting harmoniously into his universe, as Emerson drew attention to in his essay 'Self-Reliance' (1841): 'And truly it demands something godlike in him who has cast off the common motives of humanity and has ventured to trust himself for a taskmaster.'

Thoreau demonstrated a more practical application of these notions in *Walden* (1854), where he describes poetically his

two-year retirement in the woods outside Concord, Massachusetts.

But the ideas of Transcendentalism reached their height in the work of Walt Whitman (1819-1892). In his long series of poems, *Leaves of Grass* (1855), Whitman created an image for himself as the prophetic, heroic poet of America. He adopts as a symbol of his artistic inspiration the humblest and most democratic of natural growths—grass. He sees the great poet as being an 'equable man' who will speak in 'words simple as grass'; thereby making his achievement one which every man of the New World could equal:

I celebrate myself, and sing myself.
And what I assume you shall assume,
For every atom belonging to me as
good belongs to you.

291

Above and right: It was New England countryside such as this to which the poet Emily Dickinson (1830-86), pictured right, responded by 'spreading wide my narrow hands/To gather Paradise'. Her poems are intensely personal expressions of her feelings about God, immortality, nature and her fellow men. They speak, too, of a life of loneliness: 'The soul selects her own society,/Then shuts the door;/To her different majority/Present no more.'

Whitman sees himself as a minstrel (his poems are often called 'songs') whose job it is to sing the praises of America. As he developed and his vision spread to encompass and embrace all aspects of American society he enlarged *Leaves of Grass* to include more and more poems— the 1860 version contained 124 new poems and many revisions; the fifth edition of 1872 includes his Civil War poems.

The 'dark' writers

Major writers who took a more pessimistic view of man in the New World include Edgar Allan Poe (1809-1849), Hawthorne and Melville. Like the Transcendentalists, Poe believed in the power of the imagination to perceive unity and beauty, but unlike them he conceived the artist as being a lonely, élite figure:

> '*From childhood's hour I have not been*
> *As others were—I have not seen*
> *As others saw— . . . .*'

The search for supernal beauty undertaken by his heroes often reaches its conclusion only through madness and death. This gives a peculiar mixture of horror and exhilaration to his best-known tales of terror, which include 'The Fall of the House of Usher', 'The Pit and the Pendulum' and 'Ligeia'. Poe is also known as the father of the detective story, though it is not always recognized that his detective-hero Dupin, in stories like 'The Purloined Letter', is essentially a Romantic artist, solving the crimes largely through intuition rather than through scientific rationality, which Poe detested as much as democracy.

Nathaniel Hawthorne's work deals with the bonds between individual and society, past and present. His finest novel, *The Scarlet Letter* (1850), is an historical novel dealing with a seventeenth-century

Below: *The Steerage*, a photo of immigrants during the passage to America. British, Germans, Scandinavians and, later in the 19th century, Mediterranean and Eastern European people came in massive numbers, contributing to the rich diversity of American culture.

New England Puritan community. But this tale of adultery and its consequences is perennially topical since Hawthorne is really dealing with the nature of individual freedom versus social duty. Hawthorne owed much to the Gothic novel and one of his most important contributions to American literature (apart from his recognition of the profound influence of Puritanism on American writing) was his use of old romance traditions. He sought to use *allegory* (a story or description which, apart from its obvious meaning, contains a deeper moral or spiritual meaning) to make statements about contemporary life, to found 'a neutral territory, somewhere between the real world and fairy-land, where the Actual and the Imaginary may meet'.

Herman Melville expanded Hawthorne's materials into something more truly symbolic. In *Moby-Dick* (1851) he created the most potent symbol of the age in the ferocious white whale of the title; a beast of no colour and all colours, which he used to suggest the existence of an awesome, neutral universe. With this book, Melville showed that American literature could provide an imagination as large and complex as Shakespeare's. Melville's was a questing but sceptical vision, one which desired to believe in man's potential but feared that 'the invisible spheres were formed in fright.'

Emily Dickinson and Mark Twain

Two other figures who were important in the development of American literature were Emily Dickinson and Mark Twain. Emily Dickinson (1830-1886) wrote about 1,775 short poems which, although they dealt with basic themes such as God and nature, were remarkable for their use of fresh, vivid imagery derived from the details of New England life. Evolving an intense, personal verbal style this spinster lady created poetry of astonishing psychological truth, anticipating many developments in modern poetry.

Mark Twain (real name Samuel Clemens, 1835-1910) veered sharply between patriotism and disgust in his reactions to American society. In *Huckleberry Finn* (1885) he made his finest contribution to American literature. Huck is an uneducated but intelligent boy whose wanderings down the Mississippi are punctuated by episodes which reveal to him human dishonesty and violence but which teach him wisdom and compassion.

Twain's fundamental pessimism was developed by writers such as Stephen Crane (1871-1900), Frank Norris (1870-1902), Ambrose Bierce (1842-1914?) and Jack London (1876-1916) in the closing years of the century. Following the lead of Emile Zola, these writers concentrated on man as a creature conditioned by heredity and environment, whose illusions are absurd in a post-Darwinian world where the weakest are destroyed. Nature, in their hands, was conceived as entirely neutral, a blank back-drop to folly and violence. Such negation of Transcendental ideas was summed up in a poem by Stephen Crane:

> *A man said to the Universe:*
> *'Sir, I exist.'*
> *'However,' replied the Universe,*
> *'The fact has not created in me*
> *A sense of obligation.'*

John Hillelson Agency

Mary Evans

Colnaghi & Co Ltd.

In *The Last of the Mohicans* James Fennimore Cooper tried to portray fairly the aspirations of both Indians and white Americans. The hero is a backwoodsman who must help a grasping society to destroy his way of life and that of his Indian companion, Chingachgook.

Russian Literature

When Lev Nikolayevich Tolstoy (1828-1910) was born, the great works of modern Russian literature were few and they were known only to a select Russian public. By the time of his death—an event that was reported throughout the civilized world—Russian literature was established as one of the richest and most challenging of Europe, boasting such writers of genius as Pushkin, Turgenev, Gogol, Dostoevsky and of course Tolstoy himself.

The founding fathers

Russian writers had been given a great impetus by Alexander Pushkin (1799-1837), who with his great range of poetical and prose works—including *Evgeny Onegin* (1833), *Boris Godunov* (1831) and *The Queen of Spades* (1834)—freed the Russian language and subject-matter from its eighteenth century stiffness and artificiality. Nikolay Gogol (1809-1852) founded a very different, though still influential, strain in Russian literature with his satires exposing human pretension. These include a play, *The Government Inspector* (1836) and his

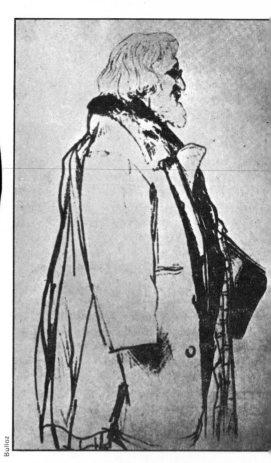

M. Pucciarelli

Above: Nikolay Gogol (1809-52) is best known for his play *The Government Inspector* **(1836) and the novel** *Dead Souls* **(1842)— brilliant satires on bureaucracy and serfdom.**

Below: Modern Russian illustration to a tale by Alexander Pushkin (1799-1837), the father of Russian literature.

Right: Ivan Turgenev (1818-1883) was the first Russian author to enjoy an international reputation. Embittered by criticism of his masterpiece *Fathers and Children* **(1862), Turgenev decided to live abroad. His novels combine current social issues with fine evocations of mood and landscape.**

Bulloz

Novosti

the range of experience that he was able to encompass and express was truly astounding. The book's immediate scope is the Napoleonic wars. Ultimately, however, it provides (as an early reviewer noted) 'a complete picture of everything in which people find their happiness and greatness, their grief and humiliation'. And its characters are observed with such insight and in such detail (one critic spoke of Tolstoy's 'psychological eavesdropping') that the reader is persuaded to accept Tolstoy's heroes and heroines into his imaginative life as intimates and friends rather than fictitious creations.

Characters reveal themselves in given situations—their words, gestures and expressions, together with their interior musings, act as the vital agents. Hardly ever does the narrator intrude or use analytical description. Tolstoy's narrative voice is heard undisguised only when he attempts to put the Napoleonic wars into perspective and turns (much to the dismay of many a reader) to an analysis of the historical process.

Heroes and heroines abound: *War and Peace* is equally concerned with life in several families, and with a wide spectrum of personalities within them. Tolstoy moves from one family to another, from Petersburg to Moscow, town to country, peace to war: his changes of focus and mood are many. Even so, the whole—immense and complex as it is and deliberately not 'rounded off'—retains a subtle organization. *War and Peace* was the product of immense labour during which the author made drafts which far outweigh the finished product in their bulk.

War and Peace was to be followed by yet another masterpiece, *Anna Karenina* (1873-7: published initially, as was its predecessor, in serial form). Tolstoy took as his starting point a real-life incident: a neighbour's mistress had committed suicide by throwing herself under a train. Tolstoy witnessed the mangled remains, and a plan which he had already discussed with his wife—to write about the circumstances of an adulteress in high society—began to take shape. Only gradually (and after the first draft had been completed) did Tolstoy begin to introduce major figures other than Anna, her husband and her lover.

It could not have been suspected at this stage that the book would concern itself as much as it eventually did with the families of Levin and Oblonsky. Yet it was by introducing these that Tolstoy was able to proceed so effectively with his exploration of the sentiment expressed in the novel's introductory sentence: 'All happy families are alike; each unhappy family is unhappy in its own way'. It is Tolstoy's reluctance to adopt any easy moral stance in respect of Anna's infidelity that gives the book its complexity and tension and ensures its lasting success.

Unlike *War and Peace*, *Anna Karenina* was set in contemporary Russia. Almost inevitably, therefore, the novel concerns itself to a considerable degree with the discussion of current social problems. In this it is at one with much of mid-nineteenth century Russian fiction. In the absence of a parliament or of an unfettered press, the writer (though himself subject to censorship) felt an obligation to offer—through his fiction—guidance on matters of public concern. Not all were able to reconcile their civic

unfinished novel *Dead Souls* (1842).

At first the young Tolstoy was uncertain whether or not to follow a literary career. As an aristocrat serving in the army he published his first work, *Childhood* (1852), even while noting in his diary 'Literature is rubbish and I should like to set down here rules and a plan for estate management'. But the immediate success of this evocation of his own childhood was enough to persuade him that there was no absolute opposition between the careers of landed aristocrat and writer. Even so, it was only in 1856, with the publication of the third of his Crimean War tales, that he revealed his authorship of these works.

Tolstoy's complete works (including his letters and his fascinating diaries) were eventually to fill ninety volumes although his devotion to extra-literary concerns, which included the manage-

ment of his estate and his several hundred serfs, increasingly occupied his time.

Childhood was to be followed by two sequels, *Boyhood* (1854) and *Youth* (1857). Neither quite lived up to the promise of the original volume, but the publication of the *Sevastopol Tales* and, especially, of *The Cossacks* (1863) meant continuing popularity for the author in the years which paved the way for his mammoth novel *War and Peace* (published 1865-9). Meanwhile Tolstoy's way of life altered; in 1862 he married and began a life centred round his family and his estate.

Tolstoy's 'War and Peace'

War and Peace, a landmark in his own development, was also a landmark in the history of the European novel. Its scope and achievement were unique and Tolstoy was in fact reluctant ever to classify it as a novel. But whatever the work's genre,

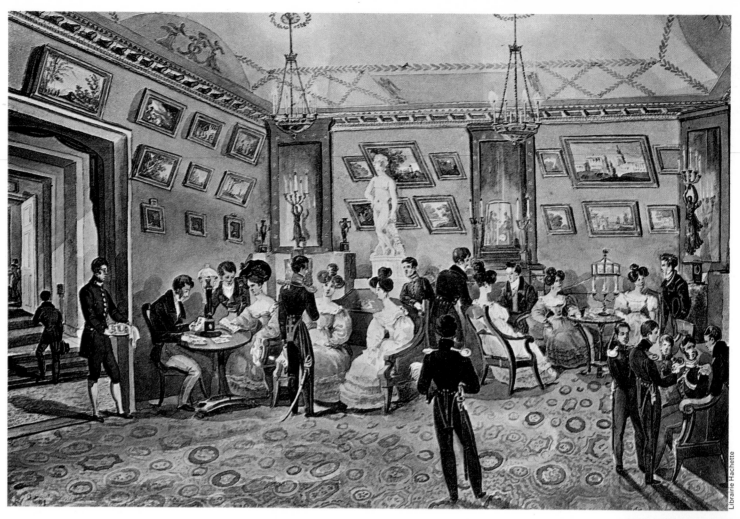

and artistic responsibilities as successfully as Tolstoy in *Anna Karenina* or Turgenev in *Fathers and Children* (1862).

Ivan Turgenev (1818-1883) excelled in the portrayal of social issues, and of the Russian intelligentsia of the mid-nineteenth century. His work is conceived on a smaller scale than Tolstoy's; its strengths are the poetic, atmospheric settings and beauty of style. Although adverse criticism greeted *Fathers and Children*, particularly its agnostic and nihilist hero Bazarov, Turgenev had already left Russia for Europe where he lived for most of his life and achieved international fame.

Aristocrat turned peasant

Tolstoy himself was soon to prefer the role of moralist, social critic and sage to that of artist, and the last thirty years of his long life were to involve a radical reassessment of his earlier achievement. Earlier, he had written: 'The aim of an artist is not to resolve a question irrefutably, but to compel people to love life in all its countless and inexhaustible manifestations'. The Tolstoy of *Anna Karenina* raises some questions more insistently than the author of *War and Peace*; but even so, unalterable solutions tend not to be advanced.

But the Tolstoy of subsequent decades is impatient of moral ambiguities. As he stated in 1887, 'It is necessary for a man to know clearly and without doubt what is good and evil, to see plainly the dividing line between them, and consequently to paint not what is, but what should be'. Thus, Tolstoy professed a revulsion against his earlier manner;

eloquently, he questioned the meaning of literature and of life itself in *Confession* (1879). In this book Tolstoy describes the religious crisis through which he passed. Rejecting orthodox religion, he sought new beliefs with which to replace it, and in works such as *What is my faith?* (1883-84) he outlined his new faith, based on his individual interpretation of the Gospels.

Much of his time was now claimed by 'estate management', though with a difference: he sought to renounce all his privileges (which were many), he dressed as a peasant and worked in the fields. Many of the writings in his new simple, instructive style, were addressed to the peasants and made effective use of their vocabulary and art forms. *The Tale of Ivan the Fool* (1885) and *Alesha Gorshok* (1905) are notable examples of such work. But the educated audience was not abandoned. *The Death of Ivan Ilyich* (1886) is a stark and moving examination of human mortality, from which—as Tolstoy hastens to point out—bourgeois prosperity provides no exemption.

The final years

However, Tolstoy's finest achievement in these later years was a work which (unlike his last novel, *Resurrection*, 1899) dispensed with some of the new certainties and simplicities. In *Khadzhi-Murat* (written 1896-1904, and published after his death), he returned to the scene and even to the manner of his earlier works, marvellously refined. That the qualities of his hero Khadzhi-Murat contradicted much that he now preached disturbed Tolstoy, but did not deflect him from his plan. He wrote this book 'on the

Above: *A St Petersburg Salon* in 1830. This watercolour painting aptly illustrates one kind of life described by Tolstoy in *War and Peace* (1865-69). Set within the framework of the Napoleonic invasions of Russia, Tolstoy's epic work contains countless characters and explores all areas of life. His immense imaginative vision and deep moral force combine to make the work pre-eminent in European literature.

Right: Chained prisoners at a Siberian labour camp (c.1885). Dostoevsky experienced the strictures of this life when he served four years hard labour from 1850-54 for the revolutionary opinions which he then held.

quiet', in a sense as an old man's treat.

But in general, Tolstoy did not spare himself. He was an unrelenting critic of the Russian state, none of whose institutions or official attitudes he felt merited respect. He preached a simplified Christian morality which was embodied in pacifism and anarchism.

He was, however, at logger-heads not only with the Russian state. The marriage which had given him inner peace to compose his greatest works had not weathered the changes of the final thirty years; worst of all, he was not at peace with himself. At the age of 82 he broke finally with his wife and family, who opposed his new views, and set off as a pilgrim for an unknown destination. He died at an obscure provincial railway station in 1910.

M. Pucciarelli

Snark

Society for Cultural Relations with the USSR

Dostoevsky's anguished world

Fyodor Dostoevsky (1821-81) is often seen as a counterbalance to Tolstoy. This man swung from revolutionary fervour to extreme patriotism and Tsarist loyalty during his lifetime: he was sentenced to execution for his radical beliefs, was at the last moment reprieved and sent instead to serve in a Siberian labour camp. His work is, like his life, concerned with extremes. Dostoevsky presents a world anguished, intense, and restless, in which the irrational aspects of man's behaviour and the theme of salvation through suffering are uppermost. The short novel *Notes from Underground* (1864) heralded his mature work: its hero, a solitary embittered clerk uncovers the dark and destructive side of man's nature.

His first great novel was *Crime and Punishment* (1866) in which a young man, Raskolnikov, rebels against society's restrictions by murdering an old woman, a pawn broker. Dostoevsky brilliantly analyzes the psychological development of Raskolnikov as he suffers under the strain of his own feelings of guilt—which finally drive him to confess to the crime.

A short novel *The Gambler* (1866), for which he drew on his own compulsive gambling, was followed by *The Idiot* (1868-69) and *The Devils* (1871-2); the first dealing with a saintly man, Prince Myshkin, whose simplicity of heart makes him powerless to deal with the destructive passions of the world; the second being an analysis of the negative, spiritually empty—and, to Dostoevsky, positively evil—mechanism of revolutionary thought. But the greatest of Dostoevsky's

achievements is probably *The Brothers Karamazov* (1879-80), which encompasses a great range and profundity of thought; Dostoevsky concentrates, in his characters, not only on universal problems and oppositions within man's psyche, but on problems confronting Russia at this crucial time in its history.

The nineteenth century certainly witnessed a golden age in Russian literature. But although its achievements are likely to remain unchallenged, the twentieth century has, in its turn, produced many distinguished and unique authors including Blok, Mandelshtam, Pasternak and Solzhenitsyn. And despite the rigours and restrictions of the Soviet period, despite the attempt to make literature the handmaid of the state, the future is far from bleak.

The Novels of Hardy, James and Conrad

To the majority of the educated British public the nineteenth century was a period of hope and optimism. The Empire, it was thought, would bring justice and Christianity to the world, and supply Britain with the raw materials that the factories would transform into a wonderful variety of goods for home consumption and foreign trade. Poverty, ignorance and disease were recognized problems, but they would be eradicated by the advance of science and the spread of wealth.

A bright new future lay ahead—or so many people thought. But those who could see a little farther were not so easily contented with such a naive view of 'progress'. In their novels Thomas Hardy, Henry James and Joseph Conrad all questioned the replacement of some older values with what they saw as shakier ones; at the same time, however, they were in their work the heralds of a new intellectual and emotional freedom. They were all aware of the creeping emotional and moral hollowness that was to become the twentieth century's greatest disease, and the biggest concern of its artists and writers. In terms of style and theme, although differing widely among themselves, these three novelists all highlight the transition from Victorian to so-called 'modern' literature.

Hardy's rural Wessex

Thomas Hardy (1840-1928) was born the son of a master mason in the Dorset village of Higher Bockhampton. He went to school in Bockhampton and Dorchester, and on leaving school at 16 he worked for the Dorchester ecclesiastical architect John Hicks until 1861. During this time he read widely, taught himself Latin and Greek and began to write verse. He became steeped in Dorset history and folklore, and was encouraged in his reading by the dialect poet William Barnes, who lived next to Hicks's office.

In 1868 he completed his first novel—*The Poor Man and the Lady*—but destroyed it later. In 1870 he was sent to work on a church in Cornwall and met Emma Gifford, his future wife. At the time he was already working on *Desperate Remedies*, his first published novel, which appeared in March 1871. Although it was described by the *Spectator* as 'a desperate remedy for a desperate purse', its publication was a great boost to Hardy's confidence, and he followed it quickly with *Under the Greenwood Tree*. This story was liked by the critics, but did not sell well. On the strength of it, however, Hardy was invited to write for the influential *Cornhill* magazine.

The serial that Hardy wrote for *Cornhill* in 1873 was *Far from the Madding Crowd* —the tempestuous (at least for the period) story of the love of three men for the beautiful and wealthy landowner Bathsheba Everdene. Although perhaps not his greatest novel it firmly established his reputation and, having been reprinted seven times by the end of 1874, gave him

Above: Portrait of Thomas Hardy (1840-1928) at the age of 63, painted by Augustus John. Hardy said of the portrait: 'I don't know whether that is how I look or not, but that is how I feel'. Bridging the 19th century and the modern age, Hardy was mourned at his death as 'the last of the great Victorians'.

Right: A 19th century Dorsetshire labourer. The old man with his smock, pipe and pint may seem a quaint and nostalgic figure today, but Hardy had no illusions about the harsh realities of peasant life. Its unhurried, rooted ways (often humorously drawn) form the rural setting of his novels.

Left: Illustrations from Hardy's novel *Tess of the D'Urbervilles* (1891): Tess sleeps on unawares as Angel Clare watches her captors close in around Stonehenge. Hardy used subject matter in *Tess* and, to a greater extent in *Jude the Obscure*, that incurred scandalized reactions from Victorian critics and institutions.

Right: The cottage at Higher Bockhampton, Dorset, where Hardy was born. In one of his earliest poems, *Domicilium*, Hardy describes the house as 'quite alone, and those tall firs / And beeches were not planted. Snakes and efts / Swarmed in summer days, and nightly bats / Would fly about our bedrooms.'

the financial security to marry Emma.

Hardy's marriage was not a great success. Perhaps Sergeant Troy in *Far from the Madding Crowd* echoes his creator's sentiments when he exclaims: 'All romance ends at marriage!' Although Hardy had longed for intimacy, when it came he felt smothered by domesticity. He and Emma did not know each other really well when they married, and they remained in separate worlds; she childless, he increasingly absorbed in his work. During the next two decades, Hardy wrote his series of fine *Wessex* novels, beginning with *The Return of the Native*, serialized in 1877, in which human destinies are played out against the natural background of Egdon Heath. The brooding presence of the heath is felt throughout the book.

The Mayor of Casterbridge (1885), Hardy's tale of the downfall of a passionate but stubborn man set against the background of the decline of the traditional rural life, owed many of its details to accounts in local newspapers—the sale of a wife, with which the book opens, still went on in remoter areas. The idea, expressed in this book, that 'happiness was but an occasional episode in the general drama of pain' is a recurring theme in Hardy. In his next novel, *The Woodlanders* (1887), Hardy began to see the cruelty of existence lying not in the universe as a whole, or in individual men, but in society. The book was greatly acclaimed, and was Hardy's own favourite.

Hardy had often complained of the prudery and false standards of 'taste' of his age, which prevented writers from

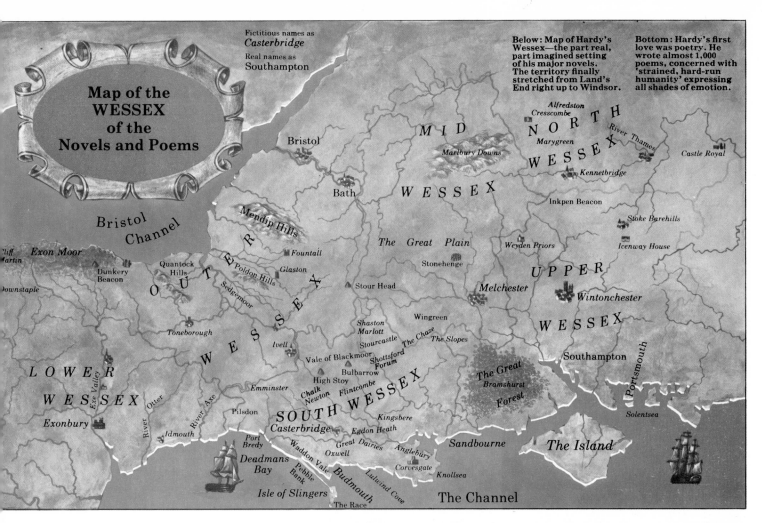

Map of the
WESSEX
of the
Novels and Poems

Fictitious names as *Casterbridge*
Real names as Southampton

Below: Map of Hardy's Wessex—the part real, part imagined setting of his major novels. The territory finally stretched from Land's End right up to Windsor.

Bottom: Hardy's first love was poetry. He wrote almost 1,000 poems, concerned with 'strained, hard-run humanity' expressing all shades of emotion.

THE SELF-UNSEEING

Here is the ancient floor,
Footworn and hollowed and thin,
Here was the former door
Where the dead feet walked in.

She sat here in her chair,
Smiling into the fire;
He who played stood there,
Bowing it higher and higher.

Childlike I danced in a dream;
Blessings emblazoned that day;
Everything glowed with a gleam;
Yet we were looking away!

telling the whole truth about human relationships. So he fought hard to have *Tess of the D'Urbervilles* published in its original form, but it was eventually with 'cynical amusement' that he re-wrote it for serialization in 1891, free of all 'offensive' matter. It was either that or refusal from all publishers. Even in its adapted form *Tess* (subtitled *A Pure Woman*, an indication of the innocence of this heroine who is seduced and finally tragically hanged) was the sensation of the year, and fulsome praise and bitter abuse were heaped on Hardy equally.

Jude the Obscure (1895) was the centre of another row, with its story of a young man 'who could not go to Oxford' and whose every ambition is defeated. Its criticism of Christian marriage—'a sordid contract, based on material convenience'

National Portrait Gallery

National Portrait Gallery

Mary Evans

Above: Henry James (1843-1916) came from a talented New York family. His elder brother William was an eminent philosopher and author of *Principles of Psychology* **and** *Varieties of Religious Experience.* **Henry James settled in Europe in 1875 and his major novels reflect the impact of European culture on Americans.**

Below: *Interior of a Palazzo in Venice* **(1899) by J. S. Sargent. Henry James stayed in the cosmopolitan society of Venice several times, in turn entranced by the 'far-shining lagoon' and depressed by the 'glutinous malodorous damp' according to the season. It was here that he wrote** *The Portrait of a Lady* **in 1881.**

Above right and far right: The Polish-born novelist Joseph Conrad (1857-1924) was brought up in the Ukraine—far from any ocean. He went to sea at the age of 17, despite the scandalized response of his relatives. Scenes such as depicted in *All Hands to the Pump* **(1889) (far right) were central to his experience.**

Right: Illustration to Conrad's novel *Typhoon* **(1902). The story was based on a very rough passage experienced by Conrad between Amsterdam and Java in 1887. The Far East was to Conrad 'absolutely riotous with life' and he absorbed every sight and event as material to be used later in his novels.**

Royal Academy

300

—and its sexual explicitness earned it widespread abuse from the contemporary arbiters of taste. To the *New York Bookman* it was 'simply one of the most objectionable books we have ever read', and W. H. Smith withdrew it from their circulating library.

The scandal caused Hardy to give up novel-writing at the age of 56 and turn his attention to poetry. His *Wessex Poems* were written over the years, but his greatest work in his later years was an epic poem, *The Dynasts*, which summed up his philosophy that the world was indeed a cruel place, where human beings were endowed with intelligence and emotions in a purposeless universe. Yet he still believed that kindness and brotherhood were possible redeeming factors.

Hardy always conveyed his themes through 'impressions' rather than 'philosophy'. The scepticism and determinism in Hardy's work underlie a vivid portrayal of rural existence, and a warm concern

for the honest appraisal of human life.

James—American and European

Henry James (1843-1916) was the second son of a large and wealthy New York family of Irish ancestry. From his earliest days he travelled widely in Europe, and never spent long in his native America.

He began to study law, but gave it up when he determined to be a writer. His first story was published when he was 22, and from then on he was a regular contributor to magazines. He visited Europe in 1869, and in London he met figures such as William Morris, Ruskin, and George Eliot, and he returned to New York full of an admiration for European art and culture which was to be reflected in his work.

James's first novel in book form, *Roderick Hudson*, was published in 1875. The story of a young American painter in Paris, his downfall, and mysterious death in the Alps, *Roderick Hudson* was very well received by the critics.

James had by this time begun to move in 'high' social and literary circles, and his work began to reflect this world. *The American* (1877) is about a rich American who falls in love with a beautiful young European aristocrat, but is prevented from marrying her by her snobbish family.

The theme of expatriate Americans is returned to in *The Europeans* (1878), in which some 'Europeanized' Americans—such as James was himself—meet their American cousins. *Daisy Miller*, published in the same year, was James's best selling book to date. By throwing together a young, unchaperoned American girl with an Italian, James was able to explore two contrasting cultures. The fine novel *Washington Square* (1881) is another story of thwarted love, in which a puritanical doctor wrecks the lives of his daughter and her lover.

James's masterpiece *The Portrait of a Lady* (1881) closed this first intensely productive period of his career. Set in Florence, Rome, and England, it is remarkable for the close observation of characters of several nationalities: the truly cosmopolitan flavour of the work develops alongside the psychological rendering of the heroine Isabel Archer.

In 1886 James produced *The Bostonians* and *The Princess Casamassima*, but both these novels of his second period went unappreciated at the time. After an unsuccessful attempt at drama, James returned to fiction. In 1897 he bought his final home, Lamb House, at Rye in Sussex, and there wrote *The Turn of the Screw* (1897), *The Wings of the Dove* (1902), *The Ambassadors* (1903) and *The Golden Bowl* (1904). For their maturity of vision these are considered major novels, but they have been criticized for their tortuous plots and convoluted prose style: Hardy, for example, felt that James had 'a ponderously warm manner of saying nothing in infinite sentences'.

Although his writings were almost completely disregarded for 30 years after his death in 1916, James's stature has increased steadily since World War II, with a recognition of his acute sense of the complexity of modern life.

Sea life and symbols

Like James an exile from his native land, Josef Teodor Kondor Korzeniowski (1856-1924), better known as Joseph Conrad, was the son of radical Polish aristocrats. Brought up in Poland, he began at the age of 16 to want to go to sea. He realized his wish in 1884, when he joined a French ship at Marseilles.

Living a life of action and adventure in his twenties, travelling to every continent, there was nothing about Conrad to suggest that he might one day become a great novelist. But all the time he was gathering an invaluable stock of experiences, as he progressed towards the master mariner's certificate he gained in 1886. It was during this decade that he began writing, and at the age of 40 was able to retire from the sea with the publication of his first novel, *Almayer's Folly* in 1895.

The rest of his life was spent in England, his adopted home, writing the novels and stories which have made him the unchallenged chronicler of the British experience with the sea. Conrad's appeal lies in his ability to tell a stirring tale, full of action and adventure, that is yet able to reveal layer upon layer of rich and symbolic meaning. It was the former quality that made his reputation during his lifetime: modern critics have emphasized the symbolic, deeply pessimistic vision of the writer.

Typical in this respect is the short novel *Heart of Darkness* (1902). Based on Conrad's own experiences in the colonial brutality of the Belgian Congo, it is at the same time a symbolic masterpiece with its powerful evocation of the emptiness of so much of human endeavour and belief in the face of a hostile wilderness.

In *Lord Jim* (1900) the outward adventure, which never lets up, is balanced against the secret inner turmoil of a man who cannot live with his own past. But Conrad's greatest work is undoubtedly *Nostromo* (1904), a wonderfully complex novel set in revolutionary South America. Its breadth and scope, and its successful blend of personal with political and historical themes, have led to deserving comparisons being made with Tolstoy's *War and Peace*.

The Beginnings of Modern Drama

Modern drama is an international rather than a national phenomenon—perhaps because the various traditions of the modern theatre sprang from many different parts of the European continent, notably France, Norway, Sweden and Russia.

In the middle of the nineteenth century, French drama dominated Europe. It was a drama in which almost everything was sacrificed to immediate theatrical effect. Its chief exponents were Victorien Sardou, Eugène Scribe and the younger Dumas who wrote the outstanding popular success of the day, *La Dame aux Camélias* (*The Lady of the Camellias*) (1852); an idealized romance on the theme of the repentant harlot. Such plays were soundly constructed but lacked plausibility, consistency or depth of character, substituted grandiose declamation for genuine emotion and melodramatic intrigue for coherent development of plot.

The new naturalism

One of the sources of modern drama arose as a reaction against the excesses of this type of drama, though it was part also of a larger change in thought and outlook which took place in late nineteenth century Europe. This reaction is usually called Naturalism and is associated with Emile Zola's dramatization of his own novel *Thérèse Raquin* (1873), some of Ibsen's earlier plays, and August Strindberg's famous play *Miss Julie* (1888).

Naturalism demanded that the drama should be, in Zola's famous phrase, 'a slice of life'—though some of its more extreme practitioners overlooked the other part of Zola's dictum, namely that the slice of life should be 'viewed through a temperament'—that is, that reality should not merely be photographically represented, but organized and interpreted by the dramatist's own vision.

Naturalistic drama placed the emphasis on the daily life of ordinary people in their normal domestic circumstances, with a credible sequence of events taking the place of sensational intrigue. It was heavily influenced by the example of novelists such as George Eliot and Balzac. The new drama required a less 'stagy' style of acting and different forms of scenic representation. These were provided by the Parisian Théatre Libre which under the direction of André Antoine presented naturalistic drama in the setting for which it was intended.

Antoine's example influenced theatrical development throughout Europe. In Germany, it led to the establishment of Brahms' Freie Buhne where Gerhart Hauptmann's realistic dramas were first presented, and in Russia it inspired Stanislavsky and the Moscow Art Theatre to produce an internationally acclaimed stage interpretation of Maxim Gorky's *The Lower Depths* (1902)—another naturalistic drama which has survived to our own day. In Britain the natural-

istic drama was championed by George Bernard Shaw (1856-1950) and the Independent Theatre of J. T. Grein, in which some of Shaw's early plays were staged.

The genius of Ibsen

Though both Henrik Ibsen (1828-1906) and August Strindberg (1849-1912) played an important part in the formation of naturalistic drama, both were dramatists of genius who soon outgrew the limitations of the new movement and developed in very different and distinctive ways.

Ibsen began his dramatic career with a raw historical melodrama, *Catiline* (1850) but fifteen years later, as a voluntary exile in Rome, he wrote *Brand*, a poetic drama full of nostalgia for his native Norway. The larger-than-life hero, derived from Scandinavian folklore, is driven by the compulsion to seek self-realization

Above: A scene from a 1937 production of *The Doll's House* by Henrik Ibsen (1828-1906) where Nora, the quiet respectable bourgeois wife momentarily breaks loose in a triumphant tarantella 'dancing as if it was a matter of life and death', as her husband remarks in amazement. The play was first produced in Ibsen's native Christiania in 1879.

Left: The British actress Maggie Smith in a modern production of Ibsen's *Hedda Gabler* (1890), a late play which explores a more symbolic world than his early work had done.

Right: Drawing of the Swedish dramatist August Strindberg (1849-1912) which captures something of the demonic power which informs plays such as *The Father* (1887) and *Miss Julie* (1888)— savage, intense studies of human frailties and the bitter enmity of the sexes.

Far right: Scene from a modern production of Strindberg's tragic expressionist drama *The Dance of Death* (1901) with Laurence Olivier.

and avoid the various snares of social constraint and domestic attachment, yet is finally destroyed by his quest.

Brand was followed in 1867 by another poetic drama, *Peer Gynt*, again featuring a folk-hero, but this time cast in a far less heroic mould. Peer Gynt is a braggart and a tell-tale, and the action of the play spans his life from early youth to his grave. The scenes are presented in a non-realistic fashion, almost as dream sequences or vivid mental images, and there is a good deal of incisive satire on such topics as commercial morality, the futility of military glory and the pettiness of many contemporary conceptions of life. But ultimately *Peer Gynt* has a breadth of vision and a compassionate understanding of human life which transcends satire. Both plays show a power of imaginative construction which goes far

Zoe Dominic

Mary Evans

Above and right: The watercolour (right) of George Bernard Shaw (1856-1950) was made in 1925 when Shaw, already a vital force in the English theatre for three decades, was at the height of his powers. The sketch brings out admirably Shaw's dramatic personality— his confidence, resolute intellect and good humour. His best-known play is perhaps *Pygmalion*. The scene (above) shows Mrs Patrick Campbell, one of the most famous actresses of her day, as Eliza Doolittle, the poor flower-seller who is 'elocuted' into elegance by the phonetician Professor Higgins. The play created a furore because of Eliza's famous line 'Not bloody likely'.

Left: Scene from the 1902 Moscow production of *The Lower Depths* by the Russian novelist and playwright Maxim Gorky (1868-1936), a powerful drama of the Moscow underworld at the turn of the century. The play's outspokenness led to Gorky's expulsion, by the Tsar, from the Imperial Academy of Russian Artists.

Above: Scene from a modern production of Chekhov's *The Three Sisters* (1901).

Below: Scene from Chekhov's *The Seagull* as produced in 1898 by the newly formed Moscow Art Theatre under the direction of Stanislavsky, who appears here in the role of Trigorin.

beyond the theatrical resources which were available to Ibsen.

After these two notable experiments, Ibsen abandoned the poetic drama in favour of plays which, on the surface, appeared to be concerned solely with social problems of the day. Between 1870 and 1882 he produced a series of plays by which he is probably best known today. They include *Pillars of Society* (1875-7), a study of the corruption and hypocrisy of small-town public life; *A Doll's House* (1878-9), a powerful indictment of the emotional and intellectual deprivation imposed on a sensitive woman by current notions of marital respectability; *Ghosts* (1881), a play on the theme of the sins of the father visited upon the children, and *An Enemy of the People* (1882), a dramatization of the conflict between a man of integrity and the corrupt society in which

he finds himself.

Plays such as these have created the conception of Ibsen as a social reformer, a conception to which Bernard Shaw gave a wide currency and one which influenced his own plays, such as *Widowers' Houses* (1885-92) and *Mrs. Warren's Profession* (1893).

But Ibsen's greatest achievement is of a very different kind, and is represented by plays of a later period. In these he attempted, often with triumphant success, to unite a highly selective realism of surface with an underlying symbolic power and depicted universal conflicts and predicaments through the portrayal of characters and settings drawn from the parochial Scandinavian society which he knew. Three of the best plays of this group are *The Wild Duck* (1883-4)— where the crippled duck in the attic is

both a real duck and a symbol of the heroine's predicament, *Rosmersholm* (1885-6) and *Hedda Gabler* (1890).

In the last phase of his career Ibsen was preoccupied by the question of the artist and his responsibility to society, to his art and to his private relationships, and explored these themes in such plays as *The Master Builder* (1891-2), *John Gabriel Borkman* (1895-8), and *When We Dead Awaken* (1897-9).

Strindberg's intense world

If Ibsen was the last great dramatist of the nineteenth century and perhaps the greatest, Strindberg was in many ways the first great one of the twentieth. After his early and highly idiosyncratic version of naturalism in *Miss Julie*, Strindberg soon developed in the direction of Expressionism, a type of drama not at all concerned with surface realism or individual characters, but with the subjective portrayal of the outer world, the inner workings of the psyche and the conflict of opposing forces. Even in *Miss Julie*, the confrontation between the restless and frustrated upper-class mistress and the vulgar, petty-minded but crudely vigorous servant is explored not so much in terms of its social implications as of a struggle between the weaker and the stronger will.

In Strindberg's other great play *The Father* (1887) the theme of the conflict of wills, this time between the husband and wife, is intensified and the characters are types rather than individuals. 'I find the joy of life in its violent and cruel struggle' Strindberg wrote at this time, and it is always a struggle for survival which engages his dramatic interest. But this struggle coloured his life, also. His pessimism and recurring sense of persecution were exacerbated by hostile critical reception of his plays and the charges of blasphemy which were brought against him. He married three times, each relationship being intense but ultimately destructive and ending in divorce, and each time Strindberg lost the custody of his children.

In later plays Strindberg moved progressively further away from realism or naturalism, dissolving the solidities of character, sequence in time and space, and cause and effect—substituting instead a free-flowing drama of dream images and repetitive patterns. Though these plays are not as frequently performed as his two earlier ones, chiefly because of the enormous technical problems involved in their presentation, they have probably been more influential (especially among German dramatists of the early twentieth century such as Georg Kaiser and Ernst Toller and American dramatists such as Elmer Rice and Eugene O'Neill) than Strindberg's more naturalistic dramas. The best of them are *Dreamplay* (1902), the *Damascus* trilogy (1898-1904) and *The Ghost Sonata* (1907).

Scenes of Russian life

Alongside Ibsen and Strindberg, the Russian Anton Chekhov (1860-1904) must be counted as one of the founding fathers of the modern theatre. Chekhov had a medical training, and his short stories as well as his plays show a scientific curiosity about facts and details as well as a doctor's compassion and understanding. His early theatrical successes were one-act farces based on the prevailing French models, two of the best of which, *The Bear* (1888) and *The Proposal* (1889), are still frequently performed.

But he is best-known for a quartet of full-length plays in which he explores, with incomparable delicacy, humour and insight, the frustrations, aspirations and crises of the Russian provincial upper class and its relations with the rest of Russian society. The first of these plays was *The Seagull* (1896) which, although it failed on its original production (in theatrical conditions utterly alien to those for which it was intended) was notably successful when produced by Stanislavsky at the Moscow Art Theatre. This was followed by *Uncle Vanya* (1899), *Three Sisters* (1901) and *The Cherry Orchard* (1904).

Chekhov's special contribution to European drama was the play of indirect action, with a simple pattern of arrival and departure and with an interest in the pressure of events on the mood of the characters rather than in the depiction of the events themselves. The apparent aimlessness and inconsequentiality of his dialogue remains faithful to the preoccupations of his characters and the inner workings of their lives, and his plays show not so much an absence of plot as a relegation of events to the background. In the twentieth-century work of such very different English playwrights as David Storey and Harold Pinter can be seen the continuing and fruitful influence of Chekhov, though his claim to lasting fame rests not on his subsequent influence but on his own unique and substantial achievement.

Above: Anton Chekhov (1860-1904) with his wife the actress Olga Knipper, who appeared in many of his plays and married him in 1901. Chekhov's achievement was to draw a delicate balance between the tragic and comic aspects of his provincial characters, living through a period of transition in Russia.

Below: Scene from the Moscow Art Theatre's production of *The Cherry Orchard* (1904), Chekhov's last play. In the centre is Chekhov's wife, who played the role of Madame Ranevsky. The plot of this play—about a family deciding whether or not to sell a cherry orchard—is subordinate to the fine interplay of characters.

Italian Opera

Music, in nineteenth-century Italy, meant opera. Opera in Europe as a whole was much more popular than it is today, and arias and overtures were quickly spread outside the opera-house by street organs, café orchestras, bands and music-hall singers. In Italy, there were very few orchestral concerts; although towards the end of the century 'quartet societies' were to be found in one or two of the largest cities, they were generally considered to be Germanic, and alien to the Italian spirit. Already in Germany opera was strongly influenced by the Romantic movement, with the *libretto* (words) reflecting the interest in the extravagant and the supernatural. But it was not until later in the century that Romanticism arrived in Italian music.

Rossini's comic operas

This delay was largely due to the dominating presence of Gioachino Rossini (1792-1868) who from about 1813 to 1829 was by far the most popular composer in Italy. An admirer of Mozart, he was a master of *opera buffa* (comic opera), which in his hands became social comedy written in a less symphonic, more lyrical style than the Austrian master's but nonetheless witty and brilliant. The virile rhythm and ornamental melody of his operas contrast strongly with the direct, plain manner which the Romantic 'back-to-nature' movement had fostered. His most celebrated comic opera is *The Barber of Seville* (1816).

During the 1820s, Rossini's interest turned to *opera seria* (a type of opera popular in the eighteenth century, with heroic or mythological settings.) The old-fashioned succession of *recitatives* (speech-like singing with orchestral or harpsichord accompaniment) and *arias* (solo songs) gives way in these works to a more flexible sequence. Rossini began to use grand *scenas* (complex solo vocal passages in several sections) with an occasional well-developed ensemble of voices; he reduced the sheerly conversational elements in the recitatives. His fame was established around Europe, and his popularity with the public ever-increasing. From about 1825 he was based in Paris, where he wrote a French comic opera *Count Ory* (1828) and *William Tell* (1829). This, his masterpiece, is a blend of the quasi-political, Romantic type of opera and the traditional Italian style. It might well have led Rossini to a new style but the composer retired immediately after this work, at the age of 37. Although he lived for nearly 40 more years, the only pieces he composed were trifles for the salon and some excellent church music.

Donizetti and Bellini

Rossini's retirement left a considerable gap in the operatic field. New operas were needed by many opera houses throughout Italy, including such large houses as La Scala in Milan and San Carlo in Naples. Two younger men, Gaetano Donizetti (1797-1848) from Bergamo and Vincenzo Bellini (1801-35) from Naples were just experienced enough to fill the bill. The two men were very different. Donizetti was of Rossini's

Above: The present-day interior of La Scala opera house, Milan. The 19th-century French writer Stendhal wrote of it: 'The Teatro alla Scala can hold three thousand five hundred spectators with the greatest of ease and comfort, and there are, if I remember rightly, two hundred and twenty boxes ... Silence is observed only at premieres; or, during subsequent performances, only while one or other of the memorable passages is being performed.' Such irreverence was not a sign of discontent; opera was immensely popular in 19th-century Italy and new operas were in constant demand.

Left: Gaetano Donizetti (1797-1848) was one of the most prolific composers of Italian opera until he was stricken with syphilis; this caused him to suffer from paralysis and mental instability during his later years. Between 1816 and 1844 he wrote some 70 operas including the sparkling comedy *Don Pasquale*.

Right: The works of Sir Walter Scott were popular with librettists at the time and Donizetti's serious opera *Lucia di Lammermoor* (1835) was based on Scott's *Bride of Lammermoor*. The opera is a vehicle for vocal display and the title role (played here by the famous singer Joan Sutherland) demands a *coloratura* soprano— a soprano with a voice suited to an extremely virtuoso, agile and florid style of singing.

306

Erich Lessing/John Hillelson Ageny

Scala

mould, being very fluent and capable of writing in all the genres—comic and serious, in the French and Italian styles. Bellini was narrower in outlook, really interested only in *opera seria*, more intense in attitude—and of a distinctly difficult disposition.

But despite the differences between the two composers, it is in their work that romanticism advanced in Italian opera. They use not only foreign and historically distant settings, but plots from Sir Walter Scott and Shakespeare, writers favoured by the Romantics. Both were essentially more masters of the dramatic situation rather than of the 'well-made' play or of rounded characters. Again the emphasis is on brilliant, decorative and precise singing. The main climax of their operas often comes in a huge ensemble, as in the magnificent sextet of Donizetti's *Lucia di Lammermoor* (1835) where the heroine expresses in front of all the main characters her feelings at being made to marry the wrong man; or the equally fine quartet with chorus in Bellini's *La Sonnambula* (1831), where the heroine's innocent habit of sleepwalking is misinterpreted by her lover and the rest of the community. Both composers were masters of filigree melody, Bellini especially so (his delicate *chromatic* decorations—the use of intervals outside the major and minor scales—were the model for Chopin's similarly textured nocturnes).

Bellini died in 1835 at a time when he was succeeding Rossini as the new European master of opera. By 1845 Donizetti's career had also ended, due to mental instability and the onset of paralysis. It is doubtful, anyway, whether he would have changed the course of Italian opera radically. By this time, however, a young composer had become known who was to do just that.

Verdi—giant of Italian opera

Giuseppe Verdi (1813-1901) was born of humble parents in a village in northern Italy. Showing early musical talent he was sent at the expense of a shopkeeper from the nearby town of Busseto, whose daughter he eventually married, to Milan. There he was refused entry to the conservatoire on the grounds of insufficient talent, and had to study privately. He returned to Busseto, where he directed the local 'philharmonic society' or wind band before gaining a modest success with an opera given in Milan. A commission for an *opera buffa* resulted. This was produced in 1840, just after Verdi had lost his young wife (whom he had married

Above: The violinist Niccolo Paganini (1782-1840) was the most famous of Italian travelling virtuosi, and the profits he made were huge. He performed feats out of the reach of ordinary players and his exploration of such things as harmonics and left-hand *pizzicato* (plucking of strings) became legendary.

Above right: Gioachino Rossini (1792-1868). Having composed two or three operas a year until he was 37, Rossini suddenly retired and lived the life of a gourmet.

Below: A 19th-century singer in the role of Rosine from Rossini's most celebrated opera *The Barber of Seville*.

307

Above: Giuseppe Verdi (1813-1901) at the age of 73. Verdi completely altered Italian opera, making it less a vehicle for formal, brilliant set pieces, and more dramatically unified. Verdi's fame rests also on a moving and powerful *Requiem* (1874), composed after the death of a friend, the great writer Manzoni.

Right: Verdi's *La Traviata* (1853) remains one of the best-loved operas, its heroine Violetta being a self-sacrificing courtesan who dies of consumption. This edition of the score is by Verdi's lifelong publisher Ricordi, who protected the composer's interests and helped to spread his fame outside Italy.

in 1836) and his two children through illness. The opera was a total flop. He was rescued from despair by his publisher Ricordi, who encouraged him to set an opera on the subject of the saving of the Jews from King Nebuchadnezzar. *Nabucco*, as it is now called, was produced in 1842.

In many ways *Nabucco* is a less subtle—certainly a less dramatically convincing—piece than those of Bellini and Donizetti, its strength lying rather in its vigorous singable choruses. One of these, 'Va pensiero', expressing the mood of the Jews in captivity, appealed to the Italian audience whose own situation under the Austrian yoke it seemed to express. It became a symbol of resistance to political oppression (it is still today virtually the Italian national anthem) and thereafter Verdi was considered a hero of the freedom movement, or *Risorgimento*. He spent the next years composing follow-up works, nearly all having a patriotic theme and grand choruses; expressive and straightforward in rhythm.

Verdi's first opera to show a substantial shift in direction was *Macbeth* (1847), in which there are still patriotic elements (such as a chorus of exiled Scottish 308 noblemen) but which reveals the com-

Verdi's works were still tuneful enough to attract the popular audience, but his interest in what was considered the macabre and even the indecent sometimes baffled the critics. The fact that in *Rigoletto* the hero (or rather anti-hero) was a hunchback and his daughter was murdered and disposed of by being carried in a sack, and that the nobleman who, according to tradition, should have been the heroic tenor was instead a seducer and brute seemed frankly horrible to some. That the heroine of *La Traviata* was a prostitute, and that the story was taken from life, was equally unusual. The original production emphasized this by playing it in contemporary dress as opposed to the distant exotic or historical settings of most operas of the time.

Verdi's genius lay in creating music powerful enough to make the plots 'live'. As well as Verdi's fine creation of atmosphere by means of matching the music to the emotions, his characters develop in a dramatically worthy way. If some are still 'pasteboard', notably Gilda in *Rigoletto*, who remains the archetypal innocent heroine, Rigoletto himself is real enough, his natural grudge against society increased by the seduction of his daughter until he becomes vicious in the final act. Violetta in *La Traviata* is still more magnificently drawn, a vivacious, unthinking woman revealing a sense of honesty and decency when her lover's father beseeches her to give up her lover for the sake of his reputation, and finally becoming a true heroine as she suffers by her sacrifice.

The triumphs of the operas of this period allowed Verdi to pick his libretti more carefully and to write fewer operas. He did not always choose wisely and though both *La Forza del Destino* (The Force of Destiny) (1862) and *Un ballo in maschera* (A Masked Ball) (1859) contain magnificent music, their libretti are unsatisfactory. But *Aida* (1871), was a complete success. Intended originally to celebrate the opening of the Suez Canal (delays prevented this), it has a patriotic and exotic background reminiscent of his early works. The subtlety of character drawing and the exploitation of situation, matched and expressed by music not only of Parisian grandeur (such as the Grand March and ballet in Act II) but of outstanding delicacy (as in the fine opening of Act III with its atmospheric depiction of a perfect evening on the banks of the Nile) were unique in Italy.

After this, Verdi's operas became even rarer and it was only the discovery of an excellent librettist that tempted him to return to the theatre. This was Arrigo Boito, himself an interesting composer with a somewhat Germanic attitude to music. Boito, however, found it difficult to complete his own works and was content to provide material for the (by now) fully acknowledged greatest composer of his country. Both loved Shakespeare and Boito created a first rate book from *Othello*.

Verdi's music for this opera (1887) carries on from that of *Aida* to become still more refined and varied. The great storm which opens the whole opera is one of the most vivid naturalistic scenes in a century which specialized in them; the character of Iago is conveyed in an aria called the 'Creed of Evil' by means not just of great melody but by a seething orchestration; while the final scene

M. Pucciarelli

Left: A scene from a Royal Opera House, Covent Garden, production of *Aida* (1871). This opera, set in ancient Egypt, heralded Verdi's last and greatest creative period. *Aida* combines a heartfelt, melodic yet orchestrally subtle score with grandeur of conception and magnificent spectacle.

Above: A scene from a 1970 production of Verdi's *Ernani* at the Rome Opera House. Written in 1844, during the time of the *Risorgimento*, it followed Verdi's first success *Nabucco* in its appeal to Italian nationalism. *Ernani* featured tuneful choruses which rapidly became popular 'hymns'.

poser's main interest as being the character study of Lady Macbeth. Her sleepwalking scene where, obsessed by her guilt, she sees again her blood-stained hands, is a marvellously orchestrated climax very different from the brilliant *scenas* of Donizetti and Bellini. Already a greater sense of dramatic continuity separates Verdi from his predecessors.

This interest in personality rather than conventional nationalistic situations is confirmed in three masterpieces, composed between 1851 and 1853. Of these *Il Trovatore* is the nearest to the old-fashioned type, the confusion of its plot saved only by the strength of its music. But both *Rigoletto* and *La Traviata* are well-constructed, being taken from plays by Victor Hugo and Alexandre Dumas respectively. Verdi here shows an absolute genius in matching drama and musical form. Gone is any suspicion of a succession of arias—neither opera has more than two or three 'set pieces'—and there is still less recitative. A new continuity is provided by ensembles and great choral scenes, often with the melody kept going in the orchestra, while the voices take that part of the melody which can fit the words.

Reg Wilson

Above: A portrait of Giacomo Puccini (1858-1924), one of the most successful of all opera composers. Although a lesser genius than Verdi, he had a gift for strong melody, realistic human situations and dramatic plots. He had a flair for theatrical effect and was a very skilful orchestrator.

Below: *Manon Lescaut* (1893) was the earliest of Puccini's operas to achieve success. This work, with American and Parisian settings, concerns two weak-willed lovers who come to disaster. Puccini's talent lay in evoking the atmosphere of situations and places rather than in developing a story.

Left: *Madame Butterfly*, the heroine from Puccini's celebrated opera of that name (1904). The story, given an exotic Oriental setting, has a contemporary theme: it deals with a foreign girl who is seduced by a visiting naval officer, who afterwards returns home and marries another.

Above: The cruel Chinese princess in *Turandot* (1917), an opera by Ferruccio Busoni (1866-1924): the story was also set by Puccini. Busoni broke away from conventional opera-writing; his anti-Romantic works are a mixture of Italian and German styles. Busoni was also a fine concert pianist and arranger.

reveals Othello's vacillating yet determined character in an astonishingly life-like way. *Othello* is perhaps the greatest 'grand opera' in the Italian vein, and although Verdi was accused of being influenced by the German Richard Wagner, largely because there are few set numbers and much of the material is given to the orchestra, in fact it is the apotheosis of Verdi's own style.

The music of Verdi's final opera, *Falstaff* (1893), a comedy based on *The Merry Wives of Windsor*, retreats from grandeur and melodrama. There are no great tunes here, the sole aim of the composer being rather to underline the words in a discreet rather than obvious manner. The work is purely Italian in its delight in character and situation rather than in the Germanic concerns for symbolism and philosophy. It is the ultimate stage in the move from a purely musical conception of opera to a dramatic one. Falstaff lives as vividly as in Shakespeare. Falstaff's last words—'All the world's a stage, and all the men and women in it merely players'—bring home the fact that nineteenth-century Italian opera is a very artificial entertainment; one which, nevertheless, offers insight into human emotion in a unique way.

Tito Gobbi as *Falstaff* in the Covent Garden production of Verdi's last opera, first produced in 1893.

Melodrama and Music Hall

Emerging as a distinct form at the end of the eighteenth century and dying out in the years following World War I, English melodrama had its heyday during the nineteenth century. It was produced wherever a stage existed, from the great royal patent theatres of Drury Lane and Covent Garden to the notorious Penny Gaffs, rough little pleasure houses which flourished amidst the poverty of London's East End and which provided entertainment at literally a penny a time.

Melodrama sacrificed probability of story for the sake of plots which relied upon rapid and thrilling action, which dealt in the most appalling catastrophes, the most harrowing situations, the most sudden of reversals. In play after play beleaguered heroines and oppressed heroes competed with remorseless villains through story-lines littered with dark imprisonments, threats of rape, murders, deadly combats, earthquakes, shipwrecks, explosions, conflagrations and the like.

The emphasis on crudely sensational types of action meant that complexity and consistency of characterization were subordinated to the demand for simple, stereotyped characters. The essential stock figures—hero, heroine, villain, old man and woman, comic man and woman—were designed to be instantly recognizable the moment they made their entrance on stage. Thus the hero (courageous, loyal, of high moral principles) was typically young and handsome and of a pleasant and open demeanour. The heroine (suffering, essentially virtuous if sometimes erring, strong-willed but still 'feminine') complemented the hero in her youth and natural beauty. For all the hero's merits, however, he presented rather a dull figure in comparison with the villain, who was often a more dynamic force—forever concocting and rearranging his dastardly schemes. Of course there were different kinds of villain, but whether a loud brigand or a more refined and calculating aristocrat, he could generally be identified by such features as the darkness of his complexion and clothes, the wicked twirling of his moustache, and by the manner in which the physical contortions of his face pointed to the imbalance of his mind.

Always true to their surface appearance, melodramatic characters lived in and acted out a world of clear moral categories; a world in which there were no confusing mixtures of vice and virtue. It was, for the audience, an escapist world: for while it stimulated excitement through its indulgence in all kinds of violence and horror the outcome of the action was almost always one in which good triumphed and order prevailed.

The subjects of melodrama

While these underlying patterns of plot and character stereotype remained unchanged throughout its history, melodrama came to draw on many different kinds of subject matter. One of the most important types of early melodrama, arising in the 1790s, was Gothic in setting and tone. Here the heroes and heroines

A SOUVENIR OF
"A ROYAL DIVORCE"
With the Compliments of W. W. KELLY

THEATRE ROYAL, SMETHWICK.
A SOLDIER'S HONOUR BY MR F. G. KIMBERLEY

'TAKE HIS SWORD AND KILL ME, RATHER THAN BRING DISGRACE UPON MY FATHER'

MONDAY, JANUARY 6th, - - SIX NIGHTS.

THE TRAITOR BY E. HILL MITCHELSON

A WRECKER OF MEN BY C. WATSON MILL

Above: A selection of programmes for 19th century melodramatic productions: their titles typify the directly emotive and sensational themes most popular with audiences.

Right: The celebrated Victorian actor Henry Irving leapt to fame through his part in *The Bells* (1871), in which he played a burgomaster haunted by the sound of the horse bells of a traveller whom he had murdered and robbed. This melodrama of crime retains Gothic elements —in the final scene, he is tried by a ghostly tribunal and sentenced to hang: choking to death, he pleads for the rope to be taken from his neck.

suffered in remote—often mountainous and forested—regions where the villains might be savage bandits or gloomy tyrants living in usurped castles. Supernatural visitation often took the form of deceased victims of the villain returning to warn the living hero of imminent danger.

Melodrama which exploited military or nautical contexts appeared almost as early as this Gothic mode. These plays traded largely on the patriotic sentiments aroused by Britain's wars with foreign powers. The typical melodramatic opposition of good to evil could be embodied in the form of the admirable British soldier opposed to a contemptible enemy.

By the second half of the century the most widely written and performed type of melodrama employed a range of 'domestic' settings. In most domestic

Left: A scene in *The
Mogul*, Drury Lane,
London, drawn by J. D.
Linton (1873). Music
halls were patronized
as much for their
convivial and relaxed
atmospheres as for the
particular shows they
staged. In this picture
not one member of the
motley audience appears
to be watching the
performance of the man
with the top hat and
cane. During the era of
their popularity,
controversy raged over
the supposed immorality
of music halls, thought
by respectable society
to be haunts of vice.
An indication of the
generally lower class,
or 'popular', appeal of
these establishments is
given here by the
glimpse of a woman
smoking a cigarette—
an activity which would
have been considered
impolite for a middle-
class lady of the time.

melodrama the family was seen as the
most indispensable of all social institutions, the destruction of which threatened
all the proper emotional and moral values
of society. One of the most consistent
themes—as in Moncrieff's *The Lear of
Private Life, or Father and Daughter*
(1820)—involved a father who is driven to
bitter mental distraction by his daughter's
elopement with a base, dishonourable
man, succeeded by a presentation of the
daughter's agonized sense of degradation
and repentance, and concluded by a
picture of the restoration of sanity and
love as parent and child are reconciled.

A significant feature of Moncrieff's play
is that the heroine is a country girl and
that London is the scene of much of her
remorseful suffering during her estrangement from home. The growth of industrial

urban society in the nineteenth century,
with its unpleasant associations of grimy
factories, slums and poverty, was
reflected in domestic melodrama's frequent identification of rural life with
virtue and of city life with vice. The
village was idealized as a place of healthy
family and social relations, representing,
to audiences drawn largely from the
smoke and deprivation of the cities, a
kind of lost paradise. The appeal of melodrama lay, of course, in its offer of a
fantasy world where such a paradise
could be regained. Among the specific
evils of city life that threatened to ruin
happy family life, gambling and drink
were the most popular as subjects for
melodrama. Vicious crime, too, was
commonly set in an urban context, as with
Pitt's *Sweeney Todd* (1847) which today

is among the most famous of melodramas.

Perhaps the most representative writer
of the high Victorian period of melodrama
was Dion Boucicault (1820-90). In the
1850s Boucicault took the sensational
aspect of melodrama to new heights of
accomplishment. His best remembered
play is *The Corsican Brothers* (1852) in
which the actor Charles Kean, known for
his 'strong' scenes, played a leading part.

The principal model for English melodrama was the French *mélodrame*. This
was a popular theatre which flowered in
the first instance because of the demand
in post-Revolutionary Paris for lurid
representations of violent class conflict.
But it soon came to embrace, under the
influence of dramatists such as Guilbert
de Pixérécourt, a variety of themes without a strictly political message.

The word *mélodrame* literally means
song—or music—drama and was used in
France to describe the manner in which
music was interspersed between dramatic
dialogue. Music remained an element in
English melodrama; but its importance
may be traced not only to the French
influence but also to the history of
licensing laws in England.

By the Licensing Act of 1737 only a
select few theatres, such as Drury Lane
and Covent Garden, held required royal
patents and were allowed to produce
serious or 'legitimate' drama. Minor
theatres were unable to trespass upon this
privilege and had to evade the problem by
converting their premises into *burletta*
houses—theatres which had by law to
include a certain amount of music and
song in their shows. This encouraged the
development of entertainment which
depended for its effect more on music
and spectacle than on the spoken word.

313

Left: An 1858 production of the pantomime *The King of the Castle*, at the Princess's Theatre, London. Pantomime descended from the *Commedia dell'Arte* tradition, first made popular in England when John Rich staged a *harlequinade* in 1728. Combining music and mime, this entertainment centred around the young lovers Harlequin and Columbine. During the next 100 years it evolved into pantomime, in which the main figure was the comic Pantaloon. This popular show persisted as a variety turn before becoming exclusively a children's Christmas entertainment.

Right: Circuses as they are known today began in the 19th century, incorporating the animal menageries, once a side-show feature at fairs.

The restrictions of the royal monopoly were broken in 1843 by a new Theatres Act but, by that time, melodrama had found a ready home in minor theatres. Although the fashionable West End theatres produced it, and while it gained a middle and upper class patronage by the end of the nineteenth century, melodrama's fundamental character was always determined by the mass working populations of the industrial cities. Melodramatic writing as such was never a 'high' literary pursuit—although melodrama does appear in the serious literature of writers such as Charles Dickens, who took a special delight in the form. However, despite its popular appeal and its association with 'illegitimate' drama, melodrama can in no way be seen as 'alternative' theatre in any subversive sense. The system of values melodrama used and endorsed was the conventional one of the established social order.

The heyday of music hall

Closely related to melodrama as a form of popular entertainment was the music hall show. Music hall had its roots in the taverns and public-houses which, during the eighteenth century, had staged—as entertainment of an 'illegitimate' sort—numerous kinds of variety turn. In the early Victorian period many taverns expanded rapidly and built halls on to the tavern proper for the purposes of singing and dancing.

Like the public house itself, music hall was a nationwide phenomenon appealing to the working class poor in the North as well as in London. Yet its real home was amidst the bustling poverty of the East End with its huge immigrant population, its busy dockland life, and all the vice that festered in the wretched slum conditions. To compensate for the struggles and hardships of their existence, people thirsted for some glamour and so they escaped to the glittering magic of the music hall, with its sentimental warmth, its solidarity and comradeship, its wine, women and song. The music halls grew up out of, shared, and portrayed a defiance of life's struggles. They caricatured familiar experiences: the joys of courtship, the trials of marriage, family life, holidays, weddings, and funerals.

As with any other popular culture, the music hall stars were immortalized, and the names of Marie Lloyd, Vesta Tilley, Eugene Stratton, Wee Georgie Wood, and 314 George Robey live on. So too the senti-

GEO. ROBEY

HEAD OF THE ROYAL ACADEMY OF MIR

Far left: George Robey (1869-1954) was one of the leading music hall stars. Although he carried on working right up to his death, Robey's powers declined steadily after the early 1920s. During his best years, he was total master of music hall technique: the eloquent patter, the frequent jokes and the rapid changes of mood.

Above left: Marie Lloyd (1870-1922) is still seen by many to epitomize the spirit of music hall as it was before World War I. At first her popularity was based on her youthful, schoolgirl songs. But with such songs as *Then You Wink The Other Eye* (shown here as a song sheet) her act became rather more risqué and she would frequently portray drunken women. An adverse critic described her as typifying 'the "knowing" female, the sophisticated young person for whom life has no secrets', with 'imperturbable self-confidence' and her 'trick of winking at every other word'.

Left: Vesta Tilley (1864-1952) rose to fame in the music hall solely on her act as a male impersonator.

Above: Harry Tate made his music hall debut in 1895: he was famed for his sporting sketches.

mental strain of the old music hall songs has lingered on, and the tear in the eye and the catch in the voice are still familiar to many.

Theatrical melodrama and true music hall declined in the face of competition from radio and cinema. The sophistication of radio and film was essentially opposed to the spontaneous originality of music hall and these vehicles of nationwide fame were death to most stage artists, who found they could not keep up with the continuous need for new material now that change, rather than familiarity, was the order of the day. Added to this, the whole fun of music hall lay in its atmosphere, the two-way relationship between the performer and his audience: radio could not cater for joking asides and amateurish slips. The turning point was World War I and the subsequent economic depression. In the thirties a new generation of entertainers and a new style of entertainment emerged.

And yet the needs which first engendered music hall are still present. There is still an urge towards direct popular entertainment, albeit in a much weakened form. In the East End many pubs still draw great crowds with their live jazz bands and small-time comedians, the northern circuit of workingmen's clubs continues to flourish, and nostalgia for 'the good old days' has led to more artificial attempts to recreate the magic of the original music hall.

315

The Romantics of Music

The nineteenth century witnessed radical changes in music. The Napoleonic Wars, following in the wake of the French Revolution, led to the disintegration of aristocratic patronage. Whereas in the eighteenth century a composer like Haydn could hope to find a comfortable living at a small court, after the devastation of the social order few princes remained who were willing or able to maintain such an establishment.

The emotional climate, too, was changing. Man's insistence on rationality had given way to his emotional cry for freedom, a return to nature, and a recognition of genius rather than well-taught talent. The artist was no longer concerned with producing a weekly cantata on demand, but instead might take years to compose a grand Mass—as with Beethoven's *Missa Solemnis*.

The nineteenth century was a time of brilliant virtuoso players. Franz Liszt (1811-86) and Frédéric Chopin (1810-49) exploited the resources of the pianoforte (made newly efficient with its delicate pedal mechanism, pearly upper notes and increased strength lent by iron frames) in a way unthinkable 30 years earlier. Niccolo Paganini (1782-1840), violinist and composer, was such a brilliant player as to be regarded almost as the devil incarnate of the violin.

A middle-class rather than aristocratic audience grew up to enjoy such music, the product of largely middle class composers: Franz Schubert (1797-1828) was the son of a schoolmaster, Robert Schumann (1810-56) the son of a bookseller, Hector Berlioz (1803-69) was from a bourgeous family and Felix Mendelssohn (1809-47) a member of a prosperous Jewish community.

The songs of Schubert and Schumann

The first manifestation of this middle class culture came in the song, known as *lied* in Germany, where it flourished. Song in the 18th century had meant an offshoot of either the religious hymn or the operatic aria. Towards the very end of the century a vogue for folksong arrived, following the Back-to-Nature movement of the literary romantics. It was Schubert who turned the simplicity of such song to sophisticated use. Although he died young, he yet managed to compose more than 600 songs, of great range and subtlety.

Some of these are obviously quasi-folksongs, with simple melodies and piano accompaniments. But Schubert's genius lay in his ability to evoke a whole mood, scene or character with the simplest of means. The mood may be happy, as in *Die Forelle* (The Trout) where the leaping of the trout is painted by a constant 'jumping' figure in the piano part: more often it is tinged with melancholy, as in most of the songs in the cycle *Die Winterreise* (The Winter Journey), 1827.

The scene evoked can be serene or conjure up a wild romantic vision, as in the setting of Goethe's ballad *Die Erlkonig*, (The Earl-King) with its constant repeated notes in the piano (an

Above: Franz Schubert (1797-1828), whose compositions took the simplicity of popular 18th Century folksongs and turned it to a new, sophisticated use. Simple themes, subtly altered, became the basis for vivid musical portraits—of a mood, a scene, a character.

Left: Printer's proof, with corrections in his own hand, of one of the compositions with which Chopin explored the new mechanical possibilities of the piano. Typically, his longer pieces have a relatively high melody line (often decorated with chromatic notes) to use the new brilliance of the upper register. The pedal mechanism helps sustain the deep bass notes, while the middle register is filled with arpeggio patterns —unfolding slowly in a sentimental piece, or fast and fierce in a study or ballad.

Right: Novelist George Sand, whose affair with Chopin was one of their era's great scandals.

Below: Chopin; portrait by Eugene Delacroix.

effect impossible on the harpsichord or early piano) giving the urgency of the man riding, in vain, to escape the ghostly Earl-King—a typical Romantic fantasm. The same lyrical beauty is found in Schubert's piano works and in the variety of chamber music he wrote, including trios, quartets, an octet, a piano quintet the *Trout*, and the *C Major* string quintet, unsurpassed for its depth and purity of feeling.

Schubert's most important successor, Robert Schumann, was to make his songs more intense and dramatic. His subject-matter is often middle class love—frustrated by convention or by early death. The melodies rarely have so simple a basis as Schubert's, and his piano parts are substantially more complex—as might be expected from one whose hopes of becoming a concert pianist were ruined by an accident to his left hand. The portrait of the young women in his cycle *Frauenliebe und leben* (Women's Love and Life),

Left: Schubert, who died too young to have reached the great opera houses and concert halls of Vienna, wrote most of his music for small gatherings of friends. These 'Schubertiads' often consisted of song recitals by his friend Vogl, with the composer himself at the piano.

Right: Carl von Weber conducts *Der Freischutz* at Covent Garden. Bigger orchestras and more complex scores led to the replacement of the director (first violinist, perhaps, or keyboard player) by a 'conductor'; Weber was among the first of these. His baton is of rolled paper; the modern wooden version did not appear until the mid-19th century.

Below: *Der Freischutz*; a contemporary drawing. In its time one of Europe's most popular and dramatic operas, it drew its simple arias and its use of the spoken word from the *singspiel* style of the later 18th Century. But in dramatic force, especially in the 'Wolf's Glen' scene, it foreshadowed the great romantic masterpieces of Wagner and Verdi.

CARL MARIA VON WEBER

R. Dazy/Ziolo

M. Pucciarelli

1840, is of a distinctly less earthy nature than Schubert's were. Nevertheless, both composers show how great issues need not be expressed in grandiose terms, how domestic life can have a fine intensity.

Chopin and Liszt

Apart from lieder, the other new field of exploration of the 1820s and 30s was piano music. Improvements in the mechanism of the instrument made it possible to give recitals on a larger scale than had been possible previously, and of several virtuosi appearing on the scene, two became famous not only as performers but also as composers: Chopin and Liszt. Although born within a year of each other and each breaking new ground in piano technique, Chopin and Liszt differed greatly in their personalities.

Frédéric Chopin, a Pole whose patriotism remained undimmed by spending all his adult life abroad, was rather a pianist for the salons of Paris than an aggressive virtuoso. He composed virtually nothing but piano music, and apart from a very few sonatas and concertos, nearly all of this was on the limited scale of the 'characteristic piece' (a musical representation of a mood or place). Chopin would take a single idea—the dance rhythms of the waltz, the Polish mazurka or polonaise, or a technical problem such as playing on the black notes—and work it out with a thoroughness hitherto unknown. The forms even of longer pieces such as the scherzos and ballades which he composed are simple: it is the subtle melodies and textures which are not. Chopin's flexibility of technique, forging new relationships between the dynamic range, the harmonies and tempi of which the piano was capable, gave him an incomparable capacity to explore each shade of a mood. For this he was probably the most influential composer for the piano

there has ever been.

In this sense, Chopin was in fact more revolutionary than Liszt, yet the public image of the latter suits him more for the revolutionary role. He was more robust than Chopin in all ways. Whereas Chopin died young after years of consumption, Franz Liszt lived long and survived innumerable crises of faith and of artistic direction. Hungarian by birth, he was an infant prodigy who throughout his life was successful in every worldly sense. His brilliance as a pianist was early established, but as a composer Liszt's gifts developed later. His works of the 1830s show less poetic imagination than Chopin's best works of the period; and there is no doubt that he learned from Chopin rather than the other way round. It was not, in fact, until he was tempted into accepting a position at the German court of Weimar in 1848 that he really began to develop in a novel way; and then it was orchestral music which stretched his genius.

At Weimar, he became the advocate of the 'modern' school of composition, that is to say, Wagner, Berlioz and their followers. Under his direction Weimar became a centre of the avant garde in a totally unexpected manner. Conducting an orchestra and dealing with music which was exploring orchestral techniques stimulated his imagination and he virtually invented a new form, the *symphonic poem*. Many of his basic ideas for this came from the music of Berlioz.

The drama and daring of Berlioz

Hector Berlioz was the odd man out of French musical life. Having quarrelled with the musical establishment in Paris as a young man, he was largely deprived of the natural way to fame in France— opera; and the energies and imagination which might have given rise to splendid

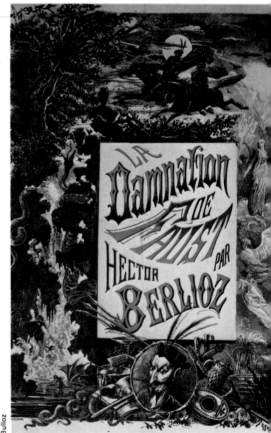

Bulloz

M. Pucciarelli

National Gallery, Berlin

grand theatrical works went instead into orchestral music. He was one of the few Frenchmen at the time to know the music of Beethoven, which proved to be a deep influence on him.

Berlioz' innovations in orchestral music were of two main kinds. The first was the concert overture, which he conceived in an operatic spirit, an example being the well known *Carnaval Romain*, used in an actual scene from his opera *Benvenuto Cellini*. The second was the *programme* symphony—'programme' music aiming to represent a mood, place or incident. His *Fantastic Symphony* (1830) borrows from Beethoven's *Pastoral* symphony the idea of a five movement work with descriptive titles for each movement; the idea of linking the whole work with a recurring theme (or *idée fixe*) is again from Beethoven, but the total effect is highly original. The story of the artist dreaming of his beloved (the *idée fixe*), eventually murdering her, being executed and being conveyed to a Witches' Sabbath, was imposed on the symphonic form; the effect is extremely vivid and highly Romantic. The passionate, theatrical quality of this work is typical of Berlioz. Perhaps the most literary of the Romantic composers, the heroes of Berlioz' music are drawn from Shakespeare, Goethe and Byron.

Berlioz' programme symphonies provided a model for other composers, notably Liszt, whose *Faust Symphony* is a fine example. Liszt's more limited essays in programme music—single movement *symphonic poems*—were, however, more consistently original and successful. These rarely tell a story; rather they create a mood inspired by a painting or a poem. The *idée fixe* or recurrent theme appears in several guises throughout the piece, usually transformed in rhythm to give variety; this allows exploration of several aspects of the mood in a way more substantial than the average concert or opera overture. Liszt's symphonic poems were a major influence on later composers and this idea of thematic transformation was used by almost every forward-looking composer for the rest of the century.

Romantic opera

Although now it seems that the major advances in music were wrought in the smaller forms, at the time it would have been in opera that most seemed to be happening. The Mecca of all forward looking composers was the Paris Opera, where Giacomo Meyerbeer (1791-1864) was the great idol. His grand spectaculars owed their popularity to the constant scenic effects—the splendid crowd scenes, the skating ballet, the massacre of the Huguenots—for which the librettos were created.

Spectacle was also an essential ingredient of the romantic operas of Carl Maria von Weber (1786-1826) whose *Der Freischutz* was one of the most famous pieces throughout Europe. But here it is the German longing for the rural life and for legendic subjects which is the basis of its romanticism. The frankly tuneful nature of many of the arias and the use of the spoken word are derived from the *singspiel* style of the later 18th century. But in fact it was only later in the century that the romantic spirit imbued opera in a sufficiently controlled way to produce great masterpieces in the work of Wagner and Verdi.

319

Wagner

With the work of Richard Wagner, Romanticism in music reached its expressive peak. This composer pushed harmony into a richness and complexity which took the traditional key system to its farthest limits. Wagner initiated developments in music which inevitably led, in the music of the composers who followed him, to the actual abandonment of what seemed an exhausted system.

Early works

Wagner was born in Leipzig in 1813. His musical education was sketchy and he first conceived of the idea of being a composer through the experience of concerts of Beethoven's music. In 1831 he had six months of formal lessons and at this time composed several works strongly influenced by Beethoven. But it was to opera—even at this early stage—that he was drawn.

In 1833 Wagner became chorus master at the Wurzburg theatre and in the following year he was made director of the Magdeburg opera company, where he wrote in 1836 *Das Liebesverbot* (*The Ban on Love*), based on Shakespeare's play *Measure for Measure*. In that year he married an actress in the company, Minna Planer, a woman who never understood Wagner's ambitions or gifts. The Magdeburg opera company came to an end soon after a disastrous production of *Das Liebesverbot* and after brief conducting appointments Wagner left for Paris. There, despite help from the immensely successful and influential composer Meyerbeer, Wagner met with no success, and he and Minna lived in miserable poverty. Despite having to earn money from hack-work Wagner managed to finish his next two operas *Rienzi* (1840) and *The Flying Dutchman* (1841) while in Paris. The first was produced with great success at Dresden and, as a result, Wagner was appointed assistant conductor there—the post was a life appointment.

The Flying Dutchman, however, was far less well received. *Rienzi* was a colourful, historically-based and nationalistic opera, far less original musically than *The Flying Dutchman* but more familiar in style to the opera-going public, who were used to Meyerbeer, Weber and Rossini—all of whom were early influen-

M. Pucciarelli

Bulloz

Above right: Scene from a 1970 production of Wagner's *The Flying Dutchman* (1841). This powerful opera was based on an ancient legend of a sailor cursed to sail the seas eternally until he finds redemption and rest through the love of a woman. The dramatic austerity of this production is in marked contrast to the elaborate and realistic early stagings of Wagner's work.

Right: A scene-painting of the Castle of the Holy Grail for Wagner's last opera *Parsifal* (1877-82). Parsifal is a 'pure fool' who, through his love, insight and ability to share the sufferings of others, saves the knights of the Holy Grail from disruption.

Above: The *music-dramas* of Richard Wagner (1813-83) embody his lifelong ideal of the spiritual redemption of man. He was also a prolific writer, on subjects ranging from racial issues to vegetarianism and anti-vivisection.

Right: Wagner wrote *Tristan and Isolde* between 1857 and 1859, during his love affair with Mathilde Wesendonk. Based on an Arthurian legend, this work concerns a consuming love which denies utterly the restraints of society: its fulfillment can only come with death. To express this, Wagner developed a musical language of equal unconstraint, in which for extended periods it is impossible to say which key the music is in. The somewhat quaint costumes of Tristan and Isolde in this 1869 Munich production seem inadequate to match the music's demonic power.

Mary Evans

ces on Wagner's music. *The Flying Dutchman* (still regularly performed today) marks the beginning of Wagner's maturity—the music is much less obviously a series of set pieces and the plot, too, has a characteristically Wagnerian theme of love's redeeming power.

Wagner was undeterred by its early lack of success and refused to turn back to the 'popular' style of *Rienzi*, despite the urgings of his wife and others. His next opera *Tannhäuser* was produced in 1845. Based on Germanic legends, its theme is the struggle between spiritual and physical love. Initially this, too, met with little success. In the meantime, Wagner was piling up debts and becoming involved with those liberal and revolutionary ideas that were to erupt, in 1848, in revolutions throughout Europe. As a result of this involvement Wagner was obliged to flee from Germany; first to Weimar, where he became friendly with Franz Liszt, and finally to Zurich in Switzerland.

Before his flight Wagner had completed a further opera *Lohengrin* (1848) and Liszt produced this with great success at Weimar. During the next few years Wagner's operas were given all over Germany, *Tannhäuser* proving especially popular. The money he gained from these successes was rapidly spent and he found himself still deeper in debt. As a result, in 1855 he spent four months conducting in London, where his music was reviled by the press (his music was described, for example, as 'unclean') even though it was well received by the public.

The transformation of opera

It was during these years of exile from Germany that Wagner first conceived what was to become his most gigantic achievement, *The Ring*—a cycle of four operas which draw on German mythology for Wagner's own symbolic purposes. By this time Wagner had fully worked out in various writings his theories concerning opera, the relationship between poetry and music, and what the future of music should be. To distinguish his operas from those of the past he called them *music-dramas*: these were not intended to be mere entertainment but works concerned with the most fundamental issues of life, playing a vital part in German national culture and providing a means of regenerating European civilization in general.

In terms of form the music-drama was quite new; no longer proceeding by the

Right: King Ludwig II of Bavaria was a sensitive, unstable man, famous for the fairy-tale castles he built in his Bavarian kingdom. He worshipped Wagner's music and was of great financial and practical assistance to the composer during his later years. At the peak of their friendship they corresponded in effusive tones; Wagner wrote to the king 'the tears of heavenliest emotion I send you' and Ludwig wrote to Wagner of 'the mighty wings of your genius in the pure ether of rapturous art'.

Below: A 19th-century scene painting of the bridal procession from *Lohengrin* (1848). This was given its first production by Liszt at Weimar in 1850. Because of its enormous and continuing popularity as a march at weddings, the music to the bridal procession has become the most famous that Wagner ever wrote.

J. L. Charmet

Interfoto Friedrich Rauch

J. L. Charmet

Left: The Ring, Wagner's greatest achievement, received its first complete performance in 1876. Made up of a cycle of four operas, The Ring plots the birth, life and destruction of a whole world, peopled by the dwarfs, giants and gods of Germanic legend. The plot is vast and has many layers of meaning. Siegfried is the hero without fear, the unwitting instrument of the gods' downfall and the end of their world. Here, in a silent film version of the Nibelungen Saga (from which Wagner drew his material), Siegfried kills the giant Fafner, who by means of the Tarnhelm (a magic helmet) has changed himself into a dragon in order to guard the Rhinegold hoard.

Bavaria

Left: The composer Franz Liszt (1811-86) with Cosima (1837-1930), his illegitimate daughter by the Italian Countess D'Agoult. Both were profound influences on Wagner's life: Liszt was one of the earliest admirers of Wagner's music and, during his period as court musician at Weimar, directed performances of *Lohengrin* and *The Flying Dutchman*. Cosima and Wagner became lovers during her marriage to Hans von Bülow, Wagner's friend and the leading conductor of his music. Bulow continued to champion Wagner's work even after his divorce from Cosima and her subsequent remarriage to Wagner.

Right: A silhouette of Wagner as conductor.

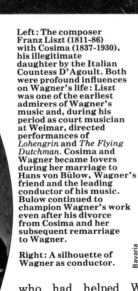

Bavaria

Above: The Bayreuth opera house in 1876. In spite of Wagner Associations, fund raising concerts and money from German municipalities, the theatre was only saved financially by King Ludwig. The strain of the venture led Wagner to remark 'Every stone in that building is red with our blood'.

alternation of set 'numbers'—arias and recitatives or spoken dialogue—but by a continuous symphonic flow, the music acting as a kind of wordless commentator upon the psychological state of the action. This was helped by Wagner's use of *Leitmotive*, literally 'leading motives' (musical themes representing a character, a force, an emotion or an object); these various themes would be developed throughout the drama in such a way that both psychological and symphonic needs were satisfied. The music-drama was to be the work of art that would combine all the arts—music, poetry, drama and, through stage presentation, the visual arts—to be created by a single artist.

To Minna's fury, it was during this period that Wagner had a love affair with Mathilde Wesendonk, the wife of a man who had helped Wagner financially. Minna and Wagner separated—Wagner going to Venice where he continued to work on *Tristan and Isolde*, an opera based on a story in Arthurian legend that he was writing simultaneously with *The Ring*. He finished *Tristan* in Lucerne in the same year (1859).

This work of almost unbearable emotional power concerns two lovers and their mystical identification of love with death. The music uses a heavily *chromatic* harmonic language (using, that is, intervals and chords built up from the chromatic scale of twelve semitones, outside the major and minor scales) sliding easily from key to key to express a fluid eroticism appropriate to the theme. It is easy to see autobiographical overtones in the two lovers' constant frustration by the powers of the society they belong to. Wagner expresses this frustration by the prolonged use of unresolved *dissonance* (a combination of notes which produce the effect of a state of tension and unrest). The enormous emotional tension arises from the need of dissonance to become *consonance* (that is for the unrest to be resolved and pass into a state of repose, or harmony) and this need is only truly fulfilled in the last bars of the whole work.

In 1861 an amnesty allowed Wagner to return to Germany; from there he went to Austria. The next few years were ones of hardship, frustration and debt for Wagner, yet during them he wrote his only comic opera, *The Mastersingers*. This work, concerning the medieval German guilds of mastersingers, is a call for German unity and for the acceptance of a renewed tradition in German music. Once again love is seen as the power which could bring this about—not the dark, self-annihilating love of *Tristan and Isolde* but a unifying life-giving love. This kind of love, and the fatal consequences of denying it for power or for wealth, is the basic theme of the *Ring* cycle, large parts of which Wagner finished during this period. When complete, *Der Ring des Nibelung* (The Ring of the Nibelung) consisted of four music dramas; *Das Rheingold* (The Rhinegold), *Die Walküre* (The Valkyrie), *Siegfried* and *Götterdämmerung* (The Twilight of the Gods). He still lacked the financial means of staging these new operas, especially as the *Ring* required the most elaborate stage effects, for example dragons, vast caverns, flooding rivers, funeral pyres, universal con-

flagrations, rainbow bridges and so on.

But, in 1864, a year in which he had been forced to flee from Vienna to escape his creditors, Wagner was befriended by the new king of Bavaria, Ludwig II. Ludwig invited the composer to Munich to realize, without any restraints or conditions, his artistic ambitions. This was not to be: Wagner's predilection for luxury, his surrounding himself with people necessary to his art, his refusal to take part in local political manoeuvrings and his notorious affair with Cosima Von Bülow (the wife of his chief conductor and Liszt's illegitimate daughter) led to an intrigue against him which finally forced Ludwig to ask him to leave. Apart from productions of earlier operas and of *Tristan and Isolde*, nothing had been accomplished. Ludwig was, however, a valuable source of finance until the end of Wagner's life. The experience gave fresh strength to Wagner's already existing conviction that he must have a special independent theatre of his own—untouched by commercial interests and away from the middle-class philistinism of the German cities.

Wagner decided upon the small town of Bayreuth as the setting for his opera house and was fortunate in finding its leading citizens in sympathy with his ideas. The foundation stone was laid on Wagner's fifty-ninth birthday, 22nd May 1872. Yet Wagner's struggles were not to be over for a further ten years, during which time the enormous debts that the theatre brought with it had continually to be paid off.

Wagner had found, in Cosima, a continuous source of encouragement; she both understood him and regarded him as her 'mission'. Before her divorce from Von Bülow, Wagner had already fathered three children by her, his own wife Minna having died in 1866. Von Bülow, although eventually in full knowledge of their affair, remained loyal to Wagner's music. Wagner and Cosima were finally married in 1870.

In 1877, Wagner began his last opera, *Parsifal*: it was first performed in 1882 and was described by the composer as a 'Sacred Festival drama'. Like *Lohengrin*, it concerns the legend of the Holy Grail (the cup from which Jesus is said to have drunk at the Last Supper). Here the *leitmotive* are all related; themes flow in and out of one another, with all the music streaming from one single transforming source wholly in accord with the mystical-religious theme of redemption by love, faith and wholeness of heart.

Wagner, with this crowning triumph and the financial future secured at last, had only one more year to live. He died in great pain on February 13 1883, as the result of a heart attack; these had become more and more frequent towards the end of his life.

Wagner's character has often been heavily criticized as being completely self-centred. Yet if his faith in himself had not been continually sustained against ignorance, malice, intrigue and poverty—and not least against his own self-doubts—his extraordinary gifts would not have been allowed an outlet in the world. The judgement may be left to Wagner himself. 'The world', he wrote, 'is taught how to behave towards all others; but how to behave towards a being of my kind—that it never can be taught, for that case occurs too rarely.' 323

Left: Arthur Rackham's illustration to Wagner's *The Rhinegold*, **the first** *Ring* **opera. The dwarf Alberich renounces love for the power which the Rhinegold will give him. He shatters the idyllic innocence of the Rhinemaidens (seen here), the guardians of the treasure, by wresting the gold from the depths of the river.**

Below: A late 19th-century poster depicting Brunnhilde, a major figure in the *Ring* **cycle. Destined to be the bride of Siegfried, she is one of the** *Valkyrie*, **the warrior-maidens fathered by Wotan, the chief god, to bear the bodies of dead heroes to Valhalla, the resting place of the gods.**

From Brahms to Mahler

The philosophy and musical ideas of Richard Wagner profoundly influenced the musical climate of Germany and Austria during the later nineteenth century. Of the two major symphonists who were Wagner's contemporaries, one, Johannes Brahms (1833-97), was cast as an opponent—the other, Anton Bruckner (1824-96), revered the master.

Johannes Brahms

Brahms was born in Hamburg, the son of a double-bass player. Some of his early years were spent playing the piano in lowly dance halls in his native city; after this he embarked on concert tours with a Hungarian violinist which widened his horizons immensely. He eventually became a friend of Robert and Clara Schumann. In these circles he was considered the natural leader of the conservatives who did not follow the Wagnerian philosophy of the *Gesamkunstwerk* (or total work of art), and his earliest works—large scale piano sonatas —take up the Beethoven tradition in their use of classical sonata form. But it was to be many years before he succeeded in writing a symphony—a form which he seems to be aiming at in his early works— so overawed was he by the works of Beethoven. His first piano concerto was inspired by Schumann's tragic death: written in D minor, the key and mood of its opening clearly looks back to Beethoven's Ninth Symphony and the last movement is equally clearly reminiscent of Beethoven's Third Piano Concerto. But in spite of this influence, it is a highly romantic, personal work full of intense emotion.

Brahms had by 1863 settled in Vienna and was making a good living partly by conducting one of the leading choral societies, partly by composition. His first symphony finally came out in 1876, and was promptly hailed as the natural successor to Beethoven's great Ninth Symphony; and indeed in its tragic opening movement and especially its finale with a hymn-like principal theme the resemblances and aims are obvious. Even so, there are many individual features; the slow movement and scherzo being more lyrically romantic, and having a gentler manner, than the more dynamic heavily accented ways of Beethoven.

Brahms wrote four symphonies in all; his last is melodious rather than dramatic in the first two movements and ends with a massive *passacaglia*, instrumental variations over a traditional *ground* (continuing) bass. This owes little to Beethoven, but more perhaps to the example of the Baroque composers. Brahms had edited some of their music, as this was the time when Bach and Handel were enjoying a revival.

It was these grand works, plus his concertos for violin and piano and the splendid one for violin with cello, that gave the composer the reputation for being the upholder of the classical tradition. In his smaller scale music, too, he kept to established forms. His songs, although lacking that gift for depicting

human character possessed by Schumann and Hugo Wolf, are often exquisite examples of marvellously expressive melody, accompanied by complex but full-sounding piano parts. The piano pieces of his later years are even more subtle, ranging in mood from the gently beautiful Intermezzo in E flat to the fierce rhapsodies in G minor and E flat which demand a real virtuosity.

Massive music of Bruckner

Brahms' older contemporary, Bruckner, was incapable of such variety but achieved, within a narrower scope, a remarkable intensity. His father, an Austrian schoolmaster, died early and he was sent to be a choir-boy at the monastery of St Florian. There he received the education of a church musician, learning counterpoint in the strict manner and the art of improvisation

on the organ. The music which he wrote up to the age of forty was virtually all for the church; grand masses which are either a mixture of archaic polyphony and modern harmonic practice, or are written for full orchestra with a dramatic or symphonic colouring.

Until this time, there is little sign that he knew much of the music of Beethoven. But in 1866 he had heard the Ninth Symphony, which affected him deeply, and three years later he produced a symphony (not included in the normal canon of Bruckner's symphonies and so called 'No. 0') that has obvious similarities to Beethoven in its sinister conclusion of the first movement. And although he withdrew this work as unsatisfactory, Bruckner devoted the rest of his life to the composition of symphonies, completing eight and leaving part of a ninth.

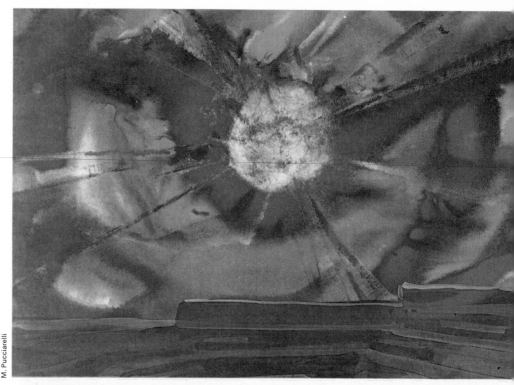

M. Pucciarelli

Reg Wilson

Above left and left: A stage set and scene from different modern productions of *Salome*, a one-act tragic opera by Richard Strauss. First produced in 1905, it was based on a play by Oscar Wilde. In music of mounting tension and tonal complexity, Strauss unfolds the erotic drama of Salome's Dance of the Seven Veils for Herod in return for the head of John the Baptist.

Right: The composer and conductor Richard Strauss (1864-1949) was a brilliant, bold orchestrator. The sensuous, lush effect of his technique is at its height in his symphonic poems. His fame rests also on his varied operas and beautiful song settings.

Above: From the extreme subjects of his early operas *Salome* and *Electra* (1909), Strauss turned to a warm, intimate comedy with *Der Rosenkavalier* (1911). Set in 18th century Vienna this is, with its bitter-sweet love plot and lush score, his most popular opera.

Right and below: The musical development of Anton Bruckner (1824-96) was late and his output the product of immense labour and effort. His 9 symphonies, 4 Masses, a *Requiem* and *Te Deum* are monumental works inspired by his devotion to God. His musical education took place at the monastery church of St Florian (below), where he was choirboy and, later, virtuoso organist.

In spite of the model of Beethoven, Bruckner was also affected by Wagner, of whose philosophical concepts he understood little, but whose techniques of creating huge musical structures from thematic fragments fascinated him. With these means Bruckner expanded symphonic movements beyond the scale conceived by his predecessors. These influences are evident in Bruckner's style, especially in his 'Wagnerian' orchestral sound: but in the shaping of his symphonies he is interested less in developing themes (as was Wagner) than in the drama created by juxtaposing melodies against one another or by unexpected changes of key. This technique, like the composer himself, sometimes seems naive; but there is a true depth of solemnity and strength in his finest works, notably in the seventh and uncompleted ninth symphonies.

SPECIES TIBI CHRISTIANE DATVR

Above: Johannes Brahms (1833-97) restrained his Romantic expression by combining it with established classical musical forms: he is musically conservative in contrast to Wagner. An immensely wide ranging composer, he wrote symphonies, overtures, concertos, chamber music, piano and choral works.

Above right: Esteem for the Austrian composer and conductor Gustav Mahler (1860-1911) has risen enormously during the 20th century. His symphonies, which employ huge forces, are gigantic in scale and use extreme *chromatic* harmonies, form a link between Wagner and the *atonality* introduced by Arnold Schoenberg.

Strauss and Mahler

Of the two giants of the later generation, Gustav Mahler (1860-1911) and Richard Strauss (1864-1949), again it was the younger who made his mark earlier and showed a more varied capacity. Strauss, the son of a player in the Munich opera orchestra, was brought up to know only such classics as Mozart and Beethoven, his father having a low opinion of the 'modernist' Wagner—who had indeed quarrelled with most of Munich's musical community. Strauss' earliest works, including a large scale *Serenade for Wind Instruments* reflect this upbringing, approaching Brahms in general manner.

In his late teens, however, Strauss discovered the Wagner-Liszt school of composition and since they had been 'forbidden fruit', took to their ways even more strongly than he might otherwise have done. He was beginning to make his way as a conductor, and his first attempts in the new style were symphonic poems after the manner of Liszt, with which he had an immediate success. Starting with *Don Juan* in 1888 these continued for about the next twenty years with such works as *Till Eulenspiegel*, *Don Quixote*, *Death and Transfiguration* and *A Hero's Life*.

If at first sight these seem the natural successors of Liszt's own works in this medium, there are a number of marked differences between them. Firstly, whereas Liszt was attempting to free himself from the classical forms, Strauss tends to return to them. For example, *Till Eulenspiegel* was described by the composer as a *rondo*, (an instrumental piece in which a theme heard at the beginning recurs between contrasting episodes and

at the end) and *Don Quixote* is certainly a set of variations.

Even more significant is the difference in emotional content. Liszt's subject matter is Romantic in its philosophic aspirations and high purpose. Strauss' is often realistic and down-to-earth. *Till Eulenspiegel*, depicting the adventures of a medieval rogue, has flashes of humour and a sense of detachment; *Don Quixote* shows the ridiculousness, as well as the pathos, of this idealist by placing him against a vivid orchestral background of braying sheep and the turning of windmills; while *A Hero's Life* shows the 'hero' to be the composer himself, fighting the critics, quarrelling with his wife, and occupied with simple everyday events—far removed from the ideal Romantic hero.

After these works, Strauss was one of the most famous composers of his time as well as being a prosperous conductor, and he now could turn his attention to opera with the certainty of achieving productions in well equipped theatres. His earliest two operas were not very successful, but the next two, *Salome* and *Elektra* were highly original. Both exploit the then current vogue for neurotic subject matter; *Salome* being a study in necrophilia, *Elektra* in matricide. Strauss set them as extended one-act dramas with no relaxation from the tension produced by extreme, dissonant chromatic harmonies derived ultimately from Wagner's *Tristan and Isolde*. They were enormously popular, partly because they quickly achieved a scandalous reputation, but it was clear that this line could be carried little further, at least by Strauss. So he turned to a less intense vein, using his love for Mozart to good effect in *Der Rosenkavalier*, a period comedy set in 18th century Vienna, with the passing of time and love as its main theme.

After the First World War Strauss appeared increasingly a figure of an earlier age, yet in his final years, when in the 1939-45 War he had lost his fortune because of the loss of income from copyrights, he had a glorious final phase of composition, writing works such as a

beautiful Oboe Concerto, a nostalgic piece for strings—*Metamorphosen*, and the marvellous *Four Last Songs* for soprano and orchestra, which seem to epitomize the passing of the romantic age.

By this time, Strauss's contemporary Gustav Mahler had been dead nearly forty years, but he probably was having more effect on the younger composers. Because he made his living as a conductor, Mahler composed comparatively little. He was musical director of the Vienna State Opera for some years and a principal conductor in New York in later life. If his career seems a reasonably successful one by ordinary standards, he felt himself to be the perennial outsider; a Jew in an anti-semetic Austria, a conductor who could never entirely get his own way in the opera house (where he had to fit in to established routine), and as a creative artist, a composer who could only indulge in his major activity during vacations.

These conflicts are expressed in his music, nine symphonies and several song cycles for singers and orchestra including *The Song of the Earth* and *Songs on the Death of Children*. He composed little which was not on an extensive scale (here he is the opposite of Brahms and Strauss), for his attitude was that a symphony must express a view of the world; and to this end, he incorporated voices—both soloists and choruses—into his symphonies to make explicit his meaning. Although he often used large resources (his eighth symphony being called *Symphony of a Thousand* because of the number of performers called for), he used them sparingly.

It is the irony of life which is expressed uniquely in his music: the desire of the modern sophisticated man for the simple pastoral existence; the artist's grandiose vision of the universe suddenly brought down to everyday life by hearing a commonplace tune; the serenity of beauty inspired only by the tragic foreboding of death. It is this contrast of the ideal and real which has endeared him to modern audiences and to many of the composers of an unstable twentieth century.

Richard Strauss's opera *Der Rosenkavalier* (The Knight of the Rose), composed in 1911, is a rich and vivid expression of 20th century Romanticism. Its theme is love and the passing of time, and its music has a glowing sensuality.

Late 19th Century French Music

The history of French music from the late nineteenth century to the mid-twentieth century is a series of reactions followed by counter-reactions. Meyerbeer and Wagner were dominating influences—'Wagner worship' in particular flourished in France towards the end of the nineteenth century. His musical language, his metaphysical and large scale aspirations often crushed French native talents too small and fragile to bear their weight. French music was often deliberately unaspiring and superficial.

The composer César Franck (1822-90) and his pupils attempted to establish a serious and genuinely French music. Franck is now remembered for the works of the last few years of his life, especially his symphony, symphonic variations for piano and orchestra, a piano quintet and a sonata for violin and piano. Franck's debt to Wagner was very great, but he sowed some of the seeds of what was to be the richest period in France's musical history. Debussy and Ravel in the nineteenth century, Messiaen and

Left: Claude Debussy (1862-1918) achieved a maturity and independence of style which marks him as the first truly great French composer after Berlioz.

Above: Set for a 1947 production of Debussy's opera *Pelléas et Mélisande*, based on the tragedy by Maeterlinck.

Right: This edition of Debussy's *La Mer* (*The Sea*) (1903-5) has as its motif a Japanese woodcut of waves. The Japanese concern with stylization and arabesque found echoes in the European art of this time and in the curling, intertwining musical shapes of *La Mer*.

Below: Nijinsky as the faun in a 1913 production of *Prelude à l'Après midi d'un Faune* (1892-4), an orchestral piece by Debussy: a sensuous evocation of a young animal bathing in afternoon heat and sunshine.

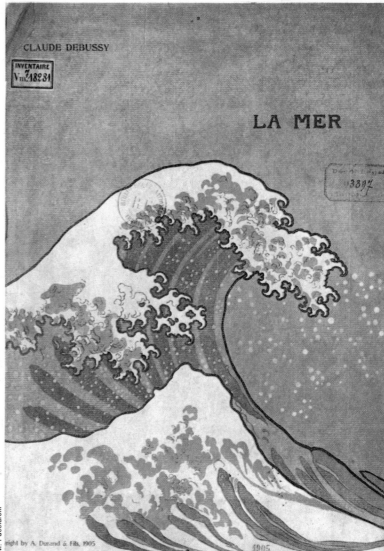

CLAUDE DEBUSSY

LA MER

even the avant-garde composer Boulez in the twentieth, have many roots in Franck's emphasis on rich harmonies, the use of dissonance to create immediate sensuous effects and a preoccupation with unity and purity of form.

Exploring new tones

Claude Debussy (1862-1918) was himself a pupil of Franck for a short time and his early string quartet (1893) uses the Franckian technique of attempting to achieve unity through the use of a single motive which constantly appears in new forms throughout the work. Debussy reacted against the pervasive Wagnerism in France: although he was deeply influenced by Wagner, he was great enough to absorb the influence into his own personal style. In fact it is even possible to regard Debussy as continuing Wagner's revolutionary treatment of harmony by breaking down and replacing in many ways the old *diatonic* system, which uses the harmonies available within the major and minor key system.

Debussy's music frequently uses masterfully contrived dissonances, often spread out through many octaves, which are beautiful and instantly appealing in themselves. He makes use, also, of exotic scales and in particular *whole tone* scales, which progress entirely in whole tones, instead of partly in whole tones and partly in semitones like the major and minor scales, and in which there is no note which presents itself as a point of rest, a 'home' or 'key' note.

Debussy had heard and been influenced by the Javanese *gamelan* orchestra of xylophone-like instruments of bronze and bamboo: a gamelan orchestra had appeared at the Paris exhibition of 1889, playing music of a non-diatonic tradition, and using highly complex rhythmic counterpoint. Debussy actually declared that it was time to abandon diatonic music.

Thus the function of dissonance in his music is not to create a tension in need of resolution, but to create an immediate harmonic lushness for the ear to revel in. His superb orchestration is also addressed to this end—the richness of sound is part of the new emphasis on the immediate enjoyment of harmonies for their own sake rather than for their function in the whole work. The more luscious the *timbre* (the quality of the sound) the more this could be achieved.

Debussy's remarkable opera *Pelléas et Mélisande* (first produced in 1902) shows his debt to Wagner while affirming his own individuality. The plot, like *Tristan and Isolde*, is concerned with two ill-fated lovers, with much symbolism in terms of light and darkness. It uses an orchestra of almost exactly the same dimension and make-up, but unlike *Tristan and Isolde*, *Pelléas* is essentially a quiet work, translucent in orchestration and avoiding big emotions and climaxes.

The majority of Debussy's other works are on a small scale. His piano music,

Above: Portraits of *Les Six*, a group of French composers who, led by the writer Jean Cocteau (1889-1963), rejected the heavy post-Romantic style and attempted to establish an independent and essentially witty French musical style.

Below: Set by the 20th-century artist Ferdinand Léger for *La Création du Monde* (1923), a ballet with music by Darius Milhaud (1892-1974). The influence of jazz and Latin American music is striking in this remarkable score.

composed from 1888 to 1915, shows his essential musical developments—an increasing harmonic richness and interest in exploiting all the resonances and colours of the modern piano, an interest in *ostinato* rhythms (that is, persistent and repeated rhythms) and the increasing importance of timbre rather than melody.

The richness of Debussy's orchestration is quite unlike the lavish post-Romantic extravagance of a composer like Richard Strauss, for example. Debussy, unlike Strauss, is not interested in narrative aspects; one of his most important orchestral works, *La Mer* (*The Sea*) (1905) has the quality of the sea itself; in its overlapping, ever-changing rhythms and currents of sound it seems to have no reference to human beings at all. The literature that Debussy was interested in was the new French poetry—itself concerned with stressing the musical and non-narrative aspects of language. It was the poet Verlaine who said, 'De la musique avant toute chose'—'Music before everything else', to emphasize the new concern with beauty of sound rather than story-telling.

Debussy associated more with artists and poets than with musicians and was perhaps as much influenced by them; he is frequently labelled an 'Impressionist' after the contemporary movement in painting. Certainly the Impressionist painters were not concerned with narrative but with the immediate appearance of things at a particular moment in time, and so developed a rapid working method: they tended, therefore, to be immensely prolific. Debussy was quite the opposite and he himself disapproved of the term as applied to his music. His music is extra-

ordinarily precise: every element has a necessary part in creating his rich, unified textures.

The audacious music of Satie

Debussy's great friend Erik Satie (1866-1925) was much more extreme in his rejection of French Wagnerism and the whole apparatus of nineteenth century Romanticism in general; rejecting even the most fundamental characteristics of Western music. His music can best be described by replacing all the usual attributes of Romanticism with their opposites: for large scale works small scale, for high seriousness flippancy and frivolity, for complex polyphony and harmony bare lines with eccentric, apparently inconsequential harmonies and in place of continuously evolving musical argument he favoured the static and repetitive. He was a very eccentric man; living in self-imposed poverty in a Paris suburb, his passion was for collecting identical suits and umbrellas.

While as a café pianist Satie met Debussy, who introduced him into artistic and intellectual circles. He met the French author Jean Cocteau (1889-1963) in 1915 and collaborated with him on the ballet *Parade*, produced by Diaghilev in 1917, with decor by Picasso. The same remarkable group produced Satie's next ballet *Mercure* (*Mercury*) (1924).

Because of his rejection of traditional Western musical forms, Satie has been hailed by twentieth century avant-garde musicians as a founding father. He certainly stands at the beginning of a strong tradition in twentieth century art which tends to debunk all accepted artistic norms. Naturally the results are

Above left: Maurice Ravel (1875-1937) was not himself a virtuoso pianist, but his solo piano music is some of the most brilliant and difficult ever written. A supreme orchestrator he transcribed much of his own piano music, including *Ma Mère L'Oye* (Mother Goose Suite).

Above: Score of *L'Enfant et les Sortilèges* (1925), Ravel's one-act opera with text by the authoress Colette, in which a naughty child is tormented—but finally forgiven—by the furniture (which comes to life), and the trees, birds and animals which he has mis-used.

EVOCATION DE PARADE

Left: Sketch of the composer Erik Satie (1866-1925) by his friend Jean Cocteau.

Below left: Set by Léon Bakst for the 1912 Diaghilev production of the ballet *Daphnis et Chloé*, with music by Ravel. Around the simple plot derived from Greek mythology, Ravel weaves a symphonic score of miraculous beauty, colour and translucence.

Above: Evocation of the ballet *Parade*. Created by Cocteau and Satie, it was produced by Diaghilev in 1917, with decor by Picasso and choreography by Leonard Massine. *Parade* contains Satie's famous and deliberately bizarre piece of orchestration using a typewriter. The same remarkable group were responsible for Satie's next ballet *Mercure* (*Mercury*) (1924).

frequently absurd, and deliberately so—his *Vexations*, for example (1892-3), is supposed to be played 840 times at each performance.

With all seriousness spurned, only the absurb or flippant is left. Thus the manifesto of the group of French composers comprising Les Six (The Six), which was drawn up by Cocteau in 1917 and was strongly influenced by Satie's music, rejected not only Wagner, but Debussy and the music of the Russians which was then making a great impact in Paris through the Ballet Russes. Instead, circus and the music hall was to be the new inspiration.

The Six did not remain together long as a group, losing its impetus during the 1920s. But each member at some time or other also attempted serious compositions. The Six comprised Auric, Durey, Tailleferre, Honegger, Milhaud and Poulenc. Only the last three are very much played: Arthur Honegger (1892-1955) is particularly known for his orchestral evocation of a powerful train, *Pacific 231* (1923), but he wrote much other worthwhile music which at present is scarcely heard at all. His later style is far from the aims of the original group, recalling Romanticism and even Wagner in its orchestral treatment. Darius Milhaud (1892-1974) was an immensely prolific composer, writing over 400 works. He ingeniously exploited *polytonality* and *polyrhythms*—the simultaneous occurrence of more than one key and more than one rhythm respectively. His ballet *La Creation du Monde* (1923) (*The Creation of the World*) makes original use of jazz and Latin American dance rhythms. Francis Poulenc (1899-1963) remained

more faithful to the aims of Les Six, but even he had a 'serious' side, mainly manifested in liturgical music. His most often heard works are the ballet music *Les Biches* (1923), his magnificent concerto in G minor for organ, strings and timpani (1938) and the piano concerto (1949).

Ravel's brilliant music

A great composer outside all groups who rejected nothing and assimilated everything in the cosmopolitan atmosphere that existed in Paris before and after the First World War was Maurice Ravel (1875-1937). Ravel was a Basque but like all the composers so far mentioned he inevitably lived in Paris, the centre of artistic life. Here numerous foreign artists had made their home, most notably the composer Igor Stravinsky, who influenced and was influenced by Ravel.

Ravel had been exposed to all the influences which shaped Debussy, including even the Javanese gamelan. In 1889 he entered the Paris Conservatory, where he studied for the unusually long time of 16 years. He believed in a rigorous musical training based on the imitation of good models and he diligently studied the scores of other composers throughout his life. His orchestration was particularly influenced by Richard Strauss and Rimsky-Korsakov. He quickly assimilated the style of Debussy and actually anticipated his development in the piano pieces *Miroirs* (Mirrors) (1905). His music also makes brilliant use of jazz and popular dance rhythms; an example of the first is in his piano concerto in G (1930-33), while both strains are present—along with almost every aspect of his musical personality—in the opera *L'Enfant et les Sortilèges* (1920-25) (*The Child and the Spells*): magical, humorous, with miraculously orchestrated sounds of animals and birds, nostalgic and child-like.

He was an immensely fastidious worker and his published compositions are only a little over 50 in number, but nearly all are enduring. Like Debussy he used exotic scale forms and modes, although he avoided whole-tone scales.

Both before and after the First World War a number of musical manifestoes in Paris proclaimed on behalf of one group or another the right to speak for all. And in counter-reaction to The Six and what was considered the general frivolity of French music at the time a group called 'The Young France' was formed with the declared aim of re-introducing into music depth, seriousness and spiritual values.

The group soon dispersed but the most important member, Olivier Messiaen (b.1908) has become the dominant French composer of this century and has had enormous international influence through a whole generation of avant-garde composers by his theorizing and personal teaching. Like Ravel his style is an idiosyncratic compound of many influences—Wagner, Debussy, Franck, Indian and Eastern music, Schoenberg, Webern, Stravinsky—and his work is dedicated to the expression of a deeply mystical sense of divine love, at work in man and nature, and expressed in the Catholic religion.

In the music of Messiaen's pupil, the composer and conductor Pierre Boulez (b.1925) the contribution which Debussy made to French music—the concern with beauty of sound and richness of texture—continues to be explored.

Chapter 6

The Twentieth Century

Evita, by Andrew Lloyd-Webber and Tim Rice. Stage musicals have been taken more seriously during the 1970's, with musical numbers carrying more of the plot instead of merely 'interrupting' the action. Stephen Sondheim, whose *Sweeney Todd* opened on Broadway in 1979, has been a leading innovator.

Modern Poetry

The poetry of the twentieth century is very different from the poetry that went before. The opening of a traditional love poem, such as these lines by Lord Byron, written at the beginning of the nineteenth century, expresses the Romantic idea of poetry:

She walks in beauty, like the night
Of cloudless climes and starry skies;
And all that's best of dark and bright
Meet in her aspect and her eyes . . .

In contrast, the opening of T. S. Eliot's poem *The Love Song of J. Alfred Prufrock* (1917), is like an act of defiance to the traditional reader:

Let us go then, you and I
When the evening is spread out
against the sky
Like a patient etherised upon a
table.

This, the poem announces, is not going to be the sort of love poem you might expect, it is going to be new, and revolutionary. The poem's use of deliberately unromantic words starts with the title. The lover is given the name of what could be an American businessman.

As the poem progresses, J. Alfred Prufrock is discovered to be a self-conscious, embarrassed, over-educated

Caboue

Radio Times Hulton Picture Library

Left: Charles Baudelaire (1821-67). Although a traditional poet using rhyme and metre, he is the father of modern poetry. He wrote, in his poems, about drugs, sex and boredom.

Above: Jeanne Duval, Baudelaire's mistress. In *Les Fleurs du Mal* (Flowers of Evil) he set out to shock. 'Folly, error, sin, avarice, occupy our minds and work on our bodies'.

Cooper-Bridgeman Library

Below left: *The Welcome* by Marc Chagall (b.1887). His paintings, based on fantasy, have their origin in folk tales and peasant traditions as does much modern poetry.

Above: W. B. Yeats in 1894. His poetry career began with romantic dreams based on Irish mythology. As a young man he behaved with a flamboyance that he felt fitted the poetic role.

Although his writing grew tougher and more modern, he never lost his flamboyance. He continued to see the poet as defying the ordinariness of the world around him.

Right: The Wheel of Fortune, from the Tarot cards, symbolizes fate. Modern poetry borrowed many images from the occult—both Yeats and Eliot used the symbols of the Tarot.

WHEEL of FORTUNE.

man, no longer young. Eliot goes on to use the striking image of the patient etherised upon a table; the evening sky clearly does not look like that. The point of the simile must be that the evening arouses in the speaker feelings of exhaustion, violence, even ugliness, which Eliot wants to express in his unconventional love poem.

A similar wish to shock the reader can be seen in the work of Eliot's friend Ezra Pound. In *Hugh Selwyn Mauberley*, an autobiographical poem with an elegy for the young men who died in World War I, he says nothing to assure us that their memory would never grow old. The poem runs as follows:

There died a myriad,
And of the best, among them,
For an old bitch gone in the teeth,
For a botched civilisation,
Charm, smiling at the good mouth,
Quick eyes gone under earth's lid,
For two gross of broken statues,
For a few thousand battered books.

Once again, a theme that traditionally suggests noble and beautiful thoughts is made to sound deliberately ugly. However, along with the comparison of civilisation as an 'old bitch' and the dismissive account of our cultural heritage, goes the haunting, lyrical description of the deaths of the young men, as if Pound wanted to set them against each other in the same poem.

Baudelaire and the Symbolists
This new way of writing poetry began with a group of French writers at the end of the nineteenth century, known as the Symbolists. They all derived, in one way or another, from the great French poet of the mid-nineteenth century, Charles Baudelaire, whose tormented yet classical and dignified poetry tried to deal with the beauty and ugliness of modern city life.

The most important of the French Symbolists were Rimbaud and Mallarmé.

Arthur Rimbaud had one of the strangest careers of all poets. Tremendously precocious, he had written all of his wild, strange poetry by the age of 19; it attempted to render a confusion of all the senses. Then, suddenly, he gave up writing, and for the rest of his life he lived as adventurer and trader in Africa and the East. He died in 1891, aged 37.

In contrast Stéphane Mallarmé (1842-98) lived a quiet, uneventful, scholarly life as a teacher, producing a small quantity of obscure but carefully polished poems, every line packed with meaning. His poems never tell stories or directly express personal feelings. He finally abandoned punctuation and experimented with irregular groups of words on a page, in an attempt to create his own poetic language.

Finally, there was Paul Valéry (1871-1945), the greatest of Mallarmé's followers, and the greatest French poet of the twentieth century. His explorations into the theories of poetry and abstract thought, his view that the modern poet has to turn ideas into the music of poetry, have provided the theoretical basis for much of the modern movement in poetry.

The Waste Land
When the young American poet T. S. Eliot (1888-1965) came to Europe in the early years of this century, he set himself the task of reshaping English poetry to make it more like French Symbolism. He wrote essays strongly influenced by Mallarmé and Valéry, and suggested that English poets turn away from their traditional models, Milton and the Romantic poets, and turn instead to John Donne, whose witty, intellectual poetry has had a great revival in the twentieth century. At the same time, he explored the possibility of juxtaposing fragments of unpolished thought, images and quotations, to express the modern sensibility more truly than the traditional lyric or narrative.

The main result of this was *The Waste Land*, dedicated to Ezra Pound, published in 1922, the most famous modern poem in English.

It was based on the legend of the Holy Grail, the part spiritual, part physical quest by King Arthur's knights for a mysterious, holy cup, which could only be reached by a knight in a state of grace. But we are only told about the Grail legend in hints and fragments: the whole method of the poem is fragmentary. It is an attempt to make us think about the world we live in in a new way, associating it with the theme of the mysterious, sterile Waste Land of the Grail story, waiting for water:

A heap of broken images, where the
sun beats,
And the dead tree gives no shelter,
the cricket no relief,
And the dry stone no sound of water.

He mixes together the teeming life of London, with the horror of a nightmare, and an anthropological ritual of death to produce haunting poetry:

There I saw one I knew, and stopped
him, crying: 'Stetson!
'You who were with me in the ships
at Mylae!
'That corpse you planted last year in
your garden,
'Has it begun to sprout? Will it
bloom this year?'

The subsequent career of T. S. Eliot came as something of a surprise to his admirers. He was converted to Christianity, leaving a record of this in another obscure, but very moving poem about a religious experience, called *Ash Wednesday* (1930). He went on to write a series of four philosophic meditations on the meaning of religion in the modern world, known as the *Four Quartets*. The poetry of T. S. Eliot never meant cutting oneself off from the past, it meant going back to the past for new models, a constant process of reinterpretation, of rediscovery, of

335

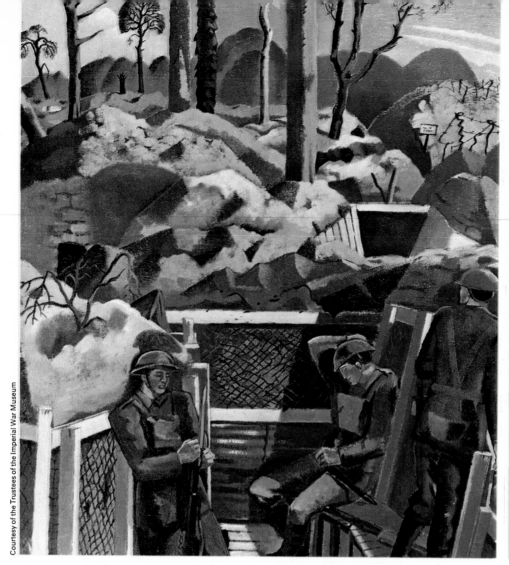

Above: Paul Nash's painting *Spring in the Trenches, Ridge Wood, 1917.* The horrors of the war forged several great poets such as Isaac Rosenberg and Wilfred Owen. Owen's statement 'My subject is war, and the pity of war. The poetry is in the pity' sums up the attitude of his generation of war poets.

Right: The first verse of W. B. Yeats' *The Second Coming,* one of the most powerful of 20th century poems. Much of it reflects Yeats' private theories on history. The poem's disturbing images still communicate to the non-specialist reader a deeply felt sense of impending anarchy and apocalypse.

Below: T. S. Eliot (1888-1965) in 1938. By then Eliot was editor of *Criterion* (an influential literary journal), a Christian convert and had written the poems which shaped modern poetry. Eliot wrote of himself 'How unpleasant to meet Mr. Eliot! With his features of clerical cut, And his brow so grim'.

Above: Portrait of Ezra Pound by Wyndham Lewis (1884-1957). Lewis, a novelist and painter—this painting is typical of his style—edited, with Pound, a review called *Blast,* which expressed the ideas of the movement then called *Vorticism,* which had right wing ideas and attacked romanticism and sentimentality.

THE SECOND COMING

Turning and turning in the
*   widening gyre*
The falcon cannot hear the falconer:
Things fall apart: the centre
*   cannot hold;*
Mere anarchy is loosed upon the
*   world,*
The blood-dimmed tide is loosed,
*   and everywhere*
The ceremony of innocence is
*   drowned:*
The best lack all conviction,
*   while the worst*
Are full of passionate intensity.

finding new meanings in past literature. That is why he has had such a huge influence, not only on how poets write, but on how readers and critics think about the whole of English literature.

Eliot's friend, Ezra Pound (1885-1972) was also producing poetry which influenced the future shape of poetry. Like Eliot, he tried to widen the horizons of English poetry by translating and adapting a great deal of foreign literature—old French, Latin, Chinese and much else. His poetry is full of quotation and deliberate reference to the past, so much so that his most ambitious work, *The Cantos,* is in places almost impenetrably obscure. Pound had a vigorous and at times beautifully lyric gift that constantly crops up even in his most difficult poetry. His eccentric views on politics and economics led him to become a great admirer of Mussolini, and his trial by the Americans for his treasonable activity during the war, which he spent in Italy, provides an example of the difficult relationship between poetry and social responsibility.

Yeats and Stevens
Despite the shock of the work produced by Eliot and Pound, other poets also helped in producing a new expression.

Both W. B. Yeats (1865-1939) and Wallace Stevens (1879-1955) produced poetry of lasting significance. Yeats, an Irishman, began by writing dreamy, haunting late-Romantic lyrics, full of Irish charm and fairy-tale, but turned to a much fiercer poetry of personal struggle, political violence and philosophic reflection in his later volumes. In a poem called *A Coat* he sums up this progression:

I made my song a coat
Covered with embroideries
Out of old mythologies
From heel to throat:
But the fools caught it
Wore it in the world's eyes
As though they'd wrought it.
Song, let them take it,
For there's more enterprise
In walking naked.

Wallace Stevens was an American who led a successful and respectable life as an insurance executive, while at the same time writing some of the most haunting and difficult poetry of our time. His finest poem is perhaps *Sunday Morning*, a marvellously dignified statement of the possible beauty of the world when no longer seen through the eyes of religion:

> *All pleasures and all pains,*
> *remembering*
> *The bough of summer and the*
> *winter branch.*
> *These are the measures destined for*
> *her soul.*

Auden and Thomas

The 1930s produced a new wave of mostly left-wing poets, who set out to deal with contemporary and political issues. Their leader was W. H. Auden (1907-1973), and his poem on the Spanish Civil War, called simply *Spain*, 1937, is one of the clearest and most famous pieces of Marxist verse ever written:

> *And the poor in their fireless*
> *lodgings, dropping the*
> *sheets*
> *Of the evening paper: 'Our day is*
> *our loss, O show us*
> *History the operator, the*
> *Organizer, Time the refreshing*
> *river.'*

Later, Auden was converted to Christianity, and his post-war verse is much less political, tending to see man as a creature of social habits best understood in religious or anthropological terms.

Dylan Thomas (1914-1953) combined Welsh gaiety and effusiveness with a technique that recalls Rimbaud. The vigour and delight he takes in playing with images is a sign of his constant energy. Thomas' most popular work is certainly his radio play *Under Milk Wood*, a portrait of a Welsh village where everyone, in however perverted a way, is in love, and in which his verbal inventiveness combined successfully with a theme of universal appeal.

New poetry in Germany

Modern poetry is an international movement. In every country of Europe, the poets of the early and mid-twentieth century were searching for new forms. A group of very gifted poets transformed German poetry. The greatest of them was Rainer Maria Rilke (1875-1926), whose *Duino Elegies* is a series of meditations on how uncomfortably man fits into the world.

Modern poetry has never been as popular with the general reader as it has with the more sophisticated poets and critics, and more traditional forms of poetry have continued to flourish alongside it. In English there has been Georgian poetry, chiefly named after anthologies published 1912-22. Its poets included Rupert Brooke (1887-1915), the epitome of golden youth who died in World War I, and the American Robert Frost, who celebrated New England in his poetry. Their work was lyrical but also realistic. Of the poets who have made their reputation since 1945, perhaps the most successful have been Philip Larkin and Ted Hughes: and the contrast between the wry lyric poems of Larkin, and the tormented violence of Hughes, shows that the conflicts of modern poetry between lyrical and violent expression is still being fought.

Below: A refugee child from the Spanish Civil War, 1936. A generation of writers were drawn into this conflict— it was seen as a war between Fascism and the Left. The novels of Ernest Hemingway, the memoirs of Arthur Koestler and George Orwell, and the poems of W. H. Auden are among the products of the war.

Right: Rainer Maria Rilke (1875-1926), the greatest modern German poet. His most significant poetry is in the *Duino Elegies* and *Sonnets to Orpheus*. Here are two typical lines from the latter: 'Everything wants to hover. And we go about like weights, lay ourselves onto everything, enraptured with gravity'.

The Modern European Novel

In the nineteenth century novelists set out first and foremost to tell a straight story and provide an objective account of the society in which they were living. The greater depth, complexity and variety which we find in the modern novel are very much the result of the influence of two modern European writers: Marcel Proust and Thomas Mann.

At first sight, it is the differences between Proust and Mann which are more striking than the similarities between them. Proust (1871-1922) was a Frenchman. He was the son of a well-known doctor and a rich, artistically gifted mother. He is famous for one immensely long novel: *A la recherche du temps perdu* (*Remembrance of Things Past*, 1913-27) the last part of which was published after his death. Mann (1875-1955) was a German, son of a wealthy grain merchant and of a Brazilian mother, and author of a much wider variety of literary works, including short stories such as *Death in Venice* (1912); *Buddenbrooks* (1924), the realistic account of the decline of a middle-class family; and an immensely comic novel, *The Confessions of Felix Krull, Confidence Man* (1954).

Travel and the cork room

The two men also led very different lives. Except for brief visits to Brittany and Venice, Proust rarely left Paris. He spent the last 15 years of his life in a room which he lined with cork to keep out the noise, and devoted himself exclusively to one task: writing his novel. Mann, in contrast, had travelled widely from his native city of Lübeck before Hitler, who came to power in 1933, began a systematic campaign against him. In 1936 he was formally expatriated and eventually forced to seek political asylum in the US. And whereas Proust never married, the almost excessively Germanic normality of Thomas Mann's personal life expressed itself in a long, happy marriage and the birth of six children.

Yet for all the differences between them, the recurring themes in the work of Proust and Mann bear out the idea that all writers, whatever their conscious intentions, tell us something about the society in which they lived. Both, for example, seem obsessed with the idea of physical illness and social decline. In Mann's *Buddenbrooks* the healthy, self-confident merchants of the eighteenth and early nineteenth centuries are replaced by weaker, neurotic, unsuccessful, sterile descendants until the family gives out completely.

It is therefore easy to see Thomas Mann as somehow expressing in his work the terrible sickness which spread across the world from Germany as a result of the two world wars. Like the immensely complicated aristocratic society of Paris which Proust analyzes in such minute detail in *Remembrance of Things Past*, Mann's secure world of Lübeck was doomed to collapse, a fate he was able to forsee, and record. And while Proust's fascination with illness is obviously linked with the asthma which plagued

338

Above left: A Tunisian café, in Paris, 1900, showing the writer André Gide (in the black hat). He struggled to free himself from his strict puritanical upbringing, and wrote lyrically about the delights of sexuality in *Les nourritures terrestres*. He was one of the first writers to defend homosexuality.

Left: *Salome* by Gustave Moreau (1826-98). Moreau specialized in elaborate fantasy scenes, and his work was admired by Proust, although Degas dismissed Moreau with 'He taught us that the Gods wore watch chains'. The theme of Salome fascinated artists and writers in the late 19th century.

Below: Literary life in Paris centred very much around the café. Pictured here at La Rotonde, meeting place for authors and painters, are Marinetti, the Italian writer, Apollinaire, the greatest French poet to write about his war experiences, and Léon Blum, a future prime minister.

Above: Paris at the races. A world chronicled by Proust in his *A la recherche du temps perdu*. Proust's great novel evokes his childhood as well as the glittering society which vanished with World War I.

Above right: Marcel Proust, photographed here on his knees, in 1892, at a party.

his life from the age of nine and provided the excuse for him to spend the last years of his life in bed, writing his novel, it also has a deep social significance. Although he died before European society made its second attempt to tear itself to pieces in World War II, his immensely sensitive nature made him realise that the ostentatiously rich and excessively self-confident middle-class world of late nineteenth century France was already declining.

In his novel Proust charts the decline which the passage of time brings to all human emotional endeavours. He also embodies the creative artist's ability to conquer time through art, by creating in his novels his own world. Proust, like all his generation, believed profoundly in art. Art was the great religion of late nineteenth century Europe, the one activity in which belief was possible after the destruction of religious faith by science, and the subsequent inability of science itself to provide the answers and explanations which it had once promised with such confidence.

Thomas Mann was almost as preoccupied with it as was Proust. He created the art-dominated writer Aschenbach in his famous short story *Death in Venice*. Art is seen as the austere religion to which Aschenbach devotes his life before his fall from grace into a more sexual and unhealthy love of the beauty of the young Polish boy Tadzio. But in Proust, art is seen more consistently and more optimistically as the one means of man's redemption, and the birth of the artistic vocation in Proust himself is linked, in one of the most famous passages in all French literature, to a specific incident in the author-narrator's life.

One day, when Marcel the narrator of *Remembrance of Things Past* is tired and depressed, he breaks off a piece of a small cake, a *petite madeleine*, dips it into a cup of lime tea, and puts it into his mouth. Suddenly, without knowing why, he is filled with ecstasy. Anxious to understand and repeat his experience, he takes another piece, but the feeling is already 339

weaker. Then, as he thinks, he realises
what has happened: the taste which he,
as a grown man, has just had of the *petite
madeleine* has exactly reproduced a
physical experience of his childhood
which his conscious mind had wholly
forgotten. When he was a little boy, his
aunt Léonie had been in the habit of
offering him just exactly such a tea-
spoonful of cake dipped in tea. The
memory of this had disappeared until the
very moment at which the precise physical
experience of tasting the *petite madeleine*
had brought it flooding back, bringing
with it the whole of his childhood and the
enchanted world in which his aunt had
lived in the little country town of
Combray.

The artistic vocation which Marcel
discovers in this moment of almost
mystical intensity comes to dominate his
whole life. For, as he realises, the physical
accidents that bring about these involun-
tary memories can never offer permanent
satisfaction. They need to be supple-
mented by the conscious and deliberate
re-creation of the past, and this can be
achieved only through art.

By going back over his life in order to
bring his experience back into existence
by writing about it, Marcel creates an
ideal world that goes beyond the world
which he knew in the past and which has
now disappeared. He brings to both his
readers and himself a kind of salvation
from time, since by participating in
Marcel's ideal world by reconstructing it
in our own minds, we too escape into a
world that time cannot touch.

Like his great contemporary André
Gide (1869-1951), Proust was a homosexual. But unlike Gide, he felt profoundly guilty of his own sexual tastes,
and satirized them mercilessly in what is
perhaps his greatest comic creation: the
Baron de Charlus. Homosexuality also
formed the subject for Thomas Mann's
best known short story, *Death in Venice*,
where the love of the writer Aschenbach
for the beautiful Polish boy Tadzio makes
him stay in Venice until he catches cholera
and dies. Both Proust and Mann, in this
respect, reflect the guilt with which
nineteenth century bourgeois society felt
at the spectacle of unorthodox sex.

Mann's exile
Again in contrast to Proust, Thomas
Mann seems more concerned with the
affairs of men in the broader political
world. He lived long enough to be a
controversial figure even for those Germans who had opposed Hitler when he
took out American nationality in 1944.
Joseph and his Brethren (1933-43), with
its insistence upon the eventual success
of the hero in saving his people, reflects
the defence which Mann put up, in his
country's darkest hour, for the best in
European culture—the traditional
humanist values of reason and civilisation.

After the defeat of Germany and the
revelation to the world of the full horrors
of Hitler's regime, Mann's *Dr Faustus*
(1947) examines the role of the artistic
and scientific thinker. In this work Mann
writes about the temptation to revert to
barbarism which constantly besieges even
the creative artist and describes the
collapse of a civilisation whose immense
intellectual achievements did not save it
from committing some of the greatest and
most systematic crimes recorded in

Anthony Crickmay

Radio Times Hulton Picture Library

Fischer Fine Art Ltd, London

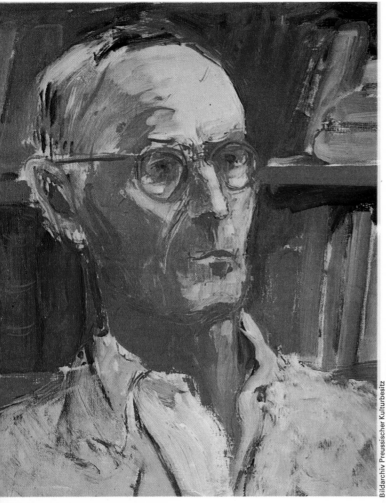

Above left: Mann's most famous short story, *Death in Venice,* has been made into an opera by Benjamin Britten. Here, Aschenbach, staying in Venice after the outbreak of cholera because of his fascination for the young Polish boy, Tadzio, is shown reacting to the news that the disease is spreading.

Far left: Thomas Mann (1875-1955), one of the greatest German novelists and short story writers. His adaptation of biblical themes in *Joseph and his Brethren* is one of the greatest modern novels. Mann sought refuge from Hitler's Germany in the US in 1939, where he wrote about the European culture which Hitler was destroying.

Left: When the Nazis seized power in Germany in 1933, they intimidated Jews and intellectuals. Scores of writers left the country either voluntarily or under duress, including Thomas Mann and his brother Heinrich, also a writer. Books by such writers as Thomas Mann, a Nobel prizewinner, who were considered subversive were publicly burnt.

Above and above right: Portrait of the writer Hermann Hesse (1877-1962) and a drawing by him. He explored in *Siddhartha* (1922) Indian philosophy and psychoanalysis. His best known novel, *Steppenwolf* (1927) deals with conflict between artist and society, and the alienation of the individual from the modern world.

human history.

It is not that Thomas Mann ever fell into the role of a preacher. The complexity and variety of his style, like the irony with which almost every idea is presented, set a constant series of puzzles to the careful reader of his work. Like Proust, he was the inheritor of the enormously rich, self-conscious and highly developed cultural tradition of Europe. He was greatly concerned with art, culture and music, as well as possessing a fierce nationalism. But his evolution from the defence of the values of his own fatherland during World War I to a wider and wiser humanism in later life is part of his development as a great writer.

Like Proust, Thomas Mann writes in a style which is complex, ornate and often difficult to understand. Proust too is a complex European in his elaborate and sophisticated style, whose immensely long sentences reproduce something of the oddness and complexity of the way we think.

The influence of Proust and Mann

With Proust and Mann, the novel finally cast off the idea that its main function was to tell a story. We rarely read such authors to find out what happened next. We read them to increase our awareness of how artists see themselves and interpret society. We read them to understand more about how our memory works and about how we too might suddenly find ourselves carried away by inner or outer forces which we cannot control. And we read them to wonder and to understand how the middle-class and aristocratic culture of late nineteenth century Europe has been changed by the

horrors of two world wars.

Proust and Thomas Mann chart for the reader how fundamentally our society has changed. It is not just a question of technological inventions. Proust had a car, saw the beginning of the aeroplane, and has some fascinating descriptions of how an anxious lover can wait for a telephone call. But the world of Proust is still one where servants were part of daily life, and where a gentleman was, above all else, someone who did not have to work for a living. Proust, of course, saw how fleeting this society was, and the very title of his novel—*Remembrance of Things Past*—indicates that the aristocratic world of late nineteenth century Paris was disappearing. Proust often takes us into a world whose social habits are as different from our own as those of the ancient Egyptians. The society that he chronicled set immense store by birth, displayed its wealth with an ostentation inconceivable nowadays, and saw as self-evidently justified a system of social ranking that divided even the aristocracy itself into many levels.

In his life time, Proust was sometimes dismissed as a snob precisely because of the concern which he showed for these exact gradings. Indeed, it is perhaps only in the last 30 years that he is seen as a curious but very real practitioner of social realism. The magnificently named ladies who set the tone of the high society of Paris's Faubourg St Germain—la duchesse de Geurmantes, la princesse de Parme—seem very far removed from us today. They have become ironic figures, just as much a symbol of social futility as the intellectuals who inhabit the sanatorium in Mann's *The Magic Mountain*.

The Developing Novel

At the end of World War I, the great moral certainties which had supported both society and art finally lay in ruins. For the arts, the impact of the war was devastating, and yet in some respects it was only the final, cataclysmic event in a long process of moral and intellectual upheaval.

Throughout the latter half of the nineteenth century, there had been signposts to the decay of the existing moral order. Religion, the central pillar, had been seriously undermined. Charles Darwin had put forward his theory of evolution, attacking the literal Biblical interpretation of man's creation; the German philosopher Nietzsche had proclaimed God was dead; in Vienna Sigmund Freud declared religious belief to be a mere figment of man's psyche, a subconscious attempt to give meaning to his life.

In Britain, the Edwardian novelists John Galsworthy and Arnold Bennett concerned themselves little with these revolutionary ideas. Even H. G. Wells, speculating about the future in early science fiction, seemed oblivious to their implications. It was left to another generation of writers to shape a radical new approach to literature, in an attempt to maintain its serious influence on changing society. However, the most influential novelists turned their attention, not to

Below: Vanessa Bell's cover illustration to one of her sister's pamphlets. The Hogarth Press, founded by Leonard and Virginia Woolf, published many works by members of the Bloomsbury circle.

Right: Virginia Woolf photographed in 1939. Her 'impressionistic' technique attempted to capture the essence of personality or mood, rather than a sequence of motivated actions. Walter Sickert's painting (below right, completed in 1915) serves as a visual reminder of the shared concern of writers and painters of the period with the dissolution of surface things and a capturing of inner reality.

Walter Sickert: a conversation. By Virginia Woolf.

The Hogarth Press one shilling & sixpence net

Above: Portrait of Lady Ottoline Morrell, a celebrated patroness of the arts. Although acquainted with the Bloomsbury Group, her circle was much wider, including Yeats, Eliot, Bertrand Russell and D. H. Lawrence.

Left: Lytton Strachey, critic and biographer, a leading member of the Bloomsbury Group, the cultured circle of intimates who denied Victorian moral and religious orthodoxy in favour of an intense artistic consciousness. The Woolfs, Clive and Vanessa Bell, Roger Fry and economist J. M. Keynes, were other central figures.

Below: Virginia Woolf and friends at Ottoline Morrell's country home.

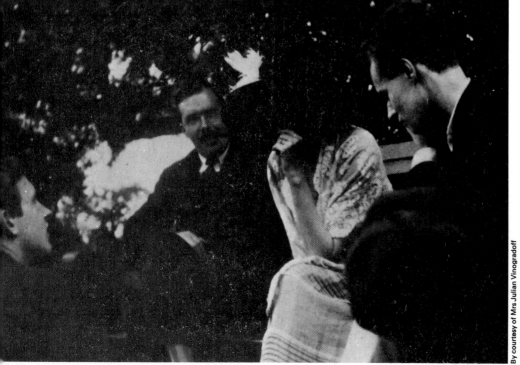

society as a whole, but to the nature of the individual and his 'inner life'.

Lawrence's 'instinct for life'

D. H. Lawrence (1885-1930) was one such writer. The son of a Nottinghamshire miner, he was brought up in the industrial Midlands. His mother encouraged him in his intellectual activities, and he won a scholarship to Nottingham University. He then worked briefly as a schoolteacher before devoting himself to full-time writing.

Lawrence was obsessed with the notion of individual integrity, feeling that man could only triumph over materialism, could only renew himself, by responding to the deepest urges of his nature. 'You can develop an instinct for life, if you will, instead of a theory of right and wrong, good and bad.' Despising bourgeois morality and social conventions, he wanted to use the novel as an instrument for regeneration.

He explored the possibilities most convincingly in his three major novels, *Sons and Lovers* (1913), *The Rainbow* (1915) and *Women in Love* (1920). The first of these is largely autobiographical, following the young Paul Morel through childhood and adolescence in a Midlands mining town. *The Rainbow* shows three generations of the Brangwen family, again in the Midlands, struggling to maintain their individuality and spiritual integrity in the face of encroaching industrial society. For Lawrence, the machine age was not only destroying man's intimate connections with the rhythms of nature, but was leading him to a way of life so alien to his needs that Western society was doomed to extinction.

The survival of the individual thus became a matter of crucial importance, and this is the reasoning behind much of Lawrence's apparent intolerance. The notion of self-sacrifice, so frequently abused in religious or patriotic appeals, was abhorrent to him, a denial of humanity. In *Women in Love*, when one of the characters accuses Birkin, Lawrence's mouthpiece, of expecting people just to do whatever they want, Birkin replies 'I think they always do. But I should like them to do the purely individual thing in themselves, which makes them act in singleness. And they only like to do the collective thing'.

In 1928 he aroused quite a scandal with *Lady Chatterley's Lover*, a novel in which the wife of a crippled industrialist is revitalized by her affair with a gamekeeper. However, his attempt to encapsulate in the novel his belief in the possibility of liberation through sex, led him into explicit sexual descriptions which brought down the rage of society upon his head. The novel was only published in full in England 30 years after his death.

Woolf's 'stream of consciousness'

Virginia Woolf (1882-1941) was another major talent of the period. More consciously literary than Lawrence, as the daughter of Sir Leslie Stephen, a distinguished writer, she was brought up in an atmosphere of refinement. Unusually for a girl of her time she was also encouraged to read widely and to discuss intellectual topics. After 1906 she became a leading figure in the famous Bloomsbury Group, which included the economist J. M. Keynes, Lytton Strachey, the biographer of *Eminent Victorians* and the novelist E. M. Forster. This group met for the purpose of discussion, celebrating 'love, the creation and enjoyment of aesthetic experience and the pursuit of knowledge.' Her life, though protected from the harsher social realities, was nonetheless intensely lived; after suffering from a kind of manic depression, she finally committed suicide by drowning.

Almost inevitably, Virginia Woolf's novels reflect the leisured society she knew best. But she was determined to explore more deeply than novelists had before. The opening sentences of her second novel *Night and Day* serve as a definition of her chosen subject matter: 'in common with many other young ladies of her class, Katherine Hilberry was pouring tea. Perhaps a fifth part of her mind was thus occupied.' Virginia Woolf felt that earlier novelists had been satisfied with that fifth part, and her task was both to delve into the other four parts and to evolve a style in which to express what she found there.

In *Jacob's Room* (1922) she attempted a major innovation by submerging not only the author's power of controlling the reader's moral response (so vital to Lawrence), but also the central character. Of Jacob's physical existence there is mention only of blue eyes, powerful hands, awkwardness and distinction. The novel is an attempt to define personality by its aura, its effect on companions and surroundings. The last chapter is a particularly clear example, for with Jacob killed during the war, the focus turns to his empty room in London, with letters scattered about, a wicker armchair, an old pair of slippers all giving clues to the nature of the former occupant.

To the Lighthouse (1927) and *The Waves* (1931) continue this attempt to capture the essence of personality; not a sequence of motivated actions but what she describes as 'a luminous halo, a semi-transparent envelope surrounding us from the beginning of consciousness to the end'. The technique is increasingly impressionistic, made up of scraps of conversation, interior monologues punctu-

National Library of Ireland

Right: A view of the Nottinghamshire countryside, dominated by the pithead wheels. Lawrence drew heavily on his Nottinghamshire background in his novels and makes frequent references to the brutalizing effects of the mines. One of his major concerns was the effect of 'modern' industrial society on the human spirit. This is an important element in his novel *The Rainbow* which centres on the experiences of a Midlands farming family at the end of the last century. Lawrence uses the arrival of railways, canals and collieries as a symbol of the challenge of broadening horizons to the instinctive vitality of inviduals once attuned to the rhythms of the land. He writes of '*the rhythmic run of the engines, startling at first, but afterwards a narcotic to the brain*', while '*the shrill whistle of the trains echoed through the heart with fearsome pleasure, announcing the far off come imminent and near*'.

Below right: a portrait of Lawrence in 1920, soon after he left England to live abroad permanently.

Left: James Joyce as a young man. Although most of his creative life was spent abroad, Joyce's youth in Ireland and his experiences of Irish life remained a major imaginative element in his work. The Martello tower (below) appears in the opening scenes of *Ulysses* as the temporary home of Stephen and Buck Mulligan.

ated with half-remembered details; the language is intense, but delicate and fluid.

Virginia Woolf's technique, often described as 'stream of consciousness', may be regarded as the literary counterpart of the kind of psychological analysis where the patient is encouraged to say whatever comes into his head, and this is considered to reveal his innermost existence. For the novelist it has the added advantage of making chronological time almost irrelevant, except as a structural device. Thus *To the Lighthouse* can deal with a period of more than ten years by describing less than two days in detail; while *The Waves* incorporates six lives into a day.

James Joyce: the greatest innovator

Perhaps the greatest experimental novelist of the century, however, was James Augustine Aloysius Joyce (1882-1941). Brought up in Ireland as the struggle for home rule was entering its decisive phase, and educated at Jesuit schools, Joyce turned his back on both Ireland and the Catholic church when he moved to Italy with his lover, Nora Barnacle. He supported her and their two children by teaching English at a language school, but devoted his energies to writing.

A Portrait of the Artist as a Young Man (1914-15), Joyce's first novel, was an almost formal purging of his adolescent experiences. Like his brilliant collection of short stories *Dubliners* (1914), the novel portrays with exceptional emotive force a series of apparently trivial incidents; each one is thus revealed as possessing unique ulterior significance—from a Jesuit sermon on damnation, to an

argument about art with a cynical friend. Like Virginia Woolf, Joyce regarded these apparently minor events as crucial to the understanding of personality.

'Ulysses' shocks the world

Joyce was, however, less restrictive in social range, more inventive in style, and far more robust in his use of language than Virginia Woolf. Copies of his greatest work, *Ulysses* (1922), were burned by the New York postal authorities and confiscated by British customs, for Joyce's sexual and scatological references were as shocking in the 1920s as Lawrence's eroticism. But *Ulysses* was published openly in Paris, and 'bootleg' translations were sold in America and Britain for ten years before the restrictions were lifted.

Unlike Lawrence, who incidentally dismissed his work as 'putrid', Joyce came to terms with the modern world. His hero, Leopold Bloom, leads a life of non-stop good intentions and petty humiliations: secretly despised as a Jew in Catholic Dublin, cuckolded by his wife Molly, and ridiculed by all who know him. It is his modest optimism in the face of such trials that earns him the mocking identification with Ulysses, the Greek hero who wandered for ten years on his way home from Troy to his faithful wife Penelope.

Bloom's journey back to the faithless Molly takes less than 24 hours, but over 400,000 words, as Joyce runs through a multitude of styles—a woman's magazine, a Socratic dialogue, a stage play—thickly peppered with allusions to literature, personalities and mythologies old and new. As an example of virtuoso writing, *Ulysses* is unrivalled; but as a novel it demands considerable mental agility from the reader. In this respect it was a sign of things to come, for *Finnegan's Wake*, Joyce's last novel; is almost inaccessible in its obscurity.

Joyce's eyes had always been weak; now they began to fail rapidly. A series of operations did little to retard the onset of blindness and much of the new work had to be dictated. Then in 1932 his daughter Lucia had a nervous breakdown. Joyce took her to the famous psychiatrist Carl Jung, who diagnosed her as schizophrenic, and told him 'you are both going to the bottom of the river, but she is falling and you are diving.' In 1936, Lucia was committed to an asylum and Joyce, reproaching himself bitterly for her fate, toiled on.

Finnegan's Wake was finally published in 1939, two years before Joyce's death. Its critical reception was both hostile and uncomprehending—which was not surprising, since the river Jung had referred to was the river of the unconscious mind, and the novel is riddled with dream images, multiple puns, made-up words and half-completed phrases. It recounts the dreams of H. C. Earwicker, a publican.

Between them, these three writers had transformed the novel in less than ten years. As a propagandist, Lawrence alone retained the traditional format of a beginning, a middle and an end—the storyteller's format. Joyce and Virginia Woolf looked beyond that, to explore the fragments of experience and the significance of the unconscious mind. But their common and greatest achievement was to accept the challenge of the new ideas, and to absorb them into the mainstream of British literature.

The American Novel

The era following World War I was a period of major revolt by young American writers. Their protest was against both the futility of the war and against the sterility and irrelevance of the prevailing techniques of writing fiction. In America itself, the traditional 'American dream' of a land of freedom, renewal and opportunity seemed to have turned irrevocably sour, and the period of disillusionment immediately following the war saw much harsh criticism from Americans about their own country's way of life.

Some of it was direct and hard-hitting; the journalist and critic H. L. Mencken, for example, indulged in ferocious 'debunking' of most aspects of American society in his influential magazine *American Mercury*. Among many young writers and artists, however, this discontent took the form of expatriation. Deserting America in favour of the experiences of Europe, a large American artistic colony inhabited the Paris of the 1920s. These men and women were the so-called 'lost generation', a phrase attributed to Gertrude Stein, a novelist and poet who was a leading figure in the Paris group. Her home became a meeting place for expatriates and visiting Americans—at various times this included such writers as Ernest Hemingway, Scott Fitzgerald, Ezra Pound, Dos Passos and Sherwood Anderson.

By all accounts, the expatriates led a fairly wild Bohemian existence. Their creative awareness was marked by a tremendous self-consciousness of themselves *as* a generation. Cut off from the aims and values of their parents, they felt alienated and set apart in a way they believed no previous generation had ever experienced. Sexual freedom, artistic freedom and individual freedom to seek out new norms and codes of behaviour were their essential values.

The experimental novels of Dos Passos
John Dos Passos was one of the most inventive experimental novelists of the inter-war years, in particular in his more radical later novels—*Manhattan Transfer* (1925) and *USA* (1930-37). Both these works are concerned with the plight of the individual under the crushing pressures of urban America. In the massive trilogy *USA*, he tries to encompass the life of the American nation between 1900 and 1921 by intermingling four distinct narrative techniques: a fragmentary chronicle of the lives of a dozen fictional characters; condensed biographies of significant American figures of the period, ranging from Edison and Ford to Frank Lloyd Wright and Valentino; 'newsreel' impressions of the nation (newspaper headlines, fragments of popular songs and so on) and what Dos Passos calls the 'Camera Eye', a stream-of-consciousness commentary on the other elements, which represents the author's viewpoint. Through this composite picture he was attempting to build up a massive indictment of an empty, materialistic society, socially and politically unjust, a picture of the corruption of the rich and success-

Above: *Armistice Night*, by George Luks, 1918. The novelist Scott Fitzgerald described the end of World War I in his short story *May Day*. '*There had been a war fought and won and the great city of the conquering people was crossed with triumphal arches and vivid with thrown flowers of red, white and blue*'. The questioning of accepted values by the post-war writers led to a new flowering of the American novel.

Right: *Baptism in Kansas*, John S. Curry, 1928. Most of the major novelists such as Hemingway, Fitzgerald and Faulkner came from country towns, and much of the strength of their writing comes from country roots.

Below: Nathaniel West (1904-40), a novelist who wrote with macabre humour and satire. His *The Day of the Locust* (1939), set in Hollywood, where West worked as a screen writer, shows an America full of freaks and violence, ending with an account of a riot at a film première. West died young and received little acclaim until after his death.

ful, the powerlessness and futility of the efforts of the poor. The overall effect of this complex collage is by no means wholly successful, but at its best it is tremendously exciting.

Hemingway's violent world
Three major writers dominate the American novel between the wars: Ernest Hemingway, Scott Fitzgerald and William Faulkner. Hemingway (1898-1961) started his career as a journalist, then volunteered to join an ambulance unit during World War I, and was severely wounded. After the war he went to Paris and started to write, and was advised there by both Gertrude Stein and Ezra Pound. The distinctive prose style which Hemingway evolved is terse and vernacular—he wished to set down the behaviour of his characters objectively, without resorting to a discussion of their thoughts and feelings. His short sentences, his avoidance of abstraction and metaphor, create a style which is in itself an expression of Hemingway's personal philosophy—an existential concern with the present moment, a feeling that the past is dead and the future indecipherable. Only the present can be controlled, however shakily. Hemingway's world is a violent, acci-

346

Collection of Whitney Museum of American Art

Collection of Whitney Museum of American Art

Courtesy of Farrar, Straus & Giroux Inc., New York

dental one where the possibilities of love and companionship are very fragile, and where man has only his own code of behaviour to rely on. His heroes, whether involved in the physical conflicts of war, bull fighting or deep-sea fishing, are frequently doomed to failure and death and can only find redemption in the manner in which they accept their fate.

Hemingway's first popular success, *Fiesta*, published in 1926, is often considered his finest novel; certainly it encapsulates many of his quintessential ideas. The scene moves from expatriate Paris to the bull fighting fiesta at Pamplona, and Hemingway superbly evokes the texture of the surface action, from the pleasures of eating, drinking or fishing to to violent ethos of the bullfight. At the core of the novel is the intolerably painful relationship between the hero Jake Barnes, an American living in Paris, and a beautiful and promiscuous Englishwoman, Lady Brett Ashley. They are unable to consummate their love because Jake is impotent, 'wounded in the war'. They and their small circle of intimates confront the emptiness of their own lives amid the intense vitality of the fiesta. All that they have to sustain them is an unspoken code of behaviour, a code which values stoicism, expertise and understatement; as Brett describes it: 'It's sort of what we have instead of religion.' Hemingway suggests that this search to achieve a mode of living is not merely a question of meaningless endurance:

> '*Perhaps as you went along you did learn something. I did not care what it was all about. All I wanted to know was how to live in it. Maybe if you found out how to live in it you learned from that what it was all about.*'

Fitzgerald and the Jazz Age

In the popular imagination, the work of F. Scott Fitzgerald (1896-1940) is for ever associated with the 'Jazz Age' of the twenties, the era which he so brilliantly evokes in his novels and short stories. It was an age he described as 'a new generation grown up to find all Gods dead, all wars fought, all faiths in man shaken.' His own life had become part of the myth: he and his wife Zelda pursued an extravagant life-style among the glittering high society of the twenties, which ended as tragically as one of his own novels, with Zelda's incurable mental illness and Fitzgerald's alcoholism and final breakdown.

Fitzgerald once said that 'the test of a first-rate intelligence is the ability to hold two opposed ideas in the mind and still retain the ability to function.' It is this very ability which underlies the greatness of his masterpiece *The Great Gatsby* (1925). Fitzgerald establishes the tensions within the central figure, Jay Gatsby, as a symbol of the tensions within 'the American Dream' itself—the tension between Gatsby's greatness as a Romantic dreamer, whose aspirations shine out against the sordid corruption and drabness around him, and Gatsby's own contribution to that corruption as a crook—a representative of the black side of American capitalism.

Daisy Buchanan is the object of Gatsby's pure and romantic passion, the embodiment of all he has aspired to and worked for. Daisy's voice 'was full of money—that was the inexhaustible charm that rose and fell in it . . . high in a white

Above: Novelist Scott Fitzgerald with his wife Zelda and daughter Scottie in Europe in the 1920s. Fitzgerald's life was as tragic as one of his own brilliant novels, with the glamorous life cracking into madness for Zelda and a breakdown and alcoholism in Fitzgerald. He sadly said at the end of his life 'I used to have a beautiful talent once. It used to be a wonderful feeling to know it was there . . . .'

Left: Ernest Hemingway in 1944. Hemingway, a former journalist, was an enormous influence both for his contemporaries and for later prose writers, with his terse style, understatement and superb dialogue. Hemingway committed suicide when he was unable to keep up the active life he loved.

Below: William Faulkner in the American South where he was born and where he created his own fictional county of Yoknapatawpha. He said, on receiving the Nobel Prize in 1950, that the writer must leave 'no room in his workshop for anything but the old verities and truths of the heart'.

palace the king's daughter, the golden girl . . .' Fitzgerald's writing here is more 'literary' than Hemingway's precisely because he is concerned to play off myth against reality, and therefore invokes literary or historical images to create his parallels.

Gatsby is one of the greatest American novels of the century, and its moving, elegaic quality, an elegy for the inevitable defeat of the great American dreamer, is perfectly captured in the last paragraph:

> '*Gatsby believed in the green light, the orgiastic future that year by year recedes before us. It eluded us then, but that's no matter—tomorrow we will run faster, stretch out our arms farther . . . . And one fine morning—*
> *So we beat on, boats against the current, borne back ceaselessly into the past.*'

Faulkner's vision of the South

William Faulkner (1897-1962) is generally regarded as the most outstanding American novelist of the twentieth century. Born in New Albany, Mississippi, in his major novels he created and stayed within his 'own little postage stamp of native soil'. This is the imaginary world of Yoknapatawpha County, Mississippi, and its county seat of Jefferson. Faulkner created for this world its own traditions and history, and concentrated on a few major families who weave in and out of his novels, the best of which include *The Sound and the Fury* (1929), *As I Lay Dying* (1930), *Light in August* (1932) and *Absalom, Absalom* (1936).

The dominant mood in his work is a pervasive sense of doom, the failure of the Southern families, their violence, egotism and incapacity for love. But the novels do not merely encapsulate the regional history of the South; rather, through the brilliance and complexity of their author's vision, they become universal comments on the nature of man's destiny and on his experience in time. The nature of his prose is intensely difficult, with seemingly endless subordinate clauses, subtle repetitions and tortuous sentence construction. But it is a medium which perfectly expresses Faulkner's sense of time as a continuum—the past can never be escaped and perpetually influences and shapes the present and the future.

The Sound and the Fury is a supreme example of Faulkner's consummate skill enforcing this awareness upon the reader. The story of the declining Compson family is told in four sections, from four different points of view; he deliberately chooses to plunge the reader into a confusing jumble of sense impressions and obscurely related events by choosing as his first narrator Benjy Compson, a congenital idiot of 33 to whom time has no meaning. The event of the moment and its past associations are to him all one; only very gradually, in the third and fourth sections, does the pattern of events become clear. Through this departure from conventional narrative, Faulkner manages to submerge our narrow concern with immediate events into a much wider, richer perspective.

The contemporary scene

American novelists since World War II have produced an astonishingly rich and varied achievement. That richness and variety must, in part, be attributed to the

Tate Gallery, London/John Webb

Above: *Harlem* **by Edward Burra, 1934, shows part of New York inhabited mainly by blacks. After World War I many blacks moved from the rural South to the northern US cities. From this migration came the 'Harlem Renaissance' of the 1920s which produced the first magazines dedicated to black writing. Talented black writers, musicians and actors soon emerged.**

Right: Novelist Norman Mailer—one of several distinguished writers to succeed in writing brilliant non-fiction. His committed account of his involvement with the peace march against the Vietnam War (*The Armies of the Night,*** 1968) is a good example.** '*A great happiness came back into the day as if finally one stood under some mythical arch in the great vault of history, helicopters buzzing about, chop-chop, and the sense of America divided on this day now liberated some undiscovered patriotism in Mailer so that he felt a sharp searing love for his country in this moment and on this day, crossing some divide in his own mind wider than the Potomac.*'

Danny Lyon/John Hillelson Agency

348

Left: *Migrant Mother, California, 1936,* by Dorothea Lange, one of the photographers of the US Farm Security Administration, who drew attention to rural poverty by recording the depression of the 1930s. The series of photographs of destitute share croppers, including this 'migrant madonna', shocked the US. Novels like Steinbeck's *The Grapes of Wrath* also focused attention on the social injustices and hardships faced by migrant farmers.

Above: Saul Bellow, regarded as one of the best American post-war novelists. Jewish, like fellow authors Bernard Malamud and Philip Roth, he has written about urban America, combining comedy with tragedy in novels like *Herzog, 1964.*

ethnic, linguistic and geographical range of the country. Jewish writers, for example, have created a paramount position for themselves in the American novel during this period: Saul Bellow, Bernard Malamud, J. D. Salinger, Philip Roth, Edward Lewis Wallant and Bruce Jay Friedman are some of the key names. Usually city-born, and often using an urban background in their novels, they write with a bitter humour born from a tradition of Jewish suffering—frequently of squalor and hurt but also of the possibilities of redemption through love.

Saul Bellow (b.1915) is generally regarded as the finest of the post-war novelists. He has written a number of accomplished novels, offering what Malcolm Bradbury has called 'a real capacity to render suffering and typify the conditions of modern life'. One of the best known, *Herzog* (1964), presents an odyssey of self-discovery by an American-Jewish intellectual. Moses Herzog faces with humour, intelligence and spirit the question of his individual identity in relation to both present society and to the whole intellectual history of the West, and he stays in the reader's mind as one of the most memorable and genuinely human heroes in contemporary fiction.

Black writers have experimented considerably in their work, which ranges from the elegant protest novels of James Baldwin to the grotesque Harlem detective novels of Chester Himes. One of the most accomplished American novels of the past 30 years, *Invisible Man* (1952), is by a black writer, Ralph Ellison. Ellison uses the journey of his unnamed black hero from the South to the North as a wickedly funny allegory of the black experience in America, but at the same time he makes a majestic plea for universal tolerance and liberty for the individual to achieve self-definition. The hero is 'invisible' because society offers him no means of self-definition; suffering rejection on all sides, he chooses to 'go underground' and remain an isolated figure.

But the theme is not one of defeat:

'. . . my world has become one of infinite possibilities . . . that much I've learned underground . . . Step outside the narrow borders of what men call reality and you step into chaos—or imagination . . . I'm invisible, not blind.'

The sixties and seventies have produced much experimentation. In one direction,

led by Tom Wolfe, writers such as Truman Capote, Norman Mailer, Hunter S. Thompson and Mary McCarthy have written 'non-fiction novels' where real people and events are described by means of well-known fictional techniques. Mailer's *The Armies of the Night* (1968), an account of the historic Vietnam peace march, locates the centre of interest in the writer as observer and participant.

Novelists such as John Barth and Thomas Pynchon have pushed fictional techniques and styles to astonishing extremes. Barth for example has written a philosophical burlesque of early American history in *The Sotweed Factor* (1960) and an epic novel about education in *Giles Goat-Boy* (1966), Both works are breathtaking pieces of parody, both learned and highly amusing. Pynchon, in *The Crying of Lot 49* (1966) and *Gravity's Rainbow* (1973), has structured strange, jokey and intellectually brilliant novels around problems in communications theory.

In keeping with the traditions of versatility manifested in American frontier history, its writers today are fearless in their determination to try out new roles and techniques. In doing so they have created possibly the most exciting and varied body of fiction in the modern world. 349

The Modern Novel

The novel is today the most popular literary form. Nineteenth century authors, such as Balzac, Dickens and Tolstoy explored every aspect of human life, and showed that the novel was a highly effective instrument with which a writer could explore human predicaments.

Even the coming of radio and television has not really affected the popularity of novels, either with authors or with the reading public. The novel is still perhaps unsurpassed as a means of embodying complex ideas in a form far more permanent than is achieved by the mass media. It is much cheaper to print a novel than to make a film or put on a play or television programme. It is consequently much easier to express unpopular ideas in a novel, especially if you live in a country where the state has complete control over the theatre, radio, television, cinema and newspapers. This is the case with the famous Russian author Alexander Solzhenitsyn (b.1918), whose depiction of life in prison camps of the Soviet Union would never have been shown on Russian television. Even then, only his first novel, *A Day in the Life of Ivan Denisovich* (1962), was published with official approval. Russian premier Nikita Khruschev allowed the book to appear as part of his campaign to discredit the regime of former dictator Joseph Stalin. But once writers are given freedom to say what they want, unjust and tyrannical regimes find it difficult to tolerate them. Solzhenitsyn's later novels about the network of forced labour camps in the Soviet Union, *The First Circle* (1968) and *Cancer Ward* (1968), were published in the teeth of official opposition, and after the award of the Nobel Prize for literature in 1970 had crowned Solzhenitsyn's literary achievement, he was deprived of his Soviet nationality and compelled to live as an exile in Switzerland.

Solzhenitsyn is not the only modern writer to have used the novel in order to make his contemproaries more acutely aware of political problems. The other Russian author to have been awarded the Nobel Prize for literature since World War II, Boris Pasternak (1891-1960), who was compelled by official pressure to decline the honour in 1958, was also out of sympathy with the totalitarian aims of post-revolutionary Russia. His *Dr Zhivago* (1957) is a plea for the private, individual values of love and poetry and an attack on the way in which all the finest hopes of the 1917 Revolution had been betrayed.

The new novel

Novelists in the West have exploited other aspects of the immense potentialities of the novel: the possibility it offers for experiments in techniques of narration, the way it can evoke characters and can juggle with time, its capacity for humour as well as for detailed analysis either of emotions or of religious and philosophical ideas. The two best known post-war German novelists form an interesting contrast, but both use the novel to comment on the state of post-war Germany. Günter Grass (b.1927) was

Above: Jean Paul Sartre (b.1925), the chief exponent of the French philosophy known as *existentialism*, which he explores in his essays, plays and in novels such as his *La Nausée (Nausea)*, 1938.

Left: Albert Camus achieved fame with his novel *L'Etranger (The Outsider)* in 1942. Camus was active in the French resistance, which he depicted allegorically in *La Peste (The Plague)*, in 1947. Alienation, the 'absurd', the problem of suffering—all recur as themes in his work.

Right: *Walking Man* by the sculptor Giacometti. His attenuated figures seem to echo Sartre's view of the perplexities and isolation of modern man in an alien universe.

Bill Brandt

Jean-Claude Francolon—Gamma/John Hillelson Agency

Galerie Maeght © by A.D.A.G.P. Paris 1977

Peter Reddaway

Top: Novelist and film director Alain Robbe-Grillet was famous during the 1950s for the novels *Les Gommes* and *La Jalousie* and for his theory that the novel should be concerned with objects, not characters. His films include *Last Year at Marienbad*.

Above: The possible plight of Soviet dissidents—painter Yury Titov, photographed in a Moscow psychiatric hospital in 1971. After public demonstrations, Titov was forcibly interned, but in 1972 he was finally allowed to emigrate. Many Soviet artists, believing the denunciation of certain Soviet practices to be a moral obligation, have had their work banned and have suffered loss of nationality and exile.

Above: Alexander Solzhenitsyn walking with Heinrich Böll at the latter's home in West Germany, after Solzhenitsyn's exile from Russia in 1975. Both men have extended the role of novelist to that of moral teacher, displaying in their work a deeply-felt social concern—both also have been Nobel Prize winners.

influenced by Beckett and the theatre of the absurd. His 1961 novel *The Tin Drum*, which made him world famous, has an epic sweep, taking its hero, a dwarf from an asylum, through his retarded childhood and the Nazi period to post-war Germany.

The grotesque humour and inventiveness of Grass seem to have little in common with the work of the equally influential novelist, Heinrich Böll. Böll's austere earnestness and careful craftsmanship (*Billiards at Half Past Nine*, 1961), charts the moral blight in post-war Germany, and the barriers between generations. His concern recently has been to find a means of overcoming the cynicism and despair he finds in modern Germany. Both Grass and Böll are writers of impressive social involvement.

The novel in France

The influential philosophers and writers Jean-Paul Sartre (b.1905) and Albert Camus (1913-60) used the novel to express their ideas on the problems of man's existence and, in the case of Sartre, to explore the possibility of political committment. Both are fundamentally concerned with the purpose of freedom and responsibility in what they consider to be a godless universe.

In France, the Nouveau Roman (or new novel) was part of the general 'new wave' movement in the arts during the 1950s. Alain Robbe-Grillet (b.1924), the most vigorous spokesman for the French 'new novelists' showed that you need not have a story or even characters in order to write fiction. It was enough, as in *Jealousy* (1957), just to describe how a man saw the walls of his bungalow, to evoke the mood of a jealous husband's reaction to his wife and a neighbour. The novelist Michel Butor (b.1925) in *Second Thoughts* (1958) told the whole story of the break-up of a love affair by having a man talk to himself in a railway carriage between Paris and Rome. Nathalie Sarraute (b.1902) experimented with presenting the fluctuations in human behaviour by describing the tiny events and details 351

Camera Press

Left: Catholic convert and upholder of controversial right wing views, Evelyn Waugh (1903-66) was a successful comic novelist. His account of army life in the trilogy *Men at Arms*, *Officers and Gentlemen* and *Unconditional Surrender* ranks among the best fiction of World War II.

Right: George Orwell (1903-50) wrote his first novel *Burmese Days* after serving with the Indian Police. During the 1930s he wrote novels denouncing capitalism but in 1945 turned to an attack on communism's tyrrany with the satire *Animal Farm*. In his masterpiece *1984* Orwell projects the political developments of the 1940s into a terrifying future in which all individual liberty has been lost. Orwell was also a brilliant critic and essayist on many themes.

Below right: Scene from the film version of Ian Fleming's short story *The Spy Who Loved Me*. The secret agent 007 James Bond, created through Fleming's novels, has become a well known cinema hero.

NATIONAL UNION OF JOURNALISTS

7 John Street, Bedford Row, London, W.C.1

'Phone: HOLborn 2258

Telegrams: Natujay Holb, London

This is to certify that

Mr. GEORGE ORWELL

of The Tribune

is a member of the ....T.+P.

Branch of the National Union of Journalists.

Leslie R. Aldous Branch Sec.

(Address) 66. Priory Gans. N.6.

Member's Sig.

which make up the passage of time.

The new novelists continued with the experimentation of the novel, following the line begun by Proust, Joyce and Beckett. Indeed the changing shape of the novel and the success which writers of this school have had, has led the influential French critic Roland Barthes to argue that what an author says and how he says it are one and the same thing.

Influences on the novel

The playright and novelist Samuel Beckett (b.1906), a Northern Irishman who lived and worked in Paris, has had a great influence on the modern novel. Beckett won the Nobel Prize in 1969, and his strange novels in which he describes the antics of creatures often barely human can be seen as the logical conclusion of the world view of his great compatriot, James Joyce (1882-1941). Like the French novelist Marcel Proust (1871-1922), Joyce too, profoundly changed writers' ideas about what the novel could be, and how a novel could express thought.

Roman Catholic novelists have produced some of the most impressive fiction of our time. In France Francois Mauriac (1885-1970) and George Bernanos (1896-1948), and in England Evelyn Waugh (1903-66) and Graham Greene (b.1904), all explored the fears, dilemmas, hopes and ideals of those who still sought to believe in the most orthodox form of Christianity. Such writers allowed political considerations and experiments in technique to come only incidentally or as an accompaniment to questions of faith.

Yet it would be wrong to see the novel as always dominated by serious ideas, whether about politics, technique of narration or religion. One of the best of modern comic novelists, P. G. Wodehouse (1882-1975) continued his creation of the world of man-about-town Bertie Wooster and Blandings Castle, home of the Earl of Emsworth and his prize pig. Kingsley Amis (b.1922) uses humour to deflate the pretensions both of academics (*Lucky Jim*, 1954) and of the English themselves (*One Fat Englishman*, 1963).

Women novelists

Women have continued to find particular inspiration in the medium of the novel. The rise of the woman novelist was begun in the nineteenth century by such giants as George Eliot and the Brontë sisters. Iris Murdoch (b.1919), a former tutor in philosophy, is one of the most prolific of modern writers. She has created novels sharply describing a confined upper middle-class, convoluted world, where the characters are involved with each other in a sexual, religious and emotional struggle (*A Fairly Honourable Defeat*, 1970). By contrast Doris Lessing (b.1919), for many years an active communist, has concentrated on the expression of political issues, the ageing woman and the conflict between generations. She has explored all these themes in *The Golden Notebook* (1962), where the heroine, Anna Wulf, keeps four notebooks 'to separate things off from each other, out of fear of chaos, of formlessness—of breakdown'.

An analysis of the woman's point of view has been taken further by women novelists in the 1970s. Such authors as Erica Jongh (*Fear of Flying*, 1974) and Kate Millett, have created sexually explicit, semi-autobiographical novels to explore the problems of modern life encountered by women.

The English novel

Several novelists in the twentieth century have turned away from depicting contemporary life, and have instead created a fantasy world of their own. J. R. R. Tolkien (1892-1976), in his trilogy *The Lord of The Rings* (1954-5) has been brilliantly successful at drawing an entirely imaginary world, peopled by vivid characters such as Frodo—a hobbit, one of a race of beings similar to, but separate from, the race of men. The book has a powerful narrative, and has worldwide popularity. William Golding (b.1911) has used the novel to present us with symbolic moral fables. In his fine *Lord of the Flies* (1954), a group of boys are stranded on a desert island, and all

352

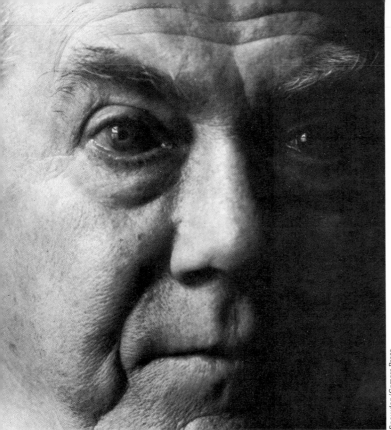

Left: Graham Greene (b.1904), novelist and dramatist, himself divides his work into serious novels and 'entertainments'. A concern with spying and betrayal typifies the entertainments, the most famous of which is *The Third Man*. Like Waugh, Greene was converted to Catholicism and his novels explore the actions of his heroes in the light of this religion, as for example in *Brighton Rock* and *The Power and the Glory*.

Right: Brought up in Rhodesia, Doris Lessing left the country for England in 1949. Her novels, among them *The Grass is Singing*, the Martha Quest series and *The Golden Notebook*, often contain an autobiographical element and are notable for their intensity and for their rigorous psychological analysis of maturing women.

Below: The Oxford professor J. R. R. Tolkien used his knowledge of Celtic, Norse and Teutonic legend in creating the complex, symbolic world of *The Hobbit* and its sequel *The Lord of the Rings*, a trilogy.

Snowdon/Camera Press

Mark Gerson/Camera Press

Snowdon/Camera Press

civilized behaviour quickly breaks down unleashing the darker aspects of human nature within each boy. Conversely, Anthony Powell (b.1905), in his long series of novels *The Music of Time*, has concentrated on depicting an upper middle class world, but uses no plot in the traditional sense: the series operates through shifts of view and the building of a web-like social structure by the narrator, himself a novelist.

The post-war novel in England produced a novement towards realism in the novel. Writers such as Angus Wilson, and John Braine interpreted this in different ways. Wilson (b.1913) began writing after recovering from a near nervous breakdown. His novels have large, almost Dickensian collections of characters whom he satirizes unmercifully (*Anglo-Saxon Attitudes*, 1956). His most ambitious novel, *No Laughing Matter* (1967), is a chronicle of a family between the two world wars, exploring with insight the motives and behaviour of the characters. John Braine (b.1922), in *Room at the Top* (1957) created the classic 'angry young man' novel, which was later successfully filmed. His hero, Joe Lampton, from a narrow working-class northern background, is determined to succeed, and this leads to conflict between his true love and success.

Few critics take detective novels or science fiction seriously, but the novels of the Belgian writer Georges Simenon give a highly evocative portrait of French provincial life and the works of John Wyndham (b.1921) or Ray Bradbury (b.1920) give a more compelling account of the possible impact of science than many learned essays. When, in 1953, Ray Bradbury wanted to warn people of the threat which science and totalitarianism held for literature, he wrote a novel called *Fahrenheit 451*: the temperature at which paper burns. Perhaps the novel will continue to survive even television because it is only through the printed word, the medium which most makes us think, that the danger to our freedom to think can really be spelt out.

Brecht

Bertolt Brecht has had a profound and lasting influence on the modern theatre. As a playwright he wrote political, Marxist-inspired plays for the people; as a director he broke with traditional theatre and developed his own spare, basic productions—known as 'epic theatre'—to remove suspense and emotion from the theatre. Predictably, the subtler Brecht tried to make the political message in his plays, the harder they became to understand. His own productions of epic theatre moved his audience to emotion and identification with his characters, often in spite of his avowed intentions.

Bertolt Brecht was born at Augsburg, Germany, in 1898. In his formative years, Brecht witnessed both the peak and the first collapse of imperialism in Europe; and in 1917, when he was 19 years old, the Russian Revolution suggested the possibility of a different way of life, a different political and economic system.

Throughout Europe, but in Germany in particular, the 1920s were a time of great political turmoil. In Germany this was expressed not only in meetings, in demonstrations and in newspapers, but also in the theatre. This renewal of creative activity stimulated a great interest in experimental drama. Major theatrical developments in the 1920s included Expressionism (based on psychology and modern art) and Neo-Realism (dealing with social themes).

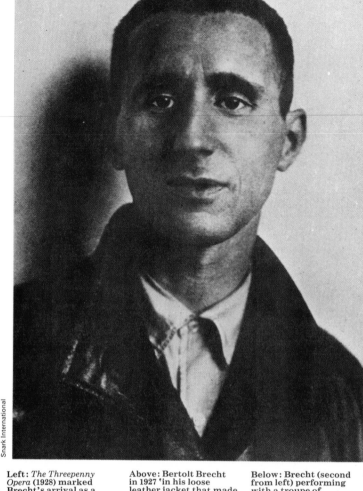

Snark International

Left: *The Threepenny Opera* (1928) marked Brecht's arrival as a major theatrical force, after its triumphant first night in Berlin. With a haunting score by Kurt Weill, the story of the robber Macheath, is an attack on the corruption of a capitalist society, and is Brecht's only truly popular success.

Above: Bertolt Brecht in 1927 'in his loose leather jacket that made him look like a cross between a truck driver and a Jesuit seminarist.' Brecht had moved in 1924 to Berlin, centre of German theatrical and political life, and had begun to study the Marxist theories that were to shape all his writing.

Below: Brecht (second from left) performing with a troupe of entertainers, Munich, 1920s. The group was led by Karl Valentin, a brilliant, ironic comic and mimic. Valentin's sharp humour influenced Brecht's work. Valentin, asked why he wore a pair of spectacles without glass, replied that it was better than nothing.

Snark International

354

Left: A photomontage of Erwin Piscator (1893-1966) outside his theatre in Berlin, 1927. He saw political propaganda as the main function of the theatre, and first evolved the theory of 'epic theatre' which Brecht also used to create a theatre which 'appeals less to the spectator's feelings than to his reason'.

Left: Max Reinhardt (1873-1943) with Lady Diana Cooper. Reinhardt was Germany's leading director and producer by the 1920s. Both Brecht and Piscator worked for him during their early years in the theatre.

Below: Kurt Weill (1900-50) and his wife Lotte Lenya (b.1901) in 1935. Weill's brilliantly ironic, yet moving music combined jazz, popular music and avante-garde musical forms. Together Weill and Brecht created a new popular opera with *The Threepenny Opera* and *Mahagonny*. Lotte Lenya brilliantly performed Brecht and Weill's work.

Above: Brecht's *Man's A Man*, 1926, foresaw the Nazis' totalitarian state. *'This evening will show how a man is being reconstructed like an auto. Even more than that: one can even turn him into a butcher . . . .'*

Brecht in Berlin

Brecht had written his first play, *Baal*, in 1918, but this was not performed until his second, *Drums in the Night* (1921), won a drama prize in Munich two years later. Both were highly Expressionistic, and in *Drums in the Night*, placards were placed in the theatre proclaiming 'Don't Stare So Romantically' and 'Every Man is Best in His Own Skin.' Brecht's development as a playwright really began, however, when he moved to Berlin in 1924. There he saw at close quarters the exciting new artistic movements in the German theatre, in particular in the work of Erwin Piscator (1893-1966).

An actor before the war, Piscator had since turned to directing and had become closely involved in left-wing politics. The tradition of the *Volksbühne*, or people's theatre, was long-established in Germany as a form of popular entertainment. Piscator, along with other left-wing directors was determined to put it to revolutionary purposes.

In 1924 Piscator was invited to join the Berliner Volksbühne, a state-funded theatre, as a director, but his militant productions caused such an uproar that he was forced to resign. Next he established a base of his own, the Piscator Theatre, where he scored a spectacular success in 1927-8 with a season of three plays. In staging one of them, *The Good Soldier Schweik*, from the comic novel by Jaroslav Hasek, about a soldier during World War I, he collaborated with Bertolt Brecht.

Working with Piscator, Brecht was gaining invaluable experience of different types of production. He had already become interested in politics—in 1926 he had begun studying Marxism at the Berlin Workers' School. Brecht was still experimenting with Expressionist forms, but Piscator's approach was to lead him in a new direction.

Partly through necessity when working with amateur groups in assembly halls around Berlin, Piscator had virtually abandoned traditional methods of staging plays. He could not use much scenery, for example, so a sign board would announce the place and time of the action. But his political purpose demanded a more elaborate technology. Piscator surrounded the stage action with as much information about society as he could.

Films and slides were projected on to the stage to tie the action into a wider context. In *Schweik*, designed by George Grosz, maps of the Czech soldier's travels and documentary film of the war were projected on to the back of the set, while the end of the play was marked by a film of endless rows of crosses in a war cemetery moving steadily closer to the audience.

Berlin was the centre for left-wing agitation, and Brecht was now devoted to some form of proletarian drama. He became increasingly active in the theatre, constantly experimenting with new ideas, but where Piscator used film to bombard his audience into submission, Brecht turned to music as a way of surprising them.

Brecht was invited to stage a production at a music festival in 1927, collaborating with a young German composer named Kurt Weill (1900-50). They produced a song-cycle, linked to a narrative about the imaginary American city of Mahagonny, which was performed by a group of actors

Above: *The White General*, 1923, by George Grosz (1893-1959). Grosz produced a powerful and satirical vision of Germany in the 1920s, during the Nazis' relentless rise to power, and the collapse of the Weimar Republic. Grosz, like Brecht, Piscator and Weill, fled from Germany when the Nazis took power.

Right: *Pillars of Society* (1926) by George Grosz. The painting shows the ruling powers: an officer, a judge, a nationalist with his reactionary paper and a Nazi. This was the society which Brecht satirized unmercifully in his plays: '*Man isn't sharp enough/He never seems to see/That it's all deceit and bluff*'.

and singers in a boxing-ring against a background of fantastic drawings projected on to a screen. The reception was passionate and divided, cheers vying with boos and whistles, which the actors returned on tin whistles supplied in advance by Brecht.

First success

The following year Brecht married the actress Helene Weigel, who performed in many of his plays. Soon afterwards he and Weill joined up again to produce *The Threepenny Opera*. Adapting John Gay's *The Beggar's Opera* (1728), Brecht used the story of Macheath the gangster and his father-in-law Peachum, the beggar king, as an image of capitalism:

'*What does a man live by? By resolutely ill-treating, cheating,*
some other bloke!
A man can only live by absolutely forgetting he's a man like
other folk!'

The excitement of the performance, inspired by the singing of Weill's wife Lotte Lenya, muted the social message of the play, but it was a triumphant success and guaranteed Brecht's place in the Berlin theatre.

These years of success as a playwright and director, however, were overshadowed by political developments. At the end of the 1920s Germany's economy slumped again and the Nazis profited more than the communists from the people's despair. In 1933 Hitler gained control of Germany. Repression of known communists was fast and ferocious; Brecht, like many other artists, was forced to leave the country immediately. He settled in the United States in 1941.

Above: A scene from *The Caucasian Chalk Circle* (1943-5), one of Brecht's masterpieces written in exile. Here a mother and foster mother dispute the ownership of a child—who can draw him out of the circle? Here, taking property and possession as a theme, Brecht created a drama of great compassion.

Below: Brecht and his wife, Helene Weigel, rehearse his masterpiece, *Mother Courage* (1939) in 1948, Brecht's comment on the horrors of war. Mother Courage survives as an itinerant trader following the armies during the Thirty Years War. One by one her three children are killed by the war, and Mother Courage is left alone.

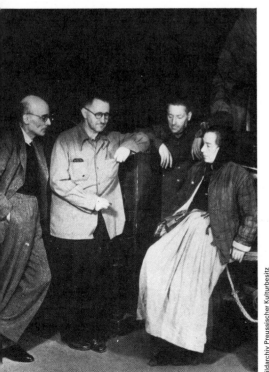

Brecht in exile

It was in exile that Brecht wrote the plays now considered to be his masterpieces: *The Life of Galileo* (1937-9), *Mother Courage* (1938-9), *The Good Woman of Setzuan* (1938-41) and *The Caucasian Chalk Circle* (1943-5). An exile for his political beliefs, he explored his ideology in a more complex and thoughtful way than had been possible while he was working full-time in the theatre. At the same time he developed his influential, theoretical approach to direction, largely as a means of explaining to actors the kind of effects he was seeking.

The Life of Galileo deals with problems directly relevant to Brecht's position at this time. The great Italian astronomer had also come into conflict with a repressive authority—the Catholic Church. The implications of astronomy in the Renaissance had threatened the very foundations of religion—as his friend Sagredo warns Galileo:

'*Can you see the Pope scribbling a note in his diary: July 10th 1610, heaven abolished? A moment ago, when you were at the telescope, I saw you tied to the stake!*'

Galileo laughs the danger off, but later, threatened with torture by the Inquisition, he recants publicly and is kept under guard. He goes on with his work in secret, however, and eventually manages to smuggle it out of Italy to be published abroad.

Brecht's treatment of this story is typical of his major works. Galileo is shown in many different lights: a scientific genius but frivolous and sensual, a great man but a coward. By denying what he knows to be true he not only betrays him-self and his pupils, he betrays the people, who are kept in subjection by the power of false ideas. The members of the audience are presented with a contradiction which they must struggle to resolve themselves, for at the end of the play their admiration for Galileo as a kind man subject to human frailty comes up against his own violent self-condemnation.

This sense of contradiction is central to Brecht's writing. Both the production of a play and the acting, he felt, should help to distance the audience from the play, so that they would look critically and unemotionally at the action rather than be absorbed in it. By using some of Piscator's devices, such as the barest possible stage properties and signboards commenting on the action, he sought to make audiences question constantly what was happening.

Similarly, by requiring his actors to perform roles rather than identify with characters, he hoped to draw the observer's attention to the fact that in real life, alternative courses of action are genuinely open. This whole technique, known as epic (or dialectic) theatre, was designed to objectify stage events. Thus, for example, if the actor playing Galileo were to win the sympathy of the audience, or dominate them, he would inevitably obscure the argument of the play; but if he performs what has been written, scene by scene, he draws attention to the problems raised by Galileo's conduct.

Brecht's seriousness did not make his plays austere, however, for he considered that the prime purpose of the theatre was to entertain. *The Caucasian Chalk Circle*, perhaps his greatest play, is also one of the most enjoyable. Throughout the play, intellectual rigour is combined with great lyrical charm, most notably in the songs which are used to knit together the various parts of the story. The play itself is introduced by a song, for Brecht wrote a prologue to *The Caucasian Chalk Circle* which makes its purpose as an instructional tale quite clear. In the prologue, two groups of workers in Azerbaijan in the Caucusus are arguing about a nearby valley. The goat herders have a traditional right to the land, but the fruit-growers claim they can make better use of it. The story of the chalk circle is told by a singer, as an example of how best to make a political decision.

In 1947 Brecht decided to leave the US after anti-communist 'witch-hunting' and returned to Berlin at the invitation of the East German Government in 1948.

The Berliner Ensemble

In 1949 Brecht formed his own company, the Berliner Ensemble, which achieved international success with Brecht's plays.

At the height of the 1950s Cold War, Brecht's reputation in the West was highly controversial. In 1954 the Ensemble won first prize at the World Theatre Festival in Paris with a production of Brecht's *The Caucasian Chalk Circle*. Just two years before his death, in 1956, Brecht had finally won recognition in the West as a major dramatist and theatrical force.

Brecht's contradictory achievements were based on his concept of theatre as a force for political change. He believed that theatre was the concern of philosophers or 'at least such philosophers who seek not only to interpret the world, but also to change it'.

Modern Opera

Although opera has largely ceased to be in the forefront of musical experimentation, all the leading twentieth century composers have contributed to it. The Viennese composer Alban Berg (1885-1935), a student of Arnold Schoenberg, was probably more innovative and influential in this field than any of his contemporaries.

Berg's first opera, *Wozzeck*, is today one of the most popular of modern operas. He worked on it from 1914 to 1921. Excerpts heard at a concert in 1924 aroused such interest that, after 137 rehearsals, it was given a stage performance by the Berlin State Opera in 1925. It was praised by some as the greatest opera since Debussy's *Pelléas et Mélisande* and was declared to be a work of genius, but the majority reaction was extremely hostile, the opera even being denounced as the ravings of a madman. The central character, Wozzeck, is an inarticulate and bullied soldier whose mind crumbles under the accumulated strain of the experiences he has to endure. He murders his mistress through obsessive jealousy and finally is drowned while searching for the murder weapon. The use of abnormal characters with a central anti-hero was itself a twentieth century coming-of-age for opera.

The opera makes use of *Sprechgesang* as developed by Schoenberg; and it is a generally atonal work, though in the remarkable orchestral passage that mourns Wozzeck's death, described by Berg as an 'invention on a key', uses a complex tonality close to Mahler. *Wozzeck* makes use of traditional forms, for example fugue, march, symphony and variation and is extremely complex and dissonant. Yet its emotional impact is immediate and Berg himself warned against approaching the opera in an analytic way: 'Nobody in the audience ought to notice anything of these various [musical forms]' instead

Brian Seed/John Hillelson Agency

Brian Seed/John Hillelson Agency

358

Left: *The Turn of the Screw* (1954) Britten's chamber opera based on Henry James' short story. The tenor, Peter Pears, who has been particularly associated with creating roles in many of Britten's operas, here plays the part of the sinister spirit of Peter Quint in the original production of the opera.

Above: The composer Benjamin Britten (1913-76) conducting at the Aldeburgh Music Festival. Born in East Anglia, Britten revealed a precocious musical talent, and soon became the foremost British composer. His decisive influence on modern music has been in his operas, which combine lyricism with drama.

Below: The Maltings, Suffolk, formerly a malt house, the concert hall of the yearly Aldeburgh Music Festival, founded by Britten and Peter Pears in 1948. The Suffolk coast, where Britten lived, provided him with much of his musical inspiration, notably for the opera *Peter Grimes*, set in a Suffolk fishing village.

in 1941, six years after Berg's death, yet it was in a far more conservative style. Britten's adherence to tonality stemmed from his natural gifts for creating memorable tunes and melodies and his admiration for similarly gifted composers of the past, such as Purcell, Mozart, Schubert, Verdi and Mahler. He was also strongly influenced by his teacher Frank Bridge in his use of *polytonality*—the use of more than one key—as well as the rhythmic and harmonic innovations of Stravinsky.

His first opera was not a success, but he was nevertheless commissioned to write another. The result was *Peter Grimes*, first performed in 1945 at Sadler's Wells in London. The opera was a tremendous success and soon played throughout Europe. The plot centres on a fisherman, Peter Grimes, an outsider of complex psychology, whose dreams and ambitions are completely at odds with his daily life. Britten's music matches the range and intensity required in a series of arias, ensembles and musical interludes. The lyrical beauty of the music ensured its popularity. Britten immeasurably raised the status of British opera and consolidated this position with subsequent works.

His next three operas are on a more modest scale and use small chamber orchestras. *The Rape of Lucretia* (1946) has a cast of six and only 12 instrumentalists. *Albert Herring* (1947) is a comic opera also on a modest scale. *Let's Make an Opera!* (1949), first performed at the Aldeburgh Festival, was intended to be sung mainly by children for children, to teach them how opera is written and produced.

In *Billy Budd* (1951) he returned to larger dimensions. The setting is aboard a British naval ship during the French Wars of 1797, and consequently uses an all-male cast. As with *Peter Grimes* the theme concerns innocence and man's inhumanity, but the musical treatment is more continuous and symphonic, with no arias or ensembles, while its emotional power is just as great.

Britten's next opera, commissioned for the coronation of Queen Elizabeth II in 1953, *Gloriana*, was however not liked by the critics. But he followed this with the successful *The Turn of the Screw* (1954) based on the famous Henry James story about the corruption of innocence. The opera brilliantly conjures up the atmosphere of menace and uncertainty in the story. After this Britten wrote *A Midsummer Night's Dream* (1960), an adaptation from the Shakespeare play, a translucent, lyrical and highly approachable score.

His next major work for voices was not an opera but a large scale setting of the Latin mass, juxtaposed with the war poems of Wilfrid Owen, *The War Requiem*. Regarded by some as his greatest work, this requiem reaches emotional heights unusual even for Britten.

After this Britten turned away again from large orchestral forces and, from 1964 to 1968, wrote three *Parables for Church Performance: Curlew River, The Burning Fiery Furnace* and *The Prodigal Son*. Each of the three church parables is introduced by *plainsong* (unaccompanied vocal lines in a free rhythm) and based upon it. The parables are conceived as being given by a monastic order so that both male and female roles are played by males. There is no conductor and the in-

Left: *Peter Grimes* tells the story of Peter Grimes, an outsider at odds with his fishing village, who is accused of ill-treating his apprentice. Grimes finally comes to terms with his own nature by committing suicide at sea. It is Britten's most popular opera, and has been performed worldwide.

Above: *Noyes Fludde* (1958) by Benjamin Britten is based on a medieval miracle play. A lighthearted and exuberant work about Noah's ark, it was brilliantly devised to be performed by children, utilizing recorders and children's voices. *Noyes Fludde* is designed for production in a church.

'everyone should be filled only by the idea of the opera, an idea which far transcends the individual fate of Wozzeck.'

His next opera, *Lulu*, was left unfinished at his death: even after seven years of almost continuous work only two acts were fully completed. *Lulu* is based entirely on a single 12-note row, but Berg's use of the 12-note technique is very flexible. The text is adapted by Berg from two dramas by Frank Wedekind and concerns the beatiful figure of Lulu who is responsible for the deaths and degradations of various lovers, but who remains true to herself; she is a corrupting force without herself being corrupt.

Britten's operas

The premiere of *Paul Bunyan*, the first opera of Benjamin Britten (1913-76) was

strumentalists take part in the action.

Britten's last opera was *Death in Venice*, based on a famous short story by Thomas Mann. Again large orchestral forces are used. Britten uses his own specially adapted 12-note techniques (as occur also in *The War Requiem*) combined with the influences from the music of Gamelan orchestras, which use fixed-note instruments and which he had heard in the Far East in 1956. The various scenes are linked by Gustav Aschenbach, the central character and a writer, in accompanied monologues whose pitch—but neither duration nor phrasing—is indicated. The opera charts Aschenbach's gradual inner disintegration and final death as part of a complex theme concerning artistic creation itself: its source, the sacrifice it exacts and the temptations that come with it.

Tippett's lyricism

Another great British opera composer, a friend and contemporary of Britten, is Michael Tippett (b.1905). Tippett was a late developer and did not produce anything which he himself regarded as significant until his thirties. His first opera—one which he still in a sense regards as the summit of his work—is *The Midsummer Marriage*, completed in 1952. The libretto is by the composer himself and it disconcerted critics by its seeming obscurity, complicated symbolism and mystical tone. The work was a failure on its first performance in 1955 but an extensively revised version was given, this time with great success, in 1968. The score is one of the most beautiful of the century, with its extraordinary, continuous, layered flow of warm lyricism. Its theme is the fundamental one of the complementary nature of the male and female principles and follows the initiation into deeper self-understanding of a couple soon to be married.

Tippett followed this with the opera *King Priam* (1962). It is based on Homer's *Iliad* and concerns Helen's seduction of Paris and Paris' tragic end, while the abstract theme is the problem of choice. The music shows a great change of style, being stark and severe in contrast to the luxury of *The Midsummer Marriage*.

His third opera *The Knot Garden* (1970), presents a still further change in style. It contains elements of both his previous musical styles fused with other elements that belong very much to contemporary life (for example, the use of an electric guitar and the quotation of the folksong *We shall overcome*).

The Ice Break (1977) is unlike all his previous operas in that it has no directly parallel developments in his non-operatic music. Like *The Knot Garden* it is very fast moving and deeply concerned with modern dilemmas and moral problems—such as racialism, violence and freedom—and again his treatment of these themes lifts them out of a merely fashionable concern, into a many-levelled, symbolic and semi-mythical world.

Janáček's Folk Operas

The Czech composer Leoš Janáček (1854-1928) has been a decisive influence on twentieth century opera. He wrote most of his greatest music after his .fiftieth year, while as an old man he became even more productive and vigorous than ever. His finest operas, *Jenufa* (1904), *Katya Kabanova* (1921), *The Cunning Little*

Zoe Dominic

EMI/Marek Grotowski

Above: *The Rise and Fall of the City of Mahagonny* (1930), an anti-capitalist satire by German composer Kurt Weill with libretto by Bertolt Brecht. Weill's music during this time was a unique blend of jazz and popular song, coupled with serious harmony and classical forms, producing a popular form of opera which reached a wide public.

Above right: *The Bassarids* (1965) by Hans Werner Henze. *The Bassarids* is Henze's last composition in a traditional operatic form. The libretto, adapted from Euripides' *The Bacchae*, concerns the introduction of the cult of Dionysus into Ancient Greece, but has as its theme the destructive effects of moral and sexual repression in any age.

Left: Krzysztof Penderecki, (b.1933), a leading avant garde composer. His compositions, like *The Devils of Loudun*, reflects his deep convictions expressed with dramatic harmonic effect.

Right: a scene from Sir Michael Tippett's *The Knot Garden* (1970). It is set in a maze-like garden which itself is a symbolic expression of the inner turmoils of the opera's characters. The maze, which according to Tippett 'continually shifts and possibly (in Act II) spins.' The theme, like all Tippett's operas, is about relationships between people and problems with contemporary life.

Zoe Dominic

Transworld

Above: Sir Michael Tippett. Besides his four operas, Tippett has also written symphonies, string quartets, piano sonatas and choral settings, developing his operatic and non-operatic music together. His music reflects his deep concern for human suffering, coupled with a sense of the possibilities of love.

Vixen (1924) and *The Makropoulos Affair* (1926) are all highly individual, full of short energetic phrases derived from his close study of speech rhythms and folk song that twist and blossom into new musical phrases in a continual interweaving of ideas. His orchestration, too, opened up new musical territory.

The Devils of Loudun

A leading Polish avant-garde composer, Krzysztof Penderecki (b.1933) has demonstrated the power and potential of modern musical techniques to express what would otherwise be unattainable in opera. His opera *The Devils of Loudun* (premiered 1969), whose libretto, by the composer, is based on a novel by Aldous Huxley, deals with the alleged demonic possession of a group of nuns in 17th century France, the appalling suffering undergone by a priest accused of originating the possession, his refusal to confess and his final martyrdom at the stake. The music wonderfully sustains and builds the accumulating terror and monstrousness. Penderecki employs sounds which until recently would not have been considered musical at all, such as whispering, scraping and hissing, as well as amplified chorus.

New directions in opera

The German composer, Hans Werner Henze (b.1926), has written ballets, symphonies, concertos and chamber music, but is best known for his operas—a form which suits his concern to express deeply held ideas and, more recently, a specifically political point of view. His music has undergone great stylistic changes and his last opera, *The Bassarids* (1965), is the culmination of his earlier style. Since the 1960s Henze's radical political sympathies have led him to find equally radical new forms of musical expression and have transformed him from a leading, but rather conservative composer, into a leading avant-garde figure.

Opera in the twentieth century has absorbed some of the techniques of avant-garde music, but has remained in a fundamentally conservative idiom. There is every indication that opera will play an increasingly important part in introducing the public to contemporary music, and in breaking down the traditional barriers between audience and performers.

Zoe Dominic

361

The New Music

The twentieth century has seen far-reaching developments in the freedom of musical form. However, these developments, made by composers like Bartók, Stravinsky and Schoenberg and his pupils, were firmly rooted in the Western musical traditions they inherited. Bartók was influenced by both his fellow composers, while Stravinsky finally became deeply committed to the methods originated by Schoenberg.

Bartók and folk music

Béla Bartók (1881-1945) was born in Hungary of a musical family and early showed musical promise. He was greatly influenced by folk music, saying that it freed him from the tyrannical use of major and minor keys. This led him to use the *chromatic scale*, basically an extension of the classical diatonic scale to include all the semitones of the musical scale. Each note of the chromatic scale was considered of equal value and could be used freely and independently.

Applying these techniques, he scored an early success with a mime play *The Wooden Prince* (1916) which enabled an earlier, yet in many ways more musically advanced and characteristic work, the opera *Bluebeard's Castle* (1911), to be performed.

Barbaric energy, the dramatic use of dissonance and rhythm, and sensuous orchestration all help the expression of the plot of Bartók's ballet *The Miraculous Mandarin* (1919), about a mysterious mandarin who in spite of various attempts to murder him, refuses to die until he gains sexual satisfaction with a prostitute. The music shows the influence of Stravinsky's *Rite of Spring*, itself part of the trend towards a kind of new primitivism emerging from the influence of African art. Jagged rhythms replaced the fluid continuous structures of the Romantic music of the late nineteenth century.

In *Music for Strings, Percussion and Celesta* (1936) and the *Sonata for Two Pianos and Percussion* (1937) Bartók explores and exploits the range of colour and rhythm in percussion instruments in exciting and unprecedented ways. His music aroused much opposition with its emphasis on rhythm and dissonance as opposed to melody. But Bartók was also a great melodist; his style gradually became more relaxed, finding room even for musical jokes and for a greater lyricism. This is particularly apparent in the works he composed in the US after migrating there in 1940 during World War II. His later works like the *Concerto for Orchestra* (1943), are all lyrical, of great beauty and far less forbidding than his earlier works. But in America Bartók was poor and suffered from ill health, and it was not until after his death that his fame as a composer was assured.

Stravinsky's new music

Unlike Bartók, Igor Stravinsky (1882-1971), one of the greatest of modern composers, showed no early talent. However, Stravinsky was fortunate in meeting the composer Rimsky-Korsakov, to whom he played some of his first attempts at composition. In spite of a decidedly low opinion of these Rimsky-Korsakov en-couraged him to continue to study music, but not to abandon law. Through Rimsky-Korsakov, Stravinsky came into contact with artists, writers and musicians and came to know the music of the then modern French composers: he was particularly impressed by the music of Debussy.

Diaghilev, the Russian impresario, heard some early works of Stravinsky in 1909 and recognized the seeds of a major talent. Diaghilev decided to commission Stravinsky to write a new ballet based on the Russian legend of the firebird: the result was *The Firebird* (1910).

First performed in Paris, it was immediately an immense success, bringing recognition to Stravinsky and marking the beginning of a new phase in modern ballet. The score is shimmering, lush and jewelled, but in the dance of the ogre Kastchei, and in other parts of the score, a new type of 'primitive' rhythmic energy makes its first appearance. In his next ballet score *Petrushka* (1911) rhythm is even more originally treated, and the orchestration is brilliant and highly coloured. *Polytonality* (the simultaneous use of two or more keys) is a notable feature of the work.

Stravinsky's next ballet, *The Rite of Spring* (1913), provoked one of the most famous musical scandals in history on its first night. A riot broke out and so much noise was created by the audience that the music itself could scarcely be heard. The work is again brilliantly orchestrated, but this time with the purpose of creating harsh and savage musical sounds. Its structure is one of great juxtaposed blocks rather than symphonic development. Its dynamic range is immense, with

Above: Schoenberg conducting. Perhaps the most influential of all modern composers, he had a strong sense of his destiny: he felt that someone *had* to innovate and once said 'No one else wanted the job, so I had to take it on'. Despite his new ideas he was a lover of, and expert on, the music of the past.

Below: A modern production of *Pierrot Lunaire* by Schoenberg. Fights broke out in the audience at the premiere in Berlin in 1912. Not only is the music atonal, but the work also employs unorthodox writing for instruments, and the poems it sets are delivered in *Sprechgesang* (speech-song).

Mary Evans Picture Library

Anthony Crickmay

Osterreichische Galerie, Vienna

Snark

Popperfoto

Below: Béla Bartók, the Hungarian composer, never received the recognition he deserved in his lifetime. He died poor in the US in 1945. In spite of hardships he never lost his fire, his integrity or his vision, and he never gave in to popular or critical taste. Soon after his death his work received wide acclaim.

Above: *The Family* by Egon Schiele (1890-1918). Schiele was just one of the many artists and thinkers to emerge from pre-World War I Vienna. These included Wittgenstein the philosopher; the composers Mahler, Berg, Schoenberg and Webern; the painters Kokoschka and Klimt; the architect Adolf Loos; and Sigmund

Freud, the founder of psychoanalysis. Viennese society was dominated by a deeply conservative middle class who saw all progress as undermining the great achievements of the past. The anti-middle class feeling of artists evident at this time throughout Europe's capitals was at its bitterest in Vienna.

Above right: A portrait of the composer Alban Berg (1885-1935) by Arnold Schoenberg, who was also a gifted Expressionist painter. Berg and Webern were pupils of Schoenberg, and their *free atonal* form of music paralleled Expressionism in the visual arts. Both were concerned with portraying emotions.

shattering climaxes and multiple sounds blasted from a huge orchestra. The score of this ballet was one of the great breakthroughs in the history of music, heralding a new musical language that had to be absorbed.

Stravinsky went on to write *Les Noces* (1914-17), using dancers and an orchestra consisting entirely of percussion—including four pianos treated percussively rather than melodically.

Stravinsky's neo-classical music

In spite of having achieved so much success with his neo-primitivism, Stravinsky turned away from it to a style which took as its model the civilized classical music of the eighteenth century. His neo-classical period lasted until the 1950s. Notable works of this period are the *Symphony of Psalms* (first performed in 1930), a religious work which looks back to Bach, and the opera *The Rake's Progress*, the culminating work of the period (first performed in 1951).

Despite this apparent reversal of style there is a continuity between his neoclassicism and his earlier style in the importance of rhythm and the structuring of works in blocks rather than employing development and transition.

He retained many of these features when, at the age of 70, he turned to *serialism* (where notes are used in an ordered series) for a new source of inspiration. In this final period he set to music many religious texts as well as other works commemorating the deaths of leading figures, often friends, like Martin Luther King Jr and President Kennedy.

Stravinsky gained many honours in his

Giraudon

Left: A costume design by Alexander Benois for Stravinsky's opera *Petrushka*. The work was written for Diaghilev's Ballet Russe, and Benois and Stravinsky were jointly responsible for the scenario. The choreography was by Fokine. First produced in Paris in 1911, it was a peak in lavishness and success even for the Ballet Russe.

Right: Stravinsky's neo-classical period closed with *The Rake's Progress*, first produced in Venice in 1951. This picture shows the 1975 Glyndebourne production of the opera with stage sets designed by David Hockney. It is based on the series of pictures by the 18th century painter and engraver William Hogarth. It is Stravinsky's only full length opera and is much influenced by Mozart, whose music he listened to constantly.

Below: A sketch of Stravinsky done by Pablo Picasso in 1920. Both artists worked for Diaghilev's Ballet Russe and their careers are often seen as parallel. They were both great innovators.

lifetime but this did not prevent him from saying that the public 'cannot and will not follow me in the progress of my musical thought'. His musical influence has been immense and widespread in the US, Europe and Russia.

Schoenberg and the 12-note row

Arnold Schoenberg had to face even greater opposition than Stravinsky or Bartók. But his musical theory has been the greatest single influence in music this century.

Schoenberg (1874-1951), was born in Vienna. His early music shows the influence of Brahms and Wagner.

Returning to Vienna, where he received much support from Mahler, Schoenberg composed the *Chamber Symphony* (1906) which employed only fifteen instruments. The style remains highly expressive but its complexity makes it a difficult work to follow; its chromaticism is so extreme that the break-up of the tonal system seems imminent and inevitable.

In 1908, Schoenberg made a crucial breakthrough in the tradition of Western music, writing his first *atonal* works. *Atonal* means literally 'not tonal' and implies that the music is not centred around any key; there is no home base to which the music must return. Instead all notes and all possible combinations of notes in chords and all possible sequences of notes or harmonies have equal validity.

The first really significant atonal composition was the final movement of Schoenberg's second string quartet (composed 1907-8). The work is already unusual for a string quartet in containing a soprano setting of a text. At the words 'I feel air from another planet' all sense of key finally dissolves. To these years of complete tonal freedom belong *Ewartung* (*Expectation*, 1909) and *Pierrot Lunaire* (1912), which used speech-song and a chamber orchestra.

The number of text settings is not coincidental in Schoenberg's music; the difficulty of deriving musical order when it seemed *any* musical order was valid was helped by the verbal order of the text.

Caboue

Strawinsky par Picasso, 1920.

Schoenberg sought for an answer to this freedom and gradually he evolved the *12-note system*—the logical outcome of his atonal developments. Schoenberg himself said it was 'a method of composing with 12 notes that are related only to one another'. All of the notes have equal status (of course in classical Western music the octave consists of only 12 notes), and the particular order or *row* chosen by the composer for a specific work must be adhered to; no note of the 12-note row can be repeated until all the others have been heard.

Schoenberg's 12-note row transforms one sequence of notes into another by applying such fixed rules as reading the row backwards or upside down, starting on any notes of the chromatic scale, so long as the original intervals of the row are preserved. Altogether there are 48 possible permutations for any given 12-note row, while combinations of these permutations are of course limitless. Schoenberg, however, insisted again and again that it is not necessary to follow

the manipulations of a 12-note row to enjoy the music.

At first Schoenberg was able to write only short pieces using this method. Its first application was in the final piece of his *Five Pieces for Piano* (opus 23, 1923). Schoenberg went on to compose large scale pieces using this method, but making use of classical forms such as sonata, fugue and suite. As he grew more used to the 12-note method his initially strict adherence to it relaxed. His works written in the US (where he had emigrated in 1933 after the Nazi rise to power) are more flexible, even allowing themselves tonal allusions, for example the *Ode to Napoleon* (1943).

Schoenberg was a great and influential teacher and one of his pupils, Anton Webern, born in Vienna (1883-1945), has been seen by many as more truly fulfilling the implications of the 12-note system. Like Schoenberg, his early work is Romantic and Wagnerian. But Webern's mature music is unparalleled for its extreme shortness, concentration and intensity—every note seems to glisten, sharp and important in itself. Only one of the *Five Pieces for Orchestra* (op. 10, 1911-13), lasts more than one minute, the fourth lasting only about 14 seconds.

The works of Webern's free atonal period are already very strictly organized, often using forms derived from his study of Renaissance music. His 12-note period sees a more radical and rigorous application of the method than that of his master Schoenberg for, unlike Schoenberg, Webern did not pour the new music into classical moulds but attempted to find new forms appropriate to it. In doing so he often anticipated what became known as *serialism*, (which extends the 12 note form of organisation to the timbre and duration of the notes), which he used in his *Symphony* (op. 21, 1928), again a very short work. Despite the frequently alleged difficulty of Webern's music he said of it: 'In 50 years at the most everyone will experience this as *their* innate music; yes, even for children it will be accessible. People will sing it.'

Leon Bakst's brilliant
sets and costumes for
Diaghilev's *Ballets
Russes* influenced
fashion and interior
design for several years.
This costume for the
ballet *Le Dieu Bleu* was
worn by Nijinsky.

Reg Wilson

Black Music

Black music is the popular term used to describe the rich and varied musical heritage of black people, both in Africa and those parts of North America and the Caribbean where they were transported as slaves. It includes not only tribal folk music but the blues, ragtime, reggae, soul and jazz—both traditional and experimental.

In African music, rhythm is of paramount importance. Instruments that are assigned a rhythmic function generally outnumber those that fulfil a melodic and harmonic role, unlike the music of the Western world.

Other features of black music are that it tends to be improvised rather than notated and to be *syncopated*, developing complex counter-rhythms and displacements of accent over a basic rhythmic pulse. And the human voice is a central reference point. Instruments attempt to achieve the flexibility and expressiveness of song and speech, instead of attempting to give the human voice the purity and accuracy of an instrument.

In the twentieth century black music has dominated the forms of popular music, which have primarily originated in the United States. But the reggae music of Jamaica has also become very popular.

The black man arrived in America subjugated as a slave, a stranger in a strange land, deprived of his own language, culture and customs. Yet the black Americans developed an enormously rich musical vocabulary, a profuse variety of musical forms to accompany every aspect of their lives—whether gay or sad, whether at work, at worship or in their brief moments of relaxation.

The work songs were unaccompanied chants and 'hollers' to be sung in the fields. The spirituals, or 'sorrow songs' as the black leader W. E. B. Dubois called them, were complex religious songs in which both resignation and a passionate desire for deliverance from the bondage of slavery were combined. Such changes of register and mood have become very characteristic of American black music, especially in the gospel tradition.

Ragtime

The first black music to achieve widespread popularity was ragtime, a gay, lilting piano style that emerged in the 1890s. A steady and generally slow rhythmic pulse was the basis for the repetition of ingratiating melodic fragments.

Its greatest exponent, Scott Joplin, the composer of the first big ragtime hit, *Maple Leaf Rag*, and many other magnificent compositions, was a tragic figure who never achieved the recognition as an artist which he rightly felt was his due. Ragtime itself was merchandized in a patronising and disparaging way, in which black people were presented as looking foolish. Only in recent years has ragtime been recognized as a major contribution to American music and been presented with dignity to enjoy a new popularity.

The blues

A music that remained closer to the experience of black people in the American South was the blues, which was much

Courtesy of Library & Museum of the Performing Arts, Lincoln Center

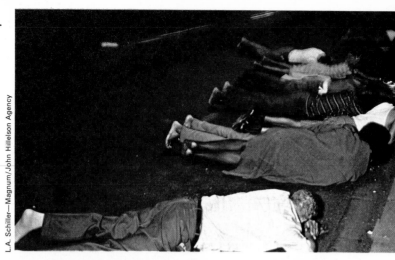

Right: Racial conflict in Watts, Los Angeles, 1964. The black American experience, from slavery to ghetto indignities, has found powerful expression in musical forms.

Below: The sheet music for the Scott Joplin composition *The Entertainer*, revived after 70 years as the theme for the 1973 film *The Sting*. When Joplin's work first appeared as sheet music and on piano rolls, it contributed to a ragtime craze. White composers were quick to imitate the style, and Joplin deplored the speeded-up hilarity the form acquired, so it is not surprising that his tempo instruction for *The Entertainer* firmly reads 'Not fast'.

L.A. Schiller—Magnum/John Hillelson Agency

THE ENTERTAINER

BY SCOTT JOPLIN

A RAGTIME TWO-STEP

Theodore Presser Company
Bryn Mawr, Pennsylvania 19010

Right: King Oliver's Creole Jazz Band. This 1920s group featured the youthful Louis Armstrong (kneeling, playing a trombone-like instrument) and his wife Lillian. King Oliver is third from left.

Below: Billie Holiday, 'Lady Day', was a jazz singer of great beauty and intensity, a tragic victim of drug addiction. Her feeling and phrasing are still being imitated.

Bottom: Bessie Smith, the 'Empress of the Blues', was its first star and remains the most important of women blues singers. A heavy drinking, hard living woman, she conveyed tremendous power in her strongly personal, lusty style.

slower to win widespread acceptance. Rightly thought of as a country music and a folk music, the blues is essentially a dialogue between the blues singer and his guitar, marked by breaks, silences and abrupt shifts of register and rhythm. Blues songs are not necessarily sad. Although they are mainly concerned with loneliness, pain and depression, they can also celebrate the joys of life. They embody a positive sense of self-assertion. The blues singer knows who he is and has the confidence to talk about himself in a way that is both revealing and self-dramatizing.

Traditionally, the blues was a man's world. But blues became popular in the US through women singers such as Ma Rainey and Bessie Smith, who first sang in tent shows with pianists and small bands. Bessie Smith, who took the blues into the concert hall, transformed the songs. They are still songs of pain and sorrow, but transformed by a tremendous power and vocal sweep that gave them an unexpected, gospel-like note of affirmation.

New Orleans jazz
The history of black music cannot be presented as a succession of musical styles superseding one another, since it is now recognized that their interrelationships are complex. Nevertheless, it is partly accurate to see the birth of New Orleans jazz as an adaptation of the ragtime style to an ensemble of cornet, clarinet, trombone, bass, guitar and drums, as it was first heard in honky-tonks and street parades.

Originally, the role assigned to the cornet or trumpet lead was a very strict one. A musician like King Oliver or Bunk Johnson did not simply carry the melodic line, he also laid down a rhythmic pattern for the other musicians to follow. But he would leave spaces for embellishments, corresponding to the ragtime right hand, by the clarinettist and trombonist.

Gradually something different emerged. A rhythm section of piano, bass and drums became responsible for the basic pulse. The collective improvisation became freer, while soloing became much more important, with solo breaks being given to each of the instrumentalists.

The greatest of the New Orleans jazz musicians, Louis Armstrong and Sidney Bechet, paradoxically contributed to the disintegration of the ensemble styles with which they were originally associated. Armstrong and Bechet swooped, uninterrupted, from melody to improvisation to melody, imposing on the music their powerful and idiosyncratic stamps.

New Orleans jazz was first popularized by a white group, the Original Dixieland Jazz Band. It was then removed further from its originators by being translated into orchestral form, most notably by band leader Paul Whiteman. With him the jazz solos of the talented white musician Bix Beiderbecke became mere desperate fragments floating in an ocean of harmonized sound.

The vital contributions to big band jazz were made by black musicians. Foremost among these were Duke Ellington, who used the tone colours of muted brass instruments and saxophones in highly imaginative and compressed orchestral tone poems such as *Harlem Airshaft* and *Ko-ko*, and Count Basie, whose jagged, interpolated piano figures against a guitar-led rhythm section were the magic 'carpet' over which blasting orchestral figures and the subtle, sinuous tenor saxophone solos of the great Lester Young could ride.

Swing and bebop
White swing bands, like that of the popular Benny Goodman, placed great emphasis on arrangements, discipline and the ability to read music. Improvisation, historically so important in black music, was assigned a minor role. This was typified by the part assigned to the highly creative trumpeter Roy Eldridge in the white Gene Krupa band—as a mere filler of holes in arrangements.

The bebop of Charlie Parker (alto saxophone) and Dizzy Gillespie (trumpet), which emerged at the end of World War II, was a deliberate reaction against this. The tunes became vehicles for incredibly complex improvisation that featured breakneck tempos, unusual harmonic progressions and instrumental virtuosity. Charlie Parker, a virtuoso tragically destroyed by heroin, became known as 'the Bird' for his literally soaring, astounding solos.

The influence of the city
In the 1940s and 1950s black music became, definitively, an urban sound, responding both to the pressures of the city and the fact that vast numbers of black people had made the exodus from the South to northern cities such as Chicago, Detroit and New York. The urban blues of Muddy Waters features an electrified guitar and a self-assertive manner, a pounding insistent beat in which all the spaces in the rural blues are filled in. It belongs to a world that is 367

David Redfern

Camera Press

Left: Duke Ellington, in a career spanning half a century, took inspired big band jazz from the dance hall to the concert stage and international recognition. He died aged 76 in 1975.

Below: The Drifters, originally a Harlem group with a gospel sound, produced a string of R&B pop classics aimed at a white teenage market. In 25 years their total line-up changes have seen Clyde McPhatter, Ben E. King, Rudy Lewis and Johnny Moore as lead singers. In 1975 they became the first black artists to perform in South Africa accompanied by white musicians before integrated audiences, a great achievement.

Above: Ray Charles with backing group. Blinded at the age of six, orphaned at 15, Charles has known troubles all his life, culminating in a prison sentence in the 1960s for possessing heroin. One of the greatest of interpretive singers, he has been a major influence on rock singers and a driving force in 'soul' music.

Right: Miles Davis. A leading jazz trumpeter from the 1950s, Davis fused jazz, rock and African elements in the late 1960s with startling effect. Many of the distinguished soloists he has led have gone on to form their own acclaimed groups, Tony Williams, Chick Corea and Herbie Hancock among them.

busier, faster and more tense.

Another characteristically urban sound is that of the black harmony group. A gospel-influenced music, this is often sentimental but highly intense through the deceptively sweet, high tenor lead. These groups include the Drifters, the Coasters and the Miracles.

In the 1950s gospel, the music of the black churches, became more and more crucial as an influence on black popular music, partly because in cities the church is an even more crucial focus of black culture. In the mid-1950s the rise of rock and roll led to the discovery by white teenagers of black rhythm and blues (R & B). But at the same time Ray Charles was recording the songs that made him famous and came to be known as soul music. His songs, such as *What'd I Say?*, were gospel influenced in style, if not in lyrical content, their 'sanctified' piano chords and their tremendous sense of theatre.

Soul music has a great emotional directness, but it also represents a wholesale borrowing of the musical traditions of the black church for the purposes of secular love. The erotic message of soul music is that body and soul are one.

By in the 1960s Berry Gordy's Tamla Motown corporation, started on a shoe-string from his home in Detroit, achieved great success with gospel-influenced pop records such as Martha and the Vandellas' *Dancing in the Street*, the Supremes' *Baby Love* and *Where Did Our Love Go?*, and the Four Tops' *Reach Out I'll Be There*. Tamla Motown records are tuneful and good to dance to. They were also very carefully produced and were conceived as a total sound.

David Redfern

Right: Tamla Motown had the top female group of the 1960s in the original Supremes with Diana Ross. After several changes in the line-up the team, shown here in the mid-1970s, finally split in 1977.

Below: Stevie Wonder is one of the most remarkable talents in contemporary music. Blind from birth, he was discovered by Tamla Motown at 12, and was a star at 13. Since then he had made many hit singles and ambitious, highly acclaimed albums acting as composer, arranger, producer, singer and multi-instrumentalist. The highest paid individual in rock, his success with both black and white audiences is unprecedented.

In the 1970s the most influential artist in the field of black music is Stevie Wonder. Born Stephen Judkins in 1950 and a star by the age of 13, Wonder has shown the consistent ability to write deceptively simple love songs such as *You are the Sunshine of My Life* as well as complex political statements such as *Living in the City* and *Village Ghetto Land*, in which he shows himself fully conscious of the indignities to which his people are still subjected. Although harmonically and instrumentally sophisticated, Wonder's music uses intricate polyrhythms in a way that brings today's black music into close alignment with the musical traditions of Africa, where it all started.

Reggae

The origins of reggae, another increasingly influential popular form, also go back to Africa by way of post-war rhythm and blues and boogie. In the 1970s reggae has become far more complex, with a switch to dramatic, electrified rhythm work and frequently powerful political lyrics. Bob Marley and the Wailers, cult figures preaching the doctrine of the Rastafarian faith and a potent force in the music scene of the mid-1970s, were the first Jamaican artists to make a real breakthrough internationally with songs such as *No Woman No Cry* and *I Shot the Sheriff*.

There is still a common world of black music in which influences pass from Africa to America and back, from New York to Jamaica and from Jamaica to New York. Black music has a rich past, a vital present and great promise for the future.

Modern Music

The music of the post-war period has absorbed many influences and raised many problems for both composer and audience. A new musical language, breaking away from the traditional tonality of Western music was established by such composers as Schoenberg and Webern at the beginning of the century, and this has been continued by modern composers Pierre Boulez and Karlheinz Stockhausen, among others.

Contemporary composers have to face unprecedented problems of language and communication, and these have increasingly been tackled using techniques made possible by recent technical advances, especially in electronics.

Electronic music

The French composer Pierre Boulez (b.1925), the German composer Karlheinz Stockhausen (b.1928) and their influential teacher Oliver Messiaen (b.1908) all wrote music in which Schoenberg's 12-note method was extended to express register, dynamics, tone colour, the number of musical events in a given time, the density of harmony and the manner in which the notes were to be played. Such pieces, like Stockhausen's piano pieces *I-IV* (1952-53), sometimes demanded an instrumental precision that was humanly impossible to realize. The initial attraction of electronic music for these composers was that such a total control over the music became technically possible.

Although electronic instruments date back to early in the century, recorded electronic music dates only from 1948 when Pierre Schaeffer began experiments at the studios of French Radio in Paris. The results became known as *musique concrète* (concrete music) because recorded sounds from everyday life were used (engines, birds, voices and so on). At first it was distinct from electronic music, which was supposed only to use pure electronic sounds, but the distinction soon broke down and all sounds began to be used together—the *concrète* sounds often modified electronically.

Electronic *synthesizers* which generated, controlled and modified sounds became widely available in the 1960s, with cheaper and smaller transistorized electronics. The latest innovation is the use of computers in synthesizing sound.

Above: The composer John Cage, with close associate, pianist David Tudor. Cage has been a tireless opponent of many of the most cherished values of Western music, and has exerted a strong influence on contemporary music. Cage has tried in his works, often performed by Tudor, to break down the traditional barriers imposed between audience and music.

Above right: The score for Cage's *Aria* (1958). The *Aria*, for any voice range, is an example of a graphic score. Horizontal lines represent time, and vertical ones pitch, while the different colours represent styles of singing chosen by the singer. These graphic representations are very general, and leave a great deal of freedom to the singer.

Right: Karlheinz Stockhausen, perhaps the most significant composer of electronic music, has also composed pieces in which players are able to explore different musical options at each performance, improvising within his basic score.

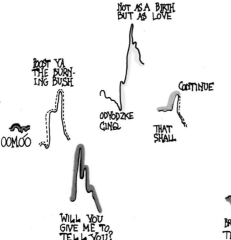

NOT AS A BIRTH
BUT AS LOVE

BOOST YA
THE BURN-
ING BUSH

CONTINUE

FAR-REMOVED

OOMOO

ODYODZKE
CINQ

THAT
SHALL

WILL YOU
GIVE ME TO,
TELL YOU?

BREAKING
THE SHELL

AT REST

Left: Pierre Boulez, as well as being an important composer of modern music, is also an influential conductor of both classical and avant garde music. Deeply concerned with the problems of modern music, Boulez has been exploring new techniques at the Institute for Acoustic and Musical Research in Paris.

Above: Composer Peter Maxwell Davies with the group who perform his works, 'The Fires of London'. They were originally founded by Maxwell Davies and another significant avant garde composer, Harrison Birtwistle. Maxwell Davies' music has been strongly influenced by Schoenberg's key work, *Pierrot Lunaire*.

Right: Cathy Beberian performing *Recital I* by Luciano Berio. Closely associated with Berio's work, she is one of the new generation of performers who bring their own creativity to the needs of the music. In *Visage* she accompanies electronic sounds with crying, laughing and sighing as well as singing.

Stockhausen and Cage

This new world of musical expression opened up for composers by electronic technology, meant that the initial interest in extended control of the music was modified by the experience of the medium itself: for example, it became possible to transform one pitch into any other, one rhythm into any other, and particularly interestingly to transform noise into pitch and vice versa. Pitch from one point of view, is enormously speeded-up rhythm, while noise is sound which has no rhythm or pitch but can be given either of these electronically.

Thus, Stockhausen could discard compositions with the 12 distinct pitches of the traditional Western division of the octave, for continuous and calculated change. His electronic tape for *Contakte* (1959) involves the continuous transformation of every element of sound. His experience of electronic music led to a new freedom of approach in his writing for live players; in an alternative version of *Contakte*, for example, performers on two pianos and percussion are able to vary their responses to the tape in every performance.

This move away from absolutely pre-determined forms to freer ones became widespread at the end of the 1950s. It was a result partly of the experience of electronic music, which could dissolve all rigid musical distinctions, and partly of the influence of new ways of conceiving the relationship between art and reality.

If any one individual can lay claim to being the source of this last influence it is the American John Cage (b.1912). Cage studied for a time with Schoenberg, who described him as an inventor rather than a composer and it is probable that he will mainly be remembered for the liberating effect of his ideas on others than for his own work.

Cage has deep sympathy with Zen Buddhism, which is strongly anti-rational in the sense that it is opposed to any divisions which exist within life, but which Western man, in particular, tends to assume are inevitable. Thus Cage attempted to deny the existence of any divisions between life and art, music and noise, choice and chance, audience and performer, and music and the other arts.

One of his most influential techniques, clearly implied by his outlook, is the use of chance. Chance music is sometimes called *aleatory*, a word coined by Pierre Boulez from the Latin 'alea' meaning dice, indicating that the throw of a dice or some other random operation governs the next musical move. Cage first began to use chance extensively in 1950. His *Imaginary Landscape No 4* (1951) uses 12 radios operated by 24 players in a random mixture. The *Concert for Piano and Orchestra* (1957-58) is different at every performance, as the soloist may play any or all the 84 different kinds of score in any order, superimposed or in fragments, and a performance may be any length.

The activities of the players are emphasized in Cage's music—*how* they are to play rather than what they are to play. One of his most famous pieces is 4′ 33″ (1952) in which a player sits at an opened piano in silence for four minutes and 33 seconds and then closes the piano. The point that Cage is attempting to make with this work is that there is music around us all the time, and the traditional rituals of the concert hall create a frame through which we hear this music. Cage has said 'This use of everyday music makes me aware of the world around me. Now I go to a cocktail party. I don't hear noise. I hear music.'

Beyond rhythm and harmony

The Polish composer Witold Lutoslawski (b.1913), after writing some fine tonal

Polish composers Lutoslawki and Penderecki have both demonstrated this, and the Hungarian Gyorgy Ligeti (b.1923) first became famous with works which rely exclusively on the effect of textures. His *Atmosphères* for large orchestra is a famous example; here there is no rhythm or harmony, only a richly sustained and constantly changing web of textures.

Berio and Boulez

A composer who exhibits a whole range of avant garde techniques in his later work is the Italian Luciano Berio (b.1925). Like his friends Boulez and Stockhausen, he too underwent the transition in his music from strict to freer forms.

His works often have a strongly theatrical element and heavily depend on the quality of the performers; the avant garde needs performers who are creators as much as interpreters. Again, like others of the avant garde, Berio sometimes re-uses, revises, re-works or comments musically upon previous output, and in the case of the *Sinfonia* (1968)—a huge collage of sound for orchestra, organ, harpsichord and piano—he uses musical quotations from other composers including Debussy, Wagner and Mahler.

Pierre Boulez began to use controlled aleatory methods in the late 1950s. His *Pli selon Pli* (literally 'fold according to fold') of 1957, a portrait of the poet Mallarmé, for soprano and orchestra, creates a series of possible musical pathways through the complex ramifications of the music. Boulez is also an eminent conductor of established nineteenth and twentieth century classics as well as of the newest music, but the standard

Left: The Beatles, the most successful group of the 1960s were to revolutionize popular music with their eclectic mixture of styles: folk, jazz, rhythm and blues, rock'n'roll, electronic music plus many more influences were worked into a unique synthesis whose appeal spanned all musical audiences.

Below: One of today's great percussionists, Stomu Yamashta. Several contemporary composers have written specially for him—including Hans Werner Henze. He is equally at home in avant garde or rock music. The strong element of theatre in his performances paved the way for his Red Buddha theatre group.

music influenced by Bartók and folk music and deciding that the 12-note technique was not for him, heard some of Cage's music in 1961. This led him to adopt a form of aleatory music which allowed a much greater degree of personal control than Cage's philosophy could have allowed. Despite this radical method, his later works are approachable and arresting, for example *Jeux Venitiens* (Venetian Games) of 1961, the first of his works to use such methods, *Trois Poemes d'Henri Michaux* (1963) and the *Cello Concerto* (1970).

The Greek composer Iannis Xenakis (b.1922), another of Messiaen's pupils, has developed his own brand of aleatory music called *stochastic* music. This is derived from a mathematical law which states that chance operations tend to a certain goal, that is they are probable rather than random. However, despite this fearsome description, his music has immediate dramatic impact and aims to express the cosmic unity he feels is in all things, including science and art.

Another outcome of the dissolution of all harmonic systems has been the increased emphasis on sheer quality of sound and texture to substitute for harmonic structure and argument. The

repertoire, in his opinion, creates a museum atmosphere and an unhealthy nostalgia and conservatism. Boulez is now head of the Institute for Acoustic and Musical Research and Coordination (IRCAM) in Paris, which aims to re-vitalize the nature of concert going and to study the implications of technological advance for music.

Pop music

Perhaps a more serious problem is the isolation of the avant garde from the average musical audience. The death of a common musical language, and the banalities of composers unable genuinely to exploit the freedoms of the present, have created a worrying gap between audience and music, wider than at any time in history.

For a time in the 1960s, pop music was claimed by some to be the genuine serious music of the age, and seemed able to bridge the gap between audience and composer. As with the avant garde, tape and electronics transformed popular music. The 1950s saw the appearance of the long-playing record (formerly the 78 rpm record had limited songs to about three minutes) and the special recording possibilities of tape enabled echo, super-imposition and special effects to be included. Such innovations were influential in the emergence of the first modern pop stars such as Elvis Presley.

Today, in most pop recordings, an engineer mixes a series of separately recorded tracks of voices, instruments or sounds into one final mix to gain the maximum clarity and effect. The primitive rhythms, the two or three chords and the

David Redfern—Photo Andrew Putler

Below: The Pink Floyd in performance, using a light show and sophisticated electronics to reproduce the effects of their records. The group produced albums from the late 1960s onwards which exploited the range of electronic effects, and occasionally almost crossed the gap between pop and 'serious' music.

Right: Mick Jagger, lead singer of the Rolling Stones, one of the successful pop groups to lead the youth revolution of the 1960s. The Stones, with their raw sound produced by massive amplifiers, are one of the few top bands renowned for their live performances, with Jagger personifying sexuality and power.

Adam Ritchie/Camera Press

simple forms that characterized rock and roll gave way to the remarkable har-monies, tempo changes and extended, often chromatic melodies of the Beatles and other groups. The Beatles did study the music of Stockhausen and Berio, and produced, in *Revolution 9* (1969), an elect-ronic piece which abandoned harmony and rhythm altogether.

The appearance of synthesizers and other devices increasingly encouraged the more inventive groups, for example Pink Floyd, to concentrate on texture and sheer sonic effect.

Thus in pop music the experience of electronics produced similar changes of emphasis, although on a different scale, as in avant garde music. Recently Steve Reich (b.1936) and Terry Riley (b.1935) have created a music (*phase music*) which appeals to both pop and avant garde audiences. Small patterns of notes are allowed gradually to overlap (go out of phase) hypnotically creating, over ex-tended periods of time (potentially in-definitely), rich harmonic and rhythmic effects as well as curious auditory illusions.

With so many experimental paths ex-plored and so many traditional barriers down, the future of contemporary music is both daunting and breathtaking.

Ballet

Ballet began as a grand, stately entertainment in the courts of early Renaissance Italy. Ballets were not then professional shows; they were performed by the aristocratic courtiers—often by the royal or ducal host as well—and, accordingly, their steps and movements were formal rather than difficult. From Italy they came to France and there, in the sixteenth century, much encouraged by the queen, the Florentine Catherine de Medici, they were the rage of the French court.

Courtly beginnings

Louis XIV derived his title of 'Sun King' from a court ballet, *Le Ballet de la Nuit*, 1653, in which he appeared—as the Sun King. Until he became too fat for it, he loved to dance; and, at least in the earlier part of his long reign, ballets were more frequent and sumptuous than ever before. In his reign, too, came the important separation between the amateur dancer and the professional. Professional male dancers had been permitted only as subsidiary characters; now they began to take over the 'noble' or leading roles and, as it would have been quite improper for ladies of the court to be partnered by these professionals, so the women began to be replaced by men *en travesti* (disguised as women). From that the next step was the arrival on the scene of actual female professional dancers.

Scala

Below left: An engraving by Jacques Callot of *La Liberazione di Tirrenio*, a typically grand court ballet performed in Florence in 1616 for the Duke of Tuscany. The dancers have come down from the stage and advance towards the Duke and his guests using a formal, stately sequence of steps. The audience is very much part of this elaborate, costly scene.

Left: A painting of Marianne Cochois, a French dancer of the 18th century. It is easy to see why, wearing such splendid but cumbersome dresses, female dancers of the period could scarcely rival their male partners in virtuosity.

Below: The famous *Pas de Quatre* performed at Her Majesty's Theatre in London on July 12, 1845. The quartet brought together Marie Taglioni, Carlotta Grisi, Fanny Cerrito and Lucile Grahn—among the greater dancers in the 'romantic' age of ballet.

Right: The costume designed by Leon Bakst for the Russian dancer Nijinsky in *L'Apres Midi d'un Faune*. This work, set to music by the French composer Debussy, was in a Greek style—not at all in ballet's tradition. This was Nijinsky's first attempt at choreography (the art of designing the steps of a ballet). It caused a sensation when first performed for the Diaghilev Company in Paris in 1912.

Freemans

Mander & Mitchenson Theatre Collection

Left: The legendary ballerina Anna Pavlova in *The Dying Swan*. This solo piece (a compound from *Swan Lake*) was made for her by the brilliant choreographer Fokine to music by Saint-Saens. She danced it first at a St Petersburg gala in 1907. Pavlova preached the beauty of classical dance at a time when Serge Diaghilev was revolutionizing ballet.

Right: Tamara Karsavina and Michel Fokine in *The Firebird* (1910). This was the first ballet composed by Igor Stravinsky, the most distinguished composer for ballet since Tchaikovsky. This production was one of the greatest successes of the Diaghilev seasons in Western Europe before World War I.

COMOEDIA

«L'APRÈS MIDI D'UN (NIJINSKY)
1er Année   Nº 1
15 Mai 1912
Numéro Exceptionnel
60 Pages
PRIX
1 fr. 50

7me Saison
des
Ballets Russes

BAKST

NIJINSKI, dans l'"Après-Midi d'un Faune"
Aquarelle originale de Léon Bakst.

In 1669 L'Academie Royale de Musique was founded, which became the Paris Opéra and, for many years, the Mecca of ballet; three years later a dancing school was added to this academy, to train performers for the opera-ballets of the Academy's famous composer-director, Jean-Baptiste Lully. The long marriage between opera and ballet had begun and ballet had started to leave the royal ballroom for the stage. The courtier and his lady, once the performers, now became the spectators of an increasingly exacting form of dance.

Pierre Beauchamps, Lully's skilful ballet-master, is credited with laying down the rule of 'the five positions', the 'turned out' foot positions which to this day are the ABC of ballet dancing. By the time of Louis XIV's death in 1715, ballet had already got the basis of its technique—and its terminology (*entrechat*, *coupé*, *cabriole*, *chassé* were steps codified by then). Ballet's technical terms have been in French ever since.

The first stars of ballet were all male because the cumbersome female attire of those times hampered virtuoso dancing. Developments in technique have often gone along with costume changes; ballet's first really famous female stars, La Camargo and Marie Sallé, were both revolutionaries in their costume. Camargo shortened her skirts to show off the brilliant foot-work which was her principal asset; and Sallé, still more progressive, danced with hair loosely dressed (instead of conventionally piled up on top) and in flowing draperies (instead of the conventional *pannier* or looped-up skirt); this enhanced the lyrical fluency which was the special attraction of her dancing.

The idea that dance should not be just an interlude between songs, as it was in the contemporary opera-ballets, but should be self-sufficient, was first put forward by the Englishman John Weaver, but not taken up in England. Jean-Georges Noverre, one of the most important figures in the history of ballet, propagated much the same ideas a few decades later in his famous *Letters on Dancing and Ballet* (1760). With his *ballets d'action* Noverre began ballet-

Michael Holford

Cauboue

making as it is known today. He put forward a new, serious approach to ballet as an art form; a dramatic spectacle in which the action and story was developed through expressive dance, with the movements more natural and the dance harmonizing with the music.

Meanwhile ballet had arrived in Russia. In 1735 a French ballet-master, Jean Baptiste Landé, set up a small ballet school in the Winter Palace of the Empress Anna Ioanova in St. Petersburg; out of it eventually grew the Imperial Russian Ballet.

In the forty years after the French Revolution ballet techniques developed considerably. Noverre's pupil Jean Dauberval produced a ballet, *La Fille Mal Gardée* (1789), which was the first to have a more or less everyday theme (the efforts of an amorous country girl to elude her repressive mother) instead of the Olympian myths which were the usual subjects of Noverre's choreography and of earlier ballets.

The splendours of romantic ballet

The new epoch of 'romantic ballet' began, abruptly and triumphantly, in 1832 with the appearance of the young Marie Taglioni at the Opéra in *La Sylphide* (devised for her by her father, Filippo). Romantic ballet was, largely, the application of Noverre's ballet d'action to the sort of theme and sentiment made fashionable by Byron, Walter Scott, Heine—about 'real' people, that is, but set in a new, romantic maze of witches, wood-nymphs and ghosts. The story in *La Sylphide* is about a Scottish crofter enchanted by a dryad and destroyed by a vengeful witch; *Giselle* is

about a Silesian peasant-girl betrayed by her lover who, after her death of a broken heart, is changed into a love-lorn spectre.

It was in the romantic period that ballerinas began to dance on tip-toe (*on point*); and, having struggled in the eighteenth century to something like equality with the male dancer, the ballerina now took over. There were creative male dancer-choreographers (choreographers are designers of dance steps) of the romantic ballet, but on stage they were subservient to such ballerinas as Taglioni, Fanny Elssler, Carlotta Grisi, Fanny Cerrito, Lucille Grahn. Significantly, this 'short list' of the top romantic ballerinas includes not one French dancer.

Italian dancers were particularly numerous among the stars of the romantic period. Italian ballet had long been eclipsed by its French offspring—but at the beginning of the nineteenth century Italian names began to loom large: Salvatore Vigano, for instance, who set the dances to Beethoven's only ballet, *The Creatures of Prometheus*, and, still more influential, Carlo Blasis, whose *Code of Terpsichore* is perhaps the most valuable treatise ever written on ballet technique.

By the 1850s Taglioni had retired; so had Elssler, Cerrito, Grisi. The age of the romantic ballet was over; so was the ascendancy of Paris and the Opéra. Of the new ballets produced there only *Coppelia* (1870), with its music by Delibes and its story about the delusion of an old doll-maker (who thinks he has brought one of his dolls to life), has become a classic.

Above left: A design by Natalia Goncharova for a peasant costume in *Le Coq d'Or* (The Golden Cockerel). This scintillating, colourful ballet, adapted from the opera by Rimsky-Korsakov, was produced by the Diaghilev Company in Paris in 1914 on a very grand scale, with singers flanking the dancing on stage.

Above: An aquatint of Nijinsky's ballet *Jeux* (1913), with music by Debussy. Nijinsky last appeared in 1917; soon after, he succumbed to mental illness, although he lived until 1950.

Below: Margot Fonteyn and Rudolf Nureyev in Frederick Ashton's ballet *Marguerite and Armand* (1963).

Anthony Crickmay

376

Below: The world-famous star Rudolf Nureyev in *Aureole*, a work by the American modern choreographer Paul Taylor; an example of the flexibility which now exists between the modern and classical roles in the ballet repertoire. Today dancers are expected to adapt to both—equally strenuous—styles.

Above: The dance of the warriors from *Spartacus*, a famous Bolshoi Ballet production of the post-war period, with music by the Russian composer Khachaturyan. With its spectacular but rather uninventive kind of classical dance, *Spartacus* is one of the most typical products of the Soviet ballet companies.

Right: *Hidden Rites* (1973), a ballet by the black American Alvin Ailey. Ailey, one of the best known dancer-choreographers in the United States, blends classical movement with 'blues' and other modern styles. His dance *Revelations*, for example, explores the world of negro spirituals.

Ballet in Imperial Russia

The aristocratic Russian capital St. Petersburg became the next centre of ballet. It was the interaction between imported talent and the enthusiastic, developing Russian 'school'—much encouraged as it was by Imperial favour—which made Russian ballet great. By the middle of the nineteenth century, Russia was itself producing fine dancers, but still the most dazzling and influential stars of Imperial Russian ballet were Italians; and the leading ballet masters-choreographers in St. Petersburg after 1850 were Frenchmen; the greatest of whom was Marius Petipa.

Petipa came to St. Petersburg in 1848, stayed till his death in 1910, aged 92, made over 50 ballets and gave to Imperial Russian ballet its grandeur and its fame. The enduring legacy from his long reign includes *Swan Lake*, and *The Nutcracker* (still the most frequently performed ballets, the world over) and *Sleeping Beauty*, all three with music composed by Tchaikovsky.

Yet despite the new grandeur and skill brought to ballet during the Imperial Russian age, it was also a time when, after the romantic liberation, ballet became fossilized. It was rigid in its patterns, utterly conventionalized in its dress, shallow (with the exception of Tchaikovsky's scores) in its music. The rule in costume was the frilly *tutu*, the short, stiffly-projecting skirt worn by every ballerina.

New directions

The much-needed revolution came at the beginning of the twentieth century, with the partnership of Michel Fokine, a budding dancer and choreographer in St. Petersburg, and Serge Diaghilev, a provincial nobleman and member of a progressive artistic group known as The World of Art. In his attempt to make the dance itself tell the story and to suit the style of dance and dress to the subject, Fokine freed classical choreography.

Diaghilev, using Fokine's choreography, the Imperial Russian dancers, the 377

Mikhail Baryshnikov and Natalia Markarova in *Don Quixote*. The dancing of this pair, both former members of the Kirov Ballet, is characterised by a superb technique, speed and elegance of line.

Above: *The Sleeping Beauty*, Nureyev's production for the English Festival Ballet of one of the great classical works which have survived from the 19th century. This is the 'White Cat' variation from the last act of the ballet.

Left: Merle Park, a ballerina with the Royal Ballet, as Juliet in *Romeo and Juliet*. Prokofiev's very fine music has made this one of the most popular of long ballets. It was first produced in Leningrad in 1940: since then many choreographic versions have been seen in the West, as well as in the Soviet Union. This production by Kenneth MacMillan (1965) is perhaps the finest.

Below: *The Fountain of Bakhchisarai* is a big, spectacular ballet, typical of the Bolshoi Company at its best. Here Maya Plissetskaya, the most famous of contemporary Soviet ballerinas, performs a characteristic Soviet-style leap in the harem scene. Her personality and brilliant technique have made her supreme in many roles.

best of music and the most progressive designers of scenery and costumes, exalted ballet to an unprecedented status among the arts. Ironically, his Ballets Russes, whose impact on Western Europe was phenomenal, were virtually unknown in Russia, for Diaghilev's company existed only by way of European tours which started in 1909; at home, meanwhile, the Imperial ballet continued in its set ways. His 'occasional' touring company became permanent and lived a gloriously inventive, precarious, exiled life in Western Europe till Diaghilev died in 1929—when it was disrupted.

But by then he had changed the face of ballet. His successive choreographers (after Fokine came Nijinsky—briefly a choreographer as well as being probably the greatest male ballet dancer ever—then Massine, Nijinska—Nijinsky's sister—and Balanchine) had widened the range of ballet to include many sorts of dance besides the traditional classical one. His dancers, though all of them classically trained, had to adapt to many novelties of style. He had enlisted eminent contemporary composers (most notably the controversial Igor Stravinsky) and such painters as Picasso, Matisse, and Braque.

Western ballet masters and dancers had brought ballet to Russia; now it was the Russians who revitalized ballet in Western Europe and inspired a growth of indigenous companies where there had been none before. In Britain a young Irishwomen, Edris Stannus, who under her stage name of Ninette de Valois had been a member of the Diaghilev Company, succeeded in founding the first British national company: Sadlers Wells, later the Royal Ballet, has become one of the finest three companies in the world. In the United States, where ballet now flourishes, the leading spirit was George Balanchine, the last of Diaghilev's choreographers and, for many years, the presiding genius of the top American company, the New York City Ballet.

Only in the Soviet Union has it been quite different. There, and in the East European countries under close Soviet influences, not only have the Diaghilevian innovations been virtually unknown but balletic inventiveness has been blighted by standardized Marxist-Leninist dogma. Some of the best dancers (Rudolf Nureyev, Makarova, Mikhail Baryshnikov) have preferred to seek their fortune—and the new choreography worthy of their skill—in the West.

The ballet which has proliferated during this century is basically classical: performed, that is, by dancers trained in the classical way—including the 'turn out' of feet, and the dancing 'on point'. That training has proved itself more adaptable and more comprehensive, as well as more exacting, than any other. And adaptable it needs to be, because the dancers so trained must nowadays take on not only classics such as *Swan Lake* and *Giselle* but also much choreography in very different, modern idioms. The American Martha Graham believes rightly that there is room, and need, for other theatrical dance-languages—her own imaginative, forceful, barefoot, modern one especially—besides that of classical ballet. But classical ballet has shown that it is the mainstream; modern theatrical dance—like folk and social dance—is its tributary.

379

The Early Cinema

The cinema in the twentieth century has grown from a peep-show at fairgrounds and music halls at the turn of the century, to an entertainment that affects millions of people.

The technology which produced the cinema developed at the end of the nineteenth century, although many inventors including Leonardo da Vinci, had tinkered with the idea of moving pictures.

What we see in the cinema as a moving picture is the result of a peculiar trick of the eye, called 'persistence of vision'. This term describes the capacity of our eyes to retain an image of whatever appears before them for a fraction of a second longer then it is actually there. 'The movies' consist of a series of still pictures projected in rapid succession. It is the persistence of vision that gives the audience the illusion of continuous movement. The phenomenon was first observed in detail by Peter Mark Roget in 1824, and demonstrated during the nineteenth century by a variety of devices. The *zoetrope*, and *stroboscope*, and the *phenakistoscope* all worked on the same principle. A series of designs showing progressive stages of a single action are flashed before the viewer, who witnesses an apparent fluid motion.

It was not suprising that men should try to combine this process with the new science of photography. In 1878 Eadweard Muybridge took a series of still photographs of a horse galloping past a line of 24 cameras. Projected in sequence they became the first 'moving pictures'. All that remained to be done was to construct a machine that would take photographs faster than ordinary still cameras.

Credit for the invention of the first successful motion picture camera is usually given to the American Thomas Edison and his assistant William Dickson. By 1894 Edison's one-minute 'living pictures' were being shown in peep-show parlours across America, but it was in France that a camera using Edison's mechanism of perforated film to hold the registration of the image was combined with a projection system, allowing the film to be shown in a theatre. In 1895 Louis and Auguste Lumière demonstrated their Cinématographe machine which could photograph and project film. They gave birth to a new word—*cinema*.

The birth of the action film

With the technical basis of the silent film established, film developed artistically throughout the next decade. The Lumière brothers' own *Train Entering A Station* (1895) caused mass panic among early cinema audiences because of the compelling realism of the effects. In Paris, 1896 also saw the first artist of the cinema, former conjuror Georges Méliès, who incorporated camera trickery and fantasy into his films. Throughout the 1900s, his bizarre imaginative serials—like *Voyage To The Moon* (1902)—made audiences accept perceptual breakthroughs much more sophisticated than those of the Lumières' literal reporting camera. As films grew in length, Méliès' showman-

Top: *Voyage to the Moon*, Georges Méliès (1902). A former magician, he was the first creative film-maker. He greatly expanded the range of the camera, at first recording theatrical illusions performed in the open air, but moving on to using lighting, specially constructed sets, and camera tricks involving double exposure of film and dissolves from one image to another.

Right: *The Cabinet of Dr Caligari* (1919), Robert Wiene. The plot told how a mysterious doctor used a sleepwalker to murder people in a small town. The nightmarish decor emerged as the chief dramatic weapon in this menacing tale of ambiguous mental instability. This film used images to express states of mind.

Below: *Nanook of the North*, by Robert Flaherty (1922). He pioneered film as an anthropological study. In 1922 a fur company financed *Nanook of the North*, a compact essay of the survival of an Eskimo and his family. Flaherty's research was exhaustive, and he would live with his subject for months before shooting a foot of film.

380

Few silent stars have maintained their popularity as long as Gloria Swanson. *Her Husband's Trademark* was released in 1922, and she still rated star billing in *Sunset Boulevard* (1950) as well as one of the *Airport* movies of the 1970's.

ship and ambition drove him far beyond the early 60 second Lumière reels, but audiences tired of him and he eventually stopped making films.

In 1903, America pioneered the modern action film. Bored with shooting single-situation shorts, cameraman Edwin S. Porter decided audiences could now make sense of a story film without long explanatory titles slowing the action. In 1903 his *The Great Train Robbery* introduced an extended narrative and crosscutting between scenes to create dramatic tension. The film was a great success with audiences and other directors began to use the idea of a continuous narrative combined with parallel and overlapping action. The action film had arrived.

The new entertainment of cinema rapidly caught the public's imagination. Thousands too poor to afford the high prices of theatre or vaudeville tickets flocked to 'nickelodeons' (price of admission 5 cents, a nickel) and demand for films and equipment far outstripped the supply from Edison's factories and studios. Competition sprang up everywhere, despite the legal battles over patents and strong-arm tactics which Edison and his General Film Company used to maintain a monopoly of film production.

The stars

In 1909, in an attempt to escape this harassment, one producer, William Selig, moved his operation to Los Angeles, suitably distant from the General Film Company's headquarters in New York, and close to the Mexican border in case of trouble. Others followed suit, and by 1912, when the Edison Company's monopoly was broken for good, the Los Angeles suburb of Hollywood was the centre of American film production. Hollywood offered sunshine, authentic locations for westerns, and cheap real estate. The first studio opened in 1911, and by the end of the decade 80 per cent of the world's films were produced in southern California. Cinema attendances soared, boosted by an uninterrupted diet of short westerns and outdoor adventures, slapstick comedy, and thriller serials.

After 1910, another element in the entertainment world emerged—the star system. Originally actors received no credit. Expected to double as technicians, they were lucky to make a living wage. But public adulation proved overwhelming, and in 1910 a crucial breakthrough occurred when 'the Biograph Girl', star of dozens of moneyspinning sentimental dramas for the studio of that name, was enticed away by Carl Laemmle, founder of Universal, with a promise of higher pay *and* her real name in the credits. Florence Lawrence became the first publicly acknowledged film star. Within a few years stars' salaries had multiplied a hundredfold, and by 1919, Mary Pickford ('America's Sweetheart') had joined her future husband, Douglas Fairbanks, and Charlie Chaplin in forming the United Artists company. Their fourth partner was D. W. Griffith the director.

Griffith (1875-1948) had a huge influence on the cinema. He introduced the extensive use of the close-up, and a recognisable modern editing style, alternating shots of varying focal length and dramatic intensity. Griffith was the master of the melodrama: he believed in relating his stories as simply as possible. Pickford

Top: *Greed* (1923) by Erich von Stroheim. It was his masterpiece, a study of the rise and fall of an immigrant. It led to a struggle between Stroheim and Irving Thalberg, studio head, for artistic control of the film.

Right: *Battleship Potemkin* (1925), Sergei Eisenstein. The famous Odessa steps sequence, a recreation of the mutiny by part of the Russian Fleet in 1905. Eisenstein combined propaganda with spectacle.

Below: *Metropolis* by Fritz Lang (1927). A frightening allegory of man's dehumanizing enslavement by machine, *Metropolis* was a landmark in cinematic effect, with its special effects and camera work.

emerged under his sensitive direction and the sisters Lillian and Dorothy Gish captivated America in *Orphans of the Storm* (1922). In sharp contrast, Griffith brought monumental force to the sprawling canvases of his epics. His *Birth Of A Nation* (1915) was one of the most influential films ever made. This film about the Civil War and its parallel effects on human beings became one of the most profitable films ever made, and finally ensured recognition of the cinema's artistic strength.

Film in Europe

The European cinema used film to abridge classics of theatre and literature down to 'one-reelers' lasting ten minutes, sometimes with famous theatrical names like Sarah Bernhardt. In 1912 Italy produced the screen's first epic, *Quo Vadis?* nearly two hours long, which was an enormous success with audiences round the world. And during World War I both sides exploited the propaganda potential of film through jingoistic newsreels from the front.

In Russia, the revolution of 1917 gave the cinema new impetus. Lenin said, 'The cinema is for us the most important of all the arts'. Young Russian filmmakers led the world in sophisticated propaganda, developing a rigorously political theory of cinema. Lev Kuleshov led the way with his *montage* (an idea expressed by different images) and experiments in editing techniques, and supervised the early Soviet newsreels of Dziga Vertov, leading documentarist of the revolutionary state. Sergei Eisenstein (1898-1948) emerged as the leading theorist and practitioner of the Russian cinema. In *Strike* (1924), *Battleship Potemkin* (1925), and *October* (1927) he restaged crucial events of the recent struggles in Russia, and used to the full aggressively dramatic camerawork, as well as his own montage system, which presented conflicting images. And in his brilliant, influential films he created stunning new visual shocks.

Expressionism flowered in Germany, exploiting horror (Robert Wiene's

Above: Valentino's death at 31 caused riots at his funeral. His rise as a star was meteoric—from the moment of his first appearance as the brilliantined lover in *Four Horsemen of the Apocalypse* (1921), all women thrilled to him. His blatant sexuality combined with balletic movements (he was once a café dancer), Latin good looks and perpetual air of cruelty enslaved and titillated millions of women. Valentino embodied the star system, with its capacity to absorb the fantasies of the mass audience.

Right: Hollywood royalty: Mary Pickford and Douglas Fairbanks at their home, Pickfair. The marriage of America's sweetheart to Douglas Fairbanks, the great screen hero, in 1920 thrilled many. Mary Pickford became a star in a succession of juvenile roles where she was curly-headed and dewy-eyed. Fairbanks was the swashbuckling, adventurous hero in many successful costume dramas. With Chaplin and D. W. Griffith they defied the big studios and formed United Artists to distribute their films.

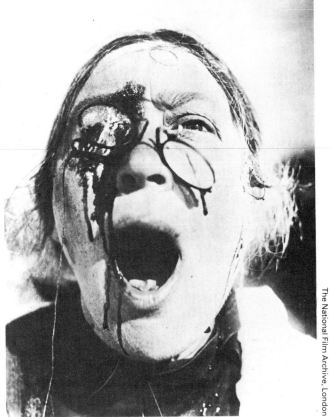

From the Odessa steps sequence in *Battleship Potemkin* (1925). Shots such as a pram bouncing down the steps, and this close-up are intercut with longer shots of the Cossacks advancing, to produce a striking example of Eisenstein's *montage* technique.

D.W. Griffith's *Intolerance* (1916) told four parallel stories – the fall of Babylon, the assassination of the Huguenots, the life of Christ, and the race to save an innocent man from the scaffold. They were intercut, all reaching their climaxes together.

Cabinet of Dr. Caligari, 1919) and science fiction (Fritz Lang's *Metropolis*, 1927) to create a nightmare world of exaggerated shape and shadow using designs from expressionist painters. F. W. Murnau's *Nosferatu* (1922) was the original screen Dracula, while *The Last Laugh* (1924) married melodrama to acid social comment, a technique perfected by G. W. Pabst, notably in *Pandora's Box* (1928). And the Dane Carl Dreyer meticulously recreated medieval France in the austere *The Passion of Joan of Arc* (1928) about the last 24 hours of Joan, perhaps the most haunting film of the whole silent era.

Hollywood

In the 1920s Hollywood consolidated its grip on world cinema. Economic logic dictated increasing centralization of American film production. The introduction of *panchromatic* film (sensitive to all colours of light) simplified lighting procedure which helped the increasingly mobile cameras to shoot more film more efficiently. Film factories emerged, reliant upon deceptively simple entertainment formulae, and a more conservative Hollywood developed the recognizable genres of modern cinema.

Right: Charlie Chaplin as the little tramp, perhaps the most durable of all cinematic images. His bowler, baggy pants and springy cane were all borrowed from others in Mack Sennett's team, and Chaplin added the moustache, fluffy hair and comic walk. His grace and superb timing came from his music hall training.

Below: Germany's earliest influence on Hollywood cinema was director F. W. Murnau's pioneering use of the mobile camera. Seen here with his crew on the set of *Sunrise* (1929), Murnau sits on a *dolly*, a platform fitted with tyres. By moving the camera forwards and around characters, this gives the film a greater freedom, and is an essential item in modern camera work.

Bottom left: *The Crowd* (1928), King Vidor. The film tapped the rich vein of individualism in the US, the drama of the common man emerging from the crowd to live his dream in the spotlight. It combined sentiment with social comment to define one of Hollywood's great themes—equality of opportunity for all.

Robert Flaherty's *Nanook Of The North* (1922), made on location in the Arctic, revealed the fascination of documentaries, charting the life of an Eskimo family. John Ford, the father of the western, rose to prominence and Howard Hawks produced the early prototypes of his masculine adventures. The American film drama of social comment started with King Vidor's *The Big Parade* (1927) and *The Crowd* (1928). Situation comedy and Hollywood's penchant for lavishly costumed period pieces were given sophistication and gloss by Ernst Lubitsch, one of many major European artists lured during the decade to the richest cinema in the world. Murnau, another German, dragged the intimate love story into the twentieth century with *Sunrise* (1927), revealing a simple purity of sentiment which remains a yardstick for American romance.

Viennese Josef Von Sternberg produced the atmospheric thrillers *Underworld* (1927), *The Dragnet* and *The Docks of New York* (1928). The 1927 *Ben Hur* used a quarter of a million 'extras'—nonspeaking personnel, as in crowd scenes—to establish the epic as Hollywood's favourite financial gamble, although Erich Von Stroheim's *Greed* (1923) remains the most fascinating monster of the period. The original print ran for nine hours, a detailed indulgence of Stroheim's gift for uncompromising realism and the tragedy of moral decline. Seven hours were cut out by its producers before release.

Comedy and Chaplin

The most persistently successful and enduring silent films were comedies. Mack Sennett's exuberant Keystone Kop two-reelers in the 1910s outlined the basic ingredients of the knockabout film comedy used ever after: violent physical action, the comic chase, a plot unburdened by complexity or characterizations, sustained at great speed as one joke moves on to another. Sennett's comics were often physical misfits—the cross-eyed Ben Turpin, the gross Fatty Arbuckle. Sennett established the tradition of enormous destruction in comedy—houses, boats and cars would be destroyed for a single 'gag'.

In 1913, Sennett first used an English comic, Charlie Chaplin, who in his first film used the props of a gentleman tramp, broken boots, bowler, baggy pants and a springy walking cane. The huge and universal popularity of the 'Little Tramp' made Chaplin one of the longest enduring stars of the cinema. Chaplin combined a restrained version of Sennett's anarchic comedy with the Victorian morality and an optimistic sentimentality derived from the tradition of English music hall, where he had begun his career. Chaplin went on to direct his own films.

Each silent comedian had his identifiable trademarks: Chaplin the baggy pants, bowler hat and cane; Harry Langdon his improbable baby face; and Harold Lloyd his thick glasses and an extraordinary ability for carrying out dangerous stunts. Buster Keaton was 'The Great Stone Face', who never smiled in his films. In *The General* (1926) and *Steamboat Bill, Jr* (1928) he took comedy to new heights. The essence of his comedy lay in his deadpan inexpressiveness in the face of repeated disasters, and in the grace with which he consistently just evaded his own impending destruction.

The birth of sound

The silent cinema, even with its usual piano or orchestral accompaniment, was an incomplete form without sound, and it was inevitable that it would disappear as soon as the problems of marrying sound to picture were solved. Four years after Warner Brothers presented their first Vitaphone 'talkie' in 1926, Hollywood had enthusiastically abandoned the obsolete silent technique. Conversion to sound created many problems: studios had to re-equip and rebuild their stages; directors and technicians had to cope with the limitations imposed by less mobile sound cameras; and many film workers, from theatre musicians to some of the most famous silent actors and comedians, found that the new medium could not accommodate their talents. But public enthusiasm for the new talking picture gave the industry, by now one of the six largest in America, the financial security that allowed it to emerge remarkably unscathed from the depression of the 1930s.

The cinema had come of age, and with the new challenge of sound, moved on to new expressions, and became the world's entertainment.

Left: Buster Keaton in *Steamboat Bill Jr* **(1927).** Keaton's comedy genius lay in his battle with his environment, rickety houses, runaway trains, the elements and their endless pointless hostility. 'The Great Stone Face' met every obstacle with serenity, absorbed in himself and not in the reactions of an incomprehensible world.

Below: In *Pandora's Box* **(1928)** G. W. Pabst etched an acid picture of social hypocrisy and decline. He used a uniform beam of light to mark his heroine's brittle success as a society mistress, and shadow to overwhelm her as a prostitute and murder victim. Pabst influenced the lighting of Hollywood melodrama.

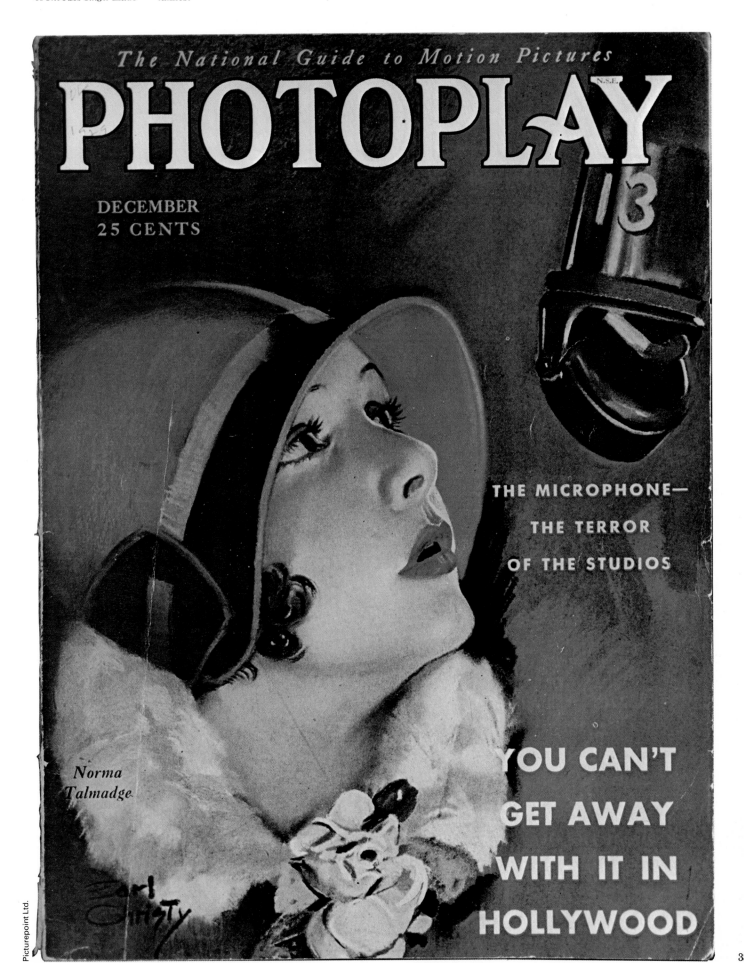

The National Guide to Motion Pictures

PHOTOPLAY

N.S.E.

DECEMBER
25 CENTS

3

THE MICROPHONE—
THE TERROR
OF THE STUDIOS

*Norma
Talmadge*

YOU CAN'T
GET AWAY
WITH IT IN
HOLLYWOOD

The Hollywood Movie

Hollywood became the centre of the US film industry during the years of the silent film. The international success of films by D. W. Griffith and others ensured Hollywood's increasing dominance of the world film market. The creation of the 'star system', on which audience loyalty depended, and the international talent which was attracted to Hollywood, both helped to create the unique character of the Hollywood film.

The first 'talkies'
Sound was being introduced in films by 1926, although the studios were uncertain at first whether to gamble on it. But in 1927 Warner Brothers released *The Jazz Singer* (a mainly silent film which incorporated some dialogue and singing). For the first time sound was used to create the plot of a full-length feature film. The Hollywood film industry was given a boost as audiences everywhere clamoured for the talkies, and *The Jazz Singer* ushered in two decades of Hollywood's undisputed dominance over world cinema.

The 1930s and 1940s were the years when the great studios reached the height of their prosperity and power. Each studio specialized in a distinctive kind of film: MGM in glamour; Paramount in sophisticated light comedy; Warner Brothers in realistic dramas; while Twentieth Century Fox's greatest asset was child star Shirley Temple, America's top box office draw in the 1930s. The studio system was committed to maintaining a large output of well-made and commercially successful films for a mass audience. The films were all made thoroughly acceptable to a family audience by the Hays Office of censorship, set up by the studios themselves to uphold traditional moral values.

The musical
One of the first places to which the Hollywood film industry turned in its attempt to fill film with sound in the late 1920s was the Broadway stage of New York. Out of this was born one of the outstanding Hollywood contributions to entertainment—the *musical*. In 1929, MGM produced *The Broadway Melody*, which was a tremendous success ('100% All Talking, 100% All Singing . . .'), and the musical was established.

Brilliant song writers such as Cole Porter and George Gershwin, were imported. A distinct film style was initiated in 1932 with *42nd Street*, introducing a score with a jazz beat and tap-dancing sequences which gave prominence to the dance director Busby Berkeley. His lavish formalized production numbers, using a mobile camera and kaleidoscopic effects featuring countless dancers, became a unique feature of the big Hollywood musical. Berkeley's *Flying Down to Rio* (1933) was also the first important film in Fred Astaire's career. The elegance of Astaire and the extravagance of Berkeley created a new sort of Hollywood film musical, with an exuberance, gaiety and style which have never been matched.

National Film Archive Stills Library/United Artists

WARNER BROS. SUPREME TRIUMPH
AL JOLSON
IN
'The JAZZ SINGER'

Left: Al Jolson in Warner Brothers' *The Jazz Singer* (1927), the first successful film to use sound—in song and dialogue. In the film Jolson prophetically said 'You ain't heard nothin' yet!' So began the race by the big studios to produce 'talkies', which revived the cinema's flagging fortunes and provided the stimulus of new subjects, and writers and actors from the theatre.

Right: Marlene Dietrich, became a star under the direction of Joseph von Sternberg in the 1930s. In his films she played a succession of *femmes fatales*, women whose erotic power men found irresistible and dangerous. Sternberg used close-ups, careful lighting and exotic settings to launch Dietrich as a star.

Below right: Vivien Leigh and Clark Gable in *Gone With The Wind* (1939), the story of America's deep south plantation society during the Civil War. The film became Hollywood's most dazzling high romance, combining the magnetic star performance of Gable with lavish sets and costumes, and the use of *Technicolor*. For many years it was the top box office success—its negative was stored in a golden canister. The film was reissued in 1968 with a new print.

Right: Greta Garbo in *Queen Christina* (1933). Here, Garbo was playing an ideal role, as the Swedish queen who abdicates for a life of her own. In *Grand Hotel* (1932) she spoke the words for ever associated with her: 'I want to be alone.' Retiring in 1941, she was never tempted back to films.

Below: *Citizen Kane*, directed by Orson Welles (1941). Welles' first film, it told the story of press magnate Kane's corruption by power and wealth. The film had a profound influence on Hollywood, with its use of many different film techniques. Elements of German Expressionism are seen in parts of the film. Welles went on to make *The Magnificent Ambersons*.

Film Preservation Bureau © 1934 MGM Corp, renewed 1961 by MGM Inc

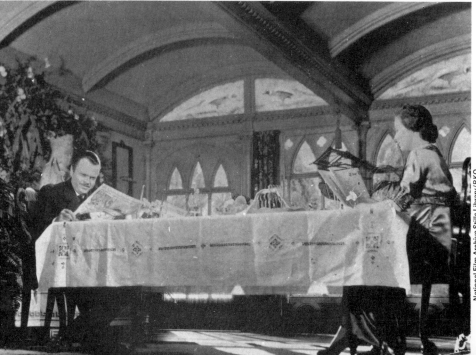

National Film Archive Stills Library/RKO

The glamour and excitement generated by Hollywood was heightened by the star system, where stars were controlled by studio publicity, and their roles carefully selected by the studios. The great stars—Clark Gable, Gary Cooper, Spencer Tracy, Greta Garbo, Bette Davis and Katherine Hepburn—were seen treading lightly through a universe of drama and romance.

Foreign imports

The American film industry benefited greatly from European artistic advances, and bought up imported talent to enhance studio prestige and growth. German-born director Ernst Lubitsch (1892-1947), for example, was brought over to Hollywood in the early 1920s. He developed a style of witty but amoral comedy films. The 'Lubitsch touch', a style of polished amoral wit, flouting conventions without shocking audiences, greatly influenced subsequent directors like Billy Wilder.

Not all foreign directors flourished: Swedish director Mauritz Stiller was invited to Hollywood by Louis B. Mayer of MGM, where he made two unsuccessful films. However, he brought with him a Swedish actress who was to become one of the screen's legendary goddesses—Greta Garbo. Garbo was built into an enigma by the studio, and her parts were chosen to exploit her mystery.

The western

Hollywood's most enduring genre was the western. The traditions of the western were already well established by the time of the introduction of sound. Originally the studios feared that the western—with its need for action rather than dialogue—would decline but directors such as John Ford, Raoul Walsh and William Wyler developed the western using sound effects, music and new big-screen techniques which ensured its popularity with the public.

Walsh's *In Old Arizona* (1929) captured the outdoor excitement with the sound of bacon crackling over a camp fire, and in *The Big Trail* (1930) he gave John Wayne his first leading role. Wayne became the archetypal western hero, being self-reliant and tough where necessary, he embodied the pioneer spirit. From 1935 the 'series western' enjoyed a brief vogue, featuring singing cowboys such as Gene Autrey. But the western did not reach a maturity of vision until the late 1930s, led by director John Ford with his brilliant film *Stagecoach* (1939), the first Ford film to star John Wayne.

In George Marshall's *Destry Rides Again* (1939) the western was debunked while maintaining the traditional style of drama and action, James Stewart parodying the typical western hero. Ford continued to make classic westerns in the postwar period with *My Darling Clementine* (1946), a loving re-creation of America's frontier myth, starring Henry Fonda as Wyatt Earp. It featured the classic shootout known as the gunfight at the OK Corral, in which Wyatt Earp, his brothers and Doc Holliday faced the Clanton gang. The western increased in seriousness in the 1940s and 1950s, using its themes as allegories of topical problems. Director Fred Zinnemann's *High Noon* (1952), where Gary Cooper played a US Marshal facing danger alone from a group of gunmen, was also a comment on the anticommunist McCarthy period in the US.

The great gangsters

The gangster film became popular during the Depression of the late 1920s and early 1930s. The stories of heroes prepared to cheat and fight their way to success touched the mood of a society in which the bare struggle for survival was a pressing reality. The greater degree of social realism in the gangster movie was a feature of the 1936 film *The Petrified Forest*. We see a disillusioned writer unable to find direction in life and a woman prepared to enter into a casual relationship with an unknown man because she is bored. Against such a background the gangster Duke Mantee, played by Humphrey Bogart, stands out as the man who is willing and able to take decisive action.

The classic phase of the gangster film lasted only for the first few years of the 1930s and is remembered for the performances of Edward G. Robinson in *Little Caesar* (1930) as the archetypal gang leader, and James Cagney in *The Public Enemy* (1931) and *Scarface* (1932) where he played small-time crooks, amoral and aggressive.

The film comedy

In the 1930s the master of film comedy was director Frank Capra, whose 'screwball' comedies were characterized by a rich vein of irreverent humour, a fast pace and eccentric characters. In his films, from *Mr Deeds goes to Town* (1936) to *It's a Wonderful Life* (1947), he produced a world turned romantic and enjoyable through the possession of a warm heart and integrity. In *It Happened One Night* (1934) Capra incorporated a subtle sexual undertone into his comedy when Claudette Colbert and Clark Gable share a bedroom. In Howard Hawks' *Bringing Up Baby* (1938) Cary Grant and Katharine Hepburn fall in love over a leopard and end up dismantling a dinosaur.

A more subversive comedy also flourished with Mae West and the Marx Brothers. Flouting every form of 'feminine' propriety Mae West ridiculed the accepted male-dominated ideas on the relationship between the sexes. Mae

National Film Archive Stills Library/United Artists

Above: *Casablanca* (1943) with Bogart and Ingrid Bergman. Set in wartime Casablanca, it tells the story of Rick Blaine, the cynical yet vulnerable owner of a bar, who finds that Bergman—his lost love— is the wife of a refugee he is reluctantly helping. The film is a superb example of Hollywood studio production.

Below: Bette Davis with romantic lead Paul Henreid in *Now Voyager* (1942). Here, Davis, in a typical 'weepie' role, has achieved beauty entirely through determination. Bette Davis was a star who became a screen beauty without conventional beauty, and whose tense acting style elevated her film scripts.

Koball Collection/United Artists

National Film Archive Stills Library/MGM © 1949 Loew's Incorporated. Copyright renewed 1976 by MGM Inc

West had her own provocative view on the subject, memorably expressed in the phrase 'It's not the man in my life, but the life in my man'. In the famous honeymoon scene from the film *My Little Chickadee* (1940), in which she co-starred with W. C. Fields (a highly gifted eccentric comic, whose wry dislike of children is captured in his comment 'No man who hates children can be all bad') Fields awaits his new wife, Mae West, in bed. West introduces a goat into the bed telling the goat 'Keep your mouth shut and let him do all the talking.'

Mae West was joined in her cynical humour by the Marx Brothers. In a series of comedies from *The Cocoanuts* (1929) to *The Big Store* (1941) Groucho's sharp dialogue ('I could dance with you till the cows come home. On second thoughts I'd rather dance with the cows till you come home'), delivered with a leer and a shambling walk, backed up by the antics of his brothers Harpo, Chico and Zeppo, poked fun at any form of social or intellectual pretension.

Welles and Citizen Kane

By the 1940s new developments were being made—and the new direction and subsequent collapse of the Hollywood film was heralded by Orson Welles' *Citizen Kane* (1941). The principal character, Charles Foster Kane (Orson Welles) was the embodiment of the entrepreneur engaged in a single-minded pursuit of material wealth and political power.

The film had a profound influence on Hollywood, as it used many innovative techniques: a script which followed events in flashbacks, enabling different characters to give their version of an event, the use of different camera lenses to make dramatic use of the film 'frame' and highlight the action of the film, and an inventive use of music. Welles, unable to establish sufficient creative control over his films, left Hollywood for Europe, but in the individuality of his handling of *Citizen Kane* he anticipated the pattern of film direction which was to emerge in subsequent decades.

The influence of Hollywood

During World War II America was the only country to continue with full scale film production, producing many brilliant escapist films including Michael Curtiz's haunting *Casablanca* (1943) and John Huston's *The Maltese Falcon* (1941), both starring Humphrey Bogart. MGM took the lead in joyous musicals, with Vincente Minnelli creating the classic musical about family life, *Meet Me in St Louis* (1944), set at the turn of the century.

In the 1950s a new naturalism was beginning to emerge. It stemmed from a combination of the effects of World War II and the desire to tackle social problems realistically, but unfortunately it coincided with Senator Joseph McCarthy's investigation into alleged communist infiltration in the film industry. This led to exile and blacklisting for many notable figures of the film world.

The departure of talent, the studios' loss of guaranteed outlets for their films and the advent of television all added to the decline of Hollywood and the great studios. Today, the evocation of the word 'Hollywood' means a glamourous locality, films characterized by realism, professionalism and style, a straightforward story and a star.

Below left: **Fred Astaire and Ginger Rogers in *The Barkleys of Broadway* (1949). Astaire and Rogers are associated with the greatest of the 1930s Hollywood musicals with their brilliant dancing and music from top songwriters. Astaire possessed an unmatched elegance, born from lengthy rehearsals.**

Above: *Dumbo*, **by Walt Disney (1941). Disney transformed the animated cartoon film from a simple comic strip to a substantial narrative form, bringing sound to cartoons. Walt Disney established his fame with the creation of Mickey Mouse in** *Steamboat Willie* **(1928), later joined by Pluto, Goofy and Donald Duck.**

Below: **Joan Crawford in** *Humouresque* **(1947). Joan Crawford was part of Hollywood's 'star system' and like many other stars played much the same part in various films. With her stern, mask-like face, and squared shoulders (created by designer Adrian), she played a succession of ruthless career women in her films.**